BCL

W9-BSZ-576

Sociological Theory
and
Modern Society

Talcott Parsons

Sociological Theory and Modern Society

New York, THE FREE PRESS
London, COLLIER-MACMILLAN LIMITED

First Printing

To the memory of

Kaspar D. Naegele

Perceptive observer, imaginative theorist,
beloved friend to very many

Preface

THE present collection of essays is the fifth that the Free Press has published by this author. (Because the 1954 edition of the *Essays in Sociological Theory* had about a 50 per cent turnover of contents as compared with the 1949 edition, I count them as two.[1]) This fact has a certain bearing on the character of my work, because these five collections comprise somewhere near half of my writings that have been published in book form, and there have been other elements of a similar character such as the introductory materials contributed to *Theories of Society.*

The prominence of such essays in my writing represents, from my point of view, a rather complex balance of continuity and discontinuity. A few of them were written without external stimulus and simply expressed the urge to "get something on paper" on a given topic. The considerable majority, however, were responses to rather specific requests to prepare papers for scientific meetings, to give lectures (usually in academic settings), to contribute to particular symposia, or to write introductions. The very fact, however, that such stimuli have, over a considerable period, impinged so consistently on an author who had gained a fairly distinctive reputation in social science, contributes a certain framework of continuity. The particular topics are certainly diverse, but they all concern various facets either of the problem of developing a coherent theoretical orientation in sociology and its most clearly related disciplines, or of using the kind of theory that was available for the interpretation of a variety of empirical social problems and phenomena, approached in rather broad terms, but approached, nevertheless, as empirical problems.

1. The other two collections are *Structure and Process in Modern Societies,* 1960, and *Social Structure and Personality,* 1964.

It is perhaps particularly important that, in line with my early concern with the relation between sociology and economics, the aforementioned stimuli and my responses to them have repeatedly taken me to and over the boundaries of sociology into a number of neighboring disciplines, not only economics, but political science, anthropology, and psychology, as well as into the interpretation of historical structures and processes. This is perhaps indicative of the importance of interdisciplinary concerns in the recent and present state of the social sciences. Furthermore, it should be clear that these "occasional" papers have borne a close relation to the broader theoretical work that has appeared primarily in the form of books written specifically to develop theoretical themes.

This combination of responding to discrete stimuli and yet attempting to use such occasions to add successively to a more comprehensive theoretical orientation and scheme and to develop an increasingly comprehensive empirical interpretation of the social scene may not be wholly idiosyncratic to one particular author but to some degree is also appropriate to the intellectual situation of a particular culture in a particular time. This is a period of rapid change and development in the social-science disciplines, not a period mainly of consolidation and codification. As part of this situation, there is a high premium on intensive communication within the most active intellectual groups; so that there has been strong pressure to participate through considering problems that are of direct interest to others and by trying one's hand at them in ways that produce smaller-scale results rather than major monographs, to say nothing of treatises. The very fact, however, that one man can contribute on this level over such a considerable range and with relatively coherent results seems to me to be an index of a major coherence in the more general movement of thought in the area. If these kinds of interchanges, of which these five volumes of essays are one type of product, continue, it seems very likely that eventually the theoretical thought involved will crystallize into solidly based and relatively formalized theoretical structures.

The present collection continues the dual orientation of its predecessors, namely a concern, on the one hand, with abstract problems of theory as such, including its history, and, on the other, the "applied" concern with the use of theory to interpret a variety of empirical phenomena, the variety of the phenomena constituting one kind of test of the generality of the theory.

The first part of the book consists of four papers dealing with the contributions of eminent figures in the background of the present phase of theoretical developments, namely Karl Marx, Émile Durkheim, and Max Weber. Part II consists of three papers dealing with the more contemporary intellectual situation at a high level of generality. I have included the paper on Pattern Variables here because of its generality in the structure of the theory of action, as compared with the more specific papers of the following section.

Part III turns to a more specific complex dealing with the dynamics of modern society. The emphasis is primarily political. Only one of the four papers, the first, is "applied" in the sense of the preceding discussion. By this criterion it could well have been included in Part IV, but has been placed here to serve as a kind of introduction to the other three more specifically theoretical papers. Finally, Part IV consists first of three primarily "applied" papers, each on a very different aspect of the empirical social world. These have been chosen from a larger list of possibilities specifically to illustrate the range of different types of social phenomena that can be analyzed fruitfully with the kind of theory under consideration. The final paper becomes more theoretical in the context of my own recently increasing concern with problems of societal evolution.

Particularly in Part III, the careful reader may note a certain amount of repetition, especially with reference to the grounding of the conception of generalized media of societal interchange. Thus certain of the relevant properties of money are reviewed in Chapters 9, 10, and 11 with considerable overlap. This of course is explained by the attempt to guide readers of three papers written for independent occasions into a line of thought that was likely to be somewhat unfamiliar to most of them. It has seemed best not to attempt to edit out this repetition in the present collection, because it might disturb the continuity of development of each of the papers in its own right. Furthermore, the importance and unfamiliarity of the idea of generalized medium and the related extension of the idea of "credit" to media other than money may perhaps warrant the extra emphasis that comes with repetition.

Following the suggestion of the Free Press, I have introduced each of the papers with a brief "Headnote" that explains the occasion for its writing and the way it fits into the general development of my work.

Talcott Parsons

CAMBRIDGE, MASS.

Contents

PART *i*

Revisiting
the Founders

CHAPTER **I**

Durkheim's Contribution to the Theory
of Integration of Social Systems

This paper was written in 1958 for the volume that appeared in 1960, edited by Kurt H. Wolff, to celebrate the centenary of Durkheim's birth in 1858. From the author's point of view, it is essentially a "revisit" paper undertaken with reference to the change and maturation of his own point of view since his extended treatment of Durkheim's work in *The Structure of Social Action* more than twenty years before. It is appropriate to place it first in the present collection partly because it was the first in actual composition of the four papers that constitute Part I, and it should be related to a number of others published elsewhere.[1]

It is also a paper that marks the beginning of an important phase of my own theoretical development. This started essentially from a new consideration of the theoretical problems posed by the integrative structures and processes in societies, this time much more directly than in the past in relationship to analysis of processes of social change. Here Durkheim's analysis, especially of the relation between mechanical and organic solidarity, has proved to be crucial. The full consequences of this development are not yet worked out. However, two theoretical discussions[2] have attempted to state them in general terms, and a number of more

1. Cf. the essays on "Durkheim," "Pareto," and "Interaction," which are to appear in the *International Encyclopedia of the Social Sciences* (forthcoming in 1967), and the paper, "Cooley and the Problem of Internalization," in the forthcoming book of essays on Cooley edited by Albert J. Riess, Jr.
2. Chapter II of *Societies: Evolutionary and Comparative Perspectives*, Prentice-Hall, Inc. (1966), and the article "Social Systems" in the *International Encyclopedia of the Social Sciences*, forthcoming in 1967.

empirical articles and chapters have utilized this perspective.[3] In particular, Durkheim's contribution to the analysis of the modern type of structurally pluralistic society has taken on new significance, the central focus being his conception of organic solidarity. Durkheim's analysis of it has, however, been considerably improved and extended by including explicit concern with role-theory and above all the plural roles in which individuals are involved in that type of society. In connection with Chapter 11, I shall remark on the relevance of this context to the analysis of generalized media of societal interchange and particularly influence in the technical sense in which the concept is used in that chapter.

I T IS appropriate at this time, just a little over one hundred years after the birth of Emile Durkheim, to take stock of his contributions to what was perhaps the central area of his theoretical interest. The development of theoretical thinking that has taken place in the intervening years enables us to achieve greater clarity in the identification and evaluation of these contributions.

It can be said, I think, that it was the problem of the integration of the social system, of what holds societies together, which was the most persistent preoccupation of Durkheim's career. In the situation of the time, one could not have chosen a more strategic focus for contributing to sociological theory. Moreover, the work Durkheim did in this field can be said to have been nothing short of epoch-making; he did not stand entirely alone, but his work was far more sharply focused and deeply penetrating than that of any other author of his time. Because of this profundity, the full implications of his work have not yet been entirely assimilated by the relevant professional groups. Furthermore, in addition to the intrinsic complexity of the subject, the rather special frame of reference of French Positivism in which he couched his analysis has made it difficult to interpret him.

The present essay will not attempt to be a scholarly review either of Durkheim's own printed work or of the secondary literature. It will rather attempt—in the light of a good many years of preoccupation with the problems for which Durkheim gave what were for his time classical formulations—to assess some of the main lines of his special contribution

3. Cf. later chapters in Societies: Evolutionary and Comparative Perspectives, and the paper in Daedalus, Winter, 1965 on "Full Citizenship for the Negro American?" and "Polarization of the World and International Order," Chapters 13 and 14 of this volume.

and to indicate the ways in which it has been both necessary and possible to try to go beyond the stage at which he left them.

✳There are two essential reference points in Durkheim's initial orientation: one is positive and the other negative. The positive is the Comtean conception of "consensus" as the focus of unity in societies. This was the primary origin of the famous concept of the *conscience collective;* this rather than any German conception of *Geist* is clearly what Durkheim had in mind. It was a sound starting point, but it was much too simple and undifferentiated to serve his purposes; primarily, perhaps, because it could not account for the fundamental phenomenon of unity in diversity, the phenomenon of the integration of a highly differentiated system.

The negative reference point is the utilitarian conception of the interplay of discrete individual interest, as first put forward by Herbert Spencer who conceived of an industrial society as a network of "contractual relations."[1] The importance of relations of contract, that is, relations in which terms are settled by some type of *ad hoc* agreement, was an immediate consequence of the division of labor which had been emphasized in the long tradition of utilitarian economics deriving from Locke and from Adam Smith's famous chapter. Durkheim made this tradition the focal point of his criticism, tackling it in one of its main citadels; and, in so doing, he raised the problem of the differentiated system which Comte had not really dealt with.

In this critique, Durkheim shows, with characteristic thoroughness and penetration, that Spencer's assumptions—which were those common to the whole liberal branch of the utilitarian tradition—failed to account for even the most elementary component of order in a system of social relations that was allegedly based on the pursuit of individual self-interest. To put it a little differently, no one had been able to answer Hobbes's fundamental question *from within the tradition,*[2] since Hobbes's own solution was palpably unacceptable. As is well known, Durkheim's emphasis is on the *institution* of contract, which at one point he char-

1. I have always considered the focal point of Durkheim's early work in this respect to lie in "Organic and Contractual Solidarity" (Book I, Chap. vii), *The Division of Labor in Society,* trans. George Simpson (Glencoe, Ill.: Free Press of Glencoe, Illinois, 1947). It starts as a critique of Spencer but actually goes clear back to Hobbes.
2. One reason for this is that the hypothetical turning-over of absolute authority to an unrestricted sovereign was empirically incompatible with the existence of the liberal governmental regimes that were a commonplace in the Western world of Durkheim's time. On this phase of the history of thought the best source is still, without question, Elie Halévy, *The Growth of Philosophic Radicalism,* trans. Mary Morris ([1901-4] New York: Macmillan Co., 1928).

acterizes as consisting in the "noncontractual elements" of contract. These
are not items agreed upon by contracting parties in the particular situation, but are norms established in the society, norms which underlie and
are independent of any particular contract. They are partly embodied in
formal law, though not necessarily only in what in a strict technical sense
is called the law of contract by jurists, and partly in more informal "un-
derstandings" and practice. The content of these norms may be summed
up as follows: They consist, first of all, in definitions of what content is
permitted and what content is prohibited in contractual agreement—in
Western society of recent times, for instance, contracts that infringe on
the personal liberty of either party or of any third party in his private
capacity are prohibited; second, in definitions of the means of securing
the assent of the other party that are legitimate and of those that are
illegitimate—in general, coercion and fraud are considered illegitimate,
however difficult it may be to draw exact borderlines; third, in definitions
of the scope and limits of responsibility which may be reasonably (or
legally) imputed to one or another party to a contractual relation, either
originally on the basis of his "capacity" to enter binding agreements—as
agent for a collectivity, for example—or subsequently on the basis of the
consequences to himself and others of the agreements made; and, fourth,
in definitions of the degree to which the interest of the society is involved
in any particular private agreement, the degree to which private contracts
bear on the interests of third parties or on those of the collectivity as a
whole.[3]

Durkheim postulated the existence of what he called organic solidarity
as a functional necessity underlying the institutionalization of contract.
This may be characterized as the integration of units, units which, in
the last analysis, are individual persons in roles, who are performing
qualitatively differentiated functions in the social system. The implication of such differentiation is that the needs of the unit cannot be met
solely by his own activities. By virtue of the specialization of his function,
the unit becomes dependent on the activities of others who must meet
the needs which are not covered by this specialized function. There is,
therefore, a special type of interdependence that is generated by this
functional differentiation. The prototype is the kind of division of labor
described by the economists. Clearly, Durkheim's conception is broader

3. Durkheim does not, of course, in his more general discussion, confine himself to
contract at the legal or other levels. He relates organic solidarity also to domestic, commercial, procedural, administrative, and constitutional law. Cf. *The Division of Labor
in Society*, p. 122.

than this. For example, he describes the differentiation of function between the sexes, in social as well as biological terms, as a case of the division of labor in his sense.

What, then, is indicated by "organic solidarity"? The most important problem in interpreting the meaning of the concept is to determine its relation to the conception of the *conscience collective*. Durkheim's primary interest is in the fact that units agree on norms because they are backed by values held in common, although the interests of the differentiated units must necessarily diverge. Durkheim's original definition of the *conscience collective* is as follows: "L'ensemble des croyances et des sentiments communs à la moyenne des membres d'une même société forme un système déterminé qui a sa vie propre; on peut l'appeler la conscience collective ou commune."[4] The keynote of this definition is, clearly, beliefs and sentiments that are held in common. This formula is essential, for it indicates that the problem of solidarity is located in the area of what may very broadly be called the motivational aspects of commitment to the society, and to conformity with the expectations institutionalized within it. Taken alone, however, it is too general to serve as more than a point of departure for an analysis of the problems of solidarity and hence of societal integration. Furthermore, Durkheim himself was seriously embarrassed by the problem of how to connect the *conscience collective* with the differentiation resulting from the division of labor.

It seems to me that Durkheim's formula needs to be further elaborated by two sets of distinctions. He himself made essential contributions to one of these, the distinction between mechanical and organic solidarity; but one of the main sources of difficulty in understanding his work is his relative neglect of the second set of distinctions, and his tendency to confuse it with the first. This second set concerns the levels of generality achieved by the cultural patterns—values, differentiated norms, collectivities, and roles—that have been institutionalized in a society. It also concerns the controls that articulate these levels and that determine the direction in which the controls operate. A discussion of the levels of generality of these four cultural patterns will provide a setting for a consideration of mechanical and organic solidarity and of the relations between them.

I think it is correct to say that in the course of his career Durkheim gradually crystallized and clarified a conviction that can be stated in terms more modern than he himself used: The structure of a society, or

4. *De la division du travail social* (Paris: Félix Alcan, 1893), p. 46.

of any human societal system, consists in (is not simply influenced by) patterns of normative culture[5] that are institutionalized in the social system and internalized (though not in identical ways) in the personalities of its individual members. The cultural patterns just outlined are the four different types of components of this structure. Elsewhere, they are referred to as "levels of generality of normative culture." Though all are institutionalized, each has a different relation to the structure and processes of the society. Societal values constitute the component which reaches the highest level of generality; for they are conceptions of the desirable society that are held in common by its members. Societal values are thus distinguished from other types of values—such as personal ones —in that the category of object evaluated is the social system and not personalities, organisms, physical systems, or cultural systems ("theories," for example).

The value system of the society is, then, the set of normative judgments held by the members of the society who define, with specific reference to their own society, what to them is a good society. In so far as this set of values is in fact held in common and is institutionalized, it is descriptive of the society as an empirical entity. This institutionalization is a matter of degree, however; for members of a going society will, to some extent, differ in their values even at the requisite level, and they will, to a certain degree, fail to act in accordance with the values they hold. But with all these qualifications, it is still correct to say that values held in common constitute the primary reference point for the analysis of a social system as an empirical system.[6]

The paramount value system is relevant to the description of the society as a whole, but it does not distinguish normative judgments which refer to differentiated parts or subsystems within the society. Therefore, when a difference of values is imputed to the two sexes, to regional groups, to class groups, and so on, one has gone from describing societal values to describing those that characterize another social system, one that should be treated analytically as a subsystem of the society of reference. When this step has been taken, it becomes essential to make another distinction, the distinction between value and differentiated norm.

5. The term "normative culture" will be used a number of times below. Here "normative" refers to any "level" of culture, the evaluative judgments of which govern or define standards and allocations at the level below. This usage is to be distinguished from those which refer to differentiated norms designating, in a particular system, one level in the hierarchy of normative culture.
6. Such a system of societal values may, of course, change over a period of time, but it is the most stable component of the social structure.

At the subsystem level, members of the society who do and who do not participate in the subsystem of reference have evaluative judgments which they apply to the qualities and performances of those members who do, as distinguished from those who do not, participate in it. These judgments are "specifications," that is, applications of the general principles of the common societal value system at a more concrete level. The expectations of behavior of those who are members of the subsystem are not the same as those of non-members. Thus, in the case of sex role, the values applying to the behavior of the two sexes are shared by both, but the norms that regulate that behavior apply differentially to the two sexes. In so far as a pattern of behavior is sex-specific, members of one sex group will conform with it, those of the other will not. This is to say that values are shared, presumptively, by all members of the most extensive relevant system; whereas norms are a function of the differentiation of socially significant behavior that is institutionalized in different parts of that system.

It follows from this that values as such do not involve a reference to a situation, or a reference to the differentiation of the units of the system in which they are institutionalized. Norms, on the other hand, make this differentiation explicit. In one respect, they are derived from the evaluative judgments that have been institutionalized in the value system; but independently of this component, they also include, as is clear in the case of legal systems, three other specifications. The first specifies the categories of units to which the norm applies; this is the problem of jurisdiction. The second specifies what the consequences will be to the unit that conforms and to the unit that does not conform to the requirements of the norm (variations in degree are, of course, possible); this is the problem of sanctions or enforcement. Finally, the third specifies that the meaning of the norm shall be interpreted in the light of the character and the situations of the units to which it applies; this constitutes the problem of interpretation, which is roughly equivalent to the appellate function in law. It should be noted that in this case the reference to the situation is confined to the one in which the unit acts vis-à-vis other units. It is thus intrasystemic. When the reference is to situations external to the system, the levels of collectivity and role structure, to be outlined later, must be brought into the picture.

Values, then, are the "normative patterns" that are descriptive of a positively evaluated social system. Norms are generalized patterns of expectation which define differentiated patterns of expectation for the differentiated kinds of units within a system. In a particular system, norms always stand at a lower level of cultural generality than do values. Put a little differently, norms can be legitimized by values, but not vice versa.

A collectivity stands at a still lower level in the hierarchy of the normative control of behavior. Subject both to the more general values of the system and to the norms regulating the behavior of the relevant differentiated types of units within the system, the normative culture of a collectivity defines and regulates a concrete system of coordinated activity that can at any given time be characterized by the commitments of specifically designated persons, and which can be understood as a specific system of collective goals in a specific situation. The functional reference of norms at the level of the collectivity is, then, no longer general, but is made specific in the particular goals, situations, and resources of the collectivity, including its "share" in the goals and resources of society. This specification of function, though it is of varying degree, emphasizes the fact that it is the goal of the collectivity which defines its level of concreteness, since the goal of a unit in a system is, in so far as the system is well integrated, the basis on which its primary function in the system is specified.

The normative character of a collective goal is precisely given by this specification of function in a system, but it is subject to given situational exigencies that are external to the system. This specification is not necessary for the definition of a norm, but it is essential for further specification at the level of the organization of the collectivity.

Collectivities constitute the essential operative units of social systems, to such an extent that where relations of cooperation and "solidarity" for a given functional unit goal do not exist within collectivities, and the function is performed by a single independent individual—by the independent artisan or professional practitioner, for example—it is legitimate to speak of this as the limiting case of the collectivity: it is a collectivity consisting of one member.

All social systems arise out of the interaction of human individuals as units. Hence the most important exigencies of the situation in which collectivities as units perform social functions are the conditions for effective performance by the constituent human individuals (including their command of physical facilities). But since the typical individual participates in more than one collectivity, the relevant structural unit is not the "total" individual or personality, but the individual in a role. In its normative aspect, then, a role may be thought of as the system of normative expectations for the performance of a participating individual in his capacity as a member of a collectivity. The role is the primary point of direct articulation between the personality of the individual and the structure of the social system.

Values, norms, and collective goals—all in some sense control, "govern," and "regulate" the behavior of individuals in roles. But only at the level of the role is the normative content of expectations specifically oriented to the exigencies presented by the personalities or "motives" of individuals (and categories of them differentiated by sex, age, level of education, place of residence, and the like) and by the organic and physical environment.

In their functioning, social systems are, of course, subject to still other exigencies. But such exigencies are not normative in the sense used in this discussion; they do not involve the orientation of persons to and through conceptions of what is desirable. Thus the sheer facts of the physical environment are simply there; they are not altered by any institutionalization of human culture, although they may, of course, be controlled through such human cultural media as technology. This control, however, involves values, norms, collectivities, and role-expectations; and, as part of the social structure, it should be analyzed in these terms.

Values, norms, collectivities, and roles are categories that are descriptive of the structural aspect of a social system only. In addition to such categories, it is necessary to analyze the system in functional terms in order to analyze processes of differentiation and the operation of these processes within a structure. Furthermore, process utilizes resources, carrying them through a series of stages of genesis, and either "consuming" them or incorporating and combining them into types of output or product, such as cultural change. The structure of institutionalized norms is the main point of articulation between these societal structures and the functional exigencies of the system. These exigencies, in turn, determine the mechanisms and categories of input and output relative to integration. Let us try to relate these considerations to the categories of mechanical and organic solidarity.

Durkheim's conception of mechanical solidarity is rooted in what I have called the system of common societal values. This is evident from the strong emphasis which he places on the relation of mechanical solidarity to the *conscience collective*. As a system of "beliefs and sentiments" that are held in common, Durkheim's *conscience collective* is more broadly defined than the system of societal values which I have given above. But it is certain that such a system is included in Durkheim's definition, and it can be argued that a system of values is the structural core of the system of beliefs and sentiments to which he refers. It should be clear, however, that Durkheim did not attempt systematically to distinguish and classify the components of the *conscience collective,* and this would seem to be essential if a satisfactory analysis of its relation to the problem of solidarity is to be made.

Such an analysis must do at least two things. In the first place, the value component must be distinguished from the others, that is, from cognitive (existential) beliefs, patterns of motivational commitment (these are close to Durkheim's "sentiments"), and patterns of legitimation of collective action (these will figure in the discussion presently). The second task involves the determination of the variations in the levels of generality and degrees of specificity of the components—of values, in particular—which eventuates in a scale corresponding to the differentiation of a society into numerous subsystems. Because of his failure to perform these two tasks, Durkheim was not able to be very exact about the relation of the *conscience collective* to mechanical solidarity, and was forced to resort to contrasting this relation with that of the *conscience collective* to organic solidarity—and this relation gave him considerable difficulty.

Mechanical solidarity is rooted in the common value component of the *conscience collective* and is an "expression" of it. Its relation to the other components is problematical. There is, however, another major aspect of mechanical solidarity, namely, its relation to the structure of the society as a collectivity. Every society is organized in terms of a paramount structure of the total system as a collectivity. In the highly differentiated modern society, this structure takes the form of governmental organization. In addition, there is, of course, an immensely complex network of lower-level collectivities, some of which are subdivisions of the governmental structure, while others are independent of it in various ways and degrees. The problem of mechanical solidarity arises wherever a collectivity is organized, but it is essential to understand what system is under consideration.

The focus of Durkheim's analysis of mechanical solidarity, in so far as it concerns the structure of the social system, lies, I suggest, in the relation between the paramount values of the society and its organization as a collectivity at the requisite level; that is, the governmental organization of the society where the system of reference is, as it is for Durkheim, the society as a whole. Mechanical solidarity is the integration of the common values of the society with the commitments of units within it to contribute to the attainment of collective goals—either negatively by refraining from action which would be felt to be disruptive of this function, or positively by taking responsibility for it.

This duality of reference is brought out with particular clarity in Durkheim's discussion of criminal law as an index or expression of mechanical solidarity. On the one hand, he makes reference to common "sentiments"; on the other, to obligations to the organized collectivity as such.[7] Also, since in all advanced societies government is the paramount agent for the application of coercion, Durkheim strongly emphasizes the role of the element of sanction in the repressive type of law. Two of the four primary functional references of a legal system noted above, legitimation and enforcement through sanctions, figure importantly in what Durkheim calls repressive law.

The preceding considerations account for the location of the phenomenon of mechanical solidarity with reference to the structure of the social system. This solidarity or integration of the system is brought about by the interplay of the system of common values, which legitimizes organization in the interest of collective goals with the commitments of units of the system (which are, in the last analysis, individual persons in roles) to loyalty and responsibility. This loyalty and responsibility are not only to the values themselves, but to the collectivity whose functioning is guided by those values and which institutionalizes them. This location in the social structure does not, however, tell us anything about the mechanisms by which the integration is generated.

Before approaching the question of the mechanisms that produce integration, it will be well to raise the corresponding question of structural location with respect to "organic solidarity." My suggestion is that, by contrast with the question of mechanical solidarity, this one does not concern the value system directly, but rather the system of institutionalized norms in relation to the structure of roles in the society. This is not putting it in Durkheim's own terms, for he did not use the concept of role that has become so important to sociological theory in the last generation. The importance of the reference to norms in his analysis is, however, entirely clear.

Furthermore, Durkheim's discussion is fully in accord with the dis-

7. "The acts that it [repressive law] prohibits and qualifies as crimes are of two sorts. Either they directly manifest very violent dissemblance between the agent who accomplishes them and the collective type, or else they offend the organ of the common conscience."—*The Division of Labor in Society,* p. 106. The context makes clear that by the "organ" Durkheim means the government.

tinction made previously between values and differentiated norms as structural components of the social system, since he so strongly emphasized the relation of organic solidarity to the differentiation of functions among units in the system, and specifically to the differentiation of expectations of behavior.[8]

Though he enumerated a number of other fields, it is also clear that there is, for Durkheim, a special relation between organic solidarity, contract, and the economic aspects of the organization of societies. This relation can, I think, provide the principal clue to the way in which roles are involved. Collectivities, it has been suggested previously, constitute the primary operative agencies for the performance of social function. The resources necessary for that performance consist, in turn, besides solidarity itself and the related patterns of "organization," in cultural resources, physical facilities, and human services. "Solidarity" cannot be treated as a component for Durkheim's purposes because it is his dependent variable; he is concerned with the conditions on which it depends. He does not treat cultural resources—knowledge, for example. He is careful, nevertheless, to take account of the role of physical facilities in discussing the institutionalization of property rights. His main concern, however, is with human services and the ways in which they can be integrated for the performance of social function.

The central problem involved here may be looked at, in the first instance, in a developmental setting. It is a general characteristic of "primitive" societies that the allocation of resources among their structurally significant units is overwhelmingly ascribed. This is most obvious in the economic sphere itself. The factors of production are controlled by units that do not have specialized economic primacy of function, and they are typically not transferable from one unit to another. Indeed, even products are seldom exchanged, and when they are, the transfer is likely to take place as a ceremonial exchange of gifts rather than in barter, as we understand it—to say nothing of market exchange. This is particularly true of labor, often thought to be the central factor of economic production.

The division of labor brings freedom from ascriptive ties regarding

8. There is, of course, a sense in which the criminal law also lays down norms. Essentially, these norms concern the minimum standards of behavior which are considered acceptable on the part of members of the society—regardless of their differentiated functions—who are not disqualified by mental incapacity, and so on. In a highly differentiated society, however, the largest body of norms increasingly concerns the relations between differentiated functions in the fields Durkheim enumerated; namely, contract, family life, commerce, administration, and the constitutional structure of the collectivity.

the utilization of consumable goods and services and the factors of production themselves. The structural location of organic solidarity thus concerns the dual problem of how the processes by which the potentially conflicting interests that have been generated can be reconciled without disruptive conflict (this leads, of course, into the Hobbesian problem), and of how the societal interest in efficient production can be protected and promoted.

Every society must, as a prerequisite of its functioning, presume some integration of the interest of units with those of the society—elsewhere I have called this the "institutional integration of motivation."[9] But by itself this is not enough. One path to further development is to use the organs of the collective attainment of goals as the agencies for defining and enforcing integration or solidarity of this type. This involves a near fusion of mechanical and organic bases of solidarity of the sort that is most conspicuous in socialistic economies. An independent basis of integration can develop, however, from the institutionalization of systems of norms and mechanisms that without centralized direction permit the allocation of fluid resources to proceed in a positively integrated manner.

This set of norms and mechanisms is organized in terms of two complementary reference points. One of these is the sociological reference to economic analysis and interests, the process by which generalized disposability of resources builds up. This concerns above all the institutionalization of contract, of property, and of the disposability of labor service through employment in occupational roles. Property and labor then become generalized resources. They can be allocated and controlled through processes which establish functionally specific claims, rather than through prior (and, therefore, in all likelihood, functionally irrelevant) bases of ascriptive claim, such as membership in a common kinship unit. This, of course, involves some sort of process of exchange among functionally differentiated units in the system.

It is an essential aspect of Durkheim's argument that this generalizability and fluid disposability of resources requires more than a freeing from irrelevant, usually ascriptive constraints. It also requires a positive institutionalization of correlative obligations and rights which are defined in terms of a normative structure. From the point of view of the definition of resources, this type of normative regulation becomes the more imperative the further removed the ultimate utilization of the resource is

9. Talcott Parsons, *The Social System* (Glencoe, Ill.: Free Press of Glencoe, Illinois, 1951), pp. 36-45.

from what may be thought of as a "natural" to-be-taken-for-granted set of rights to this utilization. From the point of view of the resource, then, a dual process is necessary: First, the resource must be "generalized"— this involves freeing it from ascriptive controls; and, second, the positive obligation to enter into the generalized allocative system must be established. Thus in a primarily ascriptive society, the equivalent of what are occupational roles in our own were filled on the basis of kinship obligations, as in the case of a son who follows his father as the proprietor and cultivator of the land held by the continuing kinship unit. In our own society, to train for an occupation in which one can compete in the labor market, and to be willing to take one's chances on finding satisfactory employment constitute a positively institutionalized obligation of the normal adult male, and of a considerable number of the members of the other sex. Therefore, there is, in a sense, a "speculative" production of labor power which precedes any specification of its channels of use. This is, of course, even more true of the control of physical facilities.

At the same time, there must also be a series of mechanisms which can determine the patterns in which such a generalized resource is utilized. As the division of labor becomes more highly developed, the proportion of such resources which are utilized in collectivities that have specific functions becomes greater. These collectivities command monetary resources which can in turn be used to contract for labor services and to provide necessary physical facilities. The institutionalization of contract is the normative system which offers access to such resources— whatever the function of the organization itself may be. The institution of property, then, regulates monetary resources and physical facilities; the institution of occupation controls human services.

It is important to note here the complex relation which exists between the economic and non-economic aspects of the constellation of factors that I am outlining. Economic production as such is only one of the primary societal functions served by the processes of production and mobilization of fluid resources through the institutionalization of contract, markets, money, property, and occupational roles. Indeed, any major function may be promoted in that way—education, health care, scientific research, and governmental administration. There are only certain special limiting cases, like the family and certain aspects of the political process, which cannot be "bureaucratized" in this sense.

At the same time, it is correct to say that the mechanisms involved here—regardless of the ultimate function that they subserve in any particular case—are primarily economic; namely, contract, markets, money, and the like. We must exercise great care, therefore, when using such a term as economic in this kind of analysis.

The generalized disposability of resources, then, is one major aspect of the functional complex which is institutionalized through organic solidarity. The other aspect concerns the standards and mechanisms by which their allocation among alternative claimant units of the social structure is worked out. Here it is clear that, within the institutional framework of contract, property, and occupation, the primary direct mechanisms concern the structuring of markets and the institutionalization of money.

This brings us back to the subtle ways in which conventional economic and non-economic elements are involved. The market may be regarded as the structural framework for the allocation of disposable resources in so far as the mechanism of this allocation is primarily freely contractual at the level of the operative organization or collectivity. Two other types of mechanism must be distinguished from this one, however. The first is administrative allotment, which is a "free" disposal of resources by those who supposedly enjoy nearly full control of them. Theoretically, this would be the case if the economy were fully socialized, for a central planning body would simply make decisions and assign budgetary quotas—indeed it might also directly distribute labor and physical facilities. The second mechanism involves negotiation between the higher agencies which hold the resources and their prospective users in such a way that political power plays a prominent part in determining the outcome whether or not governmental structures are prominently involved. An example of this would be the distribution through legislative action of public works benefits on the basis of regional and local interests, a procedure which often involves a good deal of "log-rolling."

Empirically, there is shading-off between these types. Typologically, however, in the market the bargaining powers of the contracting partners are approximately equal; neither the holders nor the utilizers of resources are simply "told" where they are to go or what they are to get; and the degree of power held by the higher level of the goal-directed organization of the relevant collectivity structure is not the decisive mechanism in the process of allocation. The market is an institutionalized mechanism which neutralizes both these potential mechanisms of allocation in a number of areas, preventing them from being the primary determinants of more detailed allocations. This means essentially that there is a hierarchy of allocative mechanisms, whose relations to each other are ordered by institutionalized norms. Among these norms are those which define the areas within which, and the occasions on which, the more "drastic" controls may and may not be allowed to supersede the "freer" mechanism of the market. Thus the taxing power of government determines a compulsory allocation of monetary resources; and certain allocations are subject to legislative control in that limitations are placed on the freedom of individual units to contract for them at will.

However, it is clearly in accord with Durkheim's views of organic solidarity to point out that within the market sphere freedom is balanced and controlled by complex sets of institutionalized norms, so that the freedoms themselves and the rights and obligations associated with them are defined in terms of such institutionalized norms. There are, in this area, two main categories of such institutionalized structures. One concerns the institutionalization of the monetary mechanism itself, the definition of the sphere of its legitimate use, and, of course, the limits of this sphere. The other concerns the institutionalization of conditions under which market transactions involving different subcategories of resources may be entered into. Let us take up the latter class of norms first.

In general terms, norms of the highest order in a modern society clearly have the status of formal legal rules and principles. They are subject to the legislative power, and the task of interpreting and administering them is the responsibility of the courts of law. For organic solidarity, as noted above, the complex of contract, property, and occupation is central; whereas leadership, authority, and what I have elsewhere called regulation are central to mechanical solidarity.

Freedom of contract, then, includes the freedom to define the conditions and limitations of the various terms which—as I have previously set forth—are involved in a contractual system with respect to the content of agreements, the means of securing assent, the scope of responsibility, and the societal interest. At both the legal and informal levels, then, these conditions and limitations vary in accordance with the societal functions performed by the contracting units, the various aspects of the situations in which they operate, and other similar considerations. Thus a private relationship between a physician and a patient, established to serve the interest of the patient's health, is sanctioned. However, the offering of certain types of health service is restricted, partly by law and partly by informal institutionalization, and may be performed only by licensed and "adequately trained" physicians; and the acceptance of such services is, if it is legitimate, restricted, in a more informal sense, to persons who are really "sick." There is abundant evidence that there is wide area in which illness is not so much an objective "condition" as a socially defined role.

Therefore, the problem of the content of contractual relations involves differentiating between role-categories that are regarded as the legitimate bearers of various social functions and those that are not. A consumer or client may contract for a very wide range of goods and services, but he is not completely free to choose the agencies with which he will contract, since institutional norms define the functions which certain agencies may perform.

In addition, the ways in which the terms of the contract are settled are institutionalized in various ways, and this influences the structure of the market. Economists have been particularly concerned with one type, the "commercial" market, where prices are arrived at on the basis of "competition," and where there is an institutionalized expectation that the right of the purveying agency to continue in operation is a function of its ability to meet expenses and to show a profit. Furthermore, it is the customer's expectation that the price he pays will cover the full cost of what he purchases. However, the structure of the market in which a large number of governmental, professional, and other services are purveyed, is quite different. Although a service may be entirely free in the monetary sense, the conditions of eligibility may be sharply defined, as in the case of those regulating admission to public hospitals. Or, as is often the case in private medical practice, there may be a sliding scale of costs, so that one participant in the contract, the patient—contrary to what is expected of the customer in the commercial market—fulfills only part of his obligation in that the fee he pays covers a portion of the costs of performing the service contracted for which ranges from far less than average unit cost to very much more.

Furthermore, there is the problem of the scope of the responsibility involved in such a relation. The Spencerian version of the idea of contract tended to assume that the question of the participants' abilities to "deliver" presented no complicated problem. The typical economic exchange in which the buyer has sufficient money and the seller sufficient goods is taken as the prototype. But this is by no means always the situation. As an illustration, let us again take a certain type of professional relationship. A sick person cannot be held responsible for ending his deplored condition simply by making a voluntary effort: his helplessness is a primary criterion by which his need of, and right to, professional service is determined. But he is responsible for recognizing his helplessness and for actively cooperating with therapeutic agencies in bringing about his recovery. These agencies, in turn, though their role may be defined in terms of technical competence, must recognize a wide variation in the capacities of individuals so that if there is a failure in certain cases, the physician is not held responsible, provided he has done his best. Another good example is found in education where because of the youth of the ignorant person, ignorance is not considered culpable. Nor is a child expected to educate himself without the help of schools. He is, however, expected to work hard in acquiring his education within the framework of the school. And some children are harder to educate than others, and failures are not treated as being always or wholly the teacher's fault. There are elaborately institutionalized norms covering fields such as these.

The protection of the interest of society in contractual relations is more diffusely institutionalized; it is, in a sense, an aspect of all the norms in this area. At the legal level, however, there are a number of provisions which enable the courts and other governmental agencies that represent the public interest to intervene in order to prevent or modify such arrangements. Because of its very nature, the institutionalization of a contractual system involves the imposition of a whole system of limitations on the powers of government. But the residual opportunities for private interests to exploit their freedom against the rest of the society require the maintenance of a delicately balanced equilibrium of integration.

The monetary mechanism is essential because, in the first place, the division of labor cannot develop very far if all exchanges are restricted to the level of barter. In a fully developed system, money has four primary functions. It serves, first, as a measure of the economic value of resources and products. It is in this connection that we speak of the gross national product as a monetary sum. Second, it serves as a standard for the rational allocation of resources, for comparing cost and outcome. Only in the "business" sector, where productive function in the economic sense has primacy, is the monetary standard the primary one applied. But in other functional areas, too, such as education or health, monetary cost is a very essential evaluative mechanism in that it is, from the point of view of the unit, the basis for evaluating one major component in the conditions necessary to accomplish whatever goal is involved, and is, from the point of view of the system at large, a measure of the sacrificed uses to which the resources in question might have been put.

It is thus essential to discriminate profitability as a measure of the worthwhileness of a function from the use of monetary cost as one component of the conditions that must be weighed in arriving at a judgment of worthwhileness. The capacity somehow to cover monetary cost, the ability to raise the money somehow, is, of course, a necessary limiting condition of those functions which require resources that are acquired through the market.

In serving as a measure and standard, money does not circulate; nothing changes hands. In performing its other two functions, however, money is a medium of exchange. In the first of these, money is an essential facility wherever the attainment of goals is dependent on resources accessible through market channels. Not only is it necessary to have it, but, it must be noted, in a highly developed market system, there is an extraordinarily wide range of choices open to the unit that possesses sufficient funds. The other mediating function of money is to serve as a reward. Here the reference is in the nature of the case comparative and relative; what counts is the amount of monetary income received by one unit or resource as compared with that received by another. It is this function of money that is the primary focus of the regulation of the process of allocation of resources, in so far as this is the result of market transactions. The basic principle is the economic one: A resource will flow to that one of the situations in which it is utilized that offers the highest relative reward, the reward being, in this case, monetary.

Here again it is essential, however, to insist on the same basic distinction which was made in connection with the standards of allocation. Money is not the sole component of the complex of rewards. It has primacy over other components only when the function of economic production has primacy over other functions, that is, in the "business" sector of the organizational and occupational system. It is essentially for this reason that the monetary remuneration for human services in that sector is higher than other sectors such as government, education, and so on. But even where other components of reward—political power, integrative acceptance or solidarity, or cultural prestige—have primacy within a given subsystem, it is essential that the monetary remuneration correspond to the quality of the services performed, as determined on the basis of the dominant criteria for that subsystem. In the academic profession, for example, contrary to the situation in the business occupations, the amount of one's income is not a valid measure of one's relative prestige in the general occupational system. Within the profession, however, and especially within the same faculty, there is strong pressure to establish a correspondence between professional competence and the salaries paid. Failure to do so is a prime source of integrative strain.

I have taken the space to discuss the relation among the allocation of fluid resources, the institutionalization of contract, property, and occupation, and the market and money in some detail because such an analysis is more comprehensive than any Durkheim was in a position to give, and thus provides a larger setting in which to evaluate the true importance of his basic insights about organic solidarity. His crucial insight is that there must be, in this area, a whole complex of institutionalized norms as a condition of the stability of a functionally differentiated system. In *De la division du travail social*, Durkheim did not go very far in analyzing the motivations underlying adherence to such norms. But he was entirely clear on one central point, namely, that this adherence on the part of the acting unit in the system could not be motivated primarily by considerations of expedient utility. This is the basic reason why the concept of the *conscience collective* as consisting in "beliefs and sentiments held in common" is of such central importance. In his later work, he took three major steps bearing on this question of motivation. Before attempting to outline these, however, it is well to discuss briefly the relation of the *conscience collective* to organic solidarity and the relation of organic and mechanical solidarity to each other.

Concerning the first of these two problems, Durkheim seems to have been genuinely confused, for he failed to clarify the structural distinction between values and norms, which I have presented earlier, and did not see that this distinction applies and is relevant equally to organic and mechanical solidarity. Instead, he got bogged down in the identification of mechanical solidarity with a lack of differentiation of structure, and hence with the similarity of roles which are personal expressions of the community of beliefs and sentiments. Consequently, he had no clear criteria for defining the relation of functionally differentiated norms to the *conscience collective*. Durkheim's treatment of the conception of the "dynamic density" of a social system and its relation to competition, represents, as Schnore has pointed out,[10] a valid attempt to solve the problem of the processes of structural differentiation, but he did not succeed in linking it to his master concept of the *conscience collective*.

It is now possible to state this fundamental relation more adequately: As noted above, the crucial component of the *conscience collective* is

10. Cf. Leo F. Schnore, "Social Morphology and Human Ecology," *American Journal of Sociology*, LXIII (1958), 620-34.

common societal values. Commitment to such values, carefully interpreted with reference to the object concerned—that is, the society as such—and to the level of generality or specification, is one major component of the general phenomenon of institutionalization. Institutionalization is, in turn, the primary basis, at the level of the integration of the social system, of Durkheim's "solidarity." But with respect to any fundamental function of the social system, values must be specified in terms of their relevance to that particular function. Furthermore, values must be brought to bear on the legitimation of the differentiated institutionalized norms that are necessary to regulate behavior in the area of that function—to regulate it, on the one hand, in relation to the concrete exigencies under which it operates, and, on the other, in relation to the interest of the society as a system. Legitimation itself, however, is not enough; in addition, there must be the functions of defining jurisdiction, of defining and administering sanctions, and of interpreting the norms themselves.

This basic complex of relationships and functions can be quite clearly worked out for the division of labor as an economic phenomenon and for the institutions clustering around it. This complex was Durkheim's primary reference; and, except for the fact that his formulation of its relation to the *conscience collective* is ambiguous, he made an excellent start on analyzing it. But he did not see that the properties of the contractual complex are directly paralleled by those of the complex involving mechanical solidarity. I have suggested that this parallel primarily concerns the relations between common values and the institutionalization of political function in the society. Here also, the values must be specified at a concrete level in order to legitimize not only society in the broadest sense, but also the type of organization which is institutionalized in it for the attainment of collective goals. This organization is, however, a differentiated functional area which in certain fundamental respects is parallel to, or cognate with, that of the mobilization of fluid resources. Furthermore, it involves differentiated structures within itself at the norm, collectivity, and role levels. Hence the relation of values to norms is essentially the same in this area as in the economic. The norms must be legitimated, but, in addition, jurisdictions must be defined, sanctions specified, and norms interpreted. The *conscience collective* does not perform these functions directly or automatically. The differentiated normative complex which centers on the institutionalization of leadership and authority parallels the complex which centers on contract, property, and occupational role in the economic area. Power is a measure and medium that in those respects which are relevant is parallel to money.[11]

Durkheim's treatment involves a further complication, namely, the problem of evolutionary sequence. He made two crucially important points in this connection. The first is that the development of the patterns of organic solidarity that are connected with an extensive division of labor presupposes the existence of a system of societal integration characterized by mechanical solidarity. The second is that the economic division of labor and an elaborated and differentiated governmental organization develop concomitantly. It is not a case of one's developing at the expense of the other.

Sound as these two insights were, Durkheim's association of mechanical solidarity with a lack of structural differentiation inclined him toward identifying this association with primitiveness in an evolutionary sense, and prevented him from making the essential connection between common values and the legitimation of the political order and organization in a more differentiated, modern type of society. The relation of modern political institutions to solidarity—very much like that of economic institutions to solidarity—was simply left hanging in the air.

I should like to suggest, therefore, a refinement of Durkheim's classification. If organic solidarity and mechanical solidarity are correlative terms, one should refer to the type of solidarity which focuses on the legitimation of political institutions, and the other to that type which focuses on economic institutions. Broadly speaking, we may say that, although the situation varies substantially with the type of social structure, both exist simultaneously in parts of the same social system, parts that can be distinguished on the basis of structure and through analysis; and there should be no general tendency for one to replace the other. The solidarity which exists prior to the development of any of the higher levels of social differentiation is not the same thing as this "political" type. The latter is closer to the principal referent of Durkheim's mechanical solidarity, but I should prefer another term—"diffuse solidarity," for ex-

11. Unfortunately, space does not permit developing this line of analysis further. Several statements, which, though brief and incomplete, are somewhat more extensive than the one found here, will be found in Talcott Parsons, "Authority, Legitimation and Political Process," in Authority, ed. Carl J. Friedrich (Cambridge, Mass.: Harvard University Press, 1958), and Talcott Parsons, " 'Voting' and the Equilibrium of the American Political System," in American Voting Behavior, ed. Eugene Burdick and Arthur J. Brodbeck (Glencoe, Ill.: Free Press of Glencoe, Illinois, 1958), Chapter 8, this volume. Max Weber's treatment of authority constitutes an essential complement to Durkheim's of mechanical solidarity.

ample. It is the common matrix out of which *both* t
emerged by a process of differentiation.

Durkheim seems to have faced a very common difficulty
with the processes of differentiation. When a component of a sy
tains the same name at a later, more highly differentiated phase in
development of the system that it had at an earlier, less differentiate
one, the component carrying the original name will have less importance
in the later phase. This follows inevitably from the fact that in the earlier
phase it may have designated one of, say, four cognate components, and
in the later phase one of eight. This diminishing of importance is often
attributed to "a loss of functions" or "a decline in strength" on the part of
the component named. Good examples in contemporary Western society
are "family" and "religion."[12] These names have been used throughout
the successive phases of our development, but the components they have
designated have not remained cognate. The modern urban family whose
function of economic production has been transferred to occupational
organizations is not cognate with the peasant household which is a principal unit of production, in addition to being, like the modern one, a
unit for the rearing of children and the regulation of personality. In its
capacity as a unit of production, the peasant family is, in fact, a "family
firm," but the term "firm" is usually not applied to it.

One qualification of this argument, touching upon the hierarchical
ordering of functions in social systems, should be made. This is that political organization, within an institutionalized framework of order, must
indeed precede, in the developmental sequence, the emergence of a
highly differentiated market type of economy. Hence there is some empirical justification, even within the framework I have sketched, for
Durkheim's saying that mechanical solidarity precedes organic solidarity.

As previously noted, in *De la division du travail social* Durkheim had
much to say about the role of institutionalized norms but little about the
character of the motivation underlying commitment to values and to
conformity with norms. However, his clear insight that the operation of
the "rational pursuit of self-interest" as interpreted in utilitarian and
economic theory does not offer an explanation of this commitment, pro-

12. I have dealt with these two cases in, respectively, *Family, Socialization and Interaction Process* (Glencoe, Ill.: Free Press of Glencoe, Illinois, 1956), Chap. i, and "Some
Reflections on Religious Organization in the United States," *Daedalus,* LXXXVII
(1958). This, and the paper from *Authority* cited in n. 11 above, are included in the
collection of my essays published under the title *Structure and Process in Modern
Societies* (Glencoe, Ill.: Free Press of Glencoe, Illinois, 1960).

vided a setting for approaching the problem. In his earlier phases, Durkheim tended to be content with the formula of "exteriority and constraint" in an interpretation which treated norms as though they were simply among the "facts of life" in the situation of the individual, a formula that did not help to solve the fundamental difficulty presented by utilitarianism. In *Le suicide,* however, and in his work on the sociology of education, he took two important steps beyond this position that I shall sketch briefly.

The first is his discovery and partial development of the idea of the internalization of values and norms. The second is the discrimination he makes, with special reference to the problem of the nature of modern "individualism" between two ranges of variation. One of these concerns types of institutionalized value-norm complexes, and is exemplified by the distinction between egoism and altruism. The other concerns the types of relations that the individual can have to whatever norms and values are institutionalized. Here the discrimination between "egoism" and "anomie" is crucial; it is parrallel to that between "altruism" and "fatalism." I shall briefly take up each in turn.

Concerning the internalization of values and norms, we may say that, within certain limits, actual behavior in the economic and political fields can be relatively well interpreted in terms of the process by which the individual adapts himself rationally to the existence of the norms and the sanctions attached to them, so that they simply become a part of the "facts of life." Durkheim saw clearly that the existence and functional indispensability of the institutionalization of these norms is independent of the interests of the units, but he did not have a theory to explain, in terms of motivation, the process by which institutions are established and maintained. His "sociologistic positivism"[13] prevented his formulating such a theory.

Durkheim was led to make his study of suicide by a paradox: According to utilitarian theory, a rising standard of living should bring about a general increase in "happiness"; however, concomitant with the certain rise in the standard of living in Western countries, there was a marked rise in the suicide rate. Why was it that as people became happier, more of them killed themselves?

It is not necessary to review here Durkheim's famous marshalling of facts and his analysis of them. What concerns us is that the decisive breakthrough in solving the paradox came about with his working out of

13. Talcott Parsons, *The Structure of Social Action* (New York: McGraw-Hill Book Co., 1937), Chaps. viii-ix.

the concept of anomie. To be sure, anomie was only one of the four components in his analysis of the reasons underlying variations in the suicide rate, but it is the decisive theoretical one in the present context.

The older view, which the early Durkheim shared, saw the goals of the action of the individual as located within his own personality, and saw social norms, which were "exterior" to him, as located in society, which was a "reality *sui generis.*" Because they were located in two different systems, the goals of the individual and the norms of society were dissociated from each other. Durkheim's concept of anomie was a formulation of his great insight that this dissociation was untenable, that the goals of the individual could not be treated as being independent of the norms and values of the society, but were, in fact, "given meaning," that is, legitimized, by these values. They must, therefore, belong to the same system. If personal goals were part of the personality, then values and norms, the *conscience collective,* must also be part of the personality. At the same time, Durkheim could not abandon the doctrine of the independence of institutional norms from the "individual." This was the very core of his conception of solidarity, and to abandon it would have meant reverting to the utilitarian position. Hence the only solution was the conception of the interpenetration of personality and social system, the conception that it must be true, in some sense, that values and norms were parts of the "individual consciousness," and were, at the same time, analytically independent of "the individual." In the earlier stages, Durkheim attempted to solve this problem by the conception that there were two "consciousnesses" within the same personality, but gradually he tended to abandon this view.

It is noteworthy that Durkheim, working in sociology, discovered essentially the same basic phenomenon of internalization and interpenetration as did Freud in his study of the personality, and that the same discovery was made independently by Charles Horton Cooley and George Herbert Mead. This convergence is, in my opinion, one of the great landmarks in the development of modern social science.

To restate Durkheim's main point concerning the operation of anomie: An individual does not commit suicide primarily because he lacks the "means" to accomplish his goals, but because his goals cannot be meaningfully integrated with the expectations which have been institutionalized in values and norms. The factors responsible for this malintegration may be social, cultural, or psychological in any combination, but the crucial point of strain concerns the meaningfulness of situations and of alternatives of action. This problem of meaning could not arise if norms and values were merely parts of the external situation and not of the actual beliefs and sentiments of the individual.

Durkheim left many problems connected with the clarification and interpretation of anomie unresolved, but his concept clearly pointed the way to a theory of the problem of social control that was not susceptible to his own criticism of utilitarianism, and could, when linked to modern psychological insight into the personality, lead to a theory of the motivation underlying conformity and deviation, and hence to a theory of the mechanisms by which solidarity is established and maintained.

On psychological grounds, it can be said that since internalized values and norms, as well as some of the components of goals, are involved in the motivation to conformity, certain crucial components of that motivation, and of the mechanisms by which it is established, maintained, and restored, are not fully or directly attributable to "reason." In other words, it is not enough merely to make clear to the actor what the situation is and what the consequences of alternative courses of action are likely to be; for the mechanisms and components of motivation, and the components of the mechanisms of social control that mirror the various aspects of this motivation, are non-rational. This puts the mechanisms of social control in a class that is different from that of the market, the ordinary exercise of political leadership and power, of legislation and of the administration—in its higher judicial aspects—of the legal system.

Those aspects of illness that can be associated with "psychic" factors, and the corresponding features of the therapeutic process that treats them, can serve as a prototype of this kind of mechanism and can be systematically related to the processes of interaction that are involved in the socialization of the child.[14] It is, however, equally clear that there is need for an elaboration of theory in this field that is parallel to that which I have previously outlined for the problem area of organic solidarity in so far as it concerns economic institutions and markets. Clearly, not all social control that is oriented to motivation concerns illness and therapy. For example, it seems very likely that the practice of law has cognate functions over a considerable area in our own society. Lawyers, however, are not therapists. The subsystem of the society that presents problems of social control to which lawyers are relevant is not an individual personality, as is the one to which physicians are relevant, but a system that involves two or more parties in their relations to the normative system which regulates all of them. Hence there is more than one attorney, and there are courts. Here the analogue of anomie is a situation in which

14. Parsons, *The Social System*, Chap. vii.

norms, and possibly the values that lie behind them, are not sufficiently well defined to place clients in a meaningful situation for action so that the pressure of this situation tends to motivate them to act "irrationally." This need not, however, imply that they have psychopathological personalities. Again it is the relational system, not the individual, which needs straightening out. It seems to me that Durkheim's own treatment of religious ritual provides another example, on which I shall remark briefly later.

It should also be noted that in following up this line of reasoning in the years following the publication of *Le suicide,* Durkheim made, in his work on education, the first major contribution to the sociological analysis of the socialization of the child.[15] It was in this connection that he was able to clarify more fully his theory of the nature of the internalization of values and norms by redefining constraint as the exercise of moral authority through the *conscience* of the individual. In this way, it became clear that the moral component of the *conscience collective* is social: first, in that it is made up of values that are common to, and shared by, the members of the society; second, in that through the process of socialization the new members of the society undergo a process by which these values are internalized; and, third, in that there are special mechanisms which reinforce the commitment to the values thus made in ways that involve the non-rational layers of the personality structure, so that deviation is counteracted by curative mechanisms. With this definition, Durkheim provided a new understanding of the operation of the social system—one which was scarcely within the purview of the Durkheim of *De la division du travail social.*

The other main contribution of *Le suicide* to the present discussion is the conception of what may be called "institutionalized individualism," at the center of which is Durkheim's concept of *égoïsme* as distinguished from anomie. This is an extension of the basic insight of *De la division du travail social,* but here Durkheim applies it in an altogether novel context and links it with the problems of social control just discussed.

Utilitarianism and with it the methodological individualism (verging on reductionism) of our intellectual tradition have tended to interpret the emphasis placed on the sphere of freedom and the expected independent achievement of the unit of a system as meaning that the unit is

15. Most notably in *L'Education morale* (Paris: Félix Alcan, 1923), and in the volume of essays, *Education and Sociology,* trans. Sherwood Fox ([1922] Glencoe, Ill.: Free Press of Glencoe, Illinois, 1956).

free from the controls of the system. It has thus reduced the importance of the integration of the system, whether positively or negatively valued. Spencerian individualism was the negation of social control in the present sense of this concept.

There is, of course, an obvious sense in which this is true, for immediate control by direct authority is incompatible with individual freedom. But there is another and deeper sense in which it is not true. An institutionalized order in which individuals are expected to assume great responsibility and strive for high achievement, and in which they are rewarded through socially organized sanctions of such behavior, cannot be accounted for by postulating the lessening of all aspects of institutionalized control. Instead, such an order, with its common values, its institutionalized norms, its sanctions and media, its mechanisms of social control, represents a particular mode of institutional structuring. It emphatically does not represent anomie, which is the weakening of control in the sense of the weakening of solidarity.

The classic empirical formulation of this point in Le suicide is in connection with the Protestant-Catholic differential. The Catholic is, in matters of religion, subjected to the direct control of the authorities of his church: he must accept official dogma on penalty of excommunication; he must accept the sacramental authority of the priest in the matter of his own salvation, and so on. The Protestant church as a collectivity does not exercise this kind of authority. A Protestant is free of these types of control. But he is not free to choose whether or not to accept such controls, for he may not, if he wishes to remain a good Protestant, relinquish his freedom to accept religious responsibility imposed on him in his direct relation to God. The obligation to accept such responsibility is legitimized by the common values of the Protestant group and is translated into norms governing behavior.

Largely for ideological reasons, this basic insight is still far from being fully assimilated into the thinking of social scientists. But there are few of Durkheim's contributions which do more in relating the theoretical approach to the analysis of social systems, to the empirical interpretation of the major features of the modern type of society.

This problem brings us around to another very important link between the two dominant themes in Durkheim's original treatment of the problems of social integration; namely, the relation between organic and mechanical solidarity. Clearly, there is a relation between the egoistic factor in suicide and organic solidarity, and between the altruistic factor and mechanical solidarity. This becomes manifest in the association between areas of the social structure in which the collectivity is tightly integrated (such as the army) and there is a high incidence of altruistic suicide, and those in which market relations predominate (the professions and business, for example) and there is a high frequency of egoistic suicide. A parallel correlation may be seen between types of societies.

However, correlations such as these raise the question of the kinds of mechanisms which are associated with the different problems of integration. Very early Durkheim emphasized the importance of the definitions of certain acts as criminal and of prescriptions for punishing them as mechanisms that reinforce mechanical solidarity. In *De la division du travail social,* he used this reinforcement primarily as a foil to highlight the contrast with the functioning of civil law in relation to organic solidarity. In this connection, his primary reference was clearly to the solidarity of the collectivity as the main structural focus of the problem of integration.

It is noteworthy that, in his last period, Durkheim came around to a field that is, in terms of the above analysis, very closely related to the problems of mechanical solidarity, but this time the relation is seen from the point of view of values rather than from that of their political implementation. I am referring to his analysis of religion in its relation to society in *Les formes élémentaires de la vie religieuse.* There are many notable features in this work, but the one of special interest here is the treatment of religious ritual as a mechanism for the reinforcement of social solidarity.

The most important link between this work and *De la division du travail social,* written twenty years earlier, is Durkheim's continuing concern with the *conscience collective.* However, in the earlier work this concept was used merely as a reference point for the analysis of the economic level of social differentiation, and the attendant problems of integration. In the later one, by contrast, the question of the primary role of the *conscience collective* in the social system as a whole comes to the center of the stage. As Durkheim treats it, ritual of the communal sort is the direct expression of the commitment of members of the collectivity—that is, the highest-level relevant social system—to the values which they hold in common. But it is, at the same time, more than just an expression of them, for it is a way in which through "dramatization" these commitments may be renewed and any tendencies to weaken them may be forestalled.

It is quite clear that religious ritual as it is conceived in this work is not directly concerned with the formulation and implementation of norms, but rather with the "inward," the internalized aspects of the systems of values and norms, with their direct involvement in the structure of personalities. Moreover, it concerns their relation to motivation in the context of the non-rational components referred to above. Therefore, in this last major phase of his work, Durkheim was clearly building on the results he had attained in his studies of suicide and education. But here for the first time he regarded the maintenance of the institutionalized value system in the society as a focus of social process, rather than as a point of reference from which to analyze other structures and processes.

There is, at the same time, an interesting return to his original reference points, for he explicitly takes up the problem of the role of the *conscience collective*—that is, of collective values—at the level of the value system, rather than at that of the structure of the concrete collectivity and of the obligations to it. Therefore, he ends up placing his original problem of organic solidarity within a more general framework of order, one in which there is a political organization which can enforce a uniform criminal law, but in which there is also a system of values which can legitimize norms that are independent of the particular political order and its "organs."

This was a major step in the differentiation of the theoretical components of the hydra-headed problem of social integration. It is perhaps significant, however, that Durkheim dealt with the problem of religious ritual in empirical detail only in the context of the primitive religions. I interpret this to mean that the old problem of the relation between the genetic and the analytical aspects of the problem of discrimination of components still plagued him. In a way, he simply drove the problem of mechanical solidarity back to a more generalized level, seeking the "origins" of repressive law in the religious commitments that are ritualized in the great tribal ceremonies. In so doing, he contributed enormously to our understanding of processes of social control at this level, an understanding that definitely included their motivational reference. But by virtue of his unfortunate confusion, he obscured rather than illuminated the problem of the relations of solidarity to the structural differentiation of modern society, the analysis of which was his original point of reference.

There is almost complete agreement that Durkheim was one of a very small company of sociological theorists who, during a critical phase in the development of the discipline, penetrated to deeper level of analysis than had been reached by any of their predecessors and who formulated the main problems on which we have been working ever since. The subject of this paper is, I think, the focal center of Durkheim's contribution to theory. He was the theorist par excellence of the problem area of social integration. He was more concerned with the primary core of the social system itself than with the relations of that system to those that border it—culture, personality, and the organism in the physical environment. In addition, he was not, in a sense, greatly concerned with problems of social structure. Though he always retained an interest in making comparative studies, he did not attempt to probe the crucial problems of comparative morphological classification so deeply as did his contemporary Max Weber.

Durkheim's central problem, the solution of which he pursued with rare persistence, was to determine the major axes around which the integrative functions and processes of a society are organized. His analysis was marred by many crudities, and there are many aspects of it which have become obsolete; but his criticism of the utilitarian tradition and his conceptions of the *conscience collective*, and of mechanical and organic solidarity—though raising many problems of interpretation—served both him and the discipline well.

The important thing about these conceptions is that they cut across the lines of the conventional structural analysis of social systems, which broke them down into political, economic, religious, and other similar categories. Only with a conceptualization such as Durkheim's was it possible to approach the problems of social integration on a level that is general enough to permit the establishment of a new theoretical orientation. The fact that he succeeded in developing this conceptualization is the basis of Durkheim's stature as a theorist.

Durkheim discovered determinate theoretical relations among a whole range of empirical subject matters which are usually parceled out among different disciplines and specialties within disciplines. In *De la division du travail social*, he established relations between law and the traditional empirical subject matter of economics, subsuming both of them under a larger theoretical perspective. He also included fruitful discussions of political matters, in which he observed that government has developed concomitantly with the economy of private enterprise. In his later work, he carried his analysis of connections into the field of psychological theory; he was driven to this by the logic of the problems he wished to solve, although he had said originally that psychological considerations are irrelevant to sociological problems. His investigations into psychological theory enabled him not only to enrich his own analysis but also to establish the basis of a remarkable convergence with Freud, thereby providing a means by which the conceptions of rationality of the economic tradition of thought and the role of the non-rational components of motivation in the psychoanalytic tradition could be linked. Finally, in his later work he analyzed the relevance of religion to the secular aspects of social organization.

This remarkable ability to see relations among fields usually treated as unconnected was possible only because Durkheim constantly kept in mind the fact that he was dealing with the problem of integration of a single system, not a congeries of discrete subsystems. He was a theorist par excellence of the functioning of systems.

In the above discussion, I have stressed many of the complications and difficulties underlying Durkheim's analyses. He was undoubtedly highly selective and was, therefore, in a sense, "biased"—take, for example, his confusing of the evolutionary and the analytical problems in relation to the status of mechanical solidarity. The structural problems can be greatly clarified by building on the tradition of Weber, and the relations to personality can be greatly clarified by mobilizing psychological knowledge which either did not exist in Durkheim's time or was contained in works in which (like the earlier ones of Freud) he showed no interest.

Such critical analysis results in considerable revision of Durkheim's positions. It does not result in refutation of them, however. It involves only extension and refinement, for Durkheim established the basic foundations for developing a fruitful theory of social integration.

CHAPTER 2

Introduction to Max Weber's
The Sociology of Religion

This chapter is much more expository than critical, particularly as
compared with both the preceding and following essays. The
occasion for its composition was the publication of the English
translation of the most systematic and generalized statement that
Weber made in the field of the sociology of religion. This was a
particularly important event, in part because so few English-
language readers knew the German original. In the absence of its
availability in English there was a strong tendency for discussion
of Weber's contributions to the sociology of religion to fall between two stools. There were the writers, mostly critics, who paid
attention primarily to the essay on the Protestant Ethic and occa-
sionally the essay on the Protestant Sects, but in either case failed
totally to see the importance of his comparative studies (Samuels-
son is the most egregious among recent cases). And there were
the scholars interested only as historians or area specialists especially in ancient China, India, or Israel.

Not only does the *Sociology of Religion* bring together in very
succinct form the whole range of Weber's interests in the field,
and systematize his conceptual apparatus, but it gives the fullest
statement of his conception of the balance between the two
basic sets of factors with which he was concerned—the cultural
traditions of religious origin and the patternings of economic and
political interests. For example, Chapter VI, entitled "Castes,
Estates, Classes, and Religion," is perhaps the most comprehensive
presentation in his writings of what, in the *Protestant Ethic*, he
referred to as "the other side of the causal chain."

With respect to my own theoretical concerns, there are two
main contexts that became paramount in working out this extended introduction, with the examination of a good deal of

"Introduction" from *The Sociology of Religion* by Max Weber translated by Ephraim
Fischo from *Wirtschaft und Gesellschaft.* Copyright © 1962 by Beacon Press. Originally
published in Great Britain by Methuen & Co. Ltd.

Weber's material that it entailed. The first was the general perspective on the theory of social and cultural evolution that it presents. This is probably the core text for Weber's sophisticated and complex views in this field. Above all, this concerns, in turn, two problems. The first is the complex balance he maintained between his ideas of phases of evolutionary sequence, bound together as they were by the process of rationalization, and his conception of of qualitative distinctions between different *directions* of societal evolution. The second was the special highlighting that Weber has given to the emergence on a worldwide basis of what Bellah calls the "historic" religions, those which, near the middle of the second millenium B.C., attained a new level of rationalization, which to me implies increased differentiation between the cultural and societal systems.

The second context of special significance to my own thinking was the question of the continuities and discontinuities of the process of religious change. As is developed in the chapter, I was greatly impressed with the very strong emphasis Weber placed in the conception of "breakthrough," especially in his conception of the role of the prophet, and I came to be much more sceptical than before of the generalizability of this conception as the main focus of sociocultural change. The implications of this altered emphasis will become evident especially in Part IV of this volume.

I N THE more than forty years since Max Weber's untimely death, recognition of his stature as one of the principal founders of modern social science, in particular modern sociology, has slowly been growing. But the magnitude of his contributions has not yet been fully appreciated; barriers to the understanding of Weber's thought are still presented by technical difficulties and by cultural resistance.

Appreciation of Weber's stature as a sociological theorist has been greatest in the United States, though Americans encounter a formidable barrier in the difference of languages and the extraordinary difficulty of Weber's German. Translations of Weber's works into English have become available piecemeal and without plan, and the technical quality of the translations has often left much to be desired. A further technical difficulty has been provided by the enormous scope of Weber's interests and contributions, a scope which makes formidable the task of critically appraising Weber's various sociological concepts and contributions. Added to these technical difficulties have been problems of understanding and problems of acceptance, which are interesting in themselves from the standpoint of the sociology of knowledge. Cultural resistance to the appreciation of Weber's work has been sufficiently formidable in the United States, but has been also the primary cause of an even greater retardation of understanding and appreciation in Continental Europe, particularly in Weber's native Germany.

The most central focus of Weber's thought lay in the field of religion, though the scope of his theoretical work extended to problems of economic organization and process, of political systems, of formal organization, and of law. His original training was in the field of historical jurisprudence, and from that he turned to historical economics. When he turned his studies toward religion, his focus was not upon religion "as such," as the theologian or church historian conceives it, but upon *the relations between* religious ideas and commitments and other aspects of human conduct, especially the economic characteristics of human conduct within a society. Weber's concern with religion was thus focused upon the *sociology* of religion. With Durkheim, who approached religion from a very different point of view, and with such modern anthropologists as Malinowski and Radcliffe-Brown, Weber inaugurated a new phase in the understanding of the relations between religious aspects and other aspects of human behavior.

The Reference Points for Weber's Sociology of Religion in His Work as a Whole

Weber's work in the sociology of religion first came to be known through his essay on the *Protestant Ethic and the Spirit of Capitalism,* which, controversial as it has been, must certainly count as one of the major landmarks of recent Western intellectual history.[1] This essay was at first received as an attempted "complete explanation" of the modern world, and especially as a counterattack against the Marxist assertion of the predominance of "material" interests in the historical process. Only gradually has it become more generally understood that in Weber's broad plan of work the book was intended as no more than an *essay* in historical-sociological interpretation. It was a fragment which provided Weber a point of departure, not a culmination, for his main contributions to the sociology of religion. Now it clearly has attained the status of a

1. As Rostow notes in *The Stages of Economic Growth,* economic historians must now "pay their respects" to the problem of the Protestant ethic, even though as individuals they have no real interest in Weber's problems.

classic, but it should be appraised as such within the context of its author's total contribution, not in isolation.

If the *Protestant Ethic* was Weber's point of departure, his immediate scholarly destination was the series of comparative monographs in the sociology of religion of which three were completed, those of Chinese religion (Confucianism and Taoism), of Indian religion (Hinduism and Buddhism), and of Ancient Judaism. All of these are now available in English translation.[2] This series was left incomplete at Weber's death. He had planned, at the very least, comparable studies of Islam, of early Christianity and of mediaeval Catholicism.

In the *Protestant Ethic,* Weber raised a set of theoretical problems in the field of human social action of the very first order of importance. The central problem was whether men's conceptions of the cosmic universe, including those of Divinity and men's religious interests within such a conceptual framework could influence or shape their concrete actions and social relationships, particularly in the very mundane field of economic action. This possibility was entertained seriously, and the question of *how* to conceive the operation of religious ideas became central. In the case of the relation between Protestantism and capitalism, the study of the operation of religious ideas led to questions of historical interpretation. But Weber early became acutely aware, as many participants in the discussion still are not, that the problem of causation involved an *analytical* problem, one of the isolation of variables and the testing of their significance in situations where they could be shown to vary independently of each other. The purely "historical" method, seeking ever more detailed knowledge of the "ideal" and "material" historical antecedents of modern economic organization, is inherently circular. It was only by establishing a methodological equivalent of experimental method, in which it is possible to hold certain factors constant, that even the beginnings of an escape from circularity was possible. Weber doubtless had many other motives for embarking upon a broad comparative study of the relations between religious orientations and social structure. But the decisive motive for his scientific method proceeded from his realization that without comparative evidence he could not hope to progress in the solution of his original central question.

2. *The Religion of China,* trans. by Hans H. Gerth (The Free Press, 1951); *Ancient Judaism,* trans. by Hans H. Gerth and Don Martindale (The Free Press, 1952); *The Religion of India,* trans. by Hans H. Gerth and Don Martindale (The Free Press, 1958).

In embarking upon comparative studies, Weber attempted to hold the factor of "economic organization" constant and to treat religious orientation as his independent variable. He sought to equate the "degrees of favorableness" of material factors to the development of capitalism. On the basis of a careful survey he judged this favorableness to be approximately equal in the European, in the Chinese, and in the Indian cases, taking account of the considerable changes within each main civilization over the long periods involved. Given the very critical differences in outcome in the three great civilizations, he then had a *prima facie* case for the importance of the religious movements as *differentiating* factors, not of course as total "explanations" of social developments. Weber repeatedly repudiated any imputation of an intent to "explain" all social developments as emanations and consequences of "idealistic" elements. His general position was as far removed from idealistic "emanationism" as it could possibly be.

Weber's orientation toward analytical methods requiring comparative studies led him to a particularly sharp break with the intellectual traditions in which he had been educated, the historical schools of social study predominant in late nineteenth-century Germany—in Weber's case, historical jurisprudence and economics. These traditions of historical social study had philosophical foundations in German Idealism, which distinguished different or opposed methods as appropriate to the natural sciences and to humanistic studies. These historical traditions rooted in Idealistic conceptions held that studies of human society and culture must be pursued by "ideographic" methods, not by the "nomothetic" methods employed in the natural sciences. Studies of human phenomena should delineate the development or unfolding of unique historical patterns, and attempt to grasp the central meanings of these unique patterns. Since these philosophical and methodological traditions were widely accepted in Weber's intellectual surroundings, it is not surprising that Weber, while publishing the *Protestant Ethic* and deciding to embark upon comparative studies, also published a series of essays[3] sharply attacking the historical methods predominant in social disciplines, especially economics. The general purport of these critical essays was Weber's insistence that in studies of society, as much as in the natural sciences, causal explanation depends upon the employment of analytical theory.

3. Collected in his *Gesammelte Aufsätze zur Wissenschaftslehre*, Verlag von J. C. B. Mohr (Paul Siebeck), 1922. Some have been translated in Shils and Finch, *Max Weber's Methodology of Science* (New York: The Free Press, 1949).

Causes of human behavior cannot be found and established without the implicit or explicit use of abstract and general concepts and propositions.

But despite Weber's sharp critique of his own intellectual background, he retained and utilized the most important susbtantive elements of the historicist and Idealist traditions. His conservation of selected historical and Idealist conceptions creates a sharp contrast between his own methodology and the positivistic reductionism then and later so prominent in France, Britain, and the United States, of which Behaviorism was an extreme manifestation.

There were two crucial foci of the historical element in Weber's work. The first was his attempt to interpret action by understanding the motives of the actor from a "subjective" point of view, that is, the investigator attempting to put himself in the actor's place. However, Weber held that this subjective interpretation does not require the complete individualization of interpretations, since there are *typical* patterns of meaning which can be abstracted from the individualized totality. This line of argument, formalized in his well-known concept of the "ideal type," was Weber's main path to the formulation of a general theory which incorporated "subjective" factors, the famous method of *Verstehen*.

The second primary focus of Weber's historicist conceptions, of particular importance in the present context, was his concern with systems of meaning (*Sinnzusammenhänge*) which could be interpreted ("understood," in Weber's special sense) and which, as definitions of situations for the actions of individuals, could be linked with individuals' "interests" (their motives in a psychological sense). Thus Weber initiated a line of theoretical analysis in many respects similar to, though in origin largely independent of, that initiated in the United States by such theorists as G. H. Mead and W. I. Thomas. Weber's "cultural complex of meanings," in one respect a system of "ideas," was also an instrument for the understanding of the action of individuals, and in this respect it was almost identical with Thomas' famous conception of the definition of the situation.

These were Weber's primary points of reference in his attempt to develop at least the beginnings of a technical body of theory in the field of social action (Weber's German technical term was *Handeln*). He was deeply committed to the need for theory. The elements of theory available to him from his intellectual environment were extremely important, yet fragmentary and seriously incomplete. He did much to extend and codify social theory, making various completely original contributions, yet his social theory at his death remained far more a beginning than an end.[4]

Weber approached problems of theory from the standpoint of an intellectual tradition that minimized the potential contribution of theory to social studies. He approached problems of theory cautiously, and primarily when theory was required for his program of empirical research. In the field of the sociology of religion he progressed from empirical studies to the development of theory, a pattern of intellectual movement he had already followed in the fields of economic and political organization. In these latter fields, he had written a considerable number of empirical monographs, especially in economic history broadly conceived,[5] before venturing into theory in the *Protestant Ethic* and in his methodological attacks upon Historicism. Only much later, in *Wirtschaft und Gesellschaft,* did he attempt to codify this material on a theoretical level. Similarly, he first pursued his program of studies in the sociology of religion through monographs. Though he engaged in a number of studies simultaneously during his most fruitful years, from time to time turning from one to another, the broad orientation of his primary attention was first toward China, then toward India, and then toward ancient Judaism. Though in these three monographic studies there is much implicit and some explicit theory, a careful and thorough critical analysis would be required to discover the general conceptual scheme Weber was applying here, and indeed there are not only serious gaps but certainly a good many inconsistencies in the implied conceptual scheme.

It was rather later in his program, though before he had reached fifty years of age, that he undertook a systematization which required far more attention to theoretical problems than he had hitherto devoted to them. It was an "external" stimulus upon Weber to which we are indebted for his systematic undertaking. This stimulus was the grandiose plan for a *Grundriss der Sozialoekonomik,* freely translated, a "General Outline of the Social and Economic Sciences," conceived by a group of

4. The incompleteness of Weber's theory of society will be apparent from what is said here of his theories in the specifically religious field. There has not in recent years, during which perspective on theory has advanced greatly, been published any comprehensive critical treatment of Weber's contributions as a theorist, in the strict sense. Bendix, in his *Max Weber: An Intellectual Portrait,* explicitly decided not to undertake the task of a comprehensive appraisal of Weber as a theorist, preferring for his purposes to concentrate upon Weber's empirical work. The present writer's *The Structure of Social Action,* especially Chapter XVII, may still be the most comprehensive analytical treatment of Weber's accomplishments in theory.
5. A number of these economic and political monographs have been collected in the volume *Gesammelte Aufsätze zur Sozial-und Wirtschafts-geschichte.*

German social scientists of which Weber was not only a member but clearly a ringleader. It was as part of this ambitious plan that Weber undertook to contribute a *general* survey of the relations between "economy and society" which took the German title of *Wirtschaft und Gesellschaft*. To this we owe the systematic, as distinguished from historical, monograph which is presented in the present volume.

The translator, Dr. Fischoff, has provided a highly illuminating account of the genesis, the general character, and the problems presented by this extraordinary work. It was not only left unfinished at Weber's death, but left in such a state that the editors could not be certain even of the general plan of the work and hence the degree to which it approached completion. The more recent and very careful work of Dr. Winckelmann, which has resulted in the latest and substantially improved German edition, has helped greatly in understanding the problem, as Dr. Fischoff shows.

Wirtschaft und Gesellschaft seems clearly to have been intended originally as a work of codification rather than a work of new empirical research or new theory, but in the hands of Weber it became much more than a codification. It was characteristic of the scope of his knowledge and thinking that several "chapters," preeminently the one on the sociology of law[6] and the present one, turned out in fact to be substantial books when nearly completed.[7] It is to this project that we owe Weber's only attempt to present a systematic account, as distinguished from a monographic case study, of his views on the sociology of religion.

In many future English-language bibliographies, there will be references to "Weber, 1962" and many readers will not stop to consider that the English translation is appearing a full half-century after the work was written. In appraising it, it is essential to keep this in mind. Weber was a scholar who avidly assembled and digested any empirical materials available in the relevant literature, within the limits of his considerable command of languages. (He did not command several of the languages most important to the study of comparative religion.) He did his unusually competent best to discover the actual facts and to correctly interpret them, over an enormous range of subject matter. But many of his detailed facts and interpretations cannot be accepted today as reliable, in part because of the very scope of his inquiries and in part because of rapid

6. Translated as *Max Weber on Law in Economy and Society*, by Rheinstein and Shils (Cambridge: Harvard Univ. Press, 1954).
7. A number of others like the one on social stratification ("Theory", Chapter IV) are clearly fragments.

progress in the sociology of religion since Weber's time. Many of his empirical generalizations, which we may call "middle-range theories," are clearly dated. Weber would have altered many of his opinions and generalizations, if he had had access to the subsequent fifty years' anthropological research into primitive religion and historical scholarship relevant to advanced religions. Given Weber's qualities as a scholar, we can be sure that he would have exploited to the limit such opportunities to improve his work.[8]

The general framework within which Weber conceived and treated, in this monograph, the problems of the sociology of religion is less likely to be dated by the contributions of the intervening half-century than is the case with many matters of specific fact, and of middle-level generalization.

Religion and the Problem of Social Evolution

Weber's perspective, especially in the sociology of religion, but elsewhere as well was basically evolutionary. This is particularly important in the light of the intellectual history of the period. After a brief and somewhat superficial flirtation of social science with the idea of evolution, under the impact of Darwinism in the biological sciences (the names of Spencer, Ward, and Summer come to mind), there developed among social scientists a sharp reaction against the idea of evolution. The evolutionary conception has made little progress in social science since Weber's time, since much of the work of historians has been particularistic, while for an entire generation most of the comparative research was carried out by anthropologists, whose thought was militantly anti-evolutionary. But it is significant that Weber and his great contemporary Emile Durkheim, the other most important founder of modern sociology, both thought in evolutionary terms.[9]

Weber had to develop a conception of primitive religion, and that is indeed the task to which he addressed himself in the first section of this book. Since Weber's time, anthropological research has enormously en-

8. As in the field of theory, in this and a number of other more empirical fields, a great service could be done by a careful appraisal of what difference it would make in Weber's interpretations and generalizations on the sociology of religion if account were taken of the materials, both specifically factual and interpretive, which have become available since Weber wrote—and of course the relevance of things available at the time which he may have neglected.

9. Cf. Robert N. Bellah, "Durkheim and History," *American Sociological Review,* Vol. 24, p. 447, 1959.

riched our knowledge in this field, though Durkheim's codification and analysis of Australian totemism remains perhaps the most eminent single monographic contribution, because it is both a great monograph and much more than that.[10] But these additions of material do not invalidate the general outline of Weber's view of primitive religion. Indeed, the convergence between Weber's and Durkheim's conceptions of primitive religion, in the absence of any apparent influence of either theorist on the other, is notable.

A first crucial point in Weber's theory is that there is no known human society without something which modern social scientists would classify as religion. Every society possesses some conceptions of a supernatural order, of spirits, gods, or impersonal forces that are different from and in some sense superior to those forces conceived as governing ordinary "natural" events, and whose nature and activities somehow give meaning to the unusual, the frustrating and the rationally impenetrable aspects of experience. The existence of the supernatural order is taken seriously, in that many concrete events of experience are attributed, in part at least, to its agency, and men devote an important part of their time and resources to regulating their relations with this order as they conceive it.

This view that belief in the supernatural is universal has been completely confirmed by modern anthropology. Religion is as much a human universal as language or an incest taboo, which is to say a kinship system. Any conception of a "natural man" who is not encumbered with such "cultural baggage" belongs to a fictional picture of prehistory, for which there is no solid evidence for the human, socially organized stage. The view that such "baggage" *ought* to be dispensed with and that rational man should "face reality" without any "superstition" is a product of sophisticated culture, in no way true of the original human condition.

Weber combined his view of the ubiquity of conceptions of the supernatural with an insight into the *symbolic character* of the conceptions of supernatural beings and their acts, although Weber did not develop this latter insight as systematically as did Durkheim. Particularly important is Weber's insistence that the conception of a supernatural order does not imply any "transcendental" goals or focus of interest for man. The aid of the supernatural is sought, so far as "primitive man" is concerned, entirely in the interest of mundane, worldly concerns: health, long life, defeat of enemies, good relations with one's own people, and

10. Emile Durkheim, *Les formes élémentaires de la vie religieuse*, 1912, translated as *The Elementary Forms of the Religious Life,* currently published by The Free Press.

the like. There are important questions about the effect of beliefs in the supernatural upon the priorities and relativities among these various mundane or "common sense" interests, but Weber does not much explore this line of problems, which we would now refer to as the field of value orientations and value integrations.

Weber's discussion of the sociology of religion, from this starting point in the universality of belief in the supernatural, proceeds to a systematic exploration of the directions in which, and the developmental paths by which, "breakthroughs" from the primitive religious state can occur. Comparative and historical evidence for the existence of such breakthroughs is sought. The possibilities are canvassed by searching back and forth between the "material" sphere of the conditions, structure and utilitarian interests of ordinary living, and the "ideal" sphere of the meanings of various conceptions of the supernatural and of other aspects of experience. Essential for the analysis of social process is Weber's emphasis upon *differentiation,* not only between the spheres, but also within each sphere to the extent that situations are differently defined with reference to action. It is methodologically important that Weber's differentiations are predominantly dichotomous; two-fold distinctions introduced for the solution of some particular problem. Weber repeatedly abstracts from the total social process some set of two principal alternatives of social structuring, after which his methodological problem is to clarify the differences and relations between these alternatives, as well as to clarify the conditions relevant to tipping the balance in one or the other direction.[11]

The concept of breakthrough is, I think, crucial. At each primary decision point, where Weber makes a primary distinction, the alternative is between a direction which makes for a source of evolutionary change in the "established" order (which Weber tended to conceptualize under the heading of traditionalism), and another direction which tends either to reinforce the established order or at least not to change it drastically. He makes a further distinction between tendencies which do and do not carry the potentiality of firmly organized "viability" under the realistic

11. This is most emphatically not to say that Weber was a partisan of the "logic of dichotomies" in either a naive or a rigid sense. Very few writers display such awareness, indeed not only awareness, but enormous knowledge, of the tremendous complexity of the empirical material and the subtleties of transition from one type to another, a circumstance which makes the reading of this material, both in the original and in translation, particularly difficult. But when one comes to try to isolate the main *logical* outline of Weber's analysis, the prominence of the pattern of dichotomization is striking. It seems to us entirely appropriate to a focus on the process of differentiation. It is also notable that this focus is shared by Weber and Durkheim.

conditions of social life (in current sociological terminology, the potentiality of effective institutionalization). Weber's *primary* interest is in religion as a source of the dynamics of social change, not religion as a reinforcement of the stability of societies.[12]

The Primary Components of a Religious System

The first of the theoretical dichotomies which Weber develops is that between the function of the magician and the function of the priest in mediating between humans and the supernatural, a dichotomy which will reappear as the distinction between magic and religion. Weber's distinction is somewhat different from the similar distinctions made by Durkheim and Malinowski. Weber's distinction is that the magician's function copes with relatively *ad hoc* interests and tensions, while the priestly function is organized into a systematic and stabilized *cult*, which is to a significant extent independent of the *ad hoc* exigencies which impinge upon the ordinary population of the society. Further, magical forces can be "forced" (*gezwungen*) to serve human needs by the magician's correct use of formulae, while religious agents must be "worshipped" or solicited. Religious forces are conceived to have an independent capacity to guide human destiny which the magical forces do not.

The range of different aspects of these problems which Weber reviews is enormous, and many penetrating observations are made along the way, such as that of the special relation between religious precepts and the later development of law in Rome. Through all this, Weber's underlying thesis is the importance of the development of conceptions of the supernatural order, the claims of this supernatural order upon human attention and performance, and the implementation of these claims through agencies which may attain a sufficient independence from the traditionally established social order to exert leverage upon that social order and change it. Already present in this underlying thesis is Weber's

12. It is probably correct to say that this is a primary difference of emphasis between Weber and Durkheim. That Weber focused his structural analysis upon process and change is of current interest, in view of the contemporary allegation that the dominant "structural-functional" trend in sociological theory channels interest toward stability and order, to the neglect of problems of change. Weber and Durkheim are usually considered intellectual ancestors of the "structural-functional" school, and however plausible the accusation against Durkheim of a "static bias" may be—I do not think it can be pressed very far, especially in the light of Bellah's analysis, *op. cit.*—it is almost impossible to make a plausible case for such a bias on Weber's part. Perhaps this allegation of a static bias proceeds from a belief held by the critics that the "real" forces of change cannot be found in the sphere of "ideas" but consist of "material" interests.

evaluative distinction between what we may call progressive and regressive changes. He holds that those changes, associated at the primitive level with priestly cults, which make for a more stringent and systematic ordering of the patterns of living are more favorable to breakthrough than are those changes which tend toward the indulgence of immediate emotional needs and pressures, which he associates with "orgiastic" components in magic and religion, but which also include needs for security.

Weber moves next, not to the problem of differentiating the roles and interests involved in the distinction between the magical and priestly functions, but to the problem of differentiating between types of normative social order based upon "religious ethics" and upon "taboo." These types represent different levels in the normative control of action, and the former type is associated with priesthood and cult, the latter type with magic. Nevertheless, many elements of taboo are empirically associated with priestly cults. The essential distinction is that taboo is concerned with the prescription and still more the proscription of specific acts, while religious ethics is more concerned to enforce a generalized orientation or pattern of action. The existence and efficacy of a religious ethic is dependent upon a conception of divinity, by no means necessarily monotheistic. According to Weber, divinities are either conceived as entering into quasi-contractual relationships with men, by which the divinities themselves assume obligations, or conceived as promulgating general laws which they expect humans to observe, much as an absolute monarch promulgates positive laws. A religious ethic is conceptualized at a higher level of generality than a system of taboo, and therefore a religious ethic is universalistic, its observance requires a high level of responsibility, and its infractions by men cannot be counteracted directly by magical punishments.

These three distinctions may be considered to formulate the main setting of the problem of religion as a force for dynamic social change, as Weber saw it. His view was that all societies at whatever level of development have had, not only secular or natural, but also supernatural elements of culture. All supernatural components have both magical and religious elements, though in widely varying proportions and relations; all have roles approximating those of magician and priest, though again with varying combinations of the components; and all have in their supernaturally sanctioned normative order elements both of a system of taboo and a system of religious ethics. With those elements and distinctions shared by the religions of all human societies, the problems of the sociology of religion become these: Under what cultural definitions of the religious situation can processes of change and breakthrough take place? Through what agencies and forms of organization can processes of change and breakthrough take place? In what situations are breakthroughs most probable?

The Process of Rationalization

Rationalization is the master conception through which cultures define their religious situation, and through which the sociology of religion must understand such cultural definitions of the situation. Rationalization comprises first the intellectual clarification, specification, and systematization of ideas. Ideas are generated by what Weber called the teleological *meanings* of man's conceptions of himself and his place in the universe, conceptions which legitimize man's orientations in and to the world and which give *meaning* to man's various goals. Such ideas imply metaphysical and theological conceptions of cosmic and moral orders, as well as man's position in relation to such wider orders.

Rationalization comprises second the normative control or sanction. This is so because the teleological reference of the ideas in question implies that human actions are goal-oriented, in means-ends terms. This in turn implies that human actions should be subject to a fundamental "hierarchy of control," and that the higher levels of this hierarchy should lie on the cultural plane. Therefore, all human societies embody references to a normative cultural order which places teleological "demands" upon men. But men's conception of the nature of this normative order is not a constant; rather, there is a differentiated variety of possible normative orders, and even a single society's conceptions of normative order change in the course of history. Weber's primary concern is the exploration of these different possible natures, and the directions these natures may take when attempting to answer by rationalizing the problems of the meaning of life. Weber's "rationalization" is thus intellectual, in that it has special reference to "existential" (though nonempirical) ideas, but is also teleological or normative, in that it places obligations on men with respect to their conduct in this life.

Third, rationalization comprises a conception of motivational commitment. The ideas in question imply, not only social and behavioral patterns, but kinds and levels of motivational commitment required for the implementation of these implied patterns. The motivational commitments include both "belief," in the sense of seriousness of commitment to the cognitive validity of the ideas, and practical commitment, in the sense of readiness to put one's own interests at stake in the service of the ideas. Here the dimension of rationalization concerns in the first instance the systematization of a pattern or program *for life as a whole,* which is given meaning by an existential conception of the universe, and within it the human condition in which this action is to be carried out.

Prophecy, Charisma, and the Process of Breakthrough

It is within this framework that the place of Weber's key concept of *prophecy* is to be understood. The prophet is above all the agent of the process of breakthrough to a higher, in the sense of more rationalized and systematized, cultural order, an order at the level of religious ethics, which in turn has implications for the nature of the society in which it becomes institutionalized. This, of course, is the focus of Weber's much-discussed concept of charisma which, though not originating with him, has become part of the common language of social and cultural discus sion mainly through his influence. For Weber the role of the religious prophet was the prototype, though not the only example, of "charismatic leadership."

There are two particularly notable points about the concept of charisma, the significance of which should be assessed in the light of the relation of the concept to the development of *conceptions* of order, that is, the cognitive aspect of the process of rationalization. The first is the focus on the *individual* person who takes the responsibility for announc-ing a break in the established normative order and declaring this break to be morally *legitimate,* thereby setting himself in significant respects in explicit opposition to the established order.[13] In order to legitimize his sponsorship of such a break the prophet must in turn invoke a source of moral authority, an imperative which leads directly into the problem of the conceptions of meaning and order. The essential question is whether it is in an evolutionary sense a higher order, a question which can only be answered in a comparative and evolutionary perspective.

It may be remarked that this individualistic emphasis in Weber's treatment of the concept of charisma has tended to obscure the fact that he treated it not *only* as a quality of an individual person, but also of a

13. The Jews of the time of Christ were preeminently a "people of the Book." Hence for Weber a prototypical expression of the prophetic attitude in this respect was the phrase, frequently reiterated in the Gospels, "It is written . . . , but I say unto you . . ." of course something in conflict with what is written.

normative *order*. The latter reference, for example, is a necessary basis
for making use of the important concepts of lineage-charisma (*Gentil-
charisma*) and charisma of office (*Amtscharisma*). In this latter context
Weber's concept of charisma is identical with Durkheim's concept of the
sacred.[14]

The second notable and closely connected point about the concept
of prophecy is Weber's insistence that, in spite of the very close connection between it and cognitive conceptions of order, there is a crucial
noncognitive aspect of it, namely that of *commitment* to the break and
the order embodied in the break. Prophecy is by no means an intellectual
exercise in metaphysical or theological speculation, but very much a case
of what Durkheim had in mind when he said of religion, *c'est de la vie
sérieuse*. This in turn is associated with the frequent violent emotionalism
of prophetic movements, sometimes—as Weber emphasizes—bordering
on the pathological.

Weber is very careful to distinguish the prophet from closely similar
types, namely the "lawgiver" and the teacher, especially in respect to
the rationalization of religious orientations. Prophets may well perform
both functions of lawgiver and teacher in addition to their prophecy;
Moses and Muhammad are famous examples of the lawgiver, and most
certainly were prophets in Weber's sense. But the essential criterion of
prophecy for Weber is whether or not the message is a call to break with
an established order; he cites the Hindu *guru* as a preeminent example of
the religious teacher who implements an established order rather than
breaking with it.

There is, however, in Weber's discussion, one type of role which involves such a break, but to which he does not apply the conception of
prophet, and this is what he calls the "mystagogue," a concept apparently
thought of as the religious counterpart of the demagogue. The essential
difference from the prophet is that the mystagogue defines his source
of legitimation primarily in magical terms, not those of a religious ethic.
He is not an agent of rationalization, but of escape from the problems of
meaning which exert pressure to rationalize, that is to establish new
levels of normative order.

Within the category of prophecy, Weber then introduces another of
his central dichotomies, namely that between exemplary and ethical

14. So prominent indeed is the individualistic aspect of charisma in most of Weber's
writings which dealt with it, that it was only in connection with the present book, and
then only on a careful second reading, that I was able to see the resemblance of Weber's
charisma in its normative social aspect to Durkheim's concept of the collective sacred,
which I described in *Structure of Social Action*, Chap. XVII.

prophecy. The exemplary prophet provides a model for a way of life which can be followed by others, embodying in a religious sense what is defined as a higher level of personal virtue. There is, however, no implication that the standards of this pattern or "way" are binding on any social community as such. The ethical prophet, on the other hand, imposes demands on certain categories of men in such a way that not only do they have an opportunity, but it is rather their *duty* to follow his precepts. These precepts in turn are defined, not so much to exhort followers to emulate the prophet's personal example, as they are to exhort them to conform with an impersonally defined normative order. Both the definition of this order and—beyond that—the reasons why acceptance of it is morally obligatory, are incorporated in the prophet's conception of the nature of his mission. This implies a very different conception of their relations to a source of legitimation on the part of the two types of prophet. The exemplary type tends to define himself as a *vessel,* as standing in some personal relation of identification with the divine, whereas the ethical prophet thinks of himself as an *instrument* of a divine will, as having a mission to promulgate an order for others which expresses that will. He himself, however, need not become personally "sanctified."

Hence the cognitive conception of the nature of divinity underlying the two types of prophecy tends to bifurcate. The conception associated with exemplary prophecy is that of an immanent, pantheistic principle of divinity, in which the prophet participates, and offers others who follow his example the opportunity to participate. But the ethical prophet tends to legitimize his teachings by reference to a transcendental conception of divinity, a conception of one or more gods who stand *outside* and above the world in which the human condition is situated, and who "legislate" for it. The religious philosophy of India represents the extreme example in the former direction, that of Judaism, Christianity, and Islam, in the latter.

The next very essential step in Weber's analytical construction is the definition of the religious community (*Gemeinde*). It is characteristic not only of primitive religion, as he sees it, but of many other types, that the organization of religion at the collectivity level is an "aspect" of the organization of the society in other functional respects, notably the political, but also of kinship and the like. There may be specialized roles like those of magician and priest, but they, together with their clientele, do not constitute an organized collectivity structurally differentiated from the rest of the society. Such persons may be "private practitioners" or they may be "functionaries" of a collectivity which is more than a religious one. The type of collectivity in which Weber is here interested is one specifically organized about religious interests as such, which is thereby distinct from other "secular" collectivities in the same society.

There is of course a close connection between the religious community and prophecy in that the type of break with an established order which Weber associates with prophecy favors the definition, both on their own part and of others, of the status of the prophet and his followers as standing in a special position different from that of non-followers. Of course the prophet may, like Moses, carry a whole "people" with him—though there may well be important defections—but the case Weber has in mind in his concept of religious community is that of a collectivity with a distinctive religious character; it is not a society, but rather a religiously specialized subgroup within a society, a "sect" or a "church."

Two particularly important problems arise at this point. The first is that of the relation of the religious leadership or specialists, in the first instance prophets, to followers who are not specialists or "virtuosos," but who are "ordinary people" in all senses except that they adhere to the special doctrine or way, or are loyal to the leader. In the religious sense these are the "laity." Weber makes much of the fact that the capacities of different types of religious movement for the effective organization of such a collectivity and in particular of the laity, vary greatly. Very broadly, exemplary prophecy tends to produce "elitist" movements of those who achieve superior religious status, and to leave the others in a status of dubious belongingness, apart from the belongingness they derive from their secular statuses. It is on the basis of ethical prophecy and an order binding on whole categories of persons that anything like a firmly organized "church" can most readily be built up.

The basic duality between magic and ethic, or emotional and rational-social, which characterizes Weber's thought throughout the book, appears in this context as the distinction between the religious community and the "sacralized polity," if we may use that term, namely the politically organized society in which the religious and the secular aspects of organization are not differentiated at the higher collectivity levels—in Western terms, a community that is both "church" and "state" at the same time.

In the entire context of the process of rationalization, Weber emphasizes the importance of the development of a *written* sacred tradition, of sacred books. The timing of its appearance is by no means a function of literacy since, for example, preservation of the oral tradition may be positively promoted in esoteric groups to protect their exclusiveness. This seems to have been the case with the Vedic tradition in India for a long period. Once there are sacred texts, however, these are subject both to continual editing and to complex processes of interpretation and tend to become the focus of specialized intellectual competence and prestige in the religious field and on the cultural level of rationalized systems of religious doctrine. Groups who have a special command of the sacred writings may then attain a special position in the religious system as a whole—the Jewish rabbis of the Talmudic tradition present a particularly salient case.

Written tradition provides a basis for further differentiation of the system precisely because it is a focus of stability which can be made independent of complete traditionalization of the status of concrete groups, notably priestly groups. One of the most important advances from this base, particularly associated with prophecy, is the development of preaching of "the Word" as distinguished from administration of the cult. Preaching, Weber holds, is a function possible only where there are prophetic definitions of the situation, and tends to be particularly prominent where ethical prophecy occurs. Another very important development of further differentiation is concern for the religious state of the individual through the "cure of souls" in various forms: confession, special spiritual exercises, special teaching and the like.

Religion and Social Status

Having thus established his main framework for analyzing the process of cultural breakthrough under religious auspices, Weber turns to consideration of the varieties of types of "soil" in which such movements may or may not be expected to grow. He extensively reviews types of social strata, examined for their sensitivity to possible prophetic, and also mystagogic, appeals, and among these he distinguishes those social strata sensitive to exemplary and to ethical prophecy.[15]

Careful consideration of this remarkable essay—in its extensiveness perhaps better termed a monograph—should end once and for all the allegation among serious scholars that Weber held a naive one-way con-

15. See Chapter VI of *The Sociology of Religion*. In the German, this section is entitled *Stände, Klassen und Religion*. It is the only part previously available to English-speaking readers, a slightly earlier translation by Christine Kayser having been included in *Theories of Society*, Parsons, Shils, Naegele, and Pitts, eds. (New York: The Free Press, 1961), Vol. II, Section B, No. 9, pp. 1138-1161.

ception of the development of human societies as the product of "ideas" without due attention to what he himself called the "other side of the causal chain." It may perhaps be called, in present terminology, a study in the sociological determinants of the "propensity to alienation." After all, what he is emphasizing as the decisive aspect of progressive (evolutionary) social change is the condition necessary to bring about what we have been calling a "break" with an established, sociologically speaking an institutionalized, order. In the earlier sections of the book he has been considering the possible nature of "stimuli" to such a break, and now he turns to the factors influencing a probable "response." It seems to be almost a truism that different societies, and different structural elements within each, will have different sensitivities to the same stimulus to break with the established order. This sensitivity is perhaps the same thing as what is now called "alienation." The alienated elements are those which are relatively "available" to be stirred by prophetic movements.

He starts with the two principal bases on which a minimum of alienation is to be expected—in each case reviewing an immense mass of comparative evidence. Those groups most likely to be strongly embedded in "traditionalism"—and here his prototypical case is that of peasants—and those most heavily involved in secular responsibility are least susceptible to prophecy or alienation. In the latter case, groups with institutionalized military functions, as feudal nobilities, figure prominently, but in a somewhat different way the concept is extended to "bureaucracies." In their very different ways, each of these types of group has a very heavy investment in maintaining the established order and "making it work," and, as Weber emphasized, the personal self-respect of the typical member is very much bound up with the completeness of his identification with this order. The case of peasantries is a kind of "base line" which is related to the whole conception of primitive societies. Weber repeatedly dwells on the close connection between peasant status and the prevalence of magical beliefs and practices, the significance of which does not require further comment in the present frame of reference. But the case of the military, extended to that of the politically responsible elements more generally, is one of great interest in the present context.

The case of the politically responsible elements is significant because of the elements of ambivalence and strain involved in their status. On the one hand there is a special "moral complexity" attached to such statuses, not least to the military because of the inherent conflicts implicit in any use of violence in relation to other human beings. Precisely

in proportion to the level of development of effective political organization, which by definition is a matter of disposal over resources, preeminently human resources whose functions cannot be traditionally
ascribed, problems arise not only of realistic capacity to command such
resources, but of *rights* to do so. Since, however, human beings, with
respect to their own services or their physical possessions, are highly
sensitive to the rights to preempt their uses, groups in a position of
political responsibility are peculiarly sensitive, not only to the amount of
power they command, in the strictly "realistic" sense of this term, but
to the basis of *legitimation* of the use of this power, which in the longer
run is a primary factor in the extent of power itself.

I think I am correct in interpreting Weber's view to be that the
"conservative" tendency among groups exercising political responsibility
is heavily determined by their need for legitimation essentially because
the use of power without regard to legitimation is possible only in the
very short run. However, in the nature of the position of such groups,
they are responsible for the more immediate consequences of their decisions. Hence, and this is a very crucial proposition, their general tendency
is to rely upon *established* sources of legitimation. This is to say, their
interest lies in attempting to stabilize, not necessarily their practical decisions, but the basis on which they can count on continuing in power
and on relative freedom from the kind of internal opposition which
would seriously impair their capacity to act. The principal effect of this
combination of factors is to give such groups a primary interest in the
stability of their sources of legitimation, precisely as a condition of their
freedom to act flexibly in current decision-making.

It may or may not be true that such groups as peasants are any freer
from tensions and frustrations than others; Weber, I think, would hesitate to suggest that they were. His point is rather that they are less likely
to seek to resolve these tensions through adherence to presumptively new
orders than are some others. He felt that they were more prone to magical mechanisms.[16]

16. This raises the question whether Weber put forward a view which was contrary to
the facts in those cases which have happened since he wrote of the roles of the peasantry, different as they were, in the Russian and the Chinese revolutions respectively.
The reasons why this is probably not so have to do with the kind of new order which
has an appeal; Weber would hold, not that peasants are immune to any sort of appeal
against currently dominant interests, but rather that they were more immune than
others to appeal to the specific kind of moral break with the pattern of the established
order which Weber was concerned with. Thus, to put it rather banally, it is easy to
mobilize peasant opposition to landowning classes, but not so easy to mobilize them

Specifically in contrast to the peasant case, Weber remarks on the regularity with which religious movements have centered in urban populations. Very notably, the early Christians were so definitely urban that the very word for non-Christian, namely pagan, originally meant simply a countryman. This of course is significant in that the major processes of social change tend to center in urban communities; they are in general less traditionalized than the rural communities.

Within urban populations there is a very great variety of social types and, Weber emphasizes, a wide range of religious propensities. Very broadly, he finds little relation between religious propensities and economic statuses as such. Above all, he is concerned to show that prophetic movements have not been primarily movements of economic protest, motivated mainly by the economic interests of the disadvantaged classes. Middle classes of various types and solid handicraft groups have been very prominent. Generally the poorest classes have not. The groups which have taken up such movements have frequently burdened themselves economically rather than improved their lot. This was the subject of an important controversy in Weber's time in Germany because certain socialist writers, notably Karl Kautsky, contended that early Christianity was essentially a proletarian movement of economic protest.

A whole range of "bourgeois" classes, in the more generic sense, constitute a particularly important type of soil for the growth of religious radicalism, if we except the lowest groups and the groups most directly involved with social responsibility, like those financiers of "politically oriented capitalism"—as Weber calls it—who stand in very close association with the more responsible groups. If I may try to state the most important favoring factors, the first type seems to be characterized by an occupational involvement which entails some order of relatively generalized rationalization of the pattern of life (*habitus* is Weber's main term). Both artisans and mercantile groups fit in this context, the first on technological grounds, the second on economic. They are identified with elements of order which cannot readily be identified with the traditionalized institutions of a society. The other type are elements that are in a status-position that reduces their level of identification with the established order—thus among artisans Weber particularly notes the apprentice and journeyman categories in connection with the very gen-

---

against a system in which landed proprietorship, large or small, is a major organizing principle. This has something to do with the fact that in both cases, after enjoying initial peasant support, the regime has had to resort to drastic reorganization of the agricultural system, in both cases apparently involving drastic conflicts with peasant groups.

eral institutionalization of "wandering," that is, of moving from place to place in search of work and experience. The most general theme is dissociation from the firmer types of anchorage in a traditional order.

Weber next turns to a very crucial problem, namely that of the dispositions of groups which have a special involvement in intellectual functions. The importance of the problem of course derives from the fact that rationalization is, in his view, the single most crucial dynamic factor in the process of change and the intellectually cognitive aspect is in turn central to rationalization. The problem concerns the relation of this implicit intellectual dynamism to the other two factors we have stressed, identification with a specifically urgent set of teleological demands on men, and the level of motivational commitment which members of the group in question may be expected to make.

His general view is that even high levels of intellectualism may, in their dynamic implications, be counteracted by sufficiently high levels of identification with an established order. The typical case is priestly intellectualism, which, above all through the rationalization of written sacred traditions, may go very far indeed toward a breakthrough, but still operate as a conservative force. This can be said of Brahmanic intellectualism in India, and to a certain extent, though with important qualifications, of Christian theologians and preeminently, in the postexilic period, of the Talmudic scholars of the Jewish Rabbinate. Very generally this is more likely to be true the higher the general social status of the intellectually inclined and trained groups, though, as in the Jewish case, pariah status may also strongly reinforce it.

There is, however, inherent dynamism in the intellectual function as such, so that in spite of such counteracting factors there may still be a radically innovative influence. In this connection Weber makes an extremely important generalization to the effect that the religious intellectualism of "elite" (*vornehm*) groups, where it does become a dynamic force, tends to work in the direction of the immanent conception of divine order, pantheism, and as we shall see presently, of seeking salvation through mystical, contemplative channels. The need for breaking with the established order, the need for "salvation" in the individual case, arises for these groups from *inner* tensions, not the pressures of the external, preeminently social situation. Rather than focusing on personal suffering or exposure to evil, this need is concerned with the question of the meaningfulness even of the *best* of fortune in worldly things— Gautama was in this respect the prototypical case. The broad conception is that intellectual breakthrough in this direction offers the opportunity for personal promotion in a scale of standing or prestige above *any* level accessible in worldly terms. Tensions involved in the feeling of meaninglessness can thus be resolved in this direction. Indeed elite intellectualism did play a central part in the development of Indian religious philosophy, and Weber mentions various other cases, notably perhaps that of Gnosticism as a movement primarily among Hellenistic intellectuals, which had it gained ascendancy, would have diverted Christianity very much in the Indian direction.

Parenthetically, it may be remarked that Weber does not say much about science, in this context, though he says a good deal about it in other contexts. Science, of course, is not directly concerned with religious problems. The interesting point, however, is that science in recent times seems to be a preeminent case of institutionalizing the dynamism of the process of rationalization, with repercussions throughout the society and culture. Moreover, scientists and the professions using applied science have become among the most important elite elements in modern society, a fact the sociological implications of which would repay a great deal of study.

On grounds such as the above, Weber concludes that in the tradition of ethical prophecy and the attempt at religiously motivated mastery over the world, a very special type of intellectualism has played a critical part. This is the intellectualism of *relatively* nonprivileged groups,[17] who for one reason or another are somewhat outside the main prestige structure of their societies. Since peasant groups are almost never bearers of a strongly intellectual tradition, the primary intellectual types are found among the urban classes which have been mentioned above, especially craftsmen and various kinds of merchants. Separateness may involve the very special pariah status of the postexilic Jews, organization in sectarian groups, or something short of that in degree of radical dissociation from the main social structure.

In any case Weber lays particular stress on three historic cases of such groups. One, of course, was the almost incredible elaboration of knowledge of the Talmudic law among Jews. To be sure the rabbis were more or less full-time specialists in such knowledge, though many of them earned a living in humble occupations. But the ordinary Jew was not too far behind, and consciously and strenuously emulated rabbinical examples. The whole Jewish community thus came to be permeated with a kind of legalistic intellectualism which, however prominent such fea-

17. Who may, in current sociological terms, be said to be affected by situations of "relative deprivation."

tures as the search for revenge and utopian chiliasm may have been, provided a special foundation for many types of later rationalization.

The second case Weber stresses was a direct beneficiary of this, namely the intellectualism of early Christian communities, whose members were on the whole people of very humble (though urban) social status. An important contingent of them were, however, converted Jews, and the status of the Bible as a whole meant mainly that the New Testament was added to the Old as an object of study. There is of course a direct link with preaching in that along with the development of the monastic orders and of the sacramental secular priesthood, a major role was played by exposition of the Christian doctrine, and, not least, exhortation to follow it.

The third case, finally, is that of the Puritans, the earlier generations in the development of ascetic Protestantism. These also, though some of their adherents and leaders were English "gentlemen," were by and large not centrally situated in the main prestige-structure. The rank and file were yeomen farmers, craftsmen, small merchants, and the like. The essential point here is their extraordinary knowledge of and concern with the details of the Bible, and the utter seriousness with which they took the theological problems which were discussed, leaning on varying interpretations of biblical texts. Almost as much as the Jews they were "people of the Book."

This is but a sample from Weber's exceedingly rich discussion of the complex relations between social status and the propensity for alienation which in turn underlies accessibility to the influence of prophetic types of religious movement. Let me emphasize that Weber's view of this problem is pluralistic. He in no way denies—rather he specifically emphasizes—that there are very important differential propensities. Thus on the negative side his discussions of peasantries and of military elites are cases in point, on the positive certain types of artisan and other "lower middle class" groups. But just as important as these concepts of predilection, is his contention that there is *no* simple one-to-one relationship between "group interests" or any other specific status-positions in the concrete social structure, and the probability that a prophetic movement will either arise or take hold. Differential patterning applies, not only to propensities, but also to the *content* of the religious orientation itself, and this can never be treated as a simple reflex of the social position of its proponents (particularly their *Interessenlage*).

Weber's analysis in this section outlines relations of interdependence and of independent variability. His most important conclusion is not the high degree to which religious developments are "determined" by their sociological contexts, on both the leadership and the followership levels, but the degree to which the social structure leaves a range of flexibility open so that when, for whatever reasons, a charismatic innovation appears, there is a limited but highly significant range of flexibility which allows the innovation an opportunity to take hold and eventually become institutionalized.

Radical Solutions of the Problem of Meaning

Having for a second time expanded his analysis of the background, Weber again turns to the problem of the basic content of religious orientations themselves. Here the question is where a "breakthrough" leads if it is pressed, precisely by intellectual reasoning, to the most radical conclusions. This leads to the problem of theodicy, which in turn is the basis of the doctrines of radical salvation which have shaped the greatest religious movements.

Here Weber employs again the basic dichotomy already outlined, between the conception of an immanent principle of divinity which is part of the world from eternity and to which in some sense man can "adapt" himself and the conception of a transcendental divinity, in principle fundamentally separate from the world, controlling it from above and, in the extreme case, conceived as having created it *ex nihilo*. Again the Brahman of Indian religious philosophy and the Semitic creator god are at the extremes. Weber held that whichever direction the process of rationalization takes, it inevitably leads to monotheism, and if divinities other than the supreme one survive in a religious system, they are conceived as in some sense subordinate to the supreme one. In this connection, he remarks that only Judaism and Islam have been monotheistic in the strictest sense, because the Christian Trinity has at least polytheistic aspects, and of course in Catholicism the angels, Mary, Satan, and even the ordinary saints have often been regarded as quasi-divinities, if not in certain phases and areas full-fledged divinities. In spite of the generality of the monotheistic trend, however, it is one of Weber's important points that the direction of the immanent conception of divinity, however monotheistic at the highest philosophical levels, is much more favorable to the retention and prominence of polytheistic elements in the total system than is the transcendental type.

Against this background Weber then deals with an aspect of the problem of meaning which is particularly important for him, and indeed is one of the main threads of his whole thought: the integrations and discrepancies between expectation systems which are institutionalized in normative orders and the actual experiences people undergo. The interest lies in what the people interpret to be the consequences *for them* and for the aspects of the human condition to which they are attached, of conformity or nonconformity with an established normative order. There are two essential dimensions of this problem. The first concerns the *level* of rationalization, a point which was built into the early distinction between taboo and religious ethic. If there is a low level of rationalization the possibility exists of a piecemeal resolution of the tensions which arise from discrepancies between normative expectations and actual experiences. This indeed comes close to Weber's very conception of magic, as the use of supernatural agency to resolve *ad hoc* elements of tension in life-situations.

The second dimension is that of discrepancy itself and its implications. Here Weber takes the fundamental position that, *regardless of the particular content of the normative order,* a major element of discrepancy is inevitable. And the more highly rationalized an order, the greater the tension, the greater the exposure of major elements of a population to experiences which are frustrating in the very specific sense, not merely that things happen and contravene their "interests," but that things happen which are "meaningless" in the sense that they *ought* not to happen. Here above all lie the problems of suffering and of evil, not merely the existence of phenomena defined in these terms, but also the prevalence of the suffering of those who do not morally deserve to suffer, the prevalence of the exposure to evil of the morally just, who thus are punished rather than rewarded for their pains, and perhaps even worse, the fact that evil consequences often will ensue from the actions of those who exactly follow the precepts of the moral law. A classic expression of the discrepancy is the saying that "the good die young and the wicked flourish as the green bay tree."

Weber postulates a basic "drive" toward meaning and the resolution of these discrepancies on the level of meaning, a drive or tendency that is often held in check by various defensive mechanisms, of which the pre-eminent one here relevant is that of magic. But whatever the situation regarding the effectiveness of this drive, there is a crucial point concerning the *direction* in which this tendency propels the development of culture. This is that the search for grounds of meaning which can resolve the discrepancies must lead to continually more "ultimate" reference points which are progressively further removed from the levels of common sense experience on which the discrepancies originally arise. The "explanations," that is, solutions to the problems of meaning, must be grounded in increasingly generalized and "fundamental" philosophical conceptions.

Given this movement toward generalized explanations, rationalization can take either of two paths. One, under the assumption of immanence, seeks to ground meaning in progressively greater extension of the time span to which it applies, and in increasingly higher "levels" of participation in the sources of ultimate "satisfaction." This is the path that in India led to the philosophies of *karma* and transmigration and to the drastic "relativizing" of the "good things of this life." The other path, under the assumption of transcendence, grounds meaning in the conception of a creation that is inherently destined—by Divine Will—to bring about a resolution of the discrepancies by creating a world and a human condition that does or will in fact accord with the prescriptions of the normative order, a "Kingdom of God on Earth."

Weber saw these two trends as culminating, at the level of moral philosophy, in the two fully consistent philosophies of moral meaning, or theodicies, which have appeared in religious history. The first of these is the doctrine of *karma*, which postulates a complete closure of the moral system over time spans altogether incommensurable with the human life span, though not strictly speaking eternal. The other consistent theodicy is the Calvinistic conception that ultimate resolution depends upon relations between an absolute, all-powerful God, whose "motives" are in principle inaccessible to finite human understanding, and a Creation, including man, which is absolutely and completely dependent on his Will.[18]

To be sure, these two theodicies resolve the problem of discrepancy by carrying it to a ground where the "moral issue" can no longer be relevant. This seems to be a special case of the general fact that logical systems must always rest on primitive postulates which cannot themselves be "proved." In Christian terms, the attempt at human justification of the Will of God presumes being above God, subjecting Him to an order which the speaker understands independently of God and God must obey.[19] Similar considerations apply in the case of *karma*.

18. The Zarathustrian conception of an eternal, in principle completely indecisive, conflict between the "Principles" of "Good" and "Evil" is logically consistent, but not so much a solution as a declaration of the philosophically insolubility of the problem.
19. The Puritan term for this presumption would be Idolatry of the Flesh.

Radical Salvation and the Orientation of Action

If one presses the theme of the necessary discrepancy between interests "in this world" and the nature of an order thought to be intrinsically capable of providing an answer in terms of truly "ultimate" meaning, the tendency is to widen the gap between the two. Hence, for those who cannot be satisfied with the "compromises" of worldly balances, there develops the need for radical solutions on a personal basis. Weber calls this the *need for salvation,* which we may describe as the need for a basis of personal legitimation which is in accord with these ultimate standards, themselves conceived as standing in essential conflict with those of *any* institutionalized worldly order.

As usual, Weber canvasses an immense range of different modes and levels of conception of the problem of salvation. All of them however, are treated as partial solutions leading up to the two radical possibilities. In both of them the conception of the "world" is central; there is no such thing as a problem of salvation except in relation to the world. The need for salvation, of course, makes sense only because the interests in the things of the world are themselves relativized, and hence of inferior value, in some sense, if not positively "evil." Along these lines then, Weber arrives at twin conceptions, first of the increased *tension* between worldly possibilities and the need to satisfy the need for "perfection," and second, of the *direction* in which resolution of the tension may be sought.

In Weber's very complex discussion the keynote is the importance of the balance between degrees of radicalism in the conception of the problem of salvation and the various devices by which radical implications can be mitigated. Among the mitigating devices, a particularly prominent place is occupied by the category already familiar from Weber's discussion of the "magical" solutions, among which the orgiastic figures prominently, which may be called a half-way station, the category of ritualized institutional dispensation of salvation. By far the most prominent example of this category is the sacramental system of the Roman Catholic church. In such cases the essential criterion is the provision of opportunity for atomized and piecemeal resolution of the tensions arising from discrepancies. The magical solutions provide a "catharsis," be it periodical or reserved for special occasions, and the sacramental system provides absolution for *particular* sins.

At this point in his study, Weber's crucial problem is the determination of the steps by which men have arrived at consideration of the *total* state of discrepancy, and hence a mode of resolution opening the possibility of a completely generalized solution of the problem, that is, the problem which in Protestant language is phrased as that of "justification." Stressing the term "systematic"—in accord with the general theme of rationalization—Weber held that there are two and only two basic directions in which this radical solution can be sought, though he was far from holding that the ultimate definition of their bases had been reached in his time.

These two generalized solutions are, stated clearly and simply, resolution of tension by escape from the conflicts of worldly existence, and resolution by active agency attempting to bring the state of the "world" in this sense into accord with the normative requirements of a *radical* religious ethic.

This dichotomy is a truism, in much the sense that the dichotomy between the alternatives of avoidance and approach is a truism in the psychology of behavior. Yet Weber's dichotomy is, in my opinion, very solidly grounded in both historical evidence and general action theory, and is truistic only in the sense in which general action theory is also truistic. Given the other elements of Weber's analysis, his dichotomy between the two ultimate or generalized resolutions of the problem of discrepancies between normative expectations and actual experiences presents an empirically applicable hypothesis, with respect to which the burden of proof rests upon him who would substitute another hypothesis.

Weber then applies this conception of dichotomy to the behavior of individuals, asking what specific *paths* are open to the seeker of radical salvation. The specification of these paths is possible by reference to a polarity of alternatives which is central in the orientation of all action, namely the polarity between resignedness in a setting of conditions and attempts to master conditions. Both resignedness and mastery are strategies to maintain or enhance personal dignity within the frame of reference. The path of mastery Weber calls *asceticism,* that of resignedness —or "adjustment," if one wishes to use that term—he calls *mysticism.* Both paths are orientations to the human condition as a whole, available to societies as well as to individuals.

Whichever path is taken by the seeker after salvation, he may still choose among various positions relative to the situational order in which he is placed. On the one hand, he may seek salvation and yet avoid a radical break with the institutional order. He remains "in the world," even if he breaks with the institutional order in some subjective way, that is, he may be—in St. Paul's phrase—"in the world but not of it." On the other hand, he may minimize contacts with the established world by becoming a solitary anchorite or by joining with others in some segregated community (the monastic solution). Weber thus derives four types of solution and of individual path, by cross-tabulating the distinction between asceticism and mysticism with the distinction between other-worldly and innerworldly positions.

Weber's primary concern is with the bases on which religious orientations can exert *leverage* toward evolutionary social change, and here is perhaps the most important single place in his analysis where this problem is brought to a head. It is his clear view that only one of the four types does in fact provide powerful leverage, but that it is in the long run a more powerful factor than any elements of economic or political interest in the usual senses. The type in question is of course *innerworldly asceticism*. Let us elucidate its character by contrast with each of the other three types.

The two otherworldly types are in the nature of the case unfavorable to this leverage. The basis of legitimation is for all four types "religious" in a sense involving high tension vis-à-vis "worldly" interests, but for the two otherworldly types the direction of endeavor is in addition *away from* any concern with the state of the world, except to the extent that it threatens to interfere with the religious interests of the individual himself. The otherworldly mystic seeks to avoid subjective "desire" because of its interference with the pursuit of salvation, which is defined as involving dissociation from the world and total loss of interest in its concerns. The otherworldly ascetic on the other hand seeks, phrased in Christian terms, "mastery" over the flesh, the capacity to control worldly motivation, but in the interest of "devotional" goals rather than worldly ones.

In innerworldly mysticism, there is no attempt to escape involvement in worldly status, but while living in and participating in the world the mystic nevertheless seeks to deprive worldly interests, including concern for the "welfare" of others, of any positive meaning or significance. (The mystic gives meaning to the "welfare" of himself and of others only in the sense that the achievement of complete indifference *is* the inner welfare, and should perhaps be achieved equally by all.)

The innerworldly ascetic, on the other hand, seeks mastery over the worldy component of his individual personality, and seeks in principle to extend this mastery to *all* aspects of the human condition. His goal is to attain mastery over the human condition as a whole. Weber saw this most significant alternative as rooted in the great transcendental-monotheistic tradition of the Semitic world in Judaism, Christianity, and

Islam, and standing in the sharpest contrast with the immanent-pantheistic traditions of India. The extreme types saw their fullest realization in ascetic Protestantism on the one hand, early Buddhism on the other. The former was the purest innerworldly asceticism, the latter the purest otherworldly mysticism.

Of particular importance in historical development was the fact that the ascetic point of view was inherently more favorable to firm collectivity formation than the mystical, which tended to a very special religious "individualism." Thus, the early Christian church was a firm and specifically differentiated religious collectivity or *Gemeinde* of which no comparable case existed on an oriental religious basis. When otherworldly asceticism developed on a Christian basis, it led to far firmer collectivity organization in the monastic orders than was the case, for example, in Buddhist monasticism. Indeed the orders provided prototypes for Christian secular society, a pattern which finally emerged most fully in ascetic Protestantism, where "every man became a monk" but lived out his "monastic" commitments in secular callings in this world.

Broadly, Weber regarded both Judaism and Islam as "inhibited" stages in the development of innerworldly asceticism, inhibited especially at the social level, above all because they remained bound by ascription, one to a traditionally defined ethnic, the other to a political community which must be "carried along" as a whole to realize the conception of a Kingdom of God on Earth. The modern way of phrasing it is that neither ever achieved the fundamental differentiation between "church" and "state." Catholic Christianity, on the other hand, was another type of way station because its sacramental system stood between the spiritual and the worldly involvements of the individual in such a way as to atomize his moral obligations as an instrument of the divine will. As Weber repeatedly says, it was possible to gain absolution for particular sins, one by one. There was hence no basic focusing of responsibility for the *total* pattern of life.

On the oriental side, Hinduism has been a kind of Indian Catholicism. It mitigated the severity of the pure Buddhist-type doctrine by supplementing it with a social sacramentalism, namely the ritual significance of caste observances, which made the spiritual fate of the individual dependent on what, in Weber's specific sense, were predominantly magical factors. Of course similar tendencies developed within the Buddhist tradition itself, notably in the *Mahayana* branch.

Though he says relatively little about them in this book, Weber seems to have regarded Confucianism and Greek "humanism" as less radical, in some sense less "religious," versions of the two basic tendencies which dominated his analysis. Confucianism was, on the background of a relatively nonrationalized culture, the institutionalization of a religious ethic of specifically *social* responsibility; it was specifically hostile to any doctrine of radical salvation. Its main cultural background was, furthermore, immanent rather than transcendent. Within its special framework it was, in Weber's classic phrase, a "rational doctrine of adaptation *to* the world," not one of "rational mastery *over* the world," which designation he reserved for ascetic Protestantism. A major indication of this, to Weber, was the failure of rationalism within the Confucian tradition to combat the magical elements of the tradition *in principle*, rather than to relativize them by declaring them to be beneath the concern of the "superior man."

The Greek, or more broadly the classical Mediterranean case, is least systematically dealt with by Weber here, though there are many more or less scattered observations about it. I believe that he viewed it as broadly parallel to the Confucian. Both, on their respective bases, represented a first main level of breakthrough of the process of rationalization, in the Confucian case that of a sacralized conception of social order, in the Greek of a cultural order, of a "rational law of nature." "Magical" elements, such as the Homeric pantheon, were fully subordinated in relation to rational laws of nature, but there was no "radical breakthrough" to the idea of an order so drastically different from the human and "natural" that there must emerge a religious ethic demanding a pattern of life drastically different in quality from even the best patterns of life in the established order.

The above is an outline of the main structure of Weber's analysis of the problem of radical salvation, the paths to it, and the implications of such commitments for orientation to "the world." This outline fails to do justice to the immense richness of Weber's discussions of the many nuances of transition and the complex compromise formations. The historical-comparative justification of Weber's main conceptual framework will doubtless long be a subject of fundamental controversy. It seems fair to say that probably no modern scholar has put forward a framework of such scope and conceptual clarity for the ordering of this central aspect of cultural and sociological analysis.

There is an important sense in which this section is the culmination of Weber's construction of a complex analytical scheme in the religious field. But since he has been dealing again here with the principal patterns of orientation themselves, he still has the task of tracing their application

to the realistic conditions of implementation, that is, of institutionalization, and along the way the kinds of conflict which are encountered by
social groups whose members have become committed to these radical
religious positions.

Types of Religious Ethics in Relation to the World

It goes without saying that any religious movement organized about a
conception of radical salvation in the nature of the case stands in a state
of high tension in its relations to an institutionalized worldly order.
Weber's concern is to analyze some of the main foci of this tension and
the ways in which the movement, particularly after its initial phases, can
cope with them.

His main point of reference is the proposition that such movements
generate an ethic of brotherly love certainly between their members, and
very generally "spilling over" to other categories, in the extreme case to
all mankind or even all living things. The Christian injunction to "love
the Lord thy God with all thy heart, and love thy neighbor as thyself" is
prototypical, and by no means confined to one religious tradition.

If it is a religion of radical salvation its reference points for brotherly
love as well as for love of God are in some sense extraworldly, though not
necessarily otherworldly in the sense of the foregoing discussion. Using a
term which Weber did not, they may be said to be "undifferentiated"
with reference to the exigencies of social organization in the world. Every
attitude and act toward one's "neighbor" should be a full expression of
religiously motivated love and should be unaffected by "practical considerations." The result is an extreme instance of what Weber called a
Gesinnungsethik, an ethic of moral sentiment rather than of responsibility for consequences. The essential question is whether such an ethic
is inherently utopian in the sense that acting fully and directly in accord
with its mandate is not compatible with the necessary conditions of the
functioning of concrete human societies.

Weber's answer to this, as to so many questions, is far from simple. It
depends on at least three considerations: the other components of the
pattern of religious orientation itself, the way it is "spelled out" in
application to social conditions, and the kind of society in question, since
this is far from being a constant. The tension is likely to be least in very
simple societies, and in specially segregated religious communities,

whether they be monastic orders or such segregated communities as the Hutterites and many other sectarian groups have formed.

A second basic difference is generated by the two main directions in which salvation may be sought. The mystical direction is connected with a tendency to declare the structure of worldly society itself to be irrelevant to true religious interests, and any concern with it to be inherently distracting from the important things. This has dual consequences. It conduces to the maximal extension of the sentiments of solidarity on the level of sentiment as such. It is probably no accident that it is on a Brahman–Hindu–Buddhist background that the radical doctrine of *ahimsa* —the prohibition of killing of any living thing, except plants of course— has arisen, and that vegetarianism is very much a virtue among high caste Hindus. The other consequence, however, is reluctance to accept any realistic conditions of implementing the ethic of brotherly love. Thus, as Weber several times emphasizes, under the strict rules of early Buddhist monasticism there was an absolute prohibition of work of any kind —unless devotions be called work—and the monk could only eat by the charity of laymen, interpreted in a very strict sense. Ideally he could not even solicit gifts of food—he could not in our sense "beg"—but was dependent on the layman's purely spontaneous recognition of his need. This is perhaps as far as the maxim "take no thought for the morrow" has ever been carried in an institution. It is hard to see how a total society could be organized on this basis and indeed, it is one of Weber's major points that this life was in principle accessible only to members of an elite.

Generally speaking the ascetic path to salvation has had a very different emphasis. It may even be said that sheer "mortification of the flesh" on an individual basis is a kind of "work" in that it is oriented to coping with the nature of worldly motives. Weber then lays great stress on the place occupied by work, that is "useful" work in a worldly sense, such as growing crops in the Benedictine Rule as an ascetic exercise. This he regarded as a case in point of the general orientation to mastery—one does not "master" a situation without reference to criteria of effectiveness in dealing with concrete conditions. Weber held that the ascetic path is inherently more likely to produce ways of dealing with realistic exigencies of human relationships than is the mystical.

Weber then reviews some of the main aspects of social organization, especially the economic aspect, from the point of view of this problem. As just noted, for the mystical tradition even the level of simple utilitarian physical production was highly problematical, but this was not so for the ascetic tradition except at the otherworldly extremes that may be said to have involved "mystical" motives. After all, as Weber repeatedly emphasized, most of the early Christians were artisans, and while they regarded the higher order of Roman society as evil, they did not so regard their simple fields of work. Questions arise, however, with advance from the simpler level of technology to the level of complex economies, involving markets and monetary exchange. Here the directness of mutual helpfulness in the simpler exchanges evaporates, and by entrusting interests to the market, one simply does not know in advance what the morally significant consequences of an act may be.[20]

The particular question to which Weber pays the most attention in this area is that of the taking of interest. In the predominantly mystical tradition it could never become a salient problem—almost by definition it belonged on the lower level from which the religious elite must disengage themselves. In the West, however, it has been a particularly central focus of problems of economic ethics. In earlier phases, taking interest has, Weber says, always been regarded as incompatible with the ethic of brotherly love. In the Western world its gradual acceptance took place only through stages involving very severe struggles. Various problems were involved, as Aristotle's famous doctrine of the "sterility" of money, the special role of the Jews and their "double ethic" in this respect, and various others. He was also particularly concerned with the history of the attitudes of the Catholic Church in this matter, the eventual upshot of which was recognition of the positive functional significance of interest-taking finance in even a "Christian society." But the Church had so involved itself in the other point of view that it could not simply "repeal" the prohibition of usury, and had to let the prohibition become a dead letter.

Weber is careful to emphasize that the usury question, and back of it the more general question of the financial aspect of capitalism, is not for him the major issue with respect to the problem of the relation of the Protestant ethic to modern economic development. Rather, the major issue is the moral legitimation of productivity and the channelling of the

20. Thus, for example, Menno Simons, the founder of the Mennonite sect, in no way disapproved the simpler concerns with worldly welfare, e.g. health, preservation of life, even comfort. The economic problem for him was the possibility that a producer who entrusted his product to the market could not guarantee the moral quality of the use to which a consumer, unknown to him, might put it. Hence he forbade all involvement where such risks might be involved. It is relatively difficult, on a Christian background, to use food unethically, hence agriculture, even in a market context, is a relatively approved occupation for Mennonites. The automobile is quite another matter. This has posed a much more serious moral problem, on which apparently there has been some "give" in recent times. The even more strictly sectarian Hutterites seem still to maintain a nearly absolute prohibition of its use.

needs of individuals for justification in the religious sense in this direction, which is the decisive point, in this context, about ascetic Protestantism. For Weber, the "typical" capitalist was not the socially elite banker, but the middle-class industrial entrepreneur.

Weber reviews extensively the ethical dilemmas posed to a religious ethic by the problems of political power, especially the role of physical force in politics. From the point of view of the pure ethic of brotherly love, the use of force is perhaps the prototypical evil. Yet violence is historically intertwined in the most complex ways with the processes of the extension of order in human societies. There have here, as well as in the economic field, been deep tensions over the status of religious groups in relation to the exigencies of the world.

In the process of its institutionalization Christianity gave religious sanction to political authority in secular society, a process which occurred in two main steps. The first step was the "Constantinian," which involved not only the conversion of a Roman emperor to Christianity, but equally the recognition by the Church, for the successors of Constantine, that an emperor could be a Christian. Later, on the basis of a much sharper *differentiation* between church and state, this sanction of political authority was symbolized by the coronation of an emperor, Charlemagne, by the Pope, an emperor whose obligation to defend his realm by military means was obviously taken for granted. The dilemmas of the use of force, and more generally of coercion by legitimate authority ultimately religiously legitimated authority—are, Weber held, inescapable. Only the main ascetic trend could develop a positive religious basis of such legitimation.

The fields of economic and political interests duly differentiated from each other, not fused as is done by Marxists, are the prototypical ones involved in the adjustment of a radical religious ethic to the exigencies of the world. In addition to these, Weber also discusses the tensions arising over the erotic sphere, and over that of art, thus manifesting an important sensitivity to problems on the one hand of the relation of the personality of the individual to its organic base, on the other hand to problems of the cultural system other than problems in the religious aspect as such. His interest in the non-religious aspects of culture is rounded out by various discussions in his work of the relation of religion to concern with science.

Weber concludes his discussion of orientations to the world, and indeed the book as a whole, with a brief and, the German editors tell us, incomplete discussion of the relevance of these problems to that of "capitalism." He makes clear that the essential point for him is not the relation between religion and capitalism in the most general formal sense of orientation to monetary profit-making. Again and again in his work he emphasizes that capitalism in this generic sense has occurred wherever the monetary mechanism itself has been developed. There are many subvarieties.

His principal interest, therefore, is not in capitalism in general but in a very special variety of it, which Weber called "rational bourgeois capitalism." This may be defined broadly as the maximization of the conception of rational effectiveness and efficiency in the organization of economic production in a market-oriented system. It includes not only profit-making, but bureaucratic organization in the interest of productivity, and various other things.

In the half-century since Weber wrote it has become increasingly clear that his main interest and focus was modern industrial society *as a whole*, not its "capitalistic" subvariety. The problem of the specific role of markets is not the essential problem from Weber's point of view, but one particularly important subproblem of the more general complex with which he was concerned. More than any other single writer in the background of our own generation, Weber gave us the primary reference points for analyzing the broad *common* patterns of modern social, political, and economic development.

As I have suggested a number of times, Weber's was the type of mind which, in an often baffling way, combined enormous sensitivity to the most complex detail with certain not only very broad, but very precisely conceived main lines of analysis. I have thought that this introduction could be most useful by attempting to highlight the main logical and substantive structures of Weber's sociology of religion, since the reader will be immersed in the detail by the mere fact of reading, and Weber does not succinctly sum up this analytical component as a whole at any point in his exposition in this book or elsewhere.

To sum up our own perspective: This book is clearly the strategically central part of a generally evolutionary view of the development of human society. It is the one in which Weber attributes prime causal significance to the factor of "religious orientation" as an initiating factor and as a differentiating factor in the process. This factor is, however, nowhere treated as automatically unfolding or "actualizing itself" except through highly complex processes of interaction with other factors and independence with them. The outcomes are always resultant from and attributable to such interaction, never to any one factor alone. Weber clearly insisted on the independent significance of the ideas which originated as solutions of the problems of meaning, and the independent significance of the "religious interests" which operate within this framework. But at the same time he made as great a single contribution to the understanding of the role of "material" factors in the process of social development as did any scholar, at least up to his time—including, it seems to me, Karl Marx.

Within this analytical framework, Weber in turn treated the development of the modern Western world, and particularly the sector of it influenced by ascetic Protestantism, as standing in the vanguard of the most important general evolutionary trend. He sees its place as having been decisively influenced by its religious background—with all the appropriate qualifications—by comparison with the other great cultural traditions. The decisive significance in the turbulent contemporary world of economic development at the industrial levels and indeed of the more modern levels of political organization, cannot be understood apart from this broader evolutionary context. As Weber insisted again and again, the problem of accounting for the origination of a pattern of cultural and social organization is fundamentally different from the problem of accounting for its diffusion from examples already established. That modern industrial society has become the primary model for the world as a whole can scarcely be doubted.

It is to be hoped that the publication of this work in English will contribute materially to a higher level of understanding of these problems of what has been happening to the human condition in the mid-twentieth century. Weber would have been the very last to claim anything like definitiveness for his own work. It seems unlikely, however, that a better assessment can be arrived at without a very thorough coming to terms with the nature and implications of Weber's work. The volume here presented is probably, for historical evaluation, the most important single segment of his work.

In spite of the soundness and scope of Weber's theoretical framework for the sociology of religion, the present day usefulness of that theoretical framework is at least partially limited by three considerations. First, the application of the framework to concrete problems requires such flexibility and such a fund of knowledge as Weber possessed. Second, the religious phenomena themselves have changed, especially in the United States, since Weber formulated his framework and his hypotheses. Third, sociological theory has in some respects advanced beyond Weber's theoretical framework. After discussing these limitations, I shall return to the basic thesis of this introduction, the enduring greatness of Weber's theoretical framework for the sociology of religion.

Weber's enormous historical erudition, as well as his high level of empirical insight and judgment, served to cover over whatever theoretical deficiencies were inherent in his conceptual framework. There is a brilliant *ad hocness* to Weber's analysis, particularly when he deals with problems of transition. Whether the problems involve a transition between types, without reference to genetic relatedness, or involve a transition in the developmental process from one phase or stage to another, such problems of transition bring to prominent attention both the difficulties inherent in Weber's conceptual framework and the brilliance with which Weber found *ad hoc* solutions to each such difficulty. But Weber's scheme itself, when applied by scholars of lesser genius than Weber, can hardly yield comparable results. This may be a principal reason why there has been relatively little cumulative development of Weber's sociological contributions. But we shall also see that sociology has developed newer and possibly better theoretical methods for dealing with the cultural phenomena which Weber treated under the concepts of "prophetic break" and "motivation."

In the fifty years since Weber wrote, much has happened in the religious situation of Christendom, and perhaps especially in the religious situation of the United States. The three dominant "faiths" of American society have come to be integrated into a single socio-religious system, a development that even in the late nineteenth century seemed highly unlikely. This system has evolved under the "historical leadership of American liberal Protestantism," but has very much involved and modified all three major faiths. For instance, the pariah status of the Jewish faith, on which Weber laid great stress, has been modified, not only through greater "toleration" of Jews by Gentiles, but also by a new level of Jewish acceptance of the *legitimacy* of the outside order in which Jews come into contact with Gentiles, especially the occupational system. For all Jews except the most rigidly orthodox, a religiously sanctioned life is no longer confined to the internal life of the Jewish community. The position of the Roman Catholic community in the United States is undergoing similar modifications, of which visible indices can be found in the broad Protestant acceptance of a Roman Catholic president, and the American Catholic hierarchy's failure to repudiate that president's expressed position on the separation between Church and State. These changes have occurred by a developmental restructuring, without a prophetic break with the established order. The basic value pattern common to all three faiths has been at least partially institutionalized at a higher level of generality, and the "privatization" of religion through denominational pluralism has been extended from the Protestant group to the whole range of faiths.[21]

Such developments in the religious situation were only beginning in Weber's time, and it would be a great deal to demand of his writings that they predict the present phase. However, the fact that the present phase was highly unlikely from Weber's point of view may be a valid index of the theoretical difficulties inherent in his position.

Weber's mode of thinking was dominated by the concept of the ideal type, which he applied to both cultural content and individual motives. He was quite right to insist, against a background of idealistic historicism, that explanatory concepts be applicable to the understandable motives of individuals. And when we consider how often the "methodological individualism" of English-speaking social scientists has led them to biopsychological reductionism, we can see that Weber was indeed right to insist that the inclusion of cultural content is indispensable to the analysis of orientations to the great problems of meaning. But it is now possible to go somewhat beyond the concept of the ideal type, by making a more sophisticated and thorough use of the concept of system.

Weber, as many "culture and personality" theorists have done since his time, tended to treat "typical motives—which for him always involved cultural "definitions of the situation"—as rigidly unchangeable entities. Thus, he used ideal types to "atomize" his material into rigid units which could only be combined and recombined in a "mechanistic" way or absorbed into higher-order "patterns." His own theoretical method suffers to some extent from the "trait atomism" of the intellectual tradition from which he came and against which he partially revolted, and his method even resembles the process of rationalization which he traces in religious phenomena. He frequently atomizes traits, and when this proves unsatisfactory, postulates unduly rigid higher-order cultural configurations.[22]

This tendency to atomize traits instead of interrelating them within

---

21. The first writer to express a clear conception of this new American religious pattern, to my knowledge, was Will Herberg in his *Protestant, Catholic, Jew* (Garden City: Doubleday, first edition 1951, second and extended edition 1960). I have dealt with some phases of the new pattern in "Some Comments on the Pattern of Religious Organization in the United States," *Daedalus*, Summer, 1959, reprinted as Chapter 10 of my volume of essays, *Structure and Process in Modern Societies* (Glencoe: Free Press, 1960).

22. The present writer has commented upon the atomism of ideal types in *The Structure of Social Action*, Chap. XVII, and on a more advanced basis in the Introduction to Weber's *Theory of Social and Economic Organization* (Glencoe: Free Press 1947).

systems appears in Weber's treatments of what we now term personality, society, and culture. Surprisingly, it is most evident in his treatment of society, even though he is thought of in the first instance as a sociologist. Though he was well versed in economic theory and contributed some of the most penetrating comments about markets that were made in his time, it is still true that his analysis of modern capitalism stressed an overly rigid typological formula of the harnessing of "bureaucratic" organization to an orientation to profit. On the one hand, he did not sufficiently analyze the articulation of these "bureaucratic" organizational units with each other.[23] On the other hand, he treated the organizational units themselves too narrowly, not taking sufficient account of the range of variation of both organizational types and the role structures within them. Most conspicuously, he failed sufficiently to recognize or analyze the roles of applied science and scientific research itself when harnessed within "bureaucratic" organizations. Less obviously, but of comparable importance, he did not adequately delineate the subtle transitions between orientation to profit-making, orientation within various "fiduciary" organizations, and orientation within public organizations. His neglect of these transitions in orientation led him to postulate a sharper dichotomy between "capitalistic" and "socialistic" forms of economic organization— as distinguished from forms of economic ideology—than the facts and trends of development warranted. The same typological rigidity makes its appearance in Weber's sociology of religion.

The theoretical difficulties caused by typological rigidity and trait atomism, covered over in many instances by Weber's enormous erudition, insight and *ad hoc* resourcefulness, come to the surface at two main points: his analyses of the prophetic *break* and of "motivation." We have seen in our review of the religious situation in the United States how gradual, cumulative, and interrelated changes can be; yet Weber seemed unable to conceive that major evolutionary steps could take place by gradual process. Such prophetic breaks as he describes have probably occurred, but he seems to have a theoretical bias toward highlighting them, to the neglect of the possibility of more gradual and cumulative processes of change. In treating phenomena of "motivation," he displays a similar theoretical bias toward hypostatizing rigid types of "motives," imputed to both individuals and classes of individuals, and paralleling the "ideal types" which are his primary units of analysis. He even reifies the famous "profit motive," though less so than has been common in the utilitarian

23. Consider the fruitfulness of Durkheim's analysis of the role of institutionalization of contract in the articulation and interrelation of organizational units.

tradition of analysis. In the field of the sociology of religion, he reifies such motives as the "need for salvation," and tends to dissociate such motives from other and more ordinary motives present at the level of individual personality. Motives are related to cultural "ideal types" in a morphological framework rather than related to other motives in the system of personality and other processes in the systems of society and culture.

Weber's scheme, in the sociology of religion and generally, which constituted a great advance in its time, has provided a foundation for further progress in sociology, and remains relevant at its broadest morphological levels. Though Weber's conceptual scheme is certainly far from complete or definitive, it seems unlikely that the broadest outline of the evolutionary pattern of the development of religious orientations, including the conception of the two basic directions of rationalization in the field of meaning, will be radically invalidated.

Difficulties seem to become more prominent as attention is focused on problems of transition, whether it be transition between types, without reference to genetic relatedness, or transition in the developmental process from one phase or stage to the next. As Weber deals with such problems, there seems to be a certain *ad hocness* when, so to speak, theoretical deficiencies are covered over by his enormous historical erudition and excellent level of empirical insight and judgment. The suggestion is that in the hands of a scholar of lesser genius than Weber, it would be very difficult to get comparable results through the use of his scheme. This may well be one principal reason for the relatively small cumulative outcome of Weber's work.

The main point is that Weber's atomism of types introduces into his analysis a rigidity which tends to suppress notice of the ranges of variation between the components included in the types. I have suggested that this typological rigidity becomes evident at two main points in Weber's analysis. First, it suppresses notice of independent variables which may account for more gradual, cumulative socio-cultural changes; and hence it leads Weber to feel that there must be abrupt shifts from one type to another. Second, typological rigidity appears in his analysis of motivation, suppressing the flexibility of transition from one motive to another, and thus tending to tie motivational categories to types of concrete social action, thereby unduly "psychologizing" the interpretation of concrete social actions in the context of analysis of the social system.

These last criticisms are not intended to derogate in any way the importance of Weber's contribution in this field, which is a permanent contribution. Indeed, if the hindsight of fifty years' development of theory in the field were not able to uncover important theoretical difficulties in such a body of thought as Weber's sociology of religion, rather than merely trivial errors of fact, this would be a sad commentary upon the progress of social science, which has in fact been real progress.

It is my view that this book is *the* most crucial contribution of our century to the comparative and evolutionary understanding of the relations between religion and society, and even of society and culture generally. But it, like any great contribution to science, is both a synthesis and a point of departure for another set of steps in the unending series of steps which constitutes the process of the improvement of knowledge.

CHAPTER 3

Evaluation and Objectivity in Social Science: An Interpretation of Max Weber's Contributions

This paper was written for the observance of the centenary of Weber's birth by the German Sociological Association, held at Heidelberg in April, 1964. It was written in English, but translated into German to be read at the meeting and was published in the *Proceedings* put out by the German Sociological Association. The English version and a French translation were published in the UNESCO *Journal of Social Science*, Vol. 17, 1965. The topic, "Evaluation and Objectivity in Social Science" was assigned to me, but it was an entirely congenial assignment. First, it provided an occasion to reconsider the meanings of Weber's two famous conceptions of "value freedom" (*Wertfreiheit*) and "value-relevance" (*Wertbeziehung*). In particular, it had not been nearly so clear to me previously that the former did not refer, as so many have claimed, to the absence of all value commitments as a norm for social scientists, but to the *differentiation* between the values of science, in the broad sense of the German *Wissenschaft*, which includes the humanistic disciplines, and the values appropriate to practical social policy. This seemed to be an essential condition of the emergence of the mature social sciences as "pure" disciplines, as distinguished from both ideologies and handmaidens of programs for "social engineering." However imperfectly this ideal has been realized since Weber's time, it remains a fundamental preference point for the development of the social sciences.

This paper also provided an occasion for reviewing the general structure of Weber's theoretical treatment of social systems.

"Evaluation and Objectivity in the Social Sciences: An Interpretation of Max Weber's Contributions" [delivered at the Weber Centennial, April, 1964] from Proceedings of the German Sociological Association, the *Deutsche Gesellschaft for Soziologie* and the *UNESCO Journal of Social Sciences*, Vol. 17, No. 1, 1965.

The systematic interrelations among the four principal divisions of his substantive work: the sociological treatment of economic processes, of political organization, of law, and of religion became much clearer than before. Above all, the central significance of the sociology of law for the design of Weber's work as a whole became conspicuous. This accorded with Weber's personal intellectual history, since he began his career in jurisprudence, but is also of major significance to his place in the general development of sociology and to the understanding of his influence. It brings him much closer to Durkheim than most interpretations of his work have recognized.

I T IS indeed both an honor and a challenge to be invited to participate in this most significant occasion, the observance of the one hundredth anniversary of the birth of Max Weber. It is also a great pleasure to revisit the University of Heidelberg, though not quite for the first time, just short of forty years after my enrollment here as a student in 1925. This was too late to know Max Weber in person, but of course his intellectual influence was all-pervasive in the Heidelberg of that time, constituting the one primary point of reference about which all theoretical and much empirical discussion in the social and cultural fields revolved. I was also privileged to know his gracious and highly intelligent widow, Marianne Weber, in particular to attend a number of her famous "sociological teas" on Sunday afternoons. It was an extraordinarily stimulating intellectual environment, participation in which was one of the most important factors in determining my whole intellectual and professional career.

I hope it is agreeable to Professor Stammer and the other members of the committee who planned this program, if I interpret my topic broadly, rather than narrowly. In the sense in which this is true of Professors Henrich and Winckelmann and many others, I am not a Max Weber scholar; in particular, a scholar of the intricate details of his methodology of science and its relation to the currents of German philosophy of his time. It seems much more appropriate for me to address myself to the broad questions of Max Weber's place in and contribution to the principal trends of development of thought in the Western world on the theoretical understanding of the problems of man in society and culture, which were both problems of his own time, seen in his perspective as a German scholar, and universal problems of all time. As an American, deeply influenced by Weber, it is doubly appropriate for me to consider his significance in this wider perspective. Moreover, I wish to see Weber's problems not only in the purely intellectual frame of reference, but also in terms of some of the social and political developments of the time to which Weber himself was so sensitive. It is my conviction that the two aspects have been very intimately connected and that a certain approach in terms of the sociology of knowledge will prove to be fruitful in understanding them.

This of course is not at all to say that the problems of the relation of values to objectivity in the social and cultural sciences, as treated by Weber, were of secondary importance. On the contrary I would attribute the greatest importance to them, perhaps, in the general intellectual development, at least as great as to that of his substantive contributions in social science. I am therefore by no means unhappy to be dealing in the first instance with the former rather than the latter, and I think it quite proper that they should be considered first in the present symposium.

To come to my central theme, I would first like to suggest that Weber's peak of intellectual maturity coincided remarkably with the outbreak of the great crisis of this century in the social and political order of the Western world, both internally and in its relation to the rest of the world of our time, namely the beginning of World War I in 1914. Fifty years of retrospect make it possible to be quite sure that this truly marked the end of an era. Politically it was the beginning of the end of the nineteenth-century system of European national states, that on the one hand has ultimately made their traditional "sovereignty" vis-à-vis each other untenable, and on the other hand has destroyed their hegemony over the rest of the world. In the first context, the Common Market and the European unification movement are sufficient indices that the old order has changed internally, the present position in the world-power system of the United States and the Soviet Union, and the ending of colonialism that the old Europe no longer plays its nineteenth-century role in relation to the rest of the world.

It is less well known, but I think equally definite and important, that the generation spanning the turn to the twentieth century saw the decisive initial steps taken in a profound intellectual and cultural transformation, the full consequences of which are even now only beginning to emerge. I would like first to discuss Weber in the context of the latter set of problems and then relate the structure of these problems and of thought about them to the trends of evolution of the social and political system.

Weber's Theoretical Reference Groups

Max Weber's intellectual home, of course, lay in the "historistic" aftermath of German Idealism as worked out in the historical schools of jurisprudence, economics, and more generally of culture, as in the work of Dilthey and of religion, as in the work of Troeltsch. The trend was, of course, to stress the internal integration and the historical individuality and uniqueness of the particular cultural system, such as Roman Law, or Renaissance Culture, or indeed "rational bourgeoise capitalism." The way in which this was done tended to accentuate the dualism already present in the Kantian position between the world of Nature and that of *Kultur* or *Geist*, involving Kant's "practical reason," human values, and problems of meaning. The cultural and social sciences, dealing with the latter realms, were thereby sharply set off against the natural, not only in terms of empirical subject matter but also of basic method and mode of conceptualization.

This position not only accentuated a distinction between the two groups of sciences. It went farther to structure the relation in favor of protecting the historical-cultural sphere against the encroachments of natural-science perspectives and methods. The implication that these were dangerous to human values was certainly present. Closely related to this problem in turn was that of the relation between the individual observer and his subject matter. As became perhaps particularly clear in the philosophy of Dilthey, the relativity inherent in the conception of the sociocultural historical individual came to involve the individual because of his involvement in it. There was, then, the threat of a socio-cultural solipsism which in some respects was more profound than the individual version propounded by Bishop Berkeley.

The crucial problem from one point of view was that of the source of leverage whereby the individual scholar or scientist and the scholarly community of which he was a part, could avoid involvement in a closed system from which there was no escape. From some perspectives the difficulty seemed to be insuperable because the understanding of motives and meanings (*Verstehen*) that were shared between observer and object, seemed to be the essence of the cultural disciplines that separated them from the natural. This was of course perhaps the most central point at which Weber made his proposals for reformulation.

The citing of these difficulties in German historicism—which incidentally have tended to be repeated a half-century later in American cultural anthropology—is by no means meant to belittle the major substantive contributions made under the aegis of the "historical schools" in various disciplines during the relevant period. They did, however, create tensions which were the starting points for Weber's special contribution.

Before attempting to characterize this, I think it will be helpful to sketch briefly the two principal alternatives to historicism that seemed to be most readily available in the intellectual situation of Weber's time. The first of these was relatively foreign to the main German tradition, though constantly close to its center of awareness. Indeed there was a strong tendency to define the main axis of the difference between German and "Western" culture in terms of the contrast between the complex just sketched and Western "rationalism," atomism, and various other terms.

In intellectual history this contrast presents too many complexities to enter into here. The most salient elements for present purposes, however, were those centering in British social thought—and American—though the United States was not at the time a very prominent focus of major intellectual movements to a central European. Here the main focus, I think, lies in the broad utilitarian movement, which had two particularly important characteristics for purposes of the present analysis. The first of these is that it tended to assimilate the natural and the sociocultural fields to each other rather than, in the German tradition, separating them. The most prominent movement in this direction centered about the development of economics as a theoretical discipline, which had become firmly established in Britain. The same general intellectual framework had much to do with the beginnings of psychology as a science. The level of economics was clearly one of the *Verstehen* of human motives, of the relation of the "wants" of individuals to the measures taken to secure their satisfaction. In theoretical terms, however, this was a sharply limited range of motives and utilitarianism also remained "atomistic"—that is to say that it had no theoretical way of establishing relations among individuals other than at the level of means and the situation of action. As such it was unstable and subject to pressures to "reductionism," the purport of which was that the relevance of the theoretical model of "natural science" tended to cover the reduction of man to what was in fact a biological organism or even a physical particle.

Considerations such as these seem to be related to the common German tendency to derogate the intellectual merits of utilitarian thought by treating it as merely an ideological expression of the "materialistic" interests of its proponents. There were, however, profoundly important intellectual problems underlying the difference between German historicism and English utilitarianism.

French social and cultural thought of the time is much more difficult to characterize. On the one hand, both positivism and rationalism of important sorts flourished in France. This circumstance is related to the German tendency at that time to treat French *Civilisation* as somehow inferior to German *Kultur*. At the same time, as developments of special interest to the sociologist have made clear, there were more readily available openings for a sociological type of development in France than in England, in the more "collectivistic" strain of French radical rather than conservative thought, that is from Rousseau, through St. Simon and Comte, to Durkheim and other contemporaries of Weber. It seems fair to say that on the whole the French situation was intermediate between the German and the British and subsequently, though not in Weber's lifetime, came to be an essential intellectual bridge between them.

The second major movement toward which Weber had to assume a position was socialist thought. As by far the most philosophical version and over the long run the most influential, it seems justified to confine attention here to Marxism. Moreover, it was the version dominant in the German intellectual situation of Weber's time, though it should not be forgotten that the split between the Communist and the Social Democratic wings did not occur in time to affect Weber's basic orientation.

In the present frame of reference, Marx presented a peculiar synthesis between the German and British patterns of thinking just outlined, which he could achieve by, in his famous phrase, "standing Hegel on his head." I understand this to mean that Marx remained basically within the main frame of reference of German philosophy in this respect: above all, he accepted a dichotomy that was not identical to that between the cultural and the natural sciences, but was obviously very closely related to it, namely between the two categories of factors operating in the field of human behavior, the *Idealfaktoren* and the *Realfaktoren*. Hegel, as an idealist, clearly thought the former to be paramount; whereas standing him on his head asserted the primacy of the other set, of the "material" interests. This could bring Marx closer to the natural sciences, as in a sense the concept "scientific socialism" suggested, but it still remained within the idealist-historicist frame of reference. It could also make possible a positive use of utilitarian economics, as a scheme for analyzing the internal dynamics of the capitalistic system in modified Ricardian terms—though remaining true to historicism, by insisting that economic theory in anything like that sense applied *only* to capitalism. To be sure, finally, Marx stopped short of pure historicism in that he shared with Hegel a teleologically-oriented scheme of the evolution of human society and culture as a whole.

My thesis is that these three intellectual movements, with reference in all cases to the problems of the sciences of human social and cultural affairs, defined the coordinates of Weber's problem. In fact he achieved a synthesis that, though refusing to accept any one of them on its own terms, ended by incorporating essential elements from all of them into a single frame of reference and leaning on this, the beginnings of a theory that was clearly on a much higher level than could be offered by any of its antecedents. Weber's innovations—in which he was not alone, but certainly in most respects preeminent, I think can best be put in terms of his "methodological" conceptions on the one hand, his substantive contributions to social science on the other. This distinction, it seems to me, is roughly equivalent to that between frame of reference and theory in the broad scientific sense.

Weber's Methodology of Social Sciences

1. WERTFREIHEIT

The concept of value freedom may be said to be the foundation of his position. It stands in sharp contrast to all three of the above views from which Weber differed. From the historicist perspective, the investigator was so firmly ascribed to his cultural position that capacity to transcend it in favor of a new level of objectivity was certainly problematical. From the Marxist point of view this embeddedness in a sociocultural system remained, but was compounded by the movement's commitment to political action in the name of the implementation of the doctrine's views of the iniquity of capitalism and the prospective glories of socialism. The case of utilitarianism is a bit more complex, but no clear line was drawn between the grounds of objectivity in empirical judgment on the one hand, and of advocacy of policies on the other, because the latter problem was reduced so completely to the level of merely individual preferences.

By contrast with all three, Weber's position is one of a much higher level of differentiation. It is not an advocacy that the social scientist abstain from all value commitments—for example, the position taken in *Wissenschaft als Beruf* makes that entirely clear. The point is rather that *in his role* as scientist a particular subvalue system must be paramount for the investigator, one in which conceptual clarity, consistency, and generality on the one hand, and empirical accuracy and verifiability on the other, are the valued outputs of the process of investigation. But the scientist is never the whole man, and the scientific community is never a whole society. It is as inconceivable that either a person or a society should be exhausted in these terms as that there should be a totally "economic" man or society. Other value components are naturally paramount in other roles of individuals and in other subsystems of the society. Value freedom I thus interpret as freedom to pursue the values of science within the relevant limits, without their being overridden by values either contradictory to or irrelevant to those of scientific investigation. At the same time it involves the renunciation of any claims that the scientist qua scientist speaks for a value position, on a broader basis of social or cultural significance than that of his science. Thus from Weber's point of view such a phrase as "scientific socialism" is just as unacceptable as "Christian Science" would be if the term science there were meant in an empirical sense. The policy orientations of political movements are *never* simple applications of scientific knowledge, but always involve value components that are analytically independent of the sciences, natural or social. Value freedom, furthermore, implies that a science need not be bound to the values of any particular historic culture.

2. WERTBEZIEHUNG

Secondly, there is a sense in which the doctrine of *Wertbeziehung* is the obverse of that of *Wertfreiheit*. The latter I have interpreted in the sense of stressing the *in*dependence of the role of scientist from other roles. The former may be interpreted as stressing their *inter*dependence. This, above all, seems to be directed against the kind of naive empiricism, according to which scientific knowledge is held to be simply a reflection of the reality of the external world, whether this empiricism be understood in the more historicist sense of involvement in the particular cultural system itself, or in that of British empiricism with its relation to utilitarianism and to cultural-trait atomism. It is an implication of the differentiation of roles between scientist and other bases of participation in both the cultural and the social systems, that the bases of interest for the posing of problems for a science should be carefully distinguished from the canons of procedure in the solution of those problems, and of the validity of propositions arrived at through following those procedures. Scientific investigation is never purely an occupation of the ivory tower and its products are not "immaculately conceived." Values for Weber may in this context be said to constitute the extrascientific source of the scientific "paternity" by virtue of which "mother science" can be fruitful. This doctrine is of course related to a number of considerations. First it may be noted that the scientist himself, as a total human being, must find his commitment to his science meaningful in terms of *his* values— it must be his calling (*Beruf*). But, secondly, science is only in a limiting case a purely individual isolated activity—it must in the nature of the case be socially organized. In this connection it is essential that it should be integrated to a degree in the value consensus of the community in which it takes place, not totally absorbed, but accorded the kind of place that is essential to its support in a broadly political sense. Without such consensus, for example, anything like a modern university system would be unthinkable. Contrary, then, to much naive cultural "isolationism" we can then say that *of course* science, including the sociocultural sciences, is oriented in terms of and dependent on the total value systems of the society and culture of the time. This almost follows from the fundamental fact that science is a human enterprise. But as noted, this interdependence is not incompatible with its essential independence.

3. CAUSAL EXPLANATION AND GENERALIZED THEORY

In the preceding two primary references of Weber's methodology of social science the problem has been that of relation to the wider culture. The next problem I wish to take up concerns a problem internal to the sciences, namely the relation between the status of natural and of cultural science. Here it seems to me that the crucial points are essentially very simple. Weber took very seriously indeed the proposition that *knowledge* in the empirical sense clearly implied the *causal explanation* of phenomena and events. Causal explanation, in turn, is simply not possible unless the particular facts are related, not merely in an historical sequence, but through analysis by means of a generalized theoretical scheme that is, in the nature of the case, abstract. Very bluntly, the conception of generalized *theory* that has developed in the great tradition of the natural sciences is an essential component of *all* empirical science. This includes not merely definitions of generalized concepts and classificatory schemes but substantive propositions about the *relations* among abstractly defined variables.

The basic fallacy of "historicism," if I am correct in interpreting Weber's view, was the idea that, through empathic "understanding" of the cultural orientations of a system alone, either it was possible to *explain* action within the system without reference to any analysis in terms of generalized theory, or explanation itself was thought irrelevant. Weber's position in repudiating both doctrines means that, in *this* crucial sense, there is no "natural" or "cultural" science, there is only science or nonscience and all empirical knowledge is scientific in so far as it is valid. It is not possible here to take the space to expound this view—only to state that it was very clearly asserted by Weber and is of the very first importance. In particular, it may be noted that Marxism still adheres basically to a position of historical relativity that is incompatible with Weber's position.

The new thing in Weber, beyond this position itself, was the claim that not only was it methodologically essential (if causal knowledge of value-oriented human action was to be achieved) to develop general analytical theory in the social sciences, but it was entirely feasible, a proposition that had been vehemently denied in the historicist tradition. Indeed Weber himself tackled this task at its very core. This seems to me to have been one primary aspect of the significance of his embarking on the famous series of comparative studies in the sociology of religion. In the essay on the Protestant Ethic he cut into the center of a major problem of "historical" explanation. In the older tradition the indicated procedure would have been to delve ever more deeply into the specific historical antecedents both of Protestantism and of capitalism in the West. Instead, Weber quite deliberately chose to develop an "experimental design" by which he studied the negative cases where "capitalism" had failed to emerge under what he showed to be comparable circumstances.[1] My essential point is that Weber chose this method not only in order to help to demonstrate his thesis about the relation between Protestantism and capitalism but *also* to show the importance and the feasibility of generalized analytical theory in the cultural sphere. His most developed product in this respect was the section on the sociology of religion in *Wirtschaft und Gesellschaft*. This is elementary theory, but for more than a generation it has been far in advance of anything else in the field. Such propositions as that stating the intimate relations be-

---

1. Of course, I refer to the two studies of religion and society in China and India respectively. The study of Ancient Judaism belongs in a different category.

tween a religious ethic and the phenomenon of prophecy, or with reference to the dispositions of different kinds of social strata to different religious orientations are examples of the propositional content of this scheme. Indeed there is a sense in which this was the major "pay-off" of Weber's new orientation, the commitment to and development of a generalized analytical science in the field precisely of the cultural content which the historicist tradition had declared completely inaccessible to such methods. This, essentially, was what Weber meant by sociology as a theoretical discipline.

4. VERSTEHEN

There was, however, one essential component of his methodology that has not yet been treated. Weber had to cope with the doctrine that the methodological dichotomy between nomothetic and ideographic orientations coincided with that between observation of "external" realities in almost the physical sense and participation with the object of observation through *Verstehen*. It is necessary to discuss this problem briefly in order to complete the methodological picture.

It can be said correctly, I think, that Weber dealt with this problem area as an integral part of his general methodology. First it was essential that he should make clear that the understanding of *both* cultural meaning-systems as such—for example, mathematical propositions—and motivational meanings "intended" by individual actors should be included. Without clarity on this point the essential bridge between cultural levels and those of the concrete actions of individuals could not have been built. The concept of *Verstehen* was, however, also intimately connected with all three of the other methodological doctrines which have just been reviewed.

First, let me suggest an important relation to the concept of *Wertbeziehung*. Not only are the nonscientific values of the investigator himself and his culture involved, but also those of the persons and collectivities which are the *objects* of his investigation. At the level of *Verstehen*, scientific investigation is basically a process of meaningful *communication*, even though, where, for example, the objects are dead, it is a one-way process. In principle, however, it would always be desirable to have the object available for interview; taking his written expressions, accounts of him by others, and so forth, is always second best—thus to have been able to interview Brutus about Caesar's death would, from the point of view of certain definitions of that event as an "historical individual," have been highly desirable.

We can now say that effective communication in human cultural-symbolic terms *always* involves the sharing of values at some level and in some respects. At the same time, however, the values shared in the nature of the case cannot be those of a total cultural *Gestalt*. If this were the case the investigator would be enclosed within a basically solipsistic system, as that problem has been already outlined. What must be conceived to be shared are value components that are relevant to the particular investigative problems, and are in principle isolable from others of the investigator's own culture. If anything, Weber seems to have underestimated the possibilities of extension of understanding on these bases, as some of his remarks on the impossibility of understanding very primitive peoples seem, in the light of the development of anthropology, to indicate. From this point of view *Verstehen*, of course, is both a method and a result of the investigative process. As method it is, as noted, inherently dependent on the sharing of values and motivational meanings between investigator and object.

The relation of these conditions to value freedom in turn is patent. *Only* the investigator who is capable of differentiating his role from that of simply a participant in his general culture can attain the perspective and the objectivity necessary to select out those elements that are essential to his scientific purposes from those of his own culture that are irrelevant to it. The science itself, that is, must have its *own* value system that articulates with the value systems of both the culture in which the investigator participates and the objects he studies. The clear implication is that of a basic *universalism* of the values involved in social science, which are not particular to any cultural complex. This seems to point to the grain of truth in Karl Mannheim's well-known doctrine about the special status of the "free intelligentsia" who were not fully bound into their cultures—however inadequate Mannheim's analysis of this phenomenon. This is one crucial sense in which Weber, as a comparative sociologist, *could not* be a radical relativist with respect to values.[2]

If, however, the *Wertbeziehung* of the social-scientific investigator is emancipated from boundness to any particular cultural complex, how is it to be conceived to be controlled by standards of genuine relevance? There is an entirely clear answer in Weber's scheme, namely by virtue of the generality of theoretical conceptualization and of the canons of empirical validity. Science is, precisely, one of the primary elements of a generalized cultural system that is most specifically governed by general

2. Cf. Dieter Henrich, *Die Einheit der Wissenschaftslehre Max Weber* 55 (Tübingen: J. C. B. Mohr, 1952).

norms, the familiar norms of objectivity both in verification of statements of empirical fact and in logical inference and analysis. Thus once
again the central importance of Weber's break with the particularism of
the historicist tradition becomes evident. The general loosening up of his
methodological position through differentiation keeps leading him back
to the view that if the values of science are to be differentiated from the
diffuser general-value complex, then if their interdependence with others
in defining relevance in the direction both of the object observed and of
the observer himself is taken into account, and finally if the crucial facts
are to be accessible through *Verstehen;* then the process as a whole must
be subject to control through general theory of the *logical* type that is
already established in the natural sciences. In *this* crucial respect Weber
aligned himself with the basic "utilitarian" tradition, especially with
British economic theory, against both historicism and Marxism. The
essential points are the basic *autonomy* of both the special values and the
technical theory of science (relative both to the general culture and to
the other value commitments of the investigator) and the priority of
these considerations over any particularities of *Verstehen* of particular
complexes of meaning or motivation.

In conclusion of this all-too-brief sketch of some problems of Weber's
methodological position, I would like to endorse emphatically the view
so clearly stated by Professor Henrich that these conceptions of Weber's
are couched at the level of the methodology of science, not that of
epistemology. Basically Weber was not concerned with the problem of
the grounds on which valid empirical science in the field of human
meaning and motivated action is or is not possible. He fundamentally
took this for granted. What he presented was an ordered account of the
structure of such knowledge and certain of its relations to the more
general culture of which it is a part. He was no more concerned with
the epistemological problem than is the modern physicist with the question of whether the physical world "really" exists, or the biologist of
whether there is any ultimate difference between living organisms and
lifeless "matter." This is perhaps the most fundamental of all the respects
in which Weber carried through a basic *differentiation* of the intellectual
tradition from which he started.[3]

3. It will be evident to the reader, especially if he is schooled in the German traditions
under consideration, that the position taken in the whole of the above discussion of
Weber's methodology diverges very considerably from that of Karl Mannheim—in
whose first seminar at Heidelberg, in the summer semester of 1927, I participated. In
it's relation both to the tradition of historicism and to Marxism, it seems to me that
Mannheim's position was retrogressive as compared with that of Weber. In this respect

Weber's Substantive Sociology

There seems to be no question of the immense importance of Weber's methodological position as I have sketched it. Yet had his writings been confined to these questions, the occasion we are here celebrating would have been far less significant than it is. Weber's methodology was meant, and in fact served, as the framework of a *substantive* contribution of the first importance. Its importance cannot be properly assessed without seeing the connection between the two.

Of course Weber had laid very extensive and substantial foundations for his substantive sociology before the methodological revolution that began with the essays on Roscher and Knies. This phase of his work was, however, as is well known, concomitant with an equally new set of substantive investigations and analysis, the first of which was the famous monograph on the *Protestant Ethic and the Spirit of Capitalism*. There is, I think, an exceedingly important set of relations between these two parts of his work.

1. SOCIOLOGY OF LAW

I should like strongly to suggest that the core of Weber's substantive sociology lies neither in his treatment of economic and political problems nor in his sociology of religion, but in his sociology of law. It is thus striking that, in *Wirtschaft und Gesellschaft,* after the very condensed statement of his methodological position, he begins immediately to outline his classification of the types and components of *normative order* in society (Section II, Part 4, beginning with the concepts of Brauch and Sitte). He comes furthermore very quickly to the concept of *legitimate* order, which is the nodal point where the concepts of law, of political authority, and of the social role of religious ethics come together.

This central emphasis is, of course, thoroughly understandable in the light of Weber's personal history, his training and early academic career in the field of jurisprudence. The tendency to dichotomize emphases as between *Idealfaktoren* and *Realfaktoren*, however, seems to have operated to obscure the continuing importance of this node; because law cannot be neatly allocated either to the one or to the other, but is the

---

I agree with the judgment of von Schelting (*Max Weber's Wissenschaftslehre*), though I would extend the criticism over a broader front than Schelting dealt with. It seems to me that Mannheim mainly made the inherent circularities of both types of position more explicit, rather than finding a way to transcend them. In addition to the schema of empirical proof which Schelting stressed so strongly, I should emphasize the role of general theoretical conceptualization. Mannheim never really faced this issue; rather than analyzing, he "delineated" the sociocultural complexes in which ideological positions, like that of German conservative thought, were rooted.

principal mediating structure between them. It is, however, very clear that Weber, precisely as a sociologist rather than a political scientist or economist, considered political and economic structures and processes not to be understandable without full analysis of their relation to normative order—witness the crucial role of the concept of authority in his political analysis. On the other hand, he did not think the analysis of religious values and meaning systems could be made relevant to understanding concrete social action without understanding how they affected conceptions of normative order and the legitimacy of its different types.[4]

It is then the very centrality of the problem of the relation between the two sets of factors in human sociocultural action that, in my opinion, underlies the centrality of the topic of law as, in advanced societies, the focus of practically significant normative order in Weber's work. It was above all by virtue of this emphasis and the substantive analyses he presented that Weber was able to develop a fundamental resolution of the dualism which kept, figuratively speaking, the Marxes and the Hegels perpetually "setting each other on their heads."[5]

Without attempting to discuss the complex problems in detail, I may suggest that the crucial focus of Weber's sociology of law lies in the concept of *formal rationality* which, though by no means confined by Weber to the field of law, was certainly particularly strongly emphasized there. The criterion of formal rationality designates a level of differentiation of the normative order at the societal level by virtue of which it can become relatively *independent* in both directions in the ideal-real series. Legal decisions then are no longer a simple application of *ethical* orientations as, for example, has tended to be the case in systems of religious law as the Jewish or the Islamic,[6] on the other hand, they can also become relatively independent of more particularistic political and economic interest constellations.

4. It is perhaps worth noting here that a primary focus of ambiguity in Marxian thought lies in the problem of the relation of legal order to the famous concept of the *Produktionsverhältnisse*. It has long seemed to me that Marx was simply unclear on the problem of how far the element of legal order in such structures, e.g., the *authority* of management in the firm, was a simple epiphenomenon of either economic interests of power position or a combination of the two. Weber's analysis came directly to grips with the core of this problem.
5. It is of course clear that the logic of this dichotomy is essentially the same as the one of heredity *versus* environment in the history of biological thought. To my mind, arguing whether the "ideal" or the "real" factors ultimately determine human action is today exactly as futile as arguing whether hereditary *or* environmental factors ultimately determine the nature of organic life. In both cases it is clearly a matter of complex interdependence among equally essential but differently operating factors.
6. Supplemented by casuistry, which often became very elaborate.

The implication of this is that, for its full effect to be felt, the system of legal norms itself must become relatively *universalistic*. It must be organized in terms of general principles so that to some significant degree particular decisions come to be derivable from these general principles when related to more particular facts. Another particularly important point is the development of procedural institutions, which emancipate the legal system from boundness to particular precepts so long as it provides procedures for arriving at legal solutions; thus though English Common Law has been less highly rationalized than Continental Roman law in systematization of legal doctrines, it has been even more highly developed on the procedural side. Finally relative independence, both from political and from religious authority, both of the judiciary and of the private legal profession, have been very important phenomena, slowly becoming more prominent in the course of legal history.

2. THE SOCIOLOGY OF POLITICAL AND ECONOMIC LIFE

As I suggested, Weber's sociology of law is an essential key to the understanding of his analysis of political and economic phenomena. The most important single link is perhaps the conception of rational-legal authority. This conception incorporates all the essentials of a highly developed legal order as just outlined, in specific relation to the organization of governmental authority and power. Under this pattern of authority political leadership is itself legally bound in the framework of something like a constitution, but equally by virtue of this legal framework it is in certain respects independent of ethical and religious control in either the traditionalistic or the charismatic senses.[7] It is then a characteristic of rational-legal authority that legitimation applies first to the legal or constitutional order itself and only through it, to the particular positions of authority that operate under it, and then to the incumbents of the positions. The concept of legitimation, therefore, is the primary link in the other direction between the legal order and, through it, the political system and the cultural system, in particular, values and religious orientations. In this respect the hallmark of both traditional and charismatic authority patterns is that neither presupposes the same order of differentiated legal system as does the rational-legal, but rather a much more

7. On a previous occasion I have attempted to show that Weber's three famous types of authority do not lie on the same level, but that the traditional and the charismatic are developmentally different from the rational-legal. Cf. my article, "Authority, Legitimation and Political Action," which appeared originally in *Nomos I: Authority* (C.J. Friedrich, Ed.) and is reprinted in my volume *Structure and Process in Modern Societies* (New York: Free Press, 1961), Chapter V.

direct legitimation of political action, on the one hand by virtue of a traditionally given diffuse status, on the other of a nontraditional assumption of moral authority. Both are, so far as they are in Weber's sense "rational" at all, cases of "substantive" rather than formal rationality.

Similar considerations apply to the economic field. As contrasted with the utilitarian tradition, it is first notable that Weber never dealt with economic problems without careful attention to their political context. Of course, in many organizational contexts, the degree of independence of economic processes and interests, either from traditionalized and diffuse *Gemeinschaft* structures, or from political authority, is low. Weber was, however, particularly interested in the situations and conditions where this independence did develop and this was to him a primary aspect of modern capitalism.

Here again the legal reference was very prominent, in particular to the institutionalization of property and contract at legal levels. In terms of Weber's empirical interests it is somewhat overshadowed by his concern with the more direct effects of commitments to a religious ethic on economic behavior, as above all in the case of the Protestant Ethic. There are, however, two things to be said in this connection. First, quite clearly the development of legal systems in the Western world, particularly perhaps in England, was closely connected with various conditions of economic development. Weber repeatedly lists a firm legal order among the most important conditions of markets and of capitalism. The keynote here is the calculability of market chances. Secondly, where this kind of condition is not present, the orientation of action to economic considerations is in the nature of the case severely limited because of its diffuse ascription to noneconomic elements such as ethnic and kinship groupings or religiously-motivated collective solidarity.

One further important conclusion emerges. In the substantive sociological sense, Weber's theoretical scheme is inherently evolutionary. The comparative emphasis is legitimate and essential. There is no simple linear process at the level dealt with even by a Comte or a Marx, and many outcomes are dependent on highly variable contingencies. Nevertheless, Weber was committed to the attempt to set forth a general picture of a "modern" type of social organization, which as it happened, emerged in its later phases primarily in the Western world, and which was qualitatively different in an evolutionary sense from anything found in other civilizations. He tended to characterize this as rational bourgeois "capitalism," but the economic stress in the designation is not sufficient or even crucial. It was, at the very least, conceived as a very comprehensive complex of institutional components, in which universalistic law and rational-legal authority, as well as profit-oriented economic enterprise, play a central part.

3. THE SOCIOLOGY OF RELIGION

The third primary part of Weber's substantive sociological contribution is in the cultural area, centering of course in his famous studies in the sociology of religion. Because they have already been mentioned a number of times only a few points above them need to be made. The first of course is to repeat that, however important Weber's historical interest in ascetic Protestantism and its relations to the rest of Christianity and to the political and economic order of Western society, the primary thrust of his concern with religion is comparative and systematic, including in the latter a pronounced evolutionary reference. I have suggested earlier that the program of comparative studies in this field was meant in part as a demonstration not only of the importance but of the feasibility of generalized analysis in the cultural field, a field which had tended to be accepted as the citadel of historicist particularism.

Secondly, there is an important problem that concerns the relative priority of Weber's treatment of religion as compared with law and with the political and economic spheres. With respect to the primary differentiating influence on the development of types of culture and society, there is no doubt that Weber assigned priority to the systems of religious orientation. Incomplete as was his study in final execution, this conclusion emerges clearly from the design and findings of his series of comparative studies in the sociology of religion. Given his evolutionary perspective, this primacy with respect to the differentiation of types of sociocultural system must of course be linked with the evolutionary strain in his thought. It seems to follow that it is in the religious sphere and, subject to that, other spheres of culture like ethical conceptions and science, that we have to seek the primary loci of the major creative innovations, whether they operate, as Weber tended to feel, by charismatic "breakthrough" or by other types of process.[8] It should, however, be made clear that this assertion of the priority of the cultural elements in

8. This general point of view is in accord with the conception that, to use the terms of current cybernetic theory, cultural systems, as primarily systems of "information" in a specific sense, are, given the requisite conditions, capable of controlling the higher "energy" systems of political and economic action. A succinct and illuminating account of the relevance of cybernetic theory to social and political systems is given in Karl W. Deutsch, *The Nerves of Government* (New York: Free Press of Glencoe, 1963), Chap. V.

certain contexts of control and differentiation of type does not imply a reversion to an idealistic emanationist point of view that denies the independent causal significance of the "real" or "material" factors. Weber is perfectly clear on the significance of the latter in general terms, and has probably made larger contributions than any single writer of his generation, if not since, to the understanding of a wide variety of detailed problems of just how they operate.

This sense of the priority of cultural factors, and hence of the sociology of religion in Weber's work, must be carefully distinguished from the sense in which I have contended that the sociology of law, as the centrally significant aspect of normative order in social systems, is the nodal center of his sociology as a whole. There is a very important and subtle relation here between the conception of the universalism, and at the same time the independence, of law and the double theme that the analyst of social systems should be objective in the sense in which its relation to the concept of *Wertfreiheit* has been discussed and should operate with generalized theoretical categories in order to do so.

Law is, as both Weber and his great French contemporary Émile Durkheim recognized, the primary structual focus of societies, the more definitely so the more advanced they are. The cultural legitimation of legal systems, however, lies in their grounding in the religious orientations of their populations and their historic antecedents. Law is thus the primary focus of the comparative and developmental analysis of societies. Interpretations of its deeper meaning, however, must rest on analysis of the cultural systems in which these meanings are grounded.

Social science, like any other rational discipline, is in the first instance grounded in culture; it is an enterprise of the human investigator in his quest for interpretation of the meanings of the human condition that are relevant to him. As such, there is a reference both to the values of scientific investigation itself, in its essentially autonomous way, and behind that to the more general value system.

The structure of the scientific discipline itself, however, the more so the more mature it becomes, is defined in terms of its theoretical uniformities and generalizations. Precisely in so far as the social sciences become autonomous relative to their philosophical and other cultural groundings, this autonomous structure is to be found in the first instance in the structure of its generalized conceptual system. Weber stood somewhat hesitantly before this conclusion and definitely did not present a "theoretical system" in a fully developed sense. He did, however, point a direction that to me is unmistakable. In any case the congruence between the structure of his methodological position and the structural relations among the components of his substantive sociology seems to me to be of first-order significance.

Weber and the Problem of Ideology

The body of this paper has been couched at the level of relatively technical, though by no means detailed, discussion of Max Weber's ideas in the fields of the methodology of social science and of his substantive sociology. We began, however, with certain major problems of the state of Western society in the present century and the relations of the prevailing patterns of social thought to these problems in the role of ideologies. In conclusion I would like to return to these themes.

First I would like to emphasize again that the three main patterns of social thought, which together constituted Weber's reference system, were at the same time technical positions on the framework of social science and foci of ideological orientations. Ideologically the idealist-historicist position may be treated as at least closely related to conservative ideologies in the European sense. These have been on the whole those which were more favorable to the old Europe and its civilization, with a certain, though by no means complete, presumption that its primary trustees should be the older aristocratic classes, particularly in their role of cultural elites. On occasion this could shift over, as in certain respects it did with the Nazis, to the view that a total "people" should become the bearers of (in a severely vulgarized version) the great tradition.

In any case, this historicist-conservative base can plausibly be contrasted with not one, but two directions of challenge to it and, from the point of view of its proponents, threats to its integrity. The older of these, which most Germans, and indeed Continental Europeans, felt to be basically "foreign" to them, was what I have called the utilitarian system, especially in the form of the ideology of "economic individualism," or more pointedly "capitalism." Here a particularly salient point is the *common* antagonism of continental conservatives *and* socialists in this ideological sense, to capitalism. The second direction of course was the socialistic, which came more and more to focus in the Marxian system.

I have already spelled out the principal respects in which Weber took a technical intellectual course that rejected acceptance of any of these three traditions, though he adopted important elements from all three.

Broadly the same can be said ideologically—with an important qualification. He was almost unequivocally antagonistic to what he conceived, in the intellectual-political situation of his time in Germany, to be both the conservative and the socialist positions; although for the former he did not unequivocally repudiate nationalism, nor for the latter the theme of "social justice." Toward the capitalistic alternative, on the other hand, he seemed to be much more markedly ambivalent. He regarded "capitalism," including bureaucratic organization, both private and governmental, as essentially the "fate" of Western society. Yet he had grave misgivings about its implications, especially in "humanistic" contexts.

I wonder whether it is going too far to suggest that this indicates a rather definite attempt to break out of the Idealist-Materialist, or Historicist-Marxist dilemma, but with a good deal of indecision about whether it was advisable and where it could lead. Clearly to him capitalism in some sense had to be accepted; but equally on a variety of grounds, scientific and ethical, the prevailing interpretations were on the one hand inadequate to the phenomenon itself, on the other out of accord with his feelings of rightness and appropriateness.

On the level of the more technical aspects of his thought, Weber clearly broke out of what I have called the "trilemma" presented by the structure of the principal currents of social thinking of his time. His resolution of the trilemma pointed in the direction of a *new* pattern of thinking in the area, of which an autonomous theoretical sociology was an essential ingredient. On this level Weber clearly converged with other parts of a major intellectual movement of his generation. Taking his contribution—which I regard as the most crucial single one—along with many others, I think it can be said that the whole intellectual-social situation has been redefined in a way that makes the principal categorizations of the late nineteenth century, many of which are still widely current, basically obsolete.[9]

I would go farther to suggest that Weber's "fourth position" could not be absorbed simply into another ideology, to compete on the same level with the other three. It is, from this point of view, no accident that it is impossible to classify Weber politically as a "conservative" in the

9. The most comprehensive treatment of this movement so far available is, to my knowledge, H. Stuart Hughes, *Consciousness and Society* (New York: Knopf, 1958). My own *Structure of Social Action* (New York: McGraw-Hill, 1937) dealt with the more directly sociological aspects, especially, besides Weber, Durkheim, and Pareto, and some of the relations to the tradition of economic individualism. Now it seems to me that particularly Freud and the American pragmatists and social psychologists, such as G. H. Mead and John Dewey, have played a very important part.

older German tradition, as a "liberal" in the economic individualist sense, or as a "socialist." His intellectual breakthrough meant, however, more than a "neutral" personal position as among these ideological positions; it was an implied assertion that the time would come when these old alignments would no longer be meaningful. To use the phrase made current in the United States recently by Daniel Bell, Weber heralded "the end of ideology" in the sense in which that concept had been so prominent in the earlier part of the present century.

It may very well be that there is a relation between this situation and the political and social situation of our time. I noted that the outbreak of World War I, just a half century ago, marked the beginning of the end of the European system of national states as that had taken shape in the nineteenth century, and of its dominance in the world. The most important single source of that loss of dominance of course has been the emergence of the two supranational units, the United States to the West and the Soviet Union to the East, which are of an order of magnitude and power altogether different from the classical national states. The rapid decline of "colonialism" can in turn be related to these changes, as can the European unification movement.

It is surely notable in this connection that the three principal intellectual positions that figured in the background of Weber's work, and that have been the foci of the principal modern ideologies, are very clearly related to the structure of the Western system. First, the idealist-historicist pattern of thought has been characteristic of the center, in the first instance of Germany, particularly Western and Southern Germany, and in different respects of France. Then clearly the utilitarian system and the ideologies of economic individualism have been most prevalent in Great Britain and, from there, the United States, at least for a considerable time. The case of Marxism may not seem to fit. With, however, its very strong emphasis on primacy of political organization—and, within that, of authoritarianism and bureaucracy of certain types—there seems to me to be more than a little affinity between Prussianism and Soviet Marxism. It is perhaps not stretching a point too far to suggest that there is a certain symmetry between the wings of the system and that, as one moved eastward from the cultural centers of Continental Europe, there has been an increase in centralized political authoritarianism which is in some sense "socialistic," whereas moving westward, the climate became increasingly "capitalistic." At any rate the ideological polarization of the cold war period has certainly been on the basis of the intellectual conflict between utilitarian individualism and Marxian socialism. I am inclined to regard this, however, as part of a still more general aspect of the situation of Western society in which Prussian authoritarianism has also been involved.

In the light of these considerations, Weber's achievement, in the crucial field of the intellectual analysis of social and cultural phenomena, of a position which clearly transcended *all* of the three ideologically-central positions in such a way as to include in relativized form contributions from all of them, takes on a special significance. It seems to me that Weber stood at a very crucial juncture in the whole development of Western civilization. He understood, as hardly any of his contemporaries did, the fact and nature of the breakup of the older system, and he contributed more than any single figure to the outline of a new intellectual orientation which promises to be of constitutive importance in defining the situation for the emerging social world.

With respect to my own country I have long felt that the designation of its social system as "capitalistic," even in Weber's highly sophisticated sense, was grossly inadequate. It seems increasingly probable that trends in the Soviet Union will make the more stereotyped conception of it as the "socialist" society just as inappropriate. In any case I cannot refrain from feeling that the emergence of the science of sociology, of which I regard Max Weber as one of the very few true founders, is a harbinger of these great changes; and that our science may well be destined to play a major role, not only in its primary task of understanding the social and cultural world we live in as object of its investigations, but, in ways which cannot now be foreseen, in actually shaping that world. In this sense it may possibly turn out to be the most important heir of the great ideologies of the turn of the last century. This possibility is perhaps the truest measure of the greatness of Max Weber.

CHAPTER 4

Some Comments on the Sociology
of Karl Marx

This is the only paper in this volume that has not been published previously. Its main substance was delivered orally at the plenary session on Karl Marx as a sociologist at the annual meeting of the American Sociological Association in August, 1965, in Chicago. The written version was composed, mainly from the notes prepared for the oral presentation, in the period just before this volume went to press.

The paper reaches back behind the period of the Weber-Durkheim convergence to discuss a critically significant chapter in the intellectual history of social science generally, and sociology in particular, which underlay that development. To me Marx built the first of the three most important bridges between the idealistic and the utilitarian traditions, into which European social thought had broadly come to be dichotomized by the turn from the eighteenth to the nineteenth century. The Marxian attempt was limited and only partially successful in scientific terms. But in addition to its own considerable contribution, it showed the urgency of the problem and did much to set the stage for later solutions. It did not stand alone in this regard, but was related, through a common grounding in utilitarianism, to anthropology (especially English anthropology), a school of thought which was not unrelated to the later contributions of Freud, since both started from the problem of extending biological thinking into the "cultural" realm.

This obviously is a case where it is particularly important to attempt to differentiate between the ideological considerations that account for the enormous impact of Marxism on the complex problems of social movements and social change in our time and Marx's contributions to the development of theory in social science. It is my view that the highly significant core of scientific contribution was one of several essential conditions of the ideological impact, but that, particularly in the later phases of the story, the scientific difficulties of accepting anything approaching an orthodox Marxian diagnosis and prognosis of the course of modern industrial societies and the process of modernization in other societies, have become so formidable that sharp formulation of the scientific problems in distinction from the ideological has become increasingly imperative.

I have attempted one other relatively extended discussion of Marx's contribution, since the very partial treatment in the *Structure of Social Action,* namely in the essay "Social Classes and Class Conflict in the Light of Recent Sociological Theory" which appeared as Chap. XV of the 1954 Edition of *Essays in Sociological Theory.* (It was written for the centenary of the Communist Manifesto in 1948, and given orally at the 1948 Meeting of the American Economic Association). In the present chapter, I have deliberately avoided overlap with this earlier paper, which dealt mainly with the "internal" problems of the Marxian theory of social stratification. The two should be evaluated together for my views of Marx's theoretical contribution to sociology.

I T SEEMS highly appropriate at this time for the American Sociological Association to devote a plenary session at its annual meeting to an evaluation of the contributions of Karl Marx as a sociologist. There is an important sense in which, although relatively few American sociologists are explicit Marxists, in a more diffused way his influence has grown in recent years as a focus of several crucial themes, notably the importance of conflict, social change, and positive political action. If anything, as Lipset and Smelser point out,[1] this more or less Marxian orientation has served as the major single reference point for opposition to the so-called "Establishment" in recent American sociology. Thus a rather mild tendency toward polarization has come to be organized about this axis. Furthermore, we have come to be engaged in considerably more active discussion than before with our colleagues in Communist countries, particularly in the Soviet Union. It was hoped that a special contribution to this dialogue would be made by the Soviet representative who was to participate in the present session, but who was, unfortunately, unable to come. The task of the present paper is not, however, to analyze these trends in contemporary sociology, but to discuss some aspects of

1. Cf. S. M. Lipset and N. J. Smelser, Eds, *Sociology: The Progress of a Decade* (Englewood Cliffs: Prentice-Hall, 1961). Introduction.

Marx's own theories in their setting in intellectual history and with reference to their bearing on current theoretical interests in sociology.

In Marx's own time, European social thought, with its still incomplete differentiation between philosophy and what we now consider social science, seems to have become rather sharply polarized. On one side were the more "empirical," mainly British, trends that were associated in philosophy with utilitarianism, and that played an essential part in the classical economics and in the "association" tradition of the early development of psychology. On the other side was philosophical idealism, centering in Germany and coming to a sharp focus in the philosophy of Hegel who presented a more radical version than Kant.

This is not the occasion to analyze the genesis of these main currents of intellectual history. In broad outline, I presume them to be sufficiently well understood so that this is unnecessary.[2] However, I should like to emphasize my view that the main frames of reference of modern social science resulted from a synthesis of elements prominent in both of these two great traditions.

I

We may approach the evaluation of Marx's significance by suggesting that he developed one of the two roughly contemporary first major attempts to synthesize these elements, the other being the emergence of anthropology. It is crucial to realize that Marx began to build his "bridge" by working from the idealistic side, attempting to formulate the principal elements that he believed had not been done justice in the idealistic tradition. The anthropological attempt started from the biological branch of the empiricist tradition—"the study of man" as a biological category— and thereby arrived at a conception of "culture," a phenomenon that had also been the main concern of the idealists.[3]

2. On utilitarianism and associated forms of thought, see especially Elie Halévy, *The Growth of Philosophical Radicalism* (London: Faber, 1927). On idealism in its social references see, above all, Ernst Troeltsch, *Der Historismus und seine Probleme* (Berlin: Heise, 1924). See also my paper "Unity and Diversity in the Modern Intellectual Disciplines," *Daedalus*, Winter, 1965, reprinted as Chapter VI in this volume.
3. Negative criticism of Marx's sociology, which will figure prominently in what follows, is couched from the perspective of hindsight with respect to both societal developments since he wrote and the potentials of the sociological theory available today. It is important to distinguish this perspective from that of evaluating his *historical* contributions to the development of modern sociology. It is also important, following especially Schumpeter, to distinguish Marx the sociologist from Marx the ideologist and leader of a revolutionary movement, even though a sharp distinction would have been uncongenial to Marx himself, and is so to contemporary Marxists.

Marx's extension beyond ground that was solid on idealistic terms into the gap vis-á-vis the empiricist traditions began with the famous "setting Hegel on his head." This consisted in reversing the primacy *within* the dichotomy that was fundamental to idealistic thought and that figured in somewhat different forms in Kant and Hegel: the dichotomy later formulated as that between ideal factors and real factors, both understood as determinants of human action in social as well as individual contexts. The Hegelian conception gave full primacy to the ideal factors, centering in the concept of "Spirit" (*Geist*), which was conceived to be a self-propelling and actualizing entity basically responsible for human development in the course of world history. The "historical materialism" of Marx consisted essentially in giving primacy to the alternative component complex *within* this dichotomy, namely the "real factors." These essentially are what we would now call economic and political. This version of "materialism" is by no means to be identified with that which postulated the *physical* world as the locus of ultimate reality and attempted to reduce all organic life and through it social and cultural phenomena to physical terms—usually as formulated in the classical mechanics. There have been attempts to consolidate the two, perhaps most notably in Lenin's book *Materialism and Empirio criticism* and in Bukharin's book *Historical Materialism.*[4] On the whole, however, the movement of thought since Marx's time has been away from their identification rather than toward it.[5]

The "pier" on the empiricist-utilitarian side of the gap with which Marx made his primary contact was the classical economics, particularly its Ricardian version, which had been strongly influenced by Malthus, and before him the tradition that eventually stemmed from Hobbes. The most essential point here is that, in contrast to the Lockean tradition marked by what Halévy called the postulate of the "natural identity of interests," this branch emphasized elements of conflict and disharmony. Moreover, by contrast with Hobbes, such elements had by this time come to be conceived as structured.[6] The basic account of the economy, however,

4. The Pavlovian school of psychology, Stalin's pronouncements on linguistics, and the former Soviet orthodoxy of Lysenko's biology and of certain theories in physics related to problems in this area. See Tucker, *The Soviet Political Mind* (New York: Praeger, 1963).
5. However, Marx seems to have first developed his materialism with such an identification in mind. This seems evident in the focus on Democritus' materialism in his doctoral thesis, but is implied in other of his earlier writings also. There is evidence that he later considered this a confusion of his youthful enthusiasm.
6. Cf. Malthus' conception of the "division of society into classes."

remained "utilitarian," postulating a rather narrow conception of individual "self-interest" and neglecting elements of both the psychology of personality and the sociology of institutions that have become prominent since then.

The point of reference for the "central span" of the bridge between the two piers was Marx's interpretation of political events in France especially those associated with the revolutionary situations of 1848 and 1870. Because, in the Revolution of over a half century before, the "bourgeoisie" had broadly won their conflict with monarchy and aristocracy, the revolutionary conflict had to be defined in terms of different political constituencies. The locus of conflict and revolt had shifted downward in the class structure, and thus made it plausible to postulate that a new conflict between bourgeoisie and proletariat was replacing the older one between aristocracy and bourgeoisie. This conflict in turn could, in Ricardian terms, be plausibly associated with the power relation inherent in the structure of the early firm as it emerged after the Industrial Revolution, as between the proprietary-managerial element and the element of propertyless wageworkers.[7]

This was undoubtedly a genuine synthesis of a high order. Hegel himself had, in his *Philosophy of Law,* outlined what he called "bourgeois society" in terms that certainly gave reference points for the conception of "material" interests. The classical economics then provided what was certainly a more sophisticated concept of self-interest. Moreover, with respect to all three of the major components of his theoretical structure, Marx rightly emphasized that the individual does not act randomly and alone, but in terms of a structured situation, the main components of which derive from the market system. It was mainly from the French political reference point that Marx derived his conceptions of the potentiality of revolutionary activism, which is the obverse of his conception of materialistic determinism.

There is another element, derived mainly from the idealistic tradition, that had both positive and negative aspects in its bearing on later sociology. This is the "historical" component in historical materialism: the conception that history is a process that is unique not only as the total outcome of phases of change, but essentially as a concatenation of unique combinations of components. This emphasis emerged with especial

7. It is important that Engels focused on this basis of conflict in his "Condition of the Working Class in England" which he wrote before coming under Marx's influence. It was the convergence that Marx recognized between this analysis and his own early analyses of social classes that evidently provided the first basis of the famous life-long collaboration.

clarity in the "historicism" that constituted the main aspect of late German idealism, at least in the areas impinging on social science, for example, in the work of Dilthey, and also many others.

This historicism was built into Hegel's philosophy in the form of the "dialectic," which postulated a qualitative difference between systems that predominated at each successive phase of an evolutionary process, and hence a sharp structural break in the transition from one to the next. The conception of dialectic also involved that of conflict. Therefore it was not a very long step to the idea that the structurally-sharp break could only be introduced by an empirical process that was revolutionary. Thus, in his "material" sphere, Marx used essentially the Hegelian conception of a succession of qualitatively different systems that were in "contradiction" with each other; the transitions being impelled by internal "contradictions" in the "outgoing" systems—the famous thesis-antithesis formula.[8]

On the most fundamental level there is perhaps no incompatibility between "ideographic" and "nomothetic" conceptualization, as this antithesis has, since Rickert, come to be called. At the level of theoretical abstraction that prevailed in Marx's day, however, the difference between the classical economics and the German historicist tradition was sharp indeed and long remained so. The classical economists were trying to formulate a generalized analysis of the processes of *economic behavior* that, subject to the relevant conditions, could be applied universally. Marx was concerned with the specific capitalist system in an historical sense, and assumed that *none* of the uniformities he analyzed as characteristic of it applied to either "feudalism" or "socialism." In this, as in certain other senses, Marx's borrowing from the utilitarian tradition was highly selective.

On this issue, the anthropological bridge[9] stood in sharp conflict with the Marxian in that, on a more or less equivalent level of concreteness, it clearly aimed at generalized, analytically universal, theoretical propo-

8. It is certainly revealing of the Hegelian background of Marxism that Marxists still prefer to speak of the "contradictions" of capitalism, as if the relation between the classes in concrete society worked out on the level of *logic*, not of the relation of economic, political, and other "interests" which are certainly not entities in a logical proposition. These interests, on Marxian premises, are not logically incompatible, but stand in realistic, "material" *conflict*. The incompatibility between the two propositions, $2 + 2 = 5$, and the set $2 + 2$ contains four integer units, is not based on a "conflict of interest" between the propositions, but is a logical contradiction.

9. This cannot be analyzed here, but see my contribution to the memorial volume for Clyde Kluckhohn, "Clyde Kluckhohn's Contribution to the Integration of the Social Sciences" in Evon Vogt and John Fischer, editors: *Essays in Anthropology* (forthcoming).

sitions. It is significant, however, that the further it advanced into the analysis of culture, the more it was tempted by the perspective of "cultural relativity." Conversely, Weber, who took idealistic formulations as his point of departure, came more and more to emphasize the importance of theoretical generalization which was not bound to particular historical "Gestalten" on either the ideal-cultural or the material levels. It will be my special thesis that a more adequate synthesis could come about only when a theoretical framework had been grounded on a higher level of abstract generality than was present in either of the two earlier attempts at synthesis. This was the case with the new synthesis in which Weber and Durkheim figured most prominently; a synthesis that is both post-Marxian and post-anthropological in the more utilitarian sense of the latter term.

II

We may now consider in more detail the principal more specific foci on which the Marxian theory concentrated in order to clarify both the elements in Marx's theory that were creative from the general theoretical point of view and the aspects in which it was destined to be superseded by subsequent developments. In this respect, it is perhaps better to move from the more microscopic elements, which were linked most closely with English economics, to the more macroscopic, which were more connected with the Hegelian philosophy of history.

The obvious starting point is the industrial firm of the early post-Industrial Revolution period. It is notable that the classical economists, particularly Ricardo, habitually used commercial agriculture for purposes of illustration. They were more concerned with the problem of capital than of labor, conceiving the latter, so far as they figured, if at all, as a process of laborers being "put to work." Marx, however, shifted attention to the "family" firm, with its components of owner-manager and propertyless wage workers. This gave Marx a convenient conception that fitted into the broader dichotomy of bourgeoisie and proletariat and also could be considered the primary source of that dichotomy. It was also, particularly in the British industry which Marx intensively studied, conveniently separated from the older aristocratic background that, in England, was heavily concentrated in the agricultural as compared to the industrial sector.

To the modern sociological eye, this was also a conspicuously *asym-*

metrical structure, not only with respect to status and power, but also with respect to other basic sociological characteristics; the "managerial" component was "familistic" and diffuse in character (indeed the proprietor was a kind of petty monarch), whereas the labor component was occupational. This asymmetry is the focus of Marx's conception of the alienation of labor, because labor in this sense had been differentiated from a *Gemeinschaft* matrix, of which the prototypes for the lower-status groups were the family farm and the artisan enterprise. It can perhaps be said that the bourgeoisie, centering for Marx on what we would now call the "business" classes, had been forced, in order to achieve status and yet maintain their differentiation from the aristocracy, to orient themselves to the market. Being in a favored position, however, this was not particularly traumatic for them; but for workers "alienation of labor" could be interpreted as directly linked to "exploitation."

Already at this level a prominent problem of Marxian theory becomes salient. Marx did not discriminate analytically between what we would now call economic and political factors but because in the special case being analyzed they seemed plausibly to operate in the *same direction* he treated them as "aspects" of the same factor. Thus, on the one hand, the firm (as "petty monarchy") put—in the mid-nineteenth century much more than now—its proprietor in a position of *power* over his employees by virtue of the functional imperative of effective management. On the other hand, the market nexus, particularly in the employer's exposure to competitive pressure in selling his products and in the weak bargaining position of workers in the labor market, tended to turn market competition in an exploitative direction. Here, Marx made the most of the intermediate phenomenon of inequality of "bargaining power" to hold that the general—and to him, short of revolutionary overturn, inescapable—trend of the system was to widen the exploitative gap. This entailed the assumption of a cumulative trend of both proletarization of those in non-managerial positions and of concentration of those in managerial positions to protect their interests. This in turn would inevitably become involved with the political structure of the society as a whole: if the "bourgeoisie" were not already essentially in control of the state, they would progressively be "forced" to assume such control, so that government in a capitalistic society would in effect become "the executive committee of the bourgeoisie."

These generalizations from the structure of the early capitalistic firm and its market involvements, if Marx intended (as surely he did) that they should be treated as the basis of concrete predictions about the course of the socioeconomic system, have been deeply invalidated by the course of events in the most advanced industrial societies—precisely those in which Marx himself expected these events to unfold.

The first set of empirical reasons for this invalidation lies in the fact that two types of intervention have proved to be feasible, both administratively and politically, and have operated to neutralize the inequality of power position between ownership-management and workers that Marx, with considerable justice, so strongly emphasized. The first of these has been the organization of workers themselves in trade unions for the protection and advancement of their own interests. The relation of union movements through labor parties and the like, to national governments has been complex. However, it can be said that such movements have developed universally in industrial societies and have substantially affected the economic position of workers. The purest type of labor movement has been that oriented primarily to "collective bargaining." Of course, this could develop only if the government were not wholly opposed to the interests of "labor." But clearly it has by no means been uniformly so. The second type of intervention has been that of government on the basis that has become familiar as the "welfare state" policy, underpinning what T. H. Marshall has called the "social" component of citizenship.[10]

It is striking that Marx, impressed as he was with the "monolithic" economic-political complex of factors centering in the capitalistic firm and the market nexus, seemed almost oblivious to the importance of the democratic extension of the franchise, which in England began in a major way with the Reform Bill of 1832 and continued right under Marx's own eyes until well into the present century. To be sure, its earlier phases, for example that of the Anti-Corn Law agitation of the 1840's, were linked to free trade and *laissez faire;* but surely the turning of the political power of the masses toward governmental welfare policies was by no means unpredictable on the basis of the social and economic situation of Marx's own time. Though in a sense it was a rather late development, by no means the least important aspect of this use of political power to redress class balances emerged in the field of mass education— again a crucial development that did not figure in the Marxian analysis.

A second basis of the failure of the Marxian predictions concerns the structure of the firm itself. As noted, Marx took as paradigmatic the simple two-class family firm and postulated a tendency for the status of the worker component to become progressively homogenized and sepa-

10. T. H. Marshall: *Class, Citizenship, and Social Development* (New York: Anchor Books, 1965).

rated more drastically from the proprietary status. With the growth of scale of operations, of advanced technology, and other factors, however, the two-class firm has given way to a quite different type of organization. The corporate legal form has facilitated the differentiation of the functions of ownership from those of management, so that the active managerial components no longer have been directly pursuing their personal financial self-interest in striving to maximize the profits of the firm. They have been operating in an occupational role, based on a form of employment which has certain structural resemblances to that of worker.

This development has been associated with a process of concentration that has substantially modified the character of market competition. The enhanced power of large firms has clearly not been used only exploitatively vis-á-vis labor—for a variety of reasons, including Henry Ford's insight into the benefits for industry of high wages, the general trend has probably been the reverse. But, above all, it has enabled firms more systematically to finance innovation and expansion by "ploughing back" profits. This in turn has been associated with the increasing involvement in industry of professional personnel, engineers, lawyers, research scientists, and the like, who clearly are neither "capitalists" nor workers in the Marxian senses. Indeed, this general tendency has been extending downward so that the components who "have nothing to lose but their chains" comprise a progressively-decreasing proportion of the total labor force. In the structure of the modern industrial firm, there is no clear basis for a neat dichotomization of interests. There is an elaborately differentiated system with many cross-cutting bases of solidarity and antagonism.

A third set of primary reasons for the invalidity of the Marxian predictions lies in the famous treatment of social classes, which showed a similar selectivity relative to the complex manifold of ingredients that a modern class system requires. First, there seems little doubt that Marx grossly underestimated the vitality of the European aristocratic classes and their capacity to play an effective part in the class system, above all in alliance with the so-called bourgeoisie, but also, to important degrees, actual fusion with them.[11] Marx seems to have been so dominated by the "logic of dichotomies" that he overhastily assumed that the triumph of the bourgeoisie meant *ipso facto* the virtual elimination of aristocracy. That this was not the case is most vividly brought out by certain contrasts between Europe and the United States; it is indeed significant that Marx paid little attention to what was happening on the western

11. Max Weber made a good deal of the *Feudalizierung der Bourgeoisie* in Germany.

side of the Atlantic, though it was clearly of the greatest importance to the future of "capitalism."[12]

Clearly European aristocracy, though highly involved with the system of ownership—shifting from land to industrial and financial bases —was, in its total position in the social structure, much more than simply an owning-exploiting class in the Marxian sense. For example, it was the primary sponsor, *after* its heyday of political ascendancy, of the main cultural developments of Western society. There were many cases of clear alliance between aristocratic and bourgeois interest in the late nineteenth-century and early twentieth-century Europe, but there were also many cases of divergence and independence of social and intellectual action. Thus the philanthropy of the early modern English merchant class was not a clear case of "exploitation" in the Marxian sense,[13] nor was the support of cultural interests by the French aristocracy in the nineteenth century a clear case of their having become crassly "bourgeois" in their orientation, promoting only class interests. Indeed, the general extent to which the movements of the sociopolitical left in the Western world have been indebted to various types of support of the older "upper classes" is a major theme of the era's history.

Similar considerations apply at the other end of the Marxian class polarization. "Lower classes" in modern societies are by no means universally "proletarian" in the Marxian sense. Marx happened to write when the most important process of change was the industrialization and urbanization of so much of Western society, and, with it, the shift from a more "diffuse" *Gemeinschaft* type of community to involvement in the labor status in the industrial complex. Marx of course stressed the traumatic aspects of this transition. Vis-á-vis the wider social system, the central theme was "exploitation," the denial to workers of their "just due" in the distribution of wealth. A complementary traumatic theme was "alienation," the severing of diffuse ties with a solidary community that was highly romanticized. It can perhaps be said that in its aftermath this peculiar involvement of Marxism with the relation between industrial labor and peasant *Gemeinschaft* came to a head in the conflict of Stalin with Mao Tse Tung over the Chinese movement.[14]

12. Moreover, the remarks on the U.S. that appear in his letters to Wedemeyer and Sorge generally are far from the mark, even those on the Civil War, which he followed with some interest.
13. Cf. W. K. Jordan: *Philanthropy in England* (New York: Russell Sage, 1959).
14. Benjamin Schwarz: *Chinese Communism and the Rise of Mao* (Cambridge: Harvard University Press, 1951); Conrad Brandt: *Stalin's Failure in China, 1924–1927* (Cambridge: Harvard University Press, 1958).

To ignore many complications and ramifications, it can be said that the Marxian conception of polarization of society on the basis of two classes was not in fact viable as a concrete generalization and basis of prediction, if it rested on the internal structure of capitalism *alone*. In fact, the conflict thesis has been bolstered where it has recognized fusions with precapitalistic interest-constellations on *both* sides, of bourgeoisie with aristocracy on the upper side, of "proletariat" with peasantry on the lower. The common feature lies in the fact that the total *class* commitment, which is the focus of the Marxian conception of the dynamics of society, cannot be limited to the level of "interests" in the sense employed in the explicit technical theory. It must, above all, involve first the fusion of the individual in a nexus of kinship and (with it) of diffuse *status* considerations.[15] In retrospect, neither of the Marxian capitalistic classes has actually been emancipated from the "feudal" background, especially in Europe. The bourgeoisie are, as it were, in part frustrated aristocrats, and the proletarians, frustrated peasants. Each is "alienated" from the true *Gemeinschaft* base of historic European upper- and lower-class status, respectively.

If this characterization is correct,[16] it carries the theoretical implication that the conception of economic and political "interests," which was the Marxian theoretical base-line, simply is not adequate for the analysis and justification of an alleged total, dichotomous interest-split, not only in the Western industrial world, but in the world that comprises the "developing" societies as well. Here again, the case of American society is crucial, because in the first place it has never had an aristocracy or peasantry in the European sense. On the original Marxian premises, the United States should have followed the pure paradigm of class conflict far more exactly than any European society. In fact, exactly the opposite took place; it failed to become a simple "class society" in that sense.[17]

It seems very clear to me that Marx was virtually oblivious to the elements of what may be called pluralization that were already developing in the European society of his day, especially in the England in

15. Cf. Weber's distinction between class and status group in *The Theory of Social and Economic Organization*. (New York: Oxford University Press, 1947), pp. 424ff.
16. It seems to have a major bearing on the crucial phenomenon of the history of Marxism, namely the transition, initiated by Lenin, from the ideology of the revolt of the "proletariat" of the most advanced industrial societies, to that of the underdeveloped societies against "imperialism," on the one hand, of their predominantly peasant lower classes against local aristocracies, on the other. This will be discussed further.
17. Cf. Lipset: *The First New Nation* (New York: Basic Books, Inc., 1963).

which he lived. Not only were there divisions among the elements that might be called, on the one hand, "feudal" and, on the other hand, "capitalistic," consider, for example, the role of "Tory democracy" in promoting the general welfare complex. There was also the very conspicuous attachment of the "masses" to national concerns, in which they lined up with their own upper classes against the "proletariat" of other nations. The theory that this was due to the exploitative pressure of the upper classes was surely thin.

There was a certain plausibility in the view that the alliances between the upper classes and the lower classes in the two postulated systems, that is, bourgeoisie and aristocracy, proletariat and peasantry, were "naturally" given on the basis of their respective interests and in the presumption that the "feudal" elements would rapidly be absorbed. However, what I have called pluralization has by no means been confined to this order of "symbiosis." It has rather been characterized by a whole series of emerging solidarities that cross-cut the basic Marxian dichotomy, even in its extended version. A good example is the alleged "Executive Committee of the Bourgeoisie" directly supporting trade-union organization and welfare legislation, both of which strengthen the position of the proletariat in the class struggle. Surely the theory of "false consciousness" is not adequate to account for such phenomena. It smacks very much of the notorious "ad hoc hypothesis."

The difficulty surely lies at another level: that concerning the kind of theoretical scheme in the analytical sense that Marx used for explaining these phenomena. Here in its relevance to problems at the empirical core of the Marxian system, the contribution of the later "bridge" between idealism and utilitarianism that connected with Durkheim and Weber, becomes relevant.

Durkheim's early contribution concerned the market system. His essential point was that the market could not be understood in terms of the operations of simple "self-interest," but involved an institutionalization of the contractual framework. This in turn exemplified and partly determined a system of "organic solidarity" that could by no means be a simple reflection of the interests of participants. These considerations diverted attention from the interests of units to the conditions of order in a *system* of contractual relations among such units. It became quite clear, in the light of Durkheim's analysis, that the bases of even competitive uniformity depended on a factor of solidarity in such a system and could not be derived simply from the interlocking of the interests of units—as Marx certainly assumed.

A second theoretical difficulty concerns the "Weber problem." This involves explanation of the *direction* in which "self-interest" will be oriented. The utilitarian view, which was not challenged by Marx, was that it was motivated by the "hedonistic" gratifications of the individual actor, the satisfaction of wants that were essentially *dissociated* from the structure of the social system. In place of the givenness of wants in the utilitarian tradition, Weber laid special stress on an *internalized value system* that was not purely individual but was rooted in major movements at the cultural level. Weber stressed in particular the ethic of ascetic Protestantism.

The Durkheimian problem raised the question of the long-standing ambiguity in Marxian theory about the status of normative order, notably at the legal level, with respect to the distinction between the "material" base and the superstructure. Marx's inclination to work at a rather low level of analytical abstraction, reinforced by his historicism, tended to locate this element of normative order in the "relations of production," which constitute the core of the interest structure of capitalism itself. Durkheim's analysis, however, showed that the crucial institution of contract, as he called it, was analytically distinct from the interests of contracting parties and varied independently of them. Moreover, Weber's analysis of the values of the calling, as constituting direct components of the motivation of the individual—both business man and worker— though in somewhat different ways, called severely into question the assumption that the interests of participants in the firm and the market nexus were independent of religious and other cultural factors and reflected only the material base.

The essential point is that the Marxian scheme postulated, and attempted to demonstrate, that the structure of the firm, the competitive pressures of the market system, and the "material" interests of the participant individuals, all taken together, constituted a single deterministic system that was subject to inherent, though "historical," laws of development. These "laws" did not admit of independent variability among the components of this system, nor of more particular modes of interdependence between such components and components that Marx assigned to the "superstructure." This included the very dubious answer to the question of the status of legal order. Only on a higher level of abstraction, which saw *both* material base and superstructure as functions of combinations of *the same* analytically defined more generalized variables than the Marxian capitalistic interests, and so forth, could one deal with the kind of empirical difficulties that have just been noted. Moreover, this set of variables must include some that Marx would classify as nonmaterial.

III

We may now approach a second context in which Marx's theory involved a theoretically limited, and hence, I think, not legitimately generalizable, pattern of dichotomizing. This is most fully illustrated in his concern with the political movements of the left in France in the nineteenth century. The first pole of the dichotomy at issue was the determinism of the capitalistic action system, so long as it was conceived to operate at the level of the actions of individuals in the firm and in the various relevant markets. These elements of determinism operated through two kinds of mechanisms, namely the use of coercive authority by proprietors within the firm, which was effective because of the laborers' disadvantaged bargaining position, and the pressures of competition operating in market relations. Not only could the ordinary worker not afford to quit his job because of the exploitative trend operating against workers in general—the best he could hope for would be another job under much the same conditions—but the capitalist could not afford to treat his workers any better, because he would increase his costs and lose out to his competitors in selling his product. The market determinism was, of course, taken quite directly from the analysis of the economists, only the value accent being reversed. Marx emphasized not how market competition kept prices low and benefitted the consumer, but how it forced the capitalist to exploit his workers. The freedom of the individual to gratify his wants, as postulated in the utilitarian theory, was thereby effectively neutralized.

It is crucial to remember that Marxian "materialism" was not that of physical determinism which would preclude the operation of "free will" in the individual. Rather, it was the operation of a system of social relations that, it will be remembered, was specifically conceived to be "historical" and thus not general to all human society. The side of the dichotomy opposite to the deterministic side, then, was Marx's conception of the possibility of breaking through capitalistic determinism by *collective* political action.

With the great French Revolution in the background, Marx viewed the political revolts of left elements, in connection with the general disturbances of French political development, as a kind of paradigm of the possibilities of the grand proletarian revolution to come. This was to be successful, not abortive as in the French cases, and was to engulf the whole international capitalistic system. It is comprehensible that Marx and his followers tended to see the ultimate cause of the abortiveness of the French uprisings in the incompleteness of the development of capitalism in France. The proletariat had not yet developed sufficiently to topple the system. This was one of the principal grounds on which Marx labeled the ideologists of these revolts as "utopian."

These considerations throw a second light on the sense in which Marx's basic theory is neither economic nor political, but both. The conception of the deterministic system of capitalism required a political element to account for exploitation and hence the dynamic trend toward capitalism's vulnerability to revolutionary overturn. Thus, the way out of the deterministic system was conceived to follow political paths, the development of a *movement* that could have a realistic prospect of gaining central political power at the level of the nation state.

That Marxian theory implied organized political action was common to all branches of the Marxian following. The main split was over the character of that action. The moderate wing, culminating in the ideas of Bernstein in Germany, saw the developing machinery of the democratic state as presenting a realistic path to socialism through the use of party organization and electoral processes to gain power. The radical branch, which eventuated in the Communist parties, took with utmost seriousness the doctrine that the state was the Executive Committee of the Bourgeoisie and would never peacefully relinquish power to a socialist movement. The conclusion was that violent revolution was the *only* path. This view strongly accentuated the tendency to dichotomize, this time between freedom and determinism.

Here, what I have called the Durkheimian problem arose in an acute form again. This time it concerned the presence of components of normative order, first in the society within which the socialist movement arose and second in the post-revolutionary society. Clearly the democratic socialists of the Bernstein persuasion believed that even in capitalist societies the normative order of political democracy was sufficiently firm and independent of the capitalists' interests, so that it could reasonably be relied upon to provide the opportunity for the advent of socialism. If this were the case, it would seem—to the contemporary sociologist at least—very unlikely that relatively independent normative order in capitalist society would be confined to this sphere. This would imply, then, that there was more continuity between capitalist and socialist societies than the radicals acknowledged.

As it is easy to see, through hindsight, the position of the radicals raised in an acute form not only this problem, but also what I am calling the Weberian problem. One crucial aspect of the revolutionary problem was posed in Marxian theory as precisely that of how to make the transition from determinism to freedom, the famous *Sprung in die Freiheit*. The *agency* of that transition, however, had to be a political party which maximized the centralization of authority in its own organization in the interests of its political effectiveness. Once in control of a national state, then, this centralized authoritarianism had, if anything, to be tightened into the "dictatorship of the proletariat"—actually of the party as the self-appointed "vanguard" of the proletariat—in order to combat the many remaining vested interests of capitalism.

How, then, were the values and the other elements of normative order, which we now know to be essential to an ongoing society, to be introduced? The problem is the more urgent since we know that radical political dictatorship is inherently unstable. Moreover, legitimation of the party as the agent of the revolution is bound to wear thin if it is not bolstered by other sources, especially as internal resistances diminish, or can no longer be plausibly attributed to the surviving remnants of capitalism, and as new internal tensions arise. Continuing external pressure can, of course, be very helpful to such a dictatorship.

Underlying such difficulties has been the fact that Marx never questioned the adequacy of the utilitarian account of motivation in its relation to the normative components of systems of action, cultural, social, or personal. On the side of the idealistic tradition, his "materialism" precluded him from building into his system the normative elements which had been critical in that tradition, notably the ones of religious derivation which Weber emphasized.

This intellectual situation left Marx essentially in the position of postulating a "utopian" conception of harmony. This amounted to another version of the "natural identity of interests"—although, in the interest of the theory of class conflict, the Malthus-Ricardo-Marx development from utilitarian premises had stood over against the tradition of such conceptions, which derived from Locke and was carried on, for example, in John Stuart Mill and Herbert Spencer. Order in the socialist society had, then, to be attributed to the "spontaneous" goodness of its members, who, once freed from the corruptions of capitalistic interests, allegedly could not conceivably act in any antisocial manner. The "state," that is the whole machinery of coercive authority, would wither away. But then, how would the necessary coordination of the activities of individuals and subgroups, and the integration of their interests, be brought about? Marx himself was notably vague on this critical point, and the communist societies cannot be said to have presented a solution yet.

The solution of modern sociology is that in *any* society, the more complex the more so, this integration can only be brought about by the institutionalization and internalization of values that cannot be analytically attributed to the material side of the Marxian Ideal-Material dichotomy. Beyond their internalization as such, these values must legitimize a ramified system of norms, legal and otherwise, that regulate action, through attaching formal and informal sanctions to their observance, and define the situation for individuals and groups by making clear what action is expected of them.

Finally, the state does not wither away, as the Marxians maintain it must. On the contrary, as Durkheim made clear, it continues to develop,[18] assuming a form much more fully differentiated in function from other elements of the society, notably from the class structure, but also from the economy and in certain respects from the normative system including its legal elements. This differentiation, however, is contingent on the development of a kind of solidarity in the societal community that Marx asserted to be impossible under capitalist conditions because of the dichotomization of class interests, and which he did not account for under socialist conditions. The actual course of development of advanced, nonsocialist industrial societies would not suggest that Marx was fully right in their cases. But even if he were, the question would still remain of the position of the state for the long run in so-called socialist societies. It is my contention that Marxian theory gives no solution of this problem and that this is perhaps the central dilemma of its application to the actual situation in socialist societies. I see no sign that the state will eventually "wither away" in any of the societies where Communist Parties are in control.

These circumstances are connected with the problem of freedom *vs.* determinism, with which the present section of the discussion began. The theoretical problem is essentially the same as appeared in the dis-

18. The Marxian assertion of the incompatibility of a strong state with "communism" is directly comparable to the view of present day conservative capitalists that modern government is "creeping socialism." The two mistaken views stem from essentially the same intellectual difficulty, inability to understand the nature and significance of structural differentiation in modern society.

cussion of the core of complex capitalism. As we have indicated, the determinism of the capitalistic complex is not so monolithic as Marx contended. Nor is it a matter of no freedom at all versus a jump into total revolution—that rigid alternative was already rejected by the Revisionists. In fact, the capitalistic system has been transformed, partly in a socialistic direction as through welfare measures, but mainly in other ways that certainly break through the rigidities of the early capitalistic system. One of the most important has been the development of educational systems and, connected with their higher ranges, of systematic research, that have not been direct functions of either capitalistic or proletarian interests, but which certain groups have been free to promote within the framework of the system which Marx diagnosed in those terms. Many other examples could be adduced.

It might be argued that, in concentrating specifically on French examples in his studies of the political potential of the left and the causes of the failure of its early attempts, Marx somewhat stacked the cards in his favor. France in the mid-nineteenth century showed a good deal of political instability, suffering four changes of regime in the fifty-five years that followed the fall of Napoleon, in 1815, 1830, 1848, and 1870. At the same time, it seemed to show a special prevalence of class conflict in something approaching the Marxian sense. Though not without her severe internal strains and conflicts, England, in roughly the same period, was able to carry out major structural changes with minimal, if any, revolutionary episodes. Had Marx studied it closely with this concern, England presumably would not have presented such strong evidence supporting the feasibility of a general socialistic revolution. Still less would the United States. To be sure, the United States had one extremely severe internal conflict, culminating in the Civil War, but it would have been difficult to explain as a class struggle in a strict Marxian sense—even by treating the South as mainly feudal.

Finally, another major problem is illuminated by this political aspect of Marxian theory. Marx and all his followers have strongly resisted the movement to differentiate empirical scientific judgment and generalization from the direct intellectual basis of political action. They have contended that Marxian theory was itself the direct and adequate canon for formulating specific programs of action, and that adequacy by this standard was a legitimate canon for evaluating the empirical validity of a theoretical scheme in the social field—hence the formula "scientific socialism." Though more modern social science has by no means been fully unified on this issue, the predominant view seems to be closer to that of Max Weber, especially if "value freedom" (*Wertfreiheit*) be interpreted, as I have suggested in Chapter 3 of this volume, in terms of *differentiation* of the value base of scientific investigation from that of political action as such, rather than as the attempt to dissociate science from all concern with values. If this interpretation is correct, I think it justifies the statement that the refusal in Marxian theory to differentiate between judgments of scientific validity and of political advocacy is still another case of its failure to attain adequate levels of differentiation, both among components and subsystems of the societal system and among the scientific and other enterprises, as political activism, in which knowledge of society plays a part.

IV

The third main context of Marx's theoretical structure derived most directly from his Hegelian background and was rooted in Hegel's *Philosophy of History*. It is essentially a theory of social evolution of a special character, which grounds the *historistic* elements of Marx's conceptual structure. The historical uniqueness of capitalism is repeatedly invoked to justify the refusal to take the step to the higher levels of analytical abstraction that can be regarded as indispensable for transcending the Marxian level of theorizing.[19]

Marx then adopted the Hegelian dialectic formula to develop a highly ingenious analysis of both the stages and the process of social evolution. This combined the three main aspects of process, namely cumulative development, internal dichotomous conflict in each phase-system, and discontinuity from system to system. The familiar general theme was that the leading class of a phase-system becomes the primary agent of the "progressive" process of development during the relevant phase. Thus the bourgeoisie *in the capitalist phase* was the main agent of the immense increase in economic productivity through the employment of machine technology and sources of mechanical power. In order to carry out its "mission," however, such a class must enlist the services of a class which then develops an interest-position in conflict with it and becomes destined to supersede it in the next phase. Thus the "feudal" class needed the services of the bourgeoisie, for example for commerce and

19. Weber's methodological writings formulate this step classically, in orientation to German historicism generally, but very explicitly including Marx. Weber's position in this respect as well as with respect to value-freedom is discussed critically in Chapter 3 of the present volume.

finance, and the latter eventually, above all through the French Revolution, displaced their former sponsors. When the industrial phase set in, the bourgeoisie, as capitalists, needed a class of wage workers under factory discipline. This class became the proletariat which, through the predicted revolution, was to displace the bourgeoisie and introduce socialism. In the formula of the "dialectic," the "carrier-of-progress" class represented the "thesis," the dependent class that was generated by its needs for effective "relations of production," the "antithesis," and the newly emerging system, with its newly dominant class, the "synthesis."

Of course Marx was by no means oblivious to the oversimplification involved in a model of dichotomous polarization of classes. In a number of his more empirical works, particularly those dealing with political conflict in France he explicitly described differing subgroups of the French bourgeoisie. However, the logic of his general theoretical position drove him increasingly in the direction both of treating these differences as secondary and of predicting that they would progressively tend to be eliminated—for example, much of the "petty bourgeoisie" were, he held, destined to be proletarianized. Certainly, he did not develop an alternative theoretical scheme comparable to Durkheim's treatment of organic solidarity that could have done justice to the trends toward pluralization in modern societies.

The basic theoretical criticisms of the foundations of this scheme have already been stated and need only to be summarized. First, there is no generalized basis on which to postulate that all historically crucial societies will be characterized by a neatly dichotomous class structure. On Marxian premises this presumes, for every system, the dominance of a single "power elite," the position of which is grounded in the "relations of production," and the polarization of the structure relative to its position. The process of differentiation in societal change, however, is by no means confined in this simple sense to polarization between two inherently antagonistic classes. Power and its unequal distribution are phenomena of the first importance in social and political history but do not structure it in so simple a manner. Other aspects of the process of differentiation, starting for example with that between predominantly political and predominantly religious elites, cannot be fitted into this formula. In particular, the higher levels of societal differentiation are more likely to lead toward pluralization—multiple rather than single centers of power and differently structured subcategories of the relations of production.

If internal societal conflict cannot be said in general to be polarized in the Marxian sense, it follows that revolution, conceived as a simple displacement from power of the previously ascendant class and assumption of power by the previously dependent class, cannot be generalized legitimately as the one significant process of transition from one system to the next. Marx's best case was the French Revolution. But the displacement of "feudal" aristocracy from power has taken place in highly complex ways in the Western world; in England, for example, it took place without a violent revolution. Moreover, even in France it clearly did not culminate to one stroke, for aristocracy remained influential if not powerful throughout the nineteenth century.

Probably the most telling fundamental criticism, however, is the untenability of Marx's attempt to rule the ideal and normative factors out of "basic" significance in the determination of social process. Marx's vulnerability with respect to what I have called the Durkheimian and the Weberian problems has been discussed previously. In the present context, it may be added that Marx followed Hegel in another untenable contention. With hindsight we can almost ridicule Hegel's assertion that the Prussian state of his own time represented the culmination of the world-historical process of human evolution, the final "actualization" of the *Weltgeist*. Marx was in an identical position, theoretically considered, with the sole difference that his terminal system was his predicted phase, socialism—or in its ideal form "communism." It is my own view that Marx not only presents no solution of the basic problems of order and social organization that are to be expected in the coming society but, in addition, presents no acceptable rationale for the contention that it will not develop a new dichotomy of classes and that the old dialectic process will not be continued. This problem in turn relates to Marxian *political* activism, as discussed in the last section, and hence to the general problem of freedom.

These yawning gaps in the Marxian system may be attributed to the fact that his "materialism" had cut Marx off from the basic insight that freedom of action—indeed for all living systems, but particularly of and in human social systems—is a function of the *organization* of behavior and action in terms of generalized codes that permit the programming of widely varying particulars. At the human level, these are what we call *cultural* codes. It is these which underlie the normative components of societies. The ultimate paradox of Marxian theory seems to be that the success of the revolutionary movement itself, both in overthrowing the capitalistic system and in establishing socialism and eventually communism, presupposes a dominant role in the determination of human action at the point of crisis for the very components that Marxian "materialism" initially declared to constitute at best a mere "superstructure." *Only* the attribution of paramount significance to a system of cultural codes and patterns could account for the stabilization of the new communistic system and thereby stop the dialectic process. The convinced Marxian, however, can see that this is the case only by making the transition to the higher level of analytical abstraction to which we have repeatedly referred, for we contend that the normative (and hence the cultural) factors are *in fact* built into the structure of Marxian "materialism" itself.[20]

Whatever may be thought of Marx's interpretation of history up to his own time, in regard to his prediction on the macrosocial scale now under consideration, there can be no doubt, with the hindsight of the century of turbulent history since Marx's main writings were composed, that it has suffered a truly basic failure. This malprediction falls into two main categories, both of which merit some comment, as do their interrelations.

A first and very obvious one is that the Marxian analysis predicted that the revolutionary situation would develop most clearly and rapidly in the most advanced industrial countries. Even for his own day, however, Marx's writings would seem to contain an implicit admission that France, which was less "capitalistically" advanced, was in a more revolutionary state than England. In the crucial situation that led up to the Russian Revolution, Lenin clearly considered the events in Russia to constitute only a "holding operation" until the revolution occurred in the Western countries. Indeed, he expected it imminently in Germany, which by then had considerably surpassed Britain on an industrial level.

Since the critical juncture of the end of World War I and the immediately ensuing years, the development of the advanced industrial West has clearly been away from, rather than toward, the predicted proletarian revolution. Even the Fascist episodes between the wars, particularly that of German Nazism, cannot be interpreted as simply the desperate effort of the bourgeoisie to protect themselves against a prole-

20. The logic of this situation is closely parallel to that which has obtained in much of the discussion of the relations between heredity and environment. At one level, it has been discussed as concrete organism in concrete environment, to which the capitalistic nexus of firm in markets is analogous. But when the discussion shifts to the genetically determined *factors* in behavior, or in the evolutionary process, as distinguished from the factors operating environmentally on whole classes of organisms throughout their life cycles, a different analytical level must be assumed. Much of the concrete organism is explained by environmental factors just as much of the concrete firm is explained by normative factors.

tarian movement, however prominently anti-Communism figured as an ideological slogan.

The dominant trend in the highly "developed" Western societies can now clearly be seen to have been that of "pluralization" through further structural differentiation on lines cross-cutting the two-class polarization, of increasing economic productivity that has upgraded the standard of living of the *whole* population and given labor a major economic stake in the community, of the development of a new order of solidary national community that has "included" not only previous lower classes but also previously "alien" ethnic and religious groups, and of broad cultural upgrading that has been most conspicuously manifested in the development of education and scientific research.[21]

It is not unimportant that, in this connection, the United States has emerged as the paradigmatic modern industrial society. It is the one in which "class struggle" has been weakest, which has never had a strong socialist movement, and which has become, under a largely private enterprise system, the industrial giant of the modern world. However, democratic government, the welfare state, trade unionism, and, above all, education, science, and even humanistic culture play such important roles that calling it "capitalistic" in anything like the classical Marxian sense seems increasingly forced. Unless there is a drastic reversal of the major trends—which I see no reason to predict—the proletarian revolution is not likely to transpire in the United States, and is only a little more likely to transpire in Western Europe.

The other side of the picture is the shift in the socialist-communist movement from the advanced industrial societies to the more or less "underdeveloped" areas. The first major step was, of course, the Russian Revolution itself.[22] With the exception of the East European regimes, which were created directly under the aegis of Soviet military power in the aftermath of World War II, the spread of the Communist movement has been directly away from, rather than into, the main seats of advanced capitalistic industrialism. This is, of course, directly contrary to the Marxian prediction.

21. The political aspects and consequences of these processes have perhaps been most fully documented by S. M. Lipset, with special reference to what has happened to socialist and communist movements and parties. See his *Political Man* (Garden City: Doubleday, 1960) and *The First New Nation* (New York: Basic Books, 1963).
22. Ulam's recent reanalysis strongly suggests that the Bolshevik takeover in 1917 was closer to being a coup d'etat than a mass revolution, and that this has on the whole continued to be the case—not implying that the present regime lacks mass support nor that the attempt to indoctrinate the people with Marxist-Leninist ideology has been wholly unsuccessful. See Adam Ulam, *The Bolsheviks* (New York: Macmillan, 1965).

From the Russian Revolution, with the important exception just noted, the main effective spread of the Communist movement has been in the East rather than in the West. Its greatest success by far has been in China, where the movement was grounded on the political support of the peasantry, not the industrial proletariat—a matter that, as noted, originally occasioned a sharp difference of opinion between Mao and Stalin. There has followed, then, considerable Communist agitation in much of the "underdeveloped" world, most of which has been emancipated recently from the colonial rule of the Western powers.

The case of China—where the revolutionary crisis differed only quantitatively from Russia—seems to show that "oppressed" lower-class masses have constituted, internal to any given society, the main condition of opportunity for revolutionary movements, and that the specifics of capitalism in the Marxian sense have relatively little to do with it. The broadest generalization is that, starting with Russia, the "class" basis of revolution has increasingly focused in the peasantry.

Even more dramatic, however, has been the shift from regarding a class within a society to regarding the society itself as the unit that is considered to have been "exploited." The early theory of imperialism found theoretical bases in Marxism for this emphasis, to be sure; but surely Marx himself never contemplated that the proletariat would, in two stages, altogether disappear from the leadership of the revolution, first in favor of the peasantries of underdeveloped nations, and second in favor of total underprivileged societies—with the broad correlation that the *less* capitalistic, the more underprivileged the society. Perhaps the end of this "line" is the contention put forward by some "Marxists" in the underdeveloped areas, notably the Chinese, that a factor having no intrinsic connection with the relations of production, namely race and color, is the "real" basis of polarization in world society and that the ultimate revolution will place the colored peoples against the white. The Chinese Communists do not, however, seem to have taken this line consistently; I must doubt that Marxist thinking will develop the theme on a very large scale.

V

A final phase of the Marxian paradoxes deserves brief comment, namely the special appeal of Marxian theory to certain classes of *intellectuals*. Where the socialist movement was associated with a strong trade-union movement, as in Western and Central Europe in the late nineteenth century, this special role remained obscured. Perhaps Marxism's first big breach with labor came when the British Labor movement repudiated the Marxian version of socialism; but it also came when a strong socialist movement failed to appear in the United States as unionism became very strong. In Russia, union support was a factor in the revolutionary movement, but its main burden was carried by intellectuals, largely in exile and organized in *party* form, though rent with the severest factionalism.

As the appeal of Marxism has moved eastward, it has continued to move away from a union base. Its appeal has focused increasingly on certain categories of intellectuals, who have professed to speak for the masses of the underprivileged in their respective societies and, in their latest phase, for the underprivileged society as a whole.[23]

It is among the intellectuals that some serious concern with social theory is often combined with passionate commitment to particular directions of social reform. Although this paper is concerned in the first instance with the structure of Marxian theory, the preceding outline of its fate in the great ideological discussions of our time suggests certain connections between the two principal components of its appeal to intellectuals, its intrinsic merits as technical theory in social science and its functions as ideology. In my view, the latter functions have progressively become ascendant over the former and have indeed selectively changed the content of the theory by playing down or omitting elements that were originally very basic.

I have spoken of certain specific theoretical vulnerabilities of Marxian theory vis-à-vis subsequent developments in sociology. Its vulnerabilities with reference to economics are even more conspicuous. Who but a very small circle of dedicated Marxists today concerns himself with the intricacies of Marx's labor theory of value and surplus value? Even in the theory of imperialism, we now hear relatively little of the inevitability of excess production in capitalist societies and of their continual need to expand political control to find new markets. We also hear little of the inevitable collapse of capitalism because of uncontrollable economic de-

---

23. It has often been remarked that it is significant that the largest Communist parties in Western Europe are in France and Italy, which have been relatively "underdeveloped" from an industrial point of view, and not in Britain, West Germany, the Netherlands, Belgium, or Sweden. Here also, surely, Marxism's special appeal to intellectuals has played an important part. One clue to this point is the militant secularism of the Marxian movement in areas that have historically been dominated in religious matters by the Catholic church.

pression. Is it too much to say that these Marxian doctrines, however important in their time, have been rendered obsolete by technical developments in theoretical economics?

In this perspective, it is possible to identify the main components of Marxian theory that have survived primarily because of their special appeal to politically activist and radical intellectuals. The first of these is the relatively radical devaluation of the existing societies in which most of these intellectuals are involved, combined with an optimistic activism oriented toward changing the societies in the desired direction.[24] The most obvious content of this desired direction, then, is economic modernization, of which Marx himself was of course a ringing advocate. However, the more generalized, and, as indicated, I think often highly utopian, expectations of general freedom and justice are also involved.

An ideology of political activism must also focus the blame for the parlous state of the society, often eventuating in a semi-paranoid theory of conspiracy. But here the focus has gradually shifted from the capitalists as such, in Marx's strict sense, to *any* ruling classes, and then, further, from internal classes to whole foreign societies, the imperialists and colonialists. The shift to the total society makes the mobilization of nationalism possible, and from there to conflict between the races is but a short step, given certain polarizations in the modern world. In all this, the drama of dichotomy between the obstructors and the promoters of progress, the exploiters and the exploited, in short, the bad guys and the good guys, is clearly crucial ideologically. There is a deep vested interest in the conception of a *two*-class system, one class of which is wrongfully in the ascendancy but, it is held, will legitimately be displaced by the previously oppressed. That "history" is on the side of the vindication of this prophecy is a powerful stimulus to activist motivation.

It can thus be seen that Marxism gives the intellectual groups, especially those of underdeveloped societies, first, a basis of committing themselves to modernization with a primarily economic emphasis. It also justifies a sharp break with the patterns of the traditional society in question. Furthermore, because most of these countries were in colonial

24. In this connection there is today a notable disillusionment with, and turning of concern away from, Soviet Russia. Fifty years is a long time after the Revolution to have to wait for the more ideal features of the new society to appear. Moreover, the problems of establishing order and conformity which inhere in any society are all too evident in Soviet Russia today. This disillusionment with the Soviet Union seems most pronounced among members of the American "New Left" and seems to have gone a considerable distance in Western Europe. It seems likely that it has not yet gone very far in the underdeveloped countries, except where there is a strong disposition to side with the Chinese in their conflict with the Russians.

status until recently, there is great satisfaction to be derived from promoting their modernization under auspices independent of, indeed hostile to, the former Western "imperialist powers." Here of course the successful modernization of Soviet Russia provides a very useful model of what is possible.

Indeed, beyond that, Western "capitalism" may be blamed not only for the previous colonial dependency of the new states, but also for the destruction of their traditional societies. Here a critical focus is on the evils of the encouragement of "self-interest" which has been so prominent in the ideology of free enterprise. There is both the nostalgic contrast between self-interest and the *Gemeinschaft* of the often-romanticized traditional society, and the equally romanticized future socialist or communist state which also will putatively put a final end to self-interest.

Finally, the last stage of the Marxian "progression," from the internal class conflict of capitalism, through the general conflict of all exploited classes against the exploiters, to the conflict of the "imperialist" nations against the "proletarian" societies, opens the door to a special type of nationalism that may coalesce ideas of past glory with those of a glorious future. In the case of the Soviet Union, themes of glorification of the great past of Russia as the "third Rome" and the like have by no means been absent from the thinking of Soviet intellectuals.[25] In the case of China, the new position of leadership in Asia, and the challenge the Chinese have laid down to Soviet leadership in world Communism as a whole, probably link with ideas of restoration of the glories of old China as the "Middle Kingdom," the center of the civilized world.

Another link in the complex is that between the nationalistic themes just noted and the virtues of strong initiative on the part of government in the developmental process, as well as the assertion of national autonomy. Hence the Communist model of centrally-administered "plans" may have considerably greater appeal than the Western pattern of decentralized management of the economy, with of course the Soviet success being available for all to see. The United States, on the other hand, is the focus of much ambivalence. Its role in the cold war, however, tends to overshadow both its relatively nonimperialistic record and its revolutionary past as "the first new nation." It is well known that when the balance is tipped one way in overt commitment in an ambivalent motivational structure, emotional expression in favor of the overt side is likely to be particularly, perhaps forcedly intense.

25. Cf. Richard Pipes, Ed. "The Soviet Intellectuals" (*Daedalus*, Summer, 1960).

It seems highly probable that these considerations do more to explain the attraction of Marxism to intellectuals, particularly (though by no means exclusively) in the underdeveloped world, than do the strictly scientific merits of Marx's theory. They also help to explain the selectivity of present concern relative to the total corpus of Marx's ideas, the neglect of the more strictly economic theory on which Marx himself laid such store, the emphasis on the problems of imperialism and the adaptation of the basic theme of exploitation to that context.

VI

In conclusion we may return to the conception of the "bridge" that Marx built between the idealistic and the utilitarian traditions of social thought. This was a major intellectual achievement that was very much facilitated by Marx's own cosmopolitan character and experience, starting with a philosophical training in his native Germany, living for a considerable time in France and being in touch with French thought (which was indeed a "middle" element in this intellectual situation),[26] and spending the latter part of his life in England where he wrote Das Kapital.

Of course, a principal merit of the Marxian scheme was that it was not simply eclectic, but very sharply structured and consistent in its logical structure. In this connection, we may stress two of its principal features, both of which contributed greatly to its theoretical clarity, but at the same time proved to be the focus of theoretical tensions around which many of the difficulties discussed above have crystallized. The first of these is the special version of the idea of materialism which Marx adopted. Its great merit, seen in terms of intellectual history, was that it enabled him to make genuine theoretical contact with utilitarianism in general and economics in particular. The importance of this is evidenced by the deep estrangement that has been so conspicuous for so long between empiricist-utilitarian types of thought and the Hegelian type of idealism. Indeed, this has often gone so far that persons steeped in the former tradition regarded Max Weber as a "metaphysically" inclined idealist.

The second striking feature was the consistent conception, in all three of the contexts stressed here, of society as basically ruled by

26. Cf. my article on Durkheim in the *International Encyclopedia of Social Sciences.*

dichotomies, first of interest structure within the capitalist system, then of total determinism within capitalism and total freedom in the state of communism, and finally in the whole dialectic structure of the historical process as Marx viewed it. This consistency threw a very strong light on the internal tensions of developing industrial society, but at the same time its very simplicity and radicality made it particularly vulnerable to the sorts of criticism advanced here.

Two further features of Marxian theory helped to protect it against the more immediate impact of such criticism. Although both of them, from the larger point of view, were foci of Marxian difficulties, they certainly constituted advances as compared with the more naive rationalism of the pre-Marxian period. The first was the relative fusion of analytical distinctions between what we would now call the economic and the political factors or aspects of social systems. Since the strand in utilitarian thought stemming from Locke and characterized by the implicit assumption of the "natural identity of interests" had been dominant, the fusion of materialism with what we call political components,[27] carrying on the tradition of Hobbes, Malthus, and Ricardo, was a step in the direction of realism. As evidenced by the growth of trade unionism and of socialist parties, class conflict was a major reality, and the Marxian analysis was certainly an orienting approach to understanding it.

The second "protecting" feature of Marxian theory, stemming from the idealistic side, was its historicism. This also has proved to be an obstacle to further advance; yet, it was also a positive element in that it protected Marxian thought from the charge of unrealistically trying to universalize features that should be treated as characteristic only of a restricted historical epoch. Thus, it avoided the less penetrating discussions of whether "economic man" was a true and universal conception of "human nature," which figured so prominently at the turn of the century. However, it is striking that the virtues of historicism, as well as its difficulties, were shared by Marxian materialism and the idealistic schools, both being in certain respects equally critical of the utilitarian claims to the universality of its theory. Marx was the more realistic here in that he could, as noted, make genuine contact with utilitarian theory; whereas the idealists, including the later radical historicists, had to treat it as *only* the ideology of a particular era.

These features of Marxian theory could only partially and temporarily

27. On this concept cf. my paper "The Political Aspect of Social Structure and Process" in David Easton, ed., *Varieties of Political Theory* (Englewood Cliffs: Prentice-Hall, 1966).

protect it from the consequences of the fact that, at its chosen level of theoretical abstraction, it attempted to generalize too far. The "historical laws" of Marxian theory are not analytical theoretical laws comparable to those of the physical sciences. Apart from their specific vulnerabilities, which have been shown in a whole series of contexts, they are couched at too concrete a level even to be considered as analytical uniformities.

This consideration of the methodology of social science is the most important single basis of my contention that, judged by the standards of the best contemporary social-science theory, Marxian theory is obsolete. The transition to a more generalized and analytical type of theory was made by the post-Marxian generation of social theorists. Economists were particularly prominent among them, perhaps especially Marshall and Keynes, but in the sociological context the most prominent figures were Durkheim and Max Weber. Both, as we have noted, fundamentally repudiated the conceptions, first that the core variables of social systems could be confined to the economic and political interest categories, relegating other components to a "superstructure" status, and second that the critical uniformities could be confined to a historical level, so that they would have to be discovered anew for each historical system. After all, both a modern theory of social evolution, to which Durkheim made very substantial contributions, and the comparative analysis of social systems, which Weber advanced so much, would be impossible if we adhered strictly to Marxian historicism.[28]

If we accept the view that the *theoretical* content of the Marxian system was concentrated in the economic-political area, it is striking that our theoretical treatment of its principal difficulties leads directly into the three principal areas of contemporary social-system theory that were neglected by Marxian theory. The first of these concerns what I have called the "Durkheimian problem," namely the problem of the basis of order in a social system in its integration of associational relations and motivations with the normative structure of the society. This is the field we would now call that of the "societal community."[29] For modern societies in particular, it is Durkheim's conception of organic solidarity

28. To use an analogy, Marxian historicism makes the theory "capitalismocentric" in a sense not altogether different from that in which Ptolemaic astronomy was geocentric. Marxian attempts to deal with the kinds of vulnerabilities which have been reviewed consist of elaborate *ad hoc* hypotheses which are highly reminiscent of the epicycles of late Ptolemaic astronomy. The generation of Durkheim and Weber brought about what may fairly be called a "Copernican revolution" in sociological thought.
29. See my *Societies: Comparative and Evolutionary Perspectives* (Englewood Cliffs: Prentice-Hall, 1966), Chap. II.

that is crucial—it is the very thing that most sharply inhibited Marx from correctly predicting the main trend of development of the advanced industrial societies. To put it in Durkheimian terms, in place of a developing system of organic solidarity, Marx saw only two antagonistic systems of mechanical solidarity, one for each of the two principal classes of his capitalistic system. Even after the transition to socialism, there is, according to Marxian theory, the sharpest limitation on the kinds of differentiation that could promote an organically-solidary societal community, in favor of a highly authoritarian system of mechanical solidarity.

Secondly, we may say that utilitarian theory in a sense made a virtue out of refusal to develop a theory of personality, perhaps justifiably for certain limited purposes. In the course of his synthesis, Marx completely accepted the assumption of the givenness of the wants of individuals, and even, if not their randomness within the individual personality, the irrelevance of inquiries into what interconnections among them might obtain. As we have seen, this left altogether unanswered certain empirical problems of the *directionality* of orientations toward work and enterprise. Weber broke through this impasse at one major point with his conception of the importance of an "economic ethic" that was a kind of value system rooted in major cultural traditions but was also (though Weber himself was vague about this) internalized in the personality of the individual.

Weber in this respect connected with the work of his contemporary Freud, who developed the theory of individual personality to an altogether new level. It is highly significant here that Freud, starting like the anthropologists primarily from a biological frame of reference, came to include in very prominent places both internalized cultural standards (superego) and internalized social objects (ego) in his structural theory of personality.[30] There was a further convergence in this respect with the development of Durkheim's thought after his original analysis of solidarity, in his reinterpretation of the concept of constraint and in his theory of *anomie.* The parallel convergence with the American social psychology of Cooley and Mead is also noteworthy.

From this point of view, it can be said that Marxian theory was, and on the whole has remained, psychologically naive. To be sure, its strong environmentalist emphasis enabled it to avoid the crude versions of "instinctivism" and the like, but it did not develop a theory of personality

30. See my *Social Structure and Personality* (New York: Free Press, 1964), especially Chap. 4.

as interpenetrating with the social system; indeed it has been particularly concerned to avoid involvement with this type of theory.[31]

Weber, in particular, pioneered for sociology the inclusion of the cultural level of analysis in the *generalized* analytical theory of social systems. Indeed, to some, he has substituted for Marx's materialism a "religious theory of history." This, of course, is fundamentally incorrect. Weber's great achievement was not his "phenomenological" interpretations of religious orientations—many in the idealistic tradition have equaled him in that—but his analysis of the *interrelations* between cultural and societal factors, notably at the level of "interests" in the Marxian sense. This again leads to a conception of interpenetration between the societal and cultural systems, a conception that has turned out to be of the greatest importance in sociological theory at many different levels, of which I will mention only two extremes. On the one hand, Weber's own work in the comparative sociology of religion attests to the fruitfulness of this perspective in analyzing the broadest ranges of differentiation among types of society and their basic trends of development. On the other hand, such critically important phenomena of the modern world as the development of science and higher education are not readily understandable without such references to cultural factors.

By setting Hegel on his head, Marx cut himself off most drastically from this third major theoretical complex. Marxian theory had then to deal with the ensuing difficulties by the most elaborate casuistry about the senses in which the superstructure might be recognized as important in certain respects without mitigating the sense in which "in the last analysis" the material base was decisive. The relation of this whole problem area to Marxian political activism has been sufficiently discussed here. By contrast with this, the Durkheimian problem could be handled, up to a point, by maintaining a certain ambiguity with reference to the status of norms as included or not included in the relations of production. Similarly, the personality problem could be avoided by concentrating on macrosocial considerations and stretching concepts of interest to cover whatever gaps appeared.

In conclusion, it must be emphasized that the anti-Marxian position on this crucial issue—that of the status of cultural factors—has in the last generation been immensely strengthened by developments, theo-

31. It must at least be strongly questioned whether the "Pavlovian" trend of so much Soviet psychology, which of course has its many partisans in the West, can, by undercutting the "action" level of the analysis of personality to speak of a purely organic system, demonstrate that what we are here arguing is a major gap in Marxian theory is of little or no importance.

retical and empirical, in such fields as linguistics, information theory and cybernetics, and symbolic and "control" systems more generally. Of course, such developments, which far transcend the social sciences to include virtually the whole range of science, do not support Hegel *against* Marx. In terms of the present universe of discourse, they rather support Weber against both Marx and Hegel in the sense that human-action systems are seen to involve, as both independent and interdependent variables, the *whole* range of factors that were involved in the original ideal-material dichotomy—and for *every* concrete system and subsystem level. We know not only *that* the whole range is involved, but in a variety of senses specifically *how* they are involved, especially in relation to each other.

The basic conclusion seems almost obvious. Karl Marx was probably the greatest social theorist whose work fell entirely within the nineteenth century. His place in intellectual history is secure. As a theorist in the specifically scientific sense, however, he belongs to a phase of development which has been superseded. In sociology today, to be a Marxian, in the strict sense that denies any substantial theoretical progress since Marx, is not a tenable position.

PART ii

Aspects of the Contemporary
Intellectual Environment

CHAPTER 5

An Approach to the Sociology of Knowledge[1]

This paper was written for a symposium on the Sociology of Knowledge—the first in the history of the International Sociological Association—which was held at the 1959 Meeting of the ISA at Stresa, Italy, under the chairmanship of Kurt Wolff. It was published in the *Transaction* of that meeting, Vol. IV.

The paper represents an attempt to come, at least partially, to terms with the problem of the discussions about ideology which have figured so prominently in one sector of Western sociology, especially since the work of Mannheim. It attempts above all to emphasize the distinction between the level of ideology which links the conceptions of social science with the evaluation of recently past, contemporary, and prospective macroscopic social developments, and the analysis of the more basic cultural components in the social process that were at the center of Weber's sociology of religion. It should be read, at least in one perspective, in the light of its relation to the more general theoretical significance of the discussions of Chapters 2, 3, and 4.

I T SEEMS to me that the tradition most explicitly associated with the concept of the sociology of knowledge, that in which the names of Marx and Mannheim are most prominent, has operated with too undifferentiated a conceptual scheme. The main framework of the problem has grown out of the tradition of German idealist-historicist thought and has concerned the relations between what are often called *Idealfaktoren*

1. This paper constitutes a considerable condensation of the version submitted for the International Sociological Congress in Stresa, September, 1959. The difficult work of condensation has been very ably carried out, with complete fidelity to the author's meaning, by Mrs. Carolyn Cooper.

"An Approach to the Sociology of Knowledge" from *Transaction of the Fourth World Congress of Sociology* at Stresa, Italy, Vol. IV (September, 1959).

and *Realfaktoren*. The tendency has been to argue over which was the "most important," as for example in the case of Hegel's "idealism" versus Marx's "materialism," and further, to neglect adequate differentiation of the components on either side of this "equation." Connected with this tendency to dichotomous, either-or thinking has been a strong tendency not to pay adequate attention to the methodological distinction between existential and evaluative judgments, a tendency to relativize all "objectivity" to a base in values or "interests." I should rather follow Max Weber in his insistence on distinguishing between the motives for interest in problems, which is inherently value-relative, and the grounds of the validity of judgments, which in the nature of the case cannot be relative in the same sense. In attempting to emphasize this and several other distinctions I consider basic to the sociology of knowledge, my approach is grounded in Weber's views as expressed both in his essays in the methodology of social science and in his studies in the sociology of religion, but also draws on other sources, notably Durkheim's analysis of social structure in relation to the problems of social solidarity. My general position is relatively close to that taken by Werner Stark in his recent book.[2]

Some Preliminaries

In order to place in context what I consider the relevant problems of a sociology of knowledge, I should like first to sketch a framework for the analysis of all human action conceived as a system. Action, so conceived, is an ordered system of components that root in the physical world and the living organism and that are controlled by cultural patterns and symbols. For the most general analytical purposes it is necessary to break action down into four primary subsystems which I should call the cultural system, the social system, the personality of the individual, and the behavioral organism. These four constitute a hierarchical order of control in the order named, i.e. from the cultural system "down." I see the problem area ordinarily known as the sociology of knowledge as involving the interdependence and the interpenetration of what I have called the social system and the cultural system. But it should not be forgotten that the other two subsystems—personalities and biological organisms in a physical environment—are also concretely involved at every single point, for this classification is clearly analytical and not a

2. Werner Stark, *The Sociology of Knowledge* (Glencoe, Ill.: Free Press, 1958).

classification of concrete entities. *All* human behavior is concretely at the same time cultural, social, psychological, and organic. Any concrete system of interacting persons is hence above all both a social system and a cultural system at the same time; these subsystems are only analytically distinguishable, not concretely separable except so far as cultural content can, for example, be "embodied" in physical artifacts like books or works of art.

To show how the cultural system and the social system are analytically distinct even though concretely interpenetrating, let us analyze each in turn into *its* four primary subsystems.

THE SOCIAL SYSTEM[3]

A social system is that aspect of action that is organized about the *interaction* of a plurality of human individuals. Its structure consists in the patterning of the relations of the individuals, and may be analyzed on four levels of generality so far as its units are concerned: (1) Individuals in roles are organized to form what we call (2) collectivities. Both roles and collectivities, however, are subject to ordering and control by (3) norms that are differentiated according to the functions of these units and to their situations, and by (4) values that define the desirable type of system of relationships. Like the subsystems of action, these four primary structural subsystems of the social system are both analytically distinguishable and concretely interpenetrating. Thus every social system in one sense "consists in" roles organized to form one collectivity, and if it is a complex system, many subcollectivities. But every role and collectivity is "governed" by norms and values, of which each category constitutes a differentiated system.

THE CULTURAL SYSTEM

A cultural system, on the other hand, is organized about patterns of the *meaning* of objects and the "expression" of these meanings through symbols and signs. Thus the "structure of culture" consists in patterns of meaning as such, i.e., what have often been called "ideas," "forms," etcetera. I would like to suggest four basic structural components (i.e., units) of cultural systems: (1) patterns of empirical existential ideas, defining the conceptual schemes in which empirical objects are "cognized"; (2) patterns of expressive symbolization defining the "forms" and

3. Cf. "An Outline of the Social System," Part II of General Introduction, *Theories of Society*, Talcott Parsons, Edward A. Shils, Kaspas D. Naegele, and Jesse R. Pitts, eds. (Glencoe, Ill.: Free Press, 1961).

"styles" in which objects are cathected and symbolically represented, or through which they acquire and express emotional meaning; (3) patterns of evaluation, or the patterns through which objects are evaluated as better or worse than each other, and (4) patterns of the grounding of meaning, or the modes of orientation in and to the world in which the "major premises" of all other components of culture are grounded. Like the above classifications of action subsystems and social subsystems, this classification also constitutes a hierarchy of control.[4] Similarly, these components must be conceived as interpenetrating with each other, as always all involved, though in different modes of relation.

But culture not only has a structure; it "functions" in action. As a component of action—as when defining roles and collectivities, or the goals and interests of persons—cultural patterns do not function "automatically" by some kind of "self-actualization" or "emanation," but only through integration with the other components of action, most importantly through what has come to be called institutionalization in the social system and internalization in the personality.

THE INSTITUTIONALIZATION OF VALUES IN THE SOCIAL SYSTEM

The primary focus of articulation between the social system and the cultural system is the institutionalization of patterns of evaluation from the cultural system into the social system to constitute its topmost controlling component. Thus every social system, even a total society, has a paramount value-pattern. This in turn is differentiated, by a process I shall call "specification," to constitute values for the various differentiated and segmented subsystems of the larger system.

The concept of institutionalization is not confined to values in its relevance. The other three cultural components—empirical existential ideas, expressive symbols, and groundings of meaning—are also institutionalized, but they do not all have the same kind of relation to the social systems that are their "bearers." Though they ordinarily play secondary parts in most subsystems of a society, they can play a primary part in special types of subsystems that cannot subsist independently of the society. Thus for example, what I call the grounding of meaning is the primary

4. In one sense this classification is organized about the subject-object relationship. Seen from this point of view, empirical existential ideas and expressive symbol systems are patternings of the meaning *of objects*. Evaluative patterns and the grounding of meaning, on the other hand, put primacy in the orienting activity of the actor *as* subject: they are patternings of orientation which may be classified in such a way as to cut across any classification of the objects to which they are oriented.

On the general basis of this classification, cf. "Culture and the Social System," Introduction to Part IV of *Theories of Society, op. cit.*

cultural component of religious collectivities, while the patterning of empirical knowledge is the primary cultural component of universities.

Values I conceive to be, in Clyde Kluckhohn's phrase, "conceptions of the desirable"[5] which I interpret to mean definitions of the directions of action-commitment that are prescribed in the culture. The institutionalization of values is, sociologically considered, a complex matter; it constitutes an area of interpenetration of cultural and social systems. As components of the cultural system, values must be related to the rest of that cultural system, and hence to the modes of institutionalization of these other three cultural components. Secondly, however, as components of the social system itself, they must be related to the noncultural components of social-system functioning in such ways as to regulate the mechanisms by which social process occurs. Hence we need a double paradigm; on the one hand, one that places institutionalized values in the context of the rest of the institutionalized cultural system, and on the other hand, a paradigm that places the value components in their relations to the noncultural components of the social system.

FIRST PARADIGM: RELATING VALUES
TO THE OTHER CULTURAL COMPONENTS

As mentioned above, institutionalization of values in a society requires their specification to different subsystems of the society. On the highest level of cultural generality, values are couched in terms that are relevant to the comparative evaluation of different categories of object, both social and nonsocial. On the social level of specification, however, these more general bases of comparison are taken for granted and what is compared in different categories of social object. A societal-value system, then, is the evaluative preference for a given type of society as compared to others. Further specification will lead to the conception of desirable types of subsystems within what is evaluated as a good society, in each case taking account of the place of the subsystem within the society.

Empirical ideas. For these evaluations to take place, however, there must be some basis for discriminating empirically between the properties which are more and less highly evaluated. This means that the same cultural system must include, along with a value system, a set of empirical conceptions of the nature of the social systems and subsystems that are

5. Clyde Kluckhohn, "Values and Value-Orientations in the Theory of Action: An Exploration in Definition and Classification," in Talcott Parsons and Edward A. Shils (eds.), *Toward a General Theory of Action* (Cambridge: Harvard University Press, 1951), esp. p. 395.

being evaluated, *and,* explicitly or implicitly, a set of empirical conceptions of the differences from and similarities to other social systems, historical or contemporary or even potentially occurring, that are differently evaluated.

It is in the *relation* between institutionalized values and empirical conceptions of the evaluated social systems that the problem of ideology arises. Clearly the actual evaluation of current social facts may vary on a positive-negative axis. Hence a whole society's value system may condemn certain aspects of a social status quo, such as crime and illness; these are by definition things the prevalence of which ought to be reduced. On the other hand, different groups within a society may evaluate the same social facts differently, resulting, for instance, in a bifurcation into "conservative" and "radical" values and ideologies.

Grounding of meaning. Because values are always problematical with respect to their legitimation, societies also institutionalize patterns of meaning in terms of which their values "make sense." Here too there is a problem of specification in that there are different levels at which the problems of meaning can be raised. The one that is most directly relevant here is the meaning of the obligations and commitments of collectivities such as the nation or profit-making business firms. It is a question of how the evaluation, positive or negative, can be backed by some sort of answer to the question why this evaluation should be accepted. In the most general terms, this meaning-complex is institutionalized in the religious system of the culture, but on occasion it may be a very prominent component in ideological systems which act as "political religions."

Expressive symbolization. Finally, all social action requires motivational commitment on the part of individuals. No system of values can be adequately institutionalized unless it is integrated with a patterning of appropriate rewards and punishments that are contingent on various courses of behavior and hence the *meanings* of the objects, *individual* and *collective,* that reward and punish. Culturally these rewards involve the whole realm of expressive symbolization, and institutionalized patterns of style and taste are of course central to it. By definition, the moral component of institutionalized values must be distinguished from the reward component, but this does not negate the great importance of the relationship between them.

In my view, all four of these components of a cultural system are closely interdependent, so that no one of them can be institutionalized without important institutional questions being raised about the other three. But sociologists have historically tended to see the relation between values and empirical facts in terms of the problem of ideology, while the relation between grounds of meaning and personal motivation, as it was treated by Weber, has been seen as a problem of religious interests. Both pairs of relationships are rightly the concern of a sociology of knowledge, in my opinion, but in this paper I shall, for reasons of space, confine my attention to the former.

SECOND PARADIGM: RELATING VALUES
TO NONCULTURAL COMPONENTS

The second paradigm referred to above concerns the problem of institutionalization at the level of functioning of the social system itself. Institutionalized values may of course be undermined at the cultural level, by changes focusing at any one or any combination of the four components just discussed, for instance by questioning the grounding of meaning, or by questioning the empirical tenability of conditions alleged to be necessary for implementing the values. Given legitimation through articulation with the cultural system, however, the institutionalization of values depends further on relative effectiveness in meeting the noncultural conditions of their implementation.

Norms. First there is the need for spelling out the general values in terms of sufficiently specific operative norms that can adequately define the situation for the different categories of actors in the society. One might say that the value system must become incorporated in a "constitution," formal or informal, for individual commitment to values is not alone adequate to their implementation.

Collectivities. The second basic condition concerns the functions of the many types of collectivities within a society. Just as values need to be legitimated, so in turn they must, through legal or informal norms, legitimate the goals of different categories of collectivities, provided that the collectivities function so as to contribute to the maintenance and/or development of the society.

Roles. The final major condition for the implementation of values in the social system concerns individuals in roles. Through the socialization process the necessary congruence must be established between personal interests and responsibilities to the larger system.

In sum, values are only fully institutionalized when they have become adequately articulated with a differentiated system of normative order; with legitimation of the goals and functions of collectivities; and with the motivational commitments of individuals in roles, as internalized through the process of socialization.

Where the Sociology of Knowledge Fits

As noted above, it seems to me that the main concern of the sociology of knowledge, especially in the tradition of Marx and of Mannheim, has been with the relation between two components outlined in the first of the two paradigms—between institutionalized value systems and empirical conceptions of societies and their subsystems. But in my opinion the sociology of knowledge should also (though not here) consider the relation between the cultural motivation of individuals and religious grounds of meaning, as this problem was analyzed in Max Weber's work in the sociology of religion.

The fact that Mannheim's attention was focused primarily on the former problem may have something to do with some of the ambiguities which have plagued discussion in this field, certain of which ambiguities start with the very term *Wissen*, which is the German word usually translated as "knowledge" in the phrase "sociology of knowledge." The focus has usually been on the concept of ideology as a structure of ideas, to be appropriately judged by the standards of empirical science. This clearly is at the center of Mannheim's thinking—the problem of the ways in which evaluative considerations enter into the allegedly empirical ideas current about societies, notably the societies in which the ideas themselves are produced, and how these may lead to distortion and selection and may or may not vitiate objectivity. The term *Wissen* is, however, also applicable in contexts that refer not to empirical objects, but to the grounds of meaning, in what Weber would call "religious ideas." I should like to argue that the relation of this kind of *Wissen* to the social system is altogether different from Mannheim's problem of ideology.

But while both empirical science and the grounding of meaning are alike in referring to matters of what "is," of what "exists," in analytical independence of imperatives for action, the other two cultural categories—patterns of evaluation and of expressive symbolization—are so different from both of these that it is of dubious utility to include values and expressive symbols at all as forms of "knowledge." The essential issue is whether the sociology of knowledge should be treated as the "sociology of culture" in the most general possible sense, or whether it could reasonably be restricted to the aspects of culture here singled out. I shall proceed on the assumption that this restriction is reasonable.

The Relation of Values to Empirical Science

Having pointed out two areas of study for a sociology of knowledge, I shall narrow the scope of this discussion to one of them—the relation of values to empirical knowledge. My starting point is the conception that empirical-rational knowledge is an authentically independent component of all cultural systems, even in the most definitely nonliterate societies.[6] The levels of its development of course vary enormously; modern science represents a phenomenon altogether without precedent in any other civilization. Science is characterized as a body of knowledge not only by its extension of the knowledge of facts, but just as importantly, by its *organization* of facts in terms of generalized conceptual schemes.

Empirical knowledge is, furthermore, differentiated in terms of its objects of study, notably into physical, biological, psychological, social, and cultural sciences. While it is obvious that these "levels" of the empirical world interpenetrate intimately with one another, the older forms of positivistic reductionism, which would deny any genuine theoretical significance to such distinctions of level, must be regarded as definitely out of date and superseded.

Values, as aforementioned, I understand to be *conceptions of the desirable*, applied to various objects and standing at varying levels of generality. Societal values are specified to the society itself as object; they are conceptions of the good type of society. When institutionalized, they are such conceptions as are held by the members of the society themselves, and to which they hold motivational commitments.

Within the cultural system—that is in terms of the first paradigm— values must meet certain imperatives. First, they must be *legitimized* through their relations to the ultimate grounds of meaning of the human situation. Secondly, they must be made motivationally meaningful through articulation of the desir*able* with the desir*ed*, that is, through definition of appropriate rewards. The third imperative is, however, the one of most direct concern here. This concerns the relation between values and empirical knowledge. In this connection we should keep in

6. Bronislaw Malinowski's well-known analysis in *Magic, Science and Religion* (London: Macmillan, 1925) is perhaps the best reference point for this assertion.

mind that within a culture, the mutual relation to each other of empirical science and of values is only one of several contexts in which each of these cultural categories is involved. Science is in particular also related to practical problems through its capacity for prediction and control, and to the cultural bases underlying the structure of theory. And social *values* are also related to the motivational commitments of individuals and to the grounds of the meaning of the values.

It should also be made clear at the start that value systems and systems of empirical knowledge are both graded into levels of generality. While for empirical knowledge the relevant scale is the hierarchy of the sciences from physical through biological to psychological, social, and cultural science, for values, it is the valuation of objects in these spheres, and of course in their subspheres. Therefore somewhat different problems arise according to what level of objects is being scientifically analyzed, on the one hand, and according to what level of specification in the system of values is involved, on the other. Our primary interest, in this paper, is clearly at the level of the relation between the values of the social system, on the one hand, and the scientific analysis of the social system, on the other. It is clear, further, that the social system referred to here is the total society. When we consider social classes or other subcategories of social structure, such as occupational status or ethnic groups within a society, another order of problems arises.

Bearing in mind these qualifications, we may say that there are here involved two fundamental problems—the "Kantian" problem and the "Weberian" problem. The Kantian problem relates in the first place to the basic scientific standards of empirical validity, which Weber called the "schema of empirical proof."[7] These basic standards are spelled out in three directions. The first, concerning the structure of the theoretical system, says that any inconsistency at theoretical levels is ground for questioning the validity of a given proposition, i.e., if this proposition is inconsistent with others believed to be validated. The other two sets of standards both concern particularized assertions about empirical objects. One concerns the empirical validity of the proposition, in terms of the well-known criteria of prediction and control; the other concerns the theoretical significance of the particular statement of fact. Put in the

7. Cf. Weber, "'Objectivity' in Social Science and Social Policy," in *Max Weber on the Methodology of the Social Sciences*, Edward A. Shils and Henry A. Finch, trans. and ed. (Glencoe, Ill.: Free Press, 1949); Alexander von v. Schelting, *Max Webers Wissenschaftslehre* (Tübingen: J. C. B. Mohr, 1934); also my own *The Structure of Social Action* [1937] (second edition, Glencoe, Ill.: Free Press, 1949). Chapter XV.

simplest terms, these two essential questions about a statement of fact are, "Is it empirically true?" and "Is it scientifically important?"

Empirical proof, however, is irrelevant without some conception of *problems* relative to which empirical propositions may be formulated. I would suggest that Kant's famous categories of the understanding constitute the formulation of the most general framework of the questions which are addressed to the empirical world. These categories are at the cultural level evaluative because they concern the categorization of what, for human beings, it is important to know about the empirical world. Clearly, the Kantian categories are rooted in the highest-level grounds of the validity of empirical knowledge, in what Kant called transcendental considerations. Thus the Kantian categories represent the level which comprises the significance of knowledge in all the empirical sciences—although clearly Kant was thinking primarily of physical science; in his time, problems of social science were hardly yet receiving serious philosophical consideration. This level would thus comprise interests in *all* categories of objects—physical, biological, social, and so forth.

In what sense could it be said that the Kantian categories are relative? I think the most likely sense is an evolutionary one. It is only when empirical knowledge becomes sufficiently developed and technical that such an elaborately differentiated scheme of categories becomes relevant. Such a relativity, however, does not affect the problem of validity as such, but rather the problem of human interests, i.e., the value of knowing different kinds of answers. Interests in this sense are subject to a process of differentiation through the development of culture.[8]

What I am calling the "Weberian" problem, as distinguished from the Kantian, arises at a lower level of generality which is more immediately relevant for the sociology of knowledge. This concerns the sense in which relatively specific social-value systems (those of a particular society, or subgroup in it) affect relatively specific bodies of knowledge. Here Weber's crucial concept is "value-relevance" (*Wertbeziehung*). Essentially what Weber said was that no matter how fully any given empirical propositions are validated, their inclusion in a body of knowledge about society is never completely independent of the value perspective from which those particular questions were asked to which these propositions constitute answers.

Weber's formulation could be said to be simply a statement of con-

8. In our formal terms, this may be interpreted to mean that the canons of scientific *validity* root in the cultural complex which focuses on empirical knowledge, whereas the problem of the *importance* of empirical propositions roots in the evaluative complex.

siderations at least implicit in the Kantian position. Weber, however, had the methodological problems of social science directly in mind, so it seems that there is a significant difference of level involved. In the study of a society by its own members, there is a different order of integration between values and empirical knowledge from that which exists between values and knowledge of the physical world. This is because the institutionalized values of a society constitute not merely a basis of selective *interest in* its phenomena, but are directly constitutive of the society's structure itself. This means that a different subject-object frame of reference is involved from that in the study of the physical world. The object is both "out there"—in Durkheim's sense an external object—and part of the observer himself, i.e., is internalized. There is doubtless a sense in which this is also true of physical objects, but it is somehow a remoter sense.

I should, however, not hesitate to apply the general methodological canons of scientific method to social theory as well as to physical theory. The position of the observer is in principle inherently involved in conceptualization of all objects—both social and physical—even though in social science it becomes in practice so much more salient that it must be explicitly analyzed to avoid serious implicit biases.[9]

These considerations do not seem to imply the *epistemological* relativism with the possibility of which Mannheim played. That this should be so depends on the conception of a fundamental unity of human culture and of the conditions of human orientation to the world. This is to say that there are universal criteria of empirical validity, a position taken clearly, following Weber, by both von Schelting and Stark. Within this framework, there is certainly variability, but it is not random variability, because neither human values nor the human situation vary at random. They vary on definable dimensions over limited ranges, ranges which are defined by the *relations* of empirical knowledge to the other three dimensions of cultural systems we have distinguished.[10]

9. It is partly for reasons of this sort that social science develops later, in the evolution of culture, than does physical, and that successful handling of it requires higher levels of maturity in individual scientists, at least in the absence of full institutionalization. It might further be inferred that the establishment of an institutional framework for its handling was more difficult and more important than in the case of physical science.

10. It has been suggested above that there are three different bases of such variability, namely, institutionalized values, relations to the grounds of meaning, and to the interests of individuals in rewards for "acceptable" conduct. There are formal reasons to place these sets of selective factors in a hierarchy of control in the order named. For the benefit of those familiar with my analytical scheme it may be pointed out that the system of empirical knowledge is considered to be the adaptive subsystem of a system of culture.

The relativity of the empirical knowledge of social phenomena is thus not in essence, that is, epistemologically, different from the relativity of physical knowledge.[11] We can, therefore, legitimately think in terms of an ideal type of objective scientific knowledge about a society, which is subject to all the fundamental canons of science, but which in selectivity (as distinguished from distortion) of content, and in the basis of its meaning within the society, is relative to the values of that society at a given time. This set of considerations merges with those previously discussed concerning the methodology of science itself, modifying them only by introducing explicitly the sense in which the content of any science, but most particularly of social science, contains an element of relation (and hence in one sense, "relativity") to values.

The Value-Science Integrate and Ideology

What Mannheim meant by the "general" conception of ideology[12] is very close to this ideal type of social science, relativized to the nature of the society in which it has arisen and gains some kind of acceptance. Interpreted in the present terms, it seems to me that Mannheim's "general ideology" should be regarded not just as a scientific explanation of the current state of the society, but as a "value-scientific integrate" at the cultural level. This is to say it is a body of "ideas" that combine a conceptual framework for interpreting the empirical state of a society, with a set of premises from which this state is evaluated positively or nega-

---

Its basic standards will be considered to be institutionalized in turn in *its* "pattern-maintenance" subsystem and thus relatively immune from influences emanating from other cultural subsystems. Of the three types of interchange with other cultural systems, however, the interchange with the value system should have the primarily *integrative* function. The relation to the grounding of meaning, then, should be particularly concerned with goal-attainment of an empirical system, and that to the cultural patterning of the reward system should have primarily adaptive significance to it. If this formal set of relationships holds, it should follow that values should, in a cybernetic sense, control the other two sources of the variability relative to the basic cultural standards, the canons of validity. This might be regarded as a formal justification of Weber's emphasis on *value*-relevance as the primary focus of the problem of relativity of social-scientific knowledge. The formal scheme referred to here has been developed most fully so far in published form in Talcott Parsons and Neil J. Smelser, *Economy and Society* (Glencoe, Ill.: Free Press, 1956), Chapter II.

11. A point of which Weber unfortunately was not fully clear since he was deeply imbued with the methodological importance of the distinction between the natural and the sociocultural sciences which was so prominent in the German intellectual milieu of his time.

12. Karl Mannheim, *Ideology and Utopia* [1929] (New York: Harcourt, Brace, 1936), esp. p. 68, n. 2.

tively. A "general ideology" is the most directly relevant general cultural framework within which a social system can be "seen as an empirical object." It explicitly shows the relevance, besides the empirical scientific component itself, of the evaluative component, but it should not be forgotten that relations to the grounding of meanings and to expressive symbolization are also always implicitly relevant, even if they are not made explicit.

The value-science integrate, unlike Mannheim's "particular" conception which I will refer to as "ideology,"[13] should be interpreted as theoretically independent of the degree of integration of the actual social system with the values which constitute the premises of the value-science integrate. It is compatible with variations from the most "conservative" defence of the status quo to the most revolutionary repudiation of it in the name of an alternative state. Its essential criterion is consistency at the *cultural* level between empirical conceptions of the "social reality" and those evaluative patterns that define the *desirable* social system.

As we have noted, this conception does not impugn the objectivity of empirical social knowledge. It suggests that the *selection* of problems to which answers are given is a function of the values of the society in which such knowledge arises and becomes significant. In this sense, every social theory is relative to the society in which it belongs. But selection in this sense must be carefully distinguished both from a secondary type of selection and from *distortion,* which is realistically always present, but which analytically must be attributed to quite a different order of factors. Weber's concept of *Wertbeziehung,* in my opinion, adequately takes care of the concept of what may be called the "primary selectivity" involved in the value-science integrate. This is to say that even apart from limitations on the empirical resources available for validation, no social science integrated with the value system of a society can give answers to *all* the possible significant problems of societies, but only to those which have meaning within this integrate.

The more usual conception of ideology, which is close to what Mannheim meant by the "particular" conception, must be approached in terms of our *second* paradigm of institutionalization, which concerns not the sense in which different components of the institutionalized cul-

13. To avoid confusion with the more common conception of ideology (Mannheim's "particular" conception, which will be outlined below), I propose to avoid the use of the term "ideology" when referring to Mannheim's general conception, by substituting the phrase "value-science integrate."

tural system are integrated with *one another,* but the sense in which the normative culture thus institutionalized in fact determines concrete social action. What I have called the value-science integrate provides the essential set of standards for identifying a particular ideology, and the points of reference for analyzing its interdependence with those components of the social system that are by definition noncultural.

Particular ideologies deviate from the value-science integrate in two significant respects. On the one hand they involve a further *selectivity,* in that among the problems and phenomena known to be significant for the social science of the time, they select some for emphasis, and neglect or play down others. Thus the business ideology, for instance, substantially exaggerates the contribution of businessmen to the national welfare and underplays the contribution of scientists and professional men. And in the current ideology of the "intellectuals," the importance of social "pressures to conformity" is exaggerated, and institutional factors in the freedom of the individual are ignored or played down.[14]

This type of selectivity, which may be called "secondary" to distinguish it from the "primary" type referred to before, shades off into *distortion;* indeed, the distinction between them depends on the level of generality at which the problem is considered. Thus, from the point of view of a full sociological analysis of American society as a whole, the "intellectuals'" neglect of the institutionalization of freedom could be called distortion; whereas at lower levels of generality, in discussions of particular organizational or peer-group phenomena, it may be considered to be selectivity. The criterion of distortion is that statements are made about the society which by social-scientific methods can be shown to be positively in error, whereas selectivity is involved where the statements are, at the proper level, "true," but do not constitute a balanced account of the available truth. It is clear that both secondary selectivity and distortion in an ideology violate the standards of empirical social science, in a sense in which the value-science integrate does not.

If these deviations from scientific objectivity are essential criteria of an ideology in this present sense, it does not follow that values have ceased to be relevant factors. The *relation* between values and empirical beliefs about the society continues to constitute the main axis of the problem. But in considering an ideology, values must be specified to the

14. Cf. F. X. Sutton, S. E. Harris, C. Kaysen, and J. Tobin, *The American Business Creed* (Cambridge: Harvard University Press, 1956); and Clyde Kluckhohn, "Have There Been Discernible Shifts in American Values During the Past Generation?" in Elting Morison, ed. *The American Style* (New York: Harper, 1958).

level of different subsystems of the society, like businessmen or intellectuals, and the degree of their compatibility with each of the noncultural components distinguished in our second paradigm becomes problematical, whereas in the first paradigm it was not.

It should be made clear that my insistence on the indispensability of a standard of empirical validity for the analysis of ideology does not imply that such analysis is possible only when the social sciences have reached perfection. What is required is not a standard of absolute correctness, but of relative validity, since the problem of ideology arises where there is a *discrepancy* between what is believed and what can be scientifically correct. Naturally the range over which such discrepancies can be demonstrated is a function of the advancement of social science. Science and ideology can be only analytically distinguished from each other; in its development, social science differentiates out from ideology because it emerges from the same roots in common sense.

Common sense is not necessarily ideological in the present meaning of the term, for it may formulate highly condensed and simplified versions of knowledge that can be scientifically demonstrated to be correct. The standard which is relevant here is not scientific proof or form of statement, but scientific correctness (including adequacy to the relevant problems). Persons who act on common sense may be themselves quite unable to explain why it is true, but so long as it *is* correct and neither selected nor distorted relative to the relevant action problems, it is not ideological.

The preceding discussion heads up to the proposition that the *problems* of the sociology of ideology cannot be clearly stated except in the context of an explicitly *cultural* reference. Secondary selection and distortion can only be demonstrated by reference to their deviation from the cultural standards of the value-science integrate, and if there is no such selection or distortion, the empirical beliefs in question must be classed as common sense, technological knowledge, or science. But once an ideology has been clearly identified by reference to deviation from these cultural standards, then the noncultural considerations included in the second paradigm can be brought into play. Two aspects of the noncultural problem may immediately be discriminated. One is the problem of explaining the *sources* of ideological selection and distortion; its reciprocal is the problem of the *consequences* to the social system of the promulgation and acceptance of ideological beliefs.

The Sources of Ideological Selection and Distortion:
The Concept of Strain

The starting point for treatment of both of the above problems clearly lies in the relation of values to social structure through institutionalization. In terms of the second paradigm, it will be remembered, in order to be institutionalized, values have to be (1) specified not only to the society but to the relevant subsystems within the society; (2) legitimized as directly motivationally relevant to the particular groups involved and spelled out in terms of norms; (3) integrated, through the relevantly specified norms, with the goals of the collectivities concerned; and (4) integrated with the motivational commitments of individuals in roles.[15]

Since our concern in discussing ideologies is with deviance from an ideal type defined by a value-science integrate, the problem of locating the elements of deviance and their underlying sources can be broken down in terms of the above four subproblems. First, there is the possibility of malintegration of the value structure itself. This would take the form of a discrepancy in pattern between the society's higher-order values and the values of one or more relevant subsystems. This, for example, would be the case for an incompletely acculturated immigrant group that comes from a society having different values from those in the host society.

Second, even where values are adequately specified, there is the problem of defining norms the terms of which can be implemented in relatively concrete situations. Since social systems are systems of interactive *relationships* between units, a set of norms governing the action of two or more such units can never be tailored totally to the values, goals, or situation of *any one*. Norms thus have, above all, the function of integrating the "needs" of operative units with each other and of reconciling them with the needs of the system as a whole. In more detail, then, norms spell out expectations for collectivities and for persons acting in roles, and, in doing so, may bring to light discrepancies among these expectations.

Third, there may be discrepancy in the definition of the functions and goals of collectivities. A particularly prominent case has been the "profit motive" in modern Western society, which in my opinion is properly conceived as a goal of the business firm as a collectivity, not a

15. It follows from his general description of the relations of values and norms to social structure that for the operative units of that structure—collectivities and persons in roles—their position in the structure is for most purposes the same thing as their relation to the societal value system and to its various subsystems specified to the relevant levels.

"motive" of individuals. It is one of two primary institutionalized goals of firms, the other being "production" of goods and/or services. It has, of course, been an important focus of ideological preoccupation in modern society, particularly since the industrial revolution.

Finally, a discrepancy may be located at the role level in terms of the motivation of the individual. A prominent example is the problem of institutionalizing commitment to marital patterns both as "love objects" and as coleaders of the family. Thus the problem areas of sexual freedom and of divorce are foci of ideological thinking; comparable problems, though very different in specific content, concern commitment to occupational responsibilities, for instance, in discussions over the relative importance of work and leisure, such as Veblen's ironic treatment of the "leisure class."

In most concrete cases, discrepancies will exist at all four of these points, but they will have differential impacts on different groups in a society. All of them are, however, foci both of institutionalization and of internalization. Since social systems, cultural systems, and personality systems are independently variable, there will never be complete correspondence between them; some degree of discrepancy is inevitable.

Where these discrepancies can be shown to be specifically "built into" the social system, we may use the concept of *structured strain*.[16] So far as structured strain underlies ideologies, it can be said to focus on the relation between empirical conceptions of the society and its subsystems, and societal values and their subspecifications. It should be remembered, however, that the concept of strain is not in itself an explanation of ideological patterns, but a generalized label for the kind of factors to look for in working out an explanation. The above frame is meant to contribute to the interpretation of what underlies this label and its use in certain contexts.

In the previous sketch, the point of reference is the factors involved in the orientations of certain categories of individuals. Persons looked at in this way are oriented in, and to, a situation external to themselves. It is, however, the crux of social-system analysis to keep continually in the forefront of attention the fact that what is a given category of actors is a set of patterned orientations from the point of view of the persons who compose that situation, and vice versa. The distinction between orienting actors and situation is hence inherently a relative distinction, relevant only at one level of analysis. This distinction is cut across by

16. Cf. Sutton, Harris, Kaysen, and Tobin, *op.cit.*, for an important recent work which makes extensive use of this concept.

the distinction among institutionalized values, their grounding of meaning, motivational commitments, and empirical knowledge. All of these concepts apply, with different empirical content, of course, on *both* sides of the actor-situation dichotomy in any given case.

The imperatives described above for maintaining the ideal type of integration of objective social science with values entail certain balances in rates of input and output between particular roles and collectivities and other elements of the social system. The primary functional concern may be the maintenance and development of empirical knowledge, for instance, or the maintenance of values. Let us take empirical science, with special reference to social science, as an example.

STRAINS AFFECTING SOCIAL SCIENCE

The scientific community may be thought of as a social system that is organized about a type of *cultural* interest and commitment, in this case, the maintenance and extension of empirical knowledge. In analyzing such a system it is essential to distinguish clearly between institutionalized cultural standards themselves, on the one hand, and the institutionalized modes of their implementation in the corresponding social system, on the other. The first problem belongs in the first paradigm, the second in the second paradigm.[17]

Thus the cultural standards outlined above as "the schema of empirical proof" must be implemented in concrete processes of action. First, a system of scientific investigation must be organized to maximize the probability of attaining its goal of "discovery," i.e., of making possible the statement of new empirical propositions. Secondly, however, discovery can only contribute to the cultural corpus of science through a process of empirical validation, in which the criteria of objectivity are paramount. Thirdly, the contribution of the isolated proposition, however valid, is limited unless it can be fitted into generalized conceptual schemes; hence building theory is just as important in investigation as a social process as is making empirical discoveries, or validating them.

The problem now is how far and by what processes the noncultural conditions impinging on this process are successfully controlled in the interest of the cultural standards. Crucial though the creativeness of the individual scientist is, if he is to be a specialist in science, he and his

17. The scientific role must be institutionalized, but roles must fit into collectivities— in this case the most important is the university. Further, universities must enjoy freedom and encouragement under the normative order of the society. All these are steps of institutionalization *under* the cultural pattern of *valuation* of science.

family must find some basis of support in the division of labor. His incomprehensible, often uncanny and sometimes disturbing or dangerous activities and ideas must somehow be tolerated in the community. He must be provided with adequate facilities to do his work, including books and periodicals, laboratory equipment, and many other things. Scientists themselves must form a subcommunity with media of communication, modes of organization, and so on.

Clearly the basic mode of institutionalization of science in the modern Western world has come to be in the university, which provides scientists with a system of fully institutionalized occupational roles having a respected status in the community, financial support, facilities, and access to students and to a community of competent colleagues. Of course, a further highly significant development is the spilling over of science into other sectors of society, notably through its relation to the various kinds of technology employed in industry and in government.

The sociology of science, then, studies the conditions under which the cultural criteria of science can become institutionalized according to the first paradigm, and once they are institutionalized, the conditions necessary for their implementation in the concrete investigative process according to the second paradigm. Further, it deals with problems having to do with how far these scientific canons and implementing activities are accepted in the society outside the scientific community. It is in the nature of social systems that this acceptance cannot be limited to the scientific community itself; there must be articulation with more generalized values and the institutional structures in which nonscientists participate.

Broadly speaking, tolerance of the scientific attitude becomes more difficult, the closer its subject matter comes to the direct constitution of the society and the personalities of its members. It seems highly probable that it is not only for technical, but also for societal, reasons that physical science, with its more remote subject matter, has been the first branch of science to achieve a high level of development, and that the development in our own time of the sciences dealing with human action documents a crucially important development in the society itself, as well as in science. It is not too much to say that in no previous society would this development have been possible. It is a fact, however, that social science has been a recently and rapidly developing thing; thus, the full institutionalization of the more general values of science, as defining the empirical role of the social scientists, cannot be taken for granted. There are "insecurities." Social scientists may lack support for scientific standards from their university as a collectivity which, to varying degrees, may have stable commitments to the goals of science. Or their own motivational commitments may be in varying respects and degrees incomplete and ambivalent, for example, they may be more concerned with practical usefulness than they are with scientific achievement as such, or they may be overly "success" oriented. Finally, the technical state of their own field may be so imperfect that it is difficult to use genuinely technical standards to resist these pressures when the primary rewards for genuine scientific achievement—self-respect or recognition from colleagues or both—may be too sparse for full efficacy over a long period.

There are thus built-in vulnerabilities to ideological "bias" at the very core of the social-scientific endeavour itself (and indeed, in somewhat lesser degree, in all science). But beyond this, what I have called the scientific community is at best only partially insulated, both culturally and socially, from those other elements in society that in the nature of *their* structural positions cannot give primacy to scientific subvalues and standards of empirical investigation. In these outside circles, commitments to other subvalues in the society are likely to be reflected in ambivalent or negative attitudes toward the scientist's role-commitments (or, what in some respects is as disturbing, in the overidealization of the scientist as a "magician"). And the layman is likely to hold positive empirical beliefs that more or less disagree with those of scientific specialists in various fields.

This is essentially to say that the input-output balance between the scientific community and other societal subsystems is likely to be precarious, with an almost inherent tendency for strong pressures to exact "concessions" from the scientific community to these outside orientations. Underlying this situation is the fact that scientists are not as such politically powerful or in command of large economic resources; they are inherently dependent on other structural elements of the society for these resources as well as for their ultimate legitimation.

It is thus clear that members of the scientific community are in the nature of the case subject to such a complex of strains that it is not surprising if they are unable to control completely either their own belief systems or the currency of beliefs in the society at large about their fields of competence. The other side of the picture is, of course, the operation, over the long run, of self-corrective mechanisms. Empirical propositions do get validated; the valuation of truth in this area does get progressively farther institutionalized. At certain points, practical "pay-offs" result in benefits that would not be available without such knowledge. Were these positive mechanisms not operative, it would be difficult to explain why the symbol "science" is clearly a modern prestige symbol that is widely, if sometimes dubiously, appropriated, as in the phrases "Christian *Science*" or "*scientific* socialism." Without the prestige of science, this would not make sense, and it would be difficult to understand that prestige if authentic science in fact had no independent importance.

It is also to be expected in terms of our analysis that as one goes from the inner core of what is here called the scientific community toward other groups in the social structure, there should be increasing prominence of selection and distortion relative to scientifically-objective standards. Further, certain of these outside groups have special relations to selected portions of the scientific community because of their common "interests" in a particular subject matter. In the American type of society, there is first an obvious and natural relation between natural science and technology. Among the social sciences, then, a special relation obtains between the business community and economics, so that economics is peculiarly vulnerable to the operation of strains as between the scientific and the business communities. Similar considerations apply to the relations between political science and the political elements of the society, and between the legal system and academic law as a discipline. Finally, sociology, with values as a central part of its subject matter, stands in a relation of strain to those elements in the society that are particularly concerned with the guardianship of its values.

Because the strain to which the scientific community is inevitably subjected is likely to be fairly definitely structured rather than random, the chances are minimized of a completely "stark" confrontation of the scientific community with antithetical outside groups. This point calls attention to the very important role of the applied professions as "buffer institutions" in modern society. Historically, this has certainly involved the development of a professional clergy and a legal profession for the application of cultural values and norms in the social system, but more recently, the striking development is that of professions involving the application of various sciences. Medicine and engineering have taken the lead as applications of physical science, but there has been a steady spread of this development, above all to the psychological and social sciences.[18]

18. A further most important development has been the increasing structural integration of these applied professions with the university, especially through their training and through research. Cf. my paper "Some Problems Confronting Sociology as a Profession," *American Sociological Review*, 24 (August, 1959), pp. 547–559.

It is commonplace to regard these applied professions as channels through which technical knowledge, generated in the scientific or otherwise predominantly cultural community, is diffused to and applied in sectors of the society that are not primarily devoted to cultural functions. This, of course, is correct, but it is only one side of the coin. The other is the sense in which the "applied" professions act as a buffer mitigating the pressures which impinge on the cultural community and which would otherwise constitute more seriously disturbing sources of strain.

These considerations are important for the study of ideology. The applied professions should constitute particularly strategic points for the study of the balance of forces operating on the scientific underpinnings of the intellectual culture of modern society, for these are the groups whose professional training has anchored them in the academic disciplines but who at the same time are in direct contact with the related nonacademic sectors of the society.

This point may be illustrated by mentioning a few empirical problems concerning American society, without attempting to enter into their analysis. One would be the problem of why "organized medicine" has come to be ideologically so closely assimilated to the predominant business ideology, thereby tending somewhat to cut itself off from university medicine. Another would be the problem of why, as documented in a recent study, the academic profession in the social sciences has leaned politically considerably to the left of other population groups of comparable income and social-prestige status.[19] Still another would be why the "intellectuals," particularly those outside the academic core, and with humanistic, literary interests, were so attracted by an ideology emphasizing the less attractive features of "mass culture," the dangers of "conformity," and the presumptive loss of "values" in contemporary society.[20]

Consideration of the ideologies of various professions connects with the problem of the ways in which groups not specifically trained in academic disciplines are predisposed to different orders of belief systems in the relevant areas. Examples would be the beliefs of the businessman or the trade unionist about the functioning of the economy, or the beliefs of the lay public concerning methods of child rearing and elementary education. With the increasing prominence of the intellectual disciplines

19. Paul F. Lazarsfeld and Wagner Thielens, Jr., *The Academic Mind* (Glencoe, Ill.: Free Press, 1958).
20. Cf. Winston R. White, *Beyond Conformity* (New York: Free Press of Glencoe, 1961).

in such areas, however, we cannot speak of ideological-belief systems without reference to the ways "popular" beliefs attempt to articulate with those beliefs current in the relevant professional circles, which may themselves, of course, be ideologically selected and distorted.

Some Social Consequences of Ideology

We may now turn briefly from the analysis of the *determinants* of ideological patterns to the obverse problem, that of the possible *effects* on a society of the currency of different ideological patterns. Systematic theoretical analysis of the articulation between cultural and social systems is necessary for this side of the problem as it is for dealing with the determination of ideas. In such analysis the two essential points of reference are again, on the one hand, the methodological criteria for objective empirical knowledge and, on the other hand, the conception of an integrated, institutionalized system of values.

The process by which a *new* value system may become institutionalized in a society or in one or more of its subsystems is clearly one version of the "influence of ideas," though not as I see it, directly of "knowledge."[21] Here I would suggest, first, that in dealing with problems of ideology it is useful to treat the higher-level values of the society as given. Since the stability of such values is in general very important indeed for a social system, we may presume that perhaps the primary function of ideology is either to protect the stability of the institutionalized values, or conversely, in the case of a revolutionary ideology, to undermine the values, at least of such subsystems as the "upper" classes and the business community, if not of the society as a whole; the latter case would present a different order of theoretical problem.

Broadly it can be said that within Western society there is at a high level a *common* value base underlying both conservative and radical

21. This process in the social system is directly analogous to that of the internalization of values in the personality through socialization. I have attempted to deal with an important societal case in "Christianity and Modern Industrial Society" in E. A. Tiryakian, ed., *Essays in Honor of Pitirim A. Sorokin* (Glencoe, Ill.: Free Press, 1961). Chapter 12 in the present volume. A full discussion of the relation of subsystem values to the process of structural differentiation within a society is given in N. J. Smelser, *Social Change in the Industrial Revolution* (Chicago: University of Chicago Press, 1959). A paradigm for the case of personality was worked out in Talcott Parsons and James Olds, "The Mechanisms of Personality Functioning with Special Reference to Socialization," Chapter IV of Talcott Parsons and Robert F. Bales, *Family, Socialization, and Interaction Process* (Glencoe, Ill.: Free Press, 1955).

ideologies. Instead of attempting to undermine these high-level values, the radical ideology tends to assert the unacceptability of the existing society from the point of view of values which everybody takes for granted, whereas the conservative ideology tends to assert that broadly the state of the society is acceptable, and that deliberate attempts to usher in change will be dangerous. Thus, questions of empirical fact about the state of the society have become especially salient with the emergence of the "ideological age" in the last century. An illustration that a radical ideology does not seek to overthrow the *whole* value complex of Western society is to be seen in the high value which "socialism," in *common* with "capitalism," places on economic production. This circumstance is one essential consideration for explaining the fact that the more radical version of socialism tends so drastically to lose its appeal in those societies which have achieved a relatively high level of industrial development and of economic welfare for the masses.[22]

A second social function of ideology is to facilitate acceptance, in the broader society, of scientific professionals and of the bodies of empirical knowledge they "produce." In spite of an ideology's selection and distortion, which are necessarily disturbing to those professionals, it may be conceived as a mechanism which mediates between their scientific standards and the values of those nonprofessional subgroups who also have an "interest" in various scientific fields. That is, *up to a certain limit*, which should be approximately definable in empirical terms, selection and distortion can still serve the function of integrating the main bearers of scientific culture with the other groups who have an "interest" in the subject matter. But somewhere there is a threshold beyond which the effect will tend to be the opposite. In contemporary society, the location of this threshold will affect the character of various versions of "anti-intellectualism." Thus the McCarthyite version of populism, for example, seems to have been clearly beyond this threshold with respect to demands for political loyalty in a democracy under severe political pressures.

A third function of ideology, vis-à-vis the maintenance of role commitments by individuals, emerges when, in the process of structural differentiation within the framework of a relatively stable institutionalized value system, subsystem values no longer jibe sufficiently with the actual nature of those subsystems, thus raising questions about what is expected of classes of persons in different role positions in the society. When ex-

22. Cf. Seymour Martin Lipset, "Socialism—Left and Right—East and West," *Confluence,* 7 (Summer, 1958), pp. 173–192, and *Political Man* (Garden City, N.Y.: Doubleday and Co., 1960).

pectations are not adequately defined, it is impossible for performance and sanction to be accurately matched, and hence motivation to role performance is likely to be disturbed. Then, as psychological rationalization, adherence to an ideology can, within the personality, serve as a mechanism for bridging the gap. But here it is important to distinguish conceptually the consequences *for the social system* of this function of ideology, from its consequences in psychological terms *for the individual personality,* as well as more generally to discriminate between value problems at the social-system level. We might indicate the distinction by saying that ideology is a category of culture more or less institutionalized in social systems, whereas the corresponding category for the personality is rationalization in the psychoanalytic sense. The degree to which rationalizations are socially shared is in principle problematical; for ideologies it is a defining criterion. Many discussions of ideology do not make these distinctions, which in terms of the present approach are crucial.

If it is indeed the case that ideology has a special relation to the process of structural differentiation in the society, it follows that it is in turn related to the problem of organic solidarity in Durkheim's sense. Perhaps it is not too much to say, in summary, that ideology is a special manifestation of the strains associated with the increasing division of labor, and that in turn it is an integrative mechanism which operates to mitigate those strains. More specifically, the strains particularly associated with structural differentiation are those of *anomie,* again in Durkheim's sense.[23] They concern inadequate clarity in the "definition of the situation," particularly at the normative level, since this level stands between values and the more specific goals of collectivities and role obligations of their members. On the whole, I would strongly suggest that a great prevalence of ideology is a symptom that the main disturbances in a society are *not* at the highest level of institutionalized values, but rather concern the integrative problems associated with the process of differentiation.

Unfortunately it is impossible, within the limits of this paper, to take space to follow out the implications of this interpretation further with the analysis of a few concrete examples, but such an attempt would be essential to a real demonstration of the usefulness of the approach.

23. Cf. my paper, "Durkheim's Contribution to the Theory of Integration of Social Systems" in Kurt H. Wolff, ed., *Emile Durkheim, 1858–1917: A Collection of Essays, with Translations and a Bibliography* (Columbus, Ohio: Ohio State University Press, 1961), Chapter 1 in this volume.

Conclusion

This discussion has necessarily been a mere sketch of an exceedingly complicated area of problems. Its primary objective has been to try to put some problems which have grown up within the sociology of knowledge into a somewhat wider perspective made possible by the theory of action, which calls for the careful analysis of both cultural and social systems and their relations to each other. The term "knowledge" has seemed to me to refer to cognitively ordered orientations to objects, with reference both to empirical facts and to problems of meaning. The problem of ideology has been interpreted to concern the first context, especially when the social system itself is the empirical object; Weber's problem of the sociology of religious ideas concerns primarily the second context. It seems important to keep these two problem areas clearly distinct, but also to relate them as the two primary branches of the sociology of knowledge.

Both involve fundamental relations to the values institutionalized in the social system. Indeed this relation to values is the focus of the sociological problems which arise with respect to these two fundamental components of cultural systems. However, neither values nor motivational commitments and their symbolization in expressive terms are, by my definitions, legitimately referred to as forms of "knowledge." The sociology of knowledge should not be identified with the sociology of culture, which is a wider category. Only through an analysis of both social and cultural systems and of their interpenetration and interdependence, however, can an adequate sociology of knowledge be worked out.

CHAPTER 6

Unity and Diversity in the Modern Intellectual Disciplines: The Role of the Social Sciences

There is a sense in which this paper sums up and brings together the various considerations about the place of sociological theory in Western intellectual history that are central to all the preceding chapters. It was written for an issue of *Daedalus* which was organized about the problems of the relation of science and culture in the contemporary world and covered the whole range of the modern intellectual disciplines. The conferences held in connection with the issue were rather particularly concerned with the conception of the "two cultures" which had been rather dramatically set forth not long before by C. P. Snow. As a sociologist, I was particularly concerned to argue that there were, in the intellectual field, not two, but three main branches, the third of course comprising the "social" disciplines. It was in turn my concern to ground this contention in a broad sketch of Western intellectual history and to relate it to the contemporary intellectual situation. In terms of the technical concerns of sociologists, this is the most "popular" of the papers presented thus far in the volume. It was written for the more general "community of scholars," rather than for the sociological theorist as such.

THIS ESSAY will discuss the intellectual disciplines as one major aspect of contemporary culture. Roughly, I conceive their scope as comparable to that of the German term *Wissenschaft*. Perhaps their best

"Unity and Diversity in the Modern Intellectual Disciplines: The Role of the Social Sciences" reprinted from *Daedalus* (Winter, 1965).

criterion is general recognition in this country as main subjects for teaching and research in the central university faculties of Arts and Sciences.
Thus, for most purposes, the "applied" fields that predominate in professional schools are excluded,[1] as are the creative and performing arts.
Typically, the included disciplines are also organized in professional
associations, both national and international, though the networks of such
associations are extremely complex.

I will particularly address the problem of understanding the unity
and diversity exhibited by these disciplines: the principles on which they
are organized, the principles from which distinctions among them derive,
and the principles they hold sufficiently in common that their common
placement in typical "pure discipline" faculties is justified. That the intellectual disciplines can be treated as belonging together requires an
explanation salient to problems of both the conjunction of cultural disciplines and the social organization of the university system. When, in so
many respects, our society steadily becomes more specialized, why do our
universities not specialize in one field, the humanities, the natural sciences, or the social sciences, leaving the other two for other universities?
Why do such technical schools as the Massachusetts Institute of Technology tend to "round out" by strengthening their humanities and social
sciences instead of specializing in the natural sciences with increasing
rigor? Similarly, the Brookings Institution, originally conceived as a
graduate school of the social sciences, did not long survive on that specialized basis except as a research organization.

When conceived broadly enough, all the disciplines seem to share
certain normative elements, that is, standards, or values and norms that
derive from their common grounding in man's quest for knowledge.
Whether the subject materials are natural phenomena, human behavior,
or documents of the cultural heritage, in language or in stone, it is agreed
that assertions about them should be solidly grounded in objective evidence accessible, if at all possible, to the relevant scholarly public. Similarly, inferences from factual statements should follow standard canons
of logic, concepts should be precise and clear, and different statements
claiming objective grounding should be logically consistent with each
other. In social terms, scholars' assertions and evidence should be public
and exposed to the criticism of professional peers. These standards apply
no less to the humanistic disciplines than to the sciences. It is not necessarily required that a poet be logically consistent. But a scholarly critic

1. There are, however, some difficult borderline problems, such as the status of law as
an intellectual discipline.

of poetry must face the negative criticism of colleagues if his statements *about* his subject are not consistent.

These common standards of the intellectual disciplines, in which commitment to specific convictions other than procedural beliefs in their own importance and their own methodological standards is inherently tentative, suggest that a convenient distinction separates them from structures in which *commitment* takes precedence over further investigation, which necessarily places questions of how and why particular bases of commitment should be accepted above action on the bases of commitment.

Four basic areas of the latter type of commitment may be distinguished. Where empirical scientific knowledge is the primary focus, members of the applied professions must act with what knowledge is immediately available. Thus a surgeon responsible for a patient with cancer will operate to remove the malignant tissue to the best of his ability, *not* stopping for further investigation into the causes of even this particular case except insofar as he can improve his knowledge of the particular case within the available time. There seems to be a parallel line between humanistic scholarship and the "creative" arts. Like the good applied scientist, the good artist is certainly concerned with knowledge of the traditions and history of his art and with "theories" about it, but in the actual process of creation he is a practitioner, not an historical scholar or theorist. He must act upon his commitments and convictions, not primarily consider on what bases they are justified or not.

In the field of religious activity, the central concern is faith, which is a matter of commitment, not of posing a problem for investigation. The religious believer, including the clergyman, is not in the first instance a theologian or philosopher, but a practitioner, no matter how important the theological traditions of his faith may be. Finally, the distinction between investigator and practitioner has a special application, which will be more fully discussed presently, to the relation between moral culture or "values" and social action. The responsible social activist, whether high official or ordinary citizen, defender of the *status quo* or revolutionist, is not as such a moral philosopher or social scientist, but once again a practitioner.

Contrary to much received opinion, I shall base my discussion on the fact that the proper classification of disciplines now seems to be broadly *tripartite* rather than dichotomous; we have the humanities, the natural sciences, and the social sciences. The last are the latest comers and are considerably more prominent in the United States than in Great Britain, or, indeed, France. The relatively late emergence of the social sciences as a "third force" seems to be a particularly important phenomenon—a deserving focus for the following discussion.

The Philosophical Background

The modern form of the intellectual disciplines originated during the Renaissance. In that early phase, they were, variously, *secular* studies not rigidly bound to *specific* religious premises like the theological-philosophical and literary-artistic endeavors of the Middle Ages. Stimulated by their encounter with texts long since lost to them, the humanists of the West eagerly undertook to recapture the civilization of the past, its religion, philosophy, art, science, even its social organization. Beyond this, it served as a point of departure not only for new and independent creation of their own in imitation of the ancients, but for such use of the riches of antiquity as Aquinas' theological appropriation of Aristotelian philosophy.

The humanities were thus the oldest and generally most prestigeful of the intellectual disciplines. With important components of theology, philosophy, and, eventually, mathematics, they comprised the core of higher learning throughout the Western world for a very long time, maintaining a virtual monopoly which was not really broken before the middle of the nineteenth century. They thereby constituted the principal common culture of the educated classes of Europe, with history, philosophy, language, and literature gradually assuming more prominent places within the same basic framework.

The natural sciences developed notably only in the late Renaissance, after the humanistic studies had been deeply absorbed. But despite the great achievements of such figures as Galileo and Newton—and the impact of their ideas on philosophy—the natural sciences did not effectually rival the humanities in higher education and the culture of the most influential social classes until well into the nineteenth century. Thus President Charles Eliot of Harvard, the most eminent modernizer of the American university system, was "only" a chemist, and his appointment was viewed very much askance because of the relatively low repute of scientists even at that late day.

It is often said that a most distinctive feature of modern Western philosophy has been its concern with the epistemological problem, the grounding of the validity of cognitive enterprises. The great seventeenth-century synthesis certainly established a frame of reference that gave primacy to the problem in Descartes' sharp formulation of a subject-object dichotomy. This tended toward a metaphysical dualism of the knowing mind and the known external world.

Interestingly, such conceptions as Hobbes's "passions" and power or Locke's "sensations" and the association of ideas contained the germs of many outstanding later developments in psychology and the social sciences. Yet their prototype of the external world was the physical world as understood by the new physical science.[2] Thus, during its first stage, modern philosophy, as "philosophy of knowledge," concentrated on knowledge of the physical world. This comprised only part of philosophy, which was also concerned, above all, with metaphysics and its relation to theology. But with reference to empirical knowledge, the internal world of "experience," the subjective side of Descartes' dichotomy, was generally understood to be only a "position of the observer" for studying physical objects, not a category of objects for study.

It is curious—and would merit investigation in terms of the sociology and psychology of knowledge—that the priority given to knowledge of the physical world in the development of modern philosophy reverses the priorities applying to the development of the human individual's knowledge of his own environment and, it seems, the formation of empirical knowledge in early cultural evolution.

Since Freud, it has been known that the child's first structured orientation to his world occurs in the field of his *social* relationships. The "objects" involved in Freud's fundamental concept of object relations are "social" objects; persons in roles, particularly parents, and the collectivities of which they are parts and into which the child is socialized. This orientation includes an empirical cognitive component which is the foundation on which a child builds his later capacity for the scientific understanding of the empirical world. What is often interpreted as the child's "magical" thinking about the physical world probably evidences a lack of capacity to differentiate between physical and social objects.[3]

Similar things appear true of cultural evolution more generally, though, coming under the general principle that ontogeny repeats phylogeny only very broadly; the parallels are far from exact. Perhaps the best single reference on the problem is the old article by Durkheim

2. This is extremely clear, for instance, in Hobbes's deliberate construction of his social science on the model of "geometry." See the opening chapters of Thomas Hobbes, *Leviathan* (Oxford: Blackwell, 1946).
3. On this aspect of Freud, see my article, "Social Structure and the Development of Personality," reprinted as Chapter 4 of my volume, *Social Structure and Personality* (New York: Free Press, 1964).

and Mauss on the forms of primitive classification.⁴ This emphasizes, with special but not exclusive reference to the Australian aborigines, the priority of the social aspect of primitive categorization of the world, notably in the conception of spatial relations in terms of the arrangement of social units in the camp.

The Two Principal Conceptions of the Intellectual Disciplines

That these problems are crucial in an underlying sense is perhaps evidenced by the fact that the great British empiricist philosophers who most sharply crystallized the basic problems of epistemology were also greatly interested in human behavior and social phenomena—especially Hobbes and Locke in the seventeenth century and Hume in the eighteenth. Hume's essays, for example, contain outstanding insights into many fields of social analysis.⁵

This concern with both the physical and social worlds was the source of one of the most important movements from which modern social science has derived. It seems best to call the movement "utilitarian" in a sense close to Halévy's term, "philosophical radicalism,"⁶ applying to the early nineteenth century. From it grew, first and perhaps with the most solid grounding, the main outline of the science of economics, in the line running from Locke to Adam Smith to Ricardo and his successors. It is no accident that economics could be relatively easily related to a viewpoint particularly concerned with the physical world. As a practical field economics is the sphere of social action most directly concerned with articulating the social and physical worlds, especially regarding technology's place in physical production and the psychological significance of physical goods in consumption contexts. The fact that money, the generalized medium of economic transaction, is quantified in a linear continuum having a logical pattern identical with that of the principal variables of classical mechanics is particularly significant in this connection.

Social science's other principal point of emergence from a utilitarian

4. Emile Durkheim and Marcel Mauss, *Primitive Classification* (Chicago: The University of Chicago Press, 1963); French edition, 1903.
5. Just to give examples, cf. "Of Superstition and Enthusiasm," which is a kind of charter for the sociology of religion, and the essays on commerce, money, trade, public credit, interest, and taxes, which are landmarks in economics. David Hume: *Essays and Treatises,* vol. I (London: Cadell, 1793).
6. Halévy, *The Growth of Philosophical Radicalism* (Boston: Beacon Paperbacks, 1960).

base was in psychology. Here the problem involved bridging the gap between concepts of the sheer givenness of the consumption wants of individuals, a cardinal reference point for economic theory, and the problem of explaining the genesis of wants or motives.[7] Insofar as handling this problem went beyond just postulating the association of inherently discrete elements (for example, in the "association" psychology of James Mill), this frame of reference contained very strong pressures to "reduce" its psychological phenomena to more or less physical terms and lead directly into the heredity-environment dichotomy which came to dominate its biological thought. This has broadly produced the dichotomy between the "instinct" psychology of the Anglo-American tradition and "behaviorism," with its environmentalist emphasis and, hence, concern with the mechanisms of learning. The crucial point for present purposes is that the differences between the social and physical aspects of the actor's environment were not considered problematical for the purposes of this type of psychology.

Like perhaps all great intellectual movements, utilitarianism had its "revolutionary underground" subverting the neat, orderly schemes of the main trend. The greatest of its representatives were probably Hobbes, one of its chief founders, and Malthus. Both were deeply concerned with the problem of the grounding of elementary social order, something which Locke took for granted.[8] The problems they posed were destined to play in various ways a critical part in breaking the closed system which gave the physical world, as conceived by early modern science, essential priority in the whole theory of possible empirical knowledge.

It will be remembered that this basically epistemological phase of modern philosophy took its departure from the Cartesian dichotomy of knowing subject and known object, and the attempt to relate them to each other. The empiricist-utilitarian phase of the movement seems to have retained a relatively simple version of this frame of reference, essentially treating its "subjective" side *only* as a point of reference and then concerning itself with objects treatable as involved *only* on the objective side. For the physical world this seemed quite appropriate, but it presented difficulties for the study of human behavior. It seems that the economists' insistence on the *givenness* of wants, involving *de facto* assumptions of their randomness, was in the first instance a way of avoiding the apparently hopeless complications of considering the knowing,

7. James Olds, *The Growth and Structure of Motives* (Glencoe: The Free Press, 1954).
8. Talcott Parsons, *The Structure of Social Action* (New York: McGraw-Hill, 1937).

wanting subject as also belonging to the objective category and requiring analysis on its merits. The complications derived from the fact that the Cartesian dichotomy had then to be conceived as being not singly but doubly salient. There were, concretely, no longer only knowing subjects on the one hand and known or observed objects on the other hand, but there were also entities in both positions at the same time. Insofar as they were both, how could specific structured properties of their different aspects relate to each other? It does not seem too harsh to say that the history of utilitarian thought has involved an elaborate evasion of this problem. The favorite device has been to hold, implicitly if not explicitly, that the subject-as-object in fact has no determinate structure. Insofar as it exists empirically at all, it consists only of given wants which, so far as they do not reflect physical realities, may safely be treated as random.

Kant, Hegel, and German Idealism

The alternative treatment of the problem was embarked upon, with all its enormous hazards, by the idealistic movement. The first step was taken by Kant. He focused in the first instance on the skeptical consequences which Hume drew from the conception of an uncontrolled impact of sense impressions from all phases of the action situation impinging on a knowing subject as equally valid "experience." Kant's answer was that order could be grounded in the field of what he called empirical knowledge only by a sharp *restriction* of the conception of empirical knowledge to what he called the field of phenomena, which in effect meant the physical world in the sense of the relevance of Newtonian theory. This world could be ordered in terms of the combination of the forms of intuition, namely Euclidean space and linear time, and the categories of *the understanding* among which causality appeared with special prominence.

This realm constituted only a small part of the legitimate concerns of human interest. Kant, however, threw everything else into one basket. To the realm of phenomenal determinism, he contrasted the realm of freedom. To that of theoretical understanding, he contrasted that of *practical* reason. In this connection, one of his principal concerns was with the status of theology, which he radically denied could be a rational, theoretical discipline. Thus the realms of theoretical understanding and practical commitment were radically dissociated, the latter having radical precedence for all realms of human concern other than natural science.

Important as this was in setting the whole frame of reference for the modern intellectual world, it was very substantially modified in its subsequent development. The next major step was introduced by Kant's successor, Hegel, and consisted in a highly ambitious attempt to order the subjective side of the dichotomy in terms of the conception of *objectiver Geist*, or spirit, as it can sometimes be translated. The important concept here is in the objective element—that is, that what are now often called cultural patterns, namely ideas, norms, or, more diffusely, "orientations," are treatable as *objects* of observation and rigorous analysis rather than merely as ways of locating the ultimate reference point for knowledge of phenomenal objects in Kant's sense.

Although he reintroduced the conception that the world of *Geist* belonged to that of objects, Hegel did not simply assimilate it to the physical world, but rather formulated its characteristics in a special way of the greatest importance for the future. "Ideal" objects were considered authentically objects, but they were to be treated conceptually in exclusively "historical" terms. The conception historical contained two primary components. One was that the historical object stood in a developmental sequence cognizance of which was essential to knowledge of it. The other asserted the object's uniqueness and, hence, in certain respects, its incomparability with other empirical entities.

Hegel himself built this into a grand scheme of the philosophy of history, interpreted as a process of the "unfolding" of the world spirit (*Weltgeist*) through the agency of human action. This had the greatest importance as one of the principal early versions of the general idea of evolution, antedating Darwin by nearly half a century. It also integrated the ideas of conflict and progress through the conception of the dialectic process in the famous formula of thesis-antithesis-synthesis.

Two themes involved in the aftermath, however, especially concern us. The first is the insistence that the field of human "subjective" concerns, of meanings, must be conceptualized in ideographic as distinguished from generalized and analytical terms. Secondly, the implications of the dissociation between the realms of the physical (and in Kant's sense phenomenal) and of the "ideal" were pressed so radically that a certain duality of determinisms tended to emerge in the contention that each "realm" functioned according to its own unique necessities and in the failure to consider clearly how the "realms" interacted with each other. The dialectic conception of the ultimate unity of conflict and integration was a third major theme which, however, may be considered secondary.

A complex set of variations on the theme of Cartesian dualism seems to have developed. We have not stressed the common philosophical concern with the difference between mind and matter, but rather the problems close to the issues of the development of social science. The social terms of the utilitarian tradition evidently emerged from what, contrary to Kant's view, were the inherently open boundaries of the physical world as conceived by early modern science and philosophy. The utilitarian tendency was to assimilate analysis of human behavior as closely to that of physical objects as seemed feasible. The case of the logical structure of early economic theory is paradigmatic. The consequence was the extension into the behavioral realm of conceptions of the scientific treatment of a world of objects in a way which left the status of knowing subjects highly equivocal in this context.

The Kantian statement cut off this tendency to extension sharply. It radically shifted the problem to the field of the noumenal, which we can equate with essentially humanistic concerns, in German terminology, of *Geist*. Here the crucial questions concerned whether and in what sense the idea of science, conceived roughly as a compromise between the Western emphasis on physical science and the broader German conception of *Wissenschaft* (roughly equivalent to discipline in English), could find an application in the intellectual world of the idealistic movement. That it did so must be interpreted in terms of the operation of the imperatives of intellectual discipline, the general values of integrity in intellectual objectivity and generality, in the subject matters of subjectively meaningful human concerns. Another process of "extension," parallel to the utilitarian extension of the paradigm of physical science, occurred here.

The sharpness of the Kantian dichotomy could not be expected to endure without modification. One reason lay in the fact that each of the the two great traditions issued in an extremism having a profound bearing on the future structure of the intellectual diciplines. On the utilitarian side, it took the form of the pervasive physicalist reductionism that tended to hold that only the natural sciences, on the model of classical mechanics, could yield valid empirical knowledge in any sense. On the idealistic side, there was a corresponding radicalism that in a sense considered Hegel too "rationalistic" in attempting to formulate laws of the development of the *Weltgeist*. In the Germany of the late nineteenth century, Hegelianism thus gave way to radical "historicism," the conception of the universe as comprised of discrete, empirically observable "historical individuals" which were, however, in principle incomparable. The sharpest formulation of the philosophical position of historicism in this sense was probably in the work of Wilhelm Dilthey.[9]

The emergence of this radically empirical trend was associated with a major intellectual movement in Germany, namely, the rise of the "historical schools" in a whole range of disciplines concerning human affairs, not only in history itself, but also in law, economics, and the cultural fields. This in turn involved a great deal of meticulous and detailed scholarship. The pull of this scholarship, as contrasted with the tendency to generalize, seems to have been responsible for a major division which appeared within this tradition and formed an exceedingly important background for the work, among others, of Max Weber.

This was the division between the atomistic and holistic trends within historicism. The first tended to break down the phenomena into minimum units and treat each as maximally independent of all others. The second tended to treat whole civilizations or epochs of history as unified entities. For the latter, the untranslatable German word *Gestalt* seems to be the best single characterization.

Very clearly, this entire mode of thinking tended to assimilate the whole sphere of human concerns to the model of the humanities. Indeed, it carried this emphasis to an extreme comparable in certain respects to the extremism of physical reductionism. The attempt to relate the two main conceptions of knowledge to each other systematically was perhaps carried farthest by Heinrich Rickert, who discussed the basic distinction between the problems of knowledge in the natural sciences and those in the *Kulturwissenschaften*.[10] Contrary to the generalizing analytical characteristics of conceptualization in the former, the latter were characterized by emphasizing the individuality of each phenomenon and therefore its inherent incomparability with others.

Movements Toward Synthesis

The two patterns of extremism, physical reductionism and historicist uniqueness and ultimate givenness, could not completely dominate the field for long, however prominently their theses still reverberate. Three main movements toward a synthesis soon appeared and have played an important part in the intellectual history of the last century.

9. Wilhelm Dilthey, *Einleitung in die Geisteswissenschaften* (Leipzig: Duncker und Humblot, 1883).
10. Heinrich Rickert, *Über die Grenzen der Naturwissenschaftlichen Begriffsbildung,* 5th edition (Tübingen: J. C. B. Mohr, 1929).

The first of these can hardly be called a movement at all. Yet it has certainly contributed importantly to the present definition of the situation. On the Western, more "empiricist" side, it has involved a combination of biological and "humanistic" emphases. Its essential keynote is a concern with the phenomena of organization—and the fact that this emphasis directs attention to patterns of relationship rather than to units in the sense of the individual particle. The trend sketched above which united physics and classical economics generally gave primary consideration to units, that is, the wants of individuals were the particles of the economic system. Biology, however, with its concern for organization and structure, tends to emphasize "forms" or patterns, in the first instance as anatomical traits. Seen in this context, the emergence of Darwinism was a culmination rather than an origin—these emphases were "in the air."

From this viewpoint, "human biology," the concern with organizational traits, can move very readily from anatomy and physiology to the behavioral and cultural levels. Indeed, there is a long tradition connecting "natural history" with an historical approach to the study of human artifacts and "ways of doing things," viewed in terms of their meanings and functions, and social institutions.

This seems to be the origin of the predominantly Anglo-American discipline of anthropology. Its self-definition, the "science of man," was conceived in a biological frame of reference as comparable to branches of biology, such as ornithology or ichthyology, which studied other sectors of the organic world. In this respect, there was nothing unusual in the specialization on humanity, except that biologically it was very limited in time and variety, there being only one human species. Such study, however, inevitably led into the human traits which were separable from man's genetically organic constitution, which anthropologists have designated generically as his "culture." Anthropology then had to define its concern as the "environmental" side of the human equation, with reference to distinctively human behavioral phenomena, if "culture" could be considered to characterize these.

Within this definition, however, the anthropological concern was with "traits," not with particles. This was a radically different focus from that of the utilitarian economists, because traits were elements in the organization of human relationships, not properties of the individual human being. There was a much less direct correspondence with the logical structure of the physical theory of the day. In fact, the crucial point for present purposes is that this background of anthropology permitted a direct convergence with the trait particularism of the German historical tradition. This convergence was most directly mediated by Franz Boas, the most influential figure in American anthropology in the first part of this century. It is significant both that Boas was a physicist before becoming an anthropologist and that he was German. In the light of this connection, it is not surprising that anthropology also developed the alternative position within ideographic historicism in the idea of a total "culture" as a unified *Gestalt*. This occurred most prominently in the work of Ruth Benedict, whose book title, *Patterns of Culture,* gave a classic expression to this viewpoint.

The second, largely contemporaneous, though somewhat earlier, synthesis was developed by Karl Marx. It involved building a bridge between the prehistoricist Hegelian works and the utilitarian aspects of the empiricist tradition.

All the emphasis in Marxian theory on "materialism" refers primarily to a contrast with "ideal" in the Hegelian sense, not to matter in the more primitive Cartesian sense. The theory does not seriously treat the physical world at all, and has had severe difficulties in the biological sphere. It is primarily an attempt to redress the imbalance created by Hegelianism in its idealistic emphasis by "setting Hegel on his head," as Marx said. The significant thing here is that Marx went rather directly to theory developed from a utilitarian base, namely, classical economics in a modified Ricardian form. As we have noted, this conceptual scheme had special connections with the physical sphere, but clearly was not itself a part of physical science—and it wholly bypassed the biological level.

The crucial Marxian concept here is "material interests." These are clearly economic in the utilitarian sense, which includes the assumption of the *unproblematical* character of individuals' wants. The concept attempts to introduce determinism into the system by postulating that, in the situation of the individual in a market economy, basically only *one* line of action is open.[11] For the "Capitalist," this is maximization of profit. For the "worker," it is staving off disaster by the acceptance of employment on the available terms.

Any serious student of modern industrial societies recognizes the tremendous oversimplification inherent in this scheme—no Western society has ever been that deterministic in precisely such narrow terms. Marx and, by and large, his followers have met this problem primarily

11. Michel Crozier, *The Bureaucratic Phenomenon* (Chicago: University of Chicago Press, 1964).

by supplementing the economic element, which had the virtue of its special articulation with the physical sphere, with one which we would call political today. That is, Marx interpreted the structure of the situation in which interests in the economic sense were defined and pursued in terms of a socially-structured conflict—which he construed as class conflict. This, however, involved the use of coercive sanctions by those occupying positions of superior power, the individual capitalist vis-à-vis his workers at the level of the firm, the capitalist class conceived as basically controlling the state at the macro-social level. The Hegelian dialectic of ideas was thus translated into a dialectic of interests which were both economic and political; the two categories were not clearly differentiated from each other.

It may be said that Marx took over Hegel's conception of the pattern of historical development, but replaced the *Weltgeist* with a modified version of Ricardo, and the periphery[12] of Ricardian theory in the broad utilitarian tradition. The content of this scheme was formulated in terms of human interests in "want-satisfaction" or goal attainment, mainly at the individual level. But the paradigm of the Hegelian historical process, activated by dialectic conflict and moving through a series of stages, gave it a quite different meaning. This aspect is crucially significant because Marxian theory has never taken, with all its materialism, many steps toward giving human social behavior a generalized analytical treatment, but, on the basis of certain broad assumptions about "human nature," has relativized all problems to particular systems and historical stages of their development. For Marxians, Ricardian economic theory has been *only* the theory of capitalist economics and not an early stage of a general economic theory applicable, with others and with appropriate qualifications, to socialist societies.

Thus the Marxian synthesis, though certainly a genuine one, was incomplete in not breaking with the basic assumptions of the idealistic tradition in three respects. First, though it formulated, with heavy borrowing from utilitarian sources, the conception of material interests and gave it priority in analyzing the causal historical process, it remained historical in the ideographic sense and did not extend the conception of generalized analytical theory from the natural sphere to that of human behavior. In this respect it represents a retrogressive step relative to the great traditions of English economics from Ricardo through J. S. Mill and Marshall to Keynes.

12. In these respects, Marx was more Hobbesian and Malthusian than Lockean in stressing the potentials for disorder and conflict.

Secondly, though repudiating the specifically Hegelian conception of the determination of human behavior by the unfolding *Geist*, Marxism retained the "ideal"—"real" dichotomy of "factors," so that explanation was couched in either-or terms rather than terms of interdependence. Since Hegel's ideal factors could not explain "history," Marx tended to propound an explanation totally in terms of material factors as the only alternative. The logical resemblance of this dilemma to that between heredity and environment in biology is too patent to need further discussion.

Third and most basically, Marxian theory, by accepting, largely implicitly, the utilitarian formula of the givenness of wants, tended to cut itself off from the most important problems leading toward a synthesis of the two sides of the Kantian dichotomy. The basic question is why, having freedom of choice, people in fact opt for one, not some other, personal goal and means of attaining it. The "ideal" component is postulated as given in Marxian theory, in a sense directly comparable to that in which the wants of individuals were assumed to be given in utilitarian theory. In other words, this is the area of an intellectual "neutrality pact," which in the nature of the subject-matter is suspect of inherent instability.

The period including the turn of the last century and the early decades of this century saw extraordinary ferment in all the fields of this discussion. A critically important development was the philosophical criticism of older views concerning the status of physical theory, strongly influenced by internal developments within physics itself. This was classically stated by Whitehead, who attributed a new level of abstraction to this type of theory, the ignoring of which involved the fallacy of misplaced concreteness.[13] This was clearly a more radical conception of the relativity of references to the physical world than that formulated by Kant. It demonstrated the validity of considering the same concrete empirical phenomena from the viewpoint of various different modes of cognitive interest, not just that of understanding in the Kantian sense.

A second major trend of the period developed interests in organizational conceptions in the biological sphere at the more physiological level, as well as at the more anatomical level. This extended the conception of organization involved in the original emergence of anthropology to dynamic levels. Perhaps the most eminent figure here is W. B.

13. A. N. Whitehead, *Science and the Modern World* (New York: Macmillan Company, 1925).

Cannon,[14] the physiologist. With *homeostasis,* he conceived of a spontaneous built-in control within the organism which maintained an equilibrium state within boundaries; this concept referred more to a "pattern of functioning" like that of behavior than to an "inert" anatomical structure.

Still later, this trend of thinking established contact with that of cybernetics and information theory, which originated in the physical field of engineering more than in physics itself, but which has nevertheless grounded conceptions of an organized system maintained by integrative control mechanisms much more solidly in the *general* theory of science. This trend in the fields closest to the physical sciences has been most important to the development of a new status for the social disciplines. However, its primary references have been outside the latter field.

Another substantive field tending to bridge the traditional gap between the humanities and the natural sciences in a way directly involving the social sciences has been the science of linguistics. Language has been the citadel of humanistic studies. Indeed, German humanists in general have tended to call themselves "philologists." This is understandable, since language has been the primary medium of symbolic process and cultural communication. However, increasingly language has been subjected to analytical rather than merely historical study. Also, this trend has connected very directly with theoretical developments in the natural-science field, notably information theory. Linguistics has also had important contact with the social sciences. First there was the older French work of de Saussure and Meillet. In American anthropology in particular, Edward Sapir and Benjamin Whorf have treated linguistic evidence as a main keynote of the idea of cultural relativity. More recently, Claude Levi-Strauss has been attempting to develop general sociocultural theory from linguistic models. It is perhaps not too much to say that linguistics is becoming a discipline that is concurrently a natural science, a branch of the humanities, and a social science.

A very significant methodological convergence should be added to these substantive convergences. First, logic itself is a general resource of all intellectual disciplines—as it has become refined technically, its general relevance has become increasingly evident. Secondly, logic has tended to merge increasingly with mathematics as a preeminent tool of analysis. Then statistics, from having been an empirical art, has increas-

14. W. B. Cannon, *The Wisdom of the Body* (New York: Norton, 1932). A comparable view with reference to genetics is stated by H. S. Jennings, *The Biological Basis of Human Nature* (New York: Norton, 1930).

ingly gained mathematical foundations and extended its range of application, even into the humanistic disciplines, particularly via linguistic studies. The recent rapid development of computer techniques is a latest phase involving an application of a complex combination of these elements. The essential point is that these technical innovations cut clean across traditional divisions between disciplines. Their recent invasion of the humanities is the clearest sign that the latter cannot be regarded as inherently isolated from their "scientific" sister disciplines.

After this digression, however, we may return to the more specifically social and behavioral reference. Somewhat antedating most of the movements just sketched has been a third major synthetic development, following the anthropological and the Marxian. This, the emergence of the modern phase of sociological theory, may be considered a synthesis of a higher order than either of the other two because it has included the principal components of the other syntheses and because it has avoided the extremism of the either-or dichotomies which have plagued the other syntheses, namely, heredity-environment in the one case and ideal-material in the other.

Max Weber and Emile Durkheim

Two great figures were mainly responsible for this development, namely Max Weber, starting in Germany from a critique of the idealist-historicist tradition, and Emile Durkheim, developing in France a corresponding critique of the utilitarian tradition.[15] These two converged very significantly on a common, though broad, conceptual scheme. Let us start with Weber.

Because of the relation to the humanistic tradition, it may be illuminating to note that Weber began his intellectual career in jurisprudence under the aegis of the historical school then dominant in Germany. This is significant because, in a very important sense, the law stands squarely between the two poles of the Hegelian-Marxian spectrum so far as human behavior is concerned. Though, as noted above, legal norms, as rules and institutions, are essentially cultural in structure, they are relational patterns. As such, they are the first-line mechanisms regulating

15. See Talcott Parsons, *The Structure of Social Action* (New York: McGraw-Hill, 1937), and H. Stuart Hughes, *Consciousness and Society* (New York: Knopf, 1958), for more detailed analyses of the theoretical positions surveyed in the following. Vilfredo Pareto in sociology, Freud in psychology and the American development of social psychology, related to Pragmatism and involving James, Dewey, C. H. Cooley, G. H. Mead and W. I. Thomas, also belong in this context.

the pursuit of the type of interests which predominate in Marxian theory. Furthermore, so far as a society is concerned, law has a reference to the system as a whole, to the "public" interest, which is not shared with the "self-interest" of businesses or political "interest groups." It may also be noted that the Marxian attitude toward law has been exceedingly ambiguous. By grounding the conception of capitalistic interest in the concrete structure of the family firm, certain property institutions, and market structures regulated by institutions of contract, Marxians have generally tended to *include* basic legal institutions within the famous material factors, the relations of production. At other times, however, they have treated law as a component of the "superstructure," and thus as "determined by," rather than as a *part of*, the relations of production. The historicist pattern of thinking facilitates this ambiguity by denying the legitimacy of the abstract analytical procedures required to straighten out the problem.

From his juristic start, Weber embarked on an ambitious study of the "material" base underlying and interacting with legal institutions, mostly through various historical studies in economic organization after the genre of the historical school of economics of the time. He did so reacting against the "formalism" of much of the jurisprudence of the time, notably Rudolf Stammler's work. In his excursions into economic history, Weber did not, however, abandon the basic idea that legal norms *control* action in pursuit of interests, both economic and political.[16] Here he was very much concerned with Marxian ideas, but the retention of this fundamental position is a prime index of his refusal to become a Marxist.

A major reorientation in Weber's thought occurred after he had recovered from an incapacitating mental illness in about 1904, and was expressed in writings on a new front. Substantively the first important new work was the famous essay on the *Protestant Ethic and the Spirit of Capitalism*.[17] This dealt directly with an "ideal factor" in reference to its significance for a specific process of historical development, indeed, the one Marxian theory had spotlighted. It was undoubtedly meant to challenge the Marxian view, but *not* in the sense of "setting Hegel back on his feet." Rather, it put the problem in a frame of reference neither Hegelian nor Marxian nor historicist in Dilthey's sense.

16. Max Weber, *Max Weber on Law in Economy and Society* (Cambridge, Mass.: Harvard University Press, 1954).
17. Max Weber, *The Protestant Ethic and the Spirit of Capitalism* (New York: C. Scribner's Sons, 1930); German original, 1905.

The crucial point is that Weber's analysis, the core of which is the Protestant Ethic thesis, bridged the theoretical gap between "want" in the economic-psychological sense and "cultural patterns" in the idealistic senses. To put it simply and radically, Weber's solution was that, once cultural patterns of meaning have been internalized in the personality of an individual, they define the situation for the structuring of motives. Therefore questions of how action (including the acceptance of the goals toward which it is oriented) makes sense must be answered by reference to the meaning-system defining the situation of action. Weber then postulated, not given wants, but given cultural definitions of the situation (the human condition) which make commitment to the satisfaction of certain classes of wants intelligible. These meaning-systems, however, were the very subject matter of humanistic-cultural study.

Did this, however, constitute only a step along a line of regression that merely put the discreteness of cultural patterns, within which particular wants became meaningful, in the place of the givenness of discrete wants of individuals? At the very least, the discrimination of two levels in the want system, the concrete, satisfaction-oriented want itself and the cultural grounding of its meaning, would be a gain. But Weber's analysis went a step farther. He treated these as independently variable factors in the determination of action, which, in their mutual interrelations and in relation to other factors, could be treated as interdependent in a system. This view basically broke through the ideal-material dichotomy of idealistic thinking about human action. The answer, analogous to that of modern biology regarding the heredity-environment problem, is that *both* sets of factors are crucial, standing in complex relations of interdependence with each other.

Before Weber, the "cement" that had been holding the parts of the dichotomy in their rigid relationship was the postulate of *historical* connection in its Hegelian-Marxian version. Thus, either the ideal constellation or that of material interests constituted a *Gestalt,* which either existed or did not, as a totality. A second focus of Weber's break with the tradition was salient there. He assumed as a matter of principle that the components of such a *Gestalt* should be treated as independently variable. He set out to analyze certain of these relations by the *comparative* method, which in terms of the logic of science is the nearest empirical equivalent to the experimental method that is accessible to this subject matter.

In treating the problem of Protestantism's role in the development of capitalism, any historicist, idealist, or Marxist would have treated the problem entirely as one of the sequences in Western history from the Reformation, and its immediate antecedents, to the Industrial Revolution. But Weber, in adopting the comparative method, studied the negative cases especially. Along with the question of why modern "capitalism" developed in Europe, Weber investigated its *non*-development in other advanced civilizations. He completed extensive monographs on China and India in this connection.[18] Again, the substantive question, how far he progressed toward the empirical demonstration of his case, is not our concern here. The point is that his *method* involved an *analytical* isolation of classes of variables by comparing cases in which they demonstrably varied independently of each other.[19] In the subject matter of cultural *Gestalten* this was a very new departure.

Concurrently, in a series of essays which, in the first instance, were polemically oriented, Weber attempted a principled grounding of this new orientation in the conception of empirical knowledge as such, but particularly in the context of the social sciences.[20] As noted he anticipated writers like Whitehead in establishing that analytical abstraction was essential even to physical science. By no means does its theory, for example, in the case of classical mechanics, simply "reflect" the reality of the external world. It is selective and hence in important degrees evaluative in its concern for empirical problems and facts. Thus it is partly determined by the interests and values of the scientist, among which possibilities of controlling natural events figure prominently, but by no means exclusively. This dependence on the evaluative concerns of the investigator (which Weber called *Wertbeziehung*) had to be matched, in whatever field, natural, social, or humanistic, by a favorable evaluative orientation to problems of the empirical disciplines centering about the canons of intellectual discipline, above all for objectivity in empirical observation and for logical, clear, and precise theoretical statement and inference. This is the focus of Weber's famous doctrine of the "value-

18. Max Weber, *The Religion of China* (Glencoe: The Free Press, 1951); *The Religion of India* (Glencoe: The Free Press, 1958); the original German editions of both, posthumous.
19. Here it should be noted that the comprehensive survey of religious structures recently translated as *The Sociology of Religion* (Boston: Beacon Press, 1962), originally published as *Religionssoziologie in Wirtschaft und Gesellschaft*, 1922, unparalleled at the time in the analytical qualities of its approach, was written as a relatively independent section of a larger work on the relationships between the economy and other aspects of social structure.
20. Max Weber, *Gesammelte Aufsätze zur Wissenschaftslehre*, 2nd edition, Johannes Winckelmann, editor (Tubingen: Mohr, 1951). Selections from this work have been translated and edited by Edward A. Shils and Henry K. Finch, *The Methodology of the Social Sciences* (Glencoe: The Free Press, 1949).

freedom" of social science (*Wertfreiheit*). It does not mean, as so many have erroneously believed, that the scientist or scholar should be free of *any* values, but rather that in his professional role, he must be free to give the discipline's values priority over others, notably in Weber's mind over political commitments. In contemporary terminology, I believe he meant that the values of the intellectual disciplines must be *differentiated* from other types of values constitutive of the culture. Only on such a basis can science and scholarship be institutionalized.

As a matter of course, however, Weber also insisted on the central importance of the "empathic" understanding (*Verstehen*) of motives and patterns of meaning as this had been emphasized in the humanistic and idealistic tradition, namely, the "subjective" side of the Cartesian dichotomy. These entities, however, were now also given the full status of objects, as regards both their own internal structure and the relevance to them of analytical abstraction and abstract generalized conceptualization. In certain senses the utilitarians had prepared the way for this, but had shied away from its full consequences. They had preferred to limit this whole realm to the status of givenness under a set of restrictive assumptions, and to follow the problems of variability only in the other direction.

The *Verstehen* conception, however, was crucial to the new position because the impact of the "ideal" factors as *variables* was to be systematically studied precisely in the definite, specific structures of cultural patterns, including legal norms, and motives. Both the utilitarian and the behavioristic positions simply foreclosed this possibility with bland philosophical assumptions.

On the background of these three essential doctrines of social science methodology, Weber thus culminated his argument by asserting that the social disciplines required generalized analytical concepts and propositions. Indeed, when Weber wrote, such theory-building had already advanced considerably in economics and parts of psychology. He, however, stated this requirement very sharply and clearly while discussing the idealist and humanistic tradition. Weber's own attempts at formulation in this field primarily took the form of ideal types. Though legitimate, they have certain limitations and constitute only one of a number of the necessary theoretical components of the social sciences.

Weber thus broke cleanly with the dogma that cultural and historical materials were subject only to ideographic conceptualization as forming unique historical individuals. His most important contention was that the more advanced analytical methods of the natural sciences must be adopted in the realm of the cultural disciplines—which meant primarily the humanities, but the bridge between the natural sciences and humanities was constituted by the new social disciplines. In Weber's case, above all, economics could not be allowed to remain caught between the imperatives of a "Western" analytical definition of its scope and a German "historical" one. Indeed, it can be said that the main rationale of Weber's venture into sociology was that he saw this as the only way out of the dilemma, the only path to a synthesis of the best in the two traditions of economics that could relate both to the essentials of the "cultural" sciences.

Weber's views in this respect cannot be said to have fully prevailed as yet. They do, however, constitute a break of such magnitude that a return to the positions of Hegel or Marx, or of Dilthey or Sombart on the idealistic side is clearly out of the question. Similarly, Weber's capacity to handle the relations between cultural movements and social organization in an historical and comparative context was such that a return to utilitarian modes of thought seems equally out of the question.

This conviction is strongly reinforced by Durkheim's striking convergence with Weber, even though they were of different nationality, did not communicate with each other, and took little notice of each other's work. Significant to the convergence is the fact that Durkheim also was partially trained in jurisprudence. In his first major work, *De la division du travail social,*[21] 1893, he used law as a principal index of the structure of societies.

Durkheim's critical point of departure was a devastating critique of the utilitarian position, couched in terms of Herbert Spencer's conception of "contractual relations," but covering the whole frame of reference back to Hobbes.[22] The crucial thesis was that, from a strictly utilitarian viewpoint, it was impossible to account for *order* in social systems, which Durkheim, using a Kantian pattern of analysis, treated as a *fact,* not a possibility. Paralleling Kant's famous question about empirical knowledge, Durkheim stated that social order, in the sense contrary to a Hobbesian state of nature, in fact exists. Given this fact, how is it possible?

Durkheim thus, from the other side, came to essentially the same basic conclusion as Weber. He established a connection between the wants of individuals, as conceived in the utilitarian tradition, and the normative patterning of the social structure, particularly as analyzed in

21. Emile Durkheim: *The Division of Labor in Society* (Glencoe: The Free Press, 1949). French original, 1893.
22. *Ibid.,* Book I, Chap. VII.

law. The institution of contract was treated as analytically independent of the interests of contracting parties, but the former constituted an indispensable set of conditions for the effective satisfaction of the latter.

The basic theme of internalization of the normative patterns defining situations had, as noted, been partially worked out by Weber. It was considerably further analyzed by Durkheim in his studies of suicide and education—his famous concept of *anomie* was a name for the failure of this relation to become stabilized in the relation of a normative system to the personality of the individual. In this basic respect Durkheim converged impressively with Freud and the American social psychologists mentioned above, particularly George Herbert Mead.

Conclusion

In outlining this intellectual history, I have attempted to trace a principal path by which the intellectual disciplines, institutionalized in the central faculties of American universities, acquired the foundation of a basic unity which is nevertheless compatible with their inherent diversity. In a sense it was natural that, as modern intellectual culture emerged, the humanities and sciences should hold radically different patterns of orientation, and that the social disciplines should be substantially less well crystallized.

The growth of knowledge itself, accompanied by generalization and sophistication on both sides, exerted pressure for firmer methodological and, eventually, philosophical groundings. Indeed, this pressure may well have been an important factor in the emphasis modern philosophy has placed on epistemological concerns.

In the movement emerging from philosophical empiricism, which included the physical sciences, utilitarianism, and eventually Darwinian biology, these problems were not generally brought into sharp focus. The social disciplines developed slowly on the basis of a rather empirical, commonsense view of the task of history, utilitarian theorizing in economics and psychology, and the extension of Darwinian biology into the behavioral fields.

This history clearly illustrates the difficulty of drawing sharp boundaries to the domain of natural science within this frame of reference. One mode of extension into the social field, of which classical economics is the type case, could be stabilized only by a "walling off" against further extension by assuming the givenness of wants and their purely individual character. The development of biological thinking, however, presented still greater difficulties, because it introduced, particularly in its extension through anthropology to the human-behavioral field, the especially important conceptions of organization and relational pattern. This, in its environmental reference, eventuated in the concept of culture, which, on a utilitarian background, was a truly revolutionary concept. This too tended to be "walled off" through the trait atomist doctrine of the so-called "historical" school of British-American anthropology.

The relevant intellectual history on the background of empiricism and utilitarianism involved a gradually increasing strain in the direction of giving a more independent status to the human cultural-behavioral fields, but attended by a continuing anxiety that doing so would imply abandoning the attempt to be scientific. Kant introduced a clean break in these respects, explicitly confining science to the field of physical phenomena—only this limited area was accessible to the methods of "pure reason." Problems of how the areas of human behavior excluded from science could be treated as objects of observation and analysis thereby became acute. The idealistic movement, especially with Hegel, solved this by focusing on the conception of *Geist* as itself objectively observable through a rather different kind of "understanding" than the Kantian, namely, that conveyed by later uses of the German term *Verstehen*. The problem here was the obverse of the one posed for the utilitarian tradition, namely, not how to treat human motives or wants as independent of their conditioning substratum in the physical world or the organism, but how to relate the imperatives of ideal patterns to the exigencies of the real world in a way accounting for the realistically effective qualities of such entities in actual behavior. This orientation went through two stages: the Hegelian grand philosophy of history and the historicist particularism which keynoted the conception of the isolated historical individual.

Beginning with this orientation, Marx developed the first major bridge toward the phenomenal world, to use Kant's term. By setting Hegel on his head, he conceived of a dialectic of "material interests" which directly matched Hegel's dialectic of the *Geist* in form. This venture directly complemented the anthropological introduction of cultural pattern as a discrete elementary particle in the human field. Each intellectual movement had, in a peculiar sense, undercut the ground of the other. The anthropologists, from a naturalistic base, had come to see the "essence" of the human behavioral world in cultural-humanistic terms, whereas the Marxians, from an idealistic base, had located its essence in the interests formulated by the utilitarians. In each case, the dominant category was the one which had figured most prominently in the history of the other tradition.

Surely this was an intellectual impasse. It is in this setting that I place the movement of which the Weber-Durkheim convergence may be regarded as the core. Its most important feature was its capacity to synthesize the two great sets of intermediate categories, wants or interests, on the one side and organization and relational pattern on the other side. Culture, as well as the organism and the physical world, had become inherently involved in the human behavioral sphere. This concurrently becomes the subject of an autonomous set of intellectual disciplines, neither humanities nor natural sciences. They are cultural in that they study the cultural productions of human experience, but they are at the same time analytical, oriented to empirical understanding in the sense of science.

This chapter of intellectual history has been sketchily analyzed to help make intelligible the *three*-fold structure of the intellectual disciplines in modern academic organization. It is my contention that neither the implicit empiricist-utilitarian monistic structure, in which basically all such disciplines were conceived as monolithic, nor the idealistic dualism is tenable as a frame of reference for the modern level of sophistication in this area. The social sciences must be treated as a fully autonomous category. They are not natural sciences in the sense of excluding the categories of subjective meaning, that is, they must consider knowing subjects as objects. Nor are they humanistic-cultural in the sense that the individuality of particular meanings must take complete precedence over analytical generality and such categories as causality. The emergence of sociological theorizing in the sense outlined crystallized this synthesis more sharply than any other intellectual event of recent times.

On this basis it has at last become clear that the analytical and historical components of knowledge are just that—components, not concrete classes. First, this means specifically that generalized analytical methods have become crucial, not only to economics and behavioristic psychology, but also to the social disciplines extending much farther into the "humanistic" range, such as sociology, anthropology, law, political science, and certain aspects of history itself. Conversely, however, historical perspectives have been extended far into the normal domains of natural science. Perhaps the original crystallization of this perspective lay in "natural history's" exceedingly important role in biology. A particularly important extension of this conception went toward paleontology as the historical perspective on the whole process of organic evolution. This in turn is most intimately related to the historical aspect of geology, the "story" of the planet earth. Extension to still further ranges has become very prominent in recent times, through the historical aspect of astronomy, the history of planets, suns, and indeed galaxies.

Finally, all three sets of disciplines have their practical aspects as knowledge applied to the implementation of human values and interests, not only as fields of knowledge for its own sake. The concept of "practical reason" is not confined to any one branch of learning, but is relevant to all of them. There is, however, the essential proviso that it is exceedingly important not to confuse the two references.[23] Increasingly, this distinction seems to be becoming institutionalized in the distinction between arts and sciences faculties and the applied "professional" faculties. Equally, the underlying premises of all the intellectual disciplines require grounding at levels which are not problematic simply for the development of the individual sets of disciplines. Thus the philosophy of science is not itself a science in the sense of physics or chemistry. All the members of the triad of intellectual disciplines look both downward to the fields applying their "pure" patterns of knowledge and upward to the grounding of their premises in the more ultimate problems of the meaning of the human condition. No basic distinction can be drawn among them on either of these two counts.

23. The fields of engineering technology and somatic medicine, as applications of natural-science knowledge, and of economic policy and of the use of psychological testing in personnel selection, as applications of social science are relatively obvious. Sometimes, however, humanists make a virtue of their claim that the humanities are completely free of any taint of practicality—that they are fields of the pursuit of learning solely for its own sake. This claim may be doubted on one ground in particular. This is that for a considerable period in European history a humanistic education constituted the principal basis of the common culture of the elite classes of European Society—and indeed still does to a considerable extent. We may suggest that the "use" of the humanistic disciplines in giving its principal cultural character to the elite of a great civilization was just as much a "social" application as any of engineering or medicine. Far from being simply the erudite scholar whose studies had no relevance beyond his own esoteric self-gratification, the typical humanist has been par excellence the educator of men of understanding and character.

CHAPTER 7

Pattern Variables Revisited: A Response to Robert Dubin †

Of the papers included in this volume, this has been the most difficult to place. The first question was whether to include it at all. It is, to be sure, highly general in theoretical reference but is also restricted and, in a sense, personal, in its specific conceptualization. Because one function of this volume is to bring together a number of writings that bear on the development of my own thinking in recent years, however, it would have seemed inappropriate to omit it. Especially because it is not elsewhere published in book form.

The paper was written in response to Robert Dubin's welcome initiative to provoke discussion of a few theoretical contributions in sociology that had attracted considerable attention in previous years. In this case Dubin presented in advance a restatement of the more general frame of reference of action and its components that had figured in *Toward a General Theory of Action* and *The Social System*, headed up by the Pattern-Variable scheme. In responding, it seemed to me most appropriate to concentrate on the latter, with an attempt to evaluate its status as of 1960, nearly a decade after its first more sophisticated statement in the two publications just cited.

I think it correct to say that this paper achieves a considerable forward step in the systematization of both the pattern-variable scheme and its grounding in the general frame of reference of systems of action. This step consisted essentially in the generalization of the integration of pattern variables into the four-function paradigm. It was possible to show that the original version of this paradigm* presented in Chaps. 3 and 5 of *Working Papers in the Theory of Action* by Talcott Parsons and Robert F. Bales

† Professor Dubin's article, "Parsons' Actor: Continuities in Social Theory," is included in this volume as an appendix with the author's permission.

"Pattern Variable Revisited: A Response to Robert Dubin" from *American Sociological Review*, Vol. 25, No. 4 (August, 1960). The Dubin paper was in the same issue.

(Glencoe: Free Press, 1953), essentially consisted of integrative standards for an orientation system, and hence could be treated as belonging in the integrative subsystem of the more general system of action. This treatment served to place this use of the pattern variables systematically in its relation to the others which had figured in the *Working Papers*. So far as subsequent work has been concerned, it has both helped to define the situation for recent concern with the integrative problems of social systems, as indicated in the note to Chap. 1, and to clarify the theoretical grounding of the generalized media of societal interchange that are discussed in Part III, especially Chaps. 10 and 11.

It seemed best to include this paper in Part II, because it forms a kind of introduction and transition from the more general concerns of the first two chapters in the section, to the more specialized theoretical concerns of Part III.

Part of the ground covered in this paper is also discussed in "The Point of View of the Author," in *The Social Theories of Talcott Parsons*, Max Black, ed. (Englewood Cliffs: Prentice-Hall, 1961).

D UBIN is essentially correct in characterizing the pattern variables as a model that uses the unit act as its building block. The unit act involves the *relationship of an actor to a situation composed of objects,* and it is conceived as a choice (imputed by the theorist to the actor) among alternative ways of defining the situation. The unit act, however, does not occur independently but as one unit in the context of a wider system of actor-situation relationships; this system—including a plurality of acts—is referred to as an *action system.* The unit act is the logically minimal unit of analysis, but as such it can be conceived empirically only as a unit of an action system. Even for analysis of one discrete concrete act, an extended set of similar acts must be postulated as part of the action system—for example, those comprising a particular role. Figure 1 is a paradigm for any such action system, not only the unit act.

The Frame of Reference

The pattern variables first emerged as a conceptual scheme for classifying types of roles in social systems, starting with the distinction between professional and business roles. In this sense, the concept "actor" referred to individual human beings as personalities in roles and the analysis—as Dubin puts it—" 'looks' out to the social system from the vantage point of the actor." In *Toward a General Theory*, the scheme was substantially revised and its relevance extended from role analysis in the social system to the analysis of all types of systems of action.

Action is thus viewed as a process occurring between two structural parts of a system—actor and situation. In carrying out analysis at any level of the total action system, the concept "actor" is extended to define not only individual personalities in roles but other types of acting units —collectivities, behavioral organisms, and cultural systems. Since the term actor is used here to refer to any such acting unit, I attempt to avoid —except for purposes of analogy or illustration—psychological reference, for example, "motivation," attributed to actors as individuals. Thus "actor" can refer to a business firm in interaction with a household, or, at the cultural level, the implementation of empirical beliefs interacting with the implementation of evaluative beliefs.

Both the pattern variables and the four system problems are conceptual schemes, or sets of categories, for classifying the components of action. They provide a frame of reference within which such classification can be made. The figures presented here indicate the methods, sets of rules and procedures, that state how these categories may be used analytically; they imply *theorems*—propositions that admit of logical, not empirical, proof—which state a set of determinate relationships among the categories and, in so doing, outline a *theory* of action. The theory, then, is a set of logical relationships among categories used to classify empirical phenomena and, in empirical reference, attempts to account for whatever may be the degree of uniformity and stability of such phenomena.

The pattern variables are a conceptual scheme for classifying the components of an action system—the actor-situation relational system which comprises a plurality of unit acts. Each variable defines one property of a particular class of components. In the first instance, they distinguish between two sets of components, *orientations* and *modalities*. Orientation concerns the actor's relationship *to* the objects in his situation and is conceptualized by the two "attudinal" variables of diffuseness-specificity and affectivity-neutrality. In psychological terms, orientation refers to the actor's need for relating to the object world, to the basis of his interest in it. For other levels of analysis, of course this psychological reference must be generalized. Modality concerns the meaning *of* the object for the actor and is conceptualized by the two "object-categorization" variables of quality-performance and universalism-particularism. It refers to those aspects of the object that have meaning for the actor, given the situation. The orientation set of pattern variables "views" the relationship of actor to situation from the side of the actor or actors; the modality set views it from the side of the situation as consisting of objects. As Dubin suggests, the pattern variable of self-collectivity orientation does not belong at this level of analysis; it is placed in proper perspective below.

In classifying the components of the actor's relation to a situation, the pattern variables suggest propositions about any particular action system in terms of those components and the type of act their combination defines; thus a particular role can be characterized by the properties of universalism, performance, and so on. An action system, however, is not characterized solely by the actor's orientations and the modalities of objects significant to the actor; it is also a *structured* system with analytically independent aspects which the elementary pattern variable combinations by themselves do not take into account.

In such a structured system both actor and object share institutionalized norms, conformity with which is a condition for stability of the system. The relation between the actor's orientations and the modalities of objects in the situation cannot be random. The *Working Papers* established a non-random relationship between the two sets by matching the functionally corresponding categories on each side—universalism with specificity, particularism with diffuseness, performance with affectivity, and quality with neutrality. This matching yielded Dubin's Model II. It turned out that this arrangement converges with the classification of functional problems of systems that Bales had earlier formulated.[1] This convergence, the main subject of the *Working Papers,* opened up such a fertile range of possibilities that for several years my main attention has been given to their exploration rather than to direct concern with the scheme out of which it grew. However, it is now clear that "Model II" is not a substitute for the earlier version, in the sense that it represents the whole scheme, but rather a formulation of one particularly crucial part of a larger scheme. The following discussion places that part in the context of the larger scheme as the formulation of "integrative standards," those aspects of the action system shared by actor and object and that make the system a stable one.

1. Robert F. Bales, *Interaction Process Analysis* (Cambridge: Addison-Wesley, 1950), Chapter 2.

In analyzing the components of any particular action system, one must also consider the larger system within which that action system is embedded. The action system is related to the "external system" beyond it, which I refer to here as the *environment* of the system, as distinguished from the *situation* of the acting unit. The following analysis treats this relation of action system to environment as mediated mainly through the adaptive subsystem. The combinations of pattern variable components in that subsystem were foreshadowed in the *Working Papers* by the "auxiliary" combinations of neutrality-performance, particularism-specificity, and so on.[2] The present paper has, I believe, established the analytical independence of *these* combinations from those of the integrative standards in Model II, and goes considerably beyond the *Working Papers* in setting forth their significance for action systems.

Finally, the pattern variables—although they designate the *properties* of actor's orientations and objects' modalities in an action system—do not as such classify *types* of actors and objects. Such a typology cannot be derived from any particular action system, but only from the analysis of a range of such systems. It is this typology of actors and objects with which Dubin's left- and right-hand columns in his Table 1 is concerned. Figure 2 has incorporated this important aspect of Dubin's problem.

With references to Dubin's Table 1 [p. 524], the pattern variables themselves are discussed under what he terms the "actor's evaluation of objects." The column headed "Modalities of Objects" is admittedly redundant, for in addition to the redundancies noted by Dubin, the terms "classificatory" and "relational" are synonymous with "universalism" and "particularism," respectively, as I acknowledged in *The Social System*. In my Figure 2, Dubin's "motivational orientation" toward objects is covered by the pattern-maintenance or orientation subsystem, his "value-orientation" by the adaptive subsystem; and his "action-orientation" is characterized by the types of output of the system as a whole. [See p. 524.]

Thus the conceptual scheme of the four system-problems has added a set of rules and procedures—the basis of theorems—whereby the analysis of components of action in terms of pattern variables can be carried out by "looking down," on them, as Dubin has aptly put it, from the perspective of the action system. The action system is presented in Figure 1 so as to establish the analytical independence of the four subsystems: orientations (pattern-maintenance); modalities (goal-attain-

2. Cf. Parsons, Bales, and Shils, *op. cit.*, Chapter 5, Figure 2, p. 182.

ment); their combination characterizing the conditions of internal stability of a relational system shared by both actor and object (integration); their combination characterizing the ways in which that system is stably related to the environment (adaptation).

Following the presentation of these four subsystems, the *same* information is displayed in tabular form different from the more familiar functional "layout." This second presentation (Figure 2) is designed to "look down" on any particular action system from the perspective of the more inclusive system. At this level, the analysis of types of actors and of objects can be carried out. In addition, Figure 2 highlights the distinction between the *control* of action—that is, the scale of priorities assigned to various ways of regulating action—and the *implementation* of action —the analytical relevance involved in the distinction between structure and process.

This then is the main frame of reference of the paper's approach to the classification and analysis of the components of action. We now turn to the paradigm itself, which is altogether newly formulated from the point of view of the internal relations between its components, and is presented in Figure 1. Its form is essentially that of Dubin's Table 4, which was derived from the *Working Papers*.[3] "Model II" is treated in the paradigm as the integration subsystem of the general system. The pattern variable scheme as formulated in *Toward A General Theory*, that is, the two "attitudinal" and "object-categorization" sets, are incorporated into the "pattern-maintenance" and the "goal-attainment" subsystems, respectively. To avoid terminological confusion we follow Dubin in referring to the two sets of pattern variables as the *orientation* set and the *modality* set. The fourth block of cells, representing the adaptation subsystem, is also entirely new, and is explicated below.

We have noted above that the primary reference of the concept "actor" is to the individual personality, but that in secondary respects collectivities, behavioral organisms, and cultural systems may be conceived as actors. It is important to remember that our scheme concerns the *generalized* components of action, so that such psychological terms as "cathexis" and "identification" and "need," as used here, stand for more generalized concepts than would be applicable to actors and objects on these other levels; their reference is not confined to the personality level.

3. *Ibid.*, p. 182.

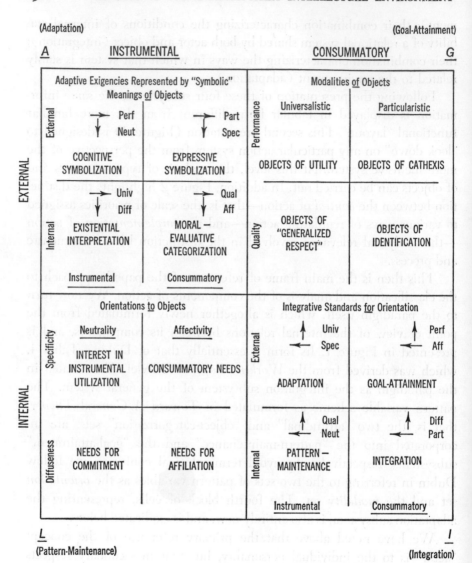

FIGURE 1. THE COMPONENTS OF ACTION SYSTEMS

The Orientation Set (Pattern-Maintenance)[4]

The *orientation base* of a system of action, may be categorized in terms of the two pattern variables, affectivity-neutrality and specificity-diffuseness. The relevant characteristic of the actor in defining his (or "its") orientation to an object or category of objects may be an "interest" in the object as a source of "consummation." This may be defined as an interest in establishing a *relation to* an object, which the actor has no incentive to change. In psychological terms, this may be phrased that the actor has a "need" for such a relationship, which can be "gratified" by its establishment. The alternative to the need for a consummatory relationship is the "need" for *help* toward the attainment of such a relationship to an object. Therefore, besides the consummatory, there is an instrumental basis of orientation to the object-world. At this point a pattern-variable "dilemma" arises because it is a fundamental assertion of our theory that consummatory and instrumental interests in objects *cannot* be maximized at the same time. The instrumental and consummatory bases are *analytically* independent.

The very discrimination of different bases of orientation of actors to objects implies that actors are conceived as systems; they are never oriented to their situations simply "as a whole," but always through specific modes of organization of independent components. From this point of view, it is always important whether the primary reference is to the *relation* of the acting system to its environment *or* to its own internal properties and equilibrium. The situation, or object-world, is in the nature of the case organized differently from the actor as system. Hence, in orientation *directly* to the situation, the specificities of differentiation among objects and their properties become salient. On the other hand, where internal "needs" of the acting system are paramount, the salience of these specificities recedes, and the orientation to objects becomes more diffuse. This is the setting in which the specificity-diffuseness variable fits. It indicates that where the "interaction surface" between actor and situation is approached, the actor's interests in objects must be more highly specified than where internal states of the acting system itself are in the forefront.

There is a pattern-variable dilemma here as well as in the instrumental-consummatory case. This is to say that the imperatives of speci-

4. There is a pattern-maintenance subsystem *below* the adaptive subsystem in the hierarchy of control of any system of action and another *above* the integrative subsystem in the series. In Figure 1 we define L as the *lower*-level case, on the basis parallel to the usage employed in relating the household to the firm in Talcott Parsons and Neil J. Smelser, *Economy and Society* (Glencoe, Ill.: Free Press, 1956), Chapter 2.

ficity and of diffuseness cannot be maximally satisfied at the same time.

The cross-classification of these two orientational pattern-variables yields a four-fold table which is presented as the pattern-maintenance subsystem (L) of Figure 1. As distinguished from the pattern variables themselves, which are rubrics of classification, this constitutes a classification of *types* of orientation to objects. This distinction has not always been clear, I believe, neither in my own work nor in that of other writers.

It will be seen that the pure type of "consummatory needs" combines affectivity and specificity of interest; it is "pure" because it can focus on the actor's relation to the *specific* discretely differentiated object. But where the basis of interest is diffuse, there must be generalization to a broader *category* of objects, so the basis of the interest is the establishment of a relation between the acting system and a wider sector of the situational object-system. We have called this a "need for affiliation," for example, for a relation of mutual "solidarity" between diffuse sectors of the acting system and the object-system.

On the instrumental side, it is apparent that the same order of distinction applies to specifically differentiated bases of interest in objects and diffuser bases. *Manipulation* of objects in the interest of consummatory gratification or even passive adaptation to them requires concern with the specificities of their properties. Hence the "interest in instrumental utilization," though affectively neutral, is also specific; interest in the *category* is not enough. Where, however, the problem is not utilization, but the place of the orientation in the internal structure of the acting system, this level of the specification of interest not only is unnecessary but, because of the independent variability of the object-situation, becomes positively obstructive. *Commitment* to the specifics of object-situations introduces a rigidity of orientation which can be highly constrictive. Commitment can be and, functionally speaking, is better organized on a diffuser level. We therefore speak of "needs for commitment" as oriented to diffuse categories of objects and their properties rather than to specific objects and properties, and as engaging more diffuse sectors of the acting system than do "interests in instrumental utilization."

The Modality Set (Goal-Attainment)

With reference to the obverse side of the action relationship, that of the modalities of objects, the modality set of pattern variables constitutes the classificatory framework—particularism and universalism, and performance and quality. Particularism in this context means that from the point of view of the action system, the most significant aspect of an object is its relation of particularity to the actor: as compared with other objects which can "intrinsically" be classified as similar to it, the significance of *this* object to the actor lies in its *inclusion* in the same interactive system. In the contrasting case of universalistic modalities, the basis of an object's meaning lies in its universalistically defined properties, hence its inclusion in classes which transcend that particular relational system. For example, when a man falls in love, it is this *particular* woman with whom the love relationship exists. He may, like some other gentlemen, prefer blondes, but he is not in love with the category, but with one particular blonde. Thus the same kind of dilemma exists here as for the two pattern variables described above—it is impossible to maximize the particularistic meaning of objects and their universalistic meaning at the same time. A man sufficiently in love with blondeness as such, who therefore pursues any blonde, cannot establish a very stable love relationship with a particular woman. That there is an important "matching" between consummatory bases of interest and particularistic meaning of objects is clear; its significance is discussed below.

A basic postulate of action theory is that the states of acting systems and those of the situational object-world in which they act are independently variable. At their "interface," then, an especially important property of objects is their probable *performance* in respect to the actors oriented to them. Recall that the prototype of the actor-object relation is social interaction, in which the "object" is also in turn an actor who does something. Thus physical objects, which do not "act," are the limiting case of objects to which the term "performance" is inherently inapplicable.

In contrast with this situation, is the meaning of objects in terms of what they "are," of their qualities defined independently of performances, which are inherently relative to situations. The internal reference of the acting system matches with interest in the qualities of objects rather than their performances, since these are presumptively more independent of direct situational exigencies.

These two classificatory rubrics—performance-quality and universalism-particularism—yield a four-fold typology of objects (or of components), seen from the perspective of their meaning to actors. This is the Goal-Attainment Subsystem (*G*) in Figure 1. This terminology is also adopted from the prototypical case of interaction of persons. Thus an object whose primary meaning is particularistic and based on its actual and expected performances, following psychoanalytic usage, may be called an "object of cathexis." It is "looked at" in terms of its potentialities for gratifying specific consummatory needs. However, if an object is defined in universalistic terms, but at the same time as a source of performances significant to the actor, it can be said to be an "object of utility," for it is viewed with respect to its potentialities in helping to bring about consummatory states of the acting system.

In contrast with both these types, objects may be treated as "objects of identification" if their meaning is both particularistic and refers essentially to what they "are" rather than what they "do." Here the objects' meaning to actors is not subject to the more detailed fluctuations which go with the meaning of cathexis.

Finally, the universalistic case, the fourth type, is called an "object of generalized respect." Here the object is categorized by the actor in universalistic terms, but also with relation to its qualities. This is the type of object which in a social context Durkheim speaks of as generating attitudes of "moral authority."[5]

Problems of Integration and Adaptation

The argument so far may be summarized: We have outlined, in terms of the present conceptual scheme, the elementary components of action and certain aspects of their interrelations. Essentially these are the components of unit acts but do not yet comprise systems of action.

First, we have assumed that all action involves the *relating* of acting units to objects in their situation. This is the basis for the fundamental distinction between components belonging to the characterization of *orienting* actors and those belonging to the *modalities* of the objects to which they are oriented—that is, between the two "sets" of elementary pattern variables. Second, we have used the elementary variables to classify types of elementary combination. The underlying assumption here is that on this level they are always analytically independent; hence the orientation set (cluster L of Figure 1) and the modality set (cluster G) are treated as mutually exclusive, each type being composed of components drawn only from one of the two sets. Third, each cell within

5. Particularly in *L'Education Morale* (Paris: Alcan, 1925). Cf. Parsons, *The Structure of Social Action* (New York: McGraw-Hill, 1937), Chapter 10. This classification of meanings of objects has been more fully set forth in Talcott Parsons, Edward A. Shils, Kaspar D. Naegele, and Jesse R. Pitts, editors, *Theories of Society* (New York: Free Press of Glencoe, 1961), Introduction to Part IV.

each cluster is composed of *only* two pattern variable designations. Fourth, what elsewhere are defined as "pattern variable opposites" never occur in the same cell. Subject to these rules, the classifications designated by the four cells in each cluster are logically exhaustive of the possibilities. We consider the fourth assumption to be the application of a fundamental theorem concerning the conditions of the stability of orientation, namely, that neither the same orientation nor the same object can be successfully defined, in a particular context or orientation, in terms of *both* alternatives without discrimination, for example, universalistically and particularistically or specifically and diffusely at the same time.

Subject to these constraints, however, we see no reason why the composition of possible types of unit acts do not exhaust the range of logically possible independent variation of the components thus formulated. But such a definition does not tell us anything about the conditions of the existence of a *system* of such unit acts other than that there are such limiting circumstances as physical and biological conditions of survival. In other words, this level of analysis describes a *population* of action-units and certain of the ways in which they are empirically ordered in relation to each other. It cannot provide an analysis of the relations of their *interaction*, which constitute a system subject to mechanisms of equilibration and change as a system through "feedback" processes—in one sense, the *organization* of the system.

To take the step to this organizational level, it is necessary to attempt to conceptualize two basic sets of "functions" which cannot be treated either as the orientations of actors or as the meanings or modalities of the objects to which they are primarily oriented. These are, first, the modes of internal *integration* of the system, that is, of the interrelations of the elementary actor-object units. This means, within our frame of reference, the normative standards on the basis of which such relations can be said to be stable. Second, there are the mechanisms by which the system as a whole is *adapted to the environment* within which it operates. Since from the point of view of orientation this environment must consist in some sense of objects, the problem is that of conceptualizing the relation between objects internal to the system and those (albeit in some sense meaningful) external to the system.

To repeat, those reviewed above constitute the full complement of elementary components of action systems. Therefore, in dealing with these two additional system functions or subsystem clusters, we do not propose to introduce additional elementary components, but rather to suggest new *combinations* of these components. On this basis the *I* and *A* clusters of cells in Figure 1 are constructed on the hypothesis that each cell of the two clusters should be defined by *one* pattern variable component drawn from each of the two elementary subsets. If this policy and the general rules formulated above are followed, the combinations represented in the two clusters will be logically exhaustive of the possibilities.

Within these rules the problem is that of the basis of allocation of the components as between the two clusters, and within each as between the cells. The governing principles for treating this problem are more fully elucidated below, following a review of the allocations themselves and some problems of the system as a whole. Here, suffice it to say, first, that internal integration is dependent on the *matching* of the function of the object for the "needs" of the orienting actor with the functional meaning with which the object is categorized. Thus in some sense the gratification of consummatory needs is dependent on the possibility of categorizing appropriate objects as objects of cathexis, and so on. Why only two of the four components which might define this matching are involved, and which two, are also explained below.

Secondly, the significance of objects external to the system is not their *actual* meaning *in* the system, but rather their *potential* meaning *for* the system—the ways in which taking cognizance of this meaning or failing to do so *may* affect the functioning of the system. With these preliminaries, we may now review schematically the actual content suggested for the cells.

The Integrative Subset

How are the formal characteristics of the *I* and *A* cells in Figure 1 to be interpreted? The integrative subset states the primary conditions of internal stability or *order* in an action system. These conditions may be formulated as follows: (1) In so far as the primary functional problem of the system, conceived either in terms of structural differentiation or temporal phases, is *adaptive*, stability is dependent on the *universalistic* categorization of the relevant objects, regardless of whether or not they have certain particularistic meanings, *and* on sufficient *specificity* in the basis of interest in these objects to exclude more diffuse considerations of orientation. (2) In so far as the primary functional problem is the *attainment* of a *goal* for the system, stability is dependent on attention to the potentialities of *performance* of the object in its relation to the actor, *and* on affective engagement of the actor in the establishment of the optimal (consummatory) relation to the object—hence the lifting of "inhibitions" on such engagement. (3) In so far as the primary functional problem is integration of the system, stability is dependent on particularistic categorization of the relevant objects (that is, to the extent that they are also actors, their inclusion in the system), *and* the maintenance of a *diffuse* basis of interest in these objects (that is, one which is not contingent on fluctuations in their specific performances or properties). (4) In so far as the primary functional problem for the system is the *maintenance* of the *pattern* of its units, stability is dependent on maintaining a categorization of the objects in terms of their *qualities* independently of their specific performances, *and* an affectively *neutral* orientation, one that is not alterable as a function of specific situational rewards.

In terms of the regulation of action, these combinations of pattern variable components define categories of *norms* governing the interaction of units in the system. Norms themselves must be differentiated. It is in the nature of an action system to be subject to a plurality of functional exigencies; no single undifferentiated normative pattern or "value" permits stability over the range of these different exigencies. Hence norms constitute a differentiated and structured subsystem of the larger system. They constitute the structural aspect of the *relational nexus* between actors and objects in their situations.

Precisely because the above propositions state conditions of stable equilibrium involving the *relations between* a plurality of elementary components, I believe that they go beyond description to state, implicitly at least, certain theorems about the consequences of variations in these relations. These theorems are considered following the discussion of the system itself.

The Adaptive Subset

In the adaptive subset, the formal bases of selection of the component combinations as we have noted, are antithetical to those used in the integrative subset. This is to say that they combine both external and internal references, and both instrumental and consummatory references.

We have termed these combinations as defining "mechanisms" for ordering the adaptive relations of a system of action to the environment in which it functions. To clarify this problem an important distinction must be made. When we referred above to the orientation of actors to objects and the related modalities or meanings of objects, we were indicating components *internal* to a system of action. Objects that are *constituents* of the system must, however, be distinguished from objects that are part of the *environment* of the system. The boundary concept which defines this distinction is "particularism;" an object categorized particularistically is defined as belonging to the system. Adaptation concerns the relations of the whole system to objects which, as such, are *not* included in it.

Adaptive mechanisms, then, must be conceived as ways of categorizing the meanings of objects universalistically, that is, independently of their actual or potential inclusion in a given system. These mechanisms are "symbolic" media, including language as the prototype, but also empirical knowledge, money, and so on. Use of the media for referring to objects and categories of objects does not *ipso facto* commit the actor to any particular relation of inclusion or exclusion relative to the objects concerned. By use of the media, however, *meanings* may be treated as *internal* to the system, whereas the objects themselves may or may not remain external. This is the basic difference from modalities, which are meanings wherein the objects themselves are defined as internal.

In this context, the pattern variable combinations of the adaptive subset may be explicated as follows: (1) In order to symbolize the *adaptive* significance of objects in the environment of an action system (for example, to "understand" them cognitively), it is necessary to categorize them in terms of what actually or potentially they "do" (*performance*), *and* to orient to them with affective *neutrality*, that is, independently of their potentialities for gratifying the actor. This "pattern" is defined as a condition for stability of an orientation to the *external* environment which can maximize "objective" understanding of the objects comprising it; adopting a term from personality analysis we may term the pattern empirical "cognitive symbolization." (2) In order to symbolize and categorize objects that are external to the system according to their significance for goal-attainment, it is necessary to focus their possible meaning on specific bases of interest or "motivation" (specificity), *and* on their potential "belongingness" in a system of meanings which also defines the system of action (particularism). This we call "expressive symbolization," the generalization of particularistic meanings to a universalistic level of significance. (3) In order to symbolize and categorize the significance of *norms* that are external to the system, it is necessary to treat them as aspects of an objectively "given" state of affairs or "order" (quality), *and* to treat them with affectivity—that is, the actor cannot be emotionally indifferent to whether or not he feels committed to the norms in question. This we name "moral-evaluative categorization." (4) In order to symbolize and categorize the significance of "sources of normative authority," it is necessary to combine a universalistic definition of the object, as having properties not dependent on its inclusion in the system, with a *diffuse* basis of interest, so that the meaning in question cannot be treated as contingent on the fluctuating relations between the orienting actor and the environment. This we call "existential interpretation."

Here another version of the external-internal distinction is important. For the first two of these—the adaptive and goal-attainment categories— refer to objects considered as such, irrespective of whether or not they are included with the acting system within a more comprehensive system. In the latter two cases, however, this question of common membership in a more comprehensive system is central. A norm is binding on a unit only in so far as the unit shares common membership with other units similarly bound. An object is a source of normative authority only so far as its authority extends to other units, defined universalistically as similarly subject to that authority. It is on these grounds that we emphasize "symbolization" in the first two cases and "categorization" in the second two.

Note that the differentiation of symbolic media according to functional significance parallels the differentiation of integrative standards. They too are results of a process of differentiating the components involved in the elementary pattern variable sets and of integrating the selected components across the orientation-modality line. As distinguished from the *internal* integration of the system, the adaptive subset refers to the system's integration with its environment as part of a more comprehensive system of action.

The Perspective of the System as a Whole

So far we have considered the elementary components which make up a system of action and two main ways in which they are related across the orientation-modality line. These components and relations, however, constitute a system which in turn functions in relation to what we call an "environment." We now consider a few aspects of the properties of this system in its environmental context. The main reference point for this analysis is a rearrangement or transformation of the items of Figure 1, as presented in Figure 2.

	STRUCTURAL CATEGORIES		CATEGORIES OF PROCESS		
	Units of Orientation to Objects (L) (Properties of Actors)	Integrative Standards (I)	Symbolic Representations of External Objects (A)	Internal Meanings of Objects (G) (Inputs-Outputs)	Outputs to Environment
L	Neut Diff NORMATIVE COMMITMENTS	Qual Neut Ground—of—meaning Anchorage PATTERN— MAINTENANCE	Diff Univ EXISTENTIAL INTERPRETATION	Univ Qual "RESPECT"	
I	Aff Diff AFFILIATIONS	Manifold of Part evaluative Diff selections INTEGRATION Allocative selection	Aff Qual MORAL— EVALUATION	Part Qual IDENTIFICATION	Responsible Action
G	Aff Spec CONSUMMATORY NEEDS	Range of Perf action—choice Aff GOAL (attainment) SELECTION	Spec Part EXPRESSIVE SYMBOLIZATION	Perf Part CATHEXIS	Expressive Action
A	Neut Spec INSTRUMENTAL CAPACITIES	Empirical— Univ cognitive Spec field ADAPTATION Means — Selection	Neut Perf COGNITIVE SYMBOLIZATION	Perf Univ UTILITY	Instrumental Action

Direction of Control ↑
Direction of Limiting Conditions ↓

Direction of Implementation *vis-à-vis* Environment ⟶
⟵ Direction of Environmental "Stimulation"

FIGURE 2. THE ACTION SYSTEM IN RELATION TO ITS ENVIRONMENT

The components in Figure 2 are the same sixteen pattern-variable combinations represented in Figure 1. However, there are two new features of the arrangement: First, each of the four major blocks of cells of Figure 1 is set forth as a column of Figure 2. Within each column the cells in turn are arranged from top to bottom in the order *L–I–G–A*. This constitutes a cybernetic hierarchy of control,[6] that is, each cell categorizes the necessary but not sufficient conditions for operation of the cell next above it in the column, and in the opposite direction, the categories of each cell control the processes categorized in the one below it.

6. Cf. Parsons *et al.*, editors, *Theories of Society, op. cit.*, General Introduction, Part II.

For instance, definition of an end or goal controls the selection of means for its attainment.

The second difference from Figure 1 is the arrangement of the columns from left to right in a serial order which, stated in functional terms, is L–I–A–G. The two left-hand columns designate the structural components of the system. The L column formulates the properties of units conceived as actors; the I column formulates the structural aspect of the relational nexus between units, that is, the norms that function as integrative standards. The two right-hand columns categorize the elements of *process* by which the system operates. The G column shows the modalities of objects from the point of view of *change* of meaning as a process of relating inputs and outputs; it brings *into* the system meaning-categorizations generated by the system. The A column formulates the components involved in the symbolic mechanisms mediating the adaptive aspect of process. Whereas the hierarchy of control places the A subset at the bottom of each column, as a column itself it is placed "inside" the system because it consists of a set of symbolized *meanings* (or "representations") of the environmental object-world outside the system, or the categorization of objects independently of their inclusion in or exclusion from the system. It therefore constitutes the *internal environment* of the system, the environment to which *units* must adapt in their relations to each other, but the actual objects symbolized constitute the external environment to which the *system* as a whole must adapt.

We have suggested that the outputs of action systems *consist in* changes in the meanings of objects. It follows that the inputs also consist in meanings of objects. What the process of action accomplishes, then, is *change* in these meanings. We assume of course that new objects and categories of objects are created in the process; these presumably are themselves action systems and their "cultural" precipitates. The distinction between changing the meaning of an old object and creating a new object thus appears to depend on the point of observation.

The modalities of objects in the G column of Figure 2 therefore may be treated as a classification of the outputs of *internal* action process, in a sense similar to the usage in economics of "value-added."[7] Thus action process, so far as it is effectively *adaptive* internally, may be said to add utility to objects—for example, utility in the economist's sense, the relevant category for social systems, also is a category of meaning in the

7. See Parsons and Smelser, *op. cit.*, Chapter 4, for a discussion of this concept; it is further developed by Smelser in *Social Change in the Industrial Revolution* (Chicago: University of Chicago Press, 1959).

present context. Action which is successfully oriented internally to *goal-attainment* leads to the enhanced cathectic value of objects in the system. Action which is successfully *integrative* leads to increased "identification-meaning"—in social systems, to solidarity with and among objects. Finally, processes of "pattern-maintenance" maintain or restore the "respect" in which the relevant system itself is held as an object in the social system; here is Durkheim's "the integrity of moral authority."

The designations to the right of the G column in Figure 2 are the "action-orientations" in the Orientation column of Dubin's Table 1 [p. 524]. We suggest that these can be treated as categories of output *to its environment* of the *system as a whole* (as distinguished from the outputs of internal process). Thus instrumental action by a system may be treated as resulting in increase in the instrumental values to it of objects *within* its environment or more inclusive system. Similarly, expressive action produces enhanced cathetic meaning of objects in the environment; and responsible action increases the integrative identification category of meaning (for example, in the social system, "moral" value). In accord with principles we have used consistently,[8] we suggest that there is no category of output for the L subsystem except in cases of change in the structure of the system.

The Classification of Objects

One further set of categories which play a part in Dubin's Table 1 needs to be accounted for—the classification of types of object as physical, social, and cultural. This problem can most conveniently be treated at the environmental level. If a given system is conceived as an actor or an action system, then a system with which it *inter*acts is a social object. We have explained why this category should be differentiated into at least two subcategories: the system organized about the single human individual, namely, personality; and the social system constituted by the interaction of a plurality of individuals. A *physical* object, then, is one with which the system does not in this sense interact, and which, standing below the action system in the hierarchy of control, is conditional to it; a *cultural* object is also one with which it does not interact, but which stands above it in the hierarchy of control, and therefore is a focus of its own control system.

However, a further principle is involved, not developed here, of

8. Cf. Parsons and Smelser, *op. cit.*

interpenetration of systems.[9] The crucial case of physical systems with which the personality interpenetrates is the behavioral organism, the physical system which constitutes the fundamental facility-base for the operation of the personality system. At the other extreme, are "acting" cultural systems, implemented through social and personal actions, which constitute the operating normative control systems of social systems. At each "end" of the control series, then, is a set of limiting conceptions of nonaction "reality." At the lower end is "purely physical" reality with which the action system does not interpenetrate, but which is only conditional to it. At the upper end is "nonempirical," perhaps "cosmic," reality with which, similarly, there is no significant interpenetration, and which is thus conceived only as an "existential ground" of operative cultural systems.

A similar classification can be worked out for the alternative case where the system in question is conceived as acting, and not as an object. Here it seems that the parallel to a cultural object is the conception of the "subject" as "knowing, feeling, and willing." At the social level, this is our concept of "actor" in the sense of participation in *interaction*. At the interpenetrating subsocial level, it is the concept of organism, as "functioning" in relation to an environment. Perhaps at a still lower level should be placed the "hereditary constitution" of a species (as distinguished from the particular organism in phylogenetic, not onto-genetic terms).

Combinations of the Components

We now return to the question of the bases of combination and allocation of the pattern variable components. A maximum number of types could be generated of course by treating the potential combinations as all those randomly possible. This procedure, however, would mean the sacrifice of connections referred to above as the *organization* of systems of action and the determinate theoretical generalizations associated with them.

We have restricted random combinations, first, by composing two cell clusters (L and G) exclusively from one or the other of the elementary sets; second, by never placing both members of a "dilemma" pair in the same cell; third, by placing only *one* component from each ele-

9. Cf. Talcott Parsons, "An Approach to Psychological Theory in Terms of the Theory of Action," in Sigmund Koch, editor, *Psychology: A Study of a Science* (New York: McGraw-Hill, 1959), Vol. 3.

mentary set in each cell of the *I* and *A* clusters; and, finally, by drawing these from "functionally cognate" cells of the elementary combination paradigms. (See Figures 1 and 2.) Within these rules of organization we have followed a further policy of selection in the allocations to the *I* and *A* clusters. In terms of the "geometry" of Figure 1, this policy involves two procedures: (1) For the *I* cluster, the distribution of the modality components is derived by keeping the "functionally cognate" reference constant and then rotating clockwise the modality axes one quarter turn, and the distribution of the orientation components is similarly decided by rotating the orientation axes in the counterclockwise direction; (2) For the *A* cluster, the direction of rotation is the reverse in each case. Thus, in the *G* cluster the distinction between universalism and particularism defines the *horizontal* axis of the paradigm, in the I cluster it assumes the *diagonal*. Put otherwise: of the *two* occurrences of each component in the *G* table only *one* of each is included in the *I* table, and these are placed in a diagonal position. The effect of this is to "shift" the relevant category from one to the other of the two positions in which it could be placed in the elementary set. The procedure never leads to "crossing over" into a "forbidden" cell; for example, universalism and particularism never "change places."

What is the meaning of these patternings? It is inherent in the organization of Figure 2 that integrative functions stand higher in the order of control than either goal-attainment or adaptive functions, which follow in that order. On grounds that cannot be fully explained here, I suggest that the horizontal and vertical axes of the paradigm state the location of the processes, conceived as interunit interchanges, which, respectively, have primarily internal adaptive significance in providing facilities to the units in question, and internal goal-attainment significance in providing rewards. Thus, the "rotation" brings about an involvement of the pattern variable components in integrative interchanges along the axes of Durkheim's "mechanical" (*L–G*) and "organic" solidarity (*A–I*).[10]

The suggestion, then, is that, relative to the elementary clusters, both *I* and *A* clusters have integrative significance. The *I* set states internal integrative *standards,* departure from which is associated with those realistic internal consequences known in interaction theory as

10. On the general problem of interchanges and their paradigmatic location, see Parsons and Smelser, *op. cit.* On the relation of the integrative interchanges to Durkheim's two types of solidarity, see Talcott Parsons, "Durkheim's Contribution to the Theory of Integration of Social Systems," in Kurt H. Wolff, editor, *Emile Durkheim 1858–1917* (Columbus: Ohio State University Press, 1960). First chapter of this volume.

"negative sanctions." The *A* set states standards of *meanings* of external objects ("cultural standards"), departure from which is associated with cultural selectivity and distortion, although not with immediately felt "sanctions."

What of the obverse "directions" of rotation? There is a double incidence of these directionalities. *Within* the clusters the rotations of the axes of the orientations and of the modalities are in opposite directions. The modalities of objects, from the point of view of a system of action, constitute ways of relating not only the acting unit but the system to the environment external to it. Hence it is an imperative of integration that, from the modality side, priority should be enjoyed by the category of meaning of the object (internally, as defining the actor-object relation) which is of primary functional significance *for the system* in the relevant context. From the orientation side, the imperative is that priority goes to the mode of orientation of primary significance to the actor in terms of its "needs." Thus, if the system function in question is adaptive, universalistic meanings take precedence over particularistic. For the actor, then, the primacy of specificity may be regarded as protecting his interest in *other* contexts of meaning of the same and other objects by limiting his commitments to the more immediately important ones.

These two designations are "functionally cognate" in that they share the characteristics of external orientation and instrumental significance. Here the rotation means that on the *A–I* axis of the integrative cluster (not of the system as a whole) the modality component in the adaptive cell is related to what in the *G* cluster is its *consummatory* "partner," whereas the orientation component is related to its *internal* partner. This is simply another way of stating the obverse directions of rotation. Put in general functional terms: the obverse relationship protects the system by giving primacy to instrumental over consummatory considerations in the adaptive context, while it protects the actor by giving primacy to external over internal considerations.

Another example from the adaptive cluster pairs the integrative cell with affectivity. From the viewpoint of the system, the significance of the object as "internalized" or institutionalized must clearly take precedence over its varying performances as oriented to the external situation. For it to serve as a standard of moral-evaluative categorization, however, there must also be affective involvement. The rotation in this case means that categorization in terms of quality is specifically distinguished from the performance component in its application to cognitive symbolization, whereas affectivity is contrasted (and thus integrated) with neutrality in the cognitive context. The formula for evaluative categorization on the modality side therefore designates internal significance, on the orientation side, consummatory significance.

The "diagonal" relations of the pattern variable pairs in the *I* and *A* clusters thus formulate the relations of combined discrimination and balance between the modality components and the orientational components. In each case the balance "protects" the categorization from confusion with its pattern variable opposite.

The same essential principles hold when the functioning of the system as a whole is considered. Here rotation in the clockwise direction designates what psychologists often call "performance" process, that is, change in the relations of the system to its environment on the assumption that its internal structure remains unchanged. The primary focus of change in this case lies in the adaptive subsystem. The counterclockwise direction of process designates "learning" processes. Here the primary focus of change centers in the internal structure of the system, in the first instance in the integrative system producing a change in its standards.

Types of Action and the Organization of Components

Another theoretical issue requires brief comment. This concerns the fact that the present analysis is mainly an analytical classification of *components* of *any* system of action, including the "unit act" as the most elementary building block of action systems.[11] Dubin, however, speaks of *types* of act. From the present point of view types must be constructed of varying combinations of components. In addition to *composition*—in terms of the presence or absence of components, or different "weights" assigned to them—there is organization of these components. We interpret the restrictions on random combination, and the clustering of pattern variable combinations in the four functional sets, to be statements of organization. The state of a system is never, in our opinion, adequately described by its "composition"—that is, by what components are present

11. The most important attempt to use essentially this conceptual scheme at the level, as I see it, of the "unit act" of the behavioral organism is James Olds' interpretation of the S–R–S sequence which has figured so prominently in behavior psychology, in action theory terms; see Olds, *The Growth and Structure of Motives* (Glencoe, Ill.: Free Press, 1956), Chapter 4. Another paradigm which seems to be more generalized, but even more precisely corresponding in logical structure with the unit act, is the TOTE unit presented by George A. Miller, Eugene Galanter, and Karl H. Pribram in *Plans and the Structure of Behavior* (New York: Holt, 1960).

in what quantities; the patterns of their relationships are equally essential. These considerations should be taken into account in attempts to develop a typology of acts from a classification of components in the act.

Another relevant point concerns the status of the pattern variable, self *versus* collectivity orientation. My present view is that this was an unduly restricted formulation of an element in the organization of action components at the level next above that designated by the primary pattern variables. In fact, Figure 1, I believe, documents four levels of organization. The first of these is represented by the L and G cells, characterized by pairs of elementary pattern-variable components—resulting in orientations and modalities, respectively. The second level is represented by the cross-combinations of elements from each pattern variable set, as shown in the I and A cells; as noted above, these are necessitated by the exigencies of differentiation and integration of the elementary combinations. The third level is the combination in turn of all of these elements into the four subsystems which have functional significance for the system as a whole, while the fourth is the organization *of* the system as a whole in relation to its environment.

The problem of the self-collectivity variable arises at the point where the I and A cells are organized into their respective subsystems. Subunits are organized into higher order "collective" units, the prototype being the organization of "members" into social collectivities. This organization takes place along the axis which distinguishes the "external" and "internal" foci in these cells. The inference is that there is another concept pair which formulates the other axis of differentiation. In the I and A cells this is termed the "instrumental-consummatory" axis, which should be placed on the same analytical level of generality as the former pattern variable.

The difference, I believe, between the two primary pattern-variable sets and this other "secondary" set—internal-external and instrumental-consummatory—is one of level of organization. The secondary set formulates the bases of relationship *across* the two primary sets, as distinguished from relations *within* each.

Some Theoretical Propositions

These restrictions on combinatorial randomness logically imply certain general propositions about the modes of interconnecting the components of a system of action. As distinguished from the exposition of a frame of reference, these are *theoretical* propositions or theorems. We are not sure that all propositions which can be derived from the logical structure of the system have been exhaustively worked out, even at this very high level of generality. But the following propositions seem to be the most significant:

1. The nature of the hierarchy of control, running from the cultural reference at the top of Figure 2 to the physical at the bottom, indicates that the *structure* of systems of action is conceived as consisting in *patterns of normative culture*. The ways in which types of action systems are differentiated, then, means that these patterns may be conceived as *internalized* in personalities and behavioral organisms, and as *institutionalized* in social and cultural systems.

2. It follows from this first proposition, plus the exposure of any system of action to plural functional exigencies, that the normative culture which constitutes its structure must be *differentiated* relative to these functional exigencies. These differentiated parts must then be integrated according to the four standards formulated in the *I* cells of Figure 1, and action oriented to the four different standards must be appropriately balanced, if the system is to remain stable. This is to say that process in the system, if it is to be compatible with the conditions of stability, must conform in some degree with the rules of a normative *order*, which is itself both differentiated and integrated.

3. For this "compliance" with the requirements of normative order to take place, the "distance" must not be too great between the structure of the acting unit and the normative requirements of its action necessitated by the functional exigencies of the system. It follows that the structure of acting units (which are objects to each other), as well as of norms, must incorporate appropriate elements of the system of normative culture—involving the internalization of "social object systems" in personalities, and the institutionalization of culturally normative systems in social systems.

4. Coordinate with the importance of order as formulated in the hierarchy of control and the place of normative culture in action systems, is the pattern of *temporal* order imposed by the functional exigencies of systems. Coordinate with the normative priority of ends is the temporal priority of means; only when the prerequisites of a consummatory goal-state have been established in the proper temporal order can the goal-state be realistically achieved. In both Figures 1 and 2, process is thus conceived in temporal terms as moving from left to right, the direction of "implementation."

5. A "law of inertia" may be stated: Change in the rate or direction of process is a consequence of *disturbance in the relations* between an actor or acting system and its situation, or the meanings of objects. If this relational system is completely stable, in this sense there is no process which is problematical for the theory of action. Whatever its source, such disturbance will always "show up" in the form of "strain" or difficulty in the attainment of valued goal states. From this point of reference may be distinguished two fundamental types of process:

(a) *"Performance" processes:* These are processes by which the disturbance is eliminated or adequately reduced through adaptive mechanisms, leaving the integrative standards—the most directly vulnerable aspect of the structure of the system—unchanged. The process may be adaptive in either the passive or the active sense, that is, through "adjusting to" changes in environmental exigencies or achieving "mastery" over them. The basic paradigm of this type of process is the means-end schema. In Figure 1 the directionality of such process is clockwise relative to the goal-focus, from *A* to *G*.

(b) *"Learning" processes* or processes of structural change in the system: Here, whatever its source, the disturbance is propagated to the integrative standards themselves and involves shifts in their symbolization and categorization and in their relative priorities. Whereas in performance processes goals are *given*, in learning processes they must be *redefined*. Relative to the goal-focus, then, the directionality of such process is counterclockwise, from *I* to *G* in Figure 1.

6. To be stable in the long run, a system of action must establish a generalized adaptive relation to its environment which is relatively emancipated from the particularities of specific goal-states. To preserve its own normative control in the face of environmental variability, it must be related *selectively* to the environment. There are two primary aspects of this adaptive relationship: (a) the level of generality of symbolic or "linguistic" organization of the orientation to environmental object-systems (the higher the level of generality the more adequate the adaptation); and (b) the ways in which the boundary of the system is drawn in terms of inclusion-exclusion of objects according to their meanings. The latter is synonymous with the conception of "control" in relevant respects. Control can thus be seen to be the active aspect of the concept of adaptation. The generalization here is that only controllable elements can be included in a system. The criterion for inclusion within an organized action system state is the action theory version of the famous "principle of natural selection." This is a fundamental generalization

about all living systems, and particularly important for action systems because they constitute a higher order of such systems.[12]

Concluding Remarks

The whole of the preceding exposition sets out a conceptual scheme, as frame of reference and as theory. It in no way purports to be an empirical contribution. Dubin, however, speaks of the importance of empirical verification of these concepts, and of their promise in this respect. There is no feature of his discussion with which I more fully agree; but the reader should not be misled to suppose that this presentation contributes to that goal. Certainly a good deal has been accomplished in this direction at various levels in my own work and in that of my collaborators as well as of many others, above all through codification with various bodies of empirical material and the conceptual schemes in terms of which they are analyzed.[13]

It should be kept in mind that the six propositions stated above are couched at a very high level of generality, deliberately designed to cover all classes of action system. Therefore it is unlikely that these propositions as such can be empirically verified at the usual operational levels. Such verification would require *specification* to lower levels, for example, the conditions of small experimental groups as a subtype of social system. Only in so far as codification reveals uniformities in the cognate features of many different types of operationally studied system do the more general theorems have a prospect of approaching rigorous empirical verification.

This specification should not be assumed to be capable of being carried out by simple "common sense"; it requires careful technical analysis through a series of concatenated steps. I believe, however, that the theory of action in its present state provides methods for successfully

12. These propositions represent a further development of the set of "laws" of action systems tentatively stated by Parsons, Bales, and Shils, *op. cit.*, Chapter 3.
13. For example: Bales' work on small groups; the work on family structure and socialization, including codification with psychoanalytic theory presented in Parsons, Robert F. Bales *et al.*, *Family, Socialization and Interaction Process* (Glencoe, Ill.: Free Press, 1955); codification with economic theory in Parsons and Smelser, *op. cit.*; and with certain problems of economic development in Smelser, *op. cit.*; codification with learning theory in Olds, *op. cit.*; the analysis of voting behavior in Parsons, "Voting and the Equilibrium of the American Political System," in Eugene Burdick and Arthur Brodbeck, editors, *American Voting Behavior* (Glencoe, Ill.: Free Press, 1958), included as chapter 8 in this volume; the relation to various aspects of psychological theory in Koch, *op. cit.*; and the essays published in Parsons, *Structure and Process in Modern Societies* (Glencoe, Ill.: Free Press, 1960), the bibliography of which contains further references.

carrying out this specification, and conversely, generalization as well *from* lower-level uniformities to higher levels. Perhaps the most important key to this possibility is the conception of *all* systems of action as systematically articulated with others along system-subsystem lines. The basic system types designated here as organisms, personalities, social systems, and cultural systems must be regarded as *sub*systems of the general category of action system. Each of these in turn is differentiated into further subsystems at different levels of elaboration. Any subsystem is articulated with other subsystems by definable categories of input-output interchange, the processes, in sufficiently highly differentiated subsystems, being mediated by symbolic-type mechanisms such as those discussed above.

In many respects, this possibility of dealing with *multiple* system references and of keeping straight the distinctions and articulations between them, has turned out to be the greatest enrichment of theoretical analysis developed from Dubin's "Model II." A "flat" conception of a single system reference which must be accepted or rejected on an all-or-none basis for the analysis of complex empirical problems, cannot possibly do justice to the formidable difficulties in the study of human action.

PART iii

*Dynamic Aspects
of Modern Society*

CHAPTER 8

"Voting" and the Equilibrium of the American Political System

With its relatively empirical reference, this paper seems to be well suited to introduce the more technically theoretical discussion of the three that follow. It was written in response to a request from Burdick and Brodbeck, coeditors of a symposium on *American Voting Behavior* (Glencoe: Free Press, 1959) to review some of the survey studies in that field from the point of view of their bearing on my theoretical interests. By far the most significant, from that point of view, seemed to me the volume *Voting*, by Berelson, Lazarsfeld, and McPhee (Chicago: University of Chicago Press, 1954), which had then been published quite recently. The data and analysis presented in this study seemed to me to present an opening for a type of generalized analysis of political processes in many ways comparable to that which the economists had developed for their field. In particular, it highlighted the importance of the pluralistic differentiatedness of American society in respects that impinge on its political processes. This perspective has been particularly important to my subsequent work in two respects. First it underlay the work on those two generalized media I have called, in my technical sense, power and influence. Second, it provided one of a number of points of reference for the analysis of the complex relations of plural groups in the societal community, a theme that is particularly important in the first three chapters of Part IV.

This paper has not previously been reprinted since its original publication in *American Voting Behavior*.

T̶HIS CHAPTER[1] concerns certain *theoretical* issues raised by the research studies that this volume as a whole discusses in a broader framework. There are two broad types of problem involved in the studies as a whole, namely (1) why a given *individual* votes as he does, and (2) how the voting process functions as part of the *social system* in which it operates. I shall focus my attention on the latter, the sociological as distinct from the psychological problem. The two are, however, so closely interwoven in the studies that some discussion of the relation between the two problems will prove necessary. I shall also, like the studies themselves, be concerned with recent presidential elections in the United States.

Because of the compactness with which *Voting*[2] presents a set of findings and interpretations that throw a great deal of light on political process in a society like ours and fit on the whole very well with a generalized analysis in terms of the theory of social systems, I shall concentrate my attention on it. To show the relation between such an analysis and the findings will be my main theme. Naturally critical questions will be raised at certain points, but I shall not anticipate them.

A framework of broad analysis of certain aspects of the structure, processes, and functional problems of the American political system will be developed, and then applied to the principal findings of the study.

A Theoretical Model of a Two-Party System

The political aspect of a social system may be thought of as centered on the generation and distribution of power. Power may, for the present purposes, be conceived as the capacity of the society to mobilize its resources in the interest of goals, defined as positively rather than permissively sanctioned by the system as a whole—goals that are "affected with a public interest." The amount of its power is an attribute of the total system and is a function of several variables. These, as I conceive them, are the *support* that can be mobilized by those exercising power, the *facilities* they have access to (notably the control of the productivity of

1. I am indebted to Samuel A. Stouffer, John W. and Matilda Riley, and Charles Drekmeier for a number of stimulating suggestions.
2. B. R. Berelson, P. F. Lazarsfeld, and W. N. McPhee, *Voting* (Chicago: University of Chicago Press, 1954).

the economy), the *legitimation* that can be accorded to the positions of the holders of power, and the relatively *unconditional loyalties* of the population to the society in its politically organized aspects. It is above all the factor of support which will be the center of concern here. In a modern, differentiated society the most important "producers" of power on the collectivity level, though by no means the sole ones, are those who hold responsible positions in what we call the structure of government—here, of course, the federal government.

An old question about power needs to be mentioned. One school of thought emphasizes power as power *over* others, with the implication that in a larger system the power held by different units must cancel out. My own emphasis is on power as capacity to get things done. Whether there is opposition or not is an empirically very important but theoretically secondary matter. My point of reference will be the *capacity of a social system to get things done in its collective interest.* Hence power involves a special problem of the *integration* of the system, including the binding of its units, individual and collective, to the necessary commitments.

Looked at in this way, the capacity to act focuses on the capacity for an agency or system of organization to make decisions responsibly, that is, with relative assurance that they can be effectively carried out. Power is essentially the basis of responsible action in this sense. The variables just mentioned are the "ingredients" of power—which can vary in quantity and combination; on them capacity for responsible action depends.

I have defined power as the capacity of a social system to mobilize resources to attain collective goals. A total society's paramount "goal" must be conceived on a very high level of abstraction. It is a function primarily of two sets of factors, the institutionalized value system of the society and the exigencies of the situation. Together they define states of affairs that need to be changed in the interest of a higher level of value-implementation. The specificity of a societal goal will vary greatly for different societies, but in any case there will be many subgoals that vary as functions of a societal development and the manifold relations of the society to the situation.

The value system of the contemporary United States centers on what may be called "instrumental activism." It is oriented to control the action situation in the interest of range and quality of adaptation, but with more economic than political emphasis. In goal definition it is highly indefinite and pluralistic, being committed to a rather general direction of progress or improvement, without any clearly defined terminal goal. Economic production is highly valued as the most immediate focus of adaptive capacity. Beyond that, however, we value particularly technology and science as means to productivity, and the maximization of opportunity for individuals and subcollectivities (manifested above all in concern with health and education). Moreover, we have a special set of attitudes toward organization and authority which might be summed up as involving, on the one hand, a pragmatic acceptance of authority in the interest of limited specifically approved goals, but, on the other hand, an objection to any pretensions of generalized superiority of status.

The over-all goal of American society (in a special technical sense) may then be tentatively defined as the *facilitation* of effective adaptive development of the society and of the societal conditions associated with it. It centers on economic development, but definitely includes the integrative conditions which are relevant. At the next lower level of specification, American society stresses the more immediate facilitation of production and the development of productivity, the effective ordering of political organization itself, the furthering of effective integration of the social system, and the promoting of conditions on the level of opportunity for operation of the system and adjustment of personalities.

The generation and allocation of power in a society occurs through a set of structures and processes, a subsystem parallel to the economy which we may call the "polity." It is essentially a functional-relational system, controlled by institutional patterns and controlling collectivities and roles.[3] The relevant institutional patterns are those governing the hierarchical ordering of social statuses, authority, and the compulsory regulation of "private" activities. The focus of the collectivity structure is clearly government, though there is a political as well as economic component in all collectivities in the society. Government is that complex of collectivities which have political *primacy*. This means that governmental organizations primarily, in their relations to the rest of the society, generate power and make it available to the rest of the society.

3. The concept of the economy used here is fully discussed in Talcott Parsons and N. J. Smelser, *Economy and Society* (Glencoe, Ill.: The Free Press, 1956). The parallel concept of the polity has not previously been discussed in print, except sketchily in the above publication. Unfortunately limitations of space make it impossible to present it here, also, except in very sketchy form. A brief discussion of these and related concepts in formal theoretical terms appears in the Technical Note appended to this chapter. Cf. also my paper "The Political Aspect of Social Structure and Process" in David Easton (ed.), *Varieties of Political Theory* (Englewood Cliffs: Prentice-Hall, 1966).

Like the economy, the polity is an analytically distinct subsystem of the society. It too is conceived to stand in relations to other parts of the society which involve the interchange of inputs and outputs over its boundaries. Of these interchanges, one is of primary importance for present purposes. It may be characterized through a comparison between the functions of government and those of the polity. On the federal level, which alone will concern us here, the main functions of government are relatively clearly set forth in the Constitution itself. The most important concern the conduct of foreign relations, the regulation of commerce between the states, the enforcement of rights (personal freedom, opportunity, property), the ensuring of justice and internal order, and the promotion of the "general welfare." Broadly, this constitutional mandate is to implement within a certain framework the goals of the society as sketched above.

The functions of the polity, as contrasted with those of government, I conceive to center in creating the conditions necessary if those assuming responsibility in government are to be able to assume and discharge this responsibility. Given the American value system these may be said to be: (1) the legitimation of the powers of government and the statuses of its various subcollectivities and offices; (2) the requisite share in the control of the basic facilities available in the society, especially control of the productivity of the economy through the establishment of "rights to intervene"; and (3) the mobilization of "support" for the assumption, by office holders in government, of leadership roles and the corresponding responsibilities for formulation of more specific goals and their implementation.[4]

The theoretical analysis of this chapter concerns the third of these conditions of responsible leadership. I shall call this the "goal-attainment" process of the polity as a system. Its goal, which must be distinguished from that of the society as a whole as sketched above, is to generate power in the political sense, that is, to mobilize "resources" that can be used to implement societal goals. There are two main levels on which this goal is (more or less effectively) achieved. The more general is the provision of effective *leadership* in the goal-specification and goal-implementation processes on the requisite collective level. The more specific is arriving at *decisions* which are binding on the society as a politically organized collectivity. For present purposes the subsystem that functions as recipient of these outputs of the polity may be referred to as the "public."

4. The reader will note that these are the variables introduced above.

We are, however, speaking of a boundary-interchange process and must be concerned not only with outputs from the polity but also with the inputs to the polity from the public—which on the one hand are essential factors in its functioning, on the other are in certain ways contingent on its performance. I should like to suggest that support (point 3) is the appropriate input category (from public to polity) which matches the outputs of provision of leadership and making of decisions. At the more general level, the support that is exchanged with and contingent upon leadership is *generalized*. It takes the form of broadly based confidence in those assuming responsibility for leadership in governmental affairs which is necessary to enable them to act with real power, that is, to make necessary and far-reaching decisions responsibly in the sense that elements of the population affected will accept the consequences. Such consequences inevitably include burdens and obligations that affect some elements adversely and bear unevenly on different groups. On the lower level of generality, the relevant type of support which corresponds to decision-making may be said to be the *advocacy of policies*. By this I mean an accepting attitude on a level more general than that of specific decisions but less general than that of an "administration" in the American or a "Government" in the British sense (which is a term of generalized support).

In the above formulation I am thinking self-consciously in terms of a parallel with the corresponding boundary-interchange of the economy, the one involved vis-à-vis the household with labor as a factor of production and the production of consumers' goods. On the higher level of generalization the primary output of the economy to the household is the production of *income* in the monetary sense—in the labor case, wage income. On the lower level it is the production of specific commodities made available to consumers. The corresponding inputs to the economy from the household are, on the high level, labor in the factor sense and, on the lower level, consumers' spending.

These relations of interchange of inputs and outputs—on the one hand, between the economy and the household—may be represented diagrammatically in a simple way as follows:[5]

5. The paradigm for this boundary-interchange of the economy (with the household in the empirically primary case) is set forth in Parsons and Smelser, *op. cit.*, Chap. 2. Cf. especially Fig. 5, p. 11. A simplified version of the general interchange paradigm is presented in the Technical Note.

* For an explanation of the notation, *A, G, I, L,* see final section of this chapter entitled, Technical Note.

I shall have this parallel in mind throughout the following analysis. It should be clearly understood, however, that it is a parallel, in the strict sense an analogy, and not an identity. Power as an output is not income in the economic sense, decisions are not commodities, support is not labor, and consumers' spending is not advocacy of policies. In an analytical sense the "public," as the source of support and advocacy of policies, is altogether different from the household, as the source of labor and consumers' spending, though members of households are at the same time parts of the public. I shall delineate the relevant characteristics of the public as we go along.[6]

Let us now attempt to apply this abstract analytical scheme to some familiar facts of American political structure. I have stated that the focus of political organization on the collectivity level is government, in our case the federal government. The boundary-interchange just outlined is that set of processes by which control of the federal government is decided, its major policies are worked out, and public attitudes toward them are influenced and brought to bear. The focus of the mechanisms by which the processes work out is what we call the party system. At the support level the most important single process on the side of the public is voting because, under our constitutional system, this decides who is to assume the primary roles of responsible leadership.

There are of course many other influences on leadership: media of opinion, behind-the-scenes persuasion and threats, financial interests, and

6. In technical analytical terms I conceive the public in this sense as an aspect of the integrative subsystem of the society. See Parsons and Smelser, *op. cit.,* pp. 51–70 and Fig. 4, p. 68.

the like. But voting is the central focus of the process of selection of leadership and hence in one sense all other influences must channel their effects *through* the voting process.

The most important fact about the American situation is the existence on the national level of the *two*-party system which, with some interruptions, has proved stable over a long period. This means that the presidency must at any given time be occupied by the candidate of one of the two parties, and that the majority party in each house of Congress has the opportunity to "organize" its house through the speakership (in the case of the House of Representatives) and chairmanships and majorities of committees. In spite of the looseness of party discipline there can be no doubt of the overwhelming importance of this two-party structure.

Within the complex of operation of the two-party system this analysis, in line with the empirical studies with which it is concerned, will be confined to the voting processes which determine the incumbency of the presidency. It is of course vital to realize that the process of electing the President, considered as a system, is only part of a larger one. It has been noted that a variety of influences operate to determine the decisions of voters. But even where the voting mechanism itself is concerned, voting for presidential candidates is only part of the voter's function and opportunity. The separation of powers means that he also votes for congressional candidates and for state and local offices.

A salient fact of American politics is that there is only a rough correlation between party votes for President and for these other offices. The looseness of party discipline and the plural voting opportunities provided in the American system mean that in no sense can the determination of the presidency be considered a *closed* system. For example, tensions generated by being forced to choose between only two candidates for President may be expressed in supporting for other offices candidates not in sympathy with the presidential candidate, or candidates of the opposing party. Empirical statements made in the following analysis should always be qualified with these considerations in mind.

Nevertheless I think it is legitimate to consider the voting process by which Presidents are elected as authentically a *social system*. It is a set of processes of action and interaction which may be treated in terms of specific modes of interdependence which can be analytically separated from other influences. Furthermore, in our system, the Presidency is the focus of integration of the political system as a whole. Of course the concrete data that will be reviewed are affected by factors emanating from outside this particular system—including the other voting processes in other subsystems of the political structure. But in principle this is true of any social system that is a subsystem of a larger one, that is, less than the total society.

To return to the substantive discussion, the main function of political organization is the facilitation of effective action on collective levels. The two-party system may be regarded as a mechanism that makes possible a certain balance between effectiveness through relative centralization of power, and mobilization of support from different sources in such a way that there is genuine contingency—the supporter is offered a real alternative.[7] Dictatorships naturally are different; their concern is to avoid losing support lest the opposition become dangerous, and there is a strong tendency to use coercive measures in coping with actual or feared opposition. But the two-party system, as has often been pointed out, makes it possible for the holders of power to be changed without upsetting the system. Naturally this depends on definite institutional conditions, notably the acceptance of electoral results by the losing side without impairment of basic loyalties, and the restraint of winners from using their power to suppress opposition. It depends overwhelmingly on the firm institutionalization of such "rules of the game."

All this I take for granted. The point of present interest is that the two-party system, as distinguished from a many-party system or one of an indefinite number of shifting factions, has certain implications for the structure of support in its relation to leadership. This way of structuring the situation forces a high level of *generalization* of support on the one side, of responsibility on the other. This is particularly true in a society with a social structure as diverse as the American, in economic, class, occupational, regional, ethnic, religious, and other terms. Support, focusing on the presidency, must be given to one of two party candidates: the alternative is a "protest" vote for a minority-party candidate, or non-participation altogether. Many votes are motivated by more particularized considerations having to do with specific interest groups, and the like. But *whatever* their motivation on lower levels of generality, all the votes have to be counted as support for the party candidate and his administration, and on some level for the power of the party in Congress. This point brings out in one context very sharply the difference in significance between the problem of the *motivation* of the individual voter, and of the *consequences* of his vote for the political system.

7. There is not, of course, at any given time a wide range of alternatives, but if the analysis of the direction of party orientation given later in this chapter is correct, it is highly important, and a wide range would be incompatible with effective political integration.

A word may now be said about the line of differentiation between the two major parties. This line is less one of ideological "principle," and more pragmatic, than is the case in European politics. A broad line can, however, be discerned. I would like to characterize this distinction as that between "right" and "left" in a sense appropriate to American conditions. The focus of the American right in this sense is the organization of the free-enterprise economy. This is by no means "conservative" in a general social sense; it is in fact the main center of dynamic development in the society. But it is *politically* conservative because the economy is institutionalized on a private-enterprise basis in such a way that positive political action can readily be defined as threatening to interfere with the conditions of operation of this type of economy.[8] Connected with the "business" interest in this sense are various other elements with a tendency to fear innovative change, notably in our recent history the rural small-town elements of a large part of the country.

The "left," on the other hand, has been the focus of those elements predisposed to favor positive action on the political level, who have been favorable to "reform" of various sorts, to control of the economy, to promotion of "welfare," and not least to "interventionism" in foreign affairs.[9] On a broad basis this distinction adequately characterizes the *main* line of distinction between Republican and Democratic tendencies. Of course the Solid South has been a special case, and at the present time major processes of realignment seem to be going on. It is my judgment, however, that the realignments will result, not in substituting a new major axis, but in reshuffling the elements involved in the support groups about the present axis. Business will continue to be the major focus of the more conservative party.

In our system the party leader, as candidate and as President, must appeal to a variety of diverse groups and interests for the support necessary to elect. He must come up with some balance involving compromises and creative syntheses. The general meaning of the aggregate of the support he receives cannot be more than the endorsement of a broad *direction* of action for the polity. More specific interests can be endorsed only as they fit the general direction; they always stand in competition with others. There can never be any "absolute" commitment to a particular interest—economic, ideological, religious, or other—because this would

8. This is by no means to say either that "business" has taken a consistently laissez-faire attitude—on many occasions it has sought help from government. But clearly the *main* trend is the one stated.
9. This is a type of intervention which is often characteristic of the right. Cf. footnote 41 this chapter.

lead to burning of bridges connecting with other elements necessary for an effective support-coalition, elements that would not "go along" with such a commitment. For example, in pre-Nazi Germany the Center party was definitely committed to represent the interests of the Catholic Church. It had considerable range for maneuver, but was prevented by this commitment from becoming a genuine national party in a religiously divided society. Similarly, an American Catholic party under our system could not conceivably become one of the two general parties.

Let us return to the parallel with the input-output boundary of the economy. What I have called the generalization of support is parallel to the "mobility of labor," the readiness to cooperate in the production of goods and services that do not themselves satisfy one's own personal needs or those of one's family. The individual worker must in an important sense relinquish control of the product of his labor. Similarly the political supporter, in our case the voter, must not claim direct control of the consequences of his vote; if he did, political support would be reduced to a "barter" basis and the political integration of a complex social system would become impossible. What then does the voter receive that is analogous to the money income of the worker? He receives the expectation that many *kinds* of measures that he approves will be implemented if his candidate wins, but without exact specification of particular policies. The directional orientation of a party candidate is a kind of political "currency" which, if he wins, will improve the probabilities that a *kind* of direct political action, over which the voter does not have direct control but which *in general* he favors, will be taken. In taking money wages for his work and relinquishing control of the product, the worker evidences "faith" that by spending the money he will be able to get something he values as much or more than the product of his work. Similarly the voter evidences faith that, if his candidate wins, the "way things will go" will be relatively in accord with his wishes, but he cannot directly control the specific decisions that will be taken.

This generalized support is, I have noted, a fundamental ingredient of power. It, along with the other ingredients, is used to help produce concrete decisions, binding on the collectivity, which are analogous to specific goods. The support is necessary because without it the decisions could not be responsible, that is, could not be made to "stick." But if the support is to be of any "use," its consequences must eventuate in concrete decisions that deal effectively with the real problems of the collectivity. The quality and quantity of these decisions and of their consequences in turn justify the acts of faith involved in giving political support. But it is the *aggregate value* of such decisions, not their particularities, which is the basis of the community's political "income" from its commitments of support.

Perhaps it is worthwhile to carry the parallel between the economic and the political one step further. The keynote of economic organization has rightly been said to be the division of labor. Through it the individual "producer" makes a sacrifice and receives a gain. The sacrifice is essentially one of self-contained independence; he can no longer meet his own needs from his own efforts and resources. The gain is one of "efficiency." He gets more by pooling competence and resources with others than if each operated alone on a self-sufficient basis. In the political case the axis is the differentiation of responsibility. The giver of support makes a sacrifice—loss of immediate control of collective decisions that affect his own interest; he "delegates" this control to the holders of power. But he also receives a gain, which is his share in the benefits of the *effectiveness* with which collective action can be taken. If the responsibility of every voter, including the President, for collective action were exactly equal, in effect *no* collective action would be taken at all. But in exchange for this gain the voter has to take his chances that the *particular* decisions in which he is most directly interested will be forthcoming.[10]

A built-in element of the conflict of interest is always present in any system of the economic division of labor—for example, the terms of the contract of employment. But this is greatly accentuated in the political case because of the commitment of the collectivity as a whole which is involved. At the leadership-support level this is, in our system, dramatized by the duality of the parties and the fact that in an immediate presidential election, what is gained by one—namely electoral victory—is by definition lost by the other. Hence there are inherently divisive potentialities in political "competition" which are not present to the same degree in economic competition. The control of such divisive potentialities is, in our society, attained through the institutionalization of the two-party system referred to above.

So far we have attempted to do two things. The first was to outline a general model of the relation between the organization of leadership and the mobilization of support in a political system. The second was to apply this to the main facts of the American two-party system so far as it involved the processes of election to the presidency. It is clear that the

---

10. Realistically, of course, neither the worker nor the voter *could* be self-sufficient. The argument is analytical, not a discussion of concrete alternatives.

operation of such a system is dependent on the firm institutionalization of the "rules of the game" by which certain standards of fairness are insured, by which the losing party accepts the legitimacy of electoral victory of the winner, and by which in turn the winners do not use the power of the state to make it impossible for the losers to have a real chance of winning in future elections.

In addition to this condition of general institutionalization, it follows, I think, from the above analysis that there are certain further conditions necessary to the successful operation of a democratic two-party system. These conditions may be stated in the following four propositions:

1) There must be mechanisms by which the average voter can come to a responsible decision that is meaningful to him. He must not, in too many cases, withdraw to nonvoting, nor be too susceptible to appeals that would be grossly disruptive of the stability of the system. Since the intellectual problems involved in a rational solution are not practicably soluble, my thesis is that the mechanisms are typically nonrational. They involve stabilization of political attitudes *in terms of association with other members of the principal solidary groups in which the voter is involved.* In terms of party affiliation this may be called "traditionalism." The traditionalistic operation of nonrational mechanisms is a condition of the stability of the system. That they root in the solidary grouping of the society follows from the fact that support is mobilized from the integration subsystem of the society.[11]

2) Pure traditionalism, however, would result in a rigidity of the system which would be incompatible both with the shift of conditions under which problems of public goal-specification and attainment must

---

11. The necessity for the operation of nonrational mechanisms may be further illustrated as follows: I have emphasized that the focusing of the decision of the electorate on two candidates forces a very high level of the generalization of support. A voter cannot, in effect, decide on highly concrete grounds, using his vote as a specific means to a specific end. However important such specific considerations may be for a given voter, the *effect* of his vote must be to contribute to the pool of general support for the candidate and party, and he cannot fail to be aware that on some level he is thrown, with respect to this pool, together with strange bedfellows who have quite different specific ends in view than his.

At the same time, to judge rationally in terms of the "welfare of the country" is an intellectual task of a very high level of complexity and difficulty. Since even the most competent technical experts in such matters, political and social scientists are far from being agreed on the better direction in a given case, how can the average voter have a competent and well-grounded opinion? This is a classic type of situation in which nonrational psychological mechanisms can be expected to operate. The voter is faced with problems to which a rational solution in the usual sense is impossible; he must fall back on mechanisms that are psychologically possible for him. But at the same time there must be some type of regulation of these mechanisms lest voters' behavior prove to be too unsettling to the society.

be posed and with the necessity, for a two-party system, that there be realistic opportunities for each party to win in its bid for leadership through the election of a President. A certain proportion of voters must shift from time to time in party allegiance, if a flexible balance is to be maintained. The data show that this takes place mainly through what has been called above the "indifference" reaction—the voting change of people under cross-pressures who show relatively low levels of interest in the campaign and have difficulty in making their decisions. This finding will be interpreted as in line with the importance of solidary groupings as foci of political loyalties. It is a mechanism which on the whole minimizes the dangers of instability, inherent in political shifting. But it is primarily a condition of effective attainment of *new* goals as they become salient.

3) Under two-party conditions a limited polarization of the electorate is essential—a choice between only two realistic alternatives is offered. This means that the inherently divisive potentialities of political power-struggle are increased. There must clearly be mechanisms which prevent this polarization from producing a progressively deepening rift in the electorate. In the subsequent discussion, it will be shown that there are two main foci of such mechanisms. First, there is the supraparty consensus referred to above, which institutionalizes the duality of party organization, prescribing rules of political fair play. Second, there is the involvement of voting with the solidary groups in the society in such a way that, though there is a correlation, there is no *exact* correspondence between political polarization and other bases of differentiation. Hence, pushing the implications of political difference too far activates the solidarities between adherents of the two parties which exist on other, nonpolitical, bases so that members of the political majority come to defend those who share other of their interests but differ from them politically. These mechanisms serve the effective integration of the system.

4) American society is not static, but dynamically evolving. The political system must be adapted to this fact and must include mechanisms of adjustment to social change. Under American conditions the main autonomous processes of social change do not operate through government, but largely through the development of the economy. The business element, which is the core of this process of change, tends to be politically conservative because positive use of the powers of government has been felt, since the early thirties, to imply interference with the

process. The left, on the other hand, is relatively residual, tending to gather together those elements in the society on whom the problems and difficulties arising from the dynamic process impinge, and who see in governmental action an opportunity to remedy their situations. There must be mechanisms in the political system which mediate the balance between right and left without running the risk that either set of elements will be oppressively overwhelmed by the other. They are mechanisms that are essential to adapt the system to *changes in the structure of the society.*

The reader will note that, with some differences, these four conditions bear a close relation to the balances on which the functioning of the system depends, as formulated by the authors of *Voting* in their final chapter. The authors speak of the balances between "involvement and indifference" and between "stability and flexibility." Both of these balances are related to each of my first two statements about conditions of functioning of the system. The relations between involvement and indifference are highly pertinent to the nature of the nonrational mechanisms on which the stability of the system depends and to the anchorage of the voter in the solidarity groupings of the society. But the same nonrational mechanisms operate in maintaining the type of flexibility which is most important in what may be called "normal" functioning. Hence, in my more detailed review of the findings of the studies, especially *Voting,* I shall treat these two together in connection with my own first two statements of conditions.

A further balance discussed by the authors is that between "consensus and cleavage." This directly concerns my third condition, that of the integrative basis of the voting system, and will be discussed under that heading. Finally, the fourth of their balances is that between "progress and conservation," as they call it. It is clear that this is essentially the same as my fourth condition which concerns adaptation to changes in the structure of the society. The fifth of their balances, that between "individualism and collectivism," seems to me to stand on a different level from the other four. It is very close to what I have called the balance between leadership responsibility and the necessity of support. This has already been discussed and will be a continuing theme throughout the remainder of the chapter.

Under the three rubrics just indicated I would now like to attempt to spell out the implications of the above analysis and relate them to some of the more detailed findings of the studies. This will both show the degree of goodness of fit between their findings and my model, and lead to a few theoretical conclusions that are not explicitly stated by the authors.

Stability, Flexibility, and the Shift of Political Allegiance

Perhaps the most striking group of findings come in the first of the three main areas: stability, flexibility, and level of interest in the campaign. These concern in a sense the status of the "independent voter"; and, from the point of view of some of the ideologies dear to intellectuals, the findings may seem rather shocking. The fact seems to be that the groups most likely to escape from the traditionalism of habitual and inherited voting patterns are those least intensely interested in the issues of the campaign. They are not particularly well informed and, indeed, often are on the margin of not voting at all. These are the groups that provide the main element of flexibility in the system, the main source of the shifters from one party to the other.[12] It is also important that these are the same kind of people who, as they report their recollection of previous voters, are most likely to have shifted allegiance between campaigns. Furthermore, intensification of the campaign tends to drive them back to their previous habits of voting.

A second very important and closely related finding is that a large proportion of the voters susceptible to shifting are people subject to "cross-pressures."[13] These are people who, in the cross-cutting status structure of our complex society, belong simultaneously to solidary groups membership in which would predispose them to vote in both of the two major directions, so that they are exposed to a role conflict. An example would be the well-to-do businessman of Irish-Catholic origin. The evidence seems to be that a considerable proportion of the people thus exposed to cross-pressures resolve their conflict by not voting at all. In any case, those who do vote make up their minds later than those not so exposed, and shift from previous allegiances more frequently.[14]

Another primary fact, of course, is that the great majority of voters are settled in their party allegiances and will not be influenced to vote for the opposing party by either the personality of the candidate or the discussion of issues. These in general include those who feel most intensely

12. Berelson, Lazarsfeld, and McPhee, *op. cit.*, Chap. 1, especially propositions stated on pp. 33–34.
13. *Ibid.*, p. 33, Proposition 6.
14. *Ibid.*, pp. 148–49.

about the outcome and take the most active part in politics at all levels.[15] This evidence, combined with other facts, seems to make clear a fundamental connection between the psychology of voting behavior and the mechanisms by which the balance of stability and flexibility are maintained which is of great interest here.

On one level we may say that the nonshifters vote "from habit" or that they are "traditionalists," but these statements do not carry us very far. Fortunately data are presented which enable us to look considerably deeper for the bases of these habits and traditions. These data show that there is a marked tendency to agree in voting preferences with certain categories of others. This is so true of the family that the authors say the family rather than the individual perhaps ought to be taken as the unit of voting behavior. The tendency to agreement then extends to friends, and somewhat less intensely to occupational associates, fellow members of ethnic and religious groups, and class associates—this last the more so in proportion to the individual's class identification.[16]

In considering the implications of these findings, let us again note that when a rational decision is not possible but at the same time there is pressure to make commitments, there has to be some stable set of reference points so that beliefs can give meaning to the commitment and people can feel "comfortable" about it. The "issues" are in general too numerous and specific to provide a focus, the individual can directly "care" about only a minority of them, and the chances are good he will disapprove of his candidate's stand on some. Furthermore, his own action can have little decisive effect on the outcome—he casts only one of millions of votes—and the direct effect of the immediate outcome on his own personal interests is usually slight.

In this situation the individual seems to vote, other things being equal, with the people whom he most directly feels to be "his own kind," who are in social status and group memberships like, and hence like-minded with, himself. It may be said that the question is not so much, on the levels of psychological determination, *for what* he is voting *as it is with whom* he is associating himself in voting. There are many questions about the specific psychological mechanisms involved in this behavior, especially because it is largely unconscious in a considerable proportion of cases. Presumably processes akin to those of natural selection have been at work. One point, however, of congruence with the social situation can be brought out. As outlined above, the relationship of

15. *Ibid.*, pp. 27, 34.
16. *Ibid.*, Chap. 6, especially p. 116.

political leadership and support must be in some sense one of mutual trust. The leader is dependent on the stability of his support in order to carry out the responsibilities he has assumed, and supporters have performed an implicit act of faith in the necessary relinquishment of control of their affairs to leadership.

Broadly the solidary groupings of a social structure are those on whose members political developments will have some sort of common impact. Probably the tightest solidary grouping in our society is the family and this seems to show the greatest cohesiveness in voting. Certainly the members of this grouping share to a high degree a "common fate" in the face of whatever vicissitudes may come and go. Occupational, ethnic, religious, class, local, and regional groupings have similar characteristics to lesser and varying degrees. I suggest that it is symbolically appropriate that, in performing an "act of faith" which establishes a relation of trust the consequences of which, however, cannot be directly controlled, a person should feel most secure in associating himself with persons who, by virtue of their real solidary relationship to him, are the ones he feels most naturally can be trusted.

In any case, whatever the more specific psychological mechanisms, the *effect* of the "pull" of the solidary groupings of the social structure on individuals, as a result of which they vote with their fellow members of such groups, is to contribute greatly to what I have called the generalization of support. As the authors of *Voting* state several times, the individual tends to vote as a group member. But it is precisely as a structure of groups that a society is stable and integrated. If people vote as members of the stably important groups of the society, this provides an element of stability in the structure of political alignments itself which matches and is a consequence of the stability of the social structure.

It was noted above that the primary problem of the generation of power was the requisite integration in a political action context of the social system in which it occurs. At the top, this integration is organized around the two-party alternative within the institutional framework of a constitutionally guaranteed set of alternatives and the opportunity for the losing side to try again. But at the bottom, the process is dependent on the statistical outcome of millions of individual acts. I have argued that the direct rational determination of those acts without intermediary "nonrational" mechanisms is out of the question. The attachment of the individual to his solidary associations as a voting reference builds the society up in a series of graduated steps from the more elementary units of the society to units that can be meaningfully related to the important issues of the day, the realistic alternatives facing the political system as a system. As a structure of political integration, the top of this structure is constituted by the two national parties. That there should be such a structure of integrations is directly deducible from general theory.[17] The clarity with which the studies have provided empirical evidence of its existence and concrete nature is impressive.

This line of argument does not, however, account for flexibility, which is also necessary to such a system. It is here that the findings about the changers and shifters and their relation to relative political indifference and to cross-pressures are so interesting and significant. In spite of the empirical difference, it can be said that the basic theme is the same. The phenomenon of cross-pressures means that many people are involved in solidary groupings which politically, and certainly in other ways, are not well integrated with each other. The potential voter is, by his solidary associations, being pulled two ways at once.

Of course the fact that these are the main sources of the shift in votes, both between elections and during campaigns, brings out the importance of group attachments for those whose voting orientation is more stable. But there are two other particularly important aspects. The first is the psychological reference: the "cross-pressure" people are the more indifferent (many on the margin of not voting at all) and make up their minds later than others.[18] Psychologically this is an understandable reaction to conflict, namely vacillation and the postponement of decision, and the tendency to withdraw from a difficult dilemma by avoiding decision altogether. These tendencies are of course facilitated by the fact that generally in American society there is little strong sanction brought to bear on nonvoters, and the ballot is secret.

There is also, secondly, an important social aspect of the phenomenon. It is through the mobility of individuals between groups and the formation of new groups (and correspondingly the weakening and eventual disappearance of old ones) that the social structure itself changes. It therefore seems legitimate to conclude that on the whole the people exposed to cross-pressures are, in terms of social structure, among those most directly involved in processes of social change. Thus, for example, the upward mobility of immigrant populations produces the Catholic of high socioeconomic status who is a type case of involve-

17. Some technical aspects of this deduction are discussed in the Technical Note.
18. Berelson, Lazarsfeld, and McPhee, *op. cit.*, p. 33.

ment in cross-pressures. Surely the result of this process will in the long run be to split the Catholic vote far more evenly between the parties than was true in the New Deal era. In the other direction, we may cite the large-scale process of migration of rural people to the industrial areas and their eventual incorporation into trade unions, a process which occurred a little earlier. The Republican predilection of many rural people thus was crossed with the Democratic predilection of many union members. On the whole one would expect the concomitant growth of industry and of unionism to produce a relatively stable increment to Democratic strength—though particularly in the light of the 1956 results, and also of facts cited in *Voting*, there must be some qualifications of this generalization. In any case, however, the cross-pressure element in its relation to social change provides the primary element of flexibility in a system which, were the factor of group solidarity too strong, might well be unduly rigid.

These facts about solidarity and its loosening through cross-pressures provide an empirical setting for the theoretical problem I posed above about the nature and significance of the levels of generalization of support.[19] This problem is very much involved in the distinction the authors of *Voting* make between what they call "position" issues and "style" issues.[20] Position issues are close to the level of what I have called binding decisions and advocacy of policies—typical examples from the 1948 campaign being revision of the Taft-Hartley Act and price control. Style issues on the other hand are closer to the ideological level and to that of "generalized support" which requires broad bases of justification—communism in government would be such an issue, though it was not yet very prominent in 1948. My essential point is that these types of issues correspond to a distinction between levels at which people are integrated in the solidary group structure of the society. Promotion of what is ordinarily called an "interest" involves acting with people who feel they have a common interest, sometimes in opposition to others.[21] It is usually thought of at a level which can be coped with by relatively specific "policies." But at this level interests are too diverse and sometimes too conflicting to serve to integrate the electorate at the level of generalized support. Hence we would expect to find symbolizations at higher levels

19. Clear insight into this problem is shown by Berelson, Lazarsfeld, and McPhee, *op. cit.*, chap. 4, with special reference to the functioning of position.
20. *Ibid.*, pp. 184–185.
21. It is interesting to note the systematic attempts of totalitarian governments to destroy the solidary groupings that mediate between individual and state.

of generalization which can come closer to setting off the two parties against each other as a whole.[22]

Consensus and Cleavage

Let us now turn to the problem of "polarization" or what Berelson *et al.* speak of as the balance between consensus and cleavage. It is important that the studies provide direct evidence of the underlying consensus that is essential if a party system is to work at all without disrupting the community, that is, polarizing it in a radical sense. This centers on the recognition that there are common "rules of the game" binding on all participants. But consensus seems to go beyond this. Though some distortion in perception of candidates and issues can be detected, it seems fair to say the notable thing is not that distortion exists, but that it is relatively small. Thus there seems to be fair agreement across party lines on the characteristics of the candidates and the relevant criteria to judge them, on what the major issues of the campaign are, on various expectations for the future, and on expectations of the voting tendencies of various blocs of voters. There is, to a fair degree, a common framework both of institutional norms and of cognitive definition of the situation.[23]

This supraparty consensus should, I think, be regarded as the top of the more general hierarchy of politically relevant solidarities. Its existence and continual reinforcement through symbolic expression should be regarded as the essential condition of the tolerance of division at the next lower level, which is the division between the major parties as such. For sociological reasons, if this division is to be considered as "tolerable," it must be based on a genuine *differentiation* of function with reference to the system as a whole. The line of division between right and left in American politics suggests a framework in which our main party structure may be interpreted. The chief problem here concerns the balance of conservation and progress, but certain problems with respect to the

22. There is a possible confusion in classifying religion as a "style" issue, if the distinction between it and position issues is meant to be more than a rather *ad hoc* empirical one. Religious groups constitute bases of solidarity just as do "economic" or local groups. They can become, especially in a system of denominational pluralism like the American, the focus of highly specific position issues. But for reasons having to do with the integration of the society, there are strong pressures against making religion an *explicit* focus of political controversy. It hence tends to become one of the things nearly everyone is "in favor of" with careful avoidance of mentioning the differences of interest between different denominational groups.

23. Berelson, Lazarsfeld, and McPhee, *op. cit.*, especially chap. 9, summarized on p. 212.

nature of the cleavage and the limitations on it need to be taken up. My broad thesis is that divisive tendencies are controlled by being placed in the context of the hierarchy of solidarities which I have outlined, so that the cleavages that develop tend to be toned down and muted on their own level and referred to higher orders of integration for resolution.

We have had a prominent recent example of the operation of this mechanism. One can scent a certain danger to this higher level consensus when, particularly in the heat of campaigns, spokesmen for the parties go beyond stating their differences from their opponents as differences of desirable directions and policies, and raise doubts about the "fitness to govern" of the opposite party and its candidates. Almost inevitably there is some of this in every campaign. On occasion it may go further, as it did in the 1952–54 period. The theme of the threat of communism was played up by the Republican extremists until it began to be applied, by inference if not explicitly, not just to certain limited allegedly subversive elements, but to the Democratic party as a whole. This culminated in McCarthy's slogan of "twenty years of treason." For a moment it seemed as though this would be taken up by the Republican moderates; a few speeches by such spokesmen as Attorney-General Brownell and Governor Dewey were couched very nearly in this vein. But this provoked a strong reaction from specifically *conservative* Democrats, such as Sam Rayburn: and in general the Republican moderates, after a brief "flirtation" with the idea, drew back sharply from it. Essentially what happened is that the vicious circle of divisive cleavage began to activate the sentiments clustering around the higher-order solidarity of the national supraparty consensus. To accuse a person of disloyalty or treason is to place him outside that consensus. To extend this accusation to one of the two major parties as such is to break national solidarity at a most critical point. It gradually became clear that at most a small fanatical minority really "meant it" in this radical sense. The anxieties aroused by this really radical implication probably had a great deal to do with making the final resolution of the McCarthy episode possible. Though this was not an explicit item in the Senate indictment, it was fundamentally McCarthy's challenge to the higher-order consensus which was the underlying basis of his censure.

Only once in our national history has such a cleavage been driven to a really disastrous point. In the events that led to the Civil War, the question of loyalty to the Union could be related to a whole series of issues and ideological symbols on which the two regional sectors of the society could divide. There were in fact real and deep differences of social structure underlying the symbols and slogans, differences that divided the population into two sufficiently equal parts. McCarthyism could not split the country in this way because it did not reflect any clear-cut *structural* division but cut across the main structural divisions. The most generalized "style" issue of the Communist threat could not split the more differentiated structural solidarities. No clear-cut line could be drawn between elements that could be activated pro and con around the Communist symbol as they were around slavery and secession. Later in this chapter I will say a little more about the nature of the disturbance that made it possible for McCarthyism to get as far as it did.

The level where the problem of cleavage and consensus next arises involves bases of solidarity not in the *first instance* political. The broad picture has already been sketched and is clearly delineated in *Voting* and the other studies. The general relationships between party alignment and socioeconomic status, occupation, ethnicity, and religion are by now well established.

Almost equally important, however, is the looseness of this relation. Shifts in the alignment are continually occurring, largely reflecting processes of change in the social structure, but with an important feedback from political action.

The very looseness of the relation between structural solidarities other than political party and the party structure itself can be said to constitute an important protection against the divisive potentialities of cleavage. The essential fact here is that most structurally important groupings in the society will contain considerable proportions of adherents of *both* parties.[24] To an important degree therefore the structural ties that bind them together on nonpolitical bases cut across their political allegiances. Hence the tendency to political cleavage will tend to be checked by a set of mechanisms that operate *below* the level of party division as well as by the more general national consensus that operates above that level. The pressure of political cleavage—by activating ties of solidarity at the more differentiated structural levels that cut across the line of cleavage—tends automatically to bring countervailing forces into play. The point of view of an individual voter is likely to be, "My fellow union member (lodge member, coreligionist, office colleague, and so forth) who is intending to vote Republican (Democratic) is in general a pretty decent guy. I just can't see how all people who hold his views can be as bad as they're made out to be." Awareness that this type of sentiment will be activated may put a certain restraint on extremism in the campaign.

24. *Ibid.,* chap. 4.

This mechanism may be said to be the obverse of what the authors of *Voting* and of *The People's Choice* call "activation."[25] In the case just described, the activation of essentially nonpolitical sentiments of solidarity acts as a brake on processes leading to divisive cleavage. Activation in the meaning of the studies, on the other hand, works as a stabilizing mechanism with reference to party alignments. It is clear that the pluralistic nature of the general social structure is so important that if nonpolitical solidarities were too strong, the necessary generalization of support which the party system requires could not be assured. The evidence from the studies seems to show that the principal direct effect of the political campaign itself on vacillating voters is to reactivate the voting preferences that predominate in the individual's past history and predominate in the solidary groups to which he is currently attached.[26]

At the psychological level this process is related to nonrational mechanisms. The very conception of rationality implies a certain ordered responsiveness to changes and shifts in the external situation. There is hence an inherent connection between nonrationality and the relative absence of such flexible *responsiveness*. If the nonrational reaction, however, is to be *ordered* it must, inherently I think, lead to a conservative response. In its impact on the individual voter the effect of the campaign is to intensify the urgency of situational stimuli. Insofar as the response is an orderly one, it has to be in terms of established patterns of voting behavior, that is, a "traditionalistic" response.

There are two main alternatives to this traditionalistic pattern of response. One is clearly delineated by the authors, the other not. The first has already been discussed as the response to cross-pressures—namely, low intensity of political interest, relative indifference, and readiness to shift political allegiance. The other, illustrated by McCarthyism, is openness to a certain type of "charismatic" appeal, to extremism and emotionalism.[27] The first is well integrated in the political system and may be said to be the normal mechanism that mediates shifts in the political balance. It is, I think, an example of what Durkheim called an "egoistic" response to strain. The second is perhaps the major type of "pathology" of our system and, if not controlled, may have highly disruptive conse-

25. Cf. especially P. F. Lazarsfeld, B. R. Berelson, and Hazel Gaudet, *The People's Choice* (2d ed.; New York: Columbia University Press, 1948), Introduction.
26. Berelson, Lazarsfeld, and McPhee, *op. cit.*, pp. 262–72, in connection with the "Fair Deal Rally."
27. This problem is discussed at greater length in the two essays on naziism in Talcott Parsons, *Essays in Sociological Theory* (2d ed.; Glencoe, Ill.: The Free Press, 1954).

quences. In Durkheim's term, it is the "anomic" response. Let us discuss each of these briefly in turn.[28]

The "indifference" reaction results when the individual, faced with a difficult conflict situation, reacts with conservative caution. Typically, he is playing with the idea of taking a new venture, of voting contrary to the voting traditions he himself has observed and/or which are observed by many of the people with whom he has important solidary ties—his relatives, friends, or associates. He hesitates, and is slow to make up his mind. If he actually does make the shift, he is likely to have been considering it since before the campaign began. But if the pressure on him is intensified through the campaign, his tendency is to retreat from his tentative overtures to the safer haven of his own accustomed pattern or that of his older and more tried associates. Finally the steps he takes are, typically, not radical ones, but from the more conservative side of the Democratic spectrum to the liberal side of the Republican or vice versa. These findings are of the first importance to the understanding of how the system functions.

By this process the voter is moving cautiously into unknown territory. He feels his way and does not actually move until sure he "has a place to go," assured that he will be accepted into the solidary groups with whom he newly identifies himself by his vote. Furthermore there is another important finding, namely that called by the authors the "breakage" effect. When the solidary groups in the voter's immediate personal environment are badly split, he is more likely to vote with the prevailing majority in the larger local community—he shifts his solidarity identification to a higher-order grouping.[29]

It is true that these tactics of the voter do not correspond to the stereotype of the classical independent voter with his sophisticated rational choice. But this newly discovered changeable voter has one trait consistent with that stereotype: he shows a kind of (albeit negative) sense of responsibility. He does not jump or panic lightly into extreme shifts of allegiance. When he does move it is cautiously and not very far. When pressed he tends to retreat to safe ground. By and large he does not rock the boat. But he is the primary agent in shifting the balance of political forces. In favorable circumstances this shift is accomplished without any deep or lasting cleavage.

28. These terms were used by Emile Durkheim in *Suicide* (Glencoe, Ill.: The Free Press, 1951), but can be generalized to include modes of reaction to strain in other fields. A third type of response illustrated by Eisenhower's special popularity will be commented on briefly later in this chapter.
29. Berelson, Lazarsfeld, and McPhee, *op. cit.,* pp. 116–17.

In addition to the considerations already brought forward it is perhaps relevant to note that voting is marginal and peripheral for the average citizen. He has many role-involvements in his sphere of private affairs and simply cannot be a sophisticated political expert. When the various factors playing on the "average voter" are combined, they add up to a relatively well-adapted set of mechanisms that facilitate shifts of balance without activating seriously divisive cleavages—as the authors of *Voting* clearly point out.

The mechanism *can*, however, get seriously out of order, and then the types of "secondary defense" just discussed become necessary. The most recent example is the McCarthyism episode; hence a few further remarks about it may be in order.[30]

By and large the people to whom McCarthyism appealed were people subject to cross-pressures, for example, members of ethnic groups of recently low but rising status, and members of other ethnic groups, such as people of German origin in the Midwest who in World War II felt a conflict between their patriotism and their German traditions.[31] It seems very likely that many of them were members of solidary groups that were severely split.[32]

It may not be amiss to suggest that they represented a second sort of "breakage effect," not into the safe haven of the majority position in the community, but in response to a violently emotional symbolic appeal, sharply dissociated from the realities of the domestic scene. The central symbol—"communism"—represented a magical danger. Behind the scenes a treasonous conspiracy allegedly threatened the security of everything American. In this context communism can be interpreted as a symbol to which many of the relatively free-floating anxieties of our society could be transferred. Above all it was anxiety-generated. Associated with it was regression to a romantically nostalgic fantasied "Americanism" from which many of the realities of the modern world were pleasantly absent—not only Communists in a literal sense, but bureaucrats, intellectuals, and various others, even in the wilder flights the income tax itself. This anomic response was not the "rational" alternative to the indifference response, but was wildly aggressive scapegoating and

30. See Talcott Parsons, "McCarthyism and American Social Tensions," *Yale Review*, Winter, 1955. Reprinted under the title "Social Strains in America," chap. 5, in Daniel Bell (ed.), *The New American Right* (New York: Criterion Books, 1955). See also the other essays in that volume.
31. This and other cross-pressure situations are discussed in S. A. Lubell, *The Future of American Politics* (New York: Harper, 1952).
32. See S. A. Stouffer, *Communism, Conformity, and Civil Liberties* (New York: Doubleday, 1955) for some evidence on these points. See also Bell, *op. cit.*

irresponsible withdrawal from disturbing reality. I suggest that too serious disturbance of the conservatism of the indifference response is likely to activate the McCarthyite type—which in content might be a "radical" rather than a "reactionary" Populism next time.[33]

In this connection it may be appropriate to make a few remarks about the phenomenon of Eisenhower popularity. This also is something of a departure from the main normal type called above the indifference pattern. Eisenhower, that is, seems to have exercised a kind of "charismatic" appeal that has shaken a certain proportion of voters out of their normal allegiances. The appeal seems to run in a "conservative" direction and may be likened to a "breakage effect," which the authors of *Voting* discussed on the level of the local community. At the present moment the country may have at the presidential level a *small* Republican majority. The mood of the country may be relatively conservative, more concerned with stability and integration than with positive action—though it is by no means certain that this is true, and even less certain that this will still be true in 1960. In any event, the Eisenhower margin of 1956 substantially exceeded such a "normal" Republican majority if it existed then.[34]

One further aspect of consensus and its relation to political balance may be discussed briefly. The authors of *Voting* seem to show some un-

33. On the historical and analytical associations of McCarthyism and Populism, see E. A. Shils, *The Torment of Secrecy* (Glencoe, Ill.: The Free Press, 1956).

34. Three types of evidence may be cited in favor of this interpretation. The first is the unusual amount of ballot-splitting of 1956 which led to the selection of a slightly Democratic Congress in the same election that produced a Republican landslide for the presidency. This strongly suggests that it is not conservatism in the party sense which alone accounts for the result. The second point is the unusual margin by which the vote of the sexes differed; when other factors are held constant, there was something like a 5 per cent excess of women's votes for Eisenhower. Generally speaking political attitudes of women tend to be more conservative than those of men, for good sociological reasons. [See S. A. Stouffer, *op. cit.*, for evidence that women's attitudes toward radicalism or nonconformity are markedly more conservative than are those of men.] But the difference was, particularly in the second Eisenhower election, substantially greater than normal. Finally, the third bit of evidence is the magnitude of the shift to Eisenhower occasioned by the international crises over Egypt and Hungary. It is authoritatively estimated that about 5 per cent of Eisenhower's vote was attributable to this shift. Hence if the international situation had been calm and if women had divided in the same ratio as men, there is a probability that Stevenson would have been elected by a small margin.

The Republican slogan of "Peace and Prosperity" expresses well the basis of the Eisenhower appeal. [In Durkheim's terms this may be said to be an "altruistic" pattern of response; a flight into identification with a national symbol relatively independent of party.] It seems to rest above all in a need to find a base of security through national solidarity in a world felt to be full of uncertainties and threats. There seems to have been a general feeling that with "Ike" in the White House things would be safer than otherwise.

certainties in their assessment of the effects of the campaign. It is, of course, striking how few votes it seems to change and how it tends to drive the vacillators back into their traditional allegiances. It is further true that, in the classical theory, the function of the campaign is to "persuade" the voter to adopt the "reasonable" position. Though it clearly does not have this effect (as it should according to the classical formula), may it not be possible that there are certain other consequences of importance?

A few straws of evidence in the findings suggest this may be true. First, it is noted that in the course of the campaign *political* bases of solidarity are strengthened at the expense of *social* bases.[35] Secondly, it was found that opinion leaders support the party position on subsidiary issues more strongly than do voters who are not opinion leaders.[36] It is also true that opinion leaders are politically more interested than others and, though dispersed throughout the social structure, are slightly higher in status than those they lead.[37] Finally, it is noted that exposure to the mass media increases interest in the campaign and strength of feeling about it, but also that voters select media matter to confirm their presuppositions.[38]

From the point of view of bringing about the main shift of political allegiances, the campaign seems relatively "functionless"; it is a "ritual." But from another point of view, if I interpret this evidence correctly, it seems to serve a very important function. This is, essentially, *to reinforce the generalization of support,* which has been shown above to be an essential condition of the functioning of a two-party democratic system.[39] Thus, first, the "social" bases of solidarity are, from the point of view of *political* integration of the society, more particularized than the political. The greater emphases on the political solidarities may thus be interpreted as a shift in the direction of generalization.

Second, the opinion leaders seem to be agents of this process in that, through supporting the party position on subsidiary issues, they serve to

35. Berelson, Lazarsfeld, and McPhee, *op. cit.,* pp. 34, 252. By political is clearly meant party bases.
36. *Ibid.,* p. 117.
37. *Ibid.,* pp. 116–117.
38. *Ibid.,* p. 251. The studies point out that the mass media are not so directly influential in getting the voter to change his political allegiance as is commonly supposed. Voters generally select campaign materials to confirm the position they hold regarding candidates and issues.
39. This is in accord with the theory of the junction of ritual advanced by Emile Durkheim in *The Elementary Forms of the Religious Life* (Glencoe, Ill.: The Free Press, 1947).

integrate the levels of generalization—what appeals to the more particularistic "interests" of special solidary groups, with what appeals to the more generalized level of the party. That the sources of such influence should be of somewhat higher social status than its objects is sociologically understandable. Generally the higher the status, the higher the level of political responsibility.

Third (and it would seem to fit the same context), the influence of the mass media works in the direction of increasing interest and strength of feeling. Interest and strength of feeling in this case concern the *outcome* of the campaign, which cannot be other than victory for one of the two major party candidates. Hence the interest and feeling become less concerned with the lower level interest-issues and more with the generalized question of which *party* is to win. Essentially this is to say that the effect of the campaign is to increase motivational commitment to the generalized support of the party, and thus to inhibit tendencies to particularistic fragmentation of the political system. The importance of this set of mechanisms is the more evident when it is considered that "when the chips are down" there is a strong tendency for people to revert to the more unproblematical loyalties. In a pluralistic, that is, highly differentiated, society like ours, this means loyalties closer to the "social" than to the "political" level of solidarity. In the major hierarchy of solidary integrations in a political reference, it means the decisions of voters are shifted closer to the "top" level of general societal integration than would otherwise happen.

Progress and Conservation

Finally, I would like to discuss briefly the balance between what the authors of *Voting* call "progress" and "conservation."

They emphasize the conservative tendencies activated by the campaign to reinforce established patterns of voting in different population groups. Yet, in the more "relaxed" periods between campaigns the newer trends, which almost by definition involve "deviance" from established patterns, establish a foothold. Usually the main question is whether this foothold is solid enough to withstand the stress of the campaign itself. In 1948 the Republican trend was not quite solid enough, but by 1952 it had become so. With all this I entirely agree.

There is, however, another aspect of the conservation-progress problem clearly brought out by the authors in one connection, though there are other important bits of evidence bearing on it in their findings which deserve further comment. This is its relation to the right-left balance of the two-party system discussed briefly above. One way of putting it is to say that (in one sense and on one level) the two-party system is a relatively "symmetrical" system, more or less evenly balanced between two trends on the most generalized level of support. From this point of view the political process has an oscillatory character, a swinging from relative predominance of one trend to that of the other and back again.

But looked at in the perspective of the dynamic development of the society, there is another aspect of this process, namely a structured relation to the general process of social change, which introduces a factor of *asymmetry* into the party structure. This aspect is, as noted above, structured in the form of division into a relatively "conservative" party in the political sense (the Republican, of course) and a relatively "liberal" party (the Democratic). I have stressed above that the conservatism of the Republican party is a conservatism in the field of *political* action; it is reluctant to sponsor too much *positive* use of governmental power for collective goals, particularly the *extension* of governmental power into areas where it has traditionally not been exercised. The Democratic party, on the other hand, has been more hospitable to positive political innovation, particularly in the fields of control of the economy, of welfare legislation, and of new commitments in foreign affairs. The traditional attitudes of the two parties in the field of government spending and fiscal policy reflect this difference.

The first bit of evidence that bears on this asymmetry is the authors' account of the type of appeal put forward by the two candidates in the 1948 campaign. As they say, Dewey stressed "style" issues that emphasized general consensus and tended to avoid controversial particularities. Truman, on the other hand, stressed "position" issues on which he advocated positive action. Dewey on the whole suggested that his election would have a quieting, unifying effect on the state of affairs, but did not stress positive new measures that needed to be taken; Truman did stress such measures, including repeal of the Taft-Hartley Act as a "new measure."[40]

The authors interpret this as the difference between a strategy appropriate to a candidate expecting to win, who hence does not wish to antagonize any important groups by advocating things they may oppose, and the strategy of one anticipating a struggle, who has to mobilize what support he can in order to come up from behind. This may well be an important factor in the difference, but I feel confident that there is an-

40. Berelson, Lazarsfeld, and McPhee, *op. cit.*, pp. 129, 251.

other aspect equally important. This is that the *conservative* party, in the sense just outlined, has broadly an interest in quieting things down politically, in damping the urgency of demands for specific and positive action. The *liberal* party, on the other hand, has an interest in arousing the public to the urgencies of action and tends to stress such action issues whenever they seem to be politically opportune.

Of course there are occasions when (rightly or wrongly) a threat to stability is felt to exist. Then there may be a demand for urgent action from the right. The "communism in government" and the "corruption" issues in 1952 are cases in point.[41] But by and large the policy of emphasizing consensus certainly has been the main Republican trend in the last three elections. Stevenson's attack on the (to him) too negative conception of the presidency by Eisenhower in the last election illustrates the point directly. Of course confirmation of this generalization would require a wider basis of fact, going back into earlier campaigns, which unfortunately has not been possible in connection with this chapter.

A second finding of the study illustrates a slightly different, though related, aspect of the right-left differentiation of the system. I have emphasized the central position of our business system in defining the relations of right and left. Differential wealth, particularly benefits to a conspicuously wealthy upper economic group, constitutes one of the most publicly salient consequences of situations favorable to the business system. This raises questions of the justice of the degree of inequality of wealth thus highlighted. Throughout our national history there has been partisan controversy about the justice and relation to national welfare of the financial rewards of the highest income groups, starting with the Jefferson-Hamilton differences. It is not surprising that the position of the wealthiest should be a target of attack from the left.

Republican voters held the view that a Republican electoral victory would benefit all classes of the society without exception, but the Democratic voters felt that a Democratic victory would benefit all classes except the wealthy.[42] This element of asymmetry in the views of adherents of the two parties is directly congruent with the interpretation of the nature of the difference between the parties, which has been put forward here. It is a special case of the general tendency of Republicans to emphasize highly general consensus, of Democrats to emphasize more specific issues that demand positive action.

41. This seems to be the most reasonable interpretation of the British-French intervention in Egypt in the fall of 1956 and indeed also, in one aspect at least, of the Soviet intervention in Hungary.
42. Berelson, Lazarsfeld, and McPhee, *op. cit.*, p. 87.

There is, finally, the interesting line of evidence bearing on the question of the right-left problem, which is presented directly in this light by the authors. They outline a very interesting conception of a time sequence in which issues come to and leave the center of political controversy. They speak of a "gateway" to political relevance.[43] Before the time is ripe, by approaching this gateway, an issue may be seen, particularly in hindsight, to be gaining in importance, but it is not politically resonant and somehow does not serve to create much interest or excitement in a campaign. Then there is an optimum time when taking up the issue pays handsome political dividends. Finally, the issue later fails to continue in the center of attention and gradually becomes "dead." It seems fair to say that "communism in government" could not have been made a central issue as early as 1948, that in 1952 it was moving into the "gateway," but that by 1956 it had become a dead issue. The Republicans not only did not, but could not, make important political capital of it as late as that—and not only because a Republican administration had been in office for four years.[44] It would be my prediction that though the issue of federal aid to public education was in the 1956 election just approaching the "gateway" but not yet close enough to be a big issue, by 1960 it will be in the middle of the gateway.

This pattern applies, I think, to issues pressed by both sides, indeed I have used one from each side as examples. But, nonetheless, as the authors themselves suggest,[45] the basic asymmetry that has appeared in the other connections applies here. The Republican issues that come through the gateway tend to be "defensive" issues, namely they tend to concern real or alleged "dangers" to the system which must be warded off. Restriction of immigration, which came to a head in 1924, is an example, as are pressures for tariff increases. The Democratic issues, on the other hand, tend to be positive innovations that require political mobilization to be put through.

The gateway theory thus formulates a very important pattern of the history of American politics, of which the element of party asymmetry is the aspect in which I am primarily interested. The central phenomenon starts with the pressing of a policy by the party of the left, in recent times the Democrats. The policy is opposed by the right, that is, the Republicans, sometimes bitterly. There are many alarmist views expressed that

43. *Ibid.*, pp. 206–12.
44. The "gateway" theory thus, rightly in my opinion, throws strong doubt on the depth of the wisdom of the anonymous Republican pundit of early 1954 who is reported as having said, "We could stay in office indefinitely just by running against Joe Stalin and Dean Acheson."
45. Cf. Berelson, Lazarsfeld, and McPhee, *op. cit.*, pp. 207–9.

the policy will ruin the country and destroy the unique virtues of the "American system." Then the measure, or a series of them, is enacted. Relatively quickly after enactment the excitement dies down, and the new situation comes to be accepted by its former opponents, for the most part with good grace, though there often is a little company of die-hards who remain irreconcilable for a long time. As the authors point out there is a spectrum of relative enthusiasm from left to right. But when the next Republican administration comes along it does not try seriously to reverse the policy or restore the *status quo ante*. There may well be some modifications of what are felt to be "abuses," but on the whole the main phenomenon is acceptance; indeed there is probably as much modest extension as paring back. The main pattern introduced by the new policy thus becomes institutionalized and an essential part of the social structure of the country.

The more obvious examples come from the fields of control of business practices and social welfare legislation. Thus the Federal Reserve Act, the Securities and Exchange Act, the Wagner Act, and the Social Security Act, were all Democratic measures—every one of which was strongly contested by the Republican party, not merely the "radical right" but the main party. Every one of them has come to be fundamentally accepted by that party with no attempt to undo the work. For example, the changes in the "charter of labor" introduced by the Taft-Hartley Act are on the whole secondary, and the present administration boasts of having extended the coverage of Social Security benefits, although their party predecessors of the 1930's widely predicted that the Act itself would destroy the moral independence of the American working population.

I am not in a position to present here a careful appraisal over a long historical period, but I think it is safe to generalize, first, that in American history the considerable majority of policies judged to have resulted in major modifications of the social structure through government action have been sponsored by the party of the left and, at the time, opposed by the party of the right.[46] Secondly, however, the majority of these policies have resulted in fully institutionalized features of the society— their consequences have come to be accepted in the society as a whole, and we have "gone on from there."

The findings of *Voting* clearly indicate that the American two-party system is a mechanism by which, at any *given* time, a relative equilibrating balance in a pluralistic society is maintained, so that conflicts and divisive tendencies are controlled and more or less fully resolved. It is

46. The administration of Theodore Roosevelt cannot be considered to have been a "typical" Republican administration in these terms.

also, seen over a period of time, a principal mechanism—though by no means the only one—by which the process of structural change in the society operates. The position of government in any modern society is such that it cannot be insulated from the broader process of social change. What happens at the governmental level both reflects these changes and is itself a major instrumentality in carrying them through. The main mechanism which adjusts the balance between the "reflection" aspect of the process and the "instrumentality" aspect is the raising and finally the resolution of issues through the operation of the party system. The essential point is that new things do "get done" and that the consequences do come to be accepted. In view of what sociologists now know of the intensity of the tensions and stresses generated by major processes of social change, the relative effectiveness of this set of mechanisms is impressive. Again, in view of the importance of this aspect for the whole process of political adjustment, the importance of the mechanisms involved in what has above been called the "conservative" or "indifference" pattern of the change of position of voters is again emphasized. There is a great deal of sociopolitical dynamite in the political process in a rapidly changing society. That it breaks over into charismatic "radicalism"—of right or left—so seldom and that these "fires" have usually been so relatively quickly extinguished, is testimony to the power of the mechanisms of social control which operate in this area. The authors of *Voting* have given us notable insight into the way these mechanisms operate.

Conclusion

It has not been possible in this chapter to review more than a sample of the rich and suggestive findings presented in *Voting*, to say nothing of the other related studies. My purpose has not, however, been to present a complete review, critical or otherwise, but to try to establish the relations between certain of these findings and a theoretical model of the operation of a two-party democratic political system. I have therefore selected for consideration the findings that seemed to be most directly relevant to the empirical problems involved in the model.

The model has been constructed essentially by extending a pattern of theoretical analysis which had been worked out in connection with the economy as a subsystem of the society, in interaction with other subsystems,[47] to the "polity" conceived as another subsystem of the society cognate with the economy. The polity in this sense is essentially the set

47. Presented in Parsons and Smelser, *op. cit.*

of societal mechanisms which makes the generation of power in the political sense possible. In constructing this model I have of course leaned heavily on the literature of political theory.

It was possible to discuss here, as specifically relevant to the voting process, only part of an as yet incomplete model. This part, however, deals with a crucial aspect of the total system, the process by which the "goal-attainment" adjustments of the polity work out through interchange with another subsystem of the society, here vaguely referred to as the "public." The interchange in question is thought of as involving, at a higher level of generalization, the interchange of "leadership" responsibility for "support," at a lower level, that of "binding decisions" for "advocacy of policies."

On the gross structural level the essential facts about the American system are that it is a constitutionally regulated, "democratic" two-party system operating in a society that is primarily oriented to growth of economic productivity and involved in a dynamic process of general internal social change as well as a highly unstable international situation. Within this framework, if the political system is, in the relation between leadership and support, to be a relatively stable one that can integrate multifarious pluralistic interests and yet adapt to changing conditions, it must, within broadly specifiable limits, have certain characteristics. By applying the model to the general structure it was possible to identify four main areas in which to look for mechanisms relevant to these functional requirements.

These, the reader will remember, concerned (1) the relations between the nonrational psychological mechanisms that must be imputed to the "average voter" and the reference points of voting decisions in the structure of solidary groupings of the society which formed the main basis of stability of the system; (2) the element of flexibility necessary to allow sufficient shift of votes to permit a two-party system to function effectively without introducing unduly disruptive elements into the system; (3) mechanisms that will organize the limited polarization that a two-party system requires and yet protect the integration of the society against too deep-seated divisive forces; and (4) mechanisms that will mediate the processes of adaptation to structural change in a rapidly evolving society.

These requirements were found to correspond very closely with four of the balances formulated by the authors of *Voting* in their final chapter. The first two of my functional requirements were related to the balances of stability and flexibility and of involvement and indifference, the third to that between consensus and cleavage, and the fourth to that between progress and conservation. The fifth of the authors' balances, between individualism and collectivism, seemed to me to correspond to the more general need for balance between effective leadership and the generalization of support which has formed the main analytical thread of the whole discussion. It hence seems to me to stand on a different level from the other four. For these reasons I organized my more detailed review of the relevant findings of *Voting* about the relation between my four propositions and the first four of the authors' balances just mentioned.

Particularly in their final chapter, but also at various points throughout the volume, the authors make generalizations from their findings which come halfway or more toward the generalizations that would have been generated deductively by use of the theoretical model with which I have been working. Hence it is not any originality of empirical insight into the workings of the American political system which I wish to claim; most of what is relevant is present and clearly stated in the book.

What is important in the present connection is rather the *fit* of these findings and conclusions with a more generalized conceptual scheme. This fit strengthens the impression from the authors' own exposition that there is an important *internal consistency* in the main structure of their findings and interpretations. In the light of the above discussion it seems to me inconceivable that the facts should be just a random collection of discrete items with no essential connection with each other. But beyond the question of internal consistency, such a fit strongly suggests the feasibility of extending a coherent analysis of the American political system in its connections with other aspects of the society, economic, institutional, and otherwise. Here I have stressed only that *theoretical* congruence exists with a part of a model for the analysis of the economy. But the political and the economic analyses are both parts of a still wider theoretical scheme that I may call a general theory of social systems.

I have attempted to take only a first step in the codification of the data of empirical studies of voting with this body of theory. These results, and of course other data, as noted, need to be fitted into other aspects of the problems of the polity. Only part of the American political system has been treated here. The American case needs to be treated in wider historical perspective and, comparatively, in relations of similarity and difference, with other political systems. Finally, of course, the political aspect of society needs to be much more systematically related to other aspects of the societies in which political systems function.

In spite of the modesty of the step here taken, it seems to me that it illustrates a kind of opportunity of which social scientists should take careful cognizance. If detailed empirical studies of the type of the voting studies can produce findings and empirical generalizations that fit as closely with deductions from highly general theory as seems to be true in this instance,[48] the prospects of a *cumulative* development of codified and systematic knowledge in this field seem to be better than they have often been thought to be. In my opinion this is not an isolated instance. Intensive work on both sides, and repeated attempts at codification, should produce important results.

Technical Note

As has several times been noted in this chapter, the main framework of the analysis it contains was not generated *ad hoc* in an attempt to interpret the results of the studies of voting behavior, but was developed independently and applied to these results. For the reader who may be interested in the technical aspects of the scheme employed, it seemed advisable to include a brief outline of the most important elements of the scheme, and their genesis.

The main background of the analysis is a generalized conceptual scheme for the analysis of social systems, which in turn is part of a still more generalized scheme for the analysis of action.[49] The basic outline of the social system scheme which is employed here was set forth first in *Working Papers in the Theory of Action.*[50] The most essential feature of this latter formulation was the merging of a scheme of "pattern variables"

48. It is of course extremely important to be clear about the sense in which I am and am not advancing a claim to a deductive anticipation of the findings of *Voting* and other studies. As I have stated it above, "it was possible to identify four main areas in which to look for mechanisms relevant to these functional requirements." Given the "gross structural facts" of the American political system, ascertainment of which does not require technical research procedures, in terms of such a "functional" model it is possible to deduce that there must be mechanisms that operate in each of these areas, and that they must operate within certain limits if the degree of stability of the system which has historically obtained is to be accounted for. In addition to these and various other sociological considerations I have postulated certain simple psychological assumptions about the limitations of rational decision-making by the individual and the kinds of psychological mechanisms that can be expected to operate where rational decision-making is impossible.

This, however, is very different from deducing the *specific* findings of the empirical research. Of course this has not been done. I have only provided certain "theoretical boxes" into which these findings can be fitted and have tested the goodness of fit in a broad way. One of the main reasons why I could not possibly have deduced the specific findings is that they must in the nature of the case be functions of whole ranges of factors not considered in my model. The model itself is necessarily abstract and deals with only part of the specifically political aspects of the concrete phenomena.

49. See Talcott Parsons and E. A. Shils, *Toward a General Theory of Action* (Cambridge, Mass.: Harvard University Press, 1951).

50. Talcott Parsons, R. F. Bales, and E. A. Shils, *Working Papers in the Theory of Action* (Glencoe, Ill.: The Free Press, 1953). See especially chaps. 3 and 5.

put forward by Parsons and Shils with a scheme of the functional requirements of social systems originally put forward by Bales.[51]

The basis of this scheme is the idea that any social system may be analyzed in terms of four logically independent functional requirements, which we formulate as *adaptation, goal-attainment, integration,* and *latent pattern-maintenance.* For these we have, for convenience, adopted the notation *A, G, I, L.* These four functional requirements were interpreted as the *dimensions* along which variations in the state of a social system could be analyzed.[52]

Within the framework of this general scheme special attention has been paid to the fact that complex social systems should be conceived as differentiated into (hence made up of) a plurality of *subsystems.* Following the general lead of biological theory we have conceived that the most promising *initial* approach to the nature of the differentiation of such subsystems, and hence of their classification, lay in the concept of function as the basis of differentiation. Starting with the conception of a highly differentiated society, this conception was applied to the idea of the *economy,* as this has been used in economic theory, and it was found that the economists' conception fitted admirably with the specifications of an adaptive subsystem of a society as worked out in terms of this general theory of social systems.[53]

The whole conception of a social system which was delineated as distinct from "situation" or "environment" external to it, has implied the existence and importance of processes of interchange between system and environment which could be formulated in terms of the concepts of input and output. But further, if the system of reference is a subsystem of a larger system, these inputs and outputs would not likely, with respect to their sources and destinations, be randomly distributed over the environment as a whole, but would have relatively specific sources and destinations capable of theoretical identification.

Since we were operating with a theoretical scheme that involved four basic functional categories, and since we had been able to treat the economy as *primarily* (in an empirical sense *never* exclusively) identified with *one* of these categories (the adaptive), it seemed sensible to attempt to work out the logic of a system in which each of the four categories was the basis of a differentiated subsystem of the society. By elementary logic each such subsystem would have three boundaries internal to the system

51. R. F. Bales, *Interaction Process Analysis* (Reading, Mass.: Addison-Wesley, 1950).
52. Parsons, Bales, and Shils, *op. cit.,* chap. 3.
53. See Parsons and Smelser, *op. cit.*

vis-à-vis each of the other three, and a fourth boundary in some sense "external" to the system. Once seen in this light, the logical requirements of this reasoning corresponded with startling exactitude to the scheme, well established in economic theory, of classification of the factors of production and the shares of income. The factors of production, that is, could be treated as categories of input into the economy from "outside" and the shares of income as categories of output from the economy to the outside.

The next analytical problem was to identify the source-destination subsystems for each input-output and to determine which was the one "external" boundary. The key to this identification turned out to be the conception of the *goal* of the economy as *production* vis-à-vis the "consumer" identified as a member of the household. The output of production was conceived to be the goal-attainment output of the economy and to go to the household, which had already[54] been identified as belonging to the "pattern-maintenance" subsystem. With two further steps, which are detailed in *Economy and Society* and hence need not be repeated here, this type of reasoning led to setting up the following paradigm[55] of boundary-interchanges between four functionally primary subsystems of a society:

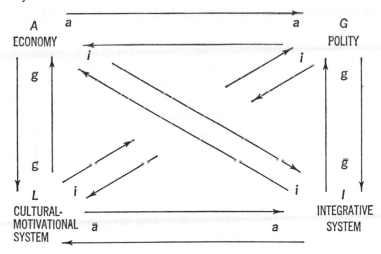

Three further implications, of special interest in the present context, followed from this. First, the category of "land" and its output cognate, "rent," clearly constituted the focus of the "external" boundary of the economy as a system. The sense in which land is a special case among

54. Cf. Parsons, Bales, and Shils, *op. cit.*, chap. 5, pp. 264 ff.
55. Parsons and Smelser, *op. cit.*, Fig. 4, p. 68.

the factors of production in economic theory corresponds directly with that in which the function of pattern-maintenance has been treated as a special case in general social system theory.[56]

Second, as had already been well established in economic theory, it was, in a sufficiently differentiated society, not possible to limit consideration to a *single* interchange of inputs and outputs at any one boundary, but it was necessary to consider a *double* interchange. In the economy-household case this is a direct consequence of the division of labor and means that the source of wage income (the employing organization) is typically not the same as the producer of most consumers' goods purchased. Hence money, as income and as a medium of exchange for the purchase of desired goods, is a necessary intermediary mechanism in an economic *system*.

Third, it became clear that the boundary-interchange between a postulated polity, as the goal-attaining subsystem of the society, and the integrative system should be theoretically cognate with that between economy and household. To put it in the terms used above, the main output of the polity to the integrative system is effective leadership, which is a form of power, and the main input into the polity from the integrative system is generalized support. Or, to put it a little differently, the *goal* of the polity is the production or generation of effective leadership and, on the less general level, of binding decisions.

It was within this framework of analysis of input-and-output relations between primary functional subsystems of the society that a beginning has been made in the attempt to work out a conception of the polity as cognate with the economy and of its goal-attainment boundary interchange, which has been the main subject of this chapter.

Certain features of the adaptive boundary of the polity were already given because it stood (in our scheme) vis-à-vis the economy. From the economic point of view it was the boundary concerned with the input of capital resources to the economy from the polity. But it proved to be a long and difficult task to formulate the categories relevant to the double boundary-interchange at the *goal-attaining* boundary of the polity which, according to the logic of our paradigm, stands vis-à-vis the integrative system and does not directly involve the economy at all. It was only here that the scheme used was fully worked out, though the categories of support and binding decisions had been worked with for some time. The scheme in its present form is obviously tentative.

The reader who has followed this rather involved theoretical argu-

56. For the detailed argument see Parsons and Smelser, *op. cit.*

ment (which he very likely cannot do without familiarity with the sources cited) may comprehend why it was so exciting to find that the results of the voting studies placed the primary basis of political support in the structure of solidary groups of the society: in our theoretical terms, *this is the integrative system* which, on the most general theoretical grounds, would be *predicted* to be the *primary* source. More generally, the deduced characteristics of a double level of interchange between polity and public turned out to fit the empirical findings of the studies with exciting exactitude.

One further technical point may finally be made: It should be clearly understood that, in terms of the technical paradigm I have used, this analysis does *not* deal with the polity as a system. The system of reference is the processes of input-output interchange between polity and integrative system (as "public"). In *Economy and Society* we dealt extensively with this type of system, the economically relevant prototype being a market. Thus we held that the interchange between economy and household may be treated as composed of two primary markets, the labor market and the market for consumers' goods. Similar logic was applied to the capital market and all of these were, in a strict sense, treated as social systems.[57]

Of course, empirically, the process of election of a President is most emphatically *not* a market in the economic sense. But in formal theoretical terms it was the paradigm worked out for the analysis of markets which proved most fruitful in analyzing the voting process. Seen in these terms, my first proposition about nonrational mechanisms in relation to solidary groupings concerned the "latent pattern-maintenance" basis of the system; the second about flexibility in pursuit of goals concerned its goal-attainment function; the third about control of divisive polarization concerned its integration; and the fourth dealing with its relation to the changing structure of the society concerned its adaptive function. These propositions are thus not arbitrary functional generalizations plucked "out of the air" and not dictated by the formal theoretical scheme, but are carefully formulated to meet the specifications of a specific generalized theoretical paradigm.

This demonstration that the voting process can be considered a social system in the fullest technical sense and can be analyzed in terms of the analytical resources of social system theory, seems to me the important contribution of this chapter.

57. Parsons and Smelser, *op. cit.,* chap. 3.

CHAPTER 9

Some Reflections on the Place of Force
in Social Process

Though published a little later, this paper was written before
Chapters 10 and 11. It was first worked out for a conference on
Internal War held at Princeton in the fall of 1961, and was published in 1964 in a volume of that title edited by Harry Eckstein.
The relation between this paper and Chapter 10 is very close,
because of the sense in which the use of force is the ultimate,
"end-of-the-line," negative situational sanction. It was consideration of the implications of the place of force as a "last resort"
which did much to pave the way for the conception of power as
a generalized medium of interchange parallel to money, with force
occupying the place parallel to monetary metal. Its most important
function, then, in relatively stable political systems, comes to be
as a "reserve" rather than an instrumentality which is expected to
be used under normal conditions.

C ONSIDERING the scope of this volume, it has seemed to me that
the most useful contribution I could make would be to attempt a general
analytical approach to examining the place of force in the operation of
social systems. This theme, of course, runs through, not only the whole
of the present volume, but a vast body of literature in the political field.
There seems, however, to be a notable lack of concerted attempts at a
general theoretical attack on the problem. This essay may, it is hoped,
provide reference points that will help make some of the more empirical
analyses more meaningful in terms of their theoretical premises and
implications.

It is conceived as an application and further development of a general conceptual scheme for the analysis of social systems. The whole scheme cannot be presented here, but an attempt will be made to present the essential assumptions on which the more circumstantial discussion is based. It should also be kept in mind that the scheme is in process of continuing development, and reference to the author's previous writings probably cannot therefore provide full elucidation of the present bases of the argument in the scheme.[1]

Force and Systems of Normative Order

This volume's concern is with internal war, and of course the hallmark of war of any sort is violence. It is perhaps worth remarking initially that the line between internal and external war is theoretically a gradual one. A relatively established "politically organized society" is clearly a "moral community" to some degree, its members sharing common norms, values, and culture—that is to say that I start with a view that repudiates the idea that any political system that rests *entirely* on self-interest, force, or a combination of them, can be stable over any considerable period of time. If the politically organized community is a moral community, however, it is equally important that at least *some* elements of moral community have generally transcended the area of political sovereignty, in the usual sense. To give only essentially trite examples, certainly the Greeks who so self-consciously distinguished themselves from barbarians constituted such a community, so that the very prevalent wars between the *polis* units were in a sense "civil wars." In more recent times, the conception of Christendom has not been a totally meaningless one, yet we are all too familiar with the prevalence of war in modern European history. Hence there is good reason to believe that a general treatment of the use of force in society will not be inapplicable simply because the internal and the external contexts of its use are radically different.

The primary reference for the concept of force—a term that I prefer, on the whole, to "violence"—is as an aspect of social interaction. Force

1. Perhaps the most useful recent publications for this background purpose are, first, Part II of the "General Introduction" to *Theories of Society*, edited by Parsons, Shils, Naegele, and Pitts (New York: The Free Press of Glencoe, 1961); second, Parsons', *Structure and Process in Modern Societies* (New York: The Free Press of Glencoe, 1960); and, third, the paper on voting referred to below (Chapter 8 above). See also two papers written subsequently to the present one: "On the Concept of Influence," *Public Opinion Quarterly* (May, 1963), and "On the Concept of Political Power," *Proceedings of the American Philosophical Society* (June, 1963). (Chapters 11 and 10 respectively of this volume.)

is a "way" not necessarily always a "means"—in which one unit in a system of social interaction may act toward another, whether the unit be an individual or a collectivity. Within this framework, then, force is the use of control of the situation in which "alter"—the unit that is the object of "ego's" action—is subjected to *physical* means to prevent him from doing something ego does not wish him to do, to "punish" him for doing something that, from ego's point of view, he should not have done (which may in turn be intended to deter him from doing similar things in the future), or to demonstrate "symbolically" the capacity of ego to control the situation, even apart from ego's specific expectations that alter may desire to do things that are undesirable from ego's point of view. I do not speak of the use of force unless the action or its "threat" is "oriented" to an alter on whom it is expected to have an impact, e.g., by frightening him or of making it impossible for him to carry out his own actual or conceivable intentions.

Seen in this perspective, the concept of force as a "way" of acting is inherently negative in its meaning to alter. It always concerns the *undesired* consequences (although from *some* points of view not taken in this discussion, they may also be desired, as in the case of martyrdom)— that alter would on the face of it like to avoid—of *his* actually or potentially acting in a certain way. Thus if ego conducts certain physical operations in his environment that may unintentionally have an injurious effect on an alter—an accident caused by negligently fast driving of a car, for example—his action does not constitute "use of force" in social action, in the present sense. Nor would we, for present purposes, treat the "forcible" holding of a child for a hypodermic injection as a use of force; it is at most only a completely marginal case.

It is the "intention" of the actor in actually using or threatening force that is our central criterion, and such intentions we have classified in three types: *deterrence* from undesired action; *punishment* for negatively valued acts actually committed; and symbolic *demonstration* of capacity to act, without orientation to specific contexts of either deterrence or intention to punish.[2] It has already become evident that this classification,

2. We have spoken of both actors and objects as either individual or collective. When we refer to a collectivity as having "intentions," they are, of course, in the *psychological* sense, the intentions of individual persons acting in roles by virtue of which their decisions can bind the collectivity. Thus a general's decision to attack may be interpreted as activating a process involving the whole collectivity—the military units he commands. For most of our purposes, it is not necessary to pursue these problems of mechanism in the relation between collectivities and individual personalities—to say that "the Third Army Group intends to attack" is not merely metaphorical.

important as it is, is cut across by another that we must keep clearly in mind.

We have stated the problem of force in the frame of reference of social interaction. Interaction, however, is a process that occurs over time, and one of its most important characteristics is that an act of ego will be a stimulus to a reaction of alter, which will in turn be the stimulus to the next act of ego, and so forth. If ego then has an ultimate intention he hopes to realize, what we usually call a "goal," he will envisage a series of "interacts" between himself and alter in the period intervening between his initiation of the process and the possible consummation of his goal. The problem of how he intends to take account of the reciprocal intentions of alter and his actions in the intermediate stages thus becomes one of the central problems.

If we take deterrence as the simplest and, in many ways, the most important of the three meanings of force, another basic distinction immediately becomes evident. On the one hand, ego may attempt to deter alter by acting so as to make his carrying out undesired intentions realistically impossible—or nearly so. We would refer to this behavior as *compulsion*. A classic example would be the arrest and imprisonment of persons whose future action is feared, without giving them any choice in the matter. The alternative to compulsion in this respect is *coercion*. By this term, we mean "threatening" to use force *if* alter carries through the presumed undesired (by ego) intentions. If alter then disregards the threat and carries out his act, the use of force against him becomes a punishment, although the primary intention of ego may still be deterrence and he may be deeply regretful at having to carry out his threats and actually to resort to force. Conversely, of course, the actual implementation of force may, although it is a punishment in the particular case, be thought of more broadly as a deterrent, both for alter's future action—he may have been "taught a lesson"—and for third parties who thereby find out what happens to noncompliers, including the lesson that ego "means it" when he says the forbidden act should not be performed. There is an important relativity between the positive and the negative here. The last statement has been phrased in terms of the performance of acts that have been forbidden. For most of the purposes of our discussion, however, it would not matter if it were an omission of acts that had been prescribed. Thus failing to pay assessed taxes is as punishable as parking under a no-parking sign. For some purposes, however, it is important to distinguish these cases, since coercive threats may not be able to motivate new commitments in exactly the same way that they can deter from abandonment of those already assumed. This problem belongs in the general context of asymmetry between positive and negative motivation, which we will take up presently.

What we will call the "demonstration case," which in this particular context is a "show of force," clearly must have the meaning of intended deterrence and not immediately of punishment. It is not, however, made contingent on specific forbidden or disapproved acts. It may then be said to be of the nature of a *warning* rather than a threat, if the distinction may be made in terms of relative diffuseness *vs.* specificity. A threat then is a direct expression of intention to impose a specific negative sanction, contingent on performance of a forbidden or disapproved act; a warning is a demonstration of the capacity and readiness to act should alter perform any of a much wider range of actions undesired by ego. The appropriate "emotion" on alter's part, in response to a threat, is fear—to a warning, anxiety. In either case, of course, the negative emotion may be overcome by "courage" or "resolution." In popular speech, we often use unrealistic absolutes—we say he had no fear at all, when we really mean that his courage was sufficient to overcome his fear.

Force and the Problem of Social Control

It is implicit in the way we have approached the problem of the use of force that the primary common element of the three components of meaning we have distinguished is *control* to which, because of the context of interaction, we may add the adjective "social." Force is a way of trying to "make sure" that alter acts in a desired manner or refrains from acting in an undesired one. We have formulated the approach in terms of ego, conceived as a *unit* in a social system, that exercises control over the actions of other units, here called "alters." One highly relevant problem is, however, to determine how this formulation is related to the mechanisms by which the actions of all units in a system are controlled —or fail to be controlled—from the point of view of the operation of the system as a system. Before approaching this problem, it is necessary to place the problem of the use of force in a more general context at the level of the interaction of units of a system.

From this point of view of control, clearly the primary meaning of force is as deterrent. Indeed, from various points of view, it can be said to be the ultimate deterrent. This statement, however, clearly refers to the context we have called "compulsion." Truly effective imprisonment, which makes escape literally impossible—a limiting case—and blocks all communication between the prisoner and possible associates, can prevent his acting as he intended. Even more drastic is the killing of alter, since dead men do not act, in our sense—at least the possibilities of escape and of communication leaks are closed by "liquidation." The indirect consequences for the actions of others of knowledge that this compulsion has been exercised, introduces many complications, of course, so that groups perfectly able to use compulsion, and ardently desiring to do so, often refrain through consideration of the indirect consequences. But this point is aside from the main argument.

The use of force as threat or warning is, of course, much more problematical even in its more immediate consequences. As threat, alter may view it in terms of cost and he may consider noncompliance quite worthwhile. As warning it may be discounted in various ways or serve only to activate resistance. In the light of these complications, it becomes imperative to consider the problem of these possibilities, of compulsion as well as of deterrence, in a wider context. The essential point is that force is only one among a number of means of controlling the action of alters coercively and, furthermore, that coercion—even by other threats than those of force—is itself only one of several modes of controlling such action at the unit-to-unit level.

Let us approach the latter problem first. We presume here a paradigm in which, on the one hand, there are two main *channels* through which ego may seek to control alter's action and, on the other hand, there are two main *modes* of such control, modes that may in turn be subdivided according to whether or not options are left open to alter.

The channels are the exercise of control over the *situation* in which alter is placed and, control over his "intentions." The second dimension, which we have called a "mode" of control, is a matter of whether ego's actual or proposed action toward alter is favorable or unfavorable from alter's point of view. On the basis of *contingency* of ego's act on alter's response to his "definition of the situation" through a threat, for example—we may distinguish four types of attempted control:

1. Situational channel, positive sanction: the offer of positive advantages to alter, conditional on his compliance with ego's wishes or "suggestions." We call this process *inducement*. Economic exchange is the prototypical case.

2. Situational channel, negative sanction: the threat of disadvantage, imposed through ego's control of alter's situation, conditional on alter's

*non*compliance with ego's wishes or suggestions. This approach is what we have called *coercion*. The use of power is the prototypical case.

3. Intentional channel, positive sanction: the offer of "good reasons" why, in the circumstances and without either offer of contingent advantages or the threat of contingent disadvantages, ego argues that it is to the "interest" of alter to comply with ego's wishes or suggestions. This mode of control we will call *persuasion*. It includes transmitting information, in addition to an appeal to alter to do what he "really wants to do."

4. Intentional channel, negative sanction: the threat or warning that, independently of any advantageous or disadvantageous changes in the situation imposed contingently by ego, it would not be "right" for alter to fail to comply with ego's suggestions on how he should act, in terms of alter's *own* standards of right action. This mode we may call *activation of commitments*. Appeal to "conscience" is the prototypical case.

Each of these types can—with respect to the time left open to alter to make a decision, ego's "tolerance" of his position and hence willingness to hear his case, etc.—be "foreshortened" in the same basic sense in which compulsion, as we have discussed it, foreshortens coercion. Compulsion thus is the limiting case where alter is in principle left no alternative; "compliance" is simply "being compelled." In the case of inducement, the element of contingency may be constricted, or even eliminated, by ego "insisting" on "doing something for" alter, whether alter likes it or not. The *gift* in the ideal-type sense, which leaves no option of refusal open, is the prototypical case. To fit our paradigm, a gift in this sense must be something of situational value, rather than a purely symbolic expression of sentiment.

As a corresponding limit to contingency in case 4, we may speak of "moral compulsion"—putting alter in such an acute "dilemma of conscience" that it is "unthinkable" for him to choose an alternative other than the one ego desires. A suitable if extreme example would be the use of hostages to control the action of an alter beyond the range of physical control. Thus if a citizen of a totalitarian society is abroad, the totalitarian authorities may try to control him by threatening to kill or torture his next of kin, whom they do physically control, unless he complies with their wishes. Bringing about the torture or death of a spouse or child by failing to comply would be, at the level in question, "unthinkable."

For reasons that we will develop later, there is a special relation between what we have called persuasion and membership in solidary groups. If this relation is accepted, we may infer that, at the *social* level with which we are directly concerned, the limit of persuasion is simply assertion of the imperative meaning of the "we" that comprises ego and alter together. At that point persuasion is no longer merely the argument that, since you are a "such-and-such," you should comply with ego's wishes, that it is to your interest to "do so and so." The pressure is sharpened instead to the point where the assertion is that "we such-and-suches *do* so and so," with the clear implication that, if you do not, you are not "really" a such-and-such. The clear implication is that the such-and-such who does not comply is subject to exclusion. This implication raises further problems, but the immediate point is the assertion that "we do" certain things, and the question is whether or not alter will go along.

Sanctions and Generalized Mechanisms of Control

According to the above paradigm, the deterrent use of force against the specific alter is an appropriate sanction in only one of the four major types of action oriented to control of an alter by an ego. That is to say, it is preeminently a means of coercion, through conditional threat and, at the extreme limit, of compulsion through the prevention of undesired action by alter. If, for the time being, we focus on coercion as a case that leaves a range of choices open to alter yet is but one of four ways of controlling him by manipulating contingent sanctions, what can we say about the place of force among the means of coercing compliance through the threat of negative sanctions and about the relation of a set of threat-sanctions to others that can conceivably control behavior?

First, a coercive threat can be that of *any* alteration in the situation in which alter acts that ego has the capacity to impose, depending on alter's compliance or noncompliance. If, however, we adhere strictly to the prime meaning of deterrence, it seems possible to designate one major dimension of variation in degrees of severity of contingent situational negative sanctions. This dimension is the *power* of alter effectively to carry out his intentions, regardless of ego's wishes—not necessarily against them, but *independently* of them. This power, which is, as we shall see, dependent on a number of other factors, is vulnerable to situational negative sanctions—which we interpret as counterpower—through the factors of capacity and opportunity for its exercise. Capacity in turn means essentially command of the facilities necessary for effective action, while opportunity is access to the support of those units that have somehow become or expect to become dependent on the output of the units in question.

Negative sanctions then, consist, in the deterrent sense, of threatened deprivations of power, or the potential for effective action resulting from capacity, opportunity, or both. On this basis, it is possible to construct a scale of degrees of deprivation of effectiveness-potential. This step will necessitate, in turn, fitting a number of factors into an ordinal scale, which is too complex a problem to enter upon here. Suffice it to say that there seem to be two main sets that can be related in a tentative way. The criterion is the capacity of alter to affect adversely the interests of ego, in the simple sense of doing what ego does not want him to do, especially, we suggest, through enlisting the cooperation of third parties. One set of factors will comprise alter's resources without special constraints on how he shall use them. Thus monetary fines reduce his financial resources but do not impose limits on how he shall use those remaining to him. The other set comprises those special constraints.

Here the critical factor seems to be deprivation of liberty. Since in social conditions the most effective action is collective action, the most important liberty is liberty to cooperate with others, to participate in collective action. Furthermore, the most important single condition of effective cooperation is communication with others. The most important deprivations of liberty are therefore those that block communication, in order to limit or prevent altogether cooperation with others.

Physical force may be an important instrument in the enforcement of *any* deprivation. It is, however, intrinsic in the deprivation itself, particularly in deprivations of liberty. Although fines and taxation are backed by force, for example, the process of implementing such sanctions by taking over financial assets is ordinarily not a forcible one. If, however, an act of enforcement is challenged, the question of what to do in case of refusal to comply arises. This question can always lead to the problem of force, for resistance can be made effective by alter, through such physical means as leaving the field commanded by ego or removing assets from it. The ultimate preventive of such evasion is force. Hence in a very broad sense we conclude that force is an "end-of-the-line" conception of a type of negative sanction that can be effective—in the context of deterrence, please note—when milder measures fail.

From this argument it *must not* be inferred that what we are calling "power" is a simple linear function of the command of physical force. In the context of deterrence, we conceive force to be a residual means that, in a showdown, is more effective than any alternative. Power, on the other hand we conceive to be a *generalized medium* for controlling action—one among others—the effectiveness of which is dependent on a variety of factors of which control of force is only one, although a strategic one in *certain* contexts. To approach the problem of the relation between the two it is necessary to go back to the general paradigm of modes of social control.

We have held that coercion is one of a family of modes of controlling action in interunit relations, the others being inducement, persuasion, and activation of commitments. Similarly we hold that what we call "power" is one of a family of *generalized media* of the interaction process. The others are *money*, what, in a special sense, we call *influence*, and the special category of *commitments*. Because of its familiarity, it is best to begin the discussion with money.

Money is generally recognized to be a medium of exchange that is generalized in the sense that it is not simply another commodity but one that is acceptable in exchange for an indefinite range of different commodities and services. The latter category, as we shall argue, raises special problems. Money may be regarded from two points of view. On one hand, it is an institutionalized medium and measure, functioning in exchange transactions within a system. In this context, it is the medium to which units are expected to resort in securing access to resources through exchange and that they are obligated to accept in the case of *bona fide* offers—a binding obligation in areas where the concept of "legal tender" applies. On the other hand, from the point of view of the unit, it is a generalized *means* of securing what is wanted through the exchange process. But the reciprocal of using money to get what one wants is willingness to accept money in exchange for relinquishing rights in valued objects—accepting a valuation in money.

In common with both these levels is the fact that money is, in the first instance, a mechanism of communication; the monetary unit therefore is clearly a *symbol*. In a special prescriptive way—as categorized by Charles Morris—it symbolizes economic productivity. The prescription comes in its property of commanding a share of this productivity, specified as a particular commodity or service according to the wishes of the spender of money. Symbolization is, however, also involved in a second way, in that the concrete instrument—for example, a dollar bill—is a symbol to the unit and "in itself" is worthless." It does not seem to be stretching matters too far to say that money is a highly specialized language, in which things "said" are not merely informative but also imperative. Money is a generalized symbolic medium of inducement, in that its offer in specific amounts is the offer of a conditional improvement of the advantageousness of alter's situation: The more money he has, the greater is his command of the immense range of utilities purchasable in the market system.

The question then arises: On what basis does the "value of money" rest? Clearly, if what is offered is a symbol, it cannot rest on the "intrinsic" worth of the object concretely offered—in the case of cash, the paper bills are virtually if not wholly worthless "in themselves." There are two directions in which this question can be followed. One is the suggestion that the symbolic object represents other concrete objects that themselves have this quality of value. This suggestion implies the continuum along which entries on certain account books, like the depositor's balance in his bank account, "represent" the cash to which he has a claim, so that he somehow "really" has not a generalized claim against the bank but instead "owns" particular dollars in cash, for which the bank acts as trustee. The cash then is also a symbol in a further series, in that it represents a "promise to pay," on the part of a bank of issue or of the government, something of still more indubitable value—a certain amount of monetary metal. Along this line of symbolic relationships then, what a dollar on deposit "means" is that it is the equivalent first of cash, then of metal. The inference is clearly that the "real" basis of the value of any kind of money is the "instrinsic" (or as the economists say, "commodity") value of given quantities of the monetary metal, usually gold, and that somehow other components of alleged value are "fictitious."

It is by now a commonplace of economics—accepted even by tough businessmen—that this description does not tell quite the whole story. There are, to be sure, circumstances in which the holder of funds who is in a position to turn them into gold is in a more secure position than the one who is not. But they are not the "normal" circumstances of monetary transaction. First, nearly the last thing an ordinary party to such transactions think of is to demand gold for hoarding in place of the other forms of money. Second, and more important, if every holder of money assets did so, the whole monetary system would collapse and with it most of the economic process.

This statement is true, of course, because the monetary metal is not itself the primary form of money but only the base on which a complex structure of credit is erected. The focus of this structure is the banking function, by virtue of which dollars do double duty. That is, the bank simply does not have—at the cash level—enough dollars at any given time to meet its commitments to its depositors. If it did, it would simply be a storage vault, not a bank, and the increase of productivity facilitated by the creation of credit would be cut off. Yet, it must be noted, every depositor has the formal right to payment in full in cash on demand. If gold were the only "good" money, there would be an enormous constriction of the general flow of exchange transactions.

The other direction in which a series of symbolic references to the value of money can be followed involves, not the solidity of the base on which the structure is erected, but the nature of the structure itself and, in particular, the functions it performs. These functions are no more derivable from the properties of gold as a metal than are the functions of good nutrition for a population derivable from the properties of a particular category of soil.

This line of analysis leads to consideration of the conditions of productivity and hence the positive significance, not only of technological efficiency, but of the division of labor and exchange. In this context, money symbolizes, as suggested, not the base of ultimate security for the isolated individual holder of funds, but the potential of productivity achievable through a *system* of productive activity. In this context, the size of the pie to be cut is a function of the general utilizability of the products of production and therefore of the fluidity of resources available for allocation among many uses, which amounts to exchangeability.

The ultimate reference in this direction is not the intrinsic "worth" of a particularized base but the ordered reliability of an organized collective system of productive activities. The primary basis of the value of money is general confidence that expectations of the productivity of the system will be realized. If, however, such a productive system is to be ordered on a social basis, it must involve an institutionalized framework of expectations, notably though by no means exclusively expectations of the fulfillment of obligations in a contractual system. It is the stability of this system of expectations and therefore the belief that the acceptor of money will not lose because of any likelihood that the system will collapse that is the main basis for establishing money as a generalized medium of exchange.

From the limited point of view of a participating unit, such a system is a case of "operation bootstrap." The rational ground for confidence in money is that others have confidence in money and that this confidence is generally shared—which confidence for the "realist" seems to provide complete demonstration of the unrealiability of all monetary systems except those restricted to solid gold. If such mutual confidence is in fact adequately institutionalized, however, it is the basis of a far higher potential of productivity than any conceivable "sound" money could be.

This argument is not merely a gratuitous digression into the common-places of economics. It is presented in order to demonstrate an exact parallel between money and power. The money held by a social unit is, we may say, the unit's capacity, through market channels under given rules of procedure, to command goods and services in exchange, which for its own reasons it desires. Correspondingly, the power of a unit is its capacity, through invoking binding obligations, to contribute to collective goals, to bring about collective goal-outputs that the "constituents" of the processes of collective action in question desire. Unlike money, it may or may not operate through the market channel, through the offer of induce-ments. But once units are brought within the relevant context of collec-tive organization, power is the medium of invoking their obligations to contribute to collective functioning. The implication of this argument is that failure to contribute as "asked" is subject to negative sanction in a sense parallel to that in which failure to accept an offer of inducement is subject to withdrawal of the offer and, potentially at least, to transfer of its benefits to a competitor.

The stability of monetary systems may be said to depend on their participants' continuing willingness to entrust their interests to a system, in the nature of which there can be no immediate, barter-like *quid pro quo* of value for every exchange. Indeed, the very meaning of money is that it is intrinsically valueless, so that there is a sense in which the acceptor of money gives up something valued for something worthless. We hold that the same principle applies to power systems. They depend on the continuing willingness of their members to entrust their stakes in and interpretations of the collective interest to an impersonal process in which binding decisions are made without the members' being in a posi-tion to control them. Giving a "mandate" to leadership is only one of a number of possibilities in this connection.

For participants in power systems, impairment of this willingness to entrust the collective interest to an institutionalized process may take the form of various levels of reservation—either of refusal to make commit-ments or withdrawal from the implementation of commitments already made. There is a continuum from full participation to total withdrawal, for example in resignation. But this continuum does not exhaust the matter. There is also the possibility of using positions *vis-à-vis* a collec-tivity—inside or outside it—to obstruct the process of collective goal-achievement.

Insofar as a member of a collectivity—or a unit in its environment—

is in a position to exercise some degree of control over it, he may be motivated to withdraw resources on which it has counted to take positive measures to obstruct its operations, a tendency that may be countered by attempts on the part of the "leadership" of the collectivity to maintain control over such resources. The meeting ground of these countertendencies seems to lie in the concept of coercion. To the extent that withdrawal of cooperation is oriented to deterrence of collective function and therefore serves as a threat of negative sanction, it is a way of coercing the collectivity—total noncontingent withdrawal through unannounced resignation is of course a case of compulsion. The strike is a clear case of coercion through contingent withdrawal. On the other side, deterrence by withdrawal may well call into play at least the contingency of coercive countermeasures, in that cooperation is obligatory in more than a "moral" sense and there are negative sanctions for failure to comply.

The attempt has been to formulate this complex in such a way that the distinction between the use of power as capacity to give binding assurances of the effectiveness of collective action, on the one hand, and the dependence on any one particular means of enforcement in case of noncompliance, on the other, stands out. Force in power systems is, we suggest, a particular means of enforcement. The question of whether it is or is not the "basis" of power is ambiguous in a sense exactly parallel to that of the question of "basing" the value of money on command of gold reserves. In the possible process of "deflationary" interaction between threats of withdrawal of contributory resources and tightening the conditions from which benefits of participation will be accorded, there is a general constriction, on the one hand, of the resources available for collective action and, on the other hand, of the degrees of freedom opened up by the availability of collective facilities of organization. Beyond this process, there is the interplay between attempts to disrupt collective operations and the attempt to forestall this disruption coercively. In this vicious circle, the threats on *both* sides readily reach the point where they become threats of force.

That is to say, in a vicious circle of threatening progressively more drastic coercive sanctions, the use of force is the end of the line. In this type of showdown, the commander of force can "protect his interests," that is he can win against those weaker in the command of force in the same sense that the controller of gold can keep his assets while those who somehow failed to secure gold lose out. Forcing the system to this point, however, means that the security of a minority is bought at the expense of a drastic deflation of the system's potential—for production in the economic case and for effective collective action in the political case. In this respect, the use of force occupies a place in power systems parallel to that of gold in monetary systems.[3]

The Relations among Money, Power, and Influence

We have suggested a parallel between money as a generalized medium of inducement and power as a generalized medium of coercion. Since they belong in the still larger families of modes of social control and generalized media that operate in the process of control, we suggest that the process of persuasion also operates through a type of generalized medium—in systems of persuasive communication that have become sufficiently differentiated so that the "barter" stage has been transcended. This medium we shall call *influence* in a special technical sense. The activation of commitments should also be so characterized. Here we can speak of *real commitments,* using the term "real" as it is used in economic theory as a contrast to "monetary." In this present paper, there will be less occasion to develop this last concept than the other three, so the reader will have to rest content with a rather truncated analysis.

The problem of influence can be better approached if a little more is said about the relations between the uses of power and of money. Money is a medium of exchange that operates precisely as a medium of social control when, with respect to the specific subject-matter at hand, the relations of ego are characterized neither by binding mutual obligations nor by a common solidarity. They are, very importantly, part of a wider system governed by a normative order and a set of values, but neither the rules nor any collective solidarity prescribe what ego and alter can expect of each other until they have entered into an agreement —the normative form par excellence being that of the contract.

The contract basically bridges the relation between inducement and coercion, and thus between money and power, in that contractual agreements, once entered into, become binding—in the extreme case, through the law of the state. Among the important types of contract is one that brings previously "free" resources within the control of a collectivity. For most purposes, these resources can be classified under three headings: physical resources, which, in an economic context, are called "commodities"; monetary resources, which include money or assets offering monetary liquidity; and human services, accessible, sociologically speaking,

3. I am indebted to Professor Karl W. Deutsch (oral communication) for this insight.

for performance in *roles*. Physical and monetary resources come to be merely "possessed" by a collectivity—the relevant institutional category is that of property—while human resources are "controlled" by authority on behalf of the collectivity, which has power over them in our strict technical sense. Collectivities can also contract to perform services, but, for the sake of simplicity, we shall confine the present discussion to the services of individuals.

The procedures by which a collectivity gains power over services or possession of property rights can vary over the whole range of the situational channel of social control as we have outlined it. At one pole is compulsion, which is typified by taxation, and among the means of compulsion may be force, although most generally it is held in reserve. At the other pole is "contribution" in the sense that resources are made available as a completely free gift—in the case of services, we say they are "voluntary." The most important middle cases are those of contract—in the physical and monetary instances, by "purchase" or loan; in that of services, by employment, which may or may not be called "purchase." Weber called this case "formally free labor," and it is, of course, the principal case in modern "bureaucratic" organization.

In the case of physical and financial possessions, a collectivity need not acquire power over them since they are not actors; there is no problem of whether or not they "comply" with ego's wishes. In the case of services, however, this aspect is crucial. The crucial factors in the exercise of power here are, on the one hand, the obligations assumed through the contract of employment and, on the other hand, the needs of the collectivity or organization as defined in terms of the exigencies for its effective operation in pursuit of the attainment of its goals.

We conceive of the transactions centering on the contract of employment as an *interchange* of power (and of economic utilities) between the performers of services and the organizations who, by employing them, utilize those services. The organization, through its executive officers, "spends" power in making commitments for the modes of utilization of the resources it controls, the implementation of which is to be carried out by employed persons. From the point of view of those persons, however, this arrangement constitutes a receipt of power. They receive "authorization" to operate *within* the organization effectively in making their "contribution" to its functioning. The input of power, which to some extent balances this output, is derived from the commitments of employed personnel to performance of services within the framework of roles in the organization. The power to operate thus acquired is then used in the framework of what we call the authority of office. When we speak of an approximate balancing of these elements, we mean it to apply to the aggregate inputs and outputs for the system of reference as a whole, not for any particular unit.

The other medium with which these interchanges are immediately articulated is that of money or resources controlled by money. In the external relations of an organization, monetary funds are the direct means of securing control over resources, both goods and services. Internally, the budget is the monetary aspect of control.[4]

The essential point to be made here is that money is the most general medium for the control of fluid resources, providing the potentiality of their acquisition through the market mechanism. Power then is the mechanism for their *mobilization* in the interest of effective collective action, which is what we mean by the process or organization of power. The bindingness of decisions, which is involved in the concept of power, and with it the involvement of negative sanctions—which must be threatened for noncompliance and actually implemented when noncompliance occurs—are conditions of effective organization.

The conditions on which these resources, particularly services, are made available to an organization must be distinguished analytically from the conditions of their utilization once committed to the organization. In the free-market situation, to take an example of the first, money takes precedence over power, particularly because of an institutionalized insulation between the internal and the external contexts. The private organization—and some that are public—is forbidden to preempt resources from outside, either by compulsion or by coercive threats. Internally, however, power takes precedence over money. Budgetary resources are allocated rather than bargained for—in the ideal type, of course—and disposition of personnel at the higher levels is by assignment through executive decision, rather than by contract. This statement does not in the least mean that we accept without reservation the dominance of the concept of "line authority" in the functioning of organizations, but the use of authority does constitute a radical difference from the prototypical market—an organization that attempted to function internally on strictly market principles would not be very effective.

Here is a good opportunity to introduce another very important point

4. This argument is an exceedingly condensed statement of a set of boundary-interchange relations, between economy and polity, as we conceive them. For a fuller discussion see "On the Concept of Political Power," Note 1, pp. 298–299 in Chapter 10 of this volume.

about the relations between power and money, which can be extended to those between positive and negative sanction systems generally. This point involves an essential *asymmetry*, which consists in the fact that the offer of a positive sanction commits the agent of the offer to implement his promise if alter complies with his wishes and accepts his offer. If it is a monetary offer, ego must pay if he is offered a commodity or service on the terms on which he and alter have agreed. In the case of negative sanctions, however, so far as they are contingent, compliance has the opposite effect. Ego is expected not to follow through with implementation of the sanction, which would indeed be a breach of faith, since the understanding was that if alter would comply, ego would refrain from imposing the threatened disadvantage on him.

There is a variety of implications of this asymmetry. One of the most important is that, when a system of normative order is functioning smoothly, the negative aspect of it is not highly visible because compliance is the rule rather than the exception. Negative sanctions therefore often remain, not only unimplemented, but only implicitly threatened. The positive sanction system, however, is highly visible, in that rewards are continually being given. The flow of monetary transactions that mean rewards may be very high, while that of the uses of power in a punitive sense may be low.

Above all, it should be remembered that, in our terms, the use of power is not to be equated with punishment, as we have defined it. The use of power is, in the unit-to-unit context, the control of alter's action through the invoking of binding obligations. If these obligations are fulfilled without resistance, there is no occasion for even threatening negative sanctions explicitly, to say nothing of actually implementing them— that is, punishing noncompliance. To speak of the holder of authority in these circumstances as not having or using power is, in our opinion, highly misleading. The question of his capacity to coerce or compel in case of noncompliance is an independent question that involves the question of handling unexpected and exceptional conditions for which the current power system may or may not be prepared. This question is parallel to that of a monetary system subjected to unusual pressures toward liquidity. Above all, the effectiveness of a power system should not be judged either by the degree to which it habitually resorts to the explicit threat of force or even by the aggregate amount of force at its disposal. The "need" for the latter may be highly variable in different power systems.

It has seemed best to deal with the case of power in a private organization first, rather than to adopt the customary focus on government, precisely because this perspective illuminates the relations between the power and the money media. Contrary to usual opinion, it may be argued that the case of government is analytically a special case. In government, the differentiation between the internal conditions of power precedence and the external conditions of market precedence is not allowed to proceed so far as in private organizations in a "liberal" society. Internally the power of government is generalized in the authority to pre-empt resources by compulsion, although it is a notable feature of such authority that in a liberal society it is normally confined to monetary resources (taxation) and physical resources (eminent domain). Only in emergencies is it extended to human services, the notable case being conscription for military service. That does not mean that market transactions are closed to government procurement in general. Employment of services plays a very big role, as do sale of commodities and of collective services to a lesser extent. The sale of financial assets in the form of government securities is, however, a major factor.

Externally, the essential point is that government maintains a particularly strict control over its own and its nationals' dealings with those of other societies through foreign trade, financial transactions, and the movement of persons. This control is, of course, an aspect of control over the territorial boundaries of a politically organized society. Again, the extensions of coercive authority and therefore the use of power by government in such connections should not be construed as definitive of such authority and power in an analytical sense, above all of the special part played by the use of force in such connections—internally in the form of police forces, externally in the form of military forces.

There is a second major area of the involvement of power besides the implementation of collective policies, as the one just discussed may be called. It is what in some political connections we have been calling the *support* system.[5] Its prototype is the democratic membership participation in the association, including the electoral aspect of governmental collectivities. Power here takes the output form of policy, distinguished from implementive—or administrative—agency, but remains within the context of membership and its responsibilities. The input of support for the

5. Cf. Parsons, " 'Voting' and the Equilibrium of the American Political System" in Eugene Burdick and Arthur J. Brodbeck, eds., *American Voting Behavior* (Glencoe, Ill.: The Free Press, 1959). Chapter 8 of this volume.

executive elements is then political support, exercised, in the fully institutionalized instance, through the voting procedure, which confers the authority of office—which we construe as power—on a leadership element. The familiar complex of capacity to act through the mobilization of binding commitments applies here, as well as in the earlier context, and it applies in both directions. Thus the "verdict of the polls" is a binding decision by the electorate; even though each individual voter may have very little power, the aggregate of votes decides.

Here, however, power does not articulate through the medium of money but through influence, as we have defined it in our technical sense. The mode of control in this case is persuasion. We have defined "persuasion" as an offer of good reasons why alter should, in his own interest, act in accord with ego's wishes. The contingent positive sanction attached to persuasion is *acceptance*, which is an attitudinal as distinct from a situational sanction.

We may speak of influence then as generalized capacity to persuade through the offer of contingent acceptance. A person or collective unit with influence is one that has high generalized persuasive capacity in controlling the action of other units. As in the cases of money and power, it is important not to infer that "need for acceptance" is typically the dominating motive for alter to allow himself to be persuaded by ego. When we speak of acceptance as the relevant type of positive sanction, we imply that it operates in the context of "belongingness," that is that those who mutually accept each other come to be bound by ties of solidarity, so that to that extent they share membership in a collectivity. To persuade, in our technical sense, is then to give alter the status of shared membership, to treat him as "one of us." In using the term "acceptance" for the appropriate positive sanction for persuasion, we wish to distinguish it from "approval," reserving the latter term for the attitudinal sanction appropriate to the activation of commitments. "Approval" in this sense has a moral connotation that "acceptance" has not. Disapproval as the negative sanction threatened by ego is correlative with guilt as alter's internal or subjective negative sanction.

There will, of course, be various conditions on which acceptance is contingent—for example, acceptance by alter in turn of certain beliefs, collective goals, or what not. The contingent bases of acceptability may be summed up under the heading of conformity with the *norms* governing the operation of the collectivity of reference. Persuasion will involve a normative reference defining the sense in which the reasons offered

are "good"; this reference may be called the *justification* of their acceptance by alter. The benefits alter then receives are those of acceptance and
consequent freedom to act within the context of membership.

The use of influence as a medium operates in support systems in two
ways. The first is in the assumption of leadership responsibility and
therefore in the solicitation of support in order to assume authority and
through it power. In highly developed democratic systems, this process is
mediated through the party as a collectivity. Candidacy for high office
and position of party leadership are identical. The candidate in soliciting
commitment of votes is asking his constituents to "join with us." The
justifications of the appeal then take the form of normative reasons why
the policy of the party is superior to that of its rivals—including, of
course, the imputed dangers of giving power to the latter. There is
plenty of room for ideological selection and distortion in this process, but
the basic reference seems to be clear.

To persons in a constituency, identification with a party—membership status need of course not always be formalized—may be regarded
as an access of influence, however small in the individual case. It may
also be regarded as involving expenditure of influence on the part of
leadership. Conversely, constituents may be viewed as exercising their
influence in attempting to persuade leadership to undertake the policies
that they advocate. This process is most visible in the attempt to influence
the leadership in power, but it also extends to that which may sometime
come to power.

Influence may then be thought of as a medium that links the power
aspect of social control with the structure of norms in the society. Group
interests are most palpably implemented in terms first of power and then
of money as modes of social control. In order for their interests to be so
implemented, however, groups must not only have access to power, but
their position must be "justified" to a greater or smaller extent within an
institutionalized system of norms—for example (but not exclusively)
at the legal level. In large-scale social systems, influence can only be exerted in major magnitudes if many join together to exert it—they must
"organize." It is solidarity in this sense that we mean when we speak
of an interest group. Moreover, any basis of solidarity becomes the basis
for an interest group when it is considered in the context of influence,
either to recruit members in the more usual mass-membership sense or to
attempt to get potential leadership to "identify" with their interests—by
acceptance of the reasons advanced for the action advocated as good, to
act in a solidary way with those who have advanced them.

It is of critical significance that in "advanced" societies, in varying ways and to varying degrees, the social structure is pluralistic, both in the sense that there are many more or less independent groups and in the sense that the typical individual has plural memberships in such groups, often highly ramified. *One* major example of the exercise of influence is the attempt to secure transfer of allegiance or solidarity from one group to a competing group. This type of attempt is a highly conspicuous feature of party systems, since electoral rules do not allow voting for two or more party candidates for the same office. This zero-sum aspect of influence does not, however, hold true in all contexts of its use. New solidarities are continually being created, which although they modify do not necessarily eliminate the old. United States participation in the United Nations, for example, is not, as some of our nationalists would have it, bought at a simple zero-sum expense of national autonomy.

We have seen that money articulates with power in the command of resources for the implementive aspects of collective function. The significance of money in the social system is not, however, confined to this context. Indeed it is less familiar to the economist than that of the production of goods for consumption and the facilitation of consumption through the system of market exchange. Similarly, influence is, we hold, articulated with power in what we have called support systems. Its place in societies is, however, by no means confined to this role. We conceive of support systems as involved with the conditions of effective collective action. The other principal context in which influence is involved is that of the evaluation of interests and the allocation of loyalties among them. In this higher-order context of justification, reference is to the system of interests rather than to implementation of more particular interests.

We have spoken of two main contexts in which we hold that power is articulated with other generalized media: money in the implementive context, influence in the supportive. There is, finally, a third and somewhat different context that must be briefly mentioned, that of *legitimation*. In our terms, legitimation is an articulation of power with real commitments. It involves essentially a question of the standing of authority—as the frame of reference or "code" of power rather than the medium of control—in terms of the institutionalized values of the society. It is concerned with "rights" to exercise atuhority, at the level of both "constitutionality" and moral right. In normative terms, legitimation is the highest order of justification, but it seems best to use the term "legitimation" to distinguish it from the normative reference of persuasion. It is the highest normative defense against the breakdown of a system of societal order within which power can operate as a medium.

The Monopoly of Force and the "Power Bank"

After this rather lengthy digression, we may now come back to certain questions of the relations between force and the power system. In the earlier part of this paper, we relied heavily on the parallel between money and power, and, in the present section, we propose to attempt to develop this parallel still further. It is a commonplace of political science that systems that are both stable and advanced—in the sense that they offer both high levels of differentiation and general political effectiveness for collective action—tend to enforce a relatively stringent monopoly of the control of organized and effective instrumentalities of force. This monopoly not only encourages the centralization of force but ensures that the constitutionally paramount organs of government are firmly in control of such force. We have here the doctrine of ultimate civilian control over the military, symbolized in the American system by the constitutional position of the president as commander in chief of all armed forces. There is perhaps no better criterion of a federal state, as distinct from a confederation, than the possession of paramount control of force by the central government.

The parallel in this case of course is the centralization of control over the monetary metal in economically advanced societies. Central banking systems, of which this control is an important aspect, have evolved late and often painfully, but they are a universal feature of advanced societies —and, of course, they are an integral part of socialist economies. Until recently—and still not unequivocally—there has been no formal prohibition against private agencies' holding gold, although an instance where such holdings were markedly superior to those of the government or central bank would certainly be considered anomalous and probably threatening and, if it tended to develop, would probably be stopped before it went much further. Such an instance would certainly, in a monetary system clearly dependent on gold to support a highly pyramidal credit system, carry with it a substantial potential for disruption, as the famous Black Friday makes clear.

Students of the subject are even more conscious that a major concentration of force in private hands has disruptive potentials because it can be used "against the public interest" or, with the opposite value-tag, as a revolutionary instrument against a decadent or iniquitous regime. The accent in this connection, however, has been on such force as a potential instrumentality of "seizing power." This potential is, of course, an important part of the picture but, as our discussion has indicated, only a part.

We have suggested that force plays a part in power systems parallel to that of gold in monetary systems. Only in one special respect is the commodity value of gold the "real basis" of the value of the dollar. Similarly, only in one special aspect is the command of physical force in a power system the "real basis" of the authority of government or the leadership of private collectivities, as the case may be. In the economic case, it is the credit system, built up primarily through the institution of banking but through several other types of mechanism, that "frees" monetary exchange from the limitations of metallic money. The "ultimate" basis of the value of its money then is the productivity of the economy.

We now suggest that there is a directly parallel set of phenomena in power systems. The primary functions of power are to facilitate the mobilization of instrumental resources like money and services and of support and the influence on which it partially depends. To repeat, this mobilization occurs through the promotion of binding obligations, the bindingness of which is symbolized by the willingness of those with power to resort to negative sanctions in case of noncompliance, sanctions that can be arranged in a rough order of severity from the threat of mild disadvantage to the drastic use of force. We have repeatedly insisted, however, that the problem of the motivation of compliance under normal conditions must not be confused with the problem of what sanctions will and will not be used in what order of severity and under what circumstances, when noncompliance occurs or is threatened. What motivation alter has for accepting or avoiding the sanctions is still a third question.

A particularly cogent set of reasons for making these distinctions lies in the existence and prominence in advanced political systems of a political analogy of the bank, which we may call, in appropriate quotation marks, the "power bank." The hallmark of the money bank is the fact that the dollars, as we noted, do double duty, remaining at the disposal of depositors while they are also at the disposal of borrowers. In the case of power, commitments to the performance of binding obligations are the analog of dollars and may be said to do double duty.

This point can be illustrated most clearly by the example of an electoral system, public or private. Members, in their capacity as voters,

may be said to have entrusted power ("deposited" it) to elected leadership, power that they reserve the right to withdraw, if not on demand, at
least at the next election. Some of this power is indeed immediately re-
turned in the form of decisions that directly satisfy constituency interests.
This return is reflected in party references to the record of benefits accruing to various categories of constituents during a term of office. In
many political systems, private as well as public, however, this return
does not exhaust the activities of leadership. The leadership also "in-
vests" a portion of its power in making commitments in what it conceives to be a larger collective interest, commitments that are in fact not
in response to the immediate demands of constituent interest groups.
Above all, these commitments tie up resources that in some sense "belong" to the constituency beyond the periods when the leadership is
formally in control of them.

     In the case of governments, the honoring of obligations assumed by
opposing parties in previous administrations, frequently in foreign affairs
but often domestically, is an indication of this phenomenon. For example,
although the appropriations are made, for the most part, formally on an
annual basis, money spent by the United States government in the
fields of scientific research and training has in fact become, to a considerable extent, a permanent obligation, in spite of the legal authority of
Congress to cut it off with a single vote. A good private example is the
ploughing back of profits by corporations without detailed authorization
by the stockholders, although the latter have the formal rights to stop it
and take the money as dividends.

     The essential point is that a "power bank," like a money bank, is, if
it is functioning well, "insolvent" at any given moment with respect to its
formal obligations, in the sense that it cannot fulfill all its legitimate
obligations if there is insistence on their fulfillment too rapidly. Even
relatively mild pressure to exceed the accustomed rate of fulfillment will
force adoption of a rigid priority system and the rapid liquidation of
some commitments that are otherwise highly desirable. Extreme pressure
will tend to bring about a serious breakdown of the power system. When
a vicious circle of "deflationary" pressure of this type gets under way, the
tendency is to bring the role of negative sanctions increasingly to the
fore and to resort to threats of sanctions of increasing severity. The "constitutional" powers can be quickly exhausted. At the end of the road lies
the resort to force in the interest of what particular groups conceive to
be their rights. The monopoly of force in the hands of government
presents special problems that will be discussed presently.

This general set of considerations constitutes what we believe to be the basis of at least one of the most important objections to the very commonly held "zero-sum" conception of the nature of power. If power were equatable with physical force or even "based on" it in a sense other than the one we have discussed, it might be more plausible to hold that the power controlled by some units in the system was necessarily subtracted from a fixed total, the balance of which was controlled by the others.

That there is a distributive aspect of power is almost obvious and is clearly implied by our comparison with money. We wish, however, to extend the parallel to the point where we postulate a set of mechanisms of expansion and contraction of the total as a function of forces operating on the level of the system as a whole, which is parallel to the phenomenon of credit in the case of money. We think that these considerations are highly relevant to the problems of the place of force and constitute some of the reasons why the complexity of the relations between power and force that we have outlined is so important.

It should also be clear from this argument that we think that the basic phenomena of power systems are dependent on the institutionalization of what ordinarily is called authority. That is to say that, for cases of the exercise of authority—in which we include the vote—compliance is both legitimately and "normally" to be expected. It is, however, in the nature of normatively regulated action that conformity with normative expectations sometimes, indeed often, fails. It is cases of this failure and the consequent possibilities of sequences of development that are the principal focus of interest for the remainder of this paper.

Power and the Internal Use of Force

We have already laid stress on the tendency to develop a monopoly of the control of force in the hands of government. It is vital to our argument that this concentration cannot, except for a limiting type, be the case with power. A monopoly of the use of power in governmental hands would be a definition of the ideal type of a totalitarian regime. It has been one of our most important contentions that power should be regarded as a circulating medium that operates throughout the society wherever organizations in the sense of collectivities exist. Of course, in this sense, the big organizations like governments, productive enterprises, and trade unions stand out conspicuously, but, in principle, families, even friendship cliques, and many other groups also have some power. In the aggregate, the power of small units may be very great, although, of course, the question of effective organization always arises.

Among those societies with highly developed organization, the modern Western, and rather particularly the American type, is characterized by pluralism.[6] Although the scale of organization is large, there are many, even among large organizations, that are more or less independent of one another. It is important not to make absolute independence in itself a criterion of pluralism. There is, moreover, a shading from the very large through many intermediate grades to the very small. Government is by no means monolithic, splintered as it is by the separation of powers, federalism (in the United States), local independence, and the internal complexity of such an immensely ramified organization as the federal executive branch. The same is true, in varying degrees, of many large private organizations.

In any complex society, more conspicuously in the more pluralistic ones, what may be called the "power structure" rests in a state of more or less stable and probably significantly shifting equilibrium. Processes of circulation operate continuously, through exchanges of commitments of resources and of opportunities for their utilization, through giving and withdrawing support for various collective goals, and through the decisions that signify commitment—not only of mobile resources, but of organizations themselves.

There is, finally, the very important point that individual persons have *plural* memberships in and commitments to collectivities. Although unevenly spread throughout a population, this plurality increases with higher differentiation of the general social structure. An increased spread of memberships implies, as one price of enhanced effectiveness, an increased potential for conflict among them or, put in obverse form, an increasingly delicate equilibrium among such loyalties.

This equilibrium both among collectivities and among loyalties to memberships—which, it should be remembered, cut across each other— is dependent on the maintenance of a level of "confidence," a factor very similar to the confidence that operates in monetary systems. In the latter, it involves the expectation of probabilities, not only of the fulfillment of contractual obligations, but also of maintenance of given rates of entering into such obligations and of relinquishing them. In the political case, it is confidence in the probability of what we have called compliance.

6. For the concept of pluralism in the present sense, see William Kornhauser, *The Politics of Mass Society* (Glencoe, Ill.: The Free Press, 1959).

This confidence centers on the fulfillment of obligations already assumed through collectivity memberships, but in a parallel to the economic case, it extends also to rates of expected acceptance of new obligations—through entry of the younger generations into the labor force and hence into employment, for example.

Although this factor is only one among several that bear on the eruption of violence in internal situations, we would like to indicate a path leading in that direction that starts from the equilibrium of authority and power relations and the conditions of its maintenance. Disturbances of this equilibrium may originate in any of a number of places—specificity of origin is not an important consideration here. The question is whether or not the immediate consequence of a disturbance is "deflationary" in the sense of its effect on the system of expectations of which the power structure is made. One general condition favorable to such deflationary influence is, of course, an overextension of power commitments, analogous to inflation in the economic sense. This problem presents a very important field of inquiry that unfortunately cannot be followed up here; that such conditions exist will simply be taken as given.

In our present context, a deflationary influence is one that leads to a demand for a binding decision or exercise of power, to which the demander has some kind of right but which is out of line with the normal expectations of operation of the system. That some units will encounter emergency conditions, as some depositors unexpectedly must withdraw their balances, is to be taken for granted. Whether the rate of imposition of such demands is abnormal is a matter for statistical estimate, unless the individual case is of overwhelming quantitative magnitude in terms of claims either on resources or on support.

Any such disturbance may, of course, be met. On the other hand, if it is not met or if the difficulty of meeting it creates a question of the capacity of the system to meet its general obligations, it *may* (not necessarily must) motivate other units to present demands they would not otherwise have presented *at this time.*[7]

If such a process once gets under way, it may enter into a vicious-circle pattern. That is, each assertion of demands for collective decision, for satisfaction of interests that would not ordinarily have been presented, will stimulate other units to assert their demands. There can then develop a *cumulative* pressure on the relevant collectivities. The general

7. The most adequate generalized analysis, including much empirical material, of the conditions under which such crises of confidence are likely to occur and under which they may be checked is presented in Neil J. Smelser, *Theory of Collective Behavior* (New York: The Free Press of Glencoe, 1963).

type of response will then be twofold. First, an increasingly stringent scale of priorities of what can and cannot be done will be set up; second, increasingly severe negative sanctions for noncompliance with collective decisions will be imposed.

With respect to the first tendency, the most important point to note is the presumption that most if not all of the demands made on collective leadership are legitimate and that, in general, their presumptive legitimacy is not dependent on specific conditions of timing and other constraints—if the analogy to the bank depositors holds up. This circumstance, once "confidence" has been sufficiently impaired, is bound to increase the pressure, since there is no formal way to make newly imposed priorities seem legitimate other than the process of "legal" pronouncement, which may or may not match the normative "sentiments" of the important groups.

With respect to the second tendency, we have already asserted that increasing severity of sanctions leads in the direction of resort to force. If pressure to fulfill demands becomes sufficiently severe and the objective possibility of fulfilling them sufficiently low, then it seems inevitable that the most vociferous insisters, who at the same time are low on the priority scale, will have to be threatened with force to deter them. Here again it must be remembered that we are positing a situation where it is objectively impossible to fulfill all the legitimate demands within a short time but where, at the same time, this incapacity is also felt to be legitimate.

The most common responses to increasing severity of sanctions are two. One is to seek security through "digging in" in a protected position, the protection of which may involve independent command of force but may also take the form of command of other resources of the most various kinds. This reaction is the withdrawal from dependence on the ramified power system, which is analogous to economic withdrawal into gold or into "real" assets—a feature of economic deflation that, interestingly, is shared with inflationary situations. The other general response is the active, aggressive attempt to *enforce* demands against the inclinations of the collective leadership. This response clearly leads in the direction of seeking capacity to implement countersanctions of severity equal to or exceeding that of those commanded by the collective leadership. Force plays a central part in any such system of countersanctions, but it should be remembered that it does not stand alone. Financial assets may be very important and, above all, influence in the technical sense in which we have used the term.

Our general argument has been deliberately couched in terms that include all collective action, governmental or private. Government, however, occupies a very special position in any developed power system. First, it is the most comprehensive level of collective organization and hence in general commands considerably larger assets than any other "interest" at most levels and in most categories, although not necessarily in all. Second, government is in a very special position in relation to the command of force, usually that of monopoly.

In what we have called the vicious circle of coercive threats, which a power-deflation may well set in motion, there may, unlike the economic case, be an inherent tendency to set up a polarity between the elements in control of the machinery of government and those in opposition to that group. In more advanced constitutional regimes, this polarity usually takes the form of a two-party system. The way of securing fulfillment of demands not approved by the party in power is to seek electoral victory against it, which of course implies waiting, perhaps for a long period, for a favorable opportunity.

Essentially a constitutional regime is marked, on the one hand, by restraint in the expectation of fulfillment of various demands and, on the other, by restraint on the coercion of the opposition by those in power. In particular, the leadership refrain from abridging the freedom to displace the incumbents from power, not only by maintaining the electoral rules, but by upholding the other normal components of political freedom like freedoms of the press, of assembly, and so forth. The opposition must be free to influence the voters, although neither they nor the incumbents should coerce or bribe them.[8]

It is when, in the vicious circle of power deflation, these restraints are broken in the interaction between incumbents and opposition that the makings of a revolutionary situation are present. We have posited a situation in which it is objectively impossible for government to satisfy all the demands presented to it. We have, moreover, argued that, though by no means all such demands need be in any sense legitimate, the type of situation we are discussing always involves a major excess of legitimate (in a "formal" sense) demands over capacity to satisfy them. This excess means that, among the unsatisfied, to whatever forces of group interest in the more "material" sense exist there will be added a sense

8. The best analysis known to us of the institutionalization of the franchise bearing on these points is Stein Rokkan, "Mass Suffrage, Secret Voting and Political Participation," *European Journal of Sociology*, II (1961), 132–152.

of normative, possibly moral, righteousness that will, as it becomes more intense, seem to justify increasing resort to more extreme measures.

At this point, certain well known generalizations about ideologies can be brought to bear. Ideologies combine an evaluative and an empirical element in the diagnosis of social situations. Because of evaluative pressures, they tend toward selectivity and sometimes toward outright distortion, both in stating the case of the proponents and attacking that of the opponents. It is typical that the former are pictured as actuated by the highest of idealistic motives, while the latter are guided by the grossest forms of self-interest. That is, ideological definition of the situation tends to get drawn into the general polarization.

A particularly important point is the question of the solidity or lack of it of the governmental monopoly of internal force. Most important, whatever the physical technology involved, a critical factor in socially effective force is always the social organization through which it is implemented. There is always some degree of dependence on the loyalties of the relevant personnel to the elements in the social structure ostensibly controlling them.

Up to a point, a pluralistic social structure can act as a very important preventive of the spread of the vicious circle of power-deflation, mainly by invoking solidarities at many points that cut across lines of incipient conflict.[9] The same type of analysis can, however, be applied at points where the vicious circle has begun to get out of control. Members of police and armed forces also have plural loyalties, among which those to their jobs do not stand alone nor necessarily predominate. Hence, even though at a given moment the sanctions against breaking away from these loyalties are very severe, there may be many critical points where mass breaking away can readily occur once a precarious equilibrium has been upset.

Connected with this point is the question of the plurality of factors in a power position, among which command of negative sanctions generally and force in particular comprise only one subset. From this point of view, a complex set of two-way forces operate around the threat and actual use of physical force. On the one hand, the use and threat of force have a set of symbolic meanings that define a penumbra of effect extending well beyond the direct effectiveness in the context of deterrence or compulsion. This statement is above all true of the meanings discussed briefly in relation to demonstration of capacity to act. On the

9. I have called attention to this factor of stability in the paper on voting cited in Note 5, p. 228. The paper is included as Chapter 8 of this volume.

one hand, exemplary uses and threats on the part of holders of force may be meant, not as specifically coercive deterrents, but merely as warnings. The same game may be played by outsiders, particularly minority opposition groups wishing to create an atmosphere of crisis. The general phenomenon of terrorism on both governmental and opposition sides seems to fit in this context.

On the other hand, a whole series of other factors are involved in willingness to resort to force and the probabilities of effectiveness once the plunge is made. In principle, all the major factors that operate on action within social systems are relevant to any such analysis. This point leads to a very important general conclusion. Social behavior in the application of physical force and in reaction to its threat or use is not subject to special "laws" of behavior. It should rather be approached by applying the generalized knowledge already available about the uniformities of such behavior to a special set of conditions, which necessitate special exigencies of effectiveness on the one hand, special modes of reaction to threat and implementation on the other. In our opinion, understanding the use of internal as well as external force is as dependent on advancement of general theoretical knowledge of the operation of social systems as on specificities of the situations peculiar to the use of force, although of course both must be pursued and adequately combined.

Conclusion

In this chapter, we have attempted an exceedingly sketchy review of a certain set of these general features of the functioning of social systems, insofar as they tend to connect with the significance of the use of force. We have viewed the problem in the general context of modes of social control and, within this context, in the light of coercion by threatening negative sanctions and of compulsion as a limiting type. In this connection, physical force appears as the ultimate instrument of coercion or compulsion, where the primary intention in its use or threat is deterrence. It also, we suggested, has the meanings of punishment and of demonstration and warning.

We then attempted to place physical force as sanction in the context, on the one hand, of a gradient of such sanctions that can be involved in the implementation of power positions and, on the other hand, of the place of coercion and power in a more comprehensive scheme of generalized media of social control. In the former context, force is the most severe in a continuum of potential deprivations of situational advantage imposed by an acting unit of reference—ego—on an alter that ego intends to control. In this context in most power systems, physical force is not the most important operative sanction but a "reserve" sanction available for emergencies. In particular, it is not likely to be resorted to internally or even directly threatened in a stable power system, except in minor instances like routine police functions in attempting to control ordinary criminals. In certain types of crisis situation, however, it may come to dominate the social scene.

We thus regard power as a generalized medium of social control. Its properties have been analyzed above all in terms of a systematic comparison with those of money. It has in common with money that it is essentially a mode of prescriptive communication. Its effectiveness is not mainly dependent on any particular base but rather on confidence, which is itself dependent on many factors in the fulfillment of interactive expectations. There is, however, an ultimate symbolic basis of security of the value of the medium: In the case of money, it is the monetary metal; in that of power, physical force. Money and power viewed in this perspective should also be related to at least two other media of comparable importance, in particular the one we have called influence.

Against this background, it is possible to see that power systems involve a phenomenon analogous to credit creation in monetary systems. This analogy implies, on the one hand, a vast extension of the range of effective collective organization, compared with a system dependent either mainly on ascriptive obligations or on more primitive sanctions like force and summary dismissal. On the other hand, it implies vulnerability to certain types of disturbance parallel to inflation and deflation in the economic case. A highly developed power system cannot meet all of its presumptively legitimate obligations all at once.

It is this particular case that we chose to illustrate the relevance of this type of analysis to the problem of internal war. We suggest that the power systems we posit are vulnerable to vicious circles of power-deflation, a vulnerability that is accentuated by the general tendency of governmental systems to polarize. In such a vicious-circle process, there will be a tendency toward the use of force, in terms of both threat and counter-threat and in terms of warnings.

CHAPTER 10

On the Concept of Political Power

An attempt to deal with political power as a generalized inter-change medium had been a central theme of my theoretical work for some time when an invitation to deliver a paper at the November, 1962 meeting of the American Philosophical Society presented a favorable opportunity for its further development. The oral presentation was much abbreviated, but the full paper was published in the *Proceedings of the American Philosophical Society*, June, 1963. It has recently been reprinted in the second edition of Bendix and Lipset, eds., *Class, Status, and Power,* (New York: The Free Press, 1966).

The paper attempts to show how the approach to the problem of the nature of power introduced here, not only fits into an analytical treatment of the polity as a societal subsystem theoretically parallel to the economy (as the economy was conceptualized in Parsons and Smelser, *Economy and Society,* New York: The Free Press, 1956), but also that this approach offers a promising way to deal with certain of the most baffling difficulties that have dogged the analysis of power in the literature of political theory. Foremost among these difficulties were the problem of specificity of conceptualization as compared with the diffuseness of conceptions which virtually equate power with all forms of capacity to gain ends (the Hobbesian approach), the problem of the relations between the coercive and the consensual aspects of power systems, the problem of the balance between the hierarchical aspects of power and the existence of egalitarian elements in the structure of political systems, and finally, what is sometimes called the "zero-sum" problem, that of whether any relational system necessarily contains only a fixed amount of power which is subject only to redistribution.

The general theoretical context of this treatment of power has, in my own work, been most fully spelled out, so far, in "The Political Aspects of Social Structure and Process," in David

"On the Concept of Political Power" reprinted from *Proceedings of the American Philosophical Society*, Vol. 107, No. 3 (June, 1963).

Easton, ed., *Varieties of Political Theory* (Englewood Cliffs: Prentice-Hall, 1966).

Power is one of the key concepts in the great Western tradition of thought about political phenomena. It is at the same time a concept on which, in spite of its long history, there is, on analytical levels, a notable lack of agreement both about its specific definition, and about many features of the conceptual context in which it should be placed. There is, however, a core complex of its meaning, having to do with the capacity of persons or collectivities "to get things done" effectively, in particular when their goals are obstructed by some kind of human resistance or opposition. The problem of coping with resistance then leads into the question of the role of coercive measures, including the use of physical force, and the relation of coercion to the voluntary and consensual aspects of power systems.

The aim of this paper is to attempt to clarify this complex of meanings and relations by placing the concept of power in the context of a general conceptual scheme for the analysis of large-scale and complex social systems, that is of societies. In doing so I speak as a sociologist rather than as a political scientist, but as one who believes that the interconnections of the principal social disciplines, including not only these two, but especially their relations to economics as well, are so close that on matters of general theory of this sort they cannot safely be treated in isolation; their interrelations must be made explicit and systematic. As a sociologist, I thus treat a central concept of political theory by selecting among the elements which have figured prominently in political theory in terms of their fit with and significance for the general theoretical analysis of society as a whole.

There are three principal contexts in which it seems to me that the difficulties of the concept of power, as treated in the literature of the last generation, come to a head. The first of these concerns its conceptual diffuseness, the tendency, in the tradition of Hobbes, to treat power as simply the generalized capacity to attain ends or goals in social relations, independently of the media employed or of the status of "authorization" to make decisions or impose obligations.[1]

1. Thus E. C. Banfield, *Political Influence* (New York: The Free Press of Glencoe, 1962), p. 348, speaks of control as the ability to cause another to give or withold action, and power as the ability to establish control over another. Similarly Robert Dahl, "The

The effect of this diffuseness, as I call it, is to treat "influence" and sometimes money, as well as coercion in various aspects, as "forms" of power, thereby making it logically impossible to treat power as a *specific* mechanism operating to bring about changes in the action of other units, individual or collective, in the processes of social interaction. The latter is the line of thought I wish to pursue.

Secondly, there is the problem of the relation between the coercive and the consensual aspects. I am not aware of any treatment in the literature which presents a satisfactory solution of this problem. A major tendency is to hold that somehow "in the last analysis" power comes down to one or the other, i.e., to "rest on" command of coercive sanctions, *or* on consensus and the will to voluntary cooperation. If going to one or the other polar solution seems to be unacceptable, a way out, taken for example by Friedrich, is to speak of each of these as different "forms" of power. I shall propose a solution which maintains that both aspects are essential, but that neither of the above two ways of relating them is satisfactory, namely subordinating either one to the other or treating them as discrete "forms."

Finally the third problem is what, since the Theory of Games, has widely come to be called the "zero-sum" problem. The dominant tendency in the literature, for example in Lasswell and C. Wright Mills, is to maintain explicitly or implicitly that power is a zero-sum phenomenon, which is to say that there is a fixed "quantity" of power in any relational system and hence any gain of power on the part of A must by definition occur by diminishing the power at the disposal of other units, B, C, D. . . . There are, of course, restricted contexts in which this condition holds, but I shall argue that it does not hold for total systems of a sufficient level of complexity.

Some General Assumptions

The initial assumption is that, within the conception of society as a system, there is an essential parallelism in theoretical structure between the conceptual schemes appropriate for the analysis of the economic and the political aspects of societies. There are four respects in which I wish

Concept of Power," *Behavioral Scientist* 2 (July, 1957), says that "A has power over B to the extent that he can get B to do something that B would not otherwise do." C. J. Friedrich takes a similar position in *Man and his Government; An Empirical Theory of Politics* (New York: McGraw-Hill, 1963).

to attempt to work out and build on this parallel, showing at the same time the crucial substantive differences between the two fields.

First "political theory" as here interpreted, which is not simply to be identified with the meaning given the term by many political scientists, is thought of as an abstract analytical scheme in the same sense in which economic theory is abstract and analytical. It is not the conceptual interpretation of any concretely complete category of social phenomena, quite definitely not those of government, though government is the area in which the political element comes nearest to having clear primacy over others. Political theory thus conceived is a conceptual scheme which deals with a restricted set of primary variables and their interrelations, which are to be found operating in all concrete parts of social systems. These variables are, however, subject to parametric conditions which constitute the values of other variables operating in the larger system which constitutes the society.

Secondly, following on this, I assume that the empirical system to which political theory in this sense applies is an analytically defined, a "functional" subsystem of a society, not for example a concrete type of collectivity. The conception of the economy of a society is relatively well defined.[2] I should propose the conception of the *polity* as the parallel empirical system of direct relevance to political theory as here advanced. The polity of a given society is composed of the ways in which the relevant components of the total system are organized with reference to one of its fundamental functions, namely effective collective action in the attainment of the goals of collectivities. Goal-attainment in this sense is the establishment of a satisfactory relation between a collectivity and certain objects in its environment which include both other collectivities and categories of personalities, e.g. "citizens." A total society must in these terms be conceived, in one of its main aspects, as a collectivity, but it is also composed of an immense variety of subcollectivities, many of which are parts not only of this society but of others.[3].

A collectivity, seen in these terms, is thus clearly not a concrete "group" but the term refers to groups, i.e. systematically related pluralities of persons, seen in the perspective of their interests in and capacities for effective collective action. The political process then is the process by

2. *Cf.* Talcott Parsons and Neil J. Smelser, *Economy and Society* (New York: The Free Press of Glencoe, 1956), Chapter I, for a discussion of this conception.
3. E.g. the American medical profession is part of American society, but also it is part of a wider medical profession which transcends this particular society, to some extent as collectivity. Interpenetration in membership is thus a feature of the relations among collectivities.

which the necessary organization is built up and operated, the goals of action are determined and the resources requisite to it are mobilized.

These two parallels to economic theory can be extended to still a third. The parallel to collective action in the political case is, for the economic, production. This conception in turn must be understood in relation to three main operative contexts. The first is adjustment to the conditions of "demand" which are conceived to be external to the economy itself, to be located in the "consumers" of the economic process. Secondly, resources must be mobilized, also from the environment of the economy, the famous factors of production. Thirdly, the internal economic process is conceived as creatively combinatorial; it is, by the "combination" of factors of production in the light of the utility of outputs, a process of creating more valuable facilities to meet the needs of consuming units than would be available to them without this combinatorial process. I wish most definitely to postulate that the logic of "value added" applies to the political sphere in the present sense.[4]

In the political case, however, the value reference is not to utility in the economic sense but to effectiveness, very precisely, I think in the sense used by C. I. Barnard.[5] For the limited purposes of political analysis as such the givenness of the goal demands of interest groups serves as the same order of factor in relation to the political system as has the corresponding givenness of consumers' wants for purposes of economic analysis—and of course the same order of qualifications on the empirical adequacy of such postulates.

Finally, fourth, political analysis as here conceived is parallel to economic in the sense that a central place in it is occupied by a generalized medium involved in the political interaction process, which is also a "measure" of the relevant values. I conceive power as such a generalized medium in a sense directly parallel in logical structure, though very different substantively, to money as the generalized medium of the economic process. It is essentially this conception of power as a generalized medium parallel to money which will, in the theoretical context sketched above, provide the thread for guiding the following analysis

4. For discussions of the conception of "value-added" in spheres of application broader than the economic alone, *cf.* Neil J. Smelser, *Social Change in the Industrial Revolution* (New York: The Free Press of Glencoe, 1959), Chapter II, pp. 7–20, and Neil J. Smelser, *Theory of Collective Behavior* (New York: The Free Press of Glencoe, 1963), Chapter II, pp. 23–47.
5. C. I. Barnard, *The Functions of the Executive* (Cambridge: Harvard University Press, 1938), Chapter V, pp. 46–64.

through the types of historic difficulty with reference to which the paper began.

The Outputs of Political Process and the Factors of Effectiveness

The logic of the combinatorial process which I hold to be common to economic theory and the type of political theory advanced here, involves a paradigm of inputs and outputs and their relations. Again we will hold that the logic is strictly parallel to the economic case, i.e. that there should be a set of political categories strictly parallel to those of the factors of production (inputs) on the one hand, the shares of income (outputs) on the other.

In the economic case, with the exception of land, the remaining three factors must be regarded as inputs from the other three cognate functional subsystems of the society, labor from what we call the "pattern-maintenance" system, capital from the polity and organization, in the sense of Alfred Marshall, from the integrative system.[6] Furthermore, it becomes clear that land is not, as a factor of production, simply the physical resource, but essentially the commitment, in value terms, of any resources to economic production in the system independent of price.

In the political case, similarly the equivalent of land is the commitment of resources to effective collective action, independent of any specifiable "pay-off" for the unit which controls them.[7] Parallel to labor is the demands or "need" for collective action as manifested in the "public" which in some sense is the constituency of the leadership of the collectivity in question—a conception which is relatively clear for the governmental or other electoral association, but needs clarification in other connections. Parallel to capital is the control of some part of the productivity of the economy for the goals of the collectivity, in a sufficiently developed economy through financial resources at the disposal of the collectivity, acquired by earnings, gift, or taxation. Finally, parallel to organization is the legitimation of the authority under which collective decisions are taken.

It is most important to note that none of these categories of input is conceived as a form of power. In so far as they involve media, it is the

6. On the rationale of these attributions, see *Economy and Society, op. cit.,* Chapter II.
7. "Pay-off" may be a deciding factor in choice between particular contexts of use, but not as to whether the resource shall be devoted to collective effectiveness at all.

media rooted in contiguous functional systems, not power as that central to the polity—e.g. control of productivity may operate through money, and constituents' demands through what I call "influence." Power then is the *means* of acquiring control of the factors in effectiveness; it is not itself one of these factors, any more than in the economic case money is a factor of production; to suppose it was, was the ancient mercantilist fallacy.

Though the analytical context in which they are placed is perhaps unfamiliar in the light of traditional political analysis, I hope it is clear that the actual categories used are well established, though there remain a number of problems of exact definition. Thus control of productivity through financing of collective action is very familiar, and the concept of "demands" in the sense of what constituents want and press for, is also very familiar.[8] The concept legitimation is used in essentially the same sense in which I think Max Weber used it in a political context.[9]

The problem of what corresponds, for the political case, to the economist's "shares of income" is not very difficult, once the essential distinction, a very old one in economic tradition, between monetary and "real" income is clearly taken into account. Our concern is with the "real" outputs of the political process—the analogue of the monetary here is output of power.

There is one, to us, critically important revision of the traditional economic treatment of outputs which must be made, namely the bracketing together of "goods and services," which then would be treated as outputs to the household as, in our technical terms, a part of the "pattern-maintenance" system. The present position is that goods, i.e., more precisely property rights in the physical objects of possession, belong in this category, but that "services," the commitment of human role-performances to an "employer," or contracting agent constitute an output, not to the household, but to the polity, the type case (though not the only one) being an employing organization in which the role-incumbent commits himself to performance of an occupational role, a job,[10] as a contribution to the effective functioning of the collectivity.

8. I have in fact adopted the term "demands" from the usage of David Easton, "An Approach to the Analysis of Political Systems," *World Politics* 9 (1957), 383–400.
9. *Cf.* Max Weber, *The Theory of Social and Economic Organization* (New York: Oxford University Press, 1947); translated by A. M. Henderson and Talcott Parsons; edited by Talcott Parsons, p. 124.
10. The cases of services concretely rendered to a household should be considered as a limiting case where the roles of consumer and employer have not become differentiated from each other.

There is, from this consideration, a conclusion which is somewhat surprising to economists, namely that service is, in the economic sense the "real" counterpart of interest as monetary income from the use of funds. What we suggest is that the political control of productivity makes it possible, through combinatorial gains in the political context, to produce a surplus above the monetary funds committed, by virtue of which under specified conditions a premium can be paid at the monetary level which, though a result of the combinatorial process as a whole, is most directly related to the output of available services as an economic phenomenon, i.e. as a "fluid resource." Seen a little differently, it becomes necessary to make a clear distinction between labor as a factor of production in the economic sense and service as an output of the economic process which is utilized in a political context, that is one of organizational or collective effectiveness.

Service, however, is not a "factor" in effectiveness, in the sense in which labor is a factor of production, precisely because it is a category of power. It is the point at which the economic utility of the human factor is matched with its potential contribution to effective collective action. Since the consumer of services is in principle the employing collectivity, it is its effectiveness for collective goals, not its capacity to satisfy the "wants" of individuals, which is the vantage point from which the utility of the service is derived. The output of power which matches the input of services to the polity, I interpret to be the "opportunity for effectiveness" which employment confers on those employed or contract offers to partners. Capital in the economic sense is one form of this opportunity for effectiveness which is derived from providing, for certain types of performances, a framework of effective organization.[11]

The second, particularly important context of "real" output of the political process is the category which, in accord with much tradition, I should like to call capacity to assume leadership responsibility. This, as a category of "real" output also is not a form of power, but this time of influence.[12] This is an output not to the economy but to what I shall call the integrative system, which in its relevance to the present context

11. In the cases treated as typical for economic analysis the collective element in capital is delegated through the *bindingness* of the contracts of loan of financial resources. To us this is a special case, employment being another, of the binding obligation assumed by an organization, whether it employs or loans, by virtue of which the recipient can be more effective than would otherwise be the case. It is not possible to go further into these complex problems here, but they will, perhaps, be somewhat illuminated by the later discussion of the place of the concept of bindingness in the theory of power.
12. See my paper "On the Concept of Influence," in *Public Opinion Quarterly* 27 (Spring, 1963), Chapter 11 in this volume.

is in the first instance the sector of the "public" which can be looked on as the "constituencies" of the collective processes under consideration. It is the group structure of the society looked at in terms of their structured interests in particular modes of effective collective action by particular collectivities. It is only through effective organization that genuine responsibility can be taken, hence the implementation of such interest demands responsibility for collective effectiveness.[13] Again it should be made quite clear that leadership responsibility is not here conceived as an output of power, though many political theorists (e.g. Friedrich) treat both leadership and, more broadly influence, as "forms" of power. The power category which regulates the output of leadership influence takes this form on the one side of binding policy decisions of the collectivity, on the other of political support from the constituency, in the type case through franchise. Policy decisions we would treat as a factor in integration of the system, not as a "consumable" output of the political process.[14]

Finally, a few words need to be said about what I have called the combinatorial process itself. It is of course assumed in economic theory that the "structures" of the factors of production on the one hand, the "demand system" for real outputs on the other hand, are independent of each other. "Utility" of outputs can only be enhanced, to say nothing of maximized, by processes of transformation of the factors in the direction of providing what is wanted as distinguished from what merely is available. The decision-making aspect of this transformative process, what is to be produced, how much and how offered for consumption, is what is meant by economic production, whereas the physical processes are not economic but "technological"; they are controlled by economic considerations, but are not themselves in an analytical sense economic.

The consequence of successful adaptation of available resources to the want or demand system is an increment in the value of the resource-stock conceived in terms of utility as a type of value. But this means recombination of the components of the resource-stock in order to adapt them to the various uses in question.

The same logic applies to the combinatorial process in the political sphere. Here the resources are not land, labor, capital, and organization, but valuation of effectiveness, control of productivity, structured demands

---

13. Here again Barnard's usage of the concept of responsibility seems to me the appropriate one. See Barnard, *op. cit.*
14. In order not to complicate things too much, I shall not enter into problem of the interchange system involving legitimation here. See my paper "Authority, Legitimation, and Political Process," in *Nomos* 1, reprinted as Chapter V of my *Structure and Process in Modern Societies* (Glencoe, Ill.: The Free Press, 1960), Chapter V, pp. 170–198.

and the patterning of legitimation. The "wants" are not for consumption in the economic sense, but for the solution of "interest" problems in the system, including both competitive problems in the allocative sense and conflict problems, as well as problems of enhancement of the total effectiveness of the system of collective organization. In this case also the "structure" of the available resources may not be assumed spontaneously to match the structure of the system of interest-demands. The increment of effectiveness in demand-satisfaction through the political process is, as in the economic case, arrived at through combinatorial decision-processes. The organizational "technology" involved is not in the analytical sense political. The demand-reference is not to discrete units of the system conceived in abstraction from the system as a whole—the "individual" consumer of the economist—but to the problem of the share of benefits and burdens to be allocated to subsystems of various orders. The "consumption" reference is to the interest-unit's place in the allocative system rather than to the independent merits of particular "needs."

The Concept of Power

The above may seem a highly elaborate setting in which to place the formal introduction of the main subject of the paper, namely the concept of power. Condensed and cryptic as the exposition may have been, however, understanding of its main structure is an essential basis for the special way in which it will be proposed to combine the elements which have played a crucial part in the main intellectual traditions dealing with the problems of power.

Power is here conceived as a circulating medium, analogous to money, within what is called the political system, but notably over its boundaries into all three of the other neighboring functional subsystems of a society (as I conceive them), the economic, integrative, and pattern-maintenance systems. Specification of the properties of power can best be approached through an attempt to delineate very briefly the relevant properties of money as such a medium in the economy.

Money is, as the classical economists said, both a medium of exchange and a "measure of value." It is symbolic in that, though measuring and thus "standing for" economic value or utility, it does not itself possess utility in the primary consumption sense—it has no "value in use" but only "in exchange," that is for possession of things having utility. The use of money is thus a mode of communication of offers, on the one hand to purchase, on the other to sell, things of utility, with and for money. It becomes an essential medium only when exchange is neither ascriptive, as exchange of gifts between assigned categories of kin, nor takes place on a basis of barter, one item of commodity or service directly for another.

In exchange for its lack of direct utility money gives the recipient four important degrees of freedom in his participation in the total exchange system. (1) He is free to spend his money for any item or combination of items available on the market which he can afford, (2) he is free to shop around among alternative sources of supply for desired items, (3) he can choose his own time to purchase, and (4) he is free to consider terms which, because of freedom of time and source he can accept or reject or attempt to influence in the particular case. By contrast, in the case of barter, the negotiator is bound to what his particular partner has or wants in relation to what he has and will part with at the particular time. The other side of the gain in degrees of freedom is of course the risk involved in the probabilities of the acceptance of money by others and of the stability of its value.

Primitive money is a medium which is still very close to a commodity, the commonest case being precious metal, and many still feel that the value of money is "really" grounded in the commodity value of the metallic base. On this base, however, there is, in developed monetary systems, erected a complex structure of credit instruments, so that only a tiny fraction of actual transactions is conducted in terms of the metal —it becomes a "reserve" available for certain contingencies, and is actually used mainly in the settlement of international balances. I shall discuss the nature of credit further in another connection later. For the moment suffice it to say that, however important in certain contingencies the availability of metallic reserves may be, no modern monetary system operates primarily with metal as the actual medium, but uses "valueless" money. Moreover, the acceptance of this "valueless" money rests on a certain institutionalized confidence in the monetary system. If the security of monetary commitments rested only on their convertibility into metal, then the overwhelming majority of them would be worthless, for the simple reason that the total quantity of metal is far too small to redeem more than a few.

One final point is that money is "good," that is works as a medium, only within a relatively defined network of market relationships which to be sure now has become world-wide, but the maintenance of which requires special measures to maintain mutual convertibility of national currencies. Such a system is on the one hand a range of exchange-potential within which money may be spent, but on the other hand, one within which certain conditions affecting the protection and management of the unit are maintained, both by law and by responsible agencies under the law.

The first focus of the concept of an institutionalized power system is, analogously, a relational system within which certain categories of commitments and obligations, ascriptive or voluntarily assumed—e.g. by contract—are treated as binding, i.e. under normatively defined conditions their fulfillment may be insisted upon by the appropriate role-reciprocal agencies. Furthermore, in case of actual or threatened resistance to "compliance," i.e. to fulfillment of such obligations when invoked, they will be "enforced" by the threat or actual imposition of situational negative sanctions, in the former case having the function of deterrence, in the latter of punishment. These are events in the situation of the actor of reference which intentionally alter his situation (or threaten to) to his disadvantage, whatever in specific content these alterations may be.

Power then is generalized capacity to secure the performance of binding obligations by units in a system of collective organization when the obligations are legitimized with reference to their bearing on collective goals and where in case of recalcitrance there is a presumption of enforcement by negative situational sanctions—whatever the actual agency of that enforcement.

It will be noted that I have used the conceptions of generalization and of legitimation in defining power. Securing possession of an object of utility by bartering another object for it is not a monetary transaction. Similarly, by my definition, securing compliance with a wish, whether it be defined as an obligation of the object or not, simply by threat of superior force, is not an exercise of power. I am well aware that most political theorists would draw the line differently and classify this as power (e.g. Dahl's definition), but I wish to stick to my chosen line and explore its implications. The capacity to secure compliance must, if it is to be called power in my sense, be generalized and not solely a function of one particular sanctioning act which the user is in a position to impose,[15] and the medium used must be "symbolic."

Secondly, I have spoken of power as involving legitimation. This is,

15. There is a certain element of generality in physical force as a negative sanction, which gives it a special place in power systems. This will be taken up later in the discussion.

in the present context, the necessary consequence of conceiving power as "symbolic," which therefore, if it is exchanged for something intrinsically valuable for collective effectiveness, namely compliance with an obligation, leaves the recipient, the performer of the obligation, with "nothing of value." This is to say, that he has "nothing" but a set of expectations, namely that in other contexts and on other occasions, he can invoke certain obligations of the part of other units. Legitimation is therefore, in power systems, the factor which is parallel to confidence in mutual acceptability and stability of the monetary unit in monetary systems.

The two criteria are connected in that questioning the legitimacy of the possession and use of power leads to resort to progressively more "secure" means of gaining compliance. These must be progressively more effective "intrinsically," hence more tailored to the particular situations of the objects and less general. Furthermore in so far as they are intrinsically effective, legitimacy becomes a progressively less important factor of their effectiveness—at the end of this series lies resort, first to various types of coercion, eventually to the use of force as the most intrinsically effective of all means of coercion.[16]

I should like now to attempt to place both money and power in the context of a more general paradigm, which is an analytical classification of ways in which, in the processes of social interaction, the actions of one unit in a system can, intentionally, be oriented to bringing about a change in what the actions of one or more other units would otherwise have been—thus all fitting into the context of Dahl's conception of power. It is convenient to state this in terms of the convention of speaking of the acting unit of reference—individual or collective—as *ego,* and the object on which he attempts to "operate" as *alter.* We may then classify the alternatives open to ego in terms of two dichotomous variables. On the one hand ego may attempt to gain his end from alter either by using some form of control over the situation in which alter is placed, actually or contingently to change it so as to increase the probability of alter acting in the way he wishes, or, alternatively, without attempting to change alter's situation, ego may attempt to change alter's intentions, i.e. he may manipulate symbols which are meaningful to alter in such a way that he tries to make alter "see" that what ego wants is a "good thing" for him (alter) to do.

16. There are complications here deriving from the fact that power is associated with *negative* sanctions and hence that, in the face of severe resistance, their effectiveness is confined to deterrence.

The second variable then concerns the type of sanctions ego may employ in attempting to guarantee the attainment of his end from alter. The dichotomy here is between positive and negative sanctions. Thus through the situational channel a positive sanction is a change in alter's situation presumptively considered by alter as to his advantage, which is used as a means by ego of having an effect on alter's actions. A negative sanction then is an alteration in alter's situation to the latter's disadvantage. In the case of the intentional channel, the positive sanction is the expression of symbolic "reasons" why compliance with ego's wishes is "a good thing" independently of any further action on ego's part, from alter's point of view, i.e. would be felt by him to be "personally advantageous," whereas the negative sanction is presenting reasons why noncompliance with ego's wishes should be felt by alter to be harmful to interests in which he had a significant personal investment and should therefore be avoided. I should like to call the four types of "strategy" open to ego respectively (1) for the situational channel, positive sanction case, "inducement"; (2) situational channel negative sanction, "coercion"; (3) intentional channel, positive sanction "persuasion," and (4) intentional channel negative sanction "activation of commitments" as shown in the following table:

Sanction type		Channel	
	Intentional	3 | 1	Situational
Positive	Persuasion		Inducement
Negative	Activation of Commitments	4 | 2	Coercion

A further complication now needs to be introduced. We think of a sanction as an intentional act on ego's part, expected by him to change his relation to alter from what it would otherwise have been. As a means of bringing about a change in alter's action, it can operate most obviously where the actual imposition of the sanction is made contingent on a future decision by alter. Thus a process of inducement will operate in two stages, first contingent offer on ego's part that, if alter will "comply" with his wishes, ego will "reward" him by the contingently promised situational change. If then alter in fact does comply, ego will perform the sanctioning act. In the case of coercion the first stage is a contingent threat that, unless alter decides to comply, ego will impose the negative sanction. If, however, alter complies, then nothing further happens, but, if he decides on noncompliance, then ego must carry out his threat, or be in a position of "not meaning it." In the cases of the intentional channel ego's first-stage act is either to predict the occurrence, or to announce his own intention of doing something which affects alter's sentiments or interests. The element of contingency enters in in that ego "argues" to alter, that if this happens, on the one hand alter should be expected to "see" that it would be a good thing for him to do what ego wants—the positive case—or that if he fails to do it it would imply an important "subjective cost" to alter. In the positive case, beyond "pointing out" if alter complies, ego is obligated to deliver the positive attitudinal sanction of approval. In the negative case, the corresponding attitudinal sanction of disapproval is implemented only for noncompliance.

It is hence clear that there is a basic asymmetry between the positive and negative sides of the sanction aspect of the paradigm. This is that, in the cases of inducement and persuasion, alter's compliance obligates ego to "deliver" his promised positive sanction, in the former case the promised advantages, in the latter his approval of alter's "good sense" in recognizing that the decision wished for by ego and accepted as "good" by alter, in fact turns out to be good from alter's point of view. In the negative cases, on the other hand, compliance on alter's part obligates ego, in the situational case, not to carry out his threat, in the intentional case by withholding disapproval to confirm to alter that his compliance did in fact spare him what to him, without ego's intervention, would have been the undesirable subjective consequences of his previous intentions, namely guilt over violations of his commitments.

Finally, alter's freedom of action in his decisions of compliance versus noncompliance is also a variable. This range has a lower limit at which the element of contingency disappears. That is, from ego's point of view, he may not say, if you do so and so, I will intervene, either by situational manipulations or by "arguments" in such and such a way, but he may simply perform an overt act and face alter with a *fait accompli*. In the case of inducement a gift which is an object of value and with respect to the acceptance of which alter is given no option is the limiting case. With respect to coercion, compulsion, that is simply imposing a disadvantageous alteration on alter's situation and then leaving it to alter to decide whether to "do something about it" is the limiting case.

The asymmetry just referred to appears here as well. As contingent it may be said that the primary meaning of negative sanctions is as means of prevention. If they are effective, no further action is required. The case of compulsion is that in which it is rendered impossible for alter to avoid the undesired action on ego's part. In the case of positive sanctions of course ego, for example in making a gift to alter, cuts himself out from benefiting from alter's performance which is presumptively advantageous to him, in the particular exchange.

Both, however, may be oriented to their effect on alter's action in future sequences of interaction. The object of compulsion may have been "taught a lesson" and hence be less disposed to noncompliance with ego's wishes in the future, as well as prevented from performance of a particular undesired act and the recipient of a gift may feel a "sense of obligation" to reciprocate in some form in the future.

So far this discussion has dealt with sanctioning acts in terms of their "intrinsic" significance both to ego and to alter. An offered inducement may thus be possession of a particular object of utility, a coercive threat, that of a particular feared loss, or other noxious experience. But just as, in the initial phase of a sequence, ego transmits his contingent intentions to alter symbolically through communication, so the sanction involved may also be symbolic, e.g. in place of possession of certain intrinsically valuable goods he may offer a sum of money. What we have called the generalized media of interaction then may be used as types of sanctions which may be analyzed in terms of the above paradigm. The factors of generalization and of legitimation of institutionalization, however, as discussed above, introduce certain complications which we must now take up with reference to power. There is a sense in which power may be regarded as the generalized medium of coercion in the above terms, but this formula at the very least requires very careful interpretation—indeed it will turn out by itself to be inadequate.

I spoke above of the "grounding" of the value of money in the commodity value of the monetary metal, and suggested that there is a corresponding relation of the "value," i.e. the effectiveness of power, to the intrinsic effectiveness of physical force as a means of coercion and, in the limiting case, compulsion.[17]

In interpreting this formula due account must be taken of the asymmetry just discussed. The special place of gold as a monetary base rests on such properties as its durability, high value in small bulk, etc., and high probability of acceptability in exchange, i.e. as means of inducement, in a very wide variety of conditions which are not dependent on an institutionalized order. Ego's primary aim in resorting to compulsion

17. I owe the insight into this parallel to Professor Karl W. Deutsch of Yale University (personal discussion).

or coercion, however, is deterrence of unwanted action on alter's part.[18] Force, therefore, is in the first instance important as the "ultimate" deterrent. It is the means which, again independent of any institutionalized system of order, can be assumed to be "intrinsically" the most effective in the context of deterrence, when means of effectiveness which *are* dependent on institutionalized order are insecure or fail. Therefore, the unit of an action system which commands control of physical force adequate to cope with any potential counter threats of force is more secure than any other in a Hobbesian state of nature.[19]

But just as a monetary system resting entirely on gold as the actual medium of exchange is a very primitive one which simply cannot mediate a complex system of market exchange, so a power system in which the only negative sanction is the threat of force is a very primitive one which cannot function to mediate a complex system of organizational coordination—it is far too "blunt" an instrument. Money cannot be only an intrinsically valuable entity if it is to serve as a generalized medium of inducement, but it must, as we have said, be institutionalized as a symbol; it must be legitimized, and must inspire "confidence" within the system—and must also within limits be deliberately managed. Similarly power cannot be only an intrinsically effective deterrent; if it is to be the generalized medium of mobilizing resources for effective collective action, and for the fulfillment of commitments made by collectivities to what we have here called their constituents; it too must be both symbolically generalized, and legitimized.

There is a direct connection between the concept of bindingness, as introduced above, and deterrence. To treat a commitment or any other form of expectation as binding is to attribute a special importance to its fulfillment. Where it is not a matter simply of maintenance of an established routine, but of undertaking new actions in changed circumstances, where the commitment is thus to undertake types of action contingent on circumstances as they develop, then the risk to be minimized is that such contingent commitments will not be carried out when the circumstances in question appear. Treating the expectation or obligation as binding is almost the same thing as saying that appropriate steps on the other side must be taken to prevent nonfulfillment, if possible. Willing-

18. "Sadistic" infliction of injury without instrumental significance to ego does not belong in this context.
19. I have attempted to develop this line of analysis of the significance of force somewhat more fully in "Some Reflections of the Role of Force in Social Relations," Chapter 9 in this volume, first published in Harry Eckstein, ed., *The Problem of Internal War* (Princeton, N.J.: Princeton University Press, 1963).

ness to impose negative sanctions is, seen in this light, simply the carrying out of the implications of treating commitments as binding, and the agent invoking them "meaning it" or being prepared to insist.

On the other hand there are areas in interaction systems where there is a range of alternatives, choice among which is optional, in the light of the promised advantageousness, situational or "intentional," of one as compared to other choices. Positive sanctions as here conceived constitute a contingent increment of relative advantageousness, situational or intentional, of the alternative ego desires alter to choose.

If in these latter areas, a generalized, symbolic medium, is to operate in place of intrinsic advantages, there must be an element of bindingness in the institutionalization of the medium itself—e.g. the fact that the money of a society is "legal tender" which must be accepted in the settlement of debts which have the status of contractual obligations under the law. In the case of money, I suggest that, for the typical acting unit in a market system, what specific undertakings he enters into is overwhelmingly optional in the above sense, but whether the money involved in the transactions is or is not "good" is not for him to judge, but his acceptance of it is binding. Essentially the same is true of the contractual obligations, typically linking monetary and intrinsic utilities, which he undertakes.

I would now like to suggest that what is in a certain sense the obverse holds true of power. Its "intrinsic" importance lies in its capacity to ensure that obligations are "really" binding, thus if necessary can be "enforced" by negative sanctions. But for power to function as a generalized medium in a complex system, that is, to mobilize resources effectively for collective action, it must be "legitimized" which in the present context means that in certain respects compliance, which is the common factor among our media, is not binding, to say nothing of being coerced, but is optional. The range within which there exists a continuous system of interlocking binding obligations is essentially that of the internal relations of an organized collectivity in our sense, and of the contractual obligations undertaken on its behalf at its boundaries.

The points at which the optional factors come to bear are, in the boundary relations of the collectivity, where factors of importance for collective functioning other than binding obligations are exchanged for such binding commitments on the part of the collectivity and *vice versa,* nonbinding outputs of the collectivity for binding commitments to it. These "optional" inputs, I have suggested above, are control of productivity of the economy at one boundary, influence through the relations between leadership and the public demands at the other.[20]

This is a point at which the dissociation of the concept of polity from exclusive relation to government becomes particularly important. In a sufficiently differentiated society, the boundary-relations of the great majority of its important units of collective organization (including some boundaries of government) are boundaries where the overwhelming majority of decisions of commitment are optional in the above sense, though once made, their fulfillment is binding. This, however, is only possible effectively within the range of a sufficiently stable, institutionalized normative order so that the requisite degrees of freedom are protected, e.g. in the fields of employment and of the promotion of interest-demands and decisions about political support.

This feature of the boundary relations of a particular political unit holds even for cases of local government, in that decisions of residence, employment, or acquisition of property within a particular jurisdiction involve the optional element, since in all these respects there is a relatively free choice among local jurisdictions, even though, once having chosen, the citizen is, for example, subject to the tax policies applying within it—and of course he cannot escape being subject to any local jurisdiction, but must choose among those available.

In the case of a "national" political organization, however, its territorial boundaries ordinarily coincide with a relative break in the normative order regulating social interaction.[21] Hence across such boundaries an ambiguity becomes involved in the exercise of power in our sense. On the one hand the invoking of binding obligations operates normally without explicit use of coercion within certain ranges where the two territorial collectivity systems have institutionalized their relations. Thus travelers in friendly foreign countries can ordinarily enjoy personal security and the amenities of the principal public accommodations, exchange of their money at "going" rates, etc. Where, on the other hand, the more general relations between national collectivities are at issue, the power system is especially vulnerable to the kind of insecurity of expectations which tends to be met by the explicit resort to threat of coercive sanctions. Such threats in turn, operating on both sides of a

20. Thus, if control of productivity operates through monetary funds, their possessor cannot "force," e.g., prospective employees to accept employment.
21. This, of course, is a relative difference. Some hazards increase the moment one steps outside his own home, police protection may be better in one local community than the next, and crossing a state boundary may mean a considerable difference in legal or actual rights.

reciprocal relationship, readily enter into a vicious circle of resort to more and more "intrinsically" effective or drastic measures of coercion, at the end of which road lies physical force. In other words, the danger of war is endemic in uninstitutionalized relations between territorially organized collectivities.

There is thus an inherent relation between both the use and the control of force and the territorial basis of organization.[22] One central condition of the integration of a power system is that it should be effective within a territorial area, and a crucial condition of this effectiveness in turn is the monopoly of control of paramount force within the area. The critical point then, at which the institutional integration of power systems is most vulnerable to strain, and to degeneration into reciprocating threats of the use of force, is between territorially organized political systems. This, notoriously, is the weakest point in the normative order of human society today, as it has been almost from time immemorial.

In this connection it should be recognized that the possession, the mutual threat, and possible use of force is only in a most proximate sense the principal "cause" of war. The essential point is that the "bottleneck" of mutual regression to more and more primitive means of protecting or advancing collective interests is a "channel" into which all elements of tension between the collective units in question may flow. It is a question of the many levels at which such elements of tension may on the one hand build up, on the other be controlled, not of any simple and unequivocal conception of the "inherent" consequences of the possession and possible uses of organized force.

It should be clear that again there is a direct parallel with the economic case. A functioning market system requires integration of the monetary medium. It cannot be a system of N independent monetary units and agencies controlling them. This is the basis on which the main range of extension of a relatively integrated market system tends to coincide with the "politically organized society," as Roscoe Pound called it, over a territorial area. International transactions require special provisions not required for domestic.

The basic "management" of the monetary system must then be integrated with the institutionalization of political power. Just as the latter depends on an effective monopoly of institutionally organized force, so monetary stability depends on an effective monopoly of basic reserves

22. *Cf.* my paper "The Principal Structures of Community," *Nomos* 2 and *Structure and Process, op. cit.,* Chapter 8. See also J. W. Hurst, *Law and Social Process in the United States* (Ann Arbor: University of Michigan Law School, 1960).

protecting the monetary unit and, as we shall see later, on centralization of control over the credit system.

The Hierarchical Aspects of Power Systems

A very critical question now arises, which may be stated in terms of a crucial difference between money and power. Money is a "measure of value," as the classical economists put it, in terms of a continuous linear variable. Objects of utility valued in money are more or less valuable than each other in numerically statable terms. Similarly, as medium of exchange, amounts of money differ in the same single dimension. One acting unit in a society has more money—or assets exchangeable for money—than another, less than, or the same.

Power involves a quite different dimension which may be formulated in terms of the conception that *A* may have power over *B*. Of course in competitive bidding the holder of superior financial assets has an advantage in that, as economists say, the "marginal utility of money" is less to him than to his competitor with smaller assets. But his "bid" is no more binding on the potential exchange partner than is that of the less affluent bidder, since in "purchasing power" all dollars are "created free and equal." There may be auxiliary reasons why the purveyor may think it advisable to accept the bid of the more affluent bidder; these, however, are not strictly economic, but concern the interrelations between money and other media, and other bases of status in the system.

The connection between the value of effectiveness—as distinguished from utility—and bindingness, implies a conception in turn of the focussing of responsibility for decisions, and hence of authority for their implementation.[23] This implies a special form of inequality of power which in turn implies a priority system of commitments. The implications of having assumed binding commitments, on the fulfillment of which spokesmen for the collectivity are prepared to insist to the point of imposing serious negative sanctions for noncompliance, are of an order of seriousness such that matching the priority system in the commitments themselves there must be priorities in the matter of which decisions take precedence over others and, back of that, of which decision-making agencies have the right to make decisions at what levels. Throughout this discussion the crucial question concerns bindingness. The reference

23. As already noted, in this area, I think the analysis of Chester I. Barnard, in *The Functions of the Executive, op. cit.,* is so outstandingly clear and cogent that it deserves the status of a classic of political theory in my specific sense. See especially Chapter X.

is to the collectivity, and hence the strategic significance of the various "contributions" on the performance of which the effectiveness of its action depends. Effectiveness for the collectivity as a whole is dependent on hierarchical ordering of the relative strategic importance of these contributions, and hence of the conditions governing the imposition of binding obligations on the contributors.

Hence the power of A over B is, in its legitimized form, the "right" of A, as a decision-making unit involved in collective process, to make decisions which take precedence over those of B, in the interest of the effectiveness of the collective operation as a whole.

The right to use power, or negative sanctions on a barter basis or even compulsion to assert priority of a decision over others, I shall, following Barnard, call authority. Precedence in this sense can take different forms. The most serious ambiguity here seems to derive from the assumption that authority and its attendant power may be understood as implying opposition to the wishes of "lower-order" echelons which hence includes the prerogative of coercing or compelling compliance. Though this is implicit, it may be that the higher-order authority and power may imply the prerogative is primarily significant as "defining the situation" for the performance of the lower-order echelons. The higher "authority" may then make a decision which defines terms within which other units in the collectivity will be expected to act, and this expectation is treated as binding. Thus a ruling by the Commissioner of Internal Revenue may exclude certain tax exemptions which units under his jurisdiction have thought taxpayers could claim. Such a decision need not activate an overt conflict between commissioner and taxpayer, but may rather "channel" the decisions of revenue agents and taxpayers with reference to performance of obligations.

There does not seem to be an essential theortical difficulty involved in this "ambiguity." We can say that the primary function of superior authority is clearly to define the situation for the lower echelons of the collectivity. The problem of overcoming opposition in the form of dispositions to noncompliance then arises from the incomplete institutionalization of the power of the higher authority holder. Sources of this may well include overstepping of the bounds of his legitimate authority on the part of this agent. The concept of compliance should clearly not be limited to "obedience" by subordinates, but is just as importantly applicable to observance of the normative order by the high echelons of authority and power. The concept of constitutionalism is the critical one at this level, namely that even the highest authority is bound in the strict sense of the concept bindingness used here, by the terms of the normative order under which he operates, e.g. holds office. Hence binding obligations can clearly be "invoked" by lower-order against higher-order agencies as well as *vice versa*.

This of course implies the relatively firm institutionalization of the normative order itself. Within the framework of a highly differentiated polity it implies, in addition to constitutionalism itself, a procedural system for the granting of high political authority, even in private, to say nothing of public organizations, and a legal framework within which such authority is legitimized. This in turn includes another order of procedural institutions within which the question of the legality of actual uses of power can be tested.

Power and Authority

The institutionalization of the normative order just referred to thus comes to focus in the concept of authority. Authority is essentially the institutional code within which the use of power as medium is organized and legitimized. It stands to power essentially as property, as an institution, does to money. Property is a bundle of rights of possession, including above all that of alienation, but also at various levels of control and use. In a highly differentiated institutional system, property rights are focused on the valuation of utility, i.e. the economic significance of the objects, e.g. for consumption or as factors of production, and this factor comes to be differentiated from authority. Thus, in European feudalism the "landlord" had both property rights in the land, and political jurisdiction over persons acting on the same land. In modern legal systems these components are differentiated from each other so the landowner is no longer the landlord; this function is taken over mainly by local political authority.

Precisely with greater differentiation the focus of the institution becomes more generalized and, while specific objects of possession of course continue to be highly important, the most important object of property comes to be monetary assets, and specific objects are valued as assets, i.e., in terms of potentials of marketability. Today we can say that rights to money assets, the ways in which these can be legitimately acquired and disposed of, the ways in which the interests of other parties must be protected, have come to constitute the core of the institution of property.[24]

Authority, then, is the aspect of a status in a system of social organization, namely its collective aspect, by virtue of which the incumbent is put in a position legitimately to make decisions which are binding, not only on himself but on the collectivity as a whole and hence its other member-units, in the sense that so far as their implications impinge on their respective roles and statuses, they are bound to act in accordance with these implications. This includes the right to insist on such action though, because of the general division of labor, the holder of authority very often is not himself in a position to "enforce" his decisions, but must be dependent on specialized agencies for this.

If, then, authority be conceived as the institutional counterpart of power, the main difference lies in the fact that authority is not a circulating medium. Sometimes, speaking loosely, we suggest that someone "gives away his property." He can give away property rights in specific possessions but not the institution of property. Similarly the incumbent of an office can relinquish authority by resigning, but this is very different from abolishing the authority of the office. Property as institution is a code defining rights in objects of possession, in the first instance physical objects, then "symbolic" objects, including cultural objects such as "ideas" so far as they are valuable in monetary terms, and of course including money itself, whoever possesses them. Authority, similarly, is a set of rights in status in a collectivity, precisely in the collectivity as actor, including most especially right to acquire and use power in that status.

The institutional stability, which is essential to the conception of a code, then for property inheres in the institutional structure of the market. At a higher level the institution of property includes rights, not only to use and dispose of particular objects of value, but to participate in the system of market transactions.

It is then essentially the institutionalized code defining rights of participation in the power system which I should like to think of as authority. It is this conception which gives us the basis for the essential distinction between the internal and the external aspects of power relative to a particular collectivity. The collectivity is, by our conception, the

24. Two particularly important manifestations of this monetization of property are, first the general legal understanding that executors of estates are not obligated to retain the exact physical inventory intact pending full statement, but may sell various items—their fiduciary obligation is focussed on the money value of the estate. Similarly in the law of contract increasing option has been given to compensate with money damages in lieu of the specific "performance" originally contracted for.

definition of the range within which a system of institutionalized rights to hold and use power can be closed. This is to say, the implications of an authoritative decision made at one point in the system can be made genuinely binding at all the other relevant points through the relevant processes of feed-back.

The hierarchical priority system of authority and power, with which this discussion started can, by this criterion, only be binding within a given particular collective system. In this sense then a hierarchy of authority—as distinguished from the sheer differences of power of other coercive capacities—must be internal to a collectively organized system in this sense. This will include authority to bind the collectivity in its relations to its environment, to persons and to other collectivities. But bindingness, legitimized and enforced through the agency of this particular collectivity, cannot be extended beyond its boundaries. If it exists at all it must be by virtue of an institutionalized normative order which transcends the particular collectivity, through contractual arrangements with others, or through other types of mutually binding obligation.

Power, Influence, Equalization, and Solidarity

It is on this basis that it may be held that at the boundaries of the collectivity the closed system of priorities is breached by "free" exercise, at the constituency or integrative boundary, of influence. Status in the collectivity gives authority to settle the terms on which power will be exchanged with influence over this boundary. The wielder of influence from outside, on the collectivity, is not bound in advance to any particular terms, and it is of the essence of use of power in the "foreign relations" of the collectivity, that authority is a right, within certain limits of discretion, to spend power in exchange for influence. This in turn can, through the offer of accepting leadership responsibility in exchange for political support, replenish the expenditure of power by a corresponding input.

By this reasoning influence should be capable of altering the priority system within the collectivity. This is what I interpret policy decision as a category of the use of power as a medium to be, the process of altering priorities in such a way that the new pattern comes to be binding on the collectivity. Similarly, the franchise must be regarded as the institutionalization of a marginal, interpenetrating status, between the main collectivity and its environment of solidary groupings in the larger system. It is the institutionalization of a marginal authority, the use of which is confined to the function of selection among candidates for leadership responsibility. In the governmental case, this is the inclusion in a common collectivity system of both the operative agencies of government and the "constituencies" on which leadership is dependent, a grant not only in a given instance of power to the latter but a status of authority with respect to the one crucial function of selection of leadership and granting them the authority of office.

In interpreting this discussion it is essential to keep in mind that a society consists, from the present point of view, not in one collectivity, but in a ramified system of collectivities. Because, however, of the basic imperatives of effective collective action already discussed, these must in addition to the pluralistic cross-cutting which goes with functional differentiation, also have the aspect of a "Chinese box" relation. There must be somewhere a paramount focus of collective authority and with it of the control of power—though it is crucial that this need not be the top of the total system of normative control, which may for example be religious. This complex of territoriality and the monopoly of force are central to this, because the closed system of enforceable bindingness can always be breached by the intervention of force.[25]

The bindingness of normative orders other than those upheld by the paramount territorial collectivity must be defined within limits institutionalized in relation to it. So far as such collectivities are not "agencies" of the state, in this sense, their spheres of "jurisdiction" must be defined in terms of a normative system, a body of law, which is binding both on government and on the nongovernmental collectivity units, though in the "last analysis" it will, within an institutionalized order either have to be enforced by government, or contrariwise, by revolutionary action against government.

Since independent control of serious, socially organized force cannot be given to "private" collectivities, their ultimate negative sanctions tend to be expulsion from membership, though many other types of sanction may be highly important.

Considerations such as these thus do not in any way eliminate or weaken the importance of hierarchical priorities within a collective

25. Since this system is the territorially organized collectivity, the state with its government, these considerations underlie the critical importance of foreign relations in the sense of the relations to other territorially organized, force-controlling collectivities, since, once internal control of force is effectively institutionalized, the danger of this kind of breach comes from the outside in this specific sense of outside. The point is cogently made by Raymond Aron.

decision-system itself. The strict "line" structure of such authority is, however, greatly modified by the interpenetration of other systems with the political, notably for our purposes the importance of technical competence. The qualifications of the importance of hierarchy apply in principle at the boundaries of the particular collective system—analytically considered—rather than internally to it. These I would interpret as defining the limits of authority. There are two main contexts in which norms of equality may be expected to modify the concrete expectations of hierarchical decision-systems, namely on the one hand, the context of influence over the right to assume power, or decision-making authority and, on the other hand, the context of access to opportunity for status as a contributing unit in the specific political system in question.

It is essential here to recall that I have treated power as a circulating medium, moving back and forth over the boundaries of the polity. The "real" outputs of the political process, and the factors in its effectiveness —in the sense corresponding to the real outputs and factors of economic production—are not in my sense "forms" of power but, in the most important cases, of financial control of economic resources, and of influence, in the meaning of the category of influence, defined as a generalized mechanism of persuasion. These are very essential elements in the total political process, but it is just as important to distinguish them from power as it is to distinguish financially valuable outputs and factors of production from money itself. They may, in certain circumstances, be exchangeable for power, but this is a very different thing from being forms of power.

The circulation of power between polity and integrative system I conceive to consist in binding policy decisions on the one hand, which is a primary factor in the integrative process, and political support on the other, which is a primary output of the integrative process. Support is exchanged, by a "public" or constituency, for the assumption of leadership responsibility, through the process of persuading those in a position to give binding support that it is advisable to do so in the particular instance—through the use of influence or some less generalized means of persuasion. In the other political "market" *vis-à-vis* the integrative system, policy decisions are given in response to interest-demands in the sense of the above discussion. This is to say that interest groups, which, it is most important to note as a concept says nothing about the moral quality of the particular interest, attempt to persuade those who hold authority in the relevant collectivity, i.e. are in a position to make binding decisions, that they should indeed commit the collectivity to the policies the influence-wielders want. In our terms this is to persuade the decision makers to use and hence "spend" some of their power for the purpose in hand. The spending of power is to be thought of, just as the spending of money, as essentially consisting in the sacrifice of alternative decisions which are precluded by the commitments undertaken under a policy. A member of the collectivity we conceive as noted to have authority to "spend" power through making binding decisions through which those outside acquire claims against the collectivity. Its authority, however, is inalienable; it can only be exercised, not "spent."

It has been suggested that policies must be hierarchically ordered in a priority system and that the power to decide among policies must have a corresponding hierarchical ordering since such decisions bind the collectivity and its constituent units. The imperative of hierarchy does not, however, apply to the other "market" of the power system in this direction, that involving the relations between leadership and political support. Here on the contrary it is a critically important fact that in the largest-scale and most highly differentiated systems, namely the leadership systems of the most "advanced" national societies, the power element has been systematically equalized through the device of the franchise, so that the universal adult franchise has been evolved in all the Western democracies.[26] Equality of the franchise which, since the consequences of its exercise are very strictly binding,[27] I classify as in fact a form of power, has been part of a larger complex of its institutionalization, which includes in addition the principle of universality—its extension to all responsible adult citizens in good standing and the secrecy of the ballot, which serves to differentiate this context of political action from other contexts of involvement, and protect it against pressures, not only from hierarchical superiors but, as Rokkan points out, from status-peers as well.

Of course the same basic principle of one member, one vote, is institutionalized in a vast number of voluntary associations, including many which are subassociations of wider collectivities, such as faculties in a university, or boards and committees. Thus the difference between a chairman or presiding officer, and an executive head is clearly marked with respect to formal authority, whatever it may be with respect to influence, by the principle that a chairman, like any other member, has

26. See, on this process, Stein Rokkan, "Mass Suffrage, Secret Voting, and Political Participation," *European Journal of Sociology* 2 (1961), 132–152.
27. I.e., the aggregate of votes, evaluated by the electoral rules, determines the incumbency of office.

only one vote. Many collectivities are in this sense "truncated" associations, e.g. in cases where fiduciary boards are self-recruiting. Nevertheless the importance of this principle of equality of power through the franchise is so great empirically that the question of how it is grounded in the structure of social systems is a crucial one.

It derives, I think, from what I should call the universalistic component in patterns of normative order. It is the value-principle that discriminations among units of a system, must be grounded in intrinsically valued differences among them, which are, for both persons and collectivities, capacities to contribute to valued societal processes. Differences of power in decision-making which mobilizes commitments, both outward in relation to the environment of the collectivity and internally, to the assignment of tasks to its members, are ideally grounded in the intrinsic conditions of effectiveness. Similarly, differences on the basis of technical competence to fulfill essential roles are grounded in the strategic conditions of effective contribution.

These considerations do not, however, apply to the functions of the choice of leadership, where this choice has been freed from ascriptive bases of right, e.g. through kinship status or some imputed "charismatic" superiority as in such a case as "white supremacy." There is a persistent pressure of the sufficiently highly valued functions or outcomes, and under this pressure there seems to have been a continual, though uneven, process of erosion of discriminations in this critical field of the distribution of power.

It may be suggested that the principle of universalistic normative organization which is immediately superordinate to that of political democracy in the sense of the universal equal franchise, is the principle of equality before the law; in the case of the American Constitution, the principle of equal protection of the laws. I have emphasized that a constitutional framework is essential to advanced collective organization, given of course levels of scale and complexity which preclude purely "informal" and traditional normative regulation. The principle in effect puts the burden of proof on the side of imposing discriminations, either in access to rights or in imposition of obligations, on the side that such discriminations are to be justified only by differences in sufficiently highly valued exigencies of operation of the system.

The principle of equality both at the level of application of the law and of the political franchise, is clearly related to a conception of the status of membership. Not all living adults have equal right to influence the affairs of all collectivities everywhere in the world, nor does an

American have equal rights with a citizen of a quite different society within its territory. Membership is in fact the application to the individual unit of the concept of boundary of a social system which has the property of solidarity, in Durkheim's sense. The equal franchise is a prerogative of members, and of course the criteria of membership can be very differently institutionalized under different circumstances.

There is an important sense in which the double interchange system under consideration here, which I have called the "support" system linking the polity with the integrative aspect of the society, is precisely the system in which power is most directly controlled, both in relation to more particularized interest-elements which seek relatively particularized policies—which of course includes wanting to prevent certain potential actions—and in relation to the more general "tone" given to the directionality of collective action by the character of the leadership elements which assume responsibility and which, in exchange, are invested, in the type case by the electoral process, with authority to carry out their responsibilities. One central feature of this control is coming to terms with the hierarchical elements inherent in power systems in the aspects just discussed. Certain value systems may of course reinforce hierarchy, but it would be my view that a universalistically oriented value system inherently tends to counteract the spread of hierarchical patterns with respect to power beyond the range felt to be functionally necessary for effectiveness.[28]

There is, however, a crucial link between the equality of the franchise and the hierarchical structure of authority within collectivities, namely the all-or-none character of the electoral process. Every voter has an equal vote in electing to an office, but in most cases only one candidate is in fact elected—the authority of office is not divided among candidates in proportion to the numbers of votes they received, but is concentrated in the successful candidate, even though the margin be very narrow, as in the U.S. presidential election of 1960. There are, of course, considerable possible variations in electoral rules, but this basic principle is as central as is that of the equality of the franchise. This principle seems to be the obverse of the hierarchy of authority.

28. Of course where conditions are sufficiently simple, or where there is sufficient anxiety about the hierarchal implications of power, the egalitarian element may penetrate far into the political decision-making system itself, with, e.g. insistence that policy-decisions, both external and internal in reference, be made by majority vote of all members, or even under a unanimity rule. The respects in which such a system— which of course realistically often involves a sharply hierarchal stratification of influence—is incompatible with effectiveness in many spheres, can be said to be relatively clear, especially for *large* collectivities.

The hierarchical character of power systems has above been sharply contrasted with the linear quantitative character of wealth and monetary assets. This has in turn been related to the fundamental difference between the exigencies of effectiveness in collective action, and the exigencies of utility in providing for the requirements of satisfying the "wants" of units. In order to place the foregoing discussion of the relations between power and influence in a comparable theoretical context, it is necessary to formulate the value-standard which is paramount in regulating the integrative function which corresponds to utility and effectiveness in the economic and political functions respectively.

This is, with little doubt, the famous concept of solidarity as formulated by Durkheim.[29] The two essential points of reference for present purposes concern the two main aspects of membership, as outlined above, the first of which concerns claims on executive authority for policy decisions which integrate the total collective interest on the one hand, the "partial" interest of a subgroup on the other. The second concerns integration of rights to a "voice" in collective affairs with the exigencies of effective leadership and the corresponding responsibility.

The principle is the "grounding" of a collective system in a consensus in the sense of the above discussion, namely an "acceptance" on the part of its members of their belonging together, in the sense of sharing, over a certain range, common interests, interests which are defined both by type, and by considerations of time. Time becomes relevant because of the uncertainty factor in all human action, and hence the fact that neither benefits nor burdens can be precisely predicted and planned for in advance; hence an effective collectivity must be prepared to absorb unexpected burdens, and to balance this, to carry out some sort of just distribution of benefits which are unexpected and/or are not attributable to the earned agency of any particular subunit.

Solidarity may then be thought of as the implementation of common values by definition of the requisite collective systems in which they are to be actualized. Collective action as such we have defined as political function. The famous problem of order, however, cannot be solved without a common normative system. Solidarity is the principle by virtue of which the commitment to norms, which is "based" in turn on values, is articulated with the formation of collectivities which are capable of

29. It is the central concept of *The Division of Labor in Society*. For my own relatively recent understanding of its significance, see "Durkheim's Contribution to the Theory of Integration of Social Systems," in Kurt Wolff, ed., *Émile Durkheim, 1858–1917* (Columbus, Ohio: Ohio State University Press, 1960), pp. 118–153, included in this volume as Chapter 1.

effective collective action. Whereas, in the economic direction, the "problem" of effective action is coping with the scarcity of available resources, including trying to facilitate their mobility, in the integrative direction it is orderly solution of competing claims, on the one hand to receive benefits—or minimize losses—deriving from memberships, on the other to influence the processes by which collective action operates. This clearly involves some institutionalization of the subordination of unit-interest to the collective in cases where the two are in conflict, actual or potential, and hence the justification of unit interests as compatible with the more extensive collective interest. A social system then possesses solidarity in proportion as its members are committed to common interests through which discrete unit interests can be integrated and the justification of conflict resolution and subordination can be defined and implemented. It defines, not the modes of implementation of these common interests through effective agency, but the standards by which such agency should be guided and the rights of various constituent elements to have a voice in the interpretation of these standards.

Power and Equality of Opportunity

We may now turn to the second major boundary of the polity, at which another order of modifications of the internal hierarchy of authority comes to focus. This is the boundary vis-à-vis the economy where the "political" interest is to secure control of productivity and services, and the economic interest lies in the collective control of fluid resources and in what we may call opportunity for effectiveness. I shall not attempt here to discuss the whole interchange complex, but will confine myself to the crucial problem of the way that here also the hierarchical structure of power can, under certain conditions, be modified in an egalitarian direction.

Productivity of the economy is in principle allocable among collective (in our sense political) claimants to its control as facilities, in linear quantitative terms. This linear quantification is achieved through the medium of money, either allocation of funds with liberty to expend them at will, or at least monetary evaluation of more specific facilities.

In a sufficiently developed system, services must be evaluated in monetary terms also, both from the point of view of rational budgeting and of the monetary cost of their employment. In terms of their utilization, however, services are "packages" of performance-capacity, which are qualitatively distinct and of unequal value as contributions to collective effectiveness. Their evaluation as facilities must hence involve an estimate of strategic significance which matches the general priority scale which has been established to regulate the internal functioning of the collectivity.

Services, however, constitute a resource to be acquired from outside the collectivity, as Weber puts it through a "formally free" contract of employment. The contracts thus made are binding on both sides, by virtue of a normative system transcending the particular collectivity, though the obligation must articulate with the internal normative order including its hierarchical aspect. But the purveyors of service are not, in advance, bound by this internal priority system and hence an exchange, which is here interpreted to operate in the first instance as between strategic significance expressed as power-potential, and the monetary value of the service, must be arrived at.

Quite clearly, when the purveyor of service has once entered into such a contract, he is bound by the aspect of its terms which articulates the service into this internal system, including the level of authority he exercises and its implications for his power position in the collectivity. If the collectivity is making in any sense a rational arrangement, this must be tailored to an estimate of the level of the value of his strategic contribution, hence his performance-capacity.

Since, however, the boundary interchange is not integral to the internal system of bindingness, the hierarchical imperatives do not apply to the opportunity aspect of this interchange on the extra-political side. This is to say that the same order of pressures of a higher-order universalistic normative system can operate here that we suggested operated to bring about equality in the franchise. Again the principle is that no particularistic discriminations are to be legitimized which are not grounded in essential functional exigencies of the system of reference.

In the case of the franchise there seems to be no inherent stopping place short of complete equality, qualified only by the minimum consideration of competence attached to fully responsible membership—excluding only minors, "defectives," through retardation and mental illness, and those morally disqualified through crime. In the service case, on the other hand, given commitments to optimum performance which in the present context can be taken for granted, the limit to the equating of universalism and equality lies in the concept of competence. Hence the principle arrived at is the famous one of equality of opportunity, by which there is equalization of access to opportunity for contribution, but selection on criteria of differential competence, both quantitative and qualitative.

Whereas the equalization of the franchise is a control on differential power "from above" in the hierarchy of control and operates mainly through the selection of leadership, equality of opportunity is (in the corresponding sense) a control from below, and operates to check particularistic tendencies which would tend to exclude sources of service which are qualified by competence to contribute, and/or to check tendencies to retain services which are inferior to those available in competition with them.

It is the combination of these two foci of universalization, the equalitarianism of upper rights to control through the franchise, and of rights to participate through service on the basis of competence, which account for the extent to which the "cumulative advantage,"[30] which might seem to be inherent in the hierarchical internal structure of power systems, often in fact fails either to materialize at all, or to be as strong as expected.

Long and complex as it is, the above discussion may be summed up as an attempted solution of the second of the three main problems with which this paper began, namely that of the relation between the coercive and the consensual aspects of the phenomenon of power. The answer is first premised on the conception of power as a specific but generalized medium of the functioning of social relationships in complex, differentiated systems of social interaction.

Power is secondly specifically associated with the bindingness of obligations to performance within a range of circumstances which may arise in a varying and changing situation. The obligations concerned are hence in some important degree generalized so that particularities under them are contingent on circumstances. The bindingness of obligations implies that they stand on a level of seriousness such that the invoking agent, ego, may be put in the position of asserting that, since he "means it" that alter must comply, he is prepared to insist on compliance. Partly then as a symbolic expression of this seriousness of "meaning it" and partly as an instrument of deterrence of noncompliance,[31] this insistence is associated with command of negative situational sanctions the application of which is frequently contingent on noncompliance, and in certain

30. Cf. C. Wright Mills, The Power Elite (New York: Oxford University Press, 1956) and my commentary in Structure and Process in Modern Societies, op. cit., Chapter 6.
31. Cf. Durkheim's famous essay, "Deux lois de l'évolution pénale," L'Année Sociologique 4(1899–1900): 65–95.

cases deterrence is achieved by compulsion. We would not speak of power where situational negative sanctions or compulsion are in no circumstances attached to noncompliance in cases where a legitimate agent insists on compliance.

Thirdly, however, power is here conceived as a generalized medium of mobilizing commitments or obligation for effective collective action. As such it ordinarily does not itself possess intrinsic effectiveness, but symbolizes effectiveness and hence the bindingness of the relevant obligations to contribute to it. The operative validity of the meaningfulness of the symbolization is not a function of any one single variable but, we argue, of two primary ones. One of these is the willingness to insist upon compliance, or at least to deter noncompliance, a line of reasoning which leads to the understanding of willingness to resort to negative sanctions, the nature of which will vary, as a function of the seriousness of the question, on the dimension of their progressively more drastic nature, in the last analysis force.

The other variable concerns the collective reference and hence the justification[32] of invoking the obligations in question in the situation. This aspect concerns the dependence of power on the institutionalization of authority and hence the rights of collective agents to mobilize performances and define them as binding obligations. This justification inherently rests on some sort of consensus among the members of the collectivity of reference, if not more broadly, with respect to a system of norms under which authority and power are legitimized on a basis wider than this particular collectivity by the values of the system. More specifically, authority is the institutionalized code within which the "language of power" is meaningful and, therefore, its use will be accepted in the requisite community, which is in the first instance the community of collective organization in our sense.

Seen in this light the threat of coercive measures, or of compulsion, without legitimation or justification, should not properly be called the use of power at all, but is the limiting case where power, losing its symbolic character, merges into an intrinsic instrumentality of securing compliance with wishes, rather than obligations. The monetary parallel is the use of a monetary metal as an instrument of barter where as a commodity it ceases to be an institutionalized medium of exchange at all.

In the history of thought there has been a very close connection between emphasis on the coercive element in power systems and on the

32. *Cf.* my paper "On The Concept of Influence," *op. cit.*, for a discussion of the concept of justification and its distinction from legitimation. Chapter 11 in this book.

hierarchical aspect of the structure of systems of authority and power. The above discussion has, I hope, helped to dissociate them by showing that this hierarchical aspect, important as it is, is only part of the structure of power systems. The view advanced is that it is an inherent aspect of the internal structure of collectivities. No collectivity, even the nation, however, stands alone as a total society since it is integrated with norms and values; subcollectivities can even less be claimed to be societies. The collectivity aspect of total social structure may in a particular case be dominant over others, but always in principle it impinges on at least two sorts of boundary-problems, namely that involved in its "support" system and that involved in the mobilization of services as sources of contribution to its functioning.

In both these cases, we have argued, quite different principles are operative from that of the hierarchy of authority, namely the equality of franchise on the one hand, equality of opportunity on the other. In both cases I envisage an interchange of power, though not of authority, over the boundary of the polity, and in neither case can the principle governing the allocation of power through this interchange be considered to be hierarchical in the line authority sense. The empirical problems here are, as elsewhere, formidable, but I definitely argue that it is illegitimate to hold that, from serious consideration of the role of power as a generalized medium, it can be inferred that there is a general trend to hierarchization in the total empirical social systems involved.[33]

The Zero-Sum Problem

We are now in a position to take up the last of the three main problems with which the discussion started, namely whether power is a zero-sum phenomenon in the sense that, in a system, a gain in power by a unit A is in the nature of the case the cause of a corresponding loss of power by other units, $B, C, D. \ldots$ The parallel with money on which we have been insisting throughout should give us clues to the answer, which clearly is, under certain circumstances yes, but by no means under all circumstances.

In the monetary case it is obvious that in budgeting the use of a fixed income, allocation to one use must be at the expense of alternative uses.

33. Failure to see this seems to me to be a major source of the utopian strain in Marxist theory, expressed above all by the expectation of the "withering away of the state." There is perhaps a parallel to the confusion connected for many centuries with the Aristotelian doctrine of the "sterility" of money.

The question is whether parallel limitations apply to an economy conceived as a total system. For long this seemed to many economists to be the case; this was the main burden of the old "quantity theory of money." The most obvious political parallel is that of the hierarchy of authority within a particular collectivity. It would seem to be obvious that, if *A*, who has occupied a position of substantial power, is demoted, and *B* takes his place, *A* loses power and *B* gains it, the total in the system remaining the same. Many political theorists like Lasswell and C. Wright Mills, generalized this to political systems as a whole.[34]

The most important and obvious point at which the zero-sum doctrine breaks down for money is that of credit-creation through commercial banking. This case is so important as a model that a brief discussion here is in order. Depositors, that is, entrust their money funds to a bank, not only for safe keeping, but as available to the bank for lending. In so doing, however, they do not relinquish any property rights in these funds. The funds are repayable by the bank in full on demand, the only normal restrictions being with respect to banking hours. The bank, however, uses part of the balances on deposit with it to make loans at interest, pursuant to which it not only makes the money available to the borrower, but in most cases assumes binding obligations not to demand repayment except on agreed terms, which in general leave the borrower undisturbed control for a stipulated period—or obligates him to specified installments of amortization. In other words, the same dollars come to do "double duty," to be treated as possessions by the depositors, who retain their property rights, and also by the banker who preempts the rights to loan them, as if they were "his." In any case there is a corresponding net addition to the circulating medium, measured by the quantity of new bank deposits created by the loans outstanding.[35]

Perhaps the best way to describe what happens is to say that there has occurred a differentiation in the functions of money and hence there are two ways of using it in the place of one. The ordinary deposit is a reserve for meeting current expenses, whether "private" or "business," which is mainly important with respect to the time element of the degrees of freedom mentioned above. From the point of view of the depositor the bank is a convenience, giving him safekeeping, the privilege of writing checks rather than using cash, etc., at a cost which is low

34. H. D. Lasswell and A. Kaplan, *Power and Society* (New Haven: Yale University Press, 1950) and Mills, *The Power Elite, op. cit.*
35. Whether this be interpreted as net addition to the medium or as increase in the velocity of circulation of the "slow" deposit funds, is indifferent, because its economic effects are the same.

because the bank earns interest through its loaning operations. From the point of view of the borrower, on the other hand, the bank is a source of otherwise unavailable funds, ideally in the economist's sense, for investment, for financing operations promising future increments of economic productivity, which would not otherwise have been feasible.

The possibility of this "miracle of loaves and fishes" of course rests on an empirical uniformity, namely that depositors do in fact, under normal circumstances, keep sufficient balances on hand—though they are not required to—so that it is safe for the bank to have substantial amounts out on loan at any given time. Underlying this basic uniformity is the fact that an individual bank will ordinarily also have access to "reserves," e.g. assets which, though earning interest, are sufficiently liquid to be realized on short notice, and in the last analysis such resources are those of a federal reserve system. The individual bank, and with it its depositors, is thus ordinarily relatively secure.

We all know, however, that this is true only so long as the system operates smoothly. A particular bank can meet unusual demands for withdrawal of deposits, but if this unusual demand spreads to a whole banking system, the result may be a crisis, which only collective action can solve. Quite clearly the expectation that all depositors should be paid, all at once, in "real" money, e.g. even "cash" to say nothing of monetary metal, cannot be fulfilled. Any monetary system in which bank credit plays an important part is in the nature of the case normally "insolvent" by that standard.

Back of these considerations, it may be said, lies an important relation between bindingness and "confidence" which is in certain respects parallel to that between coercion and consensus in relation to power, indeed one which, through the element of bindingness, involves a direct articulation between money and power. How is this parallel to be defined and how does the articulation operate?

First the banking operation depends on mutual confidence or trust in that depositors entrust their funds to the bank, knowing, if they stop to think about it, that the bank will have a volume of loans outstanding which makes it impossible to repay all deposits at once. It is well known with what hesitation, historically, many classes have been brought to trust banks at all in this simple sense—the classical case of the French peasant's insistence on putting his savings in cash under the mattress is sufficient illustration. The other side of the coin, however, is the bank's trust that its depositors will not panic to the point of in fact demanding the complete fulfillment of their legal rights.

The banker here assumes binding obligations in two directions, the honoring of both of which depends on this trust. On the one hand he has loaned money on contract which he cannot recover on demand, on the other he is legally bound to repay deposits on demand. But by making loans on binding contractual terms he is enabled to create money, which is purchasing power in the literal sense that, as noted above, the status of the monetary unit is politically guaranteed—e.g. through its position as "legal tender"—and hence the newly created dollars are "as good as" any other dollars. Hence I suggest that what makes them good in this sense is the input of power in the form of the bindingness of the contractual obligation assumed by the banker—I should classify this as opportunity for effectiveness. The bank, as collectivity, thus enjoys a "power position" by virtue of which it can give its borrowers effective control of certain types of opportunity.

It is, however, critically important that in general this grant of power is not unconditional. First it is power in its form of direct convertibility with money, and second, within that framework, the condition is that, per unit of time, there should be a surplus of money generated, the borrower can and must return more money than he received, the difference being "interest." Money, however, is a measure of productivity, and hence we may say that increasing the quantity of money in circulation is economically "functional" only if it leads after a sequence of operations over a period of time to a corresponding increase in productivity— if it does not the consequence is inflationary. The process is known as investment, and the standard of a good investment is the expected increment of productivity which, measured in money terms, is profitability. The organizational question of allocation of responsibility for decisions and payments should of course not be too directly identified with the present level of analytical argument.

It may help round out this picture if the concept of investment is related to that of "circular flow" in Schumpeter's sense.[36] The conception is that the routine functioning of economic processes is organized about the relation between producing and consuming units, we may say firms and households. So long as a series of parametric constants such as the state of demand and the coefficients of cost of production hold, this is a process in equilibrium through which money mediates the requisite decisions oriented to fixed reference points. This is precisely the case to which the zero-sum concept applies. On the one hand a fixed quantity

36. Joseph Schumpeter, The Theory of Economic Development (Cambridge: Harvard University Press, 1955), translated by Redvers Opie.

and "velocity of circulation" of the monetary medium is an essential condition of the stability of this equilibrium, whereas on the other hand, there is no place for banking operations which, through credit expansion, would change the parametric conditions.

These decisions are governed by the standard of solvency, in the sense that both producing and consuming units are normally expected to recoup their monetary expenditures, on the one hand for factors of production, on the other for consumers' goods, from monetary proceeds, on the producing side, sale of output, on the consuming, sale of factors of production, notably labor. Solvency then is a balance between monetary cost and receipts. Investment is also governed by the standard of solvency, but over a longer time period, long enough to carry out the operations necessary to bring about an increase of productivity matching the monetary obligations assumed.

There is here a crucial relation between the time-extension of the investment process and use of power to make loan contracts binding. Only if the extension of control of resources through loans creates obligations can the recipients of the loans in turn assume further obligations and expect others to assume them.

The essential principle here is that, in the sense of the hierarchy of control, a higher-order medium is used as a source of leverage to break into the "circle" of the Schumpeterian flow, giving the recipients of this power effective control of a share of fluid resources in order to divert them from the established routine channels to new uses. It is difficult to see how this could work systematically if the element of bindingness were absent either from loan contracts or from the acceptance-status of the monetary medium.

One further element of the monetary complex needs to be mentioned here. In the case of investment there is the element of time, and hence the uncertainty that projected operations aiming at increase in productivity will in fact produce either this increase or financial proceeds sufficient to repay loans plus interest in accordance with contract. In the case of the particular borrower-lender relationship this can be handled on an individual contract-solvency basis with a legally determined basis of sharing profits and/or losses. For the system, however, it creates the possibility of inflation, namely that the net effect of credit-extension may not be increase in productivity but decline in the value of the monetary unit. Furthermore, once a system involves an important component of credit, the opposite disturbance, namely deflation with a rearrangement of the meaning of the whole network of financial and credit expectations and relationships, is also a possibility. This suggests that there is, in a ramified credit economy, a set of mechanisms which, independently of particular circular flow, and credit-extension and re-payment transactions regulates the total volume of credit, rates of interest, and price-level relations in the economy.

Zero-Sum: The Case of Power

Let us now attempt to work out the parallel, and articulating, analysis for power systems. There is, I suggest, a circular flow operating between polity and economy in the interchange between factors in political effectiveness—in this case a share in control of the productivity of the economy—and an output to the economy in the form of the kind of control of resources which a loan for investment provides—though of course there are various other forms. This circular flow is controlled by the medium of power in the sense that the output of binding obligations, in particular through the commitment to perform services, broadly balances the offer of opportunity for effective performance.

The suggestion is that it is a condition of the stability of this circulation system that the inputs and outputs of power on each side should balance. This is another way of saying that it is ideally formulated as a zero-sum system, so far as power is concerned, though because it includes the investment process, the same is not true for the involvement of monetary funds in the interchanges. The political circular flow system then is conceived as the locus of the "routine" mobilization of performance expectations either through invoking obligations under old contractual— and in some cases, e.g. citizenship, ascriptive—relations, or through a stable rate of assumption of new contractual obligations, which is balanced by the liquidation, typically through fulfillment, of old ones. The balance applies to the system, of course, not to particular units.

Corresponding to utility as the value-pattern governing economic function I have put forward effectiveness as that governing political function. If it is important to distinguish utility, as the category of value to which increments are made by the combinatorial process of economic production, from solvency as the standard of satisfactory performance in handling money as the medium of economic process, then we need to distinguish effectiveness as the political value category, from a corresponding standard for the satisfactory handling of power. The best available term for this standard seems to be the success of collective goal-attainment. Where the polity is sufficiently differentiated so that power has become genuinely a generalized medium we can say that collective units are expected to be successful in the sense that the binding obligations they undertake in order to maintain and create opportunities for effectiveness, is balanced by the input of equally binding commitments to perform service, either within the collectivity in some status of employment, or for the collectivity on a contractual basis.

The unit of productive decision-making, however, is, in a sense corresponding to that applying to the household for the economic case, also expected to be successful in the sense that its expenditure of power through not only the output of services but their commitment to utilization by particular collectivities, is balanced by an input of opportunity which is dependent on collective organization, that is a unit in a position to undertake to provide opportunities which are binding on the unit.

In the light of this discussion it becomes clear that the business firm is in its aspect as collectivity in our technical sense, the case where the two standards of success and solvency coincide. The firm uses its power income primarily to maintain or increase its productivity and, as a measure of this, its money income. A surplus of power will therefore in general be exchanged for enhancement of its control of economic productivity. For a collectivity specialized in political function the primary criterion of success would be given in its power position, relative that is to other collectivities. Here there is the special problem of the meaning of the term power position. I interpret it here as relative to other collectivities in a competitive system, not as a position in an internal hierarchy of power. This distinction is of course particularly important for a pluralistic power system where government is a functionally specialized subsystem of the collectivity structure, not an approximation to the totality of that structure.[37] In somewhat corresponding fashion a collectivity specialized in integrative function would measure its success in terms of its "level of influence"—for example, as a political interest-group in the usual sense, its capacity to influence public policy decisions. A consequence of this reasoning is that such an influence group would be disposed to "give away" power, in the sense of trading it for an increment of influence. This could take the form of assuring political support, without barter-like conditions, to leadership elements which seemed to be likely to be able to exercise the kind of influence in question.

Is there then a political equivalent of the banking phenomenon, a

37. If very carefully interpreted, perhaps the old term "sovereignty" could be used to designate this standard somewhat more definitely than success.

way in which the circular flow of power comes to be broken through so as to bring about net additions to the amount of power in the system? The trend of the analytical argument indicates that there must be, and that its focus lies in the support system, that is the area of interchange between power and influence, between polity and integrative system.

First I suggest that, particularly conspicuous in the case of democratic electoral systems, political support should be conceived as a generalized grant of power which, if it leads to electoral success, puts elected leadership in a position analogous to that of the banker. The "deposits" of power made by constituents are revocable, if not at will, at the next election—a condition analogous to regularity of banking hours. In some cases election is tied to barterlike conditions of expectation of carrying out certain specific measures favored by the strategically crucial voters and only these. But particularly in a system which is pluralistic not only with reference to the composition of political support, but also to issues, such a leadership element acquires freedom to make certain types of binding decision, binding in the nature of the case on elements of the collectivity other than those whose "interest" is directly served. This freedom may be conceived to be confined to the circular flow level, which would be to say that the input of power through the channel of political support should be exactly balanced by the output through policy decisions, to interest groups which have specifically demanded these decisions.

There is, however, another component of the freedom of elected leadership which is crucial here. This is the freedom to use influence—for example through the "prestige" of office as distinguished from its specified powers—to embark on new ventures in the "equation" of power and influence. This is to use influence to create additions to the total supply of power. How can this be conceived to work?

One important point is that the relation between the media involved with respect to positive and negative sanctions is the obverse of the case of creating money through banking. There it was the use of power embodied in the binding character of loan contracts which "made the difference." Here it is the optional capacity to exert influence through persuasion. This process seems to operate through the function of leadership which, by way of the involvements it possesses with various aspects of the constituency structure of the collectivity, generates and structures new "demands" in the specific sense of demands for policy decision.

Such demands then may be conceived, in the case of the deciders, to justify an increased output of power. This in turn is made possible by the generality of the mandate of political support, the fact that it is not given on a barter basis in exchange for specific policy decisions, but once the "equation" of power and influence has been established through election, it is a mandate to do, within constitutional limits, what seems best, in the governmental case "in the public interest." Collective leadership may then be conceived as the bankers or "brokers" who can mobilize the binding commitments of their constituents in such a way that the totality of commitments made by the collectivity as a whole can be enhanced. This enhancement must, however, be justified through the mobilization of influence; it must, that is, both be felt to be in accordance with valid norms and apply to situations which "call for" handling at the level of binding collective commitments.

The critical problem of justification is, in one direction, that of consensus, of its bearing on the value-principle of solidarity as we have outlined this above. The standard therefore which corresponds to the value principle of solidarity is consensus in the sense in which that concept has been used above.

The problem then is that of a basis for breaking through the circular stability of a zero-sum power system. The crucial point is that this can only happen if the collectivity and its members are ready to assume new binding obligations over and above those previously in force. The crucial need is to justify this extension and to transform the "sentiment" that something ought to be done into a commitment to implement the sentiment by positive action, including coercive sanctions if necessary. The crucial agency of this process seems to be leadership, precisely conceived as possessing a component analytically independent of the routine power position of office, which defines the leader as the mobilizer of justifications for policies which would not be undertaken under the circular flow assumptions.

It may be suggested that the parallel to credit creation holds with respect to time-extension as well as in other respects. The increments of effectiveness which are necessary to implement new binding policies which constitute an addition to the total burden on the collectivity cannot simply be willed into being; they require organizational changes through recombinations of the factors of effectiveness, development of new agencies, procurement of personnel, new norms, and even changes in bases of legitimation. Hence leadership cannot justifiably be held responsible for effective implementation immediately, and conversely, the sources of political support must be willing to trust their leadership in the sense of not demanding immediate—by the time of the next election—"pay-off" of the power-value of their votes in their decisions dictated by their own interests.[38]

It is perhaps legitimate to call the responsibility assumed in this connection specifically leadership responsibility and distinguish it in these terms from administrative responsibility which focuses on the routine functions. In any case I should like to conceive this process of power-enhancement as strictly parallel to economic investment, in the further sense that the pay-off should be an increment to the level of collective success in the sense outlined above, that is enhanced effectiveness of collective action in valued areas which could not have been expected without risk-taking on the part of leadership in a sense parallel to entrepreneurial investment.

The operation of both governmental and nongovernmental collectivities is full of illustrations of the kind of phenomenon I have in mind, though because this type of formal analysis is somewhat unfamiliar, it is difficult to pin them down exactly. It has, for example, often been pointed out that the relation of executive responsibility to constituency-interests is very different in domestic and in foreign affairs. I suggest that the element of "political banking" in the field of foreign affairs is particularly large and that the sanction of approval of policy decisions, where it occurs, cannot infallibly be translated into votes, certainly not in the short run. Similar considerations are very frequently involved in what may be called "developmental" ventures, which cannot be expected to be "backed" by currently well-structured interests in the same sense as maintenance of current functions. The case of support of research and training is a good one since the "community of scholars" is not a very strong "pressure group" in the sense of capacity directly to influence large blocks of votes.

It would follow from these considerations that there is, in developed polities, a relatively "free-floating" element in the power system which is analogous to a credit-system. Such an element should then be subject to fluctuations on a dimension of inflation-deflation, and be in need of con-

38. Perhaps this is an unusually clear case of the relativity of the formal legal sense of the bindingness of commitments. Thus the populistic component in democratic government often ties both executive and legislative branches rather rigidly in what they can formally promise. However, there are many *de facto* obligations assumed by Government which are very nearly binding. Thus legally Congress could withdraw the totality of funds recently granted to universities for the support of scientific research and training, the formal appropriations being made year by year. Universities, however, plan very much in the expectation of maintenance of these funds and this maintenance is clearly something like a *de facto* obligation of Congress.

trols for the system as a whole, at a level above that of the activities of particular units.

The analogue of inflation seems to me to touch the credibility of the assertion of the bindingness of obligations assumed. Power, as a symbolic medium, is like money in that it is itself "worthless," but is accepted in the expectation that it can later be "cashed in," this time in the activation of binding obligations. If, however, "power-credit" has been extended too far, without the necessary organizational basis for fulfillment of expectations having been laid, then attempting to invoke the obligations will result in less than a full level of performance, inhibited by various sorts of resistance. In a collectivity undergoing disintegration the same formal office may be "worth less" than it otherwise would have been because of attrition of its basis of effectiveness. The same considerations hold when it is a case of overextension of new power-expectations without adequate provision for making them effective.

It goes without saying that a power-system in which this creditlike element is prominent is in a state analogous to the "insolvency" of a monetary system which includes an important element of actual credit, namely its commitments cannot be fulfilled all at once, even if those to whom they have been made have formally valid rights to such fulfillment. Only a strict zero-sum power system could fulfill this condition of "liquidity." Perhaps the conservatism of political ideologies makes it even more difficult to accept the legitimacy of such a situation—it is all too easy to define it as "dishonest"—than in the corresponding economic case.

There is, however, a fine line between solid, responsible and constructive political leadership which in fact commits the collectivity beyond its capacities for instantaneous fulfillment of all obligations, and reckless overextendedness, just as there is a fine line between responsible banking and "wild-catting."

Furthermore, under unusual pressures, even highly responsible leadership can be put in situations where a "deflationary" spiral sets in, in a pattern analogous to that of a financial panic. I interpret, for instance McCarthyism as such a deflationary spiral in the political field. The focus of the commitments in which the widest extension had taken place was in the international field—the United States had very rapidly come into the position of bearing the largest share of responsibility for maintenance of world political order against an expansionist Communist movement. The "loss of China" was in certain quarters a particularly traumatic experience, and the Korean war a highly charged symbol of the costs of the new stewardship.

A pluralistic political system like the American always has a large body of latent claims on the loyalty of its citizens to their government, not only for the "right sentiments" but for "sacrifices," but equally these are expected to be invoked only in genuine emergencies. The McCarthy definition of the situation was, however, that virtually anyone in a position of significant responsibility should not only recognize the "in case" priority—not necessarily by our basic values the highest—of national loyalty, but should explicitly renounce all other loyalties which might conceivably compete with that to the nation, including those to kith and kin. This was in effect a demand to liquidate all other commitments in favor of the national, a demand which in the nature of the case could not be met without disastrous consequences in many different directions. It tended to "deflate" the power system by undermining the essential basis of trust on which the influence of many elements bearing formal and informal leadership responsibilities, and which in turn sustained "power-credit," necessarily rested. Perhaps the most striking case was the allegation of communist infiltration and hence widespread "disloyalty" in the army, which was exploited to try to force the army leadership to put the commitments of all associated personnel, including e.g. research scientists, in completely "liquid" form. Two features of the McCarthy movement particularly mark it as a deflationary spiral, first the vicious circle of spreading involvement with the casting of suspicion on wider and wider circles of otherwise presumptively loyal elements in the society and secondly the surprisingly abrupt end of the spiral once the "bubble was pricked" and "confidence restored," events associated particularly with the public reaction to McCarthy's performance in the televised army hearings, and to Senator Flanders' protest on the floor of the Senate.[39]

The focus of the McCarthy disturbance may be said to have been in the influence system, in the relation between integrative and pattern-maintenance functions in the society. The primary deflationary effect was on the "credit" elements of pluralistic loyalties. This in turn would make leadership elements, not only in government but private groups, much less willing to take risks in claiming loyalties which might compete with those to government. Since, however, in the hierarchy of control the influence system is superordinate to the power system, deflation in the former is necessarily propagated to the latter. This takes in the first in-

39. I have dealt with some aspects of the McCarthy episode in "Social Strains in America," *Structure and Process,* *op. cit.,* Chapter 7, pp. 226–249. The inherent impossibility of the demand for "absolute security" in a pluralistic system is very cogently shown by Edward Shils in *The Torment of Secrecy* (Glencoe, Ill.: The Free Press, 1956), especially in Chapter VI.

stance the form of a rush to withdraw political support—which it will be remembered is here treated as a form of power—from leadership elements which could in any sense be suspected of "disloyalty." The extreme perhaps was the slogan propagated by McCarthy and played with by more responsible Republican leaders like Thomas E. Dewey, of "twenty years of treason" which impugned the loyalty of the Democratic Party as a whole. The effect was, by depriving opposition leadership of influence, to make it unsafe even to consider granting them power.

The breaking through of the zero-sum limitations of more elementary power systems opens the way to altogether new levels of collective effectiveness, but also, in the nature of the case, involves new levels of risk and uncertainty. I have already dealt briefly with this problem at the level of the particular collectivity and its extension of commitments. The problem of course is compounded for a system of collectivities because of the risk not only of particular failures, but of generalized inflationary and deflationary disturbances. There are, as we have noted, mechanisms of control which operate to regulate investment, and similarly extension of the commitments of particular collectivities, both of which have to do with the attempt to ensure responsibility, on the one hand for solvency over the long run, on the other for success of the larger "strategy" of extension. It is reasonable to suppose that beyond these, there must be mechanisms operating at the level of the system as a whole in both contexts.

In the monetary case it was the complex of central banking, credit management and their relations to governmental finance which has been seen to be the focus of these highest-level controls. In the case of power it is of course the first crucial point that there was to be some relatively paramount apex of control of the power and authority system, which we think of as in some sense the "sovereign" state.[40] This has mainly to do with the relations between what we have called justification and legitimacy, in relation to government as the highest-order tightly integrated collectivity structure—so far. This is the central focus of Weber's famous analysis of authority, but his analysis is in need of considerable exten-

40. In saying this I am very far from maintaining that "absolute" sovereignty is an essential condition of that minimal integration of political systems. On the contrary, first it is far from absolute internally, precisely because of the pluralistic character of most modern political systems and because of the openness of their boundaries in the integrative economic and other directions. Externally the relation of the territorial unit to norms and values transcending it is crucial, and steadily becoming more so. See my paper "Polarization of the World and International Order" in Quincy Wright, William M. Evan, and Morton Deutsch, eds., *Preventing World War III* (New York: Simon and Schuster, 1962), pp. 310–331, reprinted as Chapter 14 below.

sion in our sense. It seems, among other things, that he posed an unduly sharp alternative between charismatic and "routine" cases, particularly the rational-legal version of the latter. In particular it would be my view that very substantial possibilities of regulated extension of power-commitments exist within the framework of certain types of "legal" authority, especially where they are aspects of a political system which is pluralistic in general terms. These problems, however, cannot further be explored at the end of what is already a very long paper.

Conclusion

This paper has been designed as a general theoretical attack on the ancient problem of the nature of political power and its place, not only in political systems, narrowly conceived, but in the structure and processes of societies generally. The main point of reference for the attack has been the conception that the discussion of the problem in the main traditions of political thought have not been couched at a sufficiently rigorously analytical level, but have tended to treat the nation, the state, or the lower-level collectively organized "group," as the empirical object of reference, and to attempt to analyze its functioning without further basic analytical breakdown. The most conspicuous manifestation of this tendency has been the treatment of power.

The present paper takes a radically different position, cutting across the traditional lines. It takes its departure from the position of economic theory and, by inference, the asymmetry between it and the traditional political theory,[41] which has treated one as the theory of an analytically defined functional system of society—the economy—and the other as a concrete substructure, usually identified with government. Gradually the possibility has opened out both of the extension of the analytical model of economic theory to the political field and of the direct articulation of political with economic theory within the logical framework of the theory of the social system as a whole, so that the *polity* could be conceived as a functional subsystem of the society in all its theoretical fundamentals parallel to the economy.

This perspective necessarily concentrated attention on the place of money in the conception of the economy. More than that, it became increasingly clear that money was essentially a "symbolic" phenomenon

41. I myself once accepted this. *Cf. The Social System* (Glencoe, Ill.: The Free Press, 1951), Chapter V, pp. 161–163.

and hence that its analysis required a frame of reference closer to that of linguistics than of technology, i.e. it is not the intrinsic properties of gold which account for the value of money under a gold standard any more than it is the intrinsic properties of the sounds symbolized as "book" which account for the valuation of physically fixed dissertations in linguistic form. This is the perspective from which the conception of power as a *generalized symbolic medium* operating in the processes of social interaction has been set forth.

This paper has not included a survey of the empirical evidence bearing on its ramified field of problems, but my strong conviction is not only that the line of analysis adopted is consistent with the broad lines of the available empirical evidence, but that it has already shown that it can illuminate a range of empirical problems which were not well understood in terms of the more conventional theoretical positions—e.g. the reasons for the general egalitarian pressure in the evolution of the political franchise, or the nature of McCarthyism as a process of political deflationary spiral.

It does not seem necessary here to recapitulate the main outline of the argument. I may conclude with the three main points with which I began. I submit, first, that the analytical path entered upon here makes it possible to treat power in conceptually specific and precise terms and thus gets away from the theoretical diffuseness called to attention, in terms of which it has been necessary to include such a very wide variety of problematical phenomena as "forms" of power. Secondly, I think it can advance a valid claim to present a resolution of the old dilemma as to whether (in the older terms) power is "essentially" a phenomenon of coercion or of consensus. It is both, precisely because it is a phenomenon which integrates a plurality of factors and outputs of political effectiveness and is not to be identified with any one of them. Finally, light has been thrown on the famous zero-sum problem, and a definite position taken that, though under certain specific assumptions the zero-sum condition holds, these are not constitutive of power systems in general, but under different conditions systematic "extension" of power spheres without sacrifice of the power of other units is just as important a case.

These claims are put forward in full awareness that on one level there is an inherent arbitrariness in them, namely that I have defined power and a number of related concepts in my own way, which is different from many if not most of the definitions current in political theory. If theory were a matter only of the arbitrary choice of definitions and assumptions and reasoning from there, it might be permissible to leave the question at that and say simply, this is only one more personal "point of view." Any claim that it is more than that rests on the conception that the scientific understanding of societies is arrived at through a gradually developing organon of theoretical analysis and empirical interpretation and verification. My most important contention is that the line of analysis presented here is a further development of a main line of theoretical analysis of the social system as a whole, and of verified interpretation of the empirical evidence presented to that body of theory. This body of theory must ultimately be judged by its outcomes both in theoretical generality and consistency, over the whole range of social system theory, and by its empirical validity, again on levels which include not only conventionally "political" references, but their empirical interrelations with all other aspects of the modern complex society looked at as a whole.

Technical Note

The above analysis has been presented in wholly discursive terms. Many decisions about categorization and detailed steps of analysis were, however, referred to a formalized paradigm of the principal structural components and process categories and relations of a society considered as a social system. For the benefit of readers with more technical interests in social system theory it has seemed advisable to present a very brief outline of the most directly relevant parts of the general paradigm here, with a brief elucidation of its relevance to the above discussion.[42]

The structural reference points are essentially two, namely first that at a sufficiently high level of differentiation of a society, economy, polity and integrative system become empirically distinct in terms of the primacy of function of structural units e.g. there is an important structural difference between a private business firm, an administrative agency of government and a court of law. Secondly every such unit is involved in plural interchange relations with other units with respect to

42. The paradigm itself is still incomplete, and even in its present state has not been published as a whole. The first beginning statement dealing with process was made by Parsons and Smelser in *Economy and Society,* esp. Chapter II, and has been further developed in certain respects in Smelser's two subsequent books (*Social Change in the Industrial Revolution,* and *Theory of Collective Behavior*). In my own case certain aspects, which now need further revision, were published in the article "Pattern Variables Revisited" (*American Sociological Review,* August, 1960, and Chapter 7 above). Early and partial versions of application to political subject-matter are found in my contributions to Roland Young, ed., *Approaches to the Study of Politics,* and Burdick and Brodbeck, eds., *American Voting Behavior.* (Chapter 9 of this book.)

most of its functional requirements from its situation—i.e., for factor inputs—and the conditions of making its contributions to other units in the "division of labor"—i.e., disposal of "product" outputs. This order of differentiation requires *double* interchanges between all the structural components belonging to each category-pair, e.g. firms and households, firms and political agencies (not necessarily governmental, it should be remembered) etc. The double interchange situation precludes mediation of processes in terms either of ascriptive expectations or barter arrangements, or a combination of the two. It necessitates the development of generalized symbolic media, of which we have treated money, power, and influence as cases.

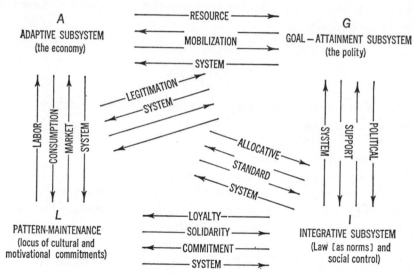

FIGURE 1. FORMAT OF THE SOCIETAL INTERCHANGE SYSTEM

At a sufficiently high level of generalized development the "governing" interchanges (in the sense of cybernetic hierarchy) take place between the media which are anchored in the various functional subsystems—as power is anchored in the polity. These media in turn serve as instrumentalities of gaining control of "lower-order" resources which are necessary for fulfillment of expectations. Thus the expenditure of money for "goods" is not, at the system or "aggregate" level (as analyzed by Keynes), acquisition of the possession of particular commodities, but consists in the generalized expectation of availability of goods on "satisfactory" market terms. This is the primary output of the economy to consumers. Similarly, when we speak of control of productivity as a factor of effectiveness, it is not managerial control of particular plants which is meant, but control of a share of general productivity of the economy through market mechanisms, without specification of particulars.

The paradigm of interchange between general media of communication is presented in Figures 1 and 2. Figure 1 simply designates the format in which this part of the paradigm is conceived. The assumptions of this format are three, none of which can be grounded or justified within the limits of the present exposition. These are (1) that the patterns of differentiation of a social system can be analyzed in terms of four primary functional categories, each of which is the focus of a primary functional subsystem of the society. As noted in the body of the essay, economy and polity are conceived to be such subsystems; (2) The primary interchange processes through which these subsystems are integrated with each other operate through generalized symbolic media of the type which I have assumed money and power to be,[43] and (3) at the level of differentiation of interest here, each interchange system is a double interchange, implying both the "alienation" of resources and products from their system of origin and the transcending of the barter level of exchange. Under these assumptions, all Figure 1 does is to portray a system of six double interchanges operating between each logically given pair among the four primary functional subsystems of a society. For convenience tentative names are given to each of these six double interchange systems.

Figure 2, then, places each of the six interchange systems on a horizontal axis, simply because they are easier to read that way. It adds to Figure 1 only by introducing names of categories, directions of flow and designations as to medium (money, power, etc.) for each of the four places in each of the six interchange systems, thus presenting twenty-four categories, each of the four basic media appearing in four "forms."

Among the six interchange sets, power as a medium is involved, by our analysis, in only three, namely the interchanges of the polity (G) with each of the other three. These are the system of "resource mobilization," *vis-à-vis* the economy, the support system which involves the input of political support and the output of decisions (*vis-à-vis* the inte-

---

43. There is a very crucial problem area which concerns the nature of the interchanges between a society as a system in our sense and its environment. This set of problems unfortunately cannot be entered into here.

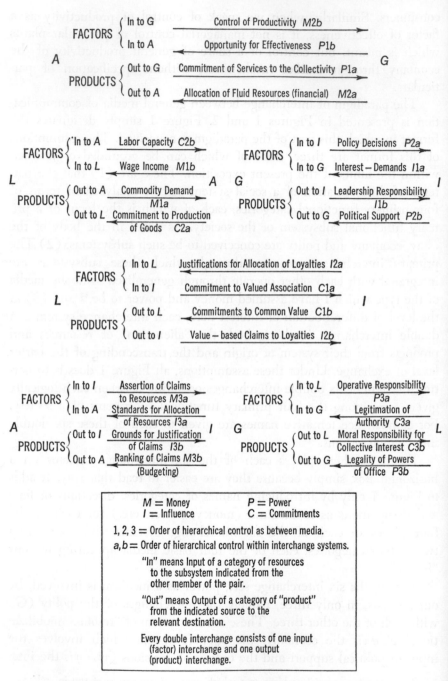

FIGURE 2. THE CATEGORIES OF SOCIETAL INTERCHANGE

grative system) and the system of legitimation, as I have called it, *vis-à-vis* the value aspect of the pattern-maintenance system. The last of these three is a special case which does not involve power as a medium, but rather the structure of the code governing authority as defining the institutionalized uses of power, hence the legitimation of authority. Primary attention can thus be given to the other two.

The categories included in the *A-G* (economy-polity, or resource mobilization) interchange can be described as "forms" of power and of money (or wealth) respectively. They will be seen to be the categories which have been used in the appropriate parts of the discursive exposition of the body of the paper. The double interchange here, as in the classic economy—or labor-consumption case, involves first one factor-interchange, namely control of productivity as factor of effectiveness exchanged for opportunity for effectiveness (in the particular case of capital, as a factor of production). Productivity is a monetary factor because it is a pool of resources controlled through monetary funds—which of course in turn can be exchanged for the particular facilities needed, notably goods and services. Opportunity, however, is a form of power in the sense discussed.

The second part of the double interchange is one of "product" outputs. This takes place between commitment of services to organization—typically through employment—which I have interpreted to be a form of power, and the allocation of fluid resources to the purveyors of service as facilities essential to the performance of their obligations—typically the control of budgeted funds, though often generalization does not extend as high as this. Thus fluid resources in the idea type case take the form of money funds.[44]

The second primary interchange system, which for convenience I shall call the support system, is that between polity and integrative system (*G-I*), which latter involves the associational aspect of group structure and solidarity in relation to the system of norms (legal and informal)—as distinguished from values. The basic difference lies in the fact that power here is interchanged not with money but with influence, and that whereas *vis-à-vis* money it was the "controlling"

44. The process of investment, which I conceive to be one very important special case of the operation of this interchange system, seems to work in such a way that the power component of a loan is a grant of opportunity, through which an increment of otherwise unavailable control of productivity is gained. The recipient of this "grant" is then, through committing (individual or collective) services, in a position to utilize these resources for increasing future economic productivity in some way. This is a special case because the resources might be used in some other way, e.g. for relieving distress or for scientific research.

medium, *vis-à-vis* influence it is controlled. This difference is symbolized by the placing of the power categories here in the outside positions whereas in the *A-G* case they were placed inside (as the monetary categories were in *L-A*).

The relevant factor interchange here is between policy decisions as a "factor of solidarity" and interest-demands as a factor of effectiveness, in the senses in which these concepts were used above. Essentially we may say that interest-demands "define the situation" for political decision-making—which of course is by no means to say that demands in their initial form are or should be simply "granted" without modifications. Like other factors they are typically transformed in the course of the political process. Correspondingly policy decisions are a factor in solidarity in that they constitute commitments for collective action on which "interested parties" within limits can count.

The interchange of "product" outputs then consists of leadership responsibility as output of the polity (a form of influence, note, *not* of power), and political support as an output of the "associational" system—in the governmental case e.g. the electorate, which is a source of the political "income" of power. It will of course be noted that the units involved in any particular case of these two interchanges typically are not the same—thus party leaders may bid for support whereas administrative officials make certain policy decisions. This type of "split" (carried out to varying degrees) is characteristic of any highly differentiated system.

Figure 3 attempts to look at the generalized media from the point of view not only of their hierarchical ordering, but of the relation between the code and message components, and the position of the latter as sanctions controlling on the one hand factors essential to the various functional subsystems, on the other hand product outputs from these subsystems. The rows are arranged from top to bottom in terms of the familiar hierarchy of control—each row designating one of the four media. The columns, on the other hand, designate components into which each medium needs to be broken down if some of the basic conditions of its operation in mediating interaction are to be understood.

In the body of the paper I have discussed the reasons for which it seems necessary to disinguish two components in the code aspect of each medium, namely what have been called the relevant value principle on the one hand, the "coordinative standard" on the other. The most familiar example concerns the paradigmatic economic case. Here the famous concept of utility seems to be the relevant value principle whereas that of solvency is the coordinative standard. Utility is the basic "meas-

COMPONENTS OF MEDIA AND INTERCHANGE RECIPROCALS / MEDIA IN HIERARCHY OF CONTROL	CODES		MESSAGES (SANCTIONS)		TYPES OF SANCTION AND OF EFFECT
	VALUE-PRINCIPLE	COORDINATION STANDARD	FACTORS CONTROLLED	PRODUCTS CONTROLLED	
			SOURCE	DESTINATION	
L COMMITMENTS	INTEGRITY	PATTERN-CONSISTENCY	WAGES A / JUSTIFICATION OF LOYALTIES I	CONSUMERS' DEMAND A / CLAIMS TO LOYALTIES I	NEGATIVE-INTENTIONAL (activation of commitments)
I INFLUENCE	SOLIDARITY	CONSENSUS	COMMITMENTS TO VALUED ASSOCIATION L / POLICY DECISIONS G	COMMITMENT TO COMMON VALUES L / POLITICAL SUPPORT G	POSITIVE-INTENTIONAL (persuasion)
G POWER	EFFECTIVENESS	SUCCESS	INTEREST-DEMANDS I / CONTROL OF PRODUCTIVITY A	LEADERSHIP RESPONSIBILITY I / CONTROL OF FLUID RESOURCES A	NEGATIVE-SITUATIONAL (securing compliance)
A MONEY	UTILITY	SOLVENCY	CAPITAL G / LABOR L	COMMITMENT OF SERVICES G / EXPECTATION OF GOODS L	POSITIVE-SITUATIONAL (inducement)

FIGURE 3. THE MEDIA AS SANCTIONS

ure" of value in the economic sense, whereas the imperative to maintain solvency is a category of norm for the guidance of units in economic action. For the political case I have adopted the concept of effectiveness in Barnard's sense as the parallel to the economist's utility. Success, for the unit in question, notably the collective case, seems to be the best available term for the corresponding coordinative standard. (Possibly, used with proper qualifications, the term sovereignty might be still more appropriate for this standard.)

At the other most important direct boundary of the polity, solidarity in Durkheim's sense seems to be the value-principle of integration which is parallel to utility and effectiveness, whereas the very important (to political theory) concept of *consensus* seems adequately to formulate the relevant integrative coordinative standard. Since they are not directly involved in the interchange systems of immediate concern here, I merely call attention to the designation of the value-principle of the pattern-maintenance system as *integrity* and the corresponding coordinative standard as *pattern-consistency*.

The A and G columns of Figure 3 then designate contexts of operation of each of the four media as sanctions, but arranged not by interchange system as in Figure 2, but by control of factor inputs and product outputs respectively. Thus money though not itself a factor of production, "controls," i.e. buys, labor and capital as the primary factors, in the A-L and the A-G interchange systems respectively, whereas for "consuming" systems money buys outputs of the economy, namely goods (in A-L) and services (in A-G) respectively.

The involvement of power is conceived to be parallel. On the one hand it "commands" the two primary mobile factors of effectiveness, namely control of productivity (in G-A) and interest-demands (in G-I) (as justified in terms of appeal to norms). On the other hand the "consumers" or beneficiaries of the outputs from the process can use power to command these outputs in the form of fluid resources (e.g. through budget allocation in G-A) and of leadership responsibility for valued goals (in G-I).

It will be noted that in Figure 3, negative and positive sanction types alternate in the hierarchy of control. Power, as the medium depending on negative situational sanctions is "sandwiched" between money (below it) with its positive situational sanctions and influence (above it) with its positive intentional sanctions.

Returning to Figure 2, power is also involved in the legitimation system (L-G), but this time as code, as aspect of authority. This may be conceived as a mechanism for linking the principles and standards in the L and G rows. What is called the assumption of operative responsibility (P3a), which is treated as a "factor of integrity" is responsibility for *success* in the implementation of the value-principles, not only of collective effectiveness, but of integrity of the paramount societal value-pattern. It may be said that the legitimation of authority (C3a) "imposes" the responsibility to attempt such success. Legality of the powers of office on the other hand (P3c), as a category of output to the polity, is an application of the standard of pattern-consistency. At the various relevant levels action may and should be taken consistent with the value-commitments. In exchange for legal authorization to take such action, the responsible office-holder must accept moral responsibility for his use of power and his decisions of interpretation (C3b).

CHAPTER 11

On the Concept of Influence

This paper was meant to be a companion piece to the paper on the concept of power. If the assumption on which the latter was grounded, that power could be treated as the same order of generalized medium as money, was correct, it would clearly be anomalous if it turned out that these two media stood alone in the functioning of social systems. Clearly money is involved in critically important relations to power, in the general area of the mobilizability of resources for political purposes. The suggested parallel involving influence concerns the mobilization of support in the political sense, though there are many further ramifications of the problem.

The occasion for attempting to pull this line of thought together was provided by an invitation to present a paper at the meeting of the *American Association for Public Opinion Research* in May, 1962. The paper was published, with commentaries by Raymond A. Bauer and James S. Coleman, in the *Public Opinion Quarterly,* Spring, 1963.

I do not feel that the analysis of influence presented in this paper is as far advanced or satisfactory as the analysis of power presented in the preceding chapter. Fuller success in working the problems through seems to me to depend on clarification of a whole range of problems concerning the integrative processes of social systems, which have been mentioned a number of times and which figure not only in a number of the chapters of this volume but also in current work.

Finally, the logic of the general conceptual scheme in which I have placed money, power, and influence calls for a fourth generalized medium, which I have been calling "generalized commitments." A range of problems concerning this medium has figured prominently in recent theoretical work, but I have not yet attempted a general statement about it—to present one is an obvious obligation for the near future.

"On the Concept of Influence" reprinted from *Public Opinion Quarterly* (Spring, 1963).

I T MAY plausibly be held that the development of research technology in the field of opinion and attitude study has outrun the development of theory. The intention of the present paper is to help to redress the balance by essaying a contribution in the theoretical area to try to bring to bear on the opinion field a more generalized conceptual scheme that has been worked out mainly in other connections.

First, let me state the main context of problems within the field on which I would like to concentrate. The first step beyond immediate description and classification of opinions is, of course, to attempt some analysis of determining factors, to answer such questions as why or under what conditions certain opinions are held or changed. It is within this area, rather than that of categories suitable for description and classification, that I wish to operate. To narrow the field still further, it is a question of whether anything can be said about *generalized* kinds of process or mechanism through the operation of which such determination, notably of change of opinions, comes about. It is as such a generalized mechanism by which attitudes or opinions are determined that I would like to conceive "influence," for the purposes of this paper.[1]

A further step in specification is to restrict my consideration to the problem of the operation of generalized mechanisms in the process of social interaction in its intentional forms. Thus, if a person's opinion has been changed by his experience of a natural event, such as a hurricane, or even by social events that could not conceivably be understood as intentionally oriented to having an effect on his opinions, such as a business depression, I shall not speak of these as "influence" in the present sense—similarly with the famous example of the alleged relation between a judge's legal opinions and the state of his digestion. Influence is a way of having an effect on the attitudes and opinions of others through intentional (though not necessarily rational) action—the effect may or may not be to change the opinion or to prevent a possible change.

1. It is taken for granted here that there is no formal standardization of terminology in this field, and that, hence, there is inevitably an element of arbitrariness involved in giving technical meaning to a term in such general usage as "influence." I make no apology for doing this, since in the social sciences the only alternative in this and many other cases is coining neologisms, the objections to which are overwhelming.

General Mechanisms of Social Interaction: The Case of Money

What, then, is meant by a generalized mechanism operating in social interaction? There are various ways of approaching this question. Language is perhaps the prototype and can serve as a major point of reference. Having an effect on the action of others, thus possibly "influencing" them, through linguistic communication, is to present them with "symbolic" experiences in place of the concrete things or objects to which the symbols refer, which they "mean." Thus, a sign, "Beware the dog," may induce caution without the passer-by's actually seeing or hearing a dog. "Intrinsically," the language symbols do not have any caution-inducing properties; the black marks on the signboard have never bitten anyone, nor have they even barked.

In the well-known formulation of Jacobsen and Halle,[2] a language must be understood to involve two aspects: on the one hand, the use of language is a process of emitting and transmitting messages, combinations of linguistic components that have specific reference to particular situations; on the other hand, language is a *code* in terms of which the particular symbols constituting any particular message "have meaning." In these terms, a message can be meaningful and hence understood only by those who "know the language," that is the code, and accept its "conventions."

Language, as that concept is generally understood, is not an isolated phenomenon. In the field of social interaction, many mechanisms have properties so similar to those of language that it is not too much to say that they *are* specialized languages. Mathematical and artistic symbol systems are cases in point, but one that is both well known and lies close to our concern is money. Hence, for my purposes, I would like to say not merely that money resembles language, but that it *is* a very specialized language, i.e. a generalized medium of communication through the use of symbols given meaning within a code.[3]

I shall therefore treat influence as a generalized medium which in turn I interpret to mean a specialized language. I should like now to attempt, using money, because of its familiarity, as an illustration, to outline a paradigm of such a generalized medium, preliminary to stating the principal properties of influence as another such medium.

2. Roman Jacobsen and Morris Halle, *Fundamentals of Language* (The Hague: Mouton & Co., 1956).
3. This perspective on money as a language is strongly suggested by the usage of the classical economists (e.g. Adam Smith, Ricardo, and J. S. Mill), when they spoke of the dual nature of money, first, as a "medium of exchange" (message transmission) and, second, as a "measure of value" (code).

Seen in this light, money is a symbolic "embodiment" of economic *value*, of what economists in a technical sense call "utility." Just as the *word* "dog" can neither bark nor bite, yet "signifies" the animal that can, so a dollar has no intrinsic utility, yet signifies commodities that do, in the special sense that it can in certain circumstances be substituted for them, and can evoke control of relations with them in the special kind of process of social interaction we call economic exchange. This means that holders of objects of utility will, on occasion, be willing to relinquish control over them for money, and, conversely, holders of money will be able to acquire, by use of the money (its "expenditure"), control over objects of utility.[4]

The economic value called utility, however, is the basis of a type of *interest* in objects in the situation of action. It defines an aspect of their actual or potential meaning, under which rubric I wish to include not only what they "are" but what they "do," if they are actors, and what can be done *with* them, such as "consuming" them in the economist's sense, if they are commodities, or "utilizing their services," if they are persons. For symbolization to take place, it is necessary for the basis of this interest to be defined with sufficient clarity and specificity, just as the category of object "dog" must be adequately defined if the linguistic symbol is to designate it unambiguously. In the case of money, this involves a very high level of generalization, since the variety of objects of utility is immense; furthermore, it means a very strict quantification on a linear scale.

In addition to the relevant category of value for human actors on the one hand, the basis of interest in objects in their situation on the other, there are two further indispensable references in the conceptualization of a generalized symbolic mechanism. One of these is to the "definition of the situation," that is the categorization of objects in the situation with reference to their bearing on the type of interest in question. In the economic-monetary case, the situation consists in "objects of utility," that is those in which actors may have an economic basis of interest. Implementation of the interest consists in acquiring control over such objects to the extent that this is a condition of "utilizing" them. The

4. It is important to note that the linguistic parallel holds here. The experience of an encounter with a ferocious dog can be "converted" into words, in that, for example, the person frightened can tell another about it in the absence of the dog and evoke in him appropriate reactions. Conversely, in our example above, linguistic warning can evoke an attitude set appropriate to dealing with such an animal in the absence of direct experience of the dog. The linguistic symbols do not have the properties either of dangerousness or of capacity to cope with danger, but they can *mediate* the action process by "orienting" an actor to danger.

"way" of acquiring such control is through exchange, which, if money is involved, may be called "market" exchange.[5]

In the case of money as a symbol, one of its meanings is clearly in the field of "procurement," of the opportunities of using it to gain access to and control over objects of utility. The first component of the situation needing definition, then, consists in the manifold objects that not only have utility but are available within the exchange system: thus certain objects of potential utility, such as full control of other human beings by owning them as chattels, are excluded in our property system. The second component concerns sources of supply, namely, units in the interaction system which, on the one hand, have control of such objects and, on the other, may be presumed to be willing to relinquish such control in exchange for other utilities, including especially money. The third component concerns the conditions on which terms of exchange can be settled, the most important one being the institutionalization of the offer of specific sums of money as a way of inducing transfer of control. And, finally, the fourth component concerns the question of the time relations involved in bringing the two ends of a chain of exchange of utilities together, for example the relinquishment of control over labor services to an employer, and the acquisition of control over consumer's goods.

By contrast with the two "pre-monetary" modes of exchange mentioned above—ascriptive and barter exchange—money introduces altogether new degrees of freedom in all four of these respects. Thus, unlike the holder of a specific commodity in surplus—relative to his own wants —who wants to barter it for another commodity, the holder of money is not bound to find a specific partner who has what he wants and wants what he has. He has the whole range of the "market system" open with respect both to the items for which he wants to spend his funds and to the sources from which he might wish to purchase each item—so long as the market for the item is not monopolized. Exceedingly important, he is not bound to any particular time, since money, unlike virtually all commodities, does not intrinsically deteriorate through time and has minimal, if any, costs of storage. Finally, he has much greater freedom to accept or reject terms, and to negotiate them.

5. There are two modes of exchange that involve levels of differentiation of the interest in utility short of what I am here calling the "market" level, namely, ascriptive exchange, the case of obligatory gifts, well known to anthropologists (cf. Marcel Mauss, *The Gift* [Glencoe, Ill.: Free Press, 1954]), and the case of barter. Both lack the involvement of a generalized medium that specifically symbolizes utility, namely, money.

These freedoms, like all freedoms, are bought at a price. Money, being a symbol, is "intrinsically" worthless. Hence, in relinquishing control of objects of "real" utility for money, one risks never gaining an equivalent in return and being "stuck" with the symbol; similarly, if one relies on a sign rather than on actually seeing a dog, one risks being fooled, either by being alerted when there is no danger at all, or by being prepared to deal with a dog when in fact a tiger is lurking in the neighborhood.

There have doubtless been heroic figures in the history of market exchange who have risked everything on a conception of the sheer *value* of money without the existence of any institutionally established normative framework of rules according to which such a medium should be used. It seems clear, however, that, without such a framework, a *system* of market exchanges in which participants will regularly put major interests into monetary assets that, in our sense, are "intrinsically" worthless can hardly be expected to function. The most elementary of these rules is the condition of reciprocity in the acceptability of money. This may be formulated as follows: He who urges money on others in exchange for "real assets" must be willing in turn to accept money from others in exchange for his assets. Only mutual acceptability can make money a functioning medium rather than simply a way of getting something for nothing. From this central point, the network of norms that we ordinarily think of as the institutions of property and contract can be worked out. This is the fourth of the basic components of the complex that constitutes a generalized medium.

If a symbol or category of symbols is to function as a generalized medium in mediating the processes of social interaction, there must therefore be, I have contended, specific definition and institutional acceptance in four basic respects: (1) a category of *value*, of respects in which needs of the acting units are at stake; (2) a category of *interest*, of properties of objects in the situation of action that are important in the light of these values; (3) a *definition of the situation*, of the features of the actual situation that can be "exploited" in the implementation of the interest; and (4) a *normative framework* of rules discriminating between legitimate and illegitimate modes of action in pursuit of the interest in question. Only with institutionalization in all four respects can the risks inherently involved in accepting the "symbolic" in lieu of the "real" be expected to be widely assumed by whole categories of acting units.

Ways of Getting Results in Interaction

Because it is highly institutionalized and hence familiar, and because the conditions of its functioning have been very thoroughly analyzed by professional economists, I have used money as the example in terms of which to elucidate the nature and conditions of a generalized medium in the sense of this paper. In approaching a fuller analysis of the primary object of our concern, influence, a next step is to attempt to place both it and money in the context of a wider family of mechanisms. It is my view that money belongs in such a family, of which another well known member is power, in the broadly political sense. These mechanisms operate in social interaction in a way that is both much more specific and more generalized than communication through language. Furthermore, they have in common the imperative mood, i.e. they are ways of "getting results" rather than only of conveying information. They face the object with a decision, calling for a response such as the acceptance or rejection of a monetary offer.

These considerations indicate the approach. Such mechanisms are ways of structuring *intentional* attempts to bring about results by eliciting the response of other actors to approaches, suggestions, etc. In the case of money, it is a matter of offers, in the case of power, of communicating decisions that activate obligations; in the case of influence, of giving reasons or "justifications" for a suggested line of action. How can these various modes of getting results be classified?

My suggestion is that there is a very simple paradigm of modes by which one acting unit—let us call him "ego"—can attempt to get results by bringing to bear on another unit, which we may call "alter," some kind of *communicative operation*: call it "pressure" if that term is understood in a nonpejorative sense.[6] It can be stated in terms of two variables, the cross-classification of which can then yield a fourfold typology. The first variable is whether ego attempts to work through potential control over the *situation* in which alter is placed and must act, or through an attempt to have an effect on alter's *intentions*, independently of changes in his situation. Let us call this the "channel" variable. Thus an offer in economic exchange operates situationally, in that it offers control either of an object of utility or of money, which in turn is exchangeable for control of such an object.

Offers are contingent—they say that, *if* alter will do something ego

6. The closest approach to this paradigm with which I am familiar from the literature is Herbert C. Kelman, "Processes of Opinion Change," *Public Opinion Quarterly*, Vol. 25 (1961), pp. 57–78.

wants done, ego in turn will do something that is situationally advantageous to alter. There is, however, the limiting case in which ego confers a situational advantage on alter without giving him any option —this would be the pure case of the gift. This element of contingency, varying to the limit of no option, applies throughout the present typology.

The second variable concerns the nature of the contingent *consequences* for alter of ego's intervention in his action-complex, that is, in one aspect, the kind of decision with which alter is faced. So far as the element of contingency is involved, this concerns whether the *sanctions* contingently imposed by ego are positive or negative in their significance to alter, that is constitute advantages or disadvantages to him. Thus, in the case of economic exchange, ego *promises* that if alter will do what he wants, he in turn will do something which alter presumably wants, that is defines as advantageous. Giving him money or control of an object of utility are prototypical cases. On the other hand, ego may attempt to get alter to do something by saying, in effect, "You must, should, or ought to do so and so." Alter may then say, "But what if I choose not to?" If ego takes this approach and "means it," he must contend that in some sense the consequences of alter's choosing noncompliance (if he can "do anything about it") will be disadvantageous to alter. If the channel is situational, this will put him in the position of having to *threaten,* contingent on noncompliance, to do something disadvantageous to alter. On the other hand, he may give alter reasons why noncompliance will, independent of ego's intervention in the situation, prove to be unacceptable, so that *intentional* noncompliance cannot make sense to alter. Here the negative sanction would be internal or intentional, and not situational so far as alter is concerned.

The limiting case where alter is given no option is, in the situational-negative combination, compulsion: ego simply structures the situation so alter *must* comply.

Cross-classification of these two variables for the case of contingency yields the set of four types shown in our table. (1) Inducement is ego's attempt to get a favorable decision from alter by an offer of situational advantages contingent on ego's compliance with his suggestions. (2) Deterrence is ego's corresponding attempt to get compliance by invoking commitments in such a way that noncompliance exposes alter to a contingent threat of suffering a situational disadvantage.[7] (3) Activation

7. This case, as well as the setting in which it fits, is much more fully discussed in my paper, "On the Concept of Political Power," *Proceedings of the American Philosophical Society*, Philadelphia, 1963 (reprinted as the preceding chapter). Generally, this is a companion piece to the present paper.

of commitments is ego's attempt to get compliance by offering reasons why it would, from alter's own point of view, be "wrong" for him to refuse to act as ego wished. And, finally, (4) persuasion is ego's attempt to get compliance by offering reasons why it would, from alter's own point of view, independent of situational advantages, "be a good thing" for him to act as ego wished.

	CHANNEL	
Sanction	Intentional	Situational
Positive	Persuasion	Inducement
Negative	Activation of commitments	Deterrence

I should now like to suggest that this simple paradigm of modes of gaining ends in social interaction is matched by a paradigm of generalized media by which, in the appropriately structured type of interaction system, an enhanced capacity to gain such ends is made possible, provided the risks of acceptance of such a medium in the requisite situation are assumed. Seen in these terms, money should be regarded as a generalized medium of inducement, and influence as a generalized medium of persuasion. I shall try presently to elucidate further what the latter conception implies, but it will be useful first to put it in the context, not only of a comparison with money, but of this still more general classification of media.

Money and influence may be conceived to operate as positive sanctions in the above sense, money through the situational, influence through the intentional, channel. The negative medium corresponding to money on the situational side is then power in the political sense; on the intentional side, the negative medium corresponding to influence is generalization of commitments. The relation between the two pairs requires some elucidation.

Inducement and persuasion are ways of eliciting positively desired responses. Imposition of sanction and response correspond here. Deterrence, on the other hand, is intended to establish an inverse relation between sanctioned act and desired response. The purely negative side is the withholding of sanction in case of "compliance." What ego desires, however, is precisely compliance, the performance of obligation. He imposes sanctions only if "forced to."

It is hence not appropriate to define power simply as a generalized medium of deterrence, but rather of mobilizing the performance of binding obligations, with the conditional implication of the imposition of negative sanctions—in the situational case, "punishment"—in case of noncompliance. The intention of ego, however, is not to punish but to secure performance. Hence, we may speak of power as generalized capacity to secure performance of binding obligations in the interest of effective collective action (goal attainment). Parallel to this, on the intentional side (so far as alter is concerned), we may speak of the generalization of commitments as the capacity, through appeal to a subjective sense of obligation, to motivate fulfillment of relevant obligations without reference to any threat of *situational* sanctions (thus differentiating it from power). In this case, however, tendencies to noncompliance will be met with evaluative expressions on ego's part (disapproval of noncompliance) that are calculated to help activate alter's sense of obligation and threaten him with guilt feelings if he fails to comply.[8] We may then insert the four generalized media in the paradigm of sanctions, as follows:

	CHANNEL	
Sanction	Intentional	Situational
Positive:		
Mode	Persuasion	Inducement
Medium	Influence	Money
Negative:		
Mode	Activation of commitments	Deterrence
Medium	Generalization of commitments	Power

Note: For readers familiar with the more general paradigm of the analysis of action on which various associates and I have worked for some years, it may be of interest to note that I conceive inducement and money to have primarily adaptive functions in the social system; deterrence and power, primarily goal-attainment functions; persuasion and influence, primarily integrative functions; and, finally, activation of commitments and the generalized commitments so activated, primarily pattern-maintenance functions.

Let us now attempt to get somewhat closer to the analysis of influence by calling attention to another aspect of the generalized media as mechanisms operating within the social system. This is the sense in which they bridge the gap between normative and factual aspects of the system in which they operate. This is to say that, from the point of view of the acting unit, whether it be individual or collectivity, there is one "direction" in which the medium serves as a means of furthering its interests, and this includes the structuring of conditions under which, in various contingencies, its interest is more or less secure. On the other

8. Ego can implement this threat through use of the *attitudinal* sanction of *disapproval*, and, in the case of compliance, by using influence he can reward alter with his *approval*.

hand, what from the acting unit's point of view are certain norms or rules to which it is subject in furthering its interest are, from the point of view of the system, a set of conditions under which process in it can be carried on stably, without disturbance to its integration and other essential functions.

In the case of money, the rock bottom of security for the unit is the possession of the proper quantity and combination of concrete objects of utility to the unit itself, namely, full "economic self-sufficiency" in terms of "real assets." The next level is possession of objects such as gold, diamonds, land, which can be exchanged in almost any contingency and the value of which is not subject to deterioration. Institutionalized money has the advantage of a far wider usefulness in exchange than such goods but the disadvantage of vulnerability to disturbances in the system. Money, however, as we have insisted, is a symbol, the "meaning" of which (in this case, its economic value) is a function of its mutual acceptability. In one direction, this acceptability is well-known to depend on its convertibility into objects of rock-bottom economic security, notably the monetary metal. Convertibility, however, is one thing, but frequent insistence on actual conversion is quite another.

The point is very simply that the insistence on actual conversion can be met only by measures that destroy the very degrees of freedom that make money an advantageous mechanism from the points of view *both* of the unit and of the system.[9] The maintenance of the degrees of freedom, however, is dependent on minimum levels of compliance with the norms of the economic complex with respect to the fulfillment of contractual obligations and the rights and obligations of property. It is by this path that we come to the conception that, while in one context the value of money rests on its "backing" by convertibility into a secure utility, for example metal, in another and probably more important context, it rests on the effective functioning of a ramified system of monetary exchanges and markets. This, in turn, is one major set of factors in the productivity of the economy of which these markets are a central part. No economist would suppose that such productivity can be created simply by adding to the supply of monetary gold.

I suggest that this duality of reference is characteristic not only of money as a mechanism, but of the whole set with which we are concerned—indeed, more broadly, of language, law, and various others. For the case of power, the basis of unit security corresponding to eco-

9. The most important reason concerns the role of banking and credit, the bearing of which on the functioning of influence will be taken up later.

nomic "real assets" consists in possession of effective means of *enforcing* compliance (that is fulfillment of wishes or performance of obligations) through implementing coercive threats or exerting compulsion. In this context, it is well known that physical force occupies a special place, a place which, it may be suggested, is parallel to monetary metal in the economic case. This is above all because force is the deterrent sanction par excellence. In turn, the most important aspect of this deterrence is very generally blocking channels of communication; for example, the most important feature of imprisonment is preventing the prisoner from communicating with others except in ways and through channels his custodians can control.

But just as possession of stocks of monetary gold cannot create a highly productive economy, so command of physical force alone cannot guarantee the effective fulfillment of ramified systems of binding obligations. The latter is dependent on such factors as the institutionalization of a system of norms in the fields of authority, and the legitimation of the power of leadership elements. The mutuality of the institutionalization of authority, on the one hand, and the acceptance of the legitimacy of its exercise, on the other, is the parallel of the mutual acceptability of "worthless" money in exchange. Clearly, the functioning of a *system* of power is preeminently dependent on the effective implementation of this normative structure. The analogue of economic productivity here may be said to be the *effectiveness of collective organization*.

Influence as a Symbolic Medium of Persuasion

Let us now attempt to apply this line of argument to the field of influence. There is a sense in which all four of the mechanisms under consideration here depend on the institutionalization of attitudes of trust. In the economic case, the actor relinquishes his interests (in commodities or labor) to the market, and the question is on what basis he can have confidence or trust that he will receive "fair value" in return for what he has relinquished. We have argued that there are two distinct foci of the problem of trust, namely, the convertibility of money into "real assets" and confidence in the functioning of the "system," which for the actor means the fulfillment of his more or less legitimate expectations from actual and potential exchange partners. Similarly, in the case of power, an actor may relinquish his coercive self-sufficiency: he cannot then defend himself adequately with his own strong right arm alone. In entrusting his security to a power *system*, there is on the one hand his possible identification with actual control of coercive means (in the last analysis, force), on the other his confidence that his expectations will be effectively fulfilled through agencies beyond his personal control, because the power *system* is effective.

In order to fit influence into this scheme, it is necessary to ask what influence symbolizes. In the case of money, it symbolized utility; in the case of power, effectiveness of collective action.[10] An answer seems to be given in our paradigm of interactive performance—sanction types. Influence is a means of *persuasion*. It is bringing about a decision on alter's part to act in a certain way because it is felt to be a "good thing" *for him*, on the one hand independently of contingent or otherwise imposed changes in his situation, on the other hand for positive reasons, not because of the obligations he would violate through noncompliance.

It then seems that, to correspond to the intrinsic "want-satisfiers," which the economist calls "goods and services," there should be a category of intrinsic "persuaders." The most obvious member of this category is "facts" from which alter can "draw his own conclusions." Ego, that is, can persuade by giving alter information which, given his situation and intentions, will lead him to make certain types of decisions.[11] It seems probable that information is indeed the proper parallel to commodities, with a special kind of information—the announcement of firm intentions of action on the part of significant others—the parallel to services.[12] Influence as a symbol, however, cannot be either of these, but must be more generalized relative to both.

The crucial thing to look for seems to be a symbolic act or component of action on ego's part which communicates a generalized intention on the basis of which trust in more specific intentions is requested and expected. This may operate in the realm of information. Here there must be some basis on which alter considers ego to be a trustworthy

10. For reasons of space, no further attempt is made here to ground this statement. Cf. my paper on political power, *op. cit.*
11. To take an extreme example, a middle-aged man might stubbornly refuse to make a will because of a kind of phantasy of immortality. If, however, a physician informed him that because of incurable cancer he had only a few months to live, this might well be enough to persuade him to make the will. This treatment of information and intentions as the primary types of intrinsic persuaders has recently been modified.
12. For many purposes, economists have bracketed "goods and services" together as the two ultimate "want-satisfiers." For certain purposes of economic sociology, however, the distinction is vital, particularly because the concept of services constitutes one perspective on labor as a factor of production. (Cf. Talcott Parsons and Neil J. Smelser, *Economy and Society* [Glencoe, Ill.: Free Press, 1956], p. 157, for a preliminary discussion of the importance of the distinction.)

source of information and "believes" him even though he is not in a position to verify the information independently—or does not want to take the trouble. It can also operate in the realm of ego's intentions, and this is indeed a crucial matter; for example, agreeing to a contract is essentially an announcement of intentions which can perhaps be fulfilled only by a long series of performances over an extended period of time.

The monetary metal is not "just" one among many commodities; it is one with certain properties that favor security and maximum exchangeability. Similarly with force as an instrument of coercion-compulsion. Is there, then, any comparable "intrinsic" source of persuasion that has a special likelihood of inspiring trust? If, in answering this question, we remember that we are dealing specifically with social interaction, it seems reasonable to suggest that the most favorable condition under which alter will trust ego's efforts to persuade him (independent of specific facts or "inherently" trustworthy intentions) will be when the two stand in a mutual relation of fundamental diffuse solidarity, when they belong together in a collectivity on such a basis that, so long as the tie holds, ego *could not* have an interest in trying to deceive alter. We may then suggest that common belongingness in a *Gemeinschaft* type of solidarity is the primary "basis" of mutual influence, and is for influence systems the equivalent of gold for monetary and force for power systems.

This, however, can be only the security *base*. Just as a ramified monetary system cannot operate with an exclusively metallic medium, so a ramified influence system would be stultified if only close *Gemeinschaft* associates ever trusted each other beyond completely concrete levels of information and binding intentions. The degrees of freedom associated with the market are here matched by those of "communication" systems, e.g., freedom of the press and the like. Like any other interchange system, the stability of a free communication system is dependent on regulation by a set of institutionalized norms corresponding to those of property and contract. These have to do with the conditions normatively regulating types of association of people with each other, the kinds of obligations assumed in making assertions and giving opinions, and the kinds of obligations involved in statements of intention. Thus, the very fundamental principle of freedom of association may be said to be the normative principle in this sphere that corresponds to freedom of contract in the sphere of market organization; in both cases, of course, the freedoms are far from absolute, being subject to such restrictions as are imposed by the interests of third parties.

What then, can be said in general about the nature of these normative references? In the case of money, the reference, within the range of freedom of contract, is to value equivalences in the utility sense. Money functions here as the measure of value, and price is a statement of the assessed value of an exchangeable item. In the case of power, the reference is to authorization, in the sense that a unit with power is, within the given limits, authorized to make decisions that bind not only himself but certain categories of others and the relevant collectivity as a whole. Thus, the vote is an exercise of power, and, subject to the electoral rules, the aggregate of votes in an election will determine bindingly the incumbency of office.

In the case of influence, I suggest that the corresponding conception should be the normative justification of generalized statements about information or intention (*not* their empirical validation). The user of influence is under pressure to justify his statements, which are intended to have an effect on alter's action, by making them correspond to norms that are regarded as binding on both.[13] With reference to items of information, justification is necessary, since influence is a symbolic medium. The function of justification is not actually to verify the items, but to provide the basis for the communicators' *right* to state them without alter's needing to verify them; for example, ego may be a technically competent "authority" in the field. With reference to intentions, justification may be regulated by various aspects of status that are regularly invoked to indicate that such intentions should prove trustworthy when stated by persons in the category in question.[14] A very important category of the justification of influence is what is ordinarily meant by "reputation." The same statement will carry more "weight" if made by someone with a high reputation for competence, for reliability, for good judgment, etc., than by someone without this reputation or with a reputation for unreliability. The common component may be called "fiduciary responsibility." A unit wields influence in proportion as, in the relevant context, its unverified declarations of information and intention are believed to be responsibly made. This is the "reputational" parallel to financial credit standing.

13. The term "justification" here refers to the level of norms. It seems useful to distinguish it from "legitimation," by which I would mean reference to the level of values. Cf. Talcott Parsons, Part II of General Introduction, in Parsons, E. Shils, K. Naegele, J. Pitts, editors, *Theories of Society* (Glencoe, Ill.: Free Press, 1961), Vol. I, pp. 43–44.
14. This, it should be noted, is independent of the assumption of formally binding obligation.

Put in familiar sociological terms, the associational base of influence may be regarded as primarily particularistic. The question is *who* the wielder is in terms of his collectivity memberships. The normative reference, however, is primarily universalistic. It is not what he is saying, which is a "content" matter, but what "right" he has to expect to be taken seriously, over and above the intrinsic cogency of what he says.

I spoke above of influence as "based" on *Gemeinschaft* solidarity, on the elementary, diffuse kind of belonging-togetherness of which, in a society like ours, the family is the prototypical case. The relevance of associatedness in collectivities is not, however, exhausted by this limiting case. Indeed, we may say that at many levels being "one of us" is a factor enhancing influence, whether it be membership in a local community, an occupational or professional group, or any one of many others. For this reason, nonmembers of groups must exercise special care in matters concerning the affairs of the group, lest they be felt to be "interfering." An obvious case is a foreigner speaking about a nation's domestic politics, especially one holding an official position at home. If this is true, then, conversely, attempting to influence is to a degree an attempt to establish a common bond of solidarity, on occasion even to bring the object of influence into common membership in a collectivity. Thus, being subject to mutual influence is to constitute a "we" in the sense that the parties have opinions and attitudes in common by virtue of which they "stand together" relative to those differing from them. There are, of course, various other conditions for establishing a full collectivity besides openness to mutual influence among its members, but we can certainly say that this is a necessary, if not sufficient, condition of a stable collectivity.

There is a very clear relation between this point and the findings of the study *Voting*, by Berelson, Lazarsfeld and McPhee, concerning the importance for voting behavior of the solidary group structures in which individuals are involved, starting with their families, but going on to occupations and ethnic, religious, and other groupings.[15] The broad presumption seems to be that a person will tend to vote with others whom he defines as "my kind of people" and that it is the "cross-pressured" groups which are mostly likely to break away from this tendency— cross-pressuring being itself a consequence of the increasing role pluralism of a complex society. Indeed, this finding was one of the most important points on which it seemed to me possible to relate empirical

15. Berelson, P. Lazarsfeld, and W. McPhee, *Voting* (Chicago: University of Chicago Press, 1954).

studies of voting behavior to the broad scheme of analysis of social interaction that has been the point of departure of the present essay.[16]

Types of Influence

We may now approach the problem of classification of types or modes of influence. Here it is essential to bear in mind that the influence system is not a closed system. On the one hand, of course, it is used to get consent to particular attitudes and opinions that are to influence what particular commodities and services are to money. In this sense, we may think of influence as a "circulating" medium. To get consent, an "opinion leader" must expend some of his influence. He must therefore carefully husband it by choosing the occasions on which to intervene and the appropriate mode of intervention. The classic type of thriftless expenditure is illustrated by the nursery story about the repetition of the cry, "Wolf! Wolf!" so that when the wolf actually came, the warning was not believed. This is to say that by wasting his influence, the author of the cry had lost his influence, that is, his capacity to convince.

The circulating character of influence as a medium can be brought out more clearly if we break it down into types, since in each context it is easier to identify the nature of the flow in both ways than if it is treated on the more general level. I should like to suggest the following tentative classification: (1) "political" influence, (2) "fiduciary" influence, (3) influence through appeal to differential loyalties, and (4) influence oriented to the interpretation of norms. The fact that, in order to characterize the last two types, it is necessary to resort to cumbrous phrases rather than succinct single-word designations indicates clearly that the subject is rather undeveloped and needs elucidation. An important guide line for interpreting the first three types lies in the convertibility of each with one of the other three types of generalized media we have discussed.

1. When speaking of political influence, I mean it in an analytical sense, but one in which there is a directly significant relation between influence and power. The prototypical structural context is that of the democratic association, whether it be in the field of government at any

16. Cf. Talcott Parsons, " 'Voting' and the Equilibrium of the American Political System," in Eugene Burdick and Arthur J. Brodbeck, editors, *American Voting Behavior* (Glencoe, Ill.: Free Press, 1959), reprinted as Chapter 8 in this volume.

one of several levels, or of private associations. The democratic association is characterized by a structure of offices the incumbents of which are authorized to take certain decisions binding on the collectivity as a whole and, hence, on its members in their respective capacities.[17] Such authorization is for action defined within constitutional norms, and there are also constitutional procedures by which incumbents of office are chosen, summed up as election and appointment.

The making of decisions binding on a collectivity I interpret to be an exercise of power, which includes the exercise of the franchise in the electoral procedure, since it is the aggregate of votes which determines who is elected to office. But both in seeking election and in office, officers and candidates are continually using other ways of getting the results they want besides the use of power in a strict sense. They are, of course, giving information and announcing intentions, in the detailed sense. They may well be offering inducements, making coercive threats outside the context of the power of office, and activating their own and others' commitments. But they are, above all, operating with influence, in our technical sense.

There are, as I conceive it, two main contexts in which this is the case. Because associations are typically differentiated on the axis of leadership-followership, we may use this axis here. One focus of influence, then, is the establishment of leadership position or reputation, either as incumbent of office or as explicit or implicit candidate, so that, for the followership in question, there will be a basis of trust going beyond the direct exercise of power, the giving of specific information and the like, and also beyond the manipulation of inducements, informal threats, etc. A leader, I suggest, must try to establish a basis on which he is trusted by a "constituency," in the symbolic sense of this discussion, so that when he "takes a position," he can count on a following "going along with him" on it, or even actively working for its implementation according to their respective capacities and roles. We often put this by saying that a leader "takes responsibility" for such positions. In any case, I would treat the concept of leadership as focusing on the use of influence, and the concept of office, on the use of power.

The other context is the obverse, that of the processes by which units not in a leadership position in the relevant respects can have and use influence oriented to having an effect on leadership. This is by and large

17. Of course, for this analysis to be relevant, the association in question need not be "fully" democratic, but this problem of ranges in degrees of democracy need not concern the present very limited discussion.

the well-known field of "interest groups," very broadly in the sense of parts of the constituencies of parties and officeholders. The influence may be used in electoral processes, trying to establish terms on which electoral support—a form of power—will be given. Or, it may play on incumbents of office by trying to influence their decisions of policy. In either case, it is the use of a basis of presumptive "trust" and, hence, "right to speak" to try to swing a balance in favor of what the influencer advocates—or opposes—relative to alternatives, whether these be candidates or policies.

Political influence, then, we would conceive as influence operating in the context of the goal-functioning of collectivities, as generalized persuasion without power—i.e., independent of the use of power or direct threat,[18]—used, on the one hand, by units either exercising or bidding for leadership position and, on the other, by nonleaders seeking to have an effect on the decisions and orientations of leaders. Though political influence is analytically independent of power, we conceive the two to be closely interconnected. Very generally, leaders expect a major share of their influence to be translated into binding support, particularly through the franchise, and constituents in turn expect an important part of theirs to be translated into binding decisions congenial to them. But the independence of influence from power means that the influence system is an open one. To tie it to power in direct, matching terms would be to reduce the power-influence relation to a barter basis, and thus destroy the element of symbolic generalization we have treated as essential.

2. The second type of influence suggested has been called "fiduciary." The relevant context here is not the effective determination of an attainment of collective goals, but the allocation of resources in a system where both collectivities and their goals are plural and the justification of each among the plural goals is problematical. The interests in control of resources and in attainment of goals are the classical instances of the operation of "interests" in social systems. In a more or less pluralistic system, the allocation of resources must, however, be subject to normative control; distributions must be justified by reference to norms more general than the mere desirability to the unit in question of getting what it wants. Furthermore, resources constitute, from the point of view of

18. Incumbents of office, though they have power, are often very careful when pleading for certain measures to make clear that they will not directly bring their power to bear in the particular case. A good example is when officeholders who are adherents of a particular party lend their influence to strictly nonpartisan causes. Thus a state governor who is a good Republican may plead for *all* the people, regardless of party, to contribute generously to the Red Cross campaign.

goal attainment, the principal opportunity factor that conditionally controls prospects of success. Hence, influence bearing on the allocation of resources is a particularly important field of trust.

There is a relation to money in this case which is in certain respects parallel to that to power in the case of political influence. This derives from the fact that, in a society in which the economy is highly differentiated relative to other elements of the social structure, money becomes the most important allocative mechanism, not only over commodities, but over human services. Hence, the focus of the fiduciary function is in the allocation of funds, because the possessor of funds is in turn in a position to claim, through market channels, control over the indicated share of "real" resources.

The interchanges we have in mind here do not constitute the use of money as a circulating medium, but rather as a measure of value. On the monetary side, an example is setting up a budget. The various interests that expect to share in a budget "assert their claims," and the budget-making agency reaches some kind of allocative ranking of these claims. This is the expression of need and of "right" in monetary terms. But both claims and accession of right in turn are subject to standards of justification, in our technical sense. These are never assertions of value as such, because the agency, dealing as it goes with scarce and allocable resources, must always consider situational exigency and competing claims. It operates, that is, at the level of norms, not of values. Those who assert claims may concretely, of course, use power to gain them; they may use inducements—in the extreme case, bribery—or various other means. But a special role is played by influence. A good example would be, in budgetary negotiations, the assertion of a highly qualified and trustworthy technical expert that to fulfill expectations he must have a certain specific minimum of resources at his disposal—an assertion that a budgetary officer, not himself an expert in the field, will find it difficult to contest. On the other hand, decisions of allocation in turn must be justified by reference to agreed standards of property priority in claims. Such standards, of course, are likely to be made most explicit where there is an unaccustomed stringency of resources and hence sacrifices must be justified. Just as the budgetary officer is often unable to judge the needs of the technical expert, so the latter, operating only in one specialized sector of the system, is not qualified to judge the urgency of the claims competing with his own. Hence the necessity for mutual influence to operate to cover this gap.

The case of a budget is the neatest case, because the relevant system is more or less closed by unitary organizational control of the resources and by power, in the strict sense, to make the allocative decisions binding. The same basic principles, however, apply in processes of allocation through free market channels. The economist's ideal of free competition is here the limiting case in which influence as an independent factor disappears. Here, then, it is in two areas that influence is most obviously operative. One is the establishment of norms by which the allocative process is regulated, as through tax legislation and the like; the other is through such modifications of "pure" market process as the involvement of voluntary contributions in allocation. The very term "fiduciary" is also most generally used for cases where certain "interested parties" cannot be expected to protect their interests without help, for example, administration of the property interests of minors by "trustees," i.e. people who can be trusted to apply acceptable standards even though their actions are not dictated by personal financial interest.

3. The third category has been called "influence through appeal to differential loyalties." Whereas in the political influence case the differentiation on the axis of leadership was the central structural focus, and in the fiduciary influence case it was the problem of allocation of scarce resources, in this case it is the pluralistic structure of memberships in society. This operates at the level both of individuals in roles and of collectivities. The more highly differentiated the society is structurally, the more every concrete unit is a responsible member of a plurality of collectivities.[19] He is therefore in a position of having to balance the claims of these plural collectivities on his loyalties, i.e. a class of his normative commitments.

For the individual, particularly the adult male, the most important case is normally the relation between kinship and occupation, since for most men it is essential to participate in both, and in modern societies they are structurally independent of each other. Generally, in a reasonably stable situation, the broad lines of allocation of obligation are institutionally settled, but there are always areas of indeterminacy and of shift in the light of changing circumstances. Moreover, our society is rapidly changing, and one of the principal aspects of such change is the rise of new collectivities, and hence loyalties to them, and the decline of old ones. A large part of the population is thus faced with decisions about whether to take on new commitments or to sacrifice old ones, or both, or to shift balances among loyalties.

19. For the collectivity as unit the relevant membership is that in more inclusive collectivities; e.g., a department is a subcollectivity in a university faculty.

The commitments we have in mind are grounded in institutionalized values, which can, for purposes of analysis, be presumed to be shared by members of a society. But it is in the nature of a differentiated society that there is an important difference between asserting, however sincerely, the desirability of a value and, on the other hand, taking personal responsibility for its implementation, since the capacities and opportunities of units for effective contribution are inherently limited, and, moreover, some kinds of attempt would infringe the prerogatives of other units. It is with this problem that the present type of influence is concerned. It is a matter of the justification of assuming particular responsibilities in particular collectivity and subcollectivity contexts.

A person, then, will be faced by manifold demands for commitment through participation in collectivities, and will often be put in a position of having to justify the allocative decisions he makes. The normative structure (of "commitments") governing such processes then involves, on the one hand, appeals to common values and, on the other, assertion of norms governing the practical decisions of allocation of commitment among plural loyalties. The categories of influence, then, are, first, the plea that an actor ought, as a practical matter, to undertake such and such a collective responsibility (not merely that it is desirable that the function be effectively performed independently of *his* commitment; that is an assertion of its value), and second, the assertion of the norms it is held should govern such decisions, again at the level of practical allocation.

In one sense, this, like the last category of influence, concerns the allocation of "resources." But what I am here referring to as loyalties are not the same kind of resource as money and power, or the concrete utilities and modes of effectiveness controlled by them. From the point of view of the unit, the question is not with what means he will implement his commitments, but *whether he will undertake the commitment in the first place*. It is not, given that he "intends" to do something, a question of *how* he is to accomplish it, but rather whether he *ought*— in our sense of justification—to undertake it at all. Commitments in this sense surely constitute a societal resource, but, in the analysis of unit action, they concern the "orientational" side, not the situational side, of the action paradigm.[20]

As noted earlier in this paper, I consider generalized commitments to

20. Cf. Talcott Parsons, "Pattern Variables Revisited," *American Sociological Review*, Vol. 25 (1960), pp. 467–483 and Chapter 7 in this volume, for an elucidation of this essential distinction.

constitute a symbolic medium operating on the interaction process in the same basic sense that money, power, and influence do. Any promise by which the actor forecloses certain alternatives may be regarded as a *particular* commitment. By invoking a *generalized* commitment, however, the actor is enabled to command a series of more particular commitments, to be in a position to "activate" them in response to appropriate circumstances as we have said above. A good example is securing the acceptance of a job offer. Commitment to the job by the prospective employee then entails a commitment to perform a complex series of more particular acts as occasion arises, including commitment to accept certain types of authority within the organization.

Being grounded in values, generalized commitments in some sense involve the "honor" of the actors concerned, the more so the more generalized they are. They therefore cannot in general be altered lightly. Nevertheless, in a pluralistic and changing society, complete rigidity of commitments would introduce an intolerable rigidity into its structure. Commitments must therefore involve priority scales of seriousness, i.e. be referred to general standards, and there must be norms defining the situations in which particular commitments may be changed, not only new ones assumed but also old ones abandoned, even where this means the breaking of promises made and accepted in good faith. A good example here is the general norm that even in occupations where rules of tenure bind the employing organization, incumbents of such positions are generally considered entitled to resign subject only to giving "reasonable" notice. The category of influence with which we are now concerned operates in this range of flexibility of commitments and concerns the relation between the justification for change and the more generalized loyalties to fulfillment of commitments made.

4. The three types of influence so far discussed deal with the relations of the normative or integrative system to the other primary functional subsystems of the society, namely, what I should call the "polity," the "economy," and the "pattern maintenance" (in a structural aspect, the value maintenance) systems respectively.[21] The fourth and final type, which was referred to as influence oriented to the interpretation of norms, is internal to the integrative system. Here the prototype is the process of interpretation of legal norms in the appellate phase of the judicial process.

21. This refers to a generalized paradigm of analysis in terms of four functional categories, elaborated more fully, for example, in the General Introduction to *Theories of Society* and in "Pattern Variables Revisited," as cited.

Since norms mediate between value commitments and particular interests and situational exigencies, they are, in formulation, in need of continual adjustment to the variations at these levels. Furthermore, since their primary function in the social system is integrative, the problem of consistency is a particularly important one. Hence, in a complex system of normative regulation, the interpretive function is highly important. A category of influence is organized about it of which the best example is the influence involved in the reputations of judges and lawyers. As in so many other fields, substantive arguments, i.e. particular justifications, of course play a central part. But there is the same need for symbolic generalization here as in the other fields. Another type of example of interpretive influence would be in the field of exegesis of ethical norms, which plays such an important part in many religious traditions.

This has been an exceedingly sketchy and tentative attempt to review a typology of the different contexts of the operation of influence. All, I think, are fields in which the general themes of the above analysis can be illustrated in sufficiently well-known terms to carry conviction of the reality and importance of the phenomena here called "influence." Let me reiterate that the critical common factor is a mechanism of persuasion that is generalized beyond appeal to particular facts, particular intentions, particular obligations and commitments, particular normative rules. The general suggestion is that, in the absence of a ramified system of influence in this sense, there would either be a much more pervasive atmosphere of distrust than in fact obtains, or the level of trust could be raised only by introducing more rigid specification as to who could be trusted in what specific ways, which would greatly limit the ranges of flexibility so important to a complex society.

Is Influence a Fixed Quantity in a Social System?

One further major topic is so essential to the general understanding of symbolic media that the discussion would be seriously incomplete without a brief treatment of it. It concerns a problem that has been particularly prominent in the history of the analysis of money and power, but the technical analysis of influence has been so primitive that it has scarcely arisen in that connection. It may be put in terms of the question whether any or all of these media are in general subject to a "zero-sum" condition of their operation.

At certain levels and in certain contexts it is obvious that this condition does hold. For a unit with fixed money income, increase of expenditure for one purpose must be balanced by reduction for one or more others. Similarly in power systems, electoral rules mean that a vote cast for one candidate must be denied to others, and persons in authority must choose between mutually incompatible alternatives in making many decisions. Important as this is, it is not, however, the whole story.

The most familiar case in the monetary field in which the zero-sum conception fails to apply is the creation of credit through banking. Money in one aspect is the most important object of property rights. Depositors in a bank in one sense "lend" their property to the bank. But, unlike most contracts of lease, they do not, even for a term, relinquish any of their rights: the main feature of a deposit is that it is repayable on demand, subject only to rules such as those regulating banking hours.

The bank, however, does not simply act as custodian for its depositors' funds. It lends a certain proportion to borrowers on contractual terms that enable the latter to "spend" them so long as they are presumptively in a position to repay at the term of the loan, and of course pay interest and any other charges. This means that *the same dollars* are functioning double as circulating media, so that the bank loans outstanding constitute a net addition to the quantity of the circulating medium.

This commonplace of economics has a very important implication. Clearly, an operating bank is in *one* important sense always formally "insolvent," in that its deposits are held on demand whereas its loans are on term. If all the depositors demand repayment at the same time, the bank cannot meet its obligations without outside resources. It usually keeps sufficient cash—and other resources—on hand to meet expected rates of withdrawal, with a margin of safety, but if it were completely "liquid," it would cease to be a bank. Financial panics are, precisely, occasions on which an abnormal rate of demand puts the bank in a difficult if not impossible position, in the extreme case forcing its "failure."

The question arises whether there are, with respect to the other media, phenomena analogous to those of banking and credit in the monetary field. The dominant opinion in the field of analysis of power seems to have been that there are not,[22] but this position has been questioned. The most appropriate context seems to be the relation between

22. For example, this seems to be the position of Harold D. Lasswell and Abraham Kaplan, *Power and Society* (New Haven: Yale University Press, 1950).

the grant of power to leadership in the democratic association and the use of that power by leadership.

Elected leaders may be said to be the recipients of a grant of power through the exercise of the franchise. This grant is, moreover, typically and in principle revocable, if not on demand, then at the end of a stated term of office, when the voter can transfer his support to a rival candidate. It could be argued, then, that this is a "deposit" of power, which is at the disposal of the depositors for the "purchase" of political benefits through the decisions made by the incumbents of office somewhere in the system, not necessarily this particular office. This would make it a "circulating" system where the amounts of power balanced.

It may be suggested, however, that this is only part of the story. Some of the power acquired through election to office may be "invested" in collective enterprises that are not direct responses to the interest-demands of constituents, and this power in turn may be utilized by agencies other than constituents. Since power is in certain circumstances convertible into money, for example through taxation, it may be suggested that some of the use of tax funds, as in the support of scientific training and research, is a process of "investment" by officeholders— in both the executive and the legislative branches—that puts the funds at the disposal of scientists and educational institutions. If the electorate, like the bank's depositors, should demand immediate and strict accounting of power, the system would, like a good bank, turn out to be "insolvent" in the sense that these commitments could not be liquidated all at once. Often, however, politicians can shrewdly estimate the latitude it is safe to assume in making commitments other than those specifically demanded by the constituents on whom they are dependent. Politically organized collectivities, including government, can probably serve as agents of creative social change mainly by virtue of this type of mechanism, namely, the creation of increments of new power, since generating direct constituency demands for these changes may involve much more serious difficulties.

It would seem logical that the same reasoning should apply to influence. The case in which the zero-sum concept should particularly apply is political influence, because, on the economic analogy, this is a kind of "circular flow" situation in which the process of eliciting collective decisions in a ramified system is mediated.[23] The economic parallel lies in the markets for consumers' goods and for labor.

23. For the concept of circular flow, cf. J. A. Schumpeter, *The Theory of Economic Development* (Cambridge, Mass.: Harvard University Press, 1934), Chap. 1.

In the field of influence, the analogy with banking and credit seems most obvious in connection with the allocation of loyalties. The postulate on which our whole analysis in this area is based is that it applies most clearly to a highly pluralistic social system in which the allocation of loyalties cannot be wholly based on direct assessment of the importance of the intrinsic issues involved, but that commitments are widely made in response to influence. If the quantity of influence is not fixed, but is expansible along the lines suggested by monetary credit, then it becomes possible for influence to operate as a mechanism by which a given capacity for power and commitments (in our technical sense) can be reallocated, in that the influence to command such commitments can be more or less directly and deliberately put in the hands of certain agencies.

My suggestion is that the principal way in which this is done in a society like the American is through voluntary associations that, unlike government even in its "democratic" aspect, are not primarily concerned with political functions—again in our technical sense. The "joiners" of such associations are analogous to depositors. They have, as we often put it, "lent their names" to the association and its leadership. But such an association often does more than simply collect increments of influence; it creates the effect of adding to the total amount of influence in circulation. This can occur in proportion as leadership exercises *independent* judgment in how to use the "name," not of individual members but of the association, to encourage commitments which they consider to be desirable, generally in quarters outside the membership itself.

Such associations may thus be considered to be a kind of "influence bank." Like money banks, they are formally "insolvent." Hence, if their members call for strict accounting—"You shall not use the name of the association without explicit consent of all the membership to the detailed implications"—this, of course, destroys the freedom of action of leaders, and leads to a deflation of "influence credit." The effect of this in turn is to deprive many agencies, dependent on the "backing" of such influence purveyors, of the basis on which they can "afford" to make important commitments. In more ordinary circumstances, however, leaders of such associations operate on a judgment of the acceptable margins of their independence. They do, in fact, make commitments of the association's name beyond the level of explicit authorization—though not of realistic expectation of "justification"—by the membership. In so doing, they add to the net amount of influence circulating in the system and have an effect on the distribution of commitments in the society in the direction of promoting the "causes" they hold to be desirable.

It should be clear from the above argument that phenomena analogous to deflation and inflation in the economic case should be found in the fields of power and influence as well. We have already indicated the direction that deflationary trends would take in these fields. In the field of power it is toward progressively increasing reliance on strict authority and coercive sanctions, culminating in the threat and use of physical force. In the field of influence it is toward undermining the basis of trust in reputations and fiduciary responsibility through increasing questioning of broader loyalties and rising insistence on narrow in-groupism.[24]

Inflationary process, on the other hand, is, for influence, the extension of claims to authoritative diagnoses of situations that cannot be validated with solid information and, on the other hand, the declaration of praiseworthy intentions that will not be backed by actual commitments when occasion arises. Unfortunately, there is no space here to develop these themes as they deserve.

It should go without saying that this essay has been very tentative indeed. It cannot claim to be more than the barest approach to the very complicated problems of this area. I hope, however, that it can serve as a useful basis not only for discussion but for the stimulation of serious research.

24. McCarthyism was a classic instance of a deflationary episode entering in the influence field, which at its culmination approached panic proportions: the demand for "absolute loyalty" was analogous to the demand for a return to the gold standard in the financial area. Cf. E. A. Shils, *The Torment of Secrecy*, and "Social Strains in America," Chap. 7 of my book of essays, *Structure and Process in Modern Societies*, (Glencoe, Ill.: Free Press, 1960).

Perspectives
in Modern Society

CHAPTER 12

Christianity and Modern Industrial Society

In its first three chapters, Part IV turns to a somewhat more "applied" level of the consideration and use of sociological theory. Their concern is more with the understanding of particular societies or societal subsystems, than with the generalized treatment of theory or "methodology" (in the German sense) which has, with the exception of Chapter 8, been the predominant interest of the preceding Chapters. For reasons of space, only a sample of essays of this type could be included in the present collection. They have been chosen to represent the types of interest and fruitfulness of the theoretical work discussed above, for empirical purposes. Chapter 15, however, stands on a somewhat different level, which will be explained in its introductory note.

The present paper represents a very general essay of the more empirical type. It was occasioned by an invitation to contribute to the volume of essays in honor of Pitirim A. Sorokin, edited by Edward A. Tiryakian, that appeared in 1963 under the title *Sociological Theory, Values, and Sociocultural Change*. Because, in the course of a long association at Harvard, my own views on this topic, being grounded in the work of Max Weber, had contrasted sharply with Professor Sorokin's conception of the development in the West of the "sensate society," it seemed appropriate to attempt to define the issue by stating my own view in the best organized and most systematic form possible.

The general perspective is that the most recent phase in the development of the relation between religiously-grounded values and the structure of secular society in the Western world could be treated as the outcome of a positively evolutionary process, the theme of which, following the conception of Troeltsch, could be interpreted as the development of the conception of a "Christian Society" (now clearly a Judeo-Christian Society) and its relatively full institutionalization. The special significance of the "Protestant

Ethic" in this general pattern has become a major focus of the analysis.

This essay fits with some others that have dealt with the religious situation of the contemporary world. "Some Comments on the Pattern of Religious Organization in the United States," which constitutes Chapter 10 of my *Structure and Process in Modern Societies* (New York: Free Press, 1960), may be taken as a basic point of reference, as may the somewhat different H. Paul Douglass Lectures for 1965, delivered in Chicago on "Religion in a Modern Pluralistic Society" (*Journal of Religious Research*). A treatment of a good deal of the subject-matter, of the present essay, but with somewhat different emphases, will be found in my article "Christianity" in the forthcoming *International Encyclopedia of the Social Sciences*.

T HE present volume is conceived as a tribute to Professor Sorokin as a distinguished elder statesman of sociology, not only in the United States but throughout the world. One of the highest achievements, particularly in a rapidly developing discipline in its early phases of development, is to serve as a generator and focus of creatively important differences of opinion. Such differences pose problems which, though not solved or in any immediate sense soluble in the generation in question, still serve to orient the thinking of professional groups. For such differences to be fruitful there must be a delicate balance of commonly accepted premises, which make a fruitful meeting of minds possible, and difference of interpretation in more particularized questions which are open to some sort of empirical test.

In the sociological profession today Professor Sorokin and the present author are probably defined predominantly as antagonists who have taken widely different views on a variety of subjects.[1] The objective of this chapter is to take explicit cognizance of one, to me crucial, field of such difference of opinion, but to attempt to place it within a framework of common problems in the hope that consideration of the difference may help others toward a fruitful solution of these problems.

In the highly empirical atmosphere of American sociology in recent times there has been a tendency to neglect the importance of the great problems of the trends of development of Western society and culture

1. *Cf.* Sorokin, *Fads and Foibles in Modern Sociology and Related Sciences* (Chicago: Henry Regnery, 1956).

in a large sense, of its place relative to the great civilizations of the Orient, and similar problems. Within this field the problem of the role of religion and its relation to social values stands in a particularly central position. In my opinion it is one of Sorokin's great services to have held these problems consistently in the forefront of concern, and to have refused to be satisfied with a sociology which did not have anything significant to say about them. In this fundamental respect Sorokin stands in the great tradition of Western sociological thought. This emphasis coincides with my own strong predilections, shaped as they were by European experience under the influences in particular of Max Weber and Durkheim.

It can, I think, safely be said that we share the convictions, first, of the enormous importance of the general evolutionary and comparative perspective in the interpretation of social phenomena and second, of the crucial role of religion and its relation to values in this large perspective. When, however, we turn to more particular problems of spelling out this context, differences of opinion emerge. A particularly important test case is that of the interpretation of the relations of religious orientation, values, and social structure in the course of that development in the modern Western world which has eventuated in modern industrialism. I propose to set over against a very schematic but I hope accurate outline of Sorokin's view, my own, which I think may be the kind of alternative which, though differing sharply from his view, may pose fruitful empirical questions on which future research may be expected to throw light. Only in this broadest contrast will I attempt to take account of the Sorokin position. My objective is not to present either a full statement or a critique of his conceptions as such, but to state my own as clearly as possible.

The heart of the Sorokin position which is relevant here I take to be his classification and use of three fundamental types of cultural orientation—the "ideational," "idealistic," and "sensate."[2] What may be called orientations in terms of the grounds of meaning on the one hand and values for social and personal conduct on the other, are treated as by and large varying together.

The ideational pattern is one which gives unquestionable primacy to transcendental and other-worldly interests in the religious sense. Reality itself is defined as ultimately beyond the reach of the senses, as

2. The most important general statements of his position are in *Social and Cultural Dynamics* (New York: American Book Company, 1937), Vol. I, Part 1, and *Society, Culture, and Personality* (New York: Harper, 1947), Part 7.

transcendental. The goal of life must be to reach the closest possible accord with the nature of transcendent reality, and the path to this must involve renunciation of all worldly interests. Broadly speaking, other-worldly asceticism and mysticism are the paths to it. The ethical component which is so prominent in Christianity generally is not missing from Sorokin's conception. It takes, however, the form on which his later work has placed increasing stress: that of altruistic love, of pure personal selfless acts of love by individuals. In this discussion I would like to differentiate this form of altruism from the *institutionalization* of Christian ethics to become part of the structure of the society itself. It is the latter with which my analysis will be concerned.

The opposite extreme to the ideational pattern is the sensate. Here the empirical, in the last analysis the "material," aspect of reality is taken as ultimately real or predominant. In practical conduct the implication of a sensate view of the world is to make the most of the opportunities of the here and now, to be concerned with worldly success, power, and—in the last analysis—to put hedonistic gratifications first of all.

The idealistic pattern is conceived as intermediate between the two, not in the sense of a simple "compromise," but rather of a synthesis which can achieve a harmonious balance between the two principal components.

This basic classification is then used as the framework for outlining a developmental pattern leading, in the history of a civilization, from ideational to idealistic predominance and in turn from idealistic to sensate. Though very generally applied, the two most important cases dealt with in Sorokin's works are the civilization of classical antiquity and that of the Christian West. In both cases there was an early ideational phase which gradually gave way to an idealistic synthesis: in the classical that of fifth-century Greece, in the Western that of the high Middle Ages. The idealistic synthesis has then proceeded to break down into an increasingly sensate phase—in the classical case the late Hellenistic and Roman periods, in the Western the modern "capitalistic" or industrial period. Sorokin tends to regard the contemporary period, exemplified particularly in the United States, but also in the Soviet Union, as close to the peak of the sensate phase of development and destined for a general breakdown comparable to that of Greco-Roman civilization before a new ideational pattern can become established.

From one point of view the general developmental trend Sorokin outlines may be described as a progressive decline in the "religiousness" of the society and culture until a radical reversal is forced by a general societal breakdown. In the Western case the phase of early Christianity was the most religious, characterized by a primarily ascetic disregard for virtually all worldly interests, and the practice of brotherly love within the Christian community itself. Correspondingly, however, Christianity in this phase had little power to organize social relationships beyond the church. With the development of the idealistic phase, however, for a time it was possible to permeate secular life with at least an approximation of Christian ethics, but the balance was precarious and broke down relatively soon.

There may well be a considerable measure of agreement up to this point. Sorokin, however, clearly regards Protestantism, compared with medieval Catholicism, as primarily a step in the general decline of religiousness, and the secularism which has been prominent since the Age of the Enlightenment as the natural further step in the same direction. It is hence on the interpretation of Protestantism in the general process of Western social development and its sequel after the Reformation period that I would like to focus my own view. It will be necessary, however, to say a few things about more general theoretical orientation, and about the earlier historical phases as background for this analysis.

An Alternative Interpretation

There are two interrelated theoretical issues which need to be discussed briefly before entering into a historical analysis. These concern factors in the structure of a religious orientation itself on the one hand and the senses in which religious orientations and their institutionalization in the social system can undergo processes of structural differentiation on the other.

In the former respect Professor Sorokin seems to think primarily in terms of a single variable which might be called "degree of religiousness." This in turn tends to be identified with transcendental orientation in the sense of *other-worldliness* as defining the acceptable field of interest and activity. This is to say that, so far as religious interests are in any sense paramount in a motivational system, the religious person will tend to renounce the world and engage so far as possible in ascetic or devotional practices or mystical contemplation and purely spontaneous acts of love, reducing his involvement in "practical" affairs which involve institutionalized obligations to a minimum. He will therefore tend to be oriented to the reduction of all desires to participate positively and actively in worldly activities like political or economic functions. By the same token, positive commitment to such worldly interests and responsibilities is taken as an index of relative lack of religious interest.

Relative to the degree of religiousness we suggest the relevance of a second variable which we think is independent. This is the one which Max Weber formulated as the variation between otherworldly and innerworldly orientation. Combined with a high degree of religiousness, the choice of one alternative leads to religious rejection of the world, the choice of the other to an orientation to mastery over the world in the name of religious values. There are further complications in the problem of a general typology of religious orientations, but suffice it to say for the present that I propose to explore the possibilities implicit in the hypothesis that Western Christianity belongs in the category of orientation which is high in degree of religiousness, with a predominantly innerworldly orientation so far as the field of expected action of the individual is concerned. In ways I shall try to explain, this applies even to early and medieval Christianity, but becomes most clearly evident in "ascetic Protestantism." I feel that this hypothesis is excluded by Sorokin's assumption that religiousness *ipso facto* implies otherworldiness, supplemented only by spontaneous altruism.

The second main theoretical point concerns the question of differentiation. I think of religion as an aspect of human action. Like all other aspects, in the course of social, cultural, and personality development it undergoes processes of differentiation in a double sense. The first of these concerns differentiation within religious systems themselves, the second the differentiation of the religious element from nonreligious elements in the more general system of action. In the latter context the general developmental trend may be said to be from fusions of religious and nonreligious components in the same action structures, to increasingly clear differentiation between multiple spheres of action.

A special problem arises when we deal with a system over a sufficiently long period of time to include two or more stages in a process of differentiation. Structural parts of the system have to be named. It is in the nature of the process of differentiation that what was one part at an earlier stage becomes two or more distinct parts at a later. The simple logical question then is whether the name applied at the earlier stage is still used to designate any one of the parts surviving at the later. If the process is one of differentiation, clearly the surviving entity which carries the same name will be narrower in scope and more "specialized" in the later than it was in the earlier stage. It will then, by mere logic, have lost function and become less important than in the earlier phase. The problem then becomes one of analyzing the continuities, not only of the component called by the same name in the different stages, e.g., *religion,* but also of the senses in which the patterns of orientation given in the earlier stages have or have not been fundamentally altered in their significance for the system as a whole, considering the exigencies of the situations in which action takes place and the complex relations of this part to the other parts of the more differentiated system, e.g., the non-religious or secular.

It is my impression that Professor Sorokin has not given sufficient weight to these considerations and has tended to measure the influence of religion, from earlier to later stages, as if it were reasonable to expect maintenance of the same "degree of inclusiveness" in the direct "definition of the situation" for action which it enjoyed in the early stage of reference. Judged by this standard the degree of religiousness of Christian society has clearly suffered a progressive decline by the mere fact that the society has become functionally a more highly differentiated system of action than was the early "primitive" church.

The Setting of the Problem: Christianity—Society

As a first step it is necessary to outline a few essentials of the nature of the early Christian church and its relations to the secular society of the time. Its structure comprised, as is well known, a very distinctive synthesis of elements derived from Judaism, Greek philosophy, the Greek conception of social organization, and of course distinctive contributions of its own.

The Hebrew and the Greek patterns had in common the conception of a solidary, religiously sanctioned social unit, the organization of which was based on values fully transcending the loyalties of kinship. In the Hebrew case it was the confederation of "tribes" bound to Jahweh and to each other by the Covenant. These units became fused into a "people" whose main orientation to life was defined in terms of the Law given to them by Jahweh, a firm collectivity structure defining its role as the fulfillment of God's commandments. In the historical course, by what precise stages need not concern us here, two crucial developments occurred. First Jahweh became a completely universal transcendental God who governed the activities not only of the people of Israel but of all mankind. Second, the people of Israel became, through the exile, depoliticized. Their religion was the essential bond of solidarity. Since this was no longer expressed in an independent political community, it was not exposed to the "secularizing" influences so importantly involved in political responsibility.

On the Greek side the *polis* was a comparable solidary confederation, in the first instance of kinship lineages. It was the "political" society almost par excellence, but one which eventually came to be based on the principle of the universalistic equality of citizens. Religiously it was oriented not to a transcendental God but to an immanent polytheism. The conception of the ultimate unity of divinity emerged in Greek civilization, but essentially as a philosophical principle the necessity of which was demonstrated by reason.

Seen against the background of Judaism and in certain respects also of the Greek component, the most important distinctive feature of Christianity of importance here was its religious individualism. In Judaism the primary religious concern was with the fate of the Jewish community as God's chosen people. In Christianity it became the fate of the individual soul; God was concerned with the salvation of individuals, not simply with the extent to which a social community as such adhered to His commandments.

This new conception of the relation of the individual soul to God might seem, given the fundamental transcendental character of the God of Judaism, to imply the virtual abandonment of concern with life in the world, to make the life of the Christian center primarily in devotional interests in preparing for the life to come. Indeed this strain in Christianity has always been a crucially important one and marks it off sharply from the main trend of Judaism. In this respect Christianity, however different its theological orientation, was closely analogous to Indian religion. But there was another aspect to Christian individualism: the fact that its adherents came to constitute a very special type of social collectivity on earth, the Christian church. The theological significance of the Christ figure as the mediator between God and man is central as defining the nature of man's relation to God, in and through the Church of Christ. It was the conception of the church which underlay the nature of the ethical conception of Christianity and was the basis from which the moral influence of Christianity could operate on secular society.

In theoretical terms this may be expressed by saying that the conception of the church, which implied the fundamental break with the Jewish law which Paul made final, constituted the *differentiation* of

Christianity as a religious system (a cultural system) from the conception of a "people" as a social system. Given the Roman ascendancy in the secular society of the time, this differentiation was expressed in the famous formula "Render unto Caesar the things that are Caesar's"— that is, the church did not claim jurisdiction over secular society as such.

At the same time this church was a solidary collectivity. The keynote here was the conception of "brothers in Christ." Its members were by no means concerned only with their respective personal salvations, but with the mission of Christ on behalf of mankind. This had the dual meaning of an obligation to extend the Christian community by proselytizing and, within it, to organize its internal relations on the basis in the first instance of mutual brotherly love.

Though, religiously speaking, this was a radically individualistic doctrine, it was not an anarchistic, but what we have come to call an "institutionalized" individualism. The Christian doctrine of the Trinity, compared with Jewish unitarianism, is intimately connected with this development. Instead of a single "line" of relationship between an ultimately transcendental God and man, God became related to man *through* the Christ figure who was both God and Man, and Christ became the head of the Church, the "essence" of which was formulated as the third person of the Trinity, the Holy Spirit.

As I interpret it, this implied, correlative with the differentiation of the church from secular society, a differentiation *within* the religious system itself, in the broadest respect between the aspect of devotion and worship on the one hand, and the aspect of the Christian's relation to his fellow men on the other. The Christian community was constituted by the fact of common faith and common worship, but the contexts in which worship was paramount were differentiated from the context of love and charity which bound the community together in bonds of human mutuality.

From the present point of view this differentiation was just as important as the first, and intimately connected with it. The Jewish law had held the individual to highly detailed prescriptions of conduct which were "rationalized" for the most part only in the sense that they were declared to be Divine commandments. Now, as a member of the church he was held to a set of principles of conduct—the obligation to act in accord with the Holy Spirit. And though obviously directly connected with his commitment to God through faith, conduct in this world could be made to a degree independent of this, above all, in the sense that detailed prescriptions of behavior were not taken as religiously given but only the general principles of ethical action. Thus action decisions in particular cases had to be left to the conscience of believers and could not be prescribed by a comprehensive religious law. The context of worship was an independent context which generated motivation to act in accord with the spirit, but was not exactly the same thing as this action.

This differentiation occurred, however, within a genuine unity. The key theological problem here was the doctrine of the Creation and whether it implied an ontological dualism. In the great formative period this came to a head in the struggle with Manichaeism, and Augustine's fundamental decision against the latter broadly settled the issue. The sphere of the church as that part of man's life on earth directly dominated by the Holy Spirit was then a point of mediation between the direct expression of Divine will through Christ and the rest of the Creation. But the implication was that this remainder of the Creation could not be governed by an ontologically independent principle of evil and was hence inherently subject to Christianization.

Thus religious individualism, in the sense in which it became institutionalized in the Christian church, represented, relative to Judaism, a new autonomy of the individual on two fronts. In his own relation to God as an object of worship, the individual was released from his ascriptive embeddedness in the Jewish community. Whatever the relation of dependence on God implied in this, it was as an individual in the religious relation that he could be saved. There was also a new autonomy in his relation to the field of human action, in the first instance as a member of the church and in his relations to his fellow members in brotherly love. The church was an association of believers, manifesting their attachment to God in their conduct in this world. The church was thus independent, not an ascribed aspect of a total society. There was hence, through these channels, a basic legitimation of the importance of life in this world, but in a situation where the church could reserve a basic independence from those aspects of secular society not felt to be permeated with the Holy Spirit.

Life in this world clearly includes human society. Indeed the church itself is clearly a social entity. But the early Christians judged the secular society of their time, that of the Roman Empire, to be ethically unacceptable, so the Christian life had to be led essentially within the church. This was connected with the Chiliastic expectation of an imminent Last Judgment. But gradually this expectation faded and the church faced the problem of continuing to live *in* the world and of attempting to come to some sort of long-run terms with the rest of the society outside itself.

I have stressed both the social character of the church and its radical break from the Jewish community because the pattern I have sketched formed a basic set of conditions under which Christian orientations could exert a kind of influence on secular society different from that which was possible to religion in the Jewish pattern. First, proselytizing on a grand scale was possible without carrying along the whole society immediately. While conversion to Judaism meant accepting full membership in the total Jewish community, a converted Christian could remain a Roman, a Corinthian, or whatever; his new social participation was confined to the church itself. There were important points at which the church potentially and actually conflicted with the societies of the time, but most of them could be solved by relative nonparticipation in "public affairs."

If in this respect the church limited its claims on its members, it also maintained a position of independence from which further influence could be exerted. It established a "place to stand" from which to exert leverage, and it developed a firm organization to safeguard that place. But the process was not to be one of absorption of the secular society into the religious community itself; it was rather one of acceptance of the fundamental *differentiation* between church and state, but the attempt to define the latter as subject to Christian principles.

There were certainly tendencies to a radical rejection of secular society in principle, but at least for the Western branch of Christianity by the time of St. Augustine the door was opened to the possibility that a Christian society as a whole could be attained. The most important vehicle for this trend was the building into Christian thought of the Greco-Roman conception of natural law. This implied a differentiation of life between spiritual and temporal spheres and a *relative* legitimation of the temporal, provided it was ordered in accordance with natural law. From this point of view, Roman society could be defined as evil, not because it was a secular society as such, but because as a society it failed to live up to norms present in its own culture.

The other principal focus of the process of Christianizing of society lay in the implications of the attempt to universalize Christian adherence within the society. Christianity was gradually transformed from a sect that remained aloof and in principle expected a Christian life only for the segregated special group of its own members into *the* church which was the trustee of the religious interests of the whole population. In proportion as this happened, persons in positions of responsibility in secular society automatically became Christians, and the question could not but arise of the relation between their church membership and their secular responsibilities. The focus of the emerging conception was that of the Christian monarch. The great symbolic event in this whole connection was the coronation of Charlemagne by the Pope. The symbolism of this event was dual. It was an act by the head of the church of legitimation of secular authority, which could be interpreted as the definitive ending of the conception of aloofness on the part of the church, of the position that it could take no moral responsibility in relation to the secular sphere. It also symbolized the acceptance by the monarch of the obligation to act, in his capacity as chief of government, as a Christian. Church and state then symbolically *shared* their commitment to Christian values.

It is not, in my opinion, correct to interpret this as the subordination of secular authority to the church. It was definitely a putting of the seal of religious legitimacy on the differentiation of the two spheres and their fundamental independence from each other as organized collectivities. But a true differentiation always involves at the same time an allegiance to common values and norms. In terms of the ultimate trusteeship of these values, the church is the higher authority. Perhaps a good analogy is the administration of the oath of office to an incoming American President by the Chief Justice of the Supreme Court. This clearly does not mean that the Chief Justice is the "real" chief of government and the President his organizational subordinate. What it means is rather that the Supreme Court is the ultimate interpreter of the Constitution, and the legitimation of presidential office by the Chief Justice is a symbolization of the subordination of the Presidency to Constitutional law, which is equally binding on the Court.

In very broad outline this seems to be the way the stage was set for the development of a process of the "Christianizing" of secular society, not, be it repeated, through absorption of secular spheres into the "religious life" in the sense of the life of the church or its religious orders, but by exerting influence on a life which remained by the church's own definition secular, hence, in the Catholic phase, religiously inferior to the highest, but still potentially at least quite definitely Christian.[3]

The first main phase was the medieval synthesis, which produced a great society and culture. But from the present point of view it must also be considered a stage in a process of development. The dynamic

3. In this general interpretation I follow in particular Ernst Troeltsch, *Social Teachings of the Christian Churches* (New York: Harper Torchbooks, 1960).

forces which led beyond the medieval pattern were in the present view inherent on both the religious and the secular sides. Brief consideration of some of the essential constituents which both went into the medieval synthesis and led beyond it will help to lay a foundation for understanding a little of the mechanisms by which a religious influence could be exerted on secular society.

First let us take the church itself. Differentiation of the church from secular society represented in one sense a renunciation of influence on secular life. There was no longer a detailed, divinely sanctioned law to prescribe all secular conduct. This may, however, be looked on as a kind of renunciation similar to that involved in a process of investment, a step toward a higher order of "productive" results in the future by a more roundabout process. Here resources are not simply mobilized to maximize short-run production. Some current resources are diverted into temporarily "unproductive" channels in uses which prepare a later production effort. To do this however, this set of resources must be protected against pressures for their immediate consumption. In the religious case the church was such a base of operations which was kept secure from absorption in the secular life of the time. Such pressures to absorption were indeed very prominent in the period after Constantine, in the West perhaps above all through the tendency of bishops to become heavily involved in secular political and economic interests.

The most important single fortress for the maintenance of the purity of religious orientation through this period was certainly the religious orders where segregated communities were devoted to a special religious life. Even this, however, had its this-worldly aspect, notably through the place taken by useful work in the Benedictine rule, which in many cases expanded into a generally high level of economic rationality. Furthermore the orders served as a highly important direct ground for the development of social organization itself; they were highly organized communities, administered in much more universalistic and less traditionalized ways than was most of the secular society of the time.

Secondly, however, that part of the church which served the laity through the secular clergy in the early medieval period underwent a major reform, significantly under monastic impetus. This of course is particularly associated with the Cluniac order and the name of Pope Gregory VII, himself a Cluniac monk. In one major aspect at least, it consisted of an extension of the monastic conception of purity of religious orientation to the roles of the secular clergy. There were two particularly important and closely related points here. One was the final defeat of the Donatist heresy and the firm establishment of the principle that priesthood was an office with powers and authority clearly separable from the person of the individual incumbent, or any particularistic network of relationships in which he might be involved. The second was the doctrine of clerical celibacy, which not only had not previously been enforced but also had not even been firmly established as a policy, and never was in the Eastern church.

These crucial reforms had two orders of significance. First, they served to consolidate and extend the independence of the church from secular influences. The particularly important extension was of course to the region of most direct and continuing contact with the laity through the secular clergy. Second, however, the structure of the medieval church came to serve, well beyond the Orders, as a model of social organization which could be extended into secular society. As Lea made so clear, in a society very largely dominated by the hereditary principle, clerical celibacy had a special significance.[4] Put in sociological terms, we may say that it made possible a social island that institutionalized a universalistic basis of role-allocation manifested in careers open to talent. The clergy was of course very far from being immune to class influence and at various times bishoprics and cardinalates were virtually monoplized by narrow circles of noble lineages. But this is not to say that the institution of celibacy and with it the barrier to inheritance of clerical office was unimportant.

There also was an intimate connection between the conception of clerical office which became crystallized in the Middle Ages and the building of much of Roman law into the structure of the church itself through canon law. In place of the relatively unrationalized and historically particularized Jewish law, the Christian church developed for its own internal use a highly rationalized and codified body of norms which underlay the legal structure of the whole subsequent development of Western society. Certainly the reception of secular Roman law in the Middle Ages could not have happened without this.

Closely related to the church's use of Roman law was the place it made for the secular intellectual culture of antiquity. There is a sense in which this was already implicit in the place taken by Greek philosophy in theology itself. It was greatly reinforced by adoption of the conception of natural law as governing the secular sphere. Its medieval phase cul-

4. H. C. Lea, *The History of Sacerdotal Celibacy* (New York: Russell and Russell, 1957).

minated in the very central place accorded to the work of Aristotle by Thomas Aquinas.

There was, however, also a structural aspect of the place of intellectual culture. Though in the earlier period it was only in the monasteries that the culture of antiquity was preserved and cultivated at all, as the medieval universities began to develop, the role of scholar and teacher assumed an important degree of independence both from the orders and from the hierarchy of the church. Though most of the schoolmen were monks, as scholars and teachers their activity was not directly controlled by their orders or chapters, nor by the bishops of the territories where they worked and taught. In terms of the crucial role of intellectual culture in later social development, notably through the rise of science, the structural basis of its independence is of an importance hardly to be exaggerated. This is perhaps the most critical single point of difference between the development of Western Christianity and of Islam, since in the latter case the influence of orthodoxy was able to suppress the independence of the scholarly class who had made such brilliant beginnings in the reception and extension of classical culture. The church's censure of Galileo should not be allowed to obscure the fact that, compared to other religious systems, Catholic Christianity made a place for an independent intellectual culture which is unique among all the great religions in their medieval phase.

There is one further important focus of the synthesis between medieval Christianity and the classical heritage. The universalism of Christianity held up a conception of a moral order for Christendom as a whole, with Christendom ideally expected eventually to comprise all mankind. This matched and was without doubt greatly influenced by the Roman conception of a universal sociopolitical order governed by a single universal system of law, a natural law coming to be institutionalized as the law of a politically organized society.

In basic Christian thinking, the Roman Empire as the secular order of the world had never ceased to exist. But since Charlemagne it could be defined as the *Holy* Roman Empire, as the normative framework of a universal Christian society. The empirical course of political development in Europe was to be such as to make this dream of unity under law in some respects progressively less realistic, at least for a very considerable period. Nevertheless the importance of the conception of a universal order should not be underestimated.

I have argued above that Christianity originally involved a cultural "marriage" between Judaic and Greco-Roman components. Though the early church repudiated the secular society of the contemporary Roman Empire, the above considerations make it quite clear that the normative aspect of classical culture was not repudiated; essentially a fundamental trusteeship of this heritage was built into the basic structure of the Christian church itself. It became the primary source from which this heritage was rediffused into the secular world and became the basis for further developments which somehow had failed to materialize in the ancient world. It is essential to my general argument here that this was a genuine integration.

Perhaps particularly from a Protestant point of view it is common to think of medieval Catholicism as mainly a pattern of compromise between a set of religious ideals and the exigencies of life in the world. It is quite true that, as Troeltsch so clearly brings out, the conception was that of a series of levels of closeness to and distance from full contact with the Divine, with the monastic life at the top. But this is not to say that positive religious sanction was withheld from everything except devotional self-sacrifice, that for example natural law was thought of merely as a concession to human weakness. Very much on the contrary, a secular world governed by natural law was thought of as ordained by God, as the part of His Creation which was to serve as the field for man's activity. Secular society was, to be sure, a field of temptation, but also of opportunity to lead a Christian life. And an essential part of the Christian life came to be the control, if not the shaping, of secular society in the interest of Christian ideals.

Professor Sorokin is quite right, I feel, in regarding this as a synthesis rather than merely a compromise. But, as noted, it is my view that this was not the end of the road, the point from which the process of religious decline started, but rather an essential station on a road which has led much farther. A few more general things about the nature of the process need to be said. The point of view I am taking here is meant to be very far indeed from any idealistic "emanationist" conception of the process of social development.

A crucial initial point is the one stressed throughout, that the church was from the beginning *itself* a special type of social organization. We do not have to think of the cultural aspect of Christianity as socially "disembodied" and suddenly, by a kind of sociological miracle, taking over the control of a society. On the contrary, it developed, survived, and exerted its influence through the same kinds of processes of interaction between cultural and social systems which operate in other connections. First, we have noted, it maintained and consolidated its independence, and developed its own internal structure. Second, it became diffused so that, within the society in which it operated, it could assume that the whole population was, in the religious sphere, subject to its jurisdiction; it successfully eliminated all organized internal religious competition—by "propaganda" and various types of more or less political process.

It had in its own social structure institutionalized a set of values. Through the universality of membership in it, it had the opportunity to play a critical part in the socialization process for all members of the society. Though not directly controlling secular social organization, at certain levels of personality its "definition of the situation" and the importance of its special sanctions could, however imperfectly, be universalized. There was much revolt and much "back-sliding," but relatively little indifference to the Christian point of view was possible. The long-run influence of such a set of forces should not be underestimated.

The church was not only an agency of reward for approved behavior and punishment of what it disapproved. It was a crucial focus of psychological support over a very wide range of human concerns—its role in administration of the *rites de passage* is a good index of this position. Finally it was a source of direct models, not only for values at the most general level, but for modes of organizing social relationship patterns at a relatively general normative level, in such fields as law, and careers open to talent.

This phase of the "Christianization" of secular society can, like others, be summed up in terms of a formula which has proved useful in other connections for the analysis of the progressive type of change in a social system.[5] Given a base in an institutionalized value system (in this case in the church) there have been three main aspects of the process. First there has been *extension* of the range of institutionalization of the values, above all through the influence on the laity through the secular clergy. Secondly, there has been a process of further *differentiation*. The church itself has become further differentiated internally in that its sacramental system has been more clearly marked off from its administrative system, and its system of prescriptions for the ethical life of Christians through the canon law more clearly differentiated from both the others. At the same time the differentiation of the church *from* secular society has become more clearly marked. There has been a process of disengagement

5. Perhaps the fullest statement of this scheme is contained in T. Parsons and W. White, "The Link between Character and Society," in S. M. Lipset and L. Loewenthal, eds., *Culture and Social Character* (New York: The Free Press of Glencoe, 1961), reprinted in my *Social Structure and Personality* (New York: Free Press, 1964).

of the church from secular society through much more stringent control of the political and economic interests of bishops and clergy, and through sacerdotal celibacy. The beginnings of a revived Roman civil law have greatly aided in this process by more clearly defining the normative order of secular society.

Finally, third, there was a process of *upgrading* in terms of fulfillment of the requirements of the value system. Internally to the church itself this is the primary meaning of its internal reform, the strengthening of its administration, the elevation of standards in the orders and among the secular clergy. Externally, it was the gradual pressure toward a higher ethical standard among the lay population. The immense lay participation in enterprises like the building of the cathedrals is the most conspicuously manifest aspect of the general wave of "religious enthusiasm" in the Middle Ages.

The Reformation Phase

Perhaps the most important principle of the relation between religion and society which was institutionalized in the Middle Ages was that of the *autonomy* of secular society, of the "state" in the medieval sense, relative to the church, but within a Christian framework. The Christianity of secular society was guaranteed, not by the subjection of secular life to a religious law, but by the *common* commitment of ecclesiastical and temporal personnel to Christian faith. The Reformation may be seen, from one point of view, as a process of the extension of this principle of autonomy[6] to the internal structure of religious organization itself, with profound consequences both for the structure of the churches and for their relation to secular society. It may be regarded as a further major step in the same line as the original Christian break with Judaism.

The essential point may be stated as the religious "enfranchisement" of the individual, often put as his coming to stand in a direct relation to God. The Catholic Church had emancipated the individual, as part of its own corporate entity, from the Jewish law and its special social community, and had given him a notable autonomy within the secular sphere. But within its own definition of the religious sphere it had kept him under a strict tutelage by a set of mechanisms of which the sacraments were the core. By Catholic doctrine the only access to Divine grace

6. By autonomy I mean here *independenec* of direct authoritarian control combined with *responsibility* defined in moral-religious terms. It is close to "theonomy" as that concept is used by Tillich.

was through the sacraments administered by a duly ordained priest. Luther broke through this tutelage to make the individual a *religiously* autonomous entity, responsible for his own religious concerns, not only in the sense of accepting the ministrations and discipline of the church but also through making his own fundamental religious commitments.

This brought faith into an even more central position than before. It was no longer the commitment to accept the particularized obligations and sacraments administered by the Church, but to act on the more general level in accordance with God's will. Like all reciprocal relation ships, this one could be "tipped" one way or the other. In the Lutheran case it was tipped far in what in certain senses may be called the "authoritarian" direction; grace was interpreted to come only from the completely "undetermined" Divine action and in no sense to be dependent on the performances of the faithful, but only on their "receptivity." In this sense Lutheranism might be felt to deprive the individual of autonomy rather than enhancing it. But this would be an incorrect interpretation. The essential point is that the individual's dependence on the *human* mediation of the church and its priesthood through the sacraments was eliminated and *as a human being* he had, under God, to rely on his own independent rseponsibility; he could not "buy" grace or absolution from a human agency empowered to dispense it. In this situation the very uncertainties of the individual's relation to God, an uncertainty driven to its extreme by the Calvinistic doctrine of predestination, could, through its definition of the situation for religious interests, produce a powerful impetus to the acceptance of individual responsibility. The more deeply felt his religious need, the sharper his sense of unworthiness, the more he had to realize that no human agency could relieve him of his responsibility; "mother" church was no longer available to protect and comfort him.

An immediate consequence was the elimination of the fundamental distinction in moral-religious quality between the religious life in the Catholic sense and life in secular "callings." It was the individual's direct relation to God which counted from the human side, his faith. This faith was not a function of any particular set of ritual or semi-magical practices, or indeed even of "discipline" except in the most general sense of living according to Christian principles. The core of the special meaning of the religious life had been the sacramental conception of the earning of "merit" and this was fundamentally dependent on the Catholic conception of the power of the sacraments.

From one point of view, that of the special powers of the *church* as a social organization, this could be regarded as a crucial loss of function, and the Lutheran conception of the fundamental religious equivalence of all callings as secularization. My interpretation, however, is in accord with Max Weber's; the more important change was not the removal of religious legitimation from the special monastic life, but rather, the endowment of secular life with a new order of religious legitimation as a field of "Christian opportunity." If the ordinary man, assumed of course to be a church member, stood in direct relation to God, and could be justified by his faith, the *whole person* could be justified, including the life he led in everyday affairs. The counterpart of eliminating the sacramental mediation of the secular priesthood was eliminating also the special virtues of the religious. It was a case of further *differentiation* within the Christian framework.

Protestantism in its Lutheran phase underwent a process, analogous to that of the early church, of relative withdrawal from direct involvement in the affairs of secular society. With the overwhelming Lutheran emphasis on faith and the importance of the individual's *subjective* sense of justification, there was, as Weber pointed out, a strong tendency to interpret the concept of the calling in a passive, traditionalist, almost Pauline sense. It was the individual's relation to his God that mattered; only in a sense of nondiscrimination was his secular calling sanctified, in that it was just as good, religiously speaking, as that of the monk.

We have, however, maintained that the conception of the generalization of a Christian pattern of life was an inherent possibility in the Christian orientation from the beginning and it came early to the fore in the Reformation period in the Calvinistic, or more broadly the ascetic, branch of the movement. Here we may say that the religious status of secular callings was extended from that of a principle of basic nondiscrimination to one of their endowment with positive instrumental significance. The key conception was that of the divine ordination of the establishment of the Kingdom of God on Earth. This went beyond the negative legitimation of secular callings to the assignment of a positive *function* to them in the divine plan.

In terms of its possibility of exerting leverage over secular society this was by far the most powerful version of the conception of the possibility of a "Christian society" which had yet appeared. First the stepwise hierarchy of levels of religious merit, so central to the Thomistic view, was eliminated by Luther. Then the individual became the focus not only of secular but also of religious responsibility emancipated from tutelary control by a sacramental church. Finally, precisely in his secular calling the individual was given a positive assignment to work in the building of the Kingdom.

The consequence of this combination was that, with one important exception, every major factor in the situation converged upon the dynamic exploitation of opportunity to change social life in the direction of conformity with religiously grounded ideals.

The basic assumption is that for Protestants the Christian commitment was no less rigorous than it had been for Catholics; if anything it was more so. In both Lutheran and Calvinistic versions the conception was one of the most rigorous submission of the individual's life to divine will. But in defining the situation for implementing this role of "creature," the Protestant position differed from the Catholic broadly as the definition of the preschool child's role relative to his parents differs from that of the school-age child's relation to his teacher. Within the family, important as the element of discipline and expectations of learning to perform are, the primary focus is on responsibility of the parents for the welfare and security of their children; the permeation of Catholic thought with familial symbolism along these lines is striking indeed.

In the school, on the other hand, the emphasis shifts. The teacher is primarily an agent of instruction, responsible for welfare, yes, but this is not the primary function; it is rather to help to equip the child for a responsible role in society when his education has been completed. To a much higher degree the question of how far he takes advantage of his opportunities becomes his own responsibility. Thus the function of the Protestant ministry became mainly a teaching function, continually holding up the Christian doctrine as a model of life to their congregations. But they no longer held a parental type of tutelary power to confer or deny the fundamentals of personal religious security.

If the analogy may be continued, the Lutheran position encouraged a more passive orientation in this situation, a leaving of the more ultimate responsibility to God, an attitude primarily of receptivity to Grace. (This is the exception referred to above—one of relatively short-run significance.) Such an attitude would tend to be generalized to worldly superiors and authorities, including both ministers and secular teachers. Ascetic Protestantism, on the other hand, though at least equally insistent on the divine origins of norms and values for life, tended to cut off this reliance on authority and place a sharper emphasis on the individual's responsibility for positive action, not just by his faith to be receptive to God's grace, but to get out and *work* in the building of the Kingdom.

This precisely excluded any special valuation of devotional exercises and put the primary moral emphasis on secular activities.

Next, this constituted a liberation in one fundamental respect from the social conservatism of the Catholic position, in that it was no longer necessary to attempt to maintain the superiority of the religious life over the secular. Hence one essential bulwark of a hierarchical ordering of society was removed. The Christian conscience rather than the doctrines and structural position of the visible Church became the focus for standards of social evaluation. This should not, however, be interpreted as the establishment of "democracy" by the Reformation. Perhaps the most important single root of modern democracy is Christian individualism. But the Reformation, in liberating the individual conscience from the tutelage of the church, took only one step toward political democracy. The Lutheran branch indeed was long particularly identified with "legitimism," and Calvinism was in its early days primarily a doctrine of a relatively rigid collective "dictatorship" of the elect in both church and state.

Third, far from weakening the elements in secular society which pointed in a direction of "modernism," the Reformation, especially in its ascetic branch, strengthened and extended them. A particularly important component was clearly law. We have emphasized the essential continuity in this respect between classical antiquity and modern Europe through the medieval church. Broadly, the revival of Roman secular law in Europe was shared between Catholic and Protestant jurisdictions; in no sense did the Reformation reverse the trend in Continental Europe to institutionalize a secular legal system. In England, however, as Pound has emphasized, Puritanism was one of the major influences on the crystallization of the common law in the most decisive period. This is very much in line with the general trends of Protestant orientation, the favoring of a system of order within which responsible individual action can function effectively. The protection of rights is only one aspect of this order; the sanctioning of responsibilities is just as important.

Perhaps most important of all is the fact that the change in the character of the church meant that, insofar as the patterns of social structure which had characterized it by contrast with the feudal elements in the medieval heritage were to be preserved, they had to become much more generalized in secular society. This is true, as noted, of a generalized and codified system of law. It is true of more bureaucratic types of organization, which developed first in the governmental field but later in economic enterprise. It is by no means least true in the field of intellectual culture. The Renaissance was initially an outgrowth of the predominantly Catholic culture of Italy, but the general revival and development of learning of the post-medieval period was certainly shared by Catholic and Protestant Europe. It is a significant fact that John Calvin was trained as a lawyer. And of course, particularly in science, ascetic Protestantism was a major force in cultural development.

It is particularly important to emphasize the breadth of the front over which the leverage of Protestantism extended because of the common misinterpretation of Max Weber's thesis on the special relation between ascetic Protestantism and capitalism. This has often been seen as though the point were that Protestantism provided a special moral justification of profit-making as such, and of that alone. In view of the deep Western ambivalence over the conception of profit, the role of ascetic Protestantism in this context could easily be interpreted as mainly a "rationalization" of the common human propensity to seek "self-interest," which is the very antithesis of religious motivation.

First, it will be recalled that Weber was quite explicit that he was not talking about profit making in general, but only about its harnessing to systematic methodical work in worldly callings in the interest of economic production through free enterprise. Weber was also well aware of a number of other facets of the same basic orientation to work in a calling, such as its basic hostility to various forms of traditionalism, including all traditional ascription of status independent of the individual, and its relation to science, a relation much further worked out by Merton.

Even Weber did not, however, in my opinion, fully appreciate the importance of the relation to the professions as a developing structural component of modern society, a component which in certain respects stands in sharp contrast to the classical orientation of economic self-interest.

The essentail point is that private enterprise in business was one special case of secular callings within a much wider context. But it was a particularly strategic case in Western development, because of the very great difficulty of emancipating economic production over a truly broad front—on the one hand from the ascriptive ties which go with such institutions as peasant agriculture and guild-type handicraft, on the other hand from the irrationalities which, from an economic point of view, are inherent in political organization, because of its inherent connection with the short-run pressures of social urgency such as defense, and because of its integration with aristocratic elements in the system of stratification which were dominated by a very different type of orientation.

There is very good reason to believe that development of the industrial revolution *for the first time* could have come about only through the primary agency of free enterprise, however dependent this was in turn on prior conditions, among the most important of which was the availability of a legal framework within which a system of contractual relations could have an orderly development. Once there has been a major breakthrough on the economic front, however, the diffusion of the patterns of social organization involved need not continue to be dependent on the same conditions.[7]

Weber's main point about the Protestant ethic and capitalism was the importance of the subordination of self-interest in the usual ideological sense to the conception of a religiously meaningful calling; only with the establishment of this component was sufficient drive mobilized to break through the many barriers which were inherent not only in the European society of the time but more generally to a more differentiated development of economic production. Basically this involves the reversal of the commonsense point of view. The latter has contended, implicitly or explicitly, that the main source of impetus to capitalistic development was the *removal* of ethical restrictions such as, for instance, the prohibition of usury. This is true within certain limits, but by far the more important point is that what is needed is a powerful motivation to innovate, to break through the barriers of traditionalism and of vested interest. It is this impetus which is the center of Weber's concern, and it is his thesis that it cannot be accounted for by any simple removal of restrictions.

However deep the ambivalence about the morality of profit-making may go, there can be little doubt that the main outcome has been a shift in social conditions more in accord with the general pattern of Christian ethics than was medieval society, provided we grant that life in this world has a positive value in itself. Not least of these is the breaking through of the population circle of high death rates and high birth rates with the attendant lengthening of the average span of life. Another crucial point is the vast extension of the sphere of order in human relationships, the lessening of the exposure of the individual to violence, to fraud and to arbitrary pressures of authority.

7. This thesis is further developed in my two essays published as Chapters III and IV of *Structure and Process in Modern Societies* (New York: The Free Press of Glencoe, 1960).

So-called material well-being has certainly never been trusted as an absolute value in the Christian or any other major religious tradition, but any acceptance of life in this world as of value entails acceptance of the value of the means necessary to do approved things effectively. Particularly at the lower end of the social scale, grinding poverty with its accompaniments of illness, premature death, and unnecessary suffering is certainly not to be taken as an inherently desirable state of affairs from a Christian point of view.

Another major theme of developments in this era which is in basic accord with Christian values is a certain strain to egalitarianism, associated with the conception of the dignity of the individual human being and the need to justify discriminations either for or against individuals and classes of them in terms of some general concept of merit or demerit. Certainly by contrast with the role of ascriptive discriminations in the medieval situation, modern society is not in this respect ethically inferior.

Also important has been the general field of learning and science. Perhaps the educational revolution of the nineteenth century was even more important in its long-run implications than was the industrial revolution of the late eighteenth century. It represents the first attempt in history to give large populations as a whole a substantial level of formal education, starting with literacy but going well beyond. Associated with this is the general cultivation of things intellectual and particularly the sciences through research. It is the marriage of the educational and industrial revolutions which provides the primary basis for the quite new level of mass well-being which is one major characteristic of the modern Western world. In both developments cultures with primarily Protestant orientations have acted as the spearheads.

The Reformation phase of Western development may be said to have culminated in the great seventeenth century, which saw the foundations of modern law and political organization so greatly advanced, the culmination of the first major phase of modern science, the main orientations of modern philosophy, and much development on the economic front. However important the Renaissance was, the great civilizational achievements of the seventeenth century as a whole are unthinkable without Protestantism. It coincided with a new level of leadership centering in predominantly Protestant northern Europe, notably England and Holland, and also with much ferment in Germany.

In spite of the very great structural differences, the essential principles governing the process by which society has become more Christianized than before were essentially the same in the Reformation period as in the earlier one. Let us recall that the Christian church from the beginning renounced the strategy of incorporation of secular society within itself, or the direct control of secular society through a religious law. It relied on the common values which bound church and secular society together, each in its own sphere, but making the Christian aspect of secular society an autonomous responsibility of Christians in their secular roles. My basic argument has been that the same fundamental principle was carried even farther in the Reformation phase. The sphere of autonomy was greatly enlarged through release of the Christian individual from the tutelage of the church. This was essentially a process of further differentiation both within the religious sphere and between it and the secular.

In all such cases there is increased objective opportunity for disregarding the values of the religious tradition and succumbing to worldly temptations. But the other side of the coin is the enhancement of motivation to religiously valued achievement by the very fact of being given more unequivocal responsibility. This process was not mainly one of secularization but one of the institutionalization of the religious responsibility of the individual through the relinquishment of tutelary authority by a "parental" church.

For purposes of this discussion the Reformation period is the most decisive one, for here it is most frequently argued, by Professor Sorokin among many others, that there was a decisive turn in the direction of secularization in the sense of abandonment of the values inherent in the Christian tradition in favor of concern with the "things of this world." As already noted, we feel that underlying this argument is a basic ambiguity about the relation of "the world" to religious orientations and that the Christian orientation is not, in the Oriental sense, an orientation of "rejection of the world" but rather in this respect mainly a source for the setting of ethical standards *for* life in this world. In line with this interpretation, the Reformation transition was not primarily one of "giving in" to the temptations of worldly interest, but rather one of extending the range of applicability and indeed in certain respects the rigor of the ethical standards applied to life in the world. It was expecting more rather than less of larger numbers of Christians in their worldly lives. It goes without saying that the content of the expectations also changed. But these changes indicated much more a change in the definition of the situation of life through changes in the structure of society than they did in the main underlying values.

Let us try to apply the same formula used in summing up the medieval phase to that of the Reformation. The most conspicuous aspect of extension was the diffusion of religious responsibility and participation in certain respects beyond the sacramentally organized church to the laity on their own responsibility. The central symbol of this was the translation of the Bible into the vernacular languages of Europe and the pressure on broad lay groups to familiarize themselves with it. The shift in the functions of the church from the sacramental emphasis to that of teaching is directly connected with this. This extension included both the elements of worship and that of responsibility for ethical conduct.

With respect to the church itself as a social system, the Reformation clearly did not involve further internal differentiation but the contrary. But it involved a major step in the differentiation of the religious organization *from* secular society. The Reformation churches, as distinguished from the sects, retained their symbiosis of interpenetration with secular political authority through the principle of Establishment. But the counterpart of what I have called the religious enfranchisement of the individual was his being freed from detailed moral tutelage by the clergy. The dropping of the sacrament of penance, the very core of Luther's revolt against the Catholic church, was central in this respect. Repentance became a matter of the individual's direct relation to God, specifically exempted from any sacramental mediation. This was essentially to say that the individual was, in matters of conscience, in prinicple accountable to no human agency, but only to God; in this sense he was *humanly* autonomous. This development tended to restrict the church to the functions of an agency for the generation of faith, through teaching and through providing a communal setting for the ritual expression of common anxiety and common faith.

There were two principal settings in which this differentiation of lay responsibility from ecclesiastical tutelage worked out. One was the direct relation to God in terms of repentance and faith. This was paramount in the Lutheran branch of the Reformation movement. The other was the primacy of moral action in the world as an instrument of the divine will, the pattern which was primary in ascetic Protestantism. In a sense in which this was impossible within the fold of Catholic unity on the level of church organization, both these movements become differentiated not only from the "parent" Catholic church but also from each other. Hence the ascetic Protestant branch, which institutionalized elements present from the beginning in Western Christian tradition, notably through Augustine, was freed from the kind of ties with other components which hindered its ascendancy as the major trend of one main branch of general Christian tradition. Clearly this is the branch which had the most direct positive influence on the complex of orientations of value which later proved to be of importance to modern industrialism.

The third point of upgrading is most conspicuous in the placing of secular callings on a plane of moral equality with the religious life itself. In crucial respects this shift increased the tension between Christian ideal and world reality. This increase of tension underlay much of the Lutheran trend to withdrawal from positive secular interests and the corresponding sectarian and mystical phenomena of the time. But once the new tension was turned into the channel of exerting leverage for the change of conduct in the secular world, above all through the imperative to work in the building of the Kingdom, it was a powerful force to moral upgrading precisely in the direction of changing social behavior in the direction of Christian ideals, not of adjustment to the given necessities of a non-Christian world.

The Denominational Phase

A common view would agree with the above argument that the Reformation itself was not basically a movement of secularization but that, in that it played a part in unleashing the forces of political nationalism and economic development—to say nothing of recent hedonism—it was the last genuinely Christian phase of Western development and that from the eighteenth century on in particular the trend had truly been one of religious decline in relation to the values of secular society. Certain trends in Weber's thinking with respect to the disenchantment of the world would seem to argue in this direction, as would Troeltsch's view that there have been only three authentic versions of the conception of a Christian society in Western history—the medieval Catholic, the Lutheran, and the Calvinistic.

Against this view I should like to present an argument for a basic continuity leading to a further phase which has come to maturity in the nineteenth and twentieth centuries, most conspicuously in the United States and coincident with the industrial and educational revolutions already referred to. From this point of view, the present system of "denominational pluralism" may be regarded as a further extension of the same basic line of institutionalization of Christian ethics which was produced both by the medieval synthesis and by the Reformation.

It is perhaps best to start with the conception of religious organization itself. Weber and Troeltsch organized their thinking on these matters within the Christian framework around the distinction between church and sect as organizational types. The church was the religious organization of the whole society which could claim and enforce the same order of jurisdiction over a total population as did the state in the secular sphere. The sect, on the other hand, was a voluntary religious association of those committed to a specifically religious life. The church type was inherently committed to the conception of an Establishment, since only through this type of integration with political authority could universal jurisdiction be upheld. The sect, on the other hand, could not establish any stable relation to secular society since its members were committed to give unequivocal primacy to their religious interests and could not admit the legitimacy of the claims of secular society, politically or otherwise, which a stable relation would entail.

This dichotomy fails to take account of an important third possibility, the denomination. As I conceive it, this shares with the church type the *differentiation* between religious and secular spheres of interest. In the same basic sense which we outlined for the medieval church, both may be conceived to be subject to Christian values, but to constitute independent foci of responsibility for their implementation. On the other hand, the denomination shares with the sect type its character as a voluntary association where the individual member is bound only by a responsible personal commitment, not by *any* factor of ascription. In the American case it is, logically I think, associated with the constitutional separation of church and state.

The denomination can thus accept secular society as a legitimate field of action for the Christian individual in which he acts on his own responsibility without organizational control by religious authority. But precisely because he is a Christian he will not simply accept everything he finds there; he will attempt to shape the situation in the direction of better conformity with Christian values. This general pattern it shares with all three of the church types, but not with the sect in Troeltsch's sense.

Two further factors are involved, however, which go beyond anything to be found in the church tradition. One of these is implicit in the voluntary principle—the acceptance of denominational pluralism—and, with it, toleration. However much there may historically have been, and still is, deep ambivalence about this problem, the genuine institutionalization of the constitutional protection of religious freedom cannot be confined to the secular side; it must be accepted as *religiously* legitimate as well. With certain qualifications this can be said to be the case in the United States today and, in somewhat more limited forms, in various other countries. From a religious point of view, this means the discrimination of two layers of religious commitment. One of these is the layer which defines the bases of denominational membership and which differentiates one denomination from another. The other is a common matrix of value-commitment which is broadly shared between denominations, and which forms the basis of the sense in which the society as a whole forms a religiously based moral community. This has, in the American case, been extended to cover a very wide range. Its core certainly lies in the institutionalized Protestant denominations, but with certain strains and only partial institutionalization, it extends to three other groups of the first importance; the Catholic church, the various branches of Judaism, and, not least important, those who prefer to remain aloof from *any* formal denominational affiliation. To deny that this underlying consensus exists would be to claim that American society stood in a state of latent religious war. Of the fact that there are considerable tensions every responsible student of the situation is aware. Institutionalization is incomplete, but the consensus is very much of a reality.

The second difference from the church tradition is a major further step in the emancipation of the individual from tutelary control by *organized* religious collectivities beyond that reached by the Reformation churches. This is the other side of the coin of pluralism, and essentially says that the rite of baptism does not commit the individual to a particular set of dogmas or a particular religious collectivity. The individual is responsible not only for managing his own relation to God through faith *within* the ascribed framework of an established church, which is the Reformation position, but for choosing that framework itself, for deciding as a mature individual *what* to believe, and *with whom* to associate himself in the organizational expression and reinforcement of his commitments. This is essentially the removal of the last vestige of coercive control over the individual in the religious sphere; he is endowed with full responsible autonomy.

That there should be a development in this direction from the position of the Reformation church seems to me to have been inherent in the Protestant position in general, in very much the same sense in which a trend to Protestantism was inherent in the medieval Catholic position. Just as Catholics tend to regard Protestantism in general as the abandonment of true religious commitment either because the extension of the voluntary principle to such lengths is held to be incompatible with a sufficiently serious commitment on the part of the church (if you are not willing to coerce people to your point of view are you yourself *really* committed to it?) or because of its legitimation of secular society so that church membership becomes only one role among many, not the primary axis of life as a whole. But against such views it is hard to see how the implicit individualism of all Christianity could be stopped, short of this doctrine of full responsible autonomy. The doctrine seems to me implicit in the very conception of faith. Asking the individual to have faith is essentially to ask him to *trust* in God. But, whatever the situation in the relation of the human to the divine, in *human* relations trust seems to have to rest on mutuality. Essentially the voluntary principle in denominationalism is extending mutuality of trust so that no *human* agency is permitted to take upon itself the authority to control the conditions under which faith is to be legitimately expected. Clearly this, like the Reformation step, involves a risk that the individual will succumb to worldly temptations. But the essential principle is not different from that involved in releasing him from sacramental control.

This is of course very far from contending that the system of denominational pluralism is equally congenial to all theological positions or that all religious groups within the tradition can fit equally well into it. There are important strains particularly in relation to the Catholic church, to Fundamentalist Protestant sects, to a lesser degree to very conservative Protestant church groups (especially Lutheran), and to the vestiges of really Orthodox Judaism. My essential contention is not that this pattern has been or can be fully universalized within Judaeo-Christianity, but that it is a genuinely Christian development, not by definition a falling away from religion. But it could not have developed without a very substantial modification of earlier positions within Protestantism. In particular it is incompatible with either strict traditional Lutheranism or strict Calvinism.

It was remarked above that the Reformation period did not usher in political democracy, but was in a sense a step toward it. There is a much closer affiliation between denominational pluralism and political democracy. But before discussing that, a comparison between the two may help illuminate the nature of the problem of how such a system of religious organization works. Legitimists for a long period have viewed with alarm the dangers of democracy since, if public policy can be determined by the majority of the irresponsible and the uninformed, how can any stability of political organization be guaranteed? There is a sense in which the classical theory of political liberalism may be said to play into the hands of this legitimist argument, since it has tended to assume that under democracy each individual made up his mind totally independently without reference to the institutionalized wisdom of any tradition.

This is not realistically the case. Careful study of voting behavior has shown that voting preferences are deeply anchored in the established involvement of the individual in the social structure. Generally speaking, most voters follow the patterns of the groups with which they are most strongly affiliated. Only when there are structural changes in the society which alter its structure of solidary groupings and expose many people to cross-pressures are major shifts likely to take place. There are, furthermore, mechanisms by which these shifts tend, in a well-institutionalized democratic system, to be orderly.[8]

I would like to suggest that similar considerations apply to a system of denominational pluralism. The importance of the family is such that it is to be taken for granted that the overwhelming majority will accept the religious affiliations of their parents—of course with varying degrees of commitment. Unless the whole society is drastically disorganized there will not be notable instability in its religious organization. But there will be an important element of flexibility and opportunity for new adjustments within an orderly system which the older church organizations, like the older political legitimacy, did not allow for.

If it is once granted that this system of religious organization is not by definiton a "falling away" from true religion, then its institutionalization of the elements of trust of the individual has, it seems to me, an important implication. On the religious side it is implicit in the pattern of toleration. Members of particular churches on the whole trust each other to be loyal to the particular collectivity. But if some should shift to another denomination it is not to be taken too tragically since the new affiliation will in most cases be included in the deeper moral community.

But such a situation could not prevail were the secular part of the system regarded as radically evil. The individual is not only trusted with reference to his religious participation, but also to lead a "decent" life in his secular concerns. Indeed I should argue, therefore, that for such a religious constitution to function, on the institutional level the society

8. Basing myself on the studies of voting behavior by Berelson, Lazarsfeld, *et al.*, I have analyzed this situation in " 'Voting' and the Equilibrium of the American Political System," in Eugene Burdick and Arthur J. Brodbeck (eds.), *American Voting Behavior* (Glencoe, Ill.: The Free Press, 1959), reprinted as Chapter 8 in this volume.

must present not a less but a more favorable field for the Christian life than did the society of earlier periods of Western history; its moral standards must in fact be higher.

There is a tendency in much religiously oriented discussion to assume that the test of the aliveness of Christian values is the extent to which "heroic" defiance of temptation or renunciation of worldly interests is empirically prevalent. This ignores one side of the equation of Christian conduct, the extent to which the "world" does or does not stand opposed to the values in question. If one argues that there has been a relative institutionalization of these values, and hence in certain respects a diminution of tension between religious ideal and actuality, he risks accusation of a Pharisaic complacency. In face of ths risk, however, I suggest that in a whole variety of respects modern society is more in accord with Christian values than its forebears have been—this is, let it be noted, a *relative* difference; the millennium definitely has not arrived.

I do not see how the extension of intra- and interdenominational trust into a somewhat greater trust in the moral quality of secular conduct would be possible were this not so. The internalization of religious values certainly strengthens character. But this is not to say that even the *average* early Christian was completely proof against worldly temptation, *independent of any support from the mutual commitments of many Christians in and through the church*. Without the assumption that this mutual support in a genuine social collectivity was of the first importance, I do not see how the general process of institutionalization of these values could have been possible at all except on the unacceptable assumption of a process of emanation of the spirit without involvement in the realistic religious interests of real persons.

However heroic a few individuals may be, no process of mass institutionalization occurs without the mediation of social solidarities and the mutual support of many individuals in commitment to a value system. The corollary of relinquishment of the organizational control of certain areas of behavior, leaving them to the responsibility of the autonomus individual, is the institutionalization of the basic conditions of carrying out this responsibility with not the elimination, but a relative minimization of, the hazard that this exposure will lead to total collapse of the relevant standards.

Let us try to sum up this fourth—denominational—phase of the line of development we have traced in terms of our threefold formula. First I would suggest that the principle of religious toleration, inherent in the system of denominational pluralism, implies a great further extension of the institutionalization of Christian values, both inside and outside the sphere of religious organization. At least it seems to me that this question poses a sharp alternative. Either there is a sharp falling away so that, in tolerating each other, the different denominations have become fellow condoners of an essentially evil situation or, as suggested above, they do in fact stand on a relatively high ethical plane so that whatever their dogmatic differences, there is no basis for drawing a drastic moral line of distinction which essentially says that the adherents of the other camp are in a moral sense not good people in a sense in which the members of our own camp are. Then the essential extension of the same principle of mutual trust into the realm of secular conduct is another part of the complex which I would like to treat as one of extension of the institutionalization of Christian values.

So far as differentiation is concerned, there are two conspicuous features of this recent situation. First, of course, the religious associations have become differentiated from each other so that, unlike in the Reformation phase (to say nothing of the Middle Ages), when there was for a politically organized society in principle only one acceptable church, adherence to which was the test of the moral quality treated as a minimum for good standing in the society, this is no longer true. The religious organization becomes a purely voluntary association, and there is an indefinite plurality of morally acceptable denominations.

This does not, however, mean that Christian ethics have become a matter of indifference in the society. It means rather that the differentiation between religious and secular spheres has gone farther than before and with it the extension of the individualistic principle inherent in Christianity to the point of the "privatizing" of formal, external religious commitment, as the Reformation made internal religious faith a matter for the individual alone. This general trend has of course coincided with an enormously proliferated process of differentiation in the structure of the society itself.

In this respect the religious group may be likened (up to a point) to the family. The family has lost many traditional functions and has become increasingly a sphere of private sentiments. There is, however, reason to believe that it is as important as ever to the maintenance of the main patterns of the society, though operating with a minimum of direct outside control. Similarly religion has become largely a private matter in which the individual associates with the group of his own choice, and in this respect has lost many functions of previous religious organizational types.

There seem to be two primary respects in which an upgrading process may be spoken of. Approaching the question from the sociological side, we may note that the development of the society has been such that it could not be operated without an upgrading of general levels of responsibility and competence, the acquisition and exercise of the latter of course implying a high sense of responsibility. This trend is a function of increase in the size of organization and the delicacy of relations of interdependence, of freedom from ascriptive bonds in many different ways, of the sheer power for destruction and evil of many of the instrumentalities of action.

Responsibility has a double aspect. The first is responsibility *of* the individual in that he cannot rely on a dependent relation to others, or to some authority, to absolve him of responsibility—this is the aspect we have been referring to as his *autonomy* in the specific sense in which the term has been used in this discussion. The other aspect is responsibility *for* and *to*, responsibility for results and to other persons and to collectivities. Here the element of mutuality inherent in Christian ethics, subject to a commonly binding set of norms and values, is the central concern.

That the general trend has been to higher orders of autonomous responsibility is, in my opinion, sociologically demonstrable.[9] The central problem then becomes that of whether the kinds of responsibility involved do or do not accord with the prescriptions of Christian ethics. This is essentially the question of whether the general trend stemming from ascetic Protestantism is basically un-Christian or not. Granting that this trend is not un-Christian, the critical *moral* problems of our day derive mainly from the fact that, since we are living in a more complicated world than ever before, which is more complicated because human initiative has been more daring and has ventured into more new realms than ever before, greater demands are being put on the human individual. He has more difficult problems, both technical and moral; he takes greater risks. Hence the possibility of failure and of the failure being his fault is at least as great as, if not greater than, it ever was.

There is a widespread view, particularly prevalent in religious circles, that our time, particularly some say in the United States, is one of unprecedented moral collapse. In these circles it is alleged that modern social development has entailed a progressive decline of moral standards which is general throughout the population. This view is clearly incompatible with the general trend of the analysis we have been making. Its most plausible grain of truth is the one just indicated, that as new and

9. *Cf.* Parsons and White, *op. cit.*, for a brief statement of the case for this view.

more difficult problems emerge, such as those involved in the possibility of far more destructive war than ever before, we do not feel morally adequate to the challenge. But to say that because we face graver problems than our forefathers faced we are doubtful of our capacity to handle them responsibly is quite a different thing from saying that, on the same levels of responsibility as those of our forefathers, we are in fact handling our problems on a much lower moral level.

Our time by and large, however, is not one of religious complacency but, particularly in the most sensitive groups in these matters, one of substantial anxiety and concern. Does not the existence of this concern stand in direct contradiction to the general line of argument I have put forward?

I think not. One element in its explanation is probably that new moral problems of great gravity have emerged in our time and that we are, for very realistic reasons, deeply concerned about them. My inclination, however, is to think that this is not the principal basis of the widespread concern.

The present discussion has, by virtue of its chosen subject, been primarily interested in the problems of the institutionalization of the values originating in Christianity as a religious movement, which have been carried forward at various stages of its development. But values— i.e., moral orientations toward the problems of life in this world—are never the whole of religion, if indeed its most central aspect. My suggestion is that the principal roots of the present religious concern do not lie in *relative* moral decline or inadequacy (relative, that is, to other periods in our society's history) but rather in problems in the other areas of religion, problems of the bases of faith and the definitions of the ultimate problems of meaning.

The very fact that the process of the integration of earlier religious values with the structure of society has gone so far as it has gone raises such problems. The element of universalism in Christian ethics inherently favors the development of a society where the different branches of Christianity cannot maintain their earlier insulation from each other. The problem of the status of Judaism has had to be raised on a new level within the structure of Western society, one which came to a very critical stage in the case of German Nazism. It is a society in which all the parochialisms of earlier religious commitments are necessarily brought into flux.

But beyond this, for the first time in history something approaching a world society is in process of emerging. For the first time in its history

Christianity is now involved in a deep confrontation with the major religious traditions of the Orient, as well as with the modern political religion of Communism.

It seems probable that a certain basic tension in relation to the "things of this world" is inherent in Christianity generally. Hence any relative success in the institutionalization of Christian values cannot be taken as final, but rather as a point of departure for new religious stock-taking. But in addition to this broad internal consideration, the confrontation on such a new basis with the non-Christian world presents a new and special situation. We are deeply committed to our own great traditions. These have tended to emphasize the exclusive possession of the truth. Yet we have also institutionalized the values of tolerance and equality of rights for all. How can we define a meaningful orientation in such a world when, in addition, the more familiar and conventional problems of suffering and evil are, if not more prevalent than ever before, at least as brought to attention through mass communications, inescapable as facts of our world?

It is the inherent tension and dynamism of Christianity and the unprecedented character of the situation we face which, to my mind, account for the intensive searching and questioning, and indeed much of the spiritual negativism, of our time. The explanation in terms of an alleged moral collapse would be far too simple, even if there were more truth in it than the evidence seems to indicate. For this would imply that we did not need new conceptions of meaning; all we would need would be to live up more fully to the standards familiar to us all. In no period of major ferment in cultural history has such a solution been adequate.

CHAPTER 13

Full Citizenship for the Negro American?

Compared to the preceding one, this paper represents an abrupt transition from a broad historical sweep to concern with a relatively specific process of change in contemporary American society. It is, however, a process of the broadest significance, not only internally to American society, but also for the much larger world situation because, to use the American Constitutional phrase, the problem of "race and color" has become so critical for the problem of integration in the world at large. In the background of this contemporary problem, of course, lies that of "creed" with respect to the religious history of Europe and its overseas offshoots. The paper, thus, deals with the three problems of ethnicity, religion, and race as sources of difficulty in the integration of American society and with some of the relations which have obtained among these three foci of difference in the present century within American society. The connection of this empirical problem area with the general theoretical problems of societal integration, as treated in a number of the preceding papers, is patent.

The paper was written as a contribution to the major effort of *Daedalus*, which included two conferences and two large issues of the Journal (Fall, 1965, and Winter, 1966), to mobilize the resources of the American intellectual community in relation to the problems of the status of the Negro in our society. The paper was published in *The Negro American*, Parsons and Clark, eds. (Boston: Houghton Mifflin Co., 1966), as well as in the journal of *Daedalus*. In my capacity as coeditor of the book, I added a brief introductory discussion, concentrating on the problem of understanding the reasons for the emergence of the civil rights issue into primary political salience in American society at that particular time.

"Full Citizenship for the Negro American?" reprinted from *Daedalus* (November, 1965).

THE DESIGNATION "second-class citizen" has often and with justice been used to describe the status of the Negro in American society. As the British sociologist T. H. Marshall has shown with particular clarity,[1] citizenship is a complicated matter that is by no means exhausted by the more literal meanings of the term "civil rights." I should like to begin this discussion with an analysis of the meaning of the concept of citizenship, leaning heavily on Marshall's work, though attempting to go beyond it in some respects. I shall then attempt to analyze some of the conditions which have been necessary to account for the progress which the Negro American has made so far toward gaining full citizenship— and which, at the same time, the society has made toward including the Negro in that status—and the further conditions which must be fulfilled if the process is to approach completion. In carrying out this analysis, I shall pay particular attention to comparing the status of the Negro with that of other groups which have in various analogous ways been discriminated against in American society. I hope that such an analysis will reveal a combination of similarities and differences which illuminates the salient features of the Negro case. Since the other groups have progressed considerably further toward full inclusion than has the Negro so far, their experience may provide certain projective guide lines for considering the Negro case. The relation of the internal change of status of the Negro American to the color problem in world affairs will also be discussed.

The concept of citizenship, as used here, refers to full membership in what I shall call the *societal community*.[2] This term refers to that aspect of the total society as a system, which forms a *Gemeinschaft*, which is the focus of solidarity or mutual loyalty of its members, and which constitutes the consensual base underlying its political integration. This membership is central to what it means to be defined, in the case of our own nation, as "an American"—hence it gives a special justification for the word order in the title of the present issue of *Dædalus*, that it is the Negro American, not vice versa. The Negro slave could have been, and certainly was called, an "American Negro"—he was resident in the United States and owned by American citizens, but was not part of the societal community in the present sense.

1. T. M. Marshall, *Class, Citizenship, and Social Development* (Garden City: Doubleday, 1964), Chap. IV.
2. Cf. Talcott Parsons, *Societies: Comparative and Evolutionary Perspectives* (Englewood Cliffs, N.J.: Prentice-Hall, 1966).

Perhaps John Rawls has formulated, in general philosophical terms, more clearly than anyone else the way in which full citizenship implies a fundamental equality of rights—not equality in *all* senses, but in the sense in which we refer to the rights of membership status in the societal community.[3]

From the unit viewpoint, societal community is a category of the commitment of members to the collectivity in which they are associated, and of the members to each other. It is the focus of loyalties which need not be absolute, indeed cannot be, but which require high priority among loyalties of the members.[4] To occupy this position the associational structure must be in accord with the common values of the society: members are committed to it because it both implements their values and organizes their interests in relation to other interests. In the latter context it is the basis for defining rules for the play of interests which make integration possible, preventing the inevitable elements of conflict from leading into vicious circles radically disruptive of the community. It is also the reference base of the standards for allocating available mobile resources in complex communities.

In all "advanced" societies, societal community is linked with political organization, but is also differentiated from it. Although all advanced societies are "politically organized," this aspect of their organization, what we ordinarily refer to, at the societal level, as government, is not identical with community in the present sense. It is precisely when the two are in some kind of conflict that revolutionary situations can arise.

The Nation as Societal Community

In modern Western history, the focus of the differentiation of the societal community lay in the emergence of the nation, hence of "nationalism." Obviously, a similar process is now going on in many parts of the world in the formation of the "new nations." There are three aspects of the emergence of the nation which I should like to note and then briefly spell out for the American case.

The first is the differentiation of criteria for belonging to the nation in contrast to membership in the more "primordial" kinship-ethnic and, often, religious groupings. Here the change is toward the establishment

3. John Rawls, "Constitutional Liberty and the Concept of Justice," in C. J. Friedrich (ed.), *Justice (Nomos VI)*, (New York: Atherton Press, 1963).
4. Edward A. Shils, *The Torment of Secrecy* (Glencoe, Ill.: Free Press, 1956).

of *associational* criteria. In the case of a total society, as politically organized, it is impossible for membership to be entirely voluntary for all, but it can move very far in this direction, that is, away from a purely ascriptive basis, and has done so. More importantly the status of citizenship comes to be institutionalized in terms independent of the ascriptive criteria just cited, for it concerns above all the "natural rights" so fundamental to American tradition.

Second, the nation is differentiated from its government. This is *not* to say they are dissociated. Rather, this differentiation involves the development of political independence by the societal community so that it is no longer ascribed to any particular governmental leadership, such as hereditary monarchy with full executive authority. The obverse of this development is that government becomes structurally independent in that it is free to mobilize within the society those resources which are relatively fluid, for example, in establishing an appointive civil service free of more partcularistic ties and in soliciting support from a range of different groups in the constituency.

Finally, the differentiation of the societal community as nation involves a shift of the integration of the three elements, community, ascriptive bases, and government, in the direction of a synthesis of citizenship and territoriality. This is necessary because the individual is anchored in residential ties, even though there is high residential mobility, because work as well as residence is located physically, and because the availability of resources is territorially anchored.[5]

For the United States, as for many other countries, the consolidation of nationhood was directly connected with a struggle for political independence. It may be said that there was sufficient ethnic and religious uniformity to make solidarity possible, but enough diversity to favor a major shift toward the associational basis of that solidarity, as compared with the European analogues. The core was surely white, Anglo-Saxon, and Protestant (WASP). The Negroes, most of whom were slaves, were not included, and the Catholic, Dutch, and Jewish minorities were so small as to be structurally almost negligible. However, one of the three components, the religious, had built-in diversity in that there were many Protestant denominations.[6] And, in spite of the prominent involvement of the Anglican church in the colonies, the non-Anglican majority was

5. Talcott Parsons, "The Principal Structures of Community," *Structure and Process in Modern Societies* (Glencoe, Ill.: Free Press, 1960).
6. Richard Niebuhr, *The Social Sources of Denominationalism* (Cleveland: World, 1957).

understandably reluctant to countenance an Anglican Establishment, particularly because of the latter's relation to England.

On the side of values, two particularly important components were the influence of the Enlightenment, with its emphasis on assuring the rights of individuals independently of their ascriptive involvements, and the fact that the most important religious groups involved were in the same broad tradition, which we tend to call "liberal Protestantism" today. The Bill of Rights is the central institutional embodiment of these components.[7]

The new American Union was, however, a *federal* union of a special sort. Though the Constitution prescribed a Republican form of government as well as other universalistic patterns, especially through the Bill of Rights, the states could and did, serve as a strong protector of the particularistic groups and institutions at many levels, from the South's "peculiar institution" before the Emancipation Proclamation and the Thirteenth Amendment to local power interests, police power, and the conservative interpretation of the Fourteenth Amendment.[8] Today we are acutely aware of how hard it has been to overcome the conception that the state was somehow "sovereign" and that we were only a confederation of states, not a federal state. In view of the difficulties of maintaining the Union, not only in the Civil War crisis, but also earlier,[9] it seems probable that this "concession" to state particularism was necessary in order to establish a union at all—*vide* the length of time it took Rhode Island to decide to join.

The essential consequence for our problem is that this version of federalism drastically limited the extent to which universalistic values and normative principles, formulated most conspicuously in the Bill of Rights, could be applied to the regulation of relations internal to a large variety of groups and collectivities. The extension of this jurisdiction has been a long process and is still far from complete. The most visible aspect of the process has been legal, based above all on the post-Civil War Amendments, the Fourteenth and Fifteenth. The legal process has been both cause and effect of a broader process of structural change in the society, several aspects of which will figure in the following discussion. A major force in this process is further societal *differentiation* in many fields, such as property rights and the development of new institutions regulating marriage and education.

7. Cf. S. M. Lipset, *The First New Nation* (New York: Basic Books, 1963).
8. Cf. Samuel Beer, "Liberalism and the National Idea," Public Affairs Conference Center, University of Chicago, 1965.
9. Seymour Martin Lipset, *The First New Nation, op. cit.*

Some of the same circumstances established quite firmly the mutual independence of government and the national community. This was a phase which underlay another main source of American strains, namely, the suspicion between the private sector and government. This has had a long-run influence on the Negro problem by minimizing certain kinds of private business support for public action in favor of the Negro. On the whole, the differentiation proceeded faster and further here than in Europe, a fact which has, on balance, contributed positively to the inclusion of the Negro as well as other groups which were originally excluded. The reason for this judgment is that the relatively open and pluralistic situation, although it provided opportunity for much obstruction, has served as a structural base for challenging and overcoming the obstruction. Above all, such structural changes as industrialization and urbanization, which ultimately undermined the obstacles, were favored.

Finally, the new nation began with a unified, territorially based control of resources and of rights, a factor which eventually contributed to the integration of its societal community. The Constitution guaranteed economic unity by prohibiting tariffs between the states and by allowing no limitations on the movement of citizens. Inherent in this guarantee was a general bias against the consolidation of local and regional particularism, even though other powerful forces worked toward it. This was of special importance because it existed in the early phase of a unique opportunity—that of occupying a territorial area of continental scope. The integration of the pattern of citizenship with that of territory in all areas under American control created a relatively uniform standard of citizenship. This meant not the neglect of sectional interests, but the positive establishment of a pattern covering all regions. The special case of the South will, of course, occupy much of our attention.

As Lipset has pointed out,[10] the United States originated as a "new nation" in a way broadly similar to those which have been emerging in our own time. It achieved independence from colonial status. It approached the pattern of association of people who came to implement their own values and goals more closely than could older nations, but it had sufficient initial cultural homogeneity to achieve its initial integration, not without serious internal struggles, but still with a certain effectiveness. This "liberal" tradition, especially as expressed in the Bill of Rights, provided a basis for other groups, culturally and ethnically more distant from those predominant in the founding generations, to be included in the national community.

10. *Ibid.*, Part I.

The consolidation of that community and the advancement of the process of differentiation of the society to the point that a strong national government could take precedence over local, state, and regional particularisms took a long time. Though the most serious crisis was settled by the outcome of the Civil War, as Samuel Beer has made clear, a new phase began in the period of the New Deal.[11] In part, this was a result of our wider sense of national responsibility in world affairs following our involvement in World War I. As we shall see, it was not unimportant that the process of inclusion of the "new immigration" reached its culmination at the same time that the Democratic party attained its new position of power in the New Deal era. It was not fortuitous that the same transitional period saw the predominant Negro political allegiance shift from the Republicans to the Democrats.

As not only the first, but probably by now the most "mature," of the "new" nations, the United States has, as Lipset emphasizes, a special opportunity to serve as a symbol of the movement of national "liberation" and to assume a role of leadership in this context. This role, in turn, has been intimately connected with the internal structure of the society with respect to liberty and equality. Of these internal standards, those of ethnicity and religion are particularly important. Unfortunately, the American role in international leadership has been severely compromised in the last generation by our competition and conflict with the Communist movement. Our hypersensitivity to the threat of internal subversion places us in danger of being identified internationally with the older European "colonial" powers and their imperialism. The relationship of these issues to race and color is patent. The suggestion will be made in this paper that the movement for inclusion of the Negro into full citizenship in the national community may prove to be a crucial aspect of this complex set of processes, and may present a great opportunity to claim a place of fuller leadership in this setting. This movement, as Rupert Emerson and Martin Kilson show in their paper, has been stimulated largely by the rise of new nonwhite nations, particularly those of Africa. It is, however, my thesis that its *main* impetus has been internal to the development of American society itself. If the movement, and the forces which favor it in the white community, can succeed substantially, this may prove to have momentous international repercussions. I shall return to this theme at the end of the paper.

I shall conclude this introduction with a brief theoretical discussion. The process by which previously excluded groups attain full citizen-

11. Samuel Beer, *op. cit.*

ship or membership in the societal community will, in this paper, be called *inclusion*. This is, as will be shown presently, a highly complex process. It will be argued that, at least under the conditions which have prevailed in American society, this has been intimately linked with the process of differentiation which has produced an increasingly *pluralistic* social structure. Not only are there many subcollectivities within the societal community, but the typical individual participates through membership in an increasingly wide variety. If interest is centered in *ethnic* groups, membership is necessarily by hereditary ascription.[12] In religious affiliation, a larger voluntary element is common, but most religious affiliations, at least to the larger groups, are *de facto* hereditary and often closely associated with ethnicity.

In a pluralistic social structure, membership in an ethnic or religious group does not determine *all* of the individual's social participations. His occupation, education, employing organization, and political affiliation may in varying degrees be independent of his ethnicity or religion. On the whole, the trend of American development has been toward increasing pluralism in this sense and, hence, increasing looseness in the connections among the components of total social status.

This trend has one particularly important implication for our purposes, namely, that it is essential to make a clear distinction between *inclusion* and *assimilation*. There may be pluralism of religious and ethnic groups among full citizens which cuts across many other involvements of the same people. The prototype was the original religious pluralism within the white Protestant group, which was built into the constitutional structure by the separation of Church and State and by religious toleration and freedom. It has subsequently been extended to include Jews and Catholics through what is usually called an "ecumenical" process.

However, because the United States was originally primarily a white Protestant society, it was often thought that inclusion was synonymous with becoming Protestant or as similar as possible to the Anglo-Saxon tradition. The developments which will be outlined below make it quite clear that this is not the case for the other white groups, and I shall argue that it need not and probably will not be so for the Negro. Full inclusion and multiple role participation are compatible with the maintenance of distinctive ethnic and/or religious identity, though not in the

12. Qualifications must be made, for example, for interethnic marriages where, with or without formal "adoption," the couple functions primarily in one group and, hence, the "inmarrying" spouse may be said to have changed ethnic affiliation, especially if the children identify clearly with the one group.

sense which is the obverse of exclusion, namely self-imposed isolation as in the case of extreme Jewish Orthodoxy.

The Components of Citizenship

T. H. Marshall, in his discussion of the development of citizenship in Great Britain noted above, distinguished three components of the status of citizenship, the *civil* (which in an American reference should perhaps be called legal), the *political*, concerned particularly with the democratic franchise, and the *social*, which refers essentially to the context we defined as "welfare" or, in the terms of our federal organization, health, education, and welfare.

Marshall establishes an important pattern of temporal sequence in the institutionalization of these three components as criteria of membership in the English national community: the civil came first, the political next, and the social last. In England, the establishment of civil rights in this relatively narrow sense was started at the time of Justice Coke in the early seventeenth century, with its consolidation of the independence of the Common Law vis-à-vis government, and extended in various phases through the eighteenth century. The political component began to emerge with the beginning of the development of the parliament's independence from the crown in the seventeenth century, which culminated in 1688. However, for the individual, its institutionalization centered in the franchise extensions of the nineteenth and twentieth centuries—from the Reform Bill of 1832 to the Women's Suffrage Act of 1918. The social component goes back to the factory acts of the nineteenth century, culminating in the enactment of the Beveridge Plan after World War II. With appropriate adaptations this pattern is applicable both to the American experience as a whole and to that of the Negro.

Before entering into this, further explanation of the meaning of these components is necessary. The civil or legal component concerns the *application* of the value system to the relevant context. This is what is particularly salient in the context of the term, *rights*. Rights indicate that members of the societal community in the normative sense "must" enjoy certain basic freedoms and securities in them. The catalogue is of course familiar. It involves security of each individual and of property, freedom of speech, religion, assembly, and association, and both substantive and procedural equality before the law—components formulated in our Constitutional tradition as "equal protection of the laws" and "due process of law." These rights are to take precedence over any particular political status or interest and over any social component such as wealth or poverty, prominence or obscurity.

It is a very long step from the constitutional and legal enactment of these rights to their effective implementation, and this process is still going on in many sectors of American society, even in some which are largely unrelated to the racial problem. But, the constitutional basis of these rights is firmly established and has served as the most important lever for exerting pressure during the earlier stages of the Negro inclusion movement. The special role of the N.A.A.C.P. has been to exploit this aspect of our citizenship structure in behalf of the Negro.

The political component concerns participation in collective goal-attainment, at the societal level in the process of government. The differentiation of government from the societal community, as noted above, implies that the average citizen is neither a governmental functionary in any usual sense nor a totally controlled subject of his government. He does, however, have rights of participation in the governmental process. These crystallize at two main points in modern politics. One is the franchise, basically the right of a formal voice in the selection of leadership—leadership being a more generalized and practicable focus than specific policies, which are decided by referendum. The other is the right to attempt to influence policy, starting with the rights of free speech and assembly, but extending to the sensitive area of "lobbying." As mediating structures, the party system and the institutionalization of mass media became involved here. The body of citizens needs "spokesmen," the potential influencer needs media for making his wishes and their gratifications known, and leaders need structural outlets for their opinions, appeals, and proposals.

The social component does not concern the opportunity to express and implement the rights derived from the societal values so much as the resources and capacities necessary for this implementation. In this connection the societal community defines and presents standards for the allocation of resources to the community as a whole and to its various sub-sectors. The obverse of this is the definition of the terms on which capacities, as matched with opportunities, can be involved in the process of inclusion. This is a special context of the problem of "qualifying" for inclusion.

There are two categories of resources which must be distinguished for our purposes. In our achievement-oriented society, one can scarcely imagine that justice would prevail if large classes of its members, through no fault of their own, were either denied opportunity for achievement (including the reaping of its rewards) or handicapped severely in gaining access to it. Given the formal status of equality in civil or legal rights and in basic political participation, these rights can be "empty" if opportunity is not equalized.

Of course, discrimination may be abolished or minimized across a whole range of opportunities, particularly in employment. But even absence of discrimination is "empty" if remediable handicaps continue to prevail. These handicaps may be randomly distributed among the categorial grouping with which this discussion is primarily concerned. But if they are linked to the status position of the excluded group, they raise the essential problem of the implementation of the rights of citizenship through the equalization of opportunity and the base from which that opportunity can be exploited.

This is where the distinction between the two categories of resources becomes essential. The first category is mainly financial. For an individual to be able to take advantage of available opportunities he must have not only the capacity but also the financial means to do so. This aspect of the social citizenship complex was paramount in the discussions and measures of public policy during the New Deal era. The second concerns the underlying capacity of the units, especially individuals and their families, to function effectively in the environment in which they are placed. At the level of the individual this concerns above all health and education. There has been so much discussion of all these themes that it is not necessary to spell them out further here. Suffice it to say that, first, increasing attention is being placed on education as the most decisive link between the individual's underlying levels of capacity and his relation to the opportunity structure.[13] Second, the concept of "welfare" is a diffuse one extending from the most elementary financial conditions of subsistence to the problem of the structure of the social environment in which disadvantaged groups are placed. This latter extension reflects the fact, firmly established by social science, that at the bottom of the social scale (as judged by the usual criteria of success, prestige, and so on) there is a vicious circle of cumulative *disadvantage*, the more marked the "competitiveness" of the society becomes. This

13. Peter F. Drucker, "Automation is not the Villain," *The New York Times Magazine,* January 10, 1965.

broad tendency is inseparable from the development of individualism, the kinds of citizenship rights we have been talking about, and related matters. It almost goes without saying that the Negro in this country is very deeply caught up in this vicious circle and that Marshall's category of social citizenship is particularly important in the present context.[14]

The three principal components of the citizenship complex seem to constitute not only a rough temporal series, but also a type of hierarchy. With all the differences between British and American societies, they have very similar values. After all, with an important infusion from the Frence Enlightenment and the Revolutionary tradition, the origin of our own values lies mainly in our British heritage.

We can then say that it is the civil or legal rights which come closest to direct implementation of the values which Myrdal formulated in his famous summary of the *"American Creed."*[15] In understanding what has been going on, it is crucial to remember that the societal commitment to this value pattern has exerted steady pressure toward its implementation in behavior and institutions, though this has often been counteracted in specific ways. These commitments, though they be genuine, cannot by themselves bring about a restructuring of the society. Attempts to implement them will inevitably encounter what Mayhew[16] has called "structural discrimination," which can be overcome only if factors other than the assertion of commitments come into play. Without them, the outcome will be either a stalemate, as it was for so long in the United States, or a traditionalist revolution restoring the ascendancy of the contravalue orientation—a prototype being post-Reconstruction Southern society.

The spread and consolidation of the legal component through judicial process rather than legislation is particularly important in view of the present situation in America. This is a step well beyond a *moral* commitment to the relevant rights, because it places the power of government presumptively behind their implementation. In Little Rock, Governor Faubus was defying not only the "decent opinion of mankind," but also a specific order of a duly constituted federal court. This dramatizes the sense in which the 1954 decision on education was a decisive landmark —yet by itself it produced only a rather paltry "tokenism" in spite of

14. Considerable evidence on these points is presented in other papers in the *Daedalus* issue, notably those by Rashi Fein, Daniel P. Moynihan, and Thomas F. Pettigrew.
15. Gunnar Myrdal, *An American Dilemma* (New York: Harper, 1944).
16. Leon Mayhew, "Law and Equal Opportunity: Anti-discrimination Laws in Massachusetts," 1964 Harvard Ph.D. dissertation.

being on the books for a full decade. Clearly something more was required, though this is not to belittle the enormous importance of the legal commitment. This Supreme Court decision was part of a much larger trend in the general development of judicial interpretation of the Constitution, of which more will be said later.

The two other principal factors are, on the one hand, the mobilization of political pressures designed to insure that the excluded group can enjoy both formal rights and actual participation in the political process and, on the other, the mobilization of the governmental apparatus to take the responsibility of implementing these rights. From this point of view, the step from the Supreme Court's espousal of Negro rights to the Civil Rights Acts of 1964 and 1965 was crucial, as has so often been remarked. Both, to be sure, obligate the government. But in the latter case the obligation has been enacted by the elected representatives of the people on the recommendation of a popularly elected President. Hence it can no longer be called the "whim" of nine men who, in the political as distinguished from the legal sense, do not "represent" anyone.[17] Of course there are still many steps which must be taken before effective implementation can be achieved, but the Civil Rights Acts clearly add a major set of social forces to the side of effective implementation.

Even if enforcement were effective, it would still be necessary to bring about the essential set of conditions concerned with qualifications for taking advantage of the opportunities offered. The newly included group must have the capacity to perform its role creditably. The mere statement that justice requires inclusion is not enough because allegations of injustice must involve the capacity factor—namely, that the excluded group could make valuable contributions but is denied the opportunity to do so. Capacity must be asserted on the part of the excluded group, and, insofar as it is not yet present, the larger community must take steps to help develop it.

The hierarchy to which we referred above concerns a relation between necessary and sufficient conditions. With reference to the Negro in the United States, I state broadly that although the institutionalization of both legal rights and political participation constitutes the necessary conditions of much further progress toward full inclusion in the societal community, this is not in itself sufficient. It also requires the implementation of the social component in such a way that the realistic handicaps, so conspicuous in the background, are reduced to the point that,

17. Even Arthur Krock, if my memory serves me, was impressed by this point.

though they cannot be expected to disappear in the short run, they become more or less manageable.

The constitution of a societal community is never static, but is continually changing over time. In my view, the main outline of the American community was established in the broad process of founding the new nation. This basic outline includes the Constitution as well as various aspects of the system as a total social process. At the same time, American society has been subject to major changes. The focus of the present essay is on changes in the composition of its membership through the inclusion of groups previously excluded, more or less unambiguously, from full membership. The Negro, both because of slavery and because of Southern regional isolation, was long kept insulated from the forces favoring inclusion. The groups with which I shall be concerned in the next section, those constituted by the "new immigration" of the turn of the century, were in a different situation.

I shall attempt to analyze the process of inclusion by using a model roughly similar to the "supply and demand" paradigm of economics. There are demands for inclusion—*both* from the excluded group and from certain elements who are already "in"—and there is a supply, which also operates on both sides of the exclusion line. Supply here refers, for the excluded groups, to their qualifications for membership, a matter of their cultural and social structures. Later I shall use the illustration that fully orthodox Judaism, with its rather strong insulation against all but the most instrumental contacts with Gentiles, constituted a formidable barrier to the inclusion of Jews in the American community. The presence of Reform Judaism in the German immigration which preceded that from Eastern Europe provided a focus for the general liberalization of the Jewish community structure. This made it far more amenable to inclusion than the Orthodox structure, as well as far more acceptable to their American hosts. On the side of the receiving community, "supply" consists in structural conditions which create institutionalized "slots" into which the newly received elements can fit, slots structured in accordance with the basic citizenship patterns of the developing community, not opportunities for crude "exploitation" by its members. Supply in this sense refers to a set of structural conditions on both sides of the "equation." This will be analyzed in terms of the factors necessary to extend and consolidate the societal community as such, that is, the commitment to association in a national community, the mobilization of political power and influence, and the establishment of the capacities which have been reviewed in the present section, as well as the underlying value-patterns which are assumed throughout.

The demand aspect concerns the *mobilization* of these factors and their consequences, again on both sides of the inclusion-exclusion boundary. It is a matter first of the existence of attitudes, in both the group "wanting in" and significant sectors of those already in, that the inclusion is normatively desirable and that it *should* be promoted, and then the transformation of these attitudes into various action programs and their implementation. Certainly, much of the actual process often occurs inconspicuously without much of a movement—this, for example, seems to have been the case for much of the inclusion of the new immigration, though by no means all of it. Nevertheless, as expression and implementation of demand in the present sense, the relevant *movements* have a very important place in our analysis.

Such movements tend to gather strength as the strain of conflict between the normative requirements for inclusion and the factual limitations on it are translated into pressures to act. Movements, however, not only express strain in this sense, but "stir things up" further. Thus, their consequences are often relatively unpredictable.[18] One tendency of this type of movement should be noted. The ultimate social grounding of the demand for inclusion lies in commitment to the values which legitimize it. The general reaction to increasing strain is to increase mobilization of such commitments. This in turn is often associated with a demand for direct, immediate, and complete action to implement the values in full. This tendency encounters a problem deriving from the fact that value-commitment, crucial as it is, is only one of the factors necessary for successful inclusion. Strengthening this factor without likewise strengthening the others may lead not to promotion of the "cause," but to a disproportionate activation of the *always-present* factors of resistance, and hence to setbacks. The activists in such movements are above all likely to become impatient with those who would pay attention to the importance of the other factors.[19]

This is the broad paradigm which the reader is requested to keep in mind in reading the sometimes involved discussion which follows.

18. Neil J. Smelser, *Theory of Collective Behavior* (New York: Free Press, 1963).
19. An almost classic instance of this is the recent impatience of the ministers, whose commitments to the values of racial equality have been impressively activated, with President Johnson, essentially because he wanted to mobilize strong political support for his more drastic proposals on voting rights before taking his own strong personal stand about the Selma crisis. The proposals were on the whole in favor of immediate and drastic federal compulsion in Alabama, regardless of the possible political costs.

The American Record on Inclusion Processes

The present crisis over the inclusion of the Negro in the American community has unique features besides its immediacy,[20] but it does not stand alone. A brief review of the larger context of related problems may prove illuminating. Two propositions will introduce the discussion. First as already noted, the core of the American community was basically white, Anglo-Saxon, and Protestant. These three terms, which have become so deeply embedded in the more popular culture, will serve as the axes of our analysis. Second, the United States, in sharp contrast to most of Europe, including our ancestral Britain, has been the proverbial land of open opportunity, welcoming all to join in building a new society in the "New World."

To be sure, this claim was never fully justified. Quite early it was made unmistakably clear that mass Oriental immigration would not be welcomed (note the Chinese exclusion act of 1882). Indeed it may be argued that the Constitutional termination of the Slave Trade was as much an effort to limit the numbers of Negroes in the territorial United States as it was a reflection of hostility to slavery as such. Nevertheless, compared with other societies, especially of that time, the U.S. was notably liberal until the 1924 immigration laws. It placed more emphasis than any other nation of, or before, its time on the view that it was indeed a voluntary association. People were here because either they or their immediate forebears *wanted* to come. And, the proportion of those who came of their own volition was extremely high for quite a long time. The fact that many were escaping from what they felt to be oppressive conditions rather than coming to positive opportunities does not change this pattern. The Negro is the exception, because his forebears were typically *brought* here as slaves.

Though various early crises of the American nation may be related to this problem, the focus of this discussion will be on the aftermath of the great wave of free immigration of the generation ending with the First World War. This was perhaps, except for the Negro, *the* great test of the norms of freedom for all comers to associate in forming a new kind of nation.[21] Most of the immigrants were a part of the so-called new immigration from Eastern and Southern Europe, and as such they violated more sharply than previous large immigrations the older WASP

20. Cf. Pettigrew, *A Profile of the Negro American* (Princeton, N.J.: Van Nostrand, 1964).
21. Oscar Handlin, *The Uprooted* (Boston: Little, Brown, 1951).

formula for the societal community; they were not only non-Anglo-Saxon, but even non-Germanic in ethnic origin, being mostly from the Latin and Slavic countries (especially Italy and Poland). Also they were predominantly Roman Catholic, except for the very large influx of Jews from Eastern Europe. In addition, the Catholics were usually peasants. Earlier, there had been a small element of German Jews, who had become relatively fully included and a larger group of English-speaking Catholics, the Irish, who were marked by a particularly sharp hostility to everything English. These two elements proved in the end to be very important mediators between the older elements and the larger masses of the new.

In this connection the WASP's generally succumbed to the temptation to define their own role on rather aristocratic terms, but on bases so tenuous that they must be considered only a pseudo-aristocracy. This occurred during the period immediately following World War I when economic prosperity was rampant and when "status-seeking" was certainly far more intensive than in the second postwar period. This is the period of the derogatory names like "wops," "polacks," and "kikes," and of the greatest prevalence of "snobbish" anti-Semitism, the deep feeling that having a Jew as a member of your club was totally unacceptable. (It is perhaps significant that such snobbishness was particularly prominent in the younger generation—in fraternities and sororities, and particularly in the Harvard Final Clubs.)

At the risk of typological oversimplification, I should like to deal with the problem of inclusion of the new immigration in terms of two categories, namely, the Jewish and the Catholic groups. It is clear that there is substantial ethnic diversity within both groups. There are not only East European Jews, who are not themselves homogenous, but also the earlier German contingent and small numbers of Spanish-Portuguese origin. The Catholic group is still more diverse. The Irish were the earliest to arrive in large numbers and have been the most influential. They spoke English, a fact which is significant particularly because they discouraged and often as bishops forbade foreign-language parochial schools. Though bringing with them a strong hostility to things English, which was reflected for generations in their tense relations with the WASP's, their long association in Ireland with English Protestantism brought the Irish brand of Catholicism much closer to Protestantism than, for example, that of most parts of Southern Europe.

Furthermore, an important part of the earlier Catholic immigration was of German origin, which was ethnically closer to the WASP's than most of the new immigration, and therefore was more fully integrated earlier. In some regions of the country, particularly the Middle West, they have played a very important part. The other two largest groups were the Italians and the Poles, which are very different from each other. There were, of course, other Slavic groups, such as the Czechs and Croats, and the two Spanish-speaking groups in the Southwest—those taken over after the Mexican war and migrants from Mexico—and, more recently, the Puerto Ricans, who have begun to diffuse beyond New York City. There are also smaller numbers which are neither Jewish nor Catholic, such as the Greeks, the Armenians, and some other groups who adhere to Orthodox churches. Finally, Protestant immigration has continued, the largest being from the British Isles and still more from English-speaking Canada.

The problem of the absorption of Jews and Catholics resulted in a genuine crisis of the American community; it was probably one of the major foci of social tension and disturbance in this century. The Immigration Act of 1924, with its system of quotas based on the composition of the population by national origin in 1890, was one striking symptom of this strain; it is significant that only now is there a serious and widely supported proposal before Congress to eliminate that egregiously discriminatory policy. The very sagacious French observer of American society at that time, André Siegfried, spoke of the "two nations" and expressed sharp doubt whether they could ever be integrated.[22]

The substantial disturbances and anxieties over the presence of such large "foreign" groups in our midst and their relations to the fears of "un-American" influence and of Communism—from the Palmer Raids and the Sacco-Vanzetti case of the 1920's to the McCarthy episode of the early 1950's—must be understood in this context.[23] Until the crescendo of McCarthyism, the ogre of "Communism" as a danger of *internal* subversion rather than of external threat was increasingly of central concern. Nevertheless it can be claimed that the main crisis over full inclusion of these groups has now passed. I shall argue that the Catholic case was the more serious of the two, and that the election of John F. Kennedy as President, accentuated by the ritual significance of the public reaction to his assassination, put a final symbolic seal on the inclusion of all Roman Catholics, not only the Irish. Perhaps it was also

22. André Siegfried, *America Comes of Age* (New York: Harcourt, Brace, 1927).
23. Talcott Parsons, "Social Strains in America" and "Postscript 1962" in Daniel Bell (ed.), *The Radical Right* (Garden City, N.Y.: Doubleday, 1964). Cf. also other essays in this volume.

symbolic that the first time Lyndon Johnson left Washington as President was to attend the funeral of a Jew in a Jewish temple, namely, that of former Senator Lehman of New York.

Neither civil rights in the legal sense nor political rights were seriously at issue in these inclusion problems. The Jewish ghetto and the status of Catholics in Britain before Catholic emancipation in the 1830's lay far in the background. The problem of acceptance lay more at the social level in the above classification than at either of the others. This we would define as the capacity and opportunity for full participation without informal discrimination, such as ineligibility for certain high political offices or relatively systematic "scapegoating." Nevertheless the problem of discrimination has been serious and, though recently it has changed greatly for the better, pockets of such discrimination remain.

It is necessary to consider briefly a difference in emphasis and, hence, symbolic involvement of these two particularly important white groups, the Jews and the Catholics. Realistically, there has never been much question of Jewish motivation and capacity for achievement in terms of social mobility in America. This applies especially to mobility through educational channels. In any case, the Jewish group, despite having had to contend with serious discrimination, has had an extraordinary success story. From lowly origins in the overwhelming proportion of cases, it has, in general, risen very high in the American social scale in about two-thirds of a century.

The Jewish problem of inclusion has been almost purely one of "acceptance" on both sides. In comparative terms, there has been relatively little serious anti-Semitism, but the Jewish community itself has been concerned about how far "assimilation" should be allowed to progress. The symbolic focus of anti-Semitism has not questioned competence— the Jew has been a *dangerous* competitor. Irrational anxiety has centered about his observance of the rules, which is to say his acceptance of the obligations of solidarity in the national community. To the more discerning, his "unscrupulousness" has not involved a lack of moral discipline, but rather a higher loyalty to an alternative community, the Jewish. In this sense the Jew has often been considered "clannish."

The Jewish community has always been of a special type. It has been a "guest" community within a host society and, therefore, notably apolitical. Its contacts with Gentiles have historically been on the economic level, with strong Jewish emphasis on their own cultural traditions—including, of course, high valuation of learning which could be transferred to the modern professions. Strong solidarity and, in Orthodox

Judaism, exclusiveness have been observed in kinship and, indeed, in all relations of intimacy. Jewish communities have been discrete and local, not organized on a national or international basis, and relatively egalitarian in their internal structure.

It seems that the conflict between Jewish and Gentile communities has been most acute where the former represented what could be interpreted as the exploitative aspect of urban society vis-à-vis the rural and parochial, as in the case of Jewish moneylenders or cattle dealers in relation to peasant communities or where, in urban settings, competition at the level of small business was most prominent.

The decline in the proportion of the American population engaged in agriculture and the development of large-scale corporate business have probably contributed to a climate favorable to inclusion. On this level the competition has not been very intense since Jewish business has centered in the small-scale proprietary fields of small business—notably the clothing industry—and certain fields of retail trade. It is very likely that the private practice professions, such as medicine and law, have been particularly congenial to the Jews who have sought higher education and that their late entry into the academic profession on a wide scale is not wholly the result of discriminatory exclusion, though that has certainly played a part.

The focus of the "problem" of anti-Semitism has been the conception of the foreignness of the Jews, of their solidarity in a community within the community, from which Gentiles could feel excluded. The pluralization of the general social structure, especially at occupational levels, and the diminishing global exclusiveness of the Jewish communities have set the stage for the progress of inclusion, since many of these groups have maintained their quite distinctive identities and considerable sense of solidarity, both among themselves and with the societies of their countries of origin.

The present essay cannot, however, attempt a generalized analysis of the ethnic and religious composition of American society, but is primarily focused on the problem of the status of the Negro American. It is my contention that, first, the Jewish group has had special significance because of its distinctive historic role and, second, the Catholic groups have been of great importance in spite of the internal ethnic diversity of the Catholic population. It is worth remarking in passing that the largest single "melting pot" in the society has probably operated within the Catholic population through extensive ethnic intermarriage, but much less so across religious lines. Within the Catholic group, the Irish have played a notable role for the reasons mentioned, with the result, among others, that there is a striking Irish predominance in the hierarchy of the American Catholic Church. For the limited purposes of this essay, I shall concentrate on these two considerations which have become the foci of two different problems and symbolic themes which can be contrasted with each other, as well as with the central issue of the Negro case.

The Jew could then be a good citizen, neighbor, business competitor, and occupational associate of the Protestant with neither relinquishing his religious identity. Religious pluralization—long under way in our society—opens the door to a conception of a basis of societal solidarity which makes all these nondiscriminatory relations possible. On the Jewish side, it should again be noted that a relaxation of the predominantly Orthodox separatism of the Jewish subcommunity has been a necessary condition. In America, the Reform movement, which stemmed from the older German-Jewish element, has been particularly important. Primarily by further development in the differentiation of roles, it has become increasingly possible for Jews to participate in more than the economic aspects of the Gentile community without having to relinquish their Jewishness. From a relatively total subsocietal community, the Jewish group has tended to evolve toward becoming a denomination in the American Protestant sense.[24] Socially, American Jews have been included very fully, but have by no means been assimilated to the same extent.[25]

In the symbolism of discrimination, the Jew has tended to serve as the prototype of "foreignness," in the sense that it is diffusely attached to a community separate from and alien to the American, and therefore presumably untrustworthy in its commitment to the latter. Compared to certain European countries, notably Germany, but also those to the South and East, the United States has had only mild attacks of anti-Semitism. The most serious was in the 1930's (Father Coughlin) and was associated with a general contraction of economic opportunity, a state in which the theme of the dangerous competition of the outsider is more easily made prominent. The more important expression of this complex has perhaps been the diffuse anxiety about foreignness and un-Americanism. The prominence of this theme would seem to fit with an earlier phase of the development of the national community away from a re-

24. Will Herberg, *Protestant, Catholic, Jew* (Garden City, N.Y.: Doubleday, 1960).
25. Thus, the rate of intermarriage with non-Jews is lower than corresponding rates for either Protestants or Catholics.

stricted ethnic-religious basis of solidarity—the famous WASP—to a more cosmopolitan one which includes many elements not qualifying on the more traditional grounds.

The next phase of strain in the openness of the American community constituted a further development of the above. If "foreigners" in general —Jews in particular—are to be accepted, should they not conform to certain requirements? In the Jewish-Protestant case there seemed to be a kind of "fair exchange," involving the non-political stance of diffusely organized communal groups on each side. The idea of a Jewish conspiracy was a rather exotic extreme of anti-Semitic phantasy since the Jews were what they were precisely because of their withdrawal from politically significant organization. One might say much the same for the American brand of Protestantism, especially that part which advocated a radical separation of Church and State. On top of this was the pluralism of American political organization, the beginnings of which go back as far as the history of this nation.[26]

It is perhaps not surprising that *any* relatively or apparently monolithic organization should be a focus of anxiety. Compared with American Protestantism, the Catholic Church was relatively monolithic and in part both was and appeared to be so because of defensive attitudes about its minority position in American society. The problem for its members was not only how far they participated in the usual roles in the American community, but also whether, in doing so, they were under the explicit authoritative control of an organization, their church, which was pursuing its own goals and policies independently of, and possibly in conflict with, the interests of the American community. Put crudely, the Catholic Church could, particularly to non-Catholic Americans, appear to be a kind of state within the state. Sensitivity to this has been heightened by the individualistic cast of American society, with its suspicion of strong central government. Indeed, for special reasons, Catholics, particularly Irish, tended to gain their mobility through governmental channels, starting with the local ones, but extending to the others. Hence they tended to strengthen Protestant suspicion of them. For this reason the symbolic show-down in the election of a Catholic to the Presidency was particularly important.

Two additional facts, besides the nature and position of the Catholic

26. It is notable that by contrast with German Nazism, American anti-Semitism has not strongly stressed the connection of Jewishness with Communism. Similarly, the anti-Communism of this cold war period has dissociated itself from anti-Semitism. Vide the role of Cohn and Schine as lieutenants of McCarthy and the fact that the name Goldwater has not been a political liability in Rightist circles.

Church, were essential here. First, as will be noted presently, the majority of the Catholic ex-peasants formed the urban lower class. In a sense they played symbolic "proletariat" to the WASP pretensions to privileged social status, a peculiar combination of the European traditions of aristocratic and "bourgeois." Second, the protection of local interests in our constitutional system opened the door, given the democratic franchise (reinforced by corruption), to organizing these new urban masses into the famous—or infamous—political machines of which New York's Tammany Hall was long a prototype. In the decisive period the leadership of these organizations, which tended to wrest immediate local political power away from the WASP element, was predominantly Irish and, of course, Catholic. Hence at a certain level—a highly salient one to the average "old" American—the Catholic Church as a state within a state seemed to have fused with an actual Catholic control of the most important system of local politics of the nation, thus compounding the felony.

The general path of resolution here has been "pluralization" in a political sense. Generally we do not have monolithic or, as Rokkan and Lipset say, "columnar"[27] blocs as major units in our political system. By their continually increasing involvement in American society at all levels, Catholics have come to be widely represented in many different sectors. They are by no means always on the same side in political decision-making. In view of the European experience, it is striking that there has been no strong move to establish a Catholic political party in the United States at either the state or national level. Obversely, the non-Catholic community has been decreasingly apt to relate to Catholics as Catholics rather than on the various other grounds, especially personal competence in specific fields, which come to be so important in the allocation of personnel through the social structure.

Whereas the integration of the Jewish group seems to have been the "simplest," at least symbolically, in that it involved only the "capacity to accept membership," sometimes through renouncing but more importantly through transcending conflicting solidarities,[28] the present case

27. Stein Rokkan and Seymour Martin Lipset, "Cleavage Structures, Party Systems, and Voter Alignments: An Introduction," in *Party Systems and Voter Alignments* (New York: Free Press, 1967).
28. On the side of supply for the receiving community, another important consideration for the Jewish case may again be emphasized. This is that the rivalrous incompatibility of the two communities—Jewish and Protestant—seems to be at its height when both sides are constituted mainly of "independent proprietors," farmers, artisans, small businessmen, and private professional practitioners. The danger of acute anti-Semitism in the American system has probably been greatly mitigated by the fact that the central

involved a further complication, namely, that the group in question might have a propensity to organize within the community for its own special ends in a way subversive of the community's delicately balanced basis of consensus. This seems clearly to be related to the more general symbol of "Communism" as a source of vague danger. The Communist system is precisely characterized by maximal commitment to effectiveness through collective organization.

What I called the American hypersensitivity to the Communist danger is connected with the problem of inclusion of the Catholic groups. The link between them is highly integrated political organization, internally on a nationwide basis but with an international base centered outside the country. It is particularly significant that the fear in the United States has been primarily of internal subversion. This may have been somewhat plausible in the 1930's, but in the cold war period the strength of the American Communist party had been reduced to practically nothing, even among intellectuals. There is a discrepancy between this internal anxiety—firmly documented in Stouffer's study[29]— and the substantially smaller concern about the really serious conflict with Communist movements in foreign affairs. Communism, however, is a symbol, the latent meanings of which include various forms of collective authority which may be felt to threaten freedom—among which the Catholic Church has figured prominently. Therefore, we can infer that the fear of Communism includes a "displaced affect," the sources of which must be sought elsewhere.

Not only was there the problem of the Catholic Church, but the relevant period, from the New Deal on, was one of rapid increase in the size and functions of the federal government. It is notable that the main internal focus of this increase lay in the strengthening of the social component of citizenship which concerned the status of the largely immigrant urban lower classes. Externally, it derived, above all, from involvement in two world wars and the attendant changes in the level of American responsibility in world affairs.

---

economic organization developed in the direction of a more highly differentiated corporate structure. In this, there is no "individual" proprietor whose interests can seem to be blocked by the competing Jew. Not unconnected with this development is that of a much broadened system of higher education, one that has changed the character of the general American elite, not least that of businessmen. Jews gradually gained access to this system and performed outstandingly in it, and, moreover, there were various structurally interstitial areas open to them, such as semi-monopolized areas of small business (for example, clothing) and, not least, the professions organized primarily on the basis of private practice.

29. Samuel Stouffer, *Communism, Conformity, and Civil Liberties* (Garden City, N.Y.: Doubleday, 1955).

In these circumstances, anti-Communism could serve as a unifying symbol for two important groups, namely the older "conservative" groups who stood in fear of and opposition to the general trend to "bigness," urbanization, and the like, and the upwardly mobile, largely Catholic, groups. The latter could claim to be more than one hundred per cent American and accuse the "liberal" elements among the WASP's of insufficient loyalty to their own country. The strongly anti-Communist stance of the Vatican before the Papacy of John XXIII presumably also strengthened this attitude.[30]

In spite of the complexities, I think it is justified to establish an equation that connects Communism symbolically with Catholicism, on the one hand, and with big government, on the other, as a focus of fears and anxieties of a large sector of the American public. It is significant that the relation to Catholicism seems to have eased greatly in the most recent period, especially since the Presidency of Kennedy. This is related to the new definition of the American Right (that is, rightward from Goldwater) as quite explicitly connecting the trend to big government and the danger of Communism. The mitigation of the anti-Communist feeling of the Catholic element—in spite of some lingerings in the South—was fundamental in Lyndon Johnson's ability to command a political consensus over such a wide band as he did in the 1964 election. The inclusion of the Catholic component in the anti-Communist syndrome seems to be parallel to the relation of anti-Semitism, again often latently, to the vaguely generalized anxiety about the "foreignness" of the new immigration as a whole, which was so prominent in the 1920's.

There is another aspect of the broadly "Catholic" inclusion problem which constitutes an important bridge to the Negro problem. The elements of the new immigration not only were different in cultural and national origin from most of their predecessors, but also occupied a different position in American society. Virtually all of them became the lower class of the large cities and industrial areas. The Jewish group escaped from this situation very rapidly, while the Catholic groups, most of whom were of peasant origin, did so more slowly. Indeed this circumstance sharply distinguished the United States from the European cases which were the prototypes for classical Marxian theory—there was hardly any indigenous "working class" here and the lower occupational roles were largely performed by immigrants whose eventual group status in the

30. Cf. my paper "Social Strains in America," in Daniel Bell (ed.), *The Radical Right, op. cit.*

society was still very uncertain. Siegfried put great stress on this fact. With a good many qualifications, it can be said that the urban Negro has inherited this status as the immigrant has moved up. He, too, is by origin predominantly a "peasant," though from the rural South, and has had to undergo many similar processes of adaptation to the urban environment.

In the Jewish case we might speak of the "foreign" community as standing "beside" the main national one. It was difficult to assign it to a hierarchical position, and it was not highly stratified internally. In proportion as the situation just outlined applied to the Catholic group, it tended to bolster the WASP position as an aristocracy in the premodern sense. This tendency was of course most accentuated in the South, particularly vis-à-vis the Negro. But it was hardly unknown in the North. Indeed, the kind of anti-Semitism which has been manifested in the exclusion of Jews from select clubs, college fraternities, residential neighborhoods, and resorts is clearly an example of this. Precisely because the Jew has been such a capable achiever by American standards, he has been excluded in order to assert a claim to a status which is not only, or sometimes not at all, linked to achievement.

In the Catholic group, this has been overcome in part by their achieving admission on the most nearly aristocratic terms. The Kennedy story illustrates this dramatically. The elder Kennedy had great wealth which was linked to local political power by his marriage to the daughter of an Irish mayor of Boston. Then not only did his son achieve political success, ultimately the summit of the Presidency, but he partially joined the circle of the WASP aristocracy by attending Harvard College and developing, with his wife, a style of living which was anything but that of peasants.[31] This is an illustration of the process of pluralization. Increasingly the Catholic populations have diffused through the social structure so that there remains little in common among them but their religion and, of course, their Americanism. The great relative growth in the urban population has helped greatly in this by reducing the distinctiveness of a predominantly urban group. The same applies to the Jews.

It was noted above that, partly in reaction to the new immigration, but also to industrialization and urbanization, the tendency toward the turn of the century and well into the present one was for the WASP's to assume something of the position of an aristocracy—a trend related to "snobbish" anti-Semitism. The Jews did a great deal to discourage this

31. Further, the sister of the President's wife married into European aristocracy, taking the title of "Princess," while remaining very close to the whole Kennedy family.

through their striking record of upward mobility, especially in educational achievement, the professions, and latterly, science and the arts. There have, however, been various symptoms of this such as the conspicuous "Anglophilism" of the upper groups in this period, which has stood in strong contrast to the Anglophobia of earlier phases of our national existence. The England particularly emphasized was that of the "Establishment," the prestige of Oxford education being a prominent symptom. In this situation, it was natural in the North for there to be greater acceptance of the status of the Negro as belonging to a "service" class in a way not too different from the trends of English colonial practice.

The upward mobility of the new immigrant groups and their increasing inclusion in the national community tended to isolate the Negro in this capacity—the virtual disappearance of Irish domestic servants is an index. Such changes as the immense broadening of the pyramid of education—so that virtually the whole age cohort has received some secondary education and a rapidly increasing proportion has been going to college and beyond—have tended to alter this situation. Thus the brief tendency to crystallize a predominantly WASP upper class has increasingly given way to a new egalitarianism—one stressing equality of opportunity, rather than of final status, but definitely covering an ever-widening ethnic-religious range. This trend has made the recent status of the Negro even more anomalous and is part of the setting of the recent phase of the inclusion process.

The Negro Case

If the predominantly Catholic part of the new immigration owed its primary status ascription in American society mainly to its lower-class status, for the Negro this has been almost wholly the case. For our purposes, color will be treated not as a direct component of the social status of the Negro—for in strict theoretical terms it is not that—but as a symbol. On relatively concrete levels, it is correct to say that individual Negroes are discriminated against in various ways solely because of their skin color. This statement is not, however, an explanation of the general phenomenon of color discrimination, as distinguished from individual cases. Unfortunately this vital distinction is often not kept firmly in mind. Our concern is with the general phenomenon.

In this context skin color symbolizes inferiority in the sense that it is purported to justify placing Negroes as a category so radically at the bottom of the scale as to be only equivocally inside the system at all. It will perhaps be illuminating to consider the problem first in connection with the difference between the South and the North.[32]

The Civil War broke out about the time of, and partly as a result of, the process of industrialization and urbanization in the North. This accentuated the difference in social structure of which slavery was a primary feature. The South was largely an agrarian society with a planter gentry at the top practicing an aristocratic style of life, and with the great mass of menial labor being done by Negro slaves. The principal class whose status was equivocal was the white group which could not pretend to gentry status, but which wanted above all to avoid being classified with the Negroes. It was something like a caste society. Though the slaves were formally emancipated as a result of the South's defeat in the war, the post-Reconstruction reaction confirmed this caste structure with the "Jim Crow" system.

Unlike the Jews and Catholics, the Southern Negro has generally had to start his rise by acquiring the most elementary components of legal and political citizenship. Through court decisions and now increasingly through legislation, this part of the task of inclusion has progressed a long way toward accomplishment. The social component is another matter—inclusion in this area is just beginning to develop, and there is no doubt that it will prove the most difficult of the three processes.

Until the First World War the Negro was scarcely a "problem" in the North, mainly because his numbers were so small. This was changed by the great migrations which began about that time, accelerated by the boll weevil havoc in Southern cotton growing. Of course, this process has now gone so far that less than half the Negro population is resident in the eleven states of the old Confederacy, and the proportion will continue to decline. Moreover, in the South there has been a great deal of migration to the cities, so that the category, Southern rural Negro— once the predominant type—is now a distinct minority.

The upward mobility of the white urban lower groups, the new immigration, has contributed to the fact that, in both North and South, the Negro is predominantly urban and lower class. Today about half of the estimated 20 per cent of Americans who are "the poor" are Negroes.[33] This classifies about 50 per cent of the Negroes as poor, whereas no other group—Irish, Italian, and so forth—has nearly that large a proportion.

In a sense the South has "infected" the North with the virus of the

32. Color, in turn, symbolizes *parentage*, since of course the skin color of Negroes varies greatly. The social criterion is that a Negro is anyone, one or both of whose parents were socially classified as a Negro.
33. Cf. Pettigrew, *op. cit.*

Negro problem, even though its meaning has been deeply changed. It was hardly to have been expected that Southerners would get very much Northern political support for maintaining the Jim Crow system intact. Even the coalition of Southern Democrats and Northern conservative Republicans has been gradually eroded to the point that, with the mounting pressure and certain general changes, it has almost disappeared. However, the "problem" is now becoming much more uniform throughout the nation—it is becoming an urban class problem.[34]

As noted above, the Jewish inclusion would probably have been much more difficult had it not been for the type of differentiation process in the economy exemplified by the growth of corporate business, and for the great development of higher education, which opened the doors of the professions to considerable numbers of Jews. Similarly, the pluralization of the political system, the breakup of the city machines as the preserves of specific groups, and the decline of the corresponding "better element" sectors of the political structure have greatly facilitated the inclusion of the Catholic groups. I should like to suggest that the "host society" has been undergoing an important process of structural change which is creating essential conditions for the inclusion not only of the Negro, but of the whole lower class in the societal community.

In an important sense, American society has been protected against the urgency of the class problem by the fact that for so long such a large proportion of its lowest socioeconomic groups has been of recent immigration status, especially in the crucially important cities which have increasingly become the structural focus of the newer society. As noted, upward mobility has greatly alleviated the potential class problems, but they are now being brought to an acute and symbolically appropriate focus by the Negro's becoming the prototypical disadvantaged category.

In the broadest terms the incipient inclusion process depends for its success on the much more effective institutionalization of Marshall's social component of citizenship. However, it comprises new movements with respect to all three of the components. It has, for example, been noted that a most important trend in the Supreme Court decisions of recent years is the extension of the Bill of Rights to the level of the states, especially through reinterpretation of the Fourteenth Amendment.[35] Many of these decisions, such as the school desegregation ruling of 1954,

34. However dramatic, episodes like that in Selma are clearly coming into the category of "mopping-up operations."
35. Erwin N. Griswold, *Law and Lawyers in the United States* (Cambridge: Harvard University Press, 1964).

have most notably affected discrimination in the South. Others, however, such as the requirement that indigent defendants accused of crime be provided with counsel (the Gideon case), apply more generally Furthermore, not only legal rights, in the narrower sense, but also political and social rights are affected. Thus the reapportionment cases profoundly affect the franchise and, with it, the distribution of political power; and the school cases impinge on the social component. They seem to imply that government is obligated to provide adequate educational facilities to the whole population—with discrimination by race being only one aspect of the present inadequacy.

Within this framework of legal rights, public policy is attempting to cope with the causes of *de facto* discrimination, not just by color but by any status of inferiority which cannot be fairly attributed to the individual himself. A certain religio-ideological grounding of this first emerged with the prominent Social Gospel movement in American Protestantism in the latter part of the nineteenth century (which, incidentally, had much to do with the establishment of sociology as an academic discipline in this country) and with its role in the development of philanthropy concerned with the disadvantaged classes. The New Deal comprised a second main phase, with the beginning of comprehensive federal social welfare legislation, including the consolidation of the legal status of trade unionism through the Wagner Act and, particularly, unemployment, old age, and other benefits. The opposition of the Supreme Court to such legislation, especially by the states, was also ended in that period. The United States now seems to be well into a third phase. Perhaps its most important feature has been the shift in concern from welfare in the narrower sense to health, education, and the nature of the urban community, focusing most acutely so far upon housing.

By the narrower sense of welfare, I mean that concerned primarily with money income. The older conceptions of lower-class status emphasized lack of financial means as the central feature of being disadvantaged. Hence, stress was put on improvement in financial status. This was reasonable especially when, as in the Great Depression, massive unemployment was the most acute condition needing a remedy. However, there has been increasing insight that poverty is a function of other factors such as poor health, both physical and—as has been emphasized more recently—mental, and certain aspects of community structure and the like.

Education has become the most salient link with the occupational system, which is, in turn, the principal basis of financial independence for the individual and his immediate family. There has been a general upgrading of education. On the one hand, this means that larger proportions of the age cohort have been attaining higher levels of education, with the results that the disadvantaged minority, especially the well-known drop-outs, has been separated from the majority with increasing sharpness. On the other hand, educational requirements for good employment have been rising at the same time—most of the present unemployment is found among the poorly-qualified groups, and educational qualifications are becoming of increasing importance in holding jobs. It seems that not only formal opportunity for a relatively good education (that is, at least through high school), but also capacity to take advantage of it, both in individual ability and in motivation, is coming to be as much a requisite of full inclusion as civil and voting rights.

Behind this, as treated in much more detail elsewhere in this issue, is the problem of the social environment of the disadvantaged, the "slum." The central concern is the vicious circle of the factors in *actual* inferior capacity for valued performance, in which poverty, bad health, low educational standards, family disorganization, delinquency, and other anti-social phenomena are mutually reinforcing. This is where the structure of the urban community itself becomes a salient problem focus. The new concern centers on the residential community. In this connection attention has been called to the fact that the Negro is disadvantaged, even beyond other slum dwellers, in many senses besides the color of his skin. First and foremost, he has been peculiarly lacking in relatively strong family organization[36] which could give strong psychological support to the individual, especially as a child. Second, this has been connected in turn with a relative weakness in "community" institutions of mutual support and solidarity, for example, of the sort which have preeminently characterized Jewish groups even before they rose significantly from their initial low status in American society. Even as the victim of the most radical discrimination of any group, the Negro has not only been forced to be subservient, but has also failed to develop, or bring with him from his Southern rural past, sufficient ingredients for socially effective self-help—a question not merely of individual qualities and initiative, but of collective solidarity and mutual support at many levels, particularly the family and the local community. The strongest Negro institutions have centered in the churches, a vital complex which must be preserved carefully against some of the disintegrating tendencies

36. Cf. remarks of Clifford Geertz in the 1964 *Daedalus* planning conference.

of urban life. The role of the churches in the civil rights movement per haps symbolizes this best and will be commented upon further below.

Some Highlights of the Inclusion Process

It is reasonable to suggest that, whatever the extent and nature of the responsibility for the many previous failures, the time is ripe for a major advance. The broad tendency of modern society, one in which America has played a rather special role, has been egalitarian in the sense of in stitutionalizing the basic rights of citizenship in all three categories sketched here.[37] This tendency has become institutionalized over an increasingly broad front, the legal development noted above being prototypical. The basic types of inequality which have continued to be tolerated—in this context rather than that of recognition and reward of achievement—have been justified, when at all, primarily in terms of "paternalistic" immunities of a variety of sectoral types, the status of the child in the family being a kind of model. In case after case, these immunities have been whittled away, so that the universalistic norms of the society have applied more and more widely. This has been true of all the main bases of particularistic solidarity, ethnicity, religion, regionalism, state's rights, and class. The "sovereignty" of the individual American state has perhaps been the most important single bulwark of these particularisms, in the first instance those of WASP's, but potentially of every group. The inclusion of the Jewish and Catholic groups as out lined above fits this paradigm.

Today, more than ever before, we are witnessing an acceleration in the emancipation of individuals of all categories from these diffuse particularistic solidarities. This must be seen as a further *differentiation* of the role-set in which the individual is involved. By being included in larger community structures, the individual need not cease to be a member of the smaller ones, but the latter must relinquish certain of the controls over him which they previously exercised. This reasoning applies to aristocratic groups as much as it does to negatively privileged ones like the Negro. We have been witnessing major steps in the extension and consolidation of the societal community.

Let me emphasize again one particularly important aspect of the present phase, that the more general insistence on the basic equalities of

37. Contrary, of course, to the temporary trend to the establishment of a WASP aristocracy.

citizenship, which is essential to the inclusion process, cuts across the status of Negro. In its deeper layers, it is a demand not for the inclusion of Negroes as such, but for the elimination of *any* category defined as inferior in itself. For a long time the status of the Negro was a peculiarly Southern problem. Then it became a national problem, but *qua* Negro. Now we are entering the phase in which it is no longer that, but the problem of eliminating status-inferiority as such, regardless of race, creed, or color. The Negro, in becoming only a "special case," even if a very salient one, loses a ground for special consideration which he has enjoyed. As the same time, he has established a position for tapping much wider bases of support than before. He can become the spokesman for the much broader category of the disadvantaged, those excluded on this egregious ground. The Negro movement, then, can become the American style "socialist" movement. This is to say that the basic demand is for full inclusion, not for domination or for equality on a basis of separateness.[38]

At the risk of repetition, I may note that the successful accomplishment of this goal of inclusion depends on a balanced mobilization of four categories of factors. The first is commitment to the values which underlie the assumption that the goal itself is desirable. This has a long history in American society and is clearly of the greatest importance. I have mentioned that it was invoked by Myrdal. Recently we have seen a notable "effervescence" (in Durkheim's sense) with respect to activation of these value-commitments at the requisite levels. Here the Negro movement has played the paramount part, but the activation has extended far beyond the movement itself. Its incidence in religious circles is especially noteworthy, not least in the way it has brought all faiths of the white community, Catholics and Jews as well as Protestants, together behind the Negro cause. The presence of Catholic nuns among the demonstrators in Selma was a new note having a significance scarcely to be overestimated.

Mere affirmation of the values is not enough. If a process of change is to be a new implementation of fundamental values, its basic direction must be articulated. This involves the development of a conception of the societal community in which all elements will be fully included in the sense of this discussion. In our own cultural background, quite different directions have also enjoyed powerful value-sanctions, even if rather

38. It could perhaps be said that the claim of Orthodox Judaism for a secure position in the host society is a case of the "separate but equal" principle. Similar things can be said of other ethnic and religious situations, for example the French minority in Canada.

insecurely. One example was the conception of the Negro as inherently inferior—indeed, in a certain version of older Calvinism now dominant in South Africa, as rightfully belonging in a subordinated status. It is the basic values, as applied to the developing conception of the American societal community, which together form the normative focus of the power of the movement.

This factor underlies the trend to implement the values by inclusion —the only tolerable solution to the enormous tensions lies in constituting a single societal community with full membership for all. This is a renewal and reinterpretation of the concept of the Union which was so central for Lincoln. No other solution is tolerable from the American point of view—hence the Black Muslims cannot gain active support in the general community. And despite much ambivalence, it seems certain that the main Negro community is committed to this outlook. The continuing mobilization of these loyalties and commitments on both sides of the racial line seems to be the second crucial factor in the general inclusion process.

It has been very common to postulate and emphasize a primary difference between the "idealists" who hope to achieve integration by asserting the values of, and a willingness for, acceptance, and the "realists" who say that *only* the mobilization of political power and economic interests will help. I should strongly repudiate this framing of alternatives. It is quite correct that the goal cannot be achieved *without* the mobilization of power and economic interests, but it does not follow that these factors are themselves sufficient. It is only a balanced combination of "ideal" and "real" factors which provides the formula for success.

In speaking of political power, I should like to conceive it here more broadly than is usual. Essential as government is, it does not stand alone in implementing major political changes. The political problems of integration involve all fields of organizational decision-making, especially for business firms to accept Negroes in employment, for colleges and universities to admit them for study, for trade unions to avoid discrimination. We have become acutely aware of the limitations of political power. Against a recalcitrant group, attempts to *enforce* compliance are all-too-often ineffective. Nevertheless, at certain crucial points its mobilization is clearly an essential factor, a factor which includes making decisions affecting inclusion processes *binding* as obligations on all members of the requisite collectivity, whether governmental or private. It is particularly important to remember that the use of power has a double effect. First, it mobilizes sanctions against recalcitrants in such ways that they may no longer be able to afford previously feasible resistance. Second, it asserts on behalf of the relevant collectivity that the policy of inclusion must be taken seriously, and hence that noncompliance will not be allowed to proceed with impunity.

Of all the factors favoring integration, economic interests are the most neutral as far as normative obligations are concerned. They involve both the extent to which receiving elements can "afford" the risks involved in taking various steps and the development of realistic capacities to do so—a theme discussed above in connection with the whole complex of inferiority of status. Perhaps most important is that without support from the other three sets of factors, economic interests and capacity to exploit economic opportunities are weak reeds. This has been made vividly clear where state governments in the deep South, backed by what seems to have been a white consensus, have adamantly opposed steps toward integration. In such cases business men simply would not move. But where the balance of the other factors shifts toward integration, economic interests on both sides can provide a powerful reinforcement of the change. It is a question of "getting over the hump."[39]

A Note on Resistance to Inclusion

In American social thinking it is regarded almost as simple common sense to emphasize primarily, when speaking of the resistance to such developments as the Negro movement for inclusion, the material vested interests of the opponents, for example, the fear of loss of real-estate values or the view that "our customers would not like dealing with a Negro receptionist," so we would lose business. Such examples themselves suggest that another set of factors is involved. The structure of vested interests is a function of the structure of values and norms underlying the relevant sphere of social interaction. We are in the midst of a process of social change in which these components, and not only the interests, are changing.

Resistance has been strongest in the white South. This is because the structure of Southern society has been more "archaic" than that of the rest of the country. It has, however, been changing very rapidly and has tended more or less to polarize around its more advanced urban, industrial, and partly intellectual sectors, on the one hand, and its more

39. It must be understood that the economic factor here includes the whole opportunity-capacity complex, which is especially important for the Negro. For this reason *primary* reliance on economic interests is clearly inadequate.

traditional rural and small town sectors, on the other. This very broad polarization is by no means peculiar to the South, but is nationwide. Thus states' rights, the resistance to reapportionment on population bases, and many other issues mark a "conservative" reaction against many of the processes of change in the society at large.

Political developments in recent years bring this situation into sharp relief. The one-party system of the South has been breaking up rapidly, creating an opportunity for the Republican party to gain a major foothold in the South. This in turn relates to the tendency of a major—and the more activist—wing of Northern Republicanism to sympathize with the whole constellation of orientation of which the Southern resistance to desegregation has been a part. Hence that part associated with, or sympathizing with, the more radical Right has been particularly attracted by what has come to be known as the "Southern strategy," which was adopted by Goldwater and his advisers in the 1964 campaign.

Nothing could bring out more sharply the impact of changes in social structure in the last generation or so. The old isolation of South and North has largely broken down. The older Republican party was largely a sectional party, which on the whole opposed the New Deal, especially institutionalization of the social component of citizenship. Now, for the reasons sketched above and others, the Negro has come to the forefront all along the line of the process of social change feared by the "conservative" elements, North and South. Indeed it may be suggested that the affinity between the Goldwaterites and the segregationist Southerners was so strong that they became almost compulsive in their urge to unite. One may suspect that shrewd political calculation played a much smaller part than did this sense of affinity. Yet the outcome of the election makes crystal-clear how impossible it is for a national party which wishes to win nationwide elections to include endorsement of the segregation system in its major policies.

An important underlying aspect of this affinity is the great prominence of Protestant Fundamentalism on both sides of the political alignment. There is strong evidence that such religious orientations are particularly marked among the Radical Right, especially in its principal stronghold of the Southwest. Certainly this is true also of the South.

The alignment of the resistance to Negro inclusion, directly or through resistance to various measures essential to its success (such as federal support of education and the war against poverty), with a *generalized* political conservatism is a highly important development. Its obverse is the alignment of the society's more progressive political forces in support of the inclusion process, again both directly and by promoting policies which will provide or strengthen its major factors. Moreover, the more serious of the resistances seem to be located politically rather far on the right, so that it is unlikely that in the near future the opponents of inclusion of the Negro can reach far enough into the political center to mobilize very large political blocks at the national level. Many resistance groups will retain power at the more local levels, but the general trend of weakening parochial particularisms seems to be working in a favorable direction. The strengthening of federal power as such is only one aspect of a much more comprehensive process.

Finally a further word should be said about the symbolization of the resistance to inclusion. I have stressed the theme of inferiority as the most central in defining the symbolic status of the Negro. If this is as important as has often been held, it follows that the main focus of anxiety involving resistance lies in the fear that the quality of the societal community will deteriorate if inferior members are admitted. Here the resemblance to fears of "debasing the currency" through irresponsible monetary management and banking is striking. Sometimes in our economic history such fears have proved justified, but over the long range the extension of credit systems and the like have contributed enormously to the productivity of the economy. The "sound money" people have on the whole fought a rear-guard action against such extensions, one which would have contributed greatly to economic retardation had it prevailed.

The process under discussion here is that of a major extension of full membership in the societal community. If it is done imprudently—as, it might be said, was the completely free immigration before World War I —it may have effects analogous to inflation. But the fears of it are just as irrational as the fears of economic modernization have been, and they can be analyzed in closely parallel terms. The most important single condition of avoiding inflationary "debasement" is the general upgrading not only of the Negro but of all elements in the population falling below the minimum acceptable standards of full citizenship.

The Negro Movement and the Problem of Negro Identity

A particularly conspicuous feature of the recent phase in the changing status of the Negro has been the emergence of a strong movement which has had very extensive and important white support, but which has struck much deeper roots in the Negro community itself than have previous phases. The emergence of the movement is a function of several factors such as the general social changes outlined above, the stimulus of the emergence of African states, the strengthening of the Negro middle classes, with their higher levels of education, and the concentration of Negro masses in the cities, primarily in the North. This essay cannot attempt a more detailed analysis of these developments. I should like rather to state a few of their implications, especially regarding the opportunities they present.

It has been remarked in several papers that the Negro group has generally had less solidarity and weaker organization than the other ethnic groups which have preceded it in gaining inclusion. The growth of the present movement seems to be both a symptom and a cause of a notable strengthening in this solidarity, which is beginning to create a more clearly defined group consciousness and sense of power and opportunity. It presents a new opportunity to shift the definition of Negro status away from its predominantly negative meaning as an oppressed group which is typically excluded and exposed to multifarious disadvantages. The problem is to develop a basis for a more positive conception of group identity in both American and world society. I should like to suggest that there is a most unusual opportunity inherent in the nature of the movement and its situation, the importance of which, however, is not yet widely appreciated.

One major point of reference is that the primary source of Negro grievance, exclusion on the basis of alleged *inherent* inferiority, is the most radical grievance entertained by any major non-WASP group, except possibly the American Indian's grievance of dispossession. It raises a clearer, more drastic *moral* issue than the other cases, one compounded by the status of the Negro's ancestors as slaves in America and by the injustice of using the "trivial" symbol of color as a primary basis of exclusion. Given the universalistic and egalitarian elements in our national traditions, both religious and Constitutional, it is difficult to find an issue which is morally more straight-forward.

It has been possible to keep the issue relatively insulated for a long time, but recent social changes as well as the movement itself have made this progressively more problematic. Now, in a period of rising economic affluence, and, it may be said, moral ambivalence both about this and about the confusions over the American position in world affairs, the nation has been presented with a notable opportunity to define a clear and *simple* issue of conscience. By and large, the reverberation of the issue in many different groups has been extensive and impressive, in spite of the tenacious resistance just reviewed. Perhaps the issue also becomes more urgent precisely because of the progress made in resolving the other issues of inclusion which we have discussed, since this leaves the Negro even more conspicuously excluded.

It seems particularly significant that white involvement has come so definitely from two sources, the churches, especially the clergy, and the students.[40] Categorizing my examples of non-Negro inclusion problems into Jews and Catholics, rather than the corresponding ethnic categories, was the result of deliberate theoretical choice, not simple convenience. I have long been convinced that the religious background of these problems has been—and remains—fundamental and that both the difficulties of inclusion and the opportunities for its success have been intimately involved with religion. One may say that, for the inclusion of the new immigrants, the problem centered in those elements of the relatively "liberal" Protestant community which were, in one way or another, involved in the tenuous WASP claim to aristocratic status.

I have noted that the processes of social change in the present century have tended increasingly to polarize the society along an axis which includes not only political conservatism in resistance to change but, closely related to this, what we call religious "fundamentalism." In the South the connection between militant segregationism and fundamentalism has been very clear,[41] and I have suggested that a broader connection was certainly evident in the Goldwater campaign.

Generally speaking, there are also important connections between

40. There is no space here to go into the reasons that the mobilization of students in the civil rights movement is so significant. I do not accept Paul Goodman's suggestion that students are the most exploited class in American society, but their position does have some similarities to that of an exploited class. Though their general prospects are good, as individuals they occupy a probationary status, being under rather strong control from their elders and their teachers. They have developed a strong subculture of their own, characterized by a "romantic" simplification of the general world—a part of the "youth culture." When politically activistic, they tend to be "radical," sometimes in a rightist as well as a leftist direction. Especially in "underdeveloped" societies, the violence of student nationalism is well known. This simplification makes them prone to a strongly moralistic stance—perhaps particularly emphasized because of the prevalence of various adult suspicions about their moral integrity. Hence, they tend to be kinds of "fundamentalists" to whom a simple moralistic issue can appeal greatly. But, by the same token, as representing the best of the future of the society, they can play an exceedingly important role in dramatizing really important moral issues. Cf. Eisenstadt, *From Generation to Generation* (Glencoe, Ill.: The Free Press, 1956), and my own article, "Youth in the Context of American Society," *Daedalus* (Winter 1961) reprinted in Erik H. Erikson ed., *Youth: Change and Challenge* (Garden City, N.Y.: Anchor Books, 1964).

41. Charles Campbell and Thomas Pettigrew, *Christians in Racial Crisis* (Washington, D.C., Public Affairs Press, 1959).

lower-class status in industrial societies, social origins in more "primitive" or "underdeveloped" social settings, particularly of a peasant type, a certain general conservatism (or, as Lipset says, "authoritarianism"), and religious fundamentalism. Indeed, one may say that the predominant kind of Catholicism among the new immigrant urban masses was a form of fundamentalism and that the liberalization of American Catholicism in the last generation is partly a function of the upward mobility and inclusion of these masses. To a degree, the Orthodoxy of so many East European Jewish immigrants was also a form of fundamentalism.

The majority of Negro Americans have been and are, religiously speaking, fundamentalists. But, this fact does not have simple consequences. Undoubtedly, in their segregated and insulated status in the rural South, it helped to motivate acceptance of their lot, as the corresponding features of Catholic and Jewish fundamentalism have done in both the peasant or ghetto circumstances of the "old countries" and in the difficult early stages of involvement in American society as first- and second-generation immigrants.

At the same time, there is the deep-seated Judeo-Christian tradition of religious motivation to preserve integrity, to assert autonomy, and eventually to seek justice through change in the structure of the situation. Here, what I am calling the more fundamentalist orientation has, in the course of history, repeatedly assumed moral leadership, in part facilitated by an unworldly lack of concern for the complexities of process in the highly differentiated societies. Fundamentalists in this sense— which includes such "secular religions" as Communism—tend to be direct-actionists, to see issues in *simple* moral terms; and about half the time they have the balance of long-run merit on their side.

However, Negro fundamentalism, like that of the previous immigrant masses, has come to be mobilized predominantly on the side of differentiation and inclusion, not of segregation and exclusion. The development of the movement has strongly activated the moral sentiments of the other groups, including very significant groups of non-Protestants. This process has quite directly *split* the fundamentalist element in American religion, with all its important *indirect* relations to politics and other contexts. The *moral* basis of opposition to change in the older and simpler order—so strongly emphasized by our latterday conservatives—is thereby gravely undermined. There has developed, significantly, a strong and sometimes very sharp dialogue on the subject of moral justification between those camps. This brings the process of restructuring the social system to the highest normative level, a level already fully structured specifically in terms of religious and social pluralism. It raises, in a form difficult to evade, the question of the moral basis of the American type of "Free Society."

I should like to emphasize the subtle combination of similarities and differences between the processes of inclusion for the groups of the new immigration and for the Negro. All three have been in certain respects "foreign." They have also come with socio-cultural patterns which have been relatively "backward" by the main standards of the new society— to put it sharply, all except Jews have been "peasants," and they have been small-town bourgeois. All three have had religio-cultural orientations which can be called "fundamentalist." Environmentally, however, all three have been plunged into a converging set of integrating influences, as the most recently arrived lower-class group in the largest urban communities.

In the other context, the three are not only distinct from each other, but constitute a series. The Jews, curiously from some points of view, have proved the easiest to include. This was not the case in Germany, with its much more hierarchical social structure. But in "individualistic" America, the principal problem was that of defining the legitimacy of, and opportunity for, cultural pluralism without prejudicing the other, more instrumental bases of participation. The Catholics had to overcome high American sensitivity to tightly organized collectivities which might be accused of "conspiracy."

In this succession, the Negro stands at the "end of the line." His is the most serious (hence in some respects, the most plausible) basis of exclusion, namely, his inherent inferiority. The relatively satisfactory— it will not in our time ever be fully so—resolution of the problem of Negro inclusion will certainly be one of the greatest achievements of American society. Moreover, the record of the movement, even up to this point, makes it clear that a very major part of the credit will go to the Negro community itself; it will be *their* achievement, certainly in the sense of direct goal-orientation to a much greater degree than is true of the groups which have already gained inclusion.

This seems to me to constitute a crucially important focus for the future of the collective Negro identity. The Negro community has the opportunity to define itself as the spearhead of one of the most important improvements in the quality of American society in its history—and to do so not only in pursuit of its own obvious self-interest, but in the fulfillment of a *moral* imperative. It is a change in American society which is deeply consonant with our moral traditions, but also one which could not come about without systematically exerted pressures and strong leadership. The resistances are quite sufficient to explain these necessities.

This role of the Negro movement and the community behind it has significance far beyond the internal American scene. The whole world has now become more or less polarized between the developed and the underdeveloped nations. This polarization largely coincides with the freeing of large areas of the world from colonial status, a process which has moved with great rapidity in recent years, and with their emancipation from inferior status in terms of both political dependence and economic and educational development. Not least, this axis also relates very closely to a color line—the Asian and African new nations are largely nonwhite.

It has been stressed above that the American Revolutionary tradition has prepared this country for a position of leadership in the movement toward equality for the new nations of the extra-European world. The internal processes of inclusion of the Jewish and Catholic elements have strengthened the American position in this respect—the vaunted promises of equal treatment have not been wholly worthless. The opportunity, then, is for the Negro to symbolize the completion of this internal process (and to give symbolic promise of the solubility of the world-wide problems) as a massively large colored group which has found its rightful place in American society and has done so very largely by its own efforts.

It has been noted above that, earlier in this century, there was a tendency to define class lines in the United States as more or less equivalent to ethnic lines, with the new immigrants forming the core of the "working class." It is probably true that the heavy influx of immigrants contributed substantially to preventing the crystallization of class divisions in the older community along the European lines stressed by Marxists as typical of "capitalist" societies. In any case, American society has certainly evolved away from, rather than toward, this Marxian model, the inclusion of the earlier immigrant groups constituting a most important aspect of the development. However discriminated against the Negro has been, he has been too small a group to constitute a full "proletariat"—indeed, within the group itself, there has been very strong resistance to this definition of their role, in spite of intensive propaganda from Communist sources.

The whole trend of development in American society constitutes the sharpest challenge to the Communist diagnosis of the modern world, and, increasingly, Western Europe has also moved in many respects in the "American" direction. These trends cannot be explained on Marxist premises. The status of the Negro has been morally the most vulnerable feature of the American society. If, as there seems to be good hope, this can be dealt with effectively, it can have a most extensive effect on the larger world situation.

This is because the Communist trend has been to redefine the crucial "class struggle" as a struggle not between classes within societies, but between exploiting and exploited societies, with the famous theory of "imperialism." Just as successful Negro inclusion will put the seal on the Marxian error in diagnosing American society, so the United States, with strong Negro participation, indeed leadership, has the opportunity to present a true alternative to the Communist pattern on a world-wide basis, one which is not bound to the stereotype of "capitalism." Because of the immensely important role of race and color in the world situation, the strategic position of the Negro American is crucial. This subcommunity of our pluralistic society has the opportunity to be *the* main symbolic spokesman of the possibility of achieving a racially, as well as religiously, nationally, and otherwise, pluralistic world society in which some kind of integration among the racial groups can be developed without a loss of identity and in terms compatible with raising the previously inferior to the status of those fundamentally equal in world citizenship.

Near the beginning of this essay, the distinction between inclusion and assimilation was stressed. The purport of this latest phase of the analysis is to suggest that to identify non-discrimination (that is, inclusion) too strongly with complete "color-blindness" might be to throw away a very precious asset, not only for the Negro, but for American society as a whole. My own view is that the healthiest line of development will not be only the preservation, but the actual building up, of the solidarity of the Negro community and of the sense that being a Negro has positive value. In the process there is the danger of cultivating separatism, as most conspicuously exemplified by the Black Muslims. But the pluralistic solution, which has been stressed throughout this discussion, is neither one of separatism—with or without equality—nor of assimilation, but one of full participation combined with the preservation of identity. The American Jewish and Catholic groups have, by and large, been able to achieve this goal.

Quite clearly, the Negro's own associations with fellow Negroes who survive the inclusion process should no longer be compulsory.[42]

42. Not only that, but the positive value of a Negro identity in the long run should not be used to justify failing to act to break up *discriminatory* segregation in the more immediate situation.

Each individual Negro should be free to associate with any non-Negro in any legal way he sees fit, and, if he so desires, to give up completely his identity as a Negro in the sense of belonging to a Negro community. But this does not mean that Negro identity should or will disappear. I should envision continuing predominance of marriages of Negroes with each other. I see no reason that some religious denominations should not be identified as "Negro churches," or that, as long as residence there is not compulsory, many neighborhoods should not continue to be mainly Negro, as many today are Jewish.

Once being a Negro loses the stigma of inferiority, I suggest, it is likely that these will cease to be salient issues. After, all, color is a *symbol* and, if the context of its historic meanings is sufficiently changed, the propect is that it will cease to be the basis of a stigma. The following schematic outline may be helpful to the reader in interpreting the preceding discussion.

Symbolic Groups in Relation to the Inclusion Problem

Focus of Anxiety	Ambiguously Included	Projected Upon
Commitments outside the community		Undefined Foreignness suspected of "un-Americanism"
High Achievement capacity plus "clannishness"	The Jews	

Common feature: diffuse foreignness. Dominant circa 1920's, but into 1930's.

Focus of Anxiety	Ambiguously Included	Projected Upon
Commitments to authoritarian, presumptively conspiratorial collectivities	Catholics	Communists

Common feature: organization which might "take over." Dominant a little later, culminating in McCarthy era.

Focus of Anxiety	Ambiguously Included	Projected Upon
Incapacity for full participation	Fundamentalists	Negroes (Color as Symbol)

Common feature: inclusion could debase the quality of citizenship. Dominant since about 1954.

Patterns for Inclusion

Jews—Foreigners: Fully differentiated participation with special reference to the occupational system—differentiating occupational status from ethnic belongingness—acceptance on one side, abandonment of "clannishness" on the other. Organic solidarity.

Catholics—Communists: Pluralization in the analytical-political sense. Movement from *altruisme* to *egoisme* in Durkheim's sense. Acceptance on both sides that citizenship is not ascribed to position in a "columnar" structure a la Rokkan and Lipset. Loyalty problem.

Fundamentalists—Negroes: Upgrading. The development of capacity for full participation after breaking the stigma of inferiority, as sinful reprobates or as biologically inferior. Symbolic animals and children.

CHAPTER 14

Polarization of the World
and International Order

This essay turns from a particular process in our own society to
the problem of the nature of the processes of integration which
appear to be going on in the world as a whole, and which offer
possibilities of a more solid basis of international order than we
have enjoyed heretofore in this century. It takes the position that
underneath the ideological conflicts that have been so prominent,
there has been emerging an important element of very broad
consensus at the level of values, centering in the complex we often
refer to as "modernization." Furthermore, on this base there is the
possibility of going beyond consensus at the level of values to the
development of more specific integrative mechanisms. In particular, given the elements of integration that have actually
existed, it is argued that the polarization which has occurred bears
some interesting resemblances to a two-party system, however important it is to be quite aware of the differences. The paper was
written for the symposium *Preventing World War III*, Quincy
Wright, William M. Evan, and Morton Deutsch, eds. (New
York: Simon and Schuster, 1962). In certain respects it is a companion and sequel to my earlier paper "Order and Community in
the International Social System" in James N. Rosenau, ed., *International Politics and Foreign Policy* (New York: Free Press,
1961).

Though the tensions clustering around the war in Viet Nam
are so prominent at present writing, it still seems justified to say
that the process of consolidation of world order through the
pluralization of interest structures and the extension and strengthening of systems of procedural norms, has made considerable head-
way since the article was written early in 1962. Perhaps the most
conspicuous field has been the relaxation of tension between the

This chapter is from *Preventing World War III: Some Proposals*. © 1962 by Quincy
Wright, William M. Evan, and Morton Deutsch. Reprinted by permission of Simon &
Schuster, Inc. It also appeared in *Berkeley Journal of Sociology* (Spring, 1961).

United States and the Soviet Union, as evidenced in the Test Ban Treaty, the Cultural Exchange Program, and various other developments. It is notable that by and large this detente has survived the confrontation over the missile bases in Cuba that took place late in 1962. A further interesting field of pluralization has been between the Soviet Union and the East European satellite states, where the term "satellite" has been coming to be decreasingly appropriate. It is perhaps not too much to assert that the burden of proof is on him who claims that the deepening of the vicious circle of conflict is the main underlying trend of the worldwide political system.

T HE GREATEST and most immediate danger to world peace stems from the bipolarization of the world community. It is wholly understandable, therefore, that this situation has been subjected to the most intensive discussion in this volume and elsewhere, and that, moreover, its threatening aspects have stood overwhelmingly at the center of attention. In this brief paper, I should like to explore the other side of this coin. For it is my contention that in certain respects these "most threatening" aspects may present an opportunity, however tenuous, to achieve a more stable system of international order.

The most obvious point of reference for the elaboration of this view is the fact that for the first time in history, we must acknowledge the existence of a world political community, at least in a relative sense. Through the development of mass media of communication, the nations of the world have become increasingly aware of their interdependence. Inevitably, important events in any major country will have rapid repercussions in all others. Indeed, any attempt to isolate a subsystem, unless that system is of minor intrinsic significance, must rely on special insulating mechanisms which impose rather rigid controls. With rapidly diminishing exceptions, we are all members of the world political community for better or worse. In the United States, there has been a growing recognition of this phenomenon during the last three decades. Interestingly, "isolationism," which was formerly a major area of debate, was not even an issue in the recent Presidential campaign; American "involvement" was taken for granted by both parties.

I am aware, of course, that the very propriety of my use of the term "world community" may be questioned, since it implies at least a rudimentary element of order. However, I maintain that polarization, in itself, implies the existence of such an element of order. While it is conceivable, of course, that this element of order is inherent in certain geopolitical constellations which have been wholly independent of the main trends in social development, the enormous diversity of societies and cultures would seem to argue against this view. "East" and "West" may merely be geographical symbols, but these symbols refer to an emergent patterning of sociocultural organization, rather than an inevitable geographically or even ideologically based conflict of interest. Indeed the ideological "battle for men's minds" constitutes a crucial factor in this argument, for an ideological conflict presupposes a common frame of reference in terms of which the ideological differences make sense.

Insofar as a conflict of orientation can be defined as "political," and insofar as it occurs within a pattern of order rather than a Hobbesian state of nature, polarization bears some similarity to the intranational two-party system. This is not to imply that such a party system now exists in the world political community. However, it does not seem beyond the realm of possibility to suggest that some of the ingredients for such a system are present.

Some Basic Components of International Order

Certain major clues emerge as to the nature of those components of international order which are currently most significant. These concern, first, the position which the Western countries have occupied in relation to the rest of the world, particularly since the eighteenth century; and second, the designation of "modernization" as the primary goal of the non-Western sector, along with various sub-goals, such as industrialization, economic development, political independence and autonomy, and the like. These developments stem from a crucial historic event, namely, the emergence in the Western world of what is known today as "industrial society" ("capitalism" is clearly too narrow a term)—in Great Britain, the United States, and Germany in the main—which came almost to full flower in the latter half of the last century, although there have been very important further developments during this century as well. Apart from the powerful "material" influence which industrialism exerts on society (whether this influence is regarded as "exploitative" or not), the concept of industrialism and its implications have been accepted almost universally.

The Implementation of a Common Set of Values

From the point of view of values, economic productivity would appear to be at the core of this pattern. Productivity has been evaluated in a variety of contexts, but a few themes have been particularly prominent. For one, economic productivity enables an improvement in living standards, along with certain concomitant benefits, in the form of higher levels of consumption, greater economic security, better health, and the like. Secondly, economic productivity has been related to autonomy, to emancipation. At this level, it has appealed to "dependent" groups; and it is in this context that it is connected with nationalism. A third and similar theme focuses on equality. As might be expected, this has involved a general challenge to the superior status of traditional elites. On the one hand, this theme has had an "internal" frame of reference, in that it pertains to territorial societies; on the other, it pertains to a demand for equal status as societies, with its bearing on political independence. The fourth important theme has been concerned with education, more specifically, its instrumental function, with respect to productivity as well as its intrinsic value.

Clearly, this broad value complex is common to both of the ideologies which today are engaged in a bitter struggle for ascendancy. Marxism grew out of Western culture during the era of emancipation from the traditionalism and "legitimism" of the European Old Regime. Its concepts stem largely from utilitarian liberalism, especially in the economic sphere; they include the political heritage of the French Revolution. The basic differences between Marxist ideology and that of the "free world" center on two points. The first, of course, involves the concept of socialism as distinguished from capitalism or free enterprise, namely, the relationship between productive organization and public authority. The second involves the interpretation of the concept of democracy, namely, the "liberal" principle of political enfranchisement and open electoral alternatives in the choice of political leadership, as opposed to guidance by a single party which assumes the trusteeship of the interests of the people. Obviously, there are other basic differences as well, such as the hostility of Communism to traditional religion, at least in principle, but important elements in the liberal world may be similarly characterized. However, on the whole, we are impressed by the fact that both of these widely divergent ideologies which, presumably, gave rise to polarization, emerged during various stages of development in the process of industrialization.

It is widely acknowledged that the recent history of the Communist movement constitutes a drastic invalidation of Marx's prediction that the revolution would originate within the most highly industrialized societies (clearly, he had England and Germany in mind). Indeed, evidence has been accumulating which would appear to indicate that the appeal of the radical left in a given society bears an inverse relation to the degree of industrialization of that society.[1] In general, the more successful industrial economies have been able to integrate their working classes into the society—with varying degrees of success, of course, and with many residual strains. In any event, this integration carries with it the legitimation of the appropriate role and status of organizational leadership and responsibility, and the recognition and reward of technical competence. The development of the Soviet Union has been in accord with these fundamental trends. On the other hand, the leftist appeal has been most effective in those instances where the structured inferiority of status, with its concomitant resentment against discrimination, exploitation, imperialism, and the like, involves not classes in the Marxian sense, but societies in the territorial-political sense.

In one sense, this phenomenon is in accord with the character and significance of Marxism, although it may not conform to its original intentions. Viewed in the perspective of later developments, I consider the most important feature of Marxism to be its assertion of the inherent fusion of economic and political factors in human societies; from the perspective of our Western society, this might be interpreted as the doctrine of politization of the economy. A process of differentiation has in fact been in progress, in more highly industrialized societies, which has decreased the relative importance of the area of such fusion. The fact that such a large proportion of the working-class vote in the United States is split between the major parties is very much a case in point. It is interesting to speculate as to what might be expected in this connection in an industrially "mature" Soviet Union, if a system of plural parties were permitted there.

As mentioned earlier, the strong interest in economic development in underdeveloped societies can be linked directly to the powerful force of nationalism. There is no question, of course, that the working classes in Western societies were more "underdeveloped" economically in Marx's time than they are at present. But the economic interests of these groups were said to cut across the main, nationally defined lines, which

1. Cf. S. M. Lipset, *Political Man* (Garden City, N.Y.: Doubleday, 1960), and my review article in *World Politics* (October, 1960).

denoted the cleavage of political interests, whereas in present so-called underdeveloped countries, economic and political interests more nearly coincide.

Theoretically, then, economics and politics comprise the two major categories of "interests." We have yet to consider their relation to systems of normative order, however. For it is a fundamental proposition of social science that no system of the "play of interests" can be considered stable, unless these interests are pursued within an institutionalized normative system—a common framework of values, of generalized norms, and of the structuring of the interests themselves.

As suggested there is a certain plausibility in the view that a primary achievement of modern industrial societies has been the resolution of the class conflict (as defined by Marx), in the sense that, insofar as they may be said to operate, internal political polarizations do not simply follow the lines of cleavage dictated by the economic interests of particular classes. Indeed, there is no clear-cut dichotomization of economic interest itself. Our problem, then, may be stated as follows: First, in the newly emergent world community, is it inevitable that the cleavage between "have" and "have-not" nations must lead to polarization? Second, is this phenomenon susceptible to those integrative processes which have, in fact, operated within successfully industrialized societies? Since the earlier Marxist assumption that integration was impossible without violent revolution has proved invalid, is it not reasonable to discount the neo-Marxist assumption that "war"—whether military or economic—between the "imperialist" nations and the "people's democracies" is equally inevitable? If we accept this view, we must then attempt to identify the mechanisms which may facilitate this integrative process.

From a sociological point of view, the process of industrialization within national societies can be interpreted as most essentially one of structural differentiation. This concept, in turn, presupposes a common normative framework, primarily at the level of values. Our first concern, then, is whether there is a common value system which at least to some extent extends across the line which separates the contemporary antagonists. Despite the older idea of a generalized cultural relativity, and an attendant ideological conflict, if the problem is defined with sufficient care there seems to be little question of the validity of this hypothesis. In each case, economic productivity on the one hand and political power (including autonomy) on the other, are the foci of concern. In societies where the status of these value components cannot be based on historical tradition, something approaching their Western evaluation has emerged, in terms of a very general set of commitments, very broadly conceived. Clearly this is historically intimately related to the overwhelmingly predominant position of the West in the areas of productivity, power, and prestige, precisely during the 'imperialist" era. In other words, even in those societies where hostility toward the West has been particularly prominent, the social equivalent of a process of identification has taken place, which might be likened to "identification with the aggressor" or what Rostow has termed the "demonstration effect."[2] In addition, there have been varying kinds and degrees of reinforcement of the existing components of other value systems.[3]

Obviously, this can hardly be said to constitute a consensus on the valuation of basic goals or meanings. Rather, it represents an instrumental consensus on the valuation of capacities, at various levels of the organization of the society, to undertake whatever activities may be deemed most important to the welfare of that society. It involves the recognition that the economic productivity of the community and its political integration—the capacity to mobilize community resources for the pursuit of collective goals without external constraints—enable new levels of possible achievement in a variety of directions. There is a hierarchical element involved here as well, in that economic "opportunity" depends on political order in a more immediate sense than political order depends on the economic status of a society. Therefore, the normative ordering of the political sphere takes a certain precedence over the regulation of its economy. I consider this the primary reason for the fact that present major conflicts are conceptualized in political terms, in spite of the ideological prominence of economic considerations.

The achievement of autonomy is clearly central to this issue. Autonomy at the national level obviously removes certain constraints which are inherent in the status of colonial dependency. However, it also creates new problems, since the potentialities of "autarchic" self-sufficiency are clearly limited. Moreover, the smaller the unit, relative to the potential system of which it may be a part, the more limited are its potentialities. These limitations can be diminished only if relevant values are institutionalized in a community which is wider than the autonomous unit. In other words, parochial interests must be subordinated to those of a more extensive (and more efficient) system. Once this subordination has been

2. See Walt W. Rostow, *Theory of Economic Growth* (Cambridge: Cambridge University Press, 1960).
3. See Robert N. Bellah, *Tokugawa Religion* (Glencoe, Ill.: The Free Press, 1958).

institutionalized, it enables a higher level of value implementation within a framework of order than would be possible if each of the subsystems involved had to go it alone as radically autonomous units. Basically, polarization may be said to stem from this phenomenon.

Given the valuation of a major type of achievement, functioning, or whatever, greater gains can be attained in the short run by freezing the problem within a relatively restricted framework of order, and insulating the system of immediate concern from the interferences and potentialities of involvement in a wider system. To adopt an economic term, the tendency to exploit this possibility of short-run effectiveness may be called "protectionism."

In this sense, the alternative to protectionism involves the risks which are a concomitant to commitment to a higher-level, more extensive system of order. In large measure, this greatly enhanced level of risk may be attributed to competitive activities, which might otherwise be excluded. Understandably, there is strong motivation to avoid such competition by operating only within the limits of a less extensive system. On the other hand, however, the potentialities of higher value implementation are equally valid arguments in favor of the more extensive system in the long run, provided certain conditions of their implementation can be realized.

In any event, we cannot fail to recognize the presence of the primary ingredient of integration as opposed to polarization: common values obtain at a certain level of the general societal system. Moreover, it is a genuinely common, albeit incomplete, system of values at the level where main conflicts come to a head. However, values constitute only one component of institutionalized order; the problem, therefore, is to strengthen the other components to the point where they begin to outweigh the divisive elements.

With regard to values, at present polarization involves those parts of the world community which have reached certain levels of attainment, as opposed to those which have not yet achieved these levels of attainment. Thus, the have-nots are faced with the problem of catching up with the haves. With respect to political power, the Communist bloc has in fact caught up, at least to some extent. With special reference to the command of military force, it is now for all practical purposes the equal of the free world. However, there is a considerable gap between the West and the Communist bloc in the economic sphere, and this is particularly evident in the standard of living of their respective populations.

In summary, then, insofar as polarization is structured about national political units, the leadership of the have-not (Communist) bloc has achieved substantial equality with respect to one component of a larger system of productivity and political effectiveness, namely, with respect to military power. But it has accomplished this by following a protectionist policy, in that other potentialities—both internal and external—have been subordinated to a restricted goal. Internally, on an economic level, the Communist bloc has used authoritarian trusteeship to concentrate its resources on building up the ingredients of national power, at the expense of the living standards of the masses,[4] and it has denied subgroups within its society a share of the power which they could exercise in a pluralistic political system. Externally, it has become oriented to protective control within its own sphere of influence, in terms of the doctrine of absolute sovereignty. However, this dual protectionism has been counteracted on the non-Communist front by a strong measure of what might be called "defensive protectionism," which is not only military, but ideological and political in the large sense, and to some extent economic as well.

In terms of ideology, the greatest threat of Communist protectionism stems from its all-encompassing goal of definitive ultimate victory for the socialist cause (although Khrushchev's famous dictum, "We will bury you," has been interpreted to imply economic superiority rather than military conquest). The counter ideology, of course, postulates the necessity of stamping out the "Communist evil." Clearly, definitive victory for either side is not the only possible choice. We have another alternative, namely, the eventual integration of both sides—and of uncommitted units as well—in a wider system of order.

In addition to common values, there are three other essential components of institutionalized order.[5] The first of these comprises a set of minimum rules through which the implications of these values are defined in practice within the system. The second component is the structure of interests, which must be differentiated at appropriate levels. The third is an ideology in which the system of reference is defined as an empirical entity, rather than an ideology concerned merely with value patterns which define directions of desirability.

The existence of a common set of values may be considered the focal

4. See Alexander Gerschenkron, "Problems and Patterns of Russian Economic Development" in Cyril Black (ed.), *The Transformation of Russian Society: Aspects of Social Change Since 1861* (Cambridge, Mass.: Harvard University Press, 1960), pp. 42–72.

5. This is a scheme developed by the author in various publications. See in particular, "An Approach to the Sociology of Knowledge," *Proceedings of the Fourth World Congress of Sociology*, IV (1961).

point for change. Three principal factors concerning these values may have a bearing on the direction of policy. The first of these is the failure to recognize the existence of such a value consensus. This lack of awareness may be due to the fact that value commitments have come to be fused with the protectionist elements of respective ideologies and practical policies. Thus, the opposition contends that only a rigid formula of socialist organization is morally acceptable; on our own side, "free enterprise" is said to be the basic moral issue with which there can be no compromise.

Obviously, this is a fundamental and delicate problem. Essentially, the task of disentangling values from other components implies that many issues which have at some point been treated as fundamental moral issues must be downgraded. Once again, the internal party system may provide a helpful point of reference. A political party may, with justification, be committed to the particular policies it favors, which are in direct contrast to those advocated by the opposition. But, in a broader sense, the party system also implies the existence of a set of value commitments of a higher order which are shared by both parties; moreover, institutional considerations must supersede party differences. In the United States, for example, loyalty to the Constitution presumably supersedes party interests, no matter how important. Admittedly it is extremely difficult to maintain this perspective in the midst of a highly emotional ideological conflict. However, it is an easier task for those whose superior positions have been established than it is for groups in the process of achieving status. My first policy recommendation, therefore, is that every effort be made to promulgate carefully considered statements of value commitments which may provide a basis for consensus among both have and have-not nations. This would require that such statements be dissociated from the specific ideological position of either of the polarized camps.

In all probability, this will also require increasing recognition of the significant status of a rather large and growing neutral group of political units not firmly committed to either side. When a nation withdraws its potential support from the forces with which it has previously been allied, whether tacitly or overtly, it is inevitable that this action must permit—and promote—neutralism. And, of course, neutralism itself can fulfill a protectionist function, in that it may incorporate a cynical approach which may have the effect, whether deliberate or not, of playing one side off against the other. At the same time, under the proper conditions, neutral forces may evince more interest than would be possible for so-called committed factions in those elements of order which transcend polarization. Although this opinion requires substantial qualification, it would seem that in this frame of reference India has come closer to achieving the position of a moral leader than any other national unit, with the possible exception of Sweden. Here again, the intranational system may serve to point up the significance of neutralism. In successful two-party systems there is likely to be an important uncommitted sector of the electorate, an independent vote. As has been noted frequently, this uncommitted sector can serve as an important check on tendencies toward extremism on either side, since the effect of such extremism is to alienate the neutral groups, and hence to throw the balance in the direction of the opposition. In summary, then, we must clarify the nature of universally held value commitments, and promulgate their effective recognition. This in turn involves maximal dissociation from the defensive ideological positions and practical policies specific to either side. Admittedly, the accomplishment of such dissociation will depend on a high level of national self-criticism and self-discipline. The proper application of social science should prove valuable in this connection.

The third factor concerns the level at which value commitments are stated. Throughout this paper I have emphasized the fact that the Communist bloc and the nations of the free world do, in fact, share certain values in common. However, this should not be interpreted to imply that these common values have ultimate standing. At present, they might best be considered as relative; however, the repudiation of value absolutism does not imply the kind of relativity which would rule out the possibility of a common measure.

To illustrate, at one phase of Western history, religion (in the historic-formal sense) was the primary focus of political conflict. Beginning with the Thirty Years War, Western Christendom has undergone a gradual process, in the course of which religious tolerance has come to be institutionalized. I cannot describe the various stages of this process here, but I think my readers will agree that it has made its greatest progress in the United States, with denominational pluralism and the separation of church and state. In a sense, the recent election of a Roman Catholic to the presidency has put a seal on the pattern.

One of the notable facts about the world situation is the broad renunciation on the part of religious groups of any attempt to further their interests through proselytizing crusades. Even in the nineteenth century the degree to which Christian missions were politically implemented by Western interests requires careful examination. Whatever level of support did exist at that time has diminished notably since; nor is this development due entirely to anticolonialism. Conversely, acceptance of the Hindu or Buddhist religion by the West is not considered a prerequisite for the maintenance of friendly relations with India or Burma. Even Islam, the non-Christian religion which is most predisposed to militant proselytizing, has not stressed this. Many other issues are involved, but the significant fact is that current polarization has taken shape at secular political levels, with only one side making a point of militant secularism. There is a lesson to be learned here, namely, that it is somewhat dangerous to be dogmatic about the exact level at which a relatively stable value consensus can be attained. It is my opinion that this value consensus will vary with time and circumstances. In addition, I think an important parallel can be drawn between the present situation and the tensions which grew out of the Peace of Westphalia, at which time the formula *cuius regio, eius religio* was established, which provided for the institutionalization of religious liberty between political units, but not within them.

To return to our present concern with political liberty, and more specifically with the generalization of the implications of a value commitment to this end, it has been claimed vociferously that autonomy is the fundamental right of territorial political units. Why should such autonomy be confined to this level of social organization, and not be extended to liberties within the political unit? Indeed, I do not believe that such a limitation is really defensible as a value position on any terms; and in fact it is not defended by the Communists on those grounds, but on ideological grounds. Their argument, which stems from the Marxist concept of stage of development, is based on the allegation that the masses cannot be permitted freedom from the tutelage of the party until the final stage of the revolution. Presumably, the "withering away of the state" (and also of the party) will bring with it a level of individual freedom—both political and in other contexts as well—which will far exceed the freedom attained by bourgeois societies. We are all familiar with this theoretical approach; I have restated it here to bring into focus one essential point, namely, that freedom is valued, however distorted the means for attaining it. We can therefore conclude that political freedom at the associational and individual levels—subject, of course, to adequate institutional regulation—constitutes an essential component of the central value complex under discussion, and that the failure of the Communist camp to recognize this component in internal matters represents a basic ideological issue which merits special treatment. From a practical point of view, we are confronted with overwhelming evidence of the importance of emphasis on the existence of a value consensus. We can establish this fact effectively only if we enunciate these values directly and if we are particularly careful to avoid ideological commitments, which are specific to particular levels of society.

The Common Observance of Procedural Norms

In the present frame of reference, norms may be defined as patterns of desirable behavior which implement values in a variety of contexts, which are differentiated according to the particular functions of the agencies concerned and the specific situations in which they operate. The agencies of primary importance for purposes of this discussion are governments; the specific situation with which we are concerned is their relationship to each other, as this bears on the question of international order or, in its broadest sense, on the question of international law.

By way of preliminary comment, I would point out that there has been considerable development, and relatively good implementation, of norms in a wide variety of spheres other than those which involve the more direct relationships between governments. I refer to the regulation of international trade, to the conventions which enable the international circulation of persons and information and the like, and to the rules which have been established for conduct on the high seas, which is outside the territorial jurisdiction of any single government. There have been certain breaks in this legal order across the line of the iron curtain, of course, and recently censorship regulations and restrictions have been imposed on persons leaving the Union of South Africa. Nevertheless, this is a component of existing order which is not to be underestimated, and which is capable of gradual extension, without incurring major controversy in the process. One of the positive heritages of colonialism lies in the fact that European standards have been extended rather widely. Perhaps in this light the restrictive policies maintained by the Communist countries[6] may be viewed as a defensive maneuver. Thus, it becomes all the more important for the countries of the free world to maintain high standards in this respect. The McCarthy episode in American history was severely damaging precisely for this reason. The

6. For example, their refusal to participate in the international copyright convention.

continuing presence of such protectionist elements in the nations of the free world should be overhauled very thoroughly.[7]

However, our discussion of the more immediately relevant category of norms—those which concern direct relations between governments—must encompass the whole complex of diplomatic usage, protocol, and immunities. Of course, under extreme stress, these break down.

The organization of the United Nations (and I refer to the League of Nations as well) may be viewed as an extension of a trend with deep historical roots. The central characteristic of this trend is the attempt to establish consensus at the procedural level. That is, the institutionalization of procedures is considered the focal growing point of systems of order at the level of norms, a feature which is shared both by legal systems, in the more technical sense, and by political systems. This is not to say that the common observance of general procedural norms will inevitably obviate conflicts as to standards of fairness, or those which refer to opportunity or methods of treatment of the case. Of course, such a procedural system undercuts the absolutism of commitment to goals by introducing problems attendant to settlement or compromise. However, there are different kinds of compromise. For our purposes, the important type is the promotion of integration, in terms of a higher normative level.

Of course, in part, procedural systems also enable coercive sanctions to enforce their norms. But coercive sanctions constitute only one component of the sanction system, and our crucial concern here does not involve the identification of specific sanctions. Rather, I wish to underscore a more basic issue, namely, the acceptance of procedural obligations.

I believe that this willingness on the part of its members to abide by the rules of procedure constitutes the central significance of the United Nations. For, in this sense, it is the embodiment of the world community. Clearly, the range within which one might compare the United Nations to a court of law is still very limited (though it certainly should be capable of extension). But, short of a court of law, the United Nations may be likened to a forum in which the participants are obliged to provide for the public statement of a case, and to permit a hearing for the opposition's objections to the case, as stated. Participation at either level implies recognition of the legitimacy and power of judgment by world opinion.

7. For example, the proposed repeal of the Connally amendment to the World Court Statute.

It is to be expected that those who are deeply committed to particular goals will be extremely ambivalent about the acceptance of procedural norms, for such acceptance carries with it the risk of defeat without all-out struggle. In light of the reluctance of the Communist bloc to compromise, the behavior of Khrushchev and his cohorts in the early fall of 1960 was significant, not because of their attempts to disturb the orderly procedure of the United Nations, but because they deemed it so important to play the game. They demanded that structural changes be made in the procedural system and in fact threatened to walk out if these demands were not met. Quite apart from the validity of these demands, I believe that the fact that polarized conflict was brought within the framework of orderly procedure was of fundamental significance, and that every effort should be made to maintain and develop this pattern. Of course, this will require shrewd assessment of the degree to which pressure can be exerted without precipitating an explosion which might wreck the whole system. Despite the problem it may pose, the existence of a procedural forum to which there is an important degree of commitment on both sides constitutes one of our most precious assets.

The significance of the United Nations as a forum will emerge in sharper focus if its similarity to a democratic electoral system and a court of law is underscored. The latter does not guarantee a satisfactory outcome for either party, or even a just outcome, but rather a fair trial. The former does not guarantee that the outcome of an election will be good for the country from the point of view of either party, but rather that the incoming administration will have the adequate support of the electorate, according to procedural rules, and thereby be enabled to take the crucial step from the status of party leadership to leadership of the polity as a whole.

Obviously, then, reliance on procedural norms inevitably means increased risk to particular partisan goals. If we expect the Communist camp to submit their vital interests to procedural norms, we must, as a corollary, accept the possibility that adherence to these norms will result in the defeat of our own interests in many instances.

In other words, the development of new systems of norms of a higher order necessarily involves the institutionalization of a willingness to take risks relative to particular goals, even very important goals. Although these risks can be confined with certain limits, they cannot be eliminated entirely. Nevertheless, this is the price we must pay for increased freedom, for the resolution of the impasse which results from the protectionist policies of antagonistic elements.[8]

The Pluralistic Structure of Interests

The third basic component of the institutionalization of a new system of order derives from the structure of what I referred to earlier as "interests." My speculations regarding this component bear a close relationship to the preceding discussion of the role of procedural norms. However, other considerations are involved as well. We are concerned here with the level of differentiation within the system of interests, with the so-called problem of pluralism.[9]

The core of the problem is contained in one facet of the contrast between the Communist system, as it operates within the current climate of polarization, and the free world. I refer to the monolithic tendency of the Communist system, that is, its tendency to include as many aspects as possible of the society in question within a single system of highly centralized control, and hence to conceive of policy as an all or-none commitment to complete success, as defined in terms of its broad goals, rather than as a commitment to attempt to integrate differentiated subinterests either internally or externally. The applicability of this definition to a national society, such as the Soviet Union, and particularly with regard to its relationship with other members of the Communist bloc, requires extensive qualification. Nevertheless, when one considers the quality of the international coalition of the free nations, whose solidarity is continually in question, the difference is striking. Furthermore, in this sense, the liberal societies are far more pluralistic internally, in ways which are undoubtedly familiar to the reader.

One of the basic attributes of a political system which has achieved a minimum level of stability is its capacity to resolve conflicts of interest; this in turn involves the structure of the system of interests. Typically, situations which require political decision-making are continually shifting. Policy issues hinge on a particular element, specific to a given situation; hence, issues change as a consequence of situational change.

In such a system, a monolithic bloc which is capable of staking its

8. An excellent example of a suggestion for a procedural device outside the framework of the United Nations is T. C. Schelling's proposal of a "special surveillance force."
9. See William Kornhauser, *The Politics of Mass Society* (Glencoe, Ill.: The Free Press, 1959), and my review article in *World Politics* (October, 1960).

whole position on a particular issue, which has grown out of a specific situation, has a built-in short-run advantage because it can afford to apply a kind of pressure that less monolithic systems cannot risk. But this short-run advantage is gained at the expense of an element of instability in the large system which is essentially a feature of rigidity, on the one hand, and of an unreadiness to contemplate drastic change, with the knowledge that such change may cause the breakdown of the whole system, on the other.

Polarization in a stable two-party system does not constitute a fundamental threat because any such disruptive tendency is counteracted by an underlying structure of pluralistic, and hence cross-cutting, solidarities. As a function of shifting situations which need to be dealt with, different balances among these structured interests can be mobilized; in other words, the sponsorship and motivation of a party are not constant, but vary, within limits, according to the situation. Interest components are enfranchised in that they have a realistic choice among a variety of alternatives to which they can lend their support. Consequently, it is exceedingly important to distinguish between polarization between monolithic blocs and polarization within a pluralistic infrastructure.

The cold war might be likened to the former type of polarization. On the one hand, the goal of the Communists is limited to the achievement of equal status. At the same time, however, in line with their deep ambivalence, they claim the right to achieve complete supremacy over the other camp. If this radical polarization is to be mitigated, our major task is to identify the process which might enable a shift in the direction of the pluralistic type of polarization, as conceptualized by the party system, and to determine the extent to which such a shift is in fact in progress.

In such a system issues must be dealt with one at a time, without too frequently posing broad questions of "confidence." Of course, in certain situations, it is possible for pluralization to operate directly between the principal protagonists. For example, in the field of cultural exchange, there has been a genuine mutual appreciation of the achievements of both sides in the natural sciences and the arts. In this area, solidarity stems from a devotion to, and recognition of, common standards. Quite possibly, the use of scientific experts to thresh out the technical problems of nuclear arms inspection would constitute a valuable application of this principle.

However, in all probability, it is with respect to pluralism that the existence of a substantial neutral bloc is most important. The process of decision-making in the world community requires that particular emphasis be placed on the expectation that the combinations in favor of one policy will differ from those which favor another. For example, it is inevitable that a major unit, such as the United States, will find itself allied with certain nations with respect to certain issues, and that these same allies may become their opponents on other issues. Ultimatums ("you are either for or against us all along the line") must be avoided at all costs. The direction of development should be pluralistic in this sense. To paraphrase the wording used by one important group of students of internal political process, the flexibility essential to the orderly adaptation of a system to variant situations involves the phenomenon of "cross-pressuring"; that is, it requires the participation of groups which have predilections in either of two alternative directions, and with respect to which the balance of interest may be expected to shift.[10]

What I have called the pluralistic structure of interests is an important ingredient of stability because it fragments the pressures which can influence the system at any one political decision point. In other words, a strong vested interest in the functioning of the larger system, as well as normative commitments, will serve to prevent untenable situations which require an ultimate and irreversible decision—in the extreme case, a declaration of war. Clearly, this implies the acceptance of the risk which is a concomitant of the subservience of individual interests to the procedural system.

One aspect of the significance of mutual nuclear deterrence is particularly relevant at this point. Nuclear war, with all of its implications of destruction for both sides, may well be the price to be paid for pressing a partisan case to the limit, so to speak. When relatively extreme measures are under consideration, a process does seem to obtain wherein the costs are counted—however subtle this process may be. Policy is thus deflected away from impulsive ultimatums to more particularized issues. This process can therefore be considered to represent one factor operating in the direction of the fragmentation which favors a pluralistic structure of interests. Moreover, it is applicable to neutral nations as well, in that the efforts on the part of the major parties to gain the allegiance of neutrals lead to a sort of stalemate which, in turn, prevents them from pushing coercive threats to extremes. Thus, competition is oriented

10. See Bernard Berelson, Paul F. Lazarsfeld, and William McPhee, *Voting: A Study of Opinion Formation in a Presidential Campaign* (Chicago: University of Chicago Press, 1954).

toward the advantages of alliance for neutral nations, rather than threats of the dire consequences of political or ideological divergence.

The Positive Function of Ideology

For present purposes, ideology refers to the formulation of an evaluative, empirical, cognitive picture of the system in question, including the form this system may possibly take in the future. It is prerequisite of stable institutionalization that there exist a strong correlation between the implications of the value system and the diagnosis of the empirical system. Moreover, those processes which will enable a closer relationship between the empirical system and value requirements must be clearly envisioned.[11]

Those who tend to treat realistic interests as the primary basis of conflict also tend to downgrade ideology to the status of an epiphenomenon which can safely be ignored. While in some respects the Communist camp appears to assert this view with great vehemence, at the same time, in another context, they insist with equal vehemence on the importance of maintaining ideological correctness. However, among the "free" nations, too, there is a school of so-called realists who profess to believe that ideology is of little consequence. In my opinion, this constitutes a serious error.

Ideology has a dual functional significance. On the one hand, it is an educational mechanism. By enlisting the fervor which accompanies a sense of mission, it greatly facilitates the process of commitment which is an essential ingredient of institutionalization. With respect to the Communists, this involves institutionalization of the values described above, which may be summarized as the trend toward modernization. That is, a radical break with the reactionary past of the societies in the enemy camp is emphasized and dramatized. Indeed, Lenin advocated the extension of this function well beyond the earlier Marxist position, in that he stressed the importance of moving directly from what Marxists called feudalism to socialism, and omitting the intermediate bourgeois capitalism stage. In this light, Communist ideology may be interpreted as a statement of the symbolic values of modernization in which symbolic, covert gestures of reconciliation are made toward both the past and the future, within the framework of expected conflict.

The first of these gestures involves the attempt to preserve the

11. See Parsons, "An Approach to the Sociology of Knowledge," *op. cit.*

integrity of the premodern system; and I believe that this is the primary significance of the symbol, socialism. In essence, the purpose of this device is to assure us that the process of differentiation which is inherent in modernization need not jeopardize the integrity of preindustrial community solidarity, provided the transition is carried out in such a way as to prevent the aggressive maneuvers of private interests, which are not bound by loyalty to such a community. Thus, this mechanism may be considered to facilitate recognition and acceptance of the risk-taking necessary for industrialization by asserting that these risks are limited to spheres of a lower order.

I would further interpret this aspect of Communist ideology as primarily defensive or protectionist in character, and hence to apply in a context which is not directly relevant to the polarized conflict. It is also very closely associated with basic anxieties about political democracy, since presumably this democracy would weaken preventive control over centrifugal tendencies in the community. The obverse of this, of course, is the defensive component of the counter-ideology, that is, the compulsive attachment to the free-enterprise formula, the fear of "creeping socialism," and the tendency to invoke authoritarian political measures, allegedly in order to safeguard our freedom.

The second component of the dual function of ideology concerns the inferior status of the rising elements, relative to those elements which are already well established. In a psychological sense, the attitude of these rising elements might be viewed as defensive; in our own frame of reference, it might be considered a variation of protectionism. Here, precisely because the core elements of the free world have already at least partially achieved the goals to which the developing nations aspire, there is a strong motivation to derogate these attainments. In ideological terms, the aim of these underdeveloped nations is not to achieve parity, but to supplant certain well-established elements of the "superior" society, for example, to substitute socialism for capitalism. The primary function of ideology in this instance is to emphasize the unique character of the socialist contribution. One rather oversimplified solution immediately comes to mind, namely, the use of opposition to maximize motivation, to define achievement as victory rather than mere goal attainment. Of course, here again the reaction of the counterideology must be considered, that is, the automatic tendency to define the success of those developing societies which are Communistically oriented as a defeat for the free world.

The direction of desirable change seems clear: ideological stresses must be minimized; those aspects of the situation which demonstrate an interest in order which transcends polarity must be underscored. One of the main themes here concerns those features which all industrial societies share in common, in contrast with previous economic and social organizations. An exposition of such features would necessarily focus on the standard of living of the masses—for obvious reasons a very sensitive area for the Communists. The features of social organization as such, particularly the differentiation of collectivities and roles, would constitute another area of focus. Still another concerns common elements at the cultural level, notably science and the arts.

This discussion has been based on an important assumption, which may seem rather vulnerable at this point. I refer to the assumption that one side has achieved a position of relative superiority in relation to the important values. The Communist goals, in terms of catching up and surpassing, may be taken as tacit proof of the validity of this assumption; however, on the other hand, their vehement assertions of the superiority of socialism and their irrational accusations of imperialism would appear to deny such gains. Thus, we must consider whether there is any prospect of dissociating these values from partisan considerations. If no such possibility exists, we must accept the fact that nonpartisanship (as opposed to the mutual unmasking of ideological biases) cannot be transcended.

The fact that common values exist which have deep roots in the great traditions of all Western culture is one focus of leverage for such dissociation. Procedural norms and the pluralistic differentiation of interests constitute mechanisms which operate in the same direction. And we have another very important resource, namely, the contribution of social science. Insofar as the development of knowledge in this sphere is genuine and not spurious, it involves the institutionalization of norms of technical competence and genuine objectivity. To date, this process has been slow, halting, and difficult, but significant progress has been made and, hopefully, will continue in the future. On the basis of a realistic assessment of the current status of industrial societies and possible future trends of development, we can detect an element of common ground. Obviously, this mechanism will not produce dramatic consequences in immediate crisis situations, but its long-run importance should not be underestimated.[12]

12. At the International Sociological Congress at Stresa, Italy, in September, 1959, the leader of the Soviet Delegation, Professor P. N. Fedosev, stated that his colleagues proposed to demonstrate the superiority of socialism by empirical research. This consti-

Summary and Conclusion

The foregoing discussion may be summarized in a series of propositions:

1. Polarization, which is the salient characteristic of the world community at present, constitutes the primary threat to peace. However, at the same tme, polarization attests to the existence of a world community and thus presents certain opportunities for the development of a more stable order within that community.

2. An effective two-party system within a relatively stable national polity constitutes a theoretical model which, while it is far from precisely applicable, is sufficiently similar to world bipolarity to provide significant clues as to methods for achieving world order.

3. The formulation of common value commitments which transcend partisan differences is one of the most important prerequisites of international order. It is my contention that, at a certain level, such a base does in fact exist in the world community, specifically with regard to the importance attached to economic development and political autonomy. This basic uniformity needs to be clearly asserted in contexts which can be dissociated from divisive ideological particularities.

4. As they are presently conceived, value concepts are too general to influence political behavior. They must be spelled out in concrete terms. Moreover, it is particularly important that they be defined in terms of norms at the level of the procedures through which they can best be implemented. A consent on the part of the opposing factions to adhere to the rules of procedure implies the assumption of risk that one's particular goal may be jeopardized, that one's adversary may be victorious with respect to particular issues. Obviously, the stronger the commitment to a particular goal, the more difficult it will become to accept this procedural risk. However, there are considerable compensations for the acceptance of such risks; these risks enable gains which would be prohibited, or at least greatly deterred, by a go-it-alone policy. At many different points in the development of social structures, this has been accomplished by processes of differentiation. It can be promoted deliberately in many ways.

5. One of the main threats to stability stems from the monolithic concentration of interests on partisan all-or-none goal striving. The mitigation of this threat is, in part, dependent on the differentiation of

---

tutes submitting one's case to an objective judgment, that of competent peers, with the implicit possibility that one may be shown to be wrong. It is another version of the supercession of intransigent assertion of particular goal-commitments, by acceptance of a procedural mechanism, including exposure to the risks inherent in such a system.

interests in a pluralistic direction, so that a sufficiently important proportion will cut across the lines of partisan division. Procedural mechanisms tend to favor this process of differentiation and hence to increase pluralism. In this connection, the existence of sufficiently strong neutral elements which can form particularized ties in either direction is important. Under the proper conditions, neutralism should not be deplored, but welcomed.

6. Ideology is essentially a defensive or protective mechanism. However, it does have important positive functions in a world community, in that it cushions the inevitable severe strains which are inherent in the process of modernization. However, its tendency toward intransigence must be counteracted. This may be accomplished by dissociating value consensus from ideological difference, on the one hand, and, on the other hand, by objective scientific diagnosis of empirical situations, which tend to be presented in selected and distorted versions in ideological discussion.

7. Progress toward institutionalizing the normative framework of the world community, and the attendant web of pluralistic interests, depends on a balanced combination of various measures which are in accord with inherent trends, rather than one dramatic set of measures. Acute crises may be handled by single dramatic measures, but this balance is essential to our prospects over the long term.

It is my opinion, therefore, that Western policy should include each of the four components formulated in propositions 3 through 6 above. These include, first, the assertion of common values in ways which minimize the self-righteous implication that only we are true to these values, that our opponents are not; second, the promotion of procedural innovations, even though by so doing we are likely to suffer defeat on particular issues; third, the promotion of those opportunities which are likely to develop ties of solidarity both with iron curtain countries on specific divergent issues, and, above all, with neutral nations, even though they may be dealing simultaneously with the opposition in regard to other issues; and, finally, the use of social science to develop the most competent analyses possible at the present state of our knowledge of social and political systems throughout the world.

The hypothesis put forth in this paper lacks specificity because it stresses the balance between a plurality of factors. Moreover, it must be regarded as a preliminary sketch, rather than the sum of a carefully developed set of proposals. I have stated repeatedly that under the proper conditions a given factor, such as the establishment of procedural norms.

or the pluralization of interests through the appeal to neutral elements, might be expected to work in the desired direction. A few suggestions as to these "proper conditions" have been delineated in the course of the discussion. But space forbids a full description of such conditions at the desired level of concreteness. (To a great extent, they probably are not known and can only be elucidated through further research.) In conclusion, then, the foregoing discussion does not purport to provide an infallible prescription for effective foreign policy. Rather, it purports to outline a theoretical framework within which, given the proper specification, a type of policy which has a better chance for success could be formulated. The careful delineation of such a policy would require a great deal of theoretical and empirical groundwork, which would obviously extend far beyond the limits of this paper.

CHAPTER 15

Evolutionary Universals in Society

Although this last paper is of a somewhat different character from the first three in Part IV; it may be said to belong with them and, in a sense, to tie together all the papers in the book. It is an attempt to formulate one major theme in the theory of societal evolution, resting on the concept of generalized adaptation, which is so central to the theory of organic evolution that it should be considered, I think, part of all evolutionary theory. The main concern is with a few complexes of social structure the emergence of which has fundamental significance for a society's advance beyond its stage of evolution at the time of their emergence. Specialized modes of cultural legitimation of societal order and social stratification are taken to be especially important for the primary steps beyond the primitive level, and four complexes, in fuller development, are especially important as underlying the modern type of society, namely, a differentiated, predominantly universalistic legal system, money and markets, "bureaucratic" organization, and the pattern of democratic association with special reference to its development at the level of government in large-scale societies.

The paper grew out of a seminar in the Theory of Social Evolution in which I collaborated with Robert N. Bellah and S. N. Eisenstadt (Visiting Professor at M.I.T. in the spring term of 1962–63, a fraction of whose time was borrowed by Harvard for the seminar). The three of us each submitted papers growing out of the seminar to the *American Sociological Review*. They were published together in the issue of June, 1964; the other papers were, Bellah's "Religious Evolution" and Eisenstadt's "Social Change, Differentiation, and Evolution." In my own work the most important closely related writings are the two small volumes in the *Foundations of Modern Sociology* Series, edited by Alex Inkeles and published by Prentice-Hall. These are entitled: *Societies, Evolutionary and Comparative Perspectives* (1966) and *The System of Modern Societies* (1968).

"Evolutionary Universals in Society" reprinted from American Sociological Review, Vol. 29, No. 3 (June, 1964).

$\mathcal{S}$LOWLY and somewhat inarticulately, emphasis in both socio-logical and anthropological quarters is shifting from a studied disinterest in problems of social and cultural evolution to a "new relativity" that relates its universals to an evolutionary framework.

The older perspectives insisted that social and cultural systems are made up of indefinitely numerous discrete "traits," that "cultures" are totally separate, or that certain broad "human" universals, like language and the incest taboo, should be emphasized. Varied as they are, these emphases have in common the fact that they divert attention from spe-cific *continuities* in patterns of social change, so that either traits or culture types must be treated as discretely unique and basically uncon-nected, and a pattern, to be considered universal, must be equally im-portant to *all* societies and cultures. Despite their ostentatious repudiation of "culture-boundness," these perspectives have been conspicuously anthropocentric in setting off problems of man's modes of life so sharply from questions of continuity with the rest of the organic world. But the emphasis on human universals has also had a kind of "levelling" in-fluence, tending to restrict attention to what is generally and essentially human, without considering gradations within the human category.

The "new relativity" removes this barrier and tries to consider human ways in direct continuity with the sub-human. It assumes that the watershed between sub-human and human does not mark a cessation of developmental change, but rather a stage in a long process that begins with many pre-human phases and continues through that watershed into our own time, and beyond. Granting a wide range of variability of types at all stages, it assumes that levels of evolutionary advancement may be empirically specified for the human as well as the pre-human phases.

Evolutionary Universals

I shall designate as an evolutionary universal any organizational development sufficiently important to further evolution that, rather than emerging only once, it is likely to be "hit upon" by various systems oper-ating under different conditions.

In the organic world, vision is a good example of an evolutionary universal. Because it mediates the input of organized information from the organism's environment, and because it deals with both the most distant and the widest range of information sources, vision is the most generalized mechanism of sensory information. It therefore has the greatest potential significance for adaptation of the organism to its environment.

The evidence is that vision has not been a "one shot" invention in organic evolution, but has evolved independently in three different phyla —the molluscs, the insects, and the vertebrates. A particularly interesting feature of this case is that, while the visual organs in the three groups are anatomically quite different and present no evolutionary continuity, biochemically all use the same mechanism involving Vitamin A, though there is no evidence that it was not independently "hit upon" three times.[1] Vision, whatever its mechanisms, seems to be a genuine prerequisite of *all* the higher levels of organic evolution. It has been lost only by very particular groups like the bats, which have not subsequently given rise to important evolutionary developments.

With reference to man and his biological potential for social and cultural evolution, two familiar evolutionary universals may be cited, namely the hands and the brain. The human hand is, of course, the primordial general-purpose tool. The combination of four mobile fingers and an opposable thumb enables it to perform an enormous variety of operations—grasping, holding, and manipulating many kinds of objects. Its location at the end of an arm with mobile joints allows it to be maneuvered into many positions. Finally, the pairing of the arm-hand organs much more than doubles the capacity of each one because it permits cooperation and a complex division of labor between them.

It is worth noting that the development of the hands and arms has been bought at a heavy cost in locomotion: man on his two legs cannot compete in speed and maneuverability with the faster four-legged species. Man, however, uses his hands for such a wide range of behavior impossible for handless species that the loss is far more than compensated. He can, for instance, protect himself with weapons instead of running away.

The human brain is less nearly unique than the hand, but its advantages over the brains of even anthropoids is so great that it is man's most distinctive organ, the most important single source of human capacity. Not only is it the primary organ for controlling complex operations, notably manual skills, and coordinating visual and auditory information, but above all it is the organic basis of the capacity to learn and manipu-

1. George Wald, "Life and Light," *Scientific American*, 201 (October, 1959), pp. 92–108.

late symbols. Hence it is the organic foundation of culture. Interestingly, this development too is bought at the sacrifice of immediate adaptive advantages. For example the brain occupies so much of the head that the jaws are much less effective than in other mammalian species—but this too is compensated for by the hands. And the large brain is partly responsible for the long period of infantile dependency because the child must learn such a large factor of its effective behavior. Hence the burden of infant care and socialization is far higher for man than for any other species.

With these organic examples in mind, the conception of an evolutionary universal may be developed more fully. It should, I suggest, be formulated with reference to the concept of adaptation, which has been so fundamental to the theory of evolution since Darwin. Clearly, adaptation should mean, not merely passive "adjustment" to environmental conditions, but rather the capacity of a living system[2] to cope with its environment. This capacity includes an active concern with mastery, or the ability to change the environment to meet the needs of the system, as well as an ability to survive in the face of unalterable features. Hence the capacity to cope with broad *ranges* of environmental factors, through adjustment or active control, or both, is crucial. Finally, a very critical point is the capacity to cope with unstable relations between system and environment, and hence with *uncertainty*. Instability here refers both to predictable variations, such as the cycle of the seasons, and to unpredictable variations, such as the sudden appearance of a dangerous predator.

An evolutionary universal, then, is a complex of structures and associated processes the development of which so increases the long-run adaptive capacity of living systems in a given class that only systems that develop the complex can attain certain higher levels of general adaptive capacity. This criterion, derived from the famous principle of natural selection, requires one major explicit qualification. The relatively disadvantaged system not developing a new universal need not be condemned to extinction. Thus some species representing all levels of organic evolution survive today—from the unicellular organisms up. The surviving lower types, however, stand in a variety of different relations to the higher. Some occupy special "niches" within which they live with limited scope, others stand in symbiotic relations to higher systems.

2. Note that the species rather than the individual organism is the major system of reference here. See George Gaylord Simpson, *The Meaning of Evolution* (New Haven: Yale University Press, 1950).

They are not, by and large, major threats to the continued existence of the evolutionary higher systems. Thus, though infectious diseases constitute a serious problem for many, bacteria are not likely to replace man as the dominant organic category, and man is symbiotically dependent on many bacterial species.

Two distinctions should be made here, because they apply most generally and throughout. The first is between the impact of an innovation when it is *first* introduced in a given species or society, and its importance as a continuing component of the system. Certain evolutionary universals in the social world, to be discussed below, initially provide their societies with major adaptive advantages over societies not developing them. Their introduction and institutionalization have, to be sure, often been attended with severe dislocations of the previous social organization, sometimes resulting in short-run losses in adaptation. Once institutionalized, however, they tend to become essential parts of later societies in the relevant lines of *development* and are seldom eliminated except by regression. But, as the system undergoes further evolution, universals are apt to generate major changes of their own, generally by developing more complex structures.

— Unlike biological genes, cultural patterns are subject to "diffusion." Hence, for the cultural level, it is necessary to add a second distinction, between the conditions under which an adaptive advantage can develop for the first time, and those favoring its adoption from a source in which it is already established.

Prerequisites of the Evolution of Culture and Society

From his distinctive organic endowment and from his capacity for and ultimate dependence on generalized learning, man derives his unique ability to create and transmit *culture*. To quote the biologist Alfred Emerson, within a major sphere of man's adaptation, the "gene" has been replaced by the "symbol."[3] Hence, it is not only the genetic constitution of the species that determines the "needs" confronting the environment, but this constitution *plus* the cultural tradition. A set of "normative expectations" pertaining to man's relation to his environment delineates the ways in which adaptation should be developed and extended. Within the relevant range, cultural innovations, especially

3. Alfred Emerson, "Homeostasis and Comparison of Systems" in Roy R. Grinker, ed., *Toward a Unified Theory of Behavior* (New York: Basic Books, 1956).

definitions of what man's life *ought* to be, thus replace Darwinian variations in genetic constitution.

Cultural "patterns" or orientations however, do not implement themselves. Properly conceived in their most fundamental aspect as "religious," they must be articulated with the environment in ways that make
effective adaptation possible. I am inclined to treat the entire orientational aspect of culture itself, in the simplest, least evolved forms, as
directly synonymous with *religion*.[4] But since a cultural system—never
any more an individual matter than a genetic pattern—is shared among
a plurality of individuals, mechanisms of *communication* must exist to
mediate this sharing. The fundamental evolutionary universal here is
language: no concrete human group lacks it. Neither communication
nor the learning processes that make it possible, however, is conceivable
without determinately organized relations among those who teach and
learn and communicate.

The evolutionary origin of *social organization* seems to be kinship.
In an evolutionary sense it is an extension of the mammalian system of
bisexual reproduction. The imperative of socialization is of course a
central corollary of culture, as is the need to establish a viable social system to "carry" the culture. From one viewpoint, the core of the kinship
system is the incest taboo, or, more generally, the rules of exogamy and
endogamy structuring relations of descent, affinity, and residence. Finally, since the cultural level of action implies the use of brain, hands, and
other organs in actively coping with the physical environment, we may
say that culture implies the existence of technology, which is, in its most
undifferentiated form, a synthesis of empirical knowledge and practical
techniques.

These four features of even the simplest action system—"religion,"
communication with language, social organization through kinship, and
technology—may be regarded as an integrated set of evolutionary universals at even the earliest human level. No known human society has
existed without *all* four in relatively definite relations to each other. In
fact, their presence constitutes the very minimum that may be said to
mark a society as truly human.

Systematic relations exist not only among these four elements themselves, but between them and the more general framework of biological
evolution. Technology clearly is the primary focus of the organization of
the adaptive relations of the human system to its physical *environment*.

4. Cf. Emile Durkheim, *The Elementary Forms of the Religious Life* (London: Allen
and Unwin, 1915).

Kinship is the social extension of the individual *organism's* basic articulation to the species through bisexual reproduction. But, through plasticity and the importance of learning, cultural and symbolic communications are integral to the human level of individual *personality* organization. *Social* relations among personalities, to be distinctively human, must be mediated by linguistic communication. Finally, the main *cultural patterns* that regulate the social, psychological, and organic levels of the total system of action are embodied (the more primitive the system, the more exclusively so) in the religious tradition, the focus of the use of symbolization to control the variety of conditions to which a human system is exposed.

Social Stratification

Two evolutionary universals are closely interrelated in the process of "breaking out" of what may be called the "primitive" stage of societal evolution. These are the development of a well-marked system of social stratification, and that of a system of explicit cultural legitimation of differentiated societal functions, preeminently the political function, independent of kinship. The two are closely connected, but I am inclined to think that stratification comes first and is a condition of legitimation of political function.

The key to the evolutionary importance of stratification lies in the role in primitive societies of *ascription* of social status to criteria of biological relatedness. The kinship nexus of social organization is intrinsically a "seamless web" of relationships which, in and of itself, contains no principle of boundedness for the system as distinguished from certain subgroups within it. Probably the earliest and most important basis of boundedness is the political criterion of territorial jurisdiction. But the economic problem of articulation with the environment, contingent on kinship as well as other groups, is also prominent in primitive societies. In the first instance this is structured primarily through place of residence, which becomes increasingly important as technological development, notably of "settled agriculture," puts a premium on definiteness and permanence of location.

For present purposes, I assume that in the society we are discussing, the population occupying a territorial area is generally endogamous, with marriage of its members to those of other territorial groups being, if it occurs, somehow exceptional, and not systematically organized.[5] Given a presumptively endogamous territorial community, comprising a plurality of purely local groups, certain general processes of internal differentiation of the society can be explained. One aspect of this tends to be a prestige difference between central or "senior" lineage groups and "cadet" groups, whether or not the differentiation is on the basis of birth.[6] Quite generally, the latter must accept less advantageous bases of subsistence, including place of residence, than the former. At least this is apt to be the case where the residence groups become foci for the control of resources and as such are sharply differentiated from more inclusive political groupings. Thus a second aspect of an increased level of functional differentiation among the structures of the society tends to be involved.

Typically, I think, kinship status, in terms of both descent criteria and relative prestige of marriage opportunities is highly correlated with relative economic advantage and political power. This is to say that, under the conditions postulated, a tendency toward *vertical* differentiation of the society as a system overrides the pressure of the seamless web of kinship to equalize the status of all units of equivalent *kinship* character. This tendency is the product of two converging forces.

On the one hand, relative advantages are differentiated: members of cadet lineages, the kinship units with lesser claims to preferment, are "forced" into peripheral positions. They move to less advantaged residential locations and accept less productive economic resources, and they are not in a position to counteract these disadvantages by the use of political power.[7]

On the other hand, the society as a system gains functional advantages by concentrating responsibility for certain functions. This concentration focuses in two areas, analytically, the political and the religious. First, the increased complexity of a society that has grown in population

5. See W. Lloyd Warner, *A Black Civilization*, 2nd ed. (New York: Harper, 1958), for an analysis showing that such boundedness can be problematic.
6. This analysis has been suggested in part by Charles Ackerman who bases himself on a variety of the recent studies of kinship systems, but, perhaps, particularly on Rodney Needham's studies of the Purums, *Structure and Sentiment* (Chicago: University of Chicago Press, 1960).
7. I am putting forward this set of differentiating factors as an ideal type. Of course, in many particular cases they may not all operate together. For example, it may frequently happen that the outer lands to which cadet lineages move are more productive than the old ones. The net effect of these discrepancies is probably a tendency toward diversity of lines of development rather than the extinction of the main one sketched here. Indeed we can go farther and say that unless this advantage of economic resources comes to be combined with such structural advantages as incorporation in a stratification system it will not lead to further evolutionary developments.

and probably territory and has become differentiated in status terms raises more difficult problems of internal order, e.g., controlling violence, upholding property and marriage rules, etc., and of defense against encroachment from outside. Second, a cultural tradition very close to both the details of everyday life and the interests and solidarities of particular groups is put under strain by increasing size and diversity. There is, then, pressure to centralize both responsibility for the symbolic systems, especially the religious, and authority in collective processes, and to redefine them in the direction of greater generality.

For the present argument, I assume that the tendencies to centralize political and religious responsibility need not be clearly differentiated in any immediate situation. The main point is that the differentiation of groups relative to an advantage-disadvantage axis tends to converge with the functional "need" for centralization of responsibility. Since responsibility and prestige seem to be inherently related in a system of institutionalized expectations, the advantaged group tends to assume, or have ascribed to it, the centralized responsibilities. It should be clear that the problem does not concern the balance between services to others and benefits accruing to the advantaged group, but the convergence of *both* sets of forces tending to the same primary structural outcome.

The development of written language can become a fundamental accelerating factor in this process, because in the nature of the case literacy cannot immediately be extended to total adult populations, and yet it confers enormous adaptive advantages. It also has a tendency to favor cultural or religious elements over the political.[8]

The crucial step in the development of a stratification system occurs when important elements in the population assume the prerogatives and functions of higher status and, at least by implication, exclude all other elements. This creates an "upper," a "leading" or, possibly, a "ruling" class set over against the "mass" of the population. Given early, or, indeed, not so early conditions, it is inevitable that membership in this upper class is primarily if not entirely based on kinship status. Thus, an individual military or other leader may go far toward establishing an important criterion of status, but in doing so he elevates the status of his lineage. He cannot dissociate his relatives from his own success, even presuming he would wish to.

Stratification in the present sense, then, is the differentiation of the population on a prestige scale of kinship units such that the distinctions

8. See Talcott Parsons, *Societies: Comparative and Evolutionary Perspectives* (Englewood Cliffs, N.J.: Prentice-Hall, 1966).

among such units, or classes of them, become hereditary to an important degree. There are reasons to assume that the early tendency, which may be repeated, leads to a *two*-class system. The most important means of consolidating such a system is upper-class endogamy. Since this repeats the primary principle which, along with territoriality, delineates the boundaries of early societies, the upper class constitutes a kind of subsociety. It is not a class, however, unless its counterpart, the lower class, is clearly included in the *same* societal community.

From this "primordial" two class system there are various possibilities for evolutionary change. Probably the most important leads to a four-class system.[9] This is based on the development of urban communities in which political-administrative functions, centralized religious and other cultural activities, and territorially specialized economic action are carried on. Thus, generalized "centers" of higher-order activity emerge, but the imperatives of social organization require that these centers, as local communities—including, for example, "provincial" centers—cannot be inhabited exclusively by upper-class people. Hence the urban upper class tends to be differentiated from the rural upper class,[10] and the urban from the rural lower class. When this occurs there is no longer a linear rank-order of classes. But so long as hereditary kinship status is a primary determinant of the individual's access to "advantages," we may speak of a stratified society; beyond the lowest level of complexity, every society is stratified.

Diffuse as its significance is, stratification is an *evolutionary* universal because the most primitive societies are not in the present sense stratified, but, beyond them, it is on two principal counts a prerequisite of a very wide range of further advances. First, what I have called a "prestige" position is a generalized prerequisite of responsible concentration of leadership. With few exceptions, those who lack a sufficiently "established" position cannot afford to "stick their necks out" in taking the responsibility for important changes. The second count concerns the availability of resources for implementing innovations. The dominance of kinship in social organization is inseparably connected with rigidity. People do what they are required to do by virtue of their kinship status. To whatever degree kinship is the basis of solidarity *within* an upper class, closure of that class by endogamy precludes kinship from being the

9. Cf. Gideon Sjoberg, *The Preindustrial City* (Glencoe, Ill.: The Free Press, 1960), Chapter 5.
10. The upper class will be primarily rural in societies that take a more or less feudal direction.

basis of upper-class claims on the services and other resources of the lower groups. So long as the latter are genuinely within the same society, which implies solidarity across the class line, relations of mutual usefulness, (e.g., patron-client relationships across class lines) on non-kin bases are possible—opening the door to universalistic definitions of merit as well as providing the upper groups with the resources to pursue their own advantages.

Social stratification in its initial development may thus be regarded as one primary condition of releasing the process of social evolution from the obstacles posed by ascription. The strong emphasis on kinship in much of the sociological literature on stratification tends to obscure the fact that the new mobility made possible by stratification is due primarily to such breaks in kinship ascription as that across class lines.

Stratification, of course, remains a major structural feature of subsequent societies and takes a wide variety of forms in their evolution. Since the general process of evolutionary change introduces a series of lines of differentiation on several bases, it is unlikely that a single simple prestige order will adequately represent the stratification system in more advanced societies. The "bourgeois" in the late European Middle Ages cannot be described simply as a "middle" class standing between the predominantly rural "feudal" classes and the peasantry. Nevertheless, stratification tends to exert a pressure to generalized hierarchization, going beyond particular bases of prestige, such as political power, special sources of wealth, etc. This is precisely because it brings these various advantages together in their relations to the diffuse status of the kinship group, and through kinship inheritance exerts pressure to continue them from generation to generation. Thus, in the transition to full modernity, stratification often becomes a predominantly conservative force in contrast to the opportunities it provides for innovation in the earlier stages.

Cultural Legitimation

Specialized cultural legitimation is, like stratification, intimately involved in the emergence from primitiveness, and certainly the two processes are related. Legitimation could, perhaps, be treated first; in certain crucial respects it is a prerequisite to the establishment of the type of prestige position referred to above. The ways in which this might be the case pose a major problem for more detailed studies of evolutionary processes. Our task here, however, is much more modest, namely to call attention to the fact that without both stratification and legitimation no major advances beyond the level of primitive society can be made.

The point of reference for the development of legitimation systems is the cultural counterpart of the seamless web of the kinship nexus with its presumptive equality of units. This is the cultural definition of the social collectivity simply as "we" who are essentially human or "people" and as such are undifferentiated, even in certain concepts of time, from our ancestors—except in certain senses from the mythical "founders"— and from contemporary "others." If the others are clearly recognized to be others (in an ideal type seamless web they would not be; they would be merely special groups of kin), they are regarded as not "really human," as strange in the sense that their relation to "us" is not comprehensible.

By explicit cultural legitimation, I mean the emergence of an institutionalized cultural definition of the society of reference, namely a referent of "we" (e.g., "We, the Tikopia" in Firth's study) which is differentiated, historically or comparatively or both, from other societies, while the merit of we-ness is asserted in a normative context. This definition has to be religious in some sense, e.g., stated in terms of a particular sacred tradition of relations to gods or holy places. It may also ascribe various meritorious features to the group, e.g., physical beauty, warlike prowess, faithful trusteeship of sacred territory or tradition, etc.[11]

This usage of the term legitimation is closely associated with Max Weber's analysis of political authority. For very important reasons the primary focus of early stages beyond the primitive is political, involving the society's capacity to carry out coordinated collective action. Stratification, therefore, is an essential condition of major advances in political effectiveness, because, as just noted, it gives the advantaged elements a secure enough position that they can accept certain risks in undertaking collective leadership.

The differentiation inherent in stratification creates new sources of strain and potential disorganization, and the use of advantaged position to undertake major innovations multiplies this strain. Especially if, as is usually the case, the authors of major social innovation are already advantaged, they require legitimation for both their actions and their posi-

11. For lack of space I shall not develop a series of examples here. Fortunately, Bellah's companion paper covers much of the relevant ground in treating the transition from primitive to archaic religion and the principal features of the latter. The basic phenomena are gods conceived as acting and impinging on human society independently of the diffuse mythological order, priesthoods, whose members are expert in regulating relations to the gods, and cults organized in relation to the gods, but not yet, Bellah points out, as bounded collectivities having memberships organized independently of "civil" status.

tions. Thus, a dynamic inherent in the development of cultural systems[12] revolves about the cultural importance of the question *why*—why such social arrangements as prestige and authority relations, and particular attendant rewards and deprivations, come about and are structured as they are. This cultural dynamic converges with the consequences of the stratification developments already outlined. Hence the crucial problem here is distributive, that of justifying advantages and prerogatives *over against* burdens and deprivations. Back of this, however, lies the problem of the meaning of the societal enterprise as a whole.

As the bases of legitimation are inherently cultural, meeting the legitimation need necessarily involves putting some kind of a premium on certain cultural services, and from this point of view there is clearly some potential advantage in specializing cultural action. Whether, under what conditions, and in what ways political and religious leadership or prestige status are differentiated from each other are exceedingly important general problems of societal evolution, but we cannot go into them here. A "God-King" may be the primary vehicle of legitimation for his own political regime, or the political "ruler" may be dependent on a priestly class that is in some degree structurally independent of his regime. But the main problems have to do with explicating the cultural basis of legitimation and institutionalizing agencies for implementing that function.

The functional argument here is essentially the same as that for stratification. Over an exceedingly wide front and relatively independently of particular cultural variations, political leaders must on the long run have not only sufficient power, but also legitimation for it. Particularly when bigger implementive steps are to be legitimized, legitimation must become a relatively explicit and, in many cases, a socially differentiated function. The combination of differentiated cultural patterns of legitimation with socially differentiated agencies is the essential aspect of the evolutionary universal legitimation.

As evolutionary universals, stratification and legitimation are associated with the developmental problems of breaking through the ascriptive nexus of kinship, on the one hand, and of "traditionalized" culture, on the other. In turn they provide the basis for differentiation of a system that has previously, in the relevant respects, been undifferentiated. Differentiation must be carefully distinguished from segmentation, i.e., from either the development of undifferentiated segmental units of any given type within the system, or the splitting off of units from the system to

12. Claude Levi-Strauss, *Totemism* (Boston: Beacon Paperbacks, 1963).

form new societies, a process that appears to be particularly common at primitive levels. Differentiation requires solidarity and integrity of the system as a whole, with both common loyalties and common normative definitions of the situation. Stratification as here conceived is a hierarchical status differentiation that cuts across the overall seamless web of kinship and occurs definitely within a single collectivity, a "societal community." Legitimation is the differentiation of cultural definitions of normative patterns from a completely embedded, taken-for-granted fusion with the social structure, accompanied by institutionalization of the explicit, culture-oriented, legitimizing function in subsystems of the society.

Legitimation, of course, continues to present functional problems at later stages of evolution. The type associated with archaic religions is bound up with the relatively particularistic, arbitrary favor of divine patrons. A crucial step, represented by Bellah's "historic" religions, relates human society to a conception of supernatural order with which men must come to terms, rather than to particular divinities. Where a divinity is involved, like Jahweh, his relations with people are conceived in terms of an order which he makes binding on them, but to which, faith assures them, he will also adhere.[13]

Bureaucratic Organization

A second pair of evolutionary universals develop, each with varying degrees of completeness and relative importance, in societies that have moved considerably past the primitive stage, particularly those with well institutionalized literacy.[14] These universals are administrative bureaucracy, which in early stages is found overwhelmingly in government, and money and markets. I shall discuss bureaucracy first because its development is likely to precede that of money and markets.

Despite the criticisms made of it, mainly in the light of the com-

13. Another problem in this field concerns the implications of the dualism, so prominent in the historical religions, between the conceptions of this world and the otherworldly ideal order, and whether an empirical society and secular action within it may be considered religiously or morally "good" when set over against the other-worldly order. A transcendence of this dualism that permits a successful relation to the supernatural order through secular action, if it is highly moral, but which nevertheless maintains the transcendence of the supernatural order over this-wordly concerns, is central in developing legitimacy for modern social structures. Cf. Ernst Troeltsch, *Social Teachings of the Christian Churches* (New York: Harper Torchbooks, 1960).

14. As a predominantly cultural innovation, literacy is not discussed here. Cf. Parsons, *Societies, op. cit.,* Chapter 1.

plexities of modern organizations, Weber's ideal type can serve as the primary point of reference for a discussion of bureaucracy.[15] Its crucial feature is the institutionalization of the *authority of office*. This means that both individual incumbents and, perhaps even more importantly, the bureaucratic organization itself, may act "officially" for, or "in the name of," the organization, which could not otherwise exist. I shall call this capacity to act, or more broadly, that to make and promulgate binding decisions, *power* in a strict analytical sense.[16]

Although backed by coercive sanctions, up to and including the use of physical force, *at the same time* power rests on the consensual solidarity of a system that includes both the users of power and the "objects" of its use. (Note that I do not say *against* whom it is used: the "against" may or may not apply.) Power in this sense is the capacity of a unit in the social system, collective or individual, to establish or activate commitments to performance that contributes to, or is in the interest of, attainment of the goals of a collectivity. It is not itself a "factor" in effectiveness, nor a "real" output of the process, but a medium of mobilization and acquisition of factors and outputs. In this respect, it is like money.

Office implies the differentiation of the role of incumbent from a person's other role-involvements, above all from his kinship roles. Hence, so far as function in the collectivity is defined by the obligations of ascriptive kinship status, the organizational status cannot be an office in the present sense. Neither of the other two types of authority that Weber discusses—traditional and charismatic—establishes this differentiation between organizational role and the "personal" status of the incumbent. Hence bureaucratic authority is always rational-legal in type. Weber's well-known proposition that the top of a bureaucratic structure cannot itself be bureaucratic may be regarded as a statement about the modes of articulation of such a structure with other structures in the society. These may involve the ascribed traditional authority of royal families, some

15. See "The Analysis of Formal Organizations," Part I of my *Structure and Process in Modern Societies* (Glencoe, Ill.: The Free Press, 1960); Peter M. Blau, "Critical Remarks on Weber's Theory of Authority," *American Political Science Review*, 57 (June, 1963), pp. 305–316, and *The Dynamics of Bureaucracy*, 2nd ed. (Chicago: University of Chicago Press, 1963); Carl J. Friedrich, ed., *Authority* (Nomos I) [Cambridge: Harvard University Press, 1958], especially Friedrich's own contribution, "Authority and Reason."
16. Cf. Talcott Parsons, "On the Concept of Political Power," *Proceedings of the American Philosophical Society*, 107 (June, 1963), pp. 232–262. Reprinted as Chapter 10 of this volume.

form of charismatic leadership, or the development of democratic associational control, to be discussed briefly below.

Internally, a bureaucratic system is always characterized by an institutionalized hierarchy of authority, which is differentiated on two axes: *level* of authority and "sphere" of competence. Spheres of competence are defined either on segmentary bases, e.g., territorially, or on functional bases, e.g., supply vs. combat units in an army. The hierarchical aspect defines the levels at which a higher authority's decisions, in case of conflict, take precedence over those of a lower authority. It is a general bureaucratic principle that the higher the level, the smaller the relative number of decision-making agencies, whether individual or collegial, and the wider the scope of each, so that at the top, in principle, a single agency must carry responsibility for *any* problems affecting the organization. Such a hierarchy is one of "pure" authority only so far as status within it is differentiated from other components of status, e.g., social class. Even with rather clear differentiation, however, position in a stratification system is likely to be highly correlated with position in a hierarchy of authority. Seldom, if ever, are high bureaucratic officials unequivocally members of the lowest social class.[17]

Externally, two particularly important boundaries pose difficulties for bureaucracies. The first has to do with recruiting manpower and obtaining facilities. In ideal type, a position in a bureaucratic organization constitutes an occupational role, which implies that criteria of eligibility should be defined in terms of competence and maximal responsibility to the organization, not to "private" interests independent of, and potentially in conflict with, those of the organization. Thus high aristocrats may put loyalty to their lineage ahead of the obligations of office, or clergymen in political office may place loyalty to the church ahead of obligation to the civil government. Also, remunerating officials and providing facilities for their functions presents a serious problem of differentiation and hence of independence. The "financing of public bodies," as Weber calls it,[18] cannot be fully bureaucratic in this sense unless payment is in money, the sources of which are outside the control of the recipients. Various forms of benefices and prebends only very imperfectly

---

17. The Ottoman Empire, where many high officials were "slaves" of the Sultan, is not an exception. In such circumstances slaves took on the status of their master's "household," and hence were outside the normal stratification system. See H.A.R. Gibb, *Studies on the Civilization of Islam* (Boston: Beacon Press, 1962).

18. Max Weber, "The Financing of Political Bodies," in *The Theory of Social and Economic Organization* (Glencoe, Ill.: The Free Press, 1947), pp. 310 ff.

meet these conditions, but modern salaries and operating budgets approximate them relatively closely.[19]

The second boundary problem concerns political support. An organization is bureaucratic so far as incumbents of its offices can function independently of the influence of elements having special "interests" in its output, except where such elements are properly involved in the definition of the organization's goals through its nonbureaucratic top. Insulation from such influence, for example through such crude channels as bribery, is difficult to institutionalize and, as is well known, is relatively rare.[20]

In the optimal case, internal hierarchy and division of functions, recruitment of manpower and facilities, and exclusion of "improper" influence, are all regulated by universalistic norms. This is implicit in the proposition that bureaucratic authority belongs to Weber's rational-legal type. Of course, in many concrete instances this condition is met very imperfectly, even in the most highly developed societies.

Bureaucracy tends to develop earliest in governmental administration primarily because even a modest approximation to the essential criteria requires a considerable concentration of power, which, as noted above, depends both on prestige and on legitimation. In the very important cases, like the *polis* of antiquity, where power is widely dispersed, private units of organization are not likely either to be large enough or to command sufficient resources to become highly bureaucratized. Perhaps the *oikos* organization of the interests of important aristocratic lineages in late antiquity constitutes one of the most important relatively early ex-

19. Problems of this type have been exceedingly common over wide ranges and long periods. Eisenstadt gives many illustrations of the loss of fluidity of resources through aristocratization and similar developments. A very important one is the ruralization of the Roman legions in the later imperial period—they became essentially a border militia. At a lower level, a particularly good example is the difficuty of institutionalizing the differentiation of occupational from familial roles for the industrial labor force. S. N. Eisenstadt, *The Political Systems of Empires* (New York: The Free Press of Glencoe, 1963), especially Chap. 3; Martin P. Nilsson, *Imperial Rome* (New York: Harcourt, Brace, 1926); Neil J. Smelser, *Social Change in the Industrial Revolution* (Chicago: University of Chicago Press, 1959).

20. The difficulty of mobilizing political support for bureaucratic regimes is exemplified by the particularly important case of the struggle between monarchs and aristocracies in early modern Europe. In spite of the obvious dangers of absolutism to the freedoms of the urban classes, the alliance between them and the monarchs was an essential way of developing sufficient support to counteract the traditionalizing influence of the aristocracies. The special place of the latter in military organization made the task of monarchies more difficult. Max Beloff, *The Age of Absolutism* (New York: Harper Torchbooks, 1962); John B. Wolf, *The Emergence of the Great Powers* (New York: Harper Torchbooks, 1962), especially chs. 4 and 7.

amples approximating private bureaucracy. The Western Church is clearly another, as are modern business firms.

The basis on which I classify bureaucracy as an evolutionary universal is very simple. As Weber said, it is the most effective large-scale administrative organization that man has invented, and there is no direct substitute for it.[21] Where capacity to carry out large-scale organized operations is important, e.g., military operations with mass forces, water control, tax administration, policing of large and heterogeneous populations, and productive enterprise requiring large capital investment and much manpower, the unit that commands effective bureaucratic organization is inherently superior to the one that does not. It is by no means the only structural factor in the adaptive capacity of social systems, but no one can deny that it is an important one. Above all, it is built on further specializations ensuing from the broad emancipation from ascription that stratification and specialized legitimation make possible.

Money and the Market Complex

Immediate effectiveness of collective function, especially on a large scale, depends on concentration of power, as noted. Power is in part a function of the mobility of the resources available for use in the interests of the collective goals in question. Mobility of resources, however, is a direct function of access to them through the market. Though the market is the most general means of such access, it does have two principal competitors. First is requisitioning through the direct application of political power, e.g., defining a collective goal as having military significance and requisitioning manpower under it for national defense. A second type of mobilization is the activation of nonpolitical solidarities and commitments, such as those of ethnic or religious membership, local community, caste, etc. The essential theme here is, "as one of us, it is your duty . . ."

The political power path involves a fundamental difficulty because of the role of explicit or implied coercion—"you contribute, or else . . ."— while the activation of non-political commitments, a category comprising at least two others, raises the issue of alternative obligations. The man appealed to in the interest of his ethnic group, may ask, "what about the problems of my family?" In contrast, market exchange avoids three dilemmas: first, that I must do what is expected or face punishment for

21. Weber, *The Theory of Social and Economic Organization, op. cit.,* p. 377.

noncompliance; second, if I do not comply, I will be disloyal to certain larger groups, identification with which is very important to my general status; third, if I do not comply, I may betray the unit which, like my family, is the primary basis of my immediate personal security.

Market exchange makes it possible to obtain resources for future action and yet avoid such dilemmas as these, because money is a generalized resource for the consumer-recipient, who can purchase "good things" regardless of his relations to their sources in other respects. Availability through the market cannot be unlimited—one should not be able to purchase conjugal love or ultimate political loyalty—but possession of physical commodities, and by extension, control of personal services by purchase, certainly can, very generally, be legitimized in the market nexus.

As a symbolic medium, money "stands for" the economic utility of the real assets for which it is exchangeable, but it represents the concrete objects so abstractly that it is neutral among the competing claims of various other orders in which the same objects are significant. It thus directs attention away from the more consummatory and, by and large, immediate significance of these objects toward their *instrumental* significance as potential means to further ends. Thus money becomes the great mediator of the instrumental use of goods and services. Markets, involving both the access of the consuming unit to objects it needs for consumption and the access of producing units to "outlets" that are not ascribed, but contingent on the voluntary decisions of "customers" to purchase, may be stabilized institutionally. Thus this universal "emancipates" resources from such ascriptive bonds as demands to give kinship expectations priority, to be loyal in highly specific senses to certain political groups, or to submit the details of daily life to the specific imperatives of religious sects.

In the money and market system, money as a medium of exchange and property rights, including rights of alienation, must be institutionalized. In general it is a further step that institutionalizes broadly an individual's contractual right to sell his services in a labor market without seriously involving himself in diffuse dependency relationships, which at lower-status levels are usually in some ways "unfree." Property in land, on a basis that provides for its alienation, presents a very important problem. Its wide extension seems, except in a very few cases, to be a late development. The institution of contract in exchange of money and goods is also a complex area of considerable variation. Finally, money itself is by no means a simple entity, and in particular the development of credit instruments, banking and the like, has many variations.[22]

These institutional elements are to a considerable degree independently variable and are often found unevenly developed. But if the main ones are sufficiently developed and integrated, the market system provides the operating units of the society, including of course its government, with a pool of disposable resources that can be applied to any of a range of uses and, within limits, can be shifted from use to use. The importance of such a pool is shown by the serious consequences of its shrinkage for even such highly organized political systems as some of the ancient empires.[23]

Modern socialist societies appear to be exceptional because, up to a point, they achieve high productivity with a relatively minimal reliance on monetary and market mechanisms, substituting bureaucracy for them. But too radical a "demonetization" has negative consequences even for such an advanced economy as that of the Soviet Union.

A principal reason for placing money and markets after bureaucracy in the present series of evolutionary universals is that the conditions of their large-scale development are more precarious. This is particularly true in the very important areas where a generalized system of universalistic norms has not yet become firmly established. Market operations, and the monetary medium itself, are inevitably highly dependent on political "protection." The very fact that the mobilization of political power, and its implementation through bureaucratic organization, is so effective generates interests against sacrificing certain short-run advantages to favor the enhanced flexibility that market systems can provide. This has been a major field of conflict historically, and it is being repeated today in underdeveloped societies. The strong tendency for developing societies to adopt a "socialistic" pattern reflects a preference for increasing productivity through governmentally controlled bureaucratic means rather than more decentralized market-oriented means.[24]

22. A useful typology of the organization of economic exchange relations, from an evolutionary point of view, is given by Neil J. Smelser, *The Sociology of Economic Life* (Englewood Cliffs, N.J.: Prentice-Hall, 1963), pp. 86–88.
23. S. N. Eisenstadt, *op. cit.* for example, makes a great deal of this factor, particularly in accounting for the gradual decline of the political power of the Byzantine Empire. This analysis is also closely related to Weber's thesis in his famous essay on the decline of the Roman Empire. Weber, however, particularly emphasized the mobility of manpower through slavery. Max Weber, "The Social Causes of the Decay of Ancient Civilization," *Journal of General Education* (October, 1950).
24. See Gregory Grossman, "The Structure and Organization of the Soviet Economy" in the *Slavic Review*, 21 (June, 1962), pp. 203–222. The constriction of the market system may also have been a major factor in the difficulties suffered by the Chinese

But in general the money and market system has undoubtedly made a fundamental contribution to the adaptive capacity of the societies in which it has developed; those that restrict it too drastically are likely to suffer from severe adaptive disadvantages in the long run.

Generalized Universalistic Norms

A feature common to bureaucratic authority and the market system is that they incorporate, and are hence dependent on, universalistic norms. For bureaucracy, these involve definitions of the powers of office, the terms of access to it, and the line dividing proper from improper pressure or influence. For money and markets, the relevant norms include the whole complex of property rights, first in commodities, later in land and in monetary assets. Other norms regulate the monetary medium and contractual relations among the parties to transactions. Here relations between contracts of service or employment and other aspects of the civil and personal statuses of the persons concerned are particularly crucial.

Up to a point, the norms governing a bureaucratic organization may be regarded as independent of those governing property or those regulating the status of private persons in the same society. As noted, however, there are also certain intrinsic connections, such as that between bureaucratic organization and the mobility of resources.[25]

Although it is very difficult to pin down just what the crucial components are, how they are interrelated, and how they develop, one can identify the development of a general legal system as a crucial aspect of societal evolution. A general legal system is an integrated system of universalistic norms, applicable to the society as a whole rather than to a few functional or segmental sectors, highly generalized in terms of principles and standards, and relatively independent of both the religious agencies that legitimize the normative order of the society and vested interest groups in the operative sector, particularly in government.

The extent to which both bureaucratic organization and market systems can develop *without* a highly generalized universalistic norma-

---

Communist regime in connection with the "Great Leap Forward" of 1958 and subsequent years. Audrey Donnithorne, "The Organization of Rural Trade in China Since 1958," *China Quarterly*, No. 8 (October–December, 1961), pp. 77–91, and Leo A. Orleans, "Problems of Manpower Absorption in Rural China," *China Quarterly*, No. 7 (July–September, 1961), pp. 69–84.

25. It goes without saying that one of the largest channels of government spending in modern societies is for the purchase of goods and services in the markets, including the payment of civil servants and military personnel.

tive order should not be underestimated. Such great Empires as the Mesopotamian, the ancient Chinese, and, perhaps the most extreme example, the Roman, including its Byzantine extension, certainly testify to this. But these societies suffered either from a static quality, failing to advance beyond certain points, or from instability leading in many cases to retrogression.[26] Although many of the elements of such a general normative order appeared in quite highly developed form in earlier societies, in my view their crystallization into a coherent system represents a distinctive new step, which more than the industrial revolution itself, ushered in the *modern* era of social evolution.[27]

The clear differentiation of secular government from religious organization has been a long and complicated process, and even in the modern world its results are unevenly developed. It has perhaps gone farthest in the sharp separation of Church and State in the United States. Bureaucracy has, of course, played an important part in this process. The secularization of government is associated with that of law, and both of these are related to the level of generality of the legal system.

Systems of law that are *directly* religiously sanctioned, treating compliance as a religious obligation, also tend to be "legalistic" in the sense of emphasizing detailed prescriptions and prohibitions, each of which is given specific Divine sanction. Preeminent examples are the Hebrew law of Leviticus, the later developments in the Talmudic tradition, and Islamic law based on the Koran and its interpretations. Legal decisions and the formulation of rules to cover new situations must then be based as directly as possible on an authoritative sacred text.

Not only does religious law as such tend to inhibit generalization of legal principle, but it also tends to favor what Weber called *substantive* over *formal* rationality.[28] The standard of legal correctness tends to be the implementation of religious precepts, not procedural propriety and consistency of general principle. Perhaps the outstanding difference between the legal systems of the other Empires, and the patterns that were developed importantly in Roman law, was the development of elements of formal rationality, which we may regard as a differentiation of legal norms out of "embeddedness" in the religious culture. The older systems —many of which still exist—tended to treat "justice" as a direct im-

26. Eisenstadt, *op. cit.*, pp. 349 ff.
27. Parsons, *Societies, op. cit.*
28. Weber, *The Theory of Social and Economic Organization, op. cit.*, pp. 184 ff., and *Max Weber on Law in Economy and Society* (Cambridge: Harvard University Press, 1954), Chap. 8.

plementation of precepts of religious and moral conduct, in terms of what Weber called *Wertrationalität*, without institutionalizing an independent system of *societal* norms, adapted to the function of social control at the societal level and integrated on its own terms. The most important foci of such an independent system are, first, some kind of "codification" of norms under principles not *directly* moral or religious, though they generally continue to be grounded in religion, and, second, the formalization of procedural rules, defining the situations in which judgments are to be made on a societal basis. Especially important is the establishment of courts for purposes other than permitting political and religious leaders to make pronouncements and "examples."[29]

Something similar can be said about what I have called operative vested interests, notably government. Advantages are to be gained, on the one hand, by binding those outside the direct control of the group in question with detailed regulation, while, on the other hand, leaving maximum freedom for the group's leadership. This duality Weber made central to his concept of traditional authority, with its sphere of traditionalized fixity, on the one hand, and that of personal prerogative, reaching its extreme form in "sultanism," on the other.[30] Both aspects are highly resistant to the type of rationalization that is essential to a generalized universalistic legal system.

Though the Chinese Empire, Hindu law (*Manu*), Babylonia, and to some extent, Islam made important beginnings in the direction I am discussing, the Roman legal system of the Imperial period was uniquely advanced in these respects. Though the early *jus civilis* was very bound religiously, this was not true to the same extent of the *jus gentium,* or of the later system as a totality. While a professional judiciary never developed, the jurisconsults in their "unofficial" status did constitute a genuine professional group, and they systematized the law very extensively, in the later phases strongly under the influence of Stoic Philosophy.[31]

Though Roman law had a variety of more or less "archaic" features, its "failure" was surely on the level of institutionalization more than in any intrinsic defect of legal content. Roman society of that period lacked the institutional capacity, through government, religious legitimation, and other channels, to integrate the immense variety of peoples and

29. Weber, *Max Weber on Law in Economy and Society, op. cit.*
30. Weber, *The Theory of Social and Economic Organization, op. cit.*
31. A handy summary of Roman legal development is "The Science of Law" by F. de Zulueta in Cyrus Bailey, ed., *The Legacy of Rome* (London: Oxford University Press, 1923).

cultures within the Empire, or to maintain the necessary economic, political, and administrative structures.[32] Roman law remained, however, the cultural reference point of all the significant later developments.

The next phase, of course, was the development of Catholic Canon Law, incorporating much of Roman law. A major characteristic of the Western Church, Canon law was not only very important in maintaining and consolidating the Church's differentiation from secular government and society, but, with the Justinian documents, it also preserved the legal tradition.

The third phase was the revival of the study of Roman secular law in Renaissance Italy and its gradual adoption by the developing national states of early modern Europe. The result was that the modern national state developed as, fundamentally, a *Rechtsstaat*. In Continental Europe, however, one fundamental limitation on this development was the degree to which the law continued to be intertwined and almost identified with government. For example, most higher civil servants were lawyers. One might ask whether this represented a "legalization of bureaucracy" or a bureaucratization of the law and the legal profession. But with elaborate bodies of law, law faculties as major constituents of every important university, and the prominence of university-trained legal professions, continental European nations certainly had well institutionalized legal systems.

In England, however, the development went, in a highly distinctive way, still farther. Although the differentiation of English Common Law from Continental Roman law had late Mediaeval roots, the crucial period was the early seventeenth century, when Justice Coke asserted the independence of the Common law from control by royal prerogative. With this, the establishment of the organizational independence of the Judiciary was the crucial symbolic development. Substantially, the Common Law came to emphasize the protection of personal rights,[33] the institution of property in private hands, and both freedom of contract and protection of contractual interests far more strongly than did the Continental law. Common Law also emphasized the development of institutions, including both the adversary system, in which parties are highly independent of the Court, and procedural protections.[34]

32. Weber, "The Social Causes of the Decay of Ancient Civilization," *op. cit.*
33. A particularly clear analysis of the fundamental principles underlying this normative order is in the paper by John Rawls, "Constitutional Liberty and the Concept of Justice," in C. J. Friedrich, ed., *Justice* (Nomos VI) [New York: Atherton Press, 1963]. Rawl's discussion is not, however, specially oriented to legal problems.
34. See Roscoe Pound, *The Spirit of the Common Law* (Boston: Beacon Paperbacks, 1963); especially Chaps. 2–4.

Significantly, these Common Law developments were integral parts of the more general development of British institutions associated with the Puritan movement,[35] including the later establishment of the independence of Parliament and the development of physical science.

This development of English Common Law, with its adoption and further development in the overseas English-speaking world, not only constituted the most advanced case of universalistic normative order, but was probably decisive for the modern world. This general type of legal order is, in my opinion, the most important single hallmark of modern society. So much is it no accident that the Industrial Revolution occurred first in England, that I think it legitimate to regard the English type of legal system as a fundamental prerequisite of the first occurrence of the Industrial Revolution.[36]

The Democratic Association

A rather highly generalized universalistic legal order is in all likelihood a necessary prerequisite for the development of the last structural complex to be discussed as universal to social evolution, the democratic association with elective leadership and fully enfranchised membership. At least this seems true of the institutionalization of this pattern in the governments of large-scale societies. This form of democratic association originated only in the late eighteenth century in the Western world and was nowhere complete, if universal adult suffrage is a criterion, until well into the present century. Of course, those who regard the Communist society as a stable and enduring type might well dispute that democratic government in this sense is an evolutionary universal. But before discussing that issue, I will outline the history and principal components of this universal.

Surely it is significant that the earliest cases of democratic government were the *poleis* of classical antiquity, which were also the primary early sources of universalistic law. The democratic *polis,* however, not only was small in scale by modern standards (note Aristotle's belief that a citizen body should never be too large to assemble within earshot of a

35. David Little, "The Logic of Order; An Examination of the Sources of Puritan-Anglican Controversy and of their Relations to Prevailing Legal Conceptions of the Corporation in the Late Sixteenth and Early Seventeenth Century in England," unpublished doctoral thesis, Harvard University, 1963.

36. It is exceedingly important here once more to distinguish the first occurrence of a social innovation from its subsequent diffusion. The latter can occur without the whole set of prerequisite societal conditions necessary for the former. Cf. my *Structure and Process in Modern Societies, op. cit.,* Chap. 3.

given speaker, of course without the aid of a public address system), but also its democratic associational aspects never included a total society. It is estimated that during the Periclean age in Athens, only about 30,000 of a total population of about 150,000 were citizens, the rest being metics and slaves. And, of course, citizen women and children were not enfranchised. Thus even in its democratic phase the *polis* was emphatically a two-class system. And under the conditions of the time, when Roman society increased in scale away from the *polis* type of situation, citizenship, at least for large proportions of the Empire's population, was bound to lose political functions almost in proportion to its gains in legal significance.

The basic principle of democratic association, however, never completely disappeared. To varying degrees and in varying forms, it survived in the *municipia* of the Roman Empire, in the Roman Senate, and in various aspects of the organization of the Christian Church, though the Church also maintained certain hierarchical aspects. Later the collegial pattern, e.g., the *college* of Cardinals, continued to be an aspect of Church structure. In the Italian and North European city-states of the late Middle Ages and early modern period, it had its place in government, for example in "senates," which though not democratically elected, were internally organized as democratic bodies. Another important case was the guild, as an association of merchants or craftsmen. In modern times there have, of course, been many different types of private association in many different fields. It is certainly safe to say that, even apart from government, the democratic association is a most prominent and important constituent of modern societies.

At the level of national government, we can speak first of the long development of Parliamentary assemblies functioning as democratic associations and legislating for the nation, whose members have been to some degree elected from fairly early times. Secondly, there has been a stepwise extension of both the franchise for electing legislative representatives and the legislative supremacy of their assemblies, following the lead of England, which developed rapidly in these respects after 1688. Later, the French and American Revolutions dramatized the conception of the total national community as essentially a democratic association in this sense.

There are four critically important components of the democratic association. First is the institutionalization of the leadership function in the form of elective office, whether occupied by individuals, executive bodies, or collegial groups like legislatures. The second is the franchise, the institutionalized participation of members in collective decision-making through the election of officers and often through voting on specific policy issues. Third is the institutionalization of procedural rules for the voting process and the determination of its outcome and for the process of "discussion" or campaigning for votes by candidates or advocates of policies. Fourth is the institutionalization of the nearest possible approximation to the voluntary principle in regard to membership status. In the private association this is fundamental—no case where membership is ascribed or compulsory can be called a "pure" democratic association. In government, however, the coercive and compulsory elements of power, as well as the recruitment of societal communities largely by birth, modify the principle. Hence universality of franchise tends to replace the voluntary membership principle.

Formalization of definite procedural rules governing voting and the counting and evaluation of votes may be considered a case of formal rationality in Weber's sense, since it removes the consequences of the act from the control of the particular actor. It limits his control to the specific act of casting his ballot, choosing among the alternatives officially presented to him. Indirectly his vote might contribute to an outcome he did not desire, e.g., through splitting the opposition to an undesirable candidate and thus actually aiding him, but he cannot control this, except in the voting act itself.

Besides such formalization, however, Rokkan has shown in his comparative and historical study of Western electoral systems, that there is a strikingly general tendency to develop three other features of the franchise.[37] The first of these is universality, minimizing if not eliminating the overlap between membership and disenfranchisement. Thus property qualifications and, most recently, sex qualifications have been removed so that now the main Western democratic polities, with minimal exceptions, have universal adult suffrage. The second is equality, eliminating "class" systems, like the Prussian system in the German Empire, in favor of the principle, one citizen, one vote.[38] Finally, secrecy of the ballot insulates the voting decision from pressures emanating from status superiors or peers that might interfere with the expression of the voter's personal preferences.

---

37. Stein Rokkan, "Mass Suffrage, Secret Voting, and Political Participation," *The European Journal of Sociology*, 2 (1961), pp. 132–152.

38. The recent decisions of the U.S. Supreme Court on legislative reapportionment also constitute an important step in this process. In the majority opinion of the decision outlawing the Georgia county unit system of voting, Justice Douglas explicitly stated that this was a direct application of the Constitutional principle of equal protection of the laws. See *The New York Times*, March 19, 1963.

Certain characteristics of elective office directly complementary to those of the franchise can be formulated. Aside from the ways of achieving office and the rules of tenure in it, they are very similar to the pattern of bureaucratic office. The first, corresponding to the formalization of electoral rules, is that conduct in office must be legally regulated by universalistic norms. Second, corresponding to the universality of the franchise, is the principle of subordinating segmental or private interests to the collective interest within the sphere of competence of the office. Third, corresponding to equality of the franchise, is the principle of accountability for decisions to a total electorate. And finally, corresponding to secrecy of the ballot, is the principle of limiting the powers of office to specified spheres, in sharp contrast to the diffuseness of both traditional and charismatic authority.

The adoption of even such a relatively specific pattern as equality of the franchise may be considered a universal tendency, essentially because, under the principle that the membership rightfully chooses both the broad orientations of collective policy and the elements having leadership privileges and responsibilities, there is, among those with minimal competence, no universalistic basis for discriminating among classes of members. As a limitation on the hierarchical structure of power within collectivities, equality of franchise is the limiting or boundary condition of the democratic association, corresponding to equality of opportunity on the bureaucratic boundary of the polity.[39]

Especially, though not exclusively, in national territorial states, the stable democratic association is notoriously difficult to institutionalize. Above all this seems to be a function of the difficulty in motivating holders of immediately effective power to relinquish their opportunities voluntarily despite the seriousness of the interest at stake—relinquishment of control of governmental machinery after electoral defeat being the most striking problem.[40] The system is also open to other serious difficulties, most notably corruption and "populist" irresponsibility, as well as *de facto* dictatorship. Furthermore, such difficulties are by no means absent in private associations, as witness the rarity of effective electoral systems in large trade unions.[41]

39. Cf. Parsons, "On the Concept of Political Power," *op. cit.* and John Rawls, *loc. cit.*
40. In the 1920's and '30's the late Professor H. J. Laski was fond of saying that no "ruling class" would *ever* relinquish its position peacefully. Yet, in the late 1940's, the British Labor government both introduced the "welfare state" and set India free without a Conservative *coup d'etat* occurring against them.
41. Seymour Martin Lipset, Martin Trow, and James Coleman, *Union Democracy* (Glencoe, Ill.: The Free Press, 1956).

The basic argument for considering democratic association a universal, despite such problems, is that, the larger and more complex a society becomes, the more important is effective political organization, not only in its administrative capacity, but also, and not least, in its support of a universalistic legal order. Political effectiveness includes both the scale and operative flexibility of the organization of power. Power, however, precisely as a generalized societal medium, depends overwhelmingly on a consensual element,[42] i.e., the ordered institutionalization and exercise of influence, linking the power system to the higher-order societal consensus at the value level.[43]

No institutional form basically different from the democratic association can, *not* specifically *legitimize* authority and power in the most general sense, but *mediate consensus in its exercise* by particular persons and groups, and in the formation of particular binding policy decisions. At high levels of structural differentiation in the society itself and in its governmental system, generalized legitimation cannot fill this gap adequately. Providing structured participation in the selection of leaders and formation of basic policy, as well as in opportunities to be heard and exert influence and to have a real choice among alternatives, is the crucial function of the associational system from this point of view.

I realize that to take this position I must maintain that communist totalitarian organization will probably not fully match "democracy" in political and integrative capacity in the long run. I do indeed predict that it will prove to be unstable and will either make adjustments in the general direction of electoral democracy and a plural party system or "regress" into generally less advanced and politically less effective forms of organization, failing to advance as rapidly or as far as otherwise may be expected. One important basis of this prediction is that the Communist Party has everywhere emphasized its function in *educating* the people for the new society.[44] In the long run its legitimacy will certainly be undermined if the party leadership continues to be unwilling to *trust* the people it has educated. In the present context, however, to trust the people is to entrust them with a share of political responsibility. This can only mean that eventually the single monolithic party must relinquish

---

42. Parsons, "On the Concept of Political Power," *loc. cit.*
43. Parsons, "On the Concept of Influence," *Public Opinion Quarterly,* 27 (Spring, 1963), pp. 37–62. (Chapter 11, this volume.)
44. Paul Hollander, "The New Man and His Enemies: A Study of the Stalinist Conceptions of Good and Evil Personified," unpublished Ph.D. dissertation, Princeton University, 1963. See also Allen Kassof's *Soviet Youth Program* (Cambridge, Mass.: Harvard University Press, 1965).

its monopoly of such responsibility. (This is not to analyze the many complex ways in which this development might proceed, but only to indicate the *direction* in which it is most likely to move and the consequences it must bear if it fails in taking that direction.)

Conclusion

This paper is not meant to present even the schematic outline of a "theory" of societal evolution. My aim is much more limited: I have selected for detailed attention and illustration an especially important type of structural innovation that has appeared in the course of social change. I have attempted to clarify the concept "evolutionary universal" by briefly discussing a few examples from organic evolution, namely, vision, the human hands, and the human brain. I have interpreted these as innovations endowing their possessors with a very substantial increase in generalized adaptive capacity, so substantial that species lacking them are relatively disadvantaged in the major areas in which natural selection operates, not so much for survival as for the opportunity to initiate further major developments.

Four features of human societies at the level of culture and social organization were cited as having universal and major significance as prerequisites for socio-cultural development: technology, kinship organization based on an incest taboo, communication based on language, and religion. Primary attention, however, was given to six organizational complexes that develop mainly at the level of social structure. The first two, particularly important for the emergence of societies from primitiveness, are stratification, involving a primary break with primitive kinship ascription, and cultural legitimation, with institutionalized agencies that are independent of a diffuse religious tradition.

Fundamental to the structure of modern societies are, taken together, the other four complexes: bureaucratic organization of collective goal-attainment, money and market systems, generalized universalistic legal systems, and the democratic association with elective leadership and mediated membership support for policy orientations. Although these have developed very unevenly, some of them going back a very long time, all are clearly much more than simple "inventions" of particular societies.

Perhaps a single theme tying them together is that differentiation and attendant reduction in ascription has caused the initial two-class system to give way to more complex structures at the levels of social stratification and the relation between social structure and its cultural legitimation. First, this more complex system is characterized by a highly generalized universalistic normative structure in all fields. Second, subunits under such normative orders have greater autonomy both in pursuing their own goals and interests and in serving others instrumentally. Third, this autonomy is linked with the probability that structural units will develop greater diversity of interests and subgoals. Finally, this diversity results in pluralization of scales of prestige and therefore of differential access to economic resources, power, and influence.[45]

Comparatively, the institutionalization of these four complexes and their interrelations is very uneven. In the broadest frame of reference, however, we may think of them as together constituting the main outline of the structural foundations of modern society. Clearly, such a combination, balanced relative to the exigencies of particular societal units, confers on its possessors an adaptive advantage far superior to the structural potential of societies lacking it. Surely the bearing of this proposition on problems of rapid "modernization" in present "underdeveloped" societies is extremely important.

Certain cultural developments such as the "philosophic breakthroughs" that produced what Bellah calls the "historic" religions or the emergence of modern science in the 16th and 17th centuries, are of significance equal to the developments discussed above. Indeed, the level of institutionalization of scientific investigation and technological application of science in the present century has become a structural complex ranking in importance with the four I have described as essential to modernity.

In closing I wish to express the hope that the reader will not be too concerned with the details of my characterizations of particular evolutionary universals, my specific judgments about their concrete historical developments, or my detailed evaluations of their importance. These parts of the paper are meant primarily for illustration. I hope he will give particular attention to the *idea* of the evolutionary universal and its grounding in the conception of generalized adaptive capacity. If this idea is sound, empirical shortcomings in its application can be remedied by research and criticism.

---

45. Lest it be forgotten, what I have called the legitimation complex represents above all the differentiation between societal and cultural systems. The maintenance and extension of this differentiation is taken for granted in the present description of developments internal to the social system.

Appendix*

Parsons' Actor: Continuities in Social Theory

ROBERT DUBIN†

Parsons' classificatory system defining the social act is analyzed for tautologies and restrictions in the relationships among its elements. This generates a set of all possible viable social acts. It is also productive to view this system as a statement of process in the act. From this standpoint, prediction of human behavior becomes possible based on the probabilities of the occurrence of each type of act.

THE PURPOSE of this paper is to develop the essential components of two models of the social act advanced by Professor Parsons and to indicate the range of their applicability in social analysis. More precisely, the tasks are: (a) to restate the models in terms of their necessary and sufficient conditions; (b) to examine some of the analytical consequences of using the particular building blocks chosen for development of the models; and (c) to evaluate the models as useful analytical tools.

We have selected for analysis Parsons' paradigm of the social act.

---

* Because Chapter 7, *Pattern Variables Revisited*, was written in response to Professor Dubin's paper on *Parsons' Actor*, it was thought it would be helpful to the reader if the latter paper were reprinted here, which has been done with the author's kind permission.
† Appreciation is expressed to the Graduate School, University of Oregon, for a grant in support of this and several related studies. In a companion paper, "Deviant Behavior and Social Structure: Continuities in Social Theory" (*American Sociological Review*, 24 [April, 1959], pp. 147–164), I have examined the use of a typology to delineate outcomes of human action. Here, I consider the typological method for establishing the units employed in building a theory. Interest in Parsons' classification was generated when, in early 1957, he visited the Center for Advanced Study in the Behavioral Sciences. Several of the sociologists then in residence were subsequently asked by colleagues to "explain" selected aspects of his thought. A first draft of this paper was one of several discussed in a seminar.

"Parsons' Actor: Continuities in Social Theory" reprinted from *American Sociological Review*, Vol. 25, No. 4 (August 1960).

This is one of several models and theoretical statements contained in *Toward a General Theory of Action*.[1] A subsequent, radically modified model of the social act is suggested in *Economy and Society*[2] and parallel writings of about the same period.

The social act has centrality in any theory of social action. Linkages between the person and the social system inevitably come under consideration whenever social action is analyzed. Parsons has addressed himself to this basic analytical problem repeatedly, and has produced two systematic models that cannot be reconciled with each other. Those employing Parsonian analysis need to be sensitive to the differences between the two models, and must choose between them when a theoretical model is used in empirical studies.

Parsons elaborated a very promising model of the social act (here called "Model I") by using social psychological building blocks. Subsequently, as his analytical attention centered on social system problems, he radically modified the paradigm of the social act (here labelled "Model II") by employing social structural elements as units of the model.

We will argue that Parsons' Model I, the social psychological one, when stripped of its tautologies, has great potential utility in two respects: (1) it describes exhaustively the set of all possible social acts; and (2) when the stages of the social act are ordered in a temporal sense, the model becomes a statement of process in social action, and can be formulated mathematically as a stochastic process.

We will also argue that Parsons' Model II, using social structural elements as units, produces an over-generalized characterization of the social act. Grounds are apparent for preferring Model I, as modified, even though a competing model was developed by Parsons himself.[3]

Model I

Table 1 represents an attempt to reproduce fully and without distortion the picture of the social act presented by Parsons and Shils in

1. Talcott Parsons and Edward A. Shils, editors (Cambridge: Harvard University Press, 1951).
2. Talcott Parsons and Neil J. Smelser (Glencoe, Ill.: Free Press, 1956).
3. It does not necessarily follow (and we certainly do not examine the issue here) that Parsons' insightful analyses of aspects of social systems must stand or fall on the adequacy of his paradigm of the social act. Parsons himself has asserted at various times that the as yet unwritten "Personality System"—essential to round out the grand schema of social action—is coordinate with the "Social System" and the "Cultural System." In this paper we are specifically concerned with examining those aspects of the "Personality System" that Parsons has found it necessary to set forth in order to make sense of the other two systems.

Toward a General Theory of Action.[4] Nowhere in the volume is the scheme set forth in this fashion. Nevertheless, it is felt that the table is a faithful outline of the substantive categories composing Parsons' model.[5]

In order fully to appreciate the analytical task he sets for himself, and his methods of solution, it is necessary to examine Parsons' view of the job of the scientist. The scientist is concerned with the systematization, for purposes of understanding, of some slice of the empirical world. Parsons distinguishes ". . . four different levels of systematization of conceptual schemes, in order of their 'primitiveness' relative to the final goals of scientific endeavor: (1) *ad hoc* classificatory systems, (2) categorical systems, (3) theoretical systems, and (4) empirical-theoretical systems."[6] Thus, Parsons' starting point for the development of a theoretical system is a workable typology of units composing a categorical system. A categorical system is distinguished by the fact that it ". . . involves a system of classes which is formed to fit the subject matter [with] sufficient complexity and articulation to duplicate . . . the interdependence of the empirical systems which are the subject matter. A categorical system, thus, is constituted by the definition of a set of interrelated elements, their interrelatedness being intrinsic to their definition."[7]

We can view Parsons' exposition of the social act as an attempt to construct just such a categorical system. Parsons is proposing the necessary and sufficient building blocks from which can be generated a theoretical system. "A categorical system in this sense is always logically prior to the laws which state further relations between its elements. . . . Insofar as specific laws can be formulated and verified, a categorical system evolves into a theoretical system. . . . But it is possible to have a categorical system or many parts of one before we have more than a rudimentary knowledge of laws."[8] Parsons' work, at the point at which we are here focusing attention, represents a transition towards such a theoretical system, and ultimately an empirical-theoretical system.

COMPONENTS OF MODEL I

Table 1 is only half the picture of action systems: in addition to the person, Parsons also points to the *collectivity* as actor. However, he never

4. Parsons and Shils, *op. cit.*, Part 2. Hereafter this work will be cited as *Action.*
5. Miriam M. Johnson served as research assistant in meticulously checking through the details of Table 1; as a former student of Parsons, she is able to capture the essence of his thought. The writer, of course, assumes full responsibility for Table 1 and the discussion of it.
6. *Action,* p. 50.
7. *Ibid.*
8. *Ibid.*

develops the content of the "Collectivity" section of Table 1 (indicated by "?"). This is an obvious incompleteness in his proposed categorical system.

Table I—Parsons' Model I of the Social Act

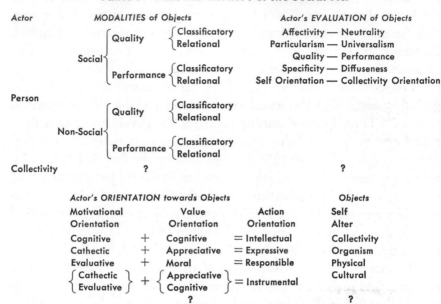

The second column of Table 1 describes the modalities of objects. "A *modality* is a property of an object; it is one of the aspects of an object in terms of which the object may be significant to an actor. Some (if not most) objects have several modalities in terms of which they may have meaning to an actor. A given actor may 'choose' to see the object only in terms of one, or a specific set of these modalities. The relevant action of the actor will be a function of the modalities he chooses."[9] The distinction between social and non-social objects is the fundamental modality for Parsons. In addition, objects are meaningful to actors in terms of the *qualities* they possess regardless of their performances, and the characteristics they display because of their *performances*.[10] Finally, objects enter the view of the actor because of their possession of *categorical attributes* meaningful in the situation of action, or because of their specific modes of *relationship* to the actor.[11] There are therefore eight

9. *Action*, p. 64.
10. *Action*, p. 65.
11. *Action*, p. 99, and Figure 6, p. 254.

possible distinctive combinations of modalities describing all objects from the actor's standpoint, as shown in Table 1.

The modalities of objects constitute Parsons' translation of the psychologist's "stimulus." Modalities are the socially significant cueing features of objects that initiate the actor's choice of a course of action. Modalities of objects, however, have to be evaluated by the actor before they trigger action. In the third column of Table 1 the evaluative choices are set forth as the well-known "pattern variables" originated by Parsons. In every situation of action, ". . . five fundamental choices . . . must be made by an actor . . . before that situation can have definitive (unambiguous) meaning for him. We have said that objects do not automatically determine the actor's 'orientation of action'; rather, a number of choices must be made before the meaning of the objects becomes definite."[12] Of course, these five fundamental choices necessary to initiate an action are between each of the members of the five pairs of pattern variables. Descriptions of the pattern variables are given in detail by Parsons and are generally well known—we will not define them here.[13]

It will be apparent that there are 32 possible ways in which the fundamental choices among the pattern variables may be made. We have already pointed out that there are eight possible distinctive combinations of object modalities. These numbers should be kept in mind for we will make important use of them presently.

Given the object modality cues, and their evaluation, the actor's orientation toward the object is then formulated on the basis of what Parsons designates as the motivational and value orientations. The elements of each of these, together with their consequences, are shown in the fourth column of Table 1. Again, the detailed definition of the six types of orientation is set forth with clarity by Parsons.[14] What is important for our purposes is that the combinations of orientation modes for the actor result in a determinate choice among four types of orientation. According to Parsons, these are intellectual, expressive, responsible, and instrumental orientations.[15]

The last column of Table 1 displays the types of objects towards which action is taken. These objects are largely self-explanatory. Parsons includes under cultural objects such items as symbols, belief systems, and

12. *Action*, p. 88.
13. *Action*, pp. 80 ff.
14. *Action*, pp. 67 ff.
15. *Action*, p. 75.

behavioral standards. A part of the category "organism," according to Parsons' depiction, consists of all living things including the self and alter as organism objects, distinct from their social definitions. It will be noted that while there are six distinctive classes of objects, each of the modalities is relevant only to sets of three. Thus, the four classes of social object modalities can only be meaningful for self, alter, or collectivity. Similarly, the four classes of non-social object modalities can only be meaningful for physical, cultural, and organism objects. Given a class of object modality as cues for action, there are only three possible object types to which it is relevant.

Table 1, then, presents the categorical system defining the components of the social act. These are the building blocks that Parsons (circa 1951) proposed as the necessary and sufficient elements for delineating the individual act.

ACTOR-TO-OBJECT PATHWAYS

With a formulation like that contained in Table 1 it becomes possible to calculate exactly the number of possible ways the person can act with respect to the object world. Each of these pathways is now recognizable as a separate type of act, at least one element of which differs from all other types of acts. Furthermore, the sum total of all such acts exhaustively defines the possible social acts derivable from the starting categorical system.

The purpose, then, of asking the simple question, "How many different possible ways are there to connect an actor with the object world?" is to describe the full range of types of social acts. There is also a secondary purpose. This system will be shown to be a representation of a stochastic process. As such, it becomes important in determining the probabilities of all outcomes of acts, given determinant choices in the early parts of the act. Thus, the particular method of formulating this categorical system turns out to be highly useful in predicting human behavior. The social act as a stochastic process is examined in the concluding sections; here the typology problem requires further analysis.

Consider the situation of a person confronting an object world differentiated only into social and non-social objects. Part of his act includes defining the object towards which action ensues. Under such circumstances, a simple series of multiplications based on Table 1 reveals that there are 3,072 (8 × 32 × 4 × 3) distinct and separate acts that might be performed. Our starting assumption of a relatively undifferentiated object world may be overly crude. Indeed, one might argue that object modalities, as triggering cues for the act, always adhere to determinant objects. Consequently, the action situation is always with reference to an object that the actor identifies as falling within one of the six object classes. We can therefore make the assumption that for any given situation of action the person and object are fixed. Under these circumstances there are 1024 (8 × 32 × 4 × 1) types of possible acts that connect them.

In the more interesting situation of ego and alter acting toward each other there are 1,048,586 (1024 × 1024) distinctive ways for the *inter-action* to take place. Perhaps Parsons, through his model, has given a substantive reality to the old saw that social phenomena are inherently complex. If we take Parsons' model of the social act literally we are confronted with genuine difficulties in grasping and retaining the multitude of act-types that result. But even here, in principle, we could allocate the task to the electronic memory of a data processing machine.

There remains, however, the task of examining Parsons' categorical system for possibilities of simplifying modifications. This can be accomplished in two fundamental ways: (a) We can discard categories in the system for various reasons, each to be explained when it is accomplished. This is done in the revision of Model I, and Parsons does it even more radically in Model II. (b) We can search for vacuous types of social acts, and through their elimination reduce the number of viable types accordingly. Parsons also uses this procedure, with the following results.

Examination of the logical reductions of categories in this system indicates, first, that the designation of quality-performance as a modality of objects and also as a pattern variable choice for the actor is tautological. It is clear in Parsons' system that this decision has to be made by the actor for his action to become determinant. Since Parsons places highest priority on the pattern variables, it seems useful to leave quality-performance among them, and remove these categories from the object modality segment of the act. Parsons himself clearly recognizes this tautology.[16]

The second logical tautology in the scheme is the inclusion of self orientation-collectivity orientation as a pattern variable, and of each of these separately as objects. Again, we follow Parsons in resolving the choice by dropping self-collectivity orientation from the pattern variables, leaving them as object categories.[17]

16. ". . . the distinction between the modalities of quality and performance, which is, of course, included in the pattern-variable scheme" (*Action*, p. 205).
17. See Parsons and Smelser, *op. cit.*, p. 36.

Table II—Revised Model I of the Social Act

Actor	MODALITIES of Objects		Actor's EVALUATION of Objects	Actor's ORIENTATION towards Objects	Objects
	Social	Classificatory	Affectivity — Neutrality	Intellectual	Self
		Relational	Particularism — Universalism	Expressive	Alter
Person			Quality — Performance	Responsible	Collectivity
	Non-Social	Classificatory	Specificity — Diffuseness	Instrumental	Organism
		Relational			Physical
					Cultural

We are now in a position to revise Model I in accordance with these simplifications. This revision is shown in Table 2. For clarity in presentation we have deleted the detailed components from the Orientation column. It should be clear that the components of motivational orientation and value orientation are understood to be the primitive elements of orientation.

In searching for vacuous types of acts logically defined by the categorical system, Parsons concludes that the affectivity choice among the pattern variables eliminates the possibility of choice between self-collectivity, and between universalism-particularism.[18] We have already suggested the elimination of self-collectivity orientation from the pattern variables for all acts. This restriction, then, has the effect of reducing the number of possible different acts that can result when affectivity is chosen below the number that can result when affective neutrality is chosen.

A second group of vacuous types of social acts is suggested by Parsons' conclusion that the quality-performance decision applies only to social objects and to organisms.[19] Thus, for physical and cultural objects the quality-performance pattern variable does not operate as a problematical choice for the actor.

The effects of eliminating tautologies and the vacuous types of social acts from this scheme are shown in Table 3. The upper portion of the table indicates that the number of types of social acts is significantly reduced by eliminating the logical tautologies in the categorical system and by subtracting the empty types resulting from the inapplicability of quality-performance choices to non-social objects. The maximum number of possible types of social acts now is 640, as contrasted with the 1,024

18. ". . . if affectivity is selected in the concrete situation instead of affective neutrality, the problems presented by pattern-variables two and three [self-collectivity orientation, and universalism-particularism] never arise" (*Action*, p. 89).
19. *Action*, p. 100, including footnote.

Table III—Number of Types of Social Acts in Model I with Tautologies Eliminated and Restrictions Imposed

Actor	Object Class		No. of Types of Social Acts
Person	Self		128
Person	Alter		128
Person	Collectivity		128
Person	Organism		128
Person	Physical*		64
Person	Cultural*		64
		Total	640
	*If "affectivity" choice is made by actor**		
Person	Self		32
Person	Alter		32
Person	Collectivity		32
Person	Organism		32
Person	Physical*		16
Person	Cultural*		16
		Total	160

* Assuming the restriction that the quality-performance decision of the actor does not apply to non-social objects, except organisms.
** Assuming the restriction that the affectivity choice eliminates the need for the choice between universalism and particularism.

ways a person and a given object can be connected in the original system. This reduction is clearly a major gain in analytical clarity, at no sacrifice to the integrity of the categorical system with which we started.

The lower section of Table 3 displays the consequences of the affectivity choice in further reducing the viable types of acts that result. It will be noted that the system yields only 160 possible different types of acts when this choice is made.

We have, of course, examined only the simplifying restrictions set forth by Parsons. It is highly probable, although beyond the scope of this paper to discuss, that other equally important simplifying modifications can be discovered. For example, it seems reasonable to conclude that expressive action necessitates the affectivity choice; that intellectual orientation flows from the affective-neutrality choice; that expressive orientation and the relational object modality go together; and that responsible orientation is the product of the neutrality and specificity choices among the pattern variables. All of these restrictions would further reduce the number of viable types of social acts, and would have the consequence of further simplifying the typology of action.

A more careful working out of all the empty types generated by this categorical system would seem to be worthwhile if the system itself has merit, as I think it has. We might reasonably expect that the number of types of social acts finally derived will turn out to be manageable.

Model II

A radical departure from Model I was presented by Parsons when he turned his attention to analyzing the social act from the standpoint of social system problems.[20] Perceiving the need to articulate social action with the requirements of a social system, Parsons started with problems of social structure and attempted to move from there to the level of the individual actor in the system. Parsons' Model I essentially "looks out" to the social system from the vantage point of the actor; his Model II "looks down" at the individual actor from the perspective of the social system.

Parsons, it is clear, remained sensitive to the need for linking actor with social system—the analytical problem always has been a critical one for him. In fact, it is not apparent that Parsons abandoned our Model I in favor of the more recent Model II. I prefer to consider the models as two coordinate solutions to the same analytical problem.

The essential difference between these two solutions lies in the units out of which the models are constructed. In Model I the social act is seen as the product of the actor's evaluations of objects and of his orientations towards them—both of which are subjective or social psychological units. In Model II, as explained directly below, the social act is viewed as a product of role definitions peculiar to the four presumably universal social system problems. Hence, the primary analytical unit becomes the system modalities from which the actor's evaluation of objects and orientation towards them are uniquely derived.

We illustrate Model II in the form presented in Table 4. This model is simplicity itself. It reveals clearly Parsons returning to the unadorned pattern variables as embodying the essence of his social psychology. This is accomplished by considering each member of four remaining pairs of pattern variables divorced from its mate as either a criterion of evaluation of objects or as a criterion of orientation towards objects.

It should be noted, first, that the portrayal of the social act in Model II attempts to establish a direct and imperative connection between the social system and the individual actor. For now the social system is introduced by way of the modalities denoting *system* problems. These modalities are the universal problems of a social system—described as

20. See Parsons and Smelser, *op. cit.*, "Technical Note," pp. 33–38. We use this source because of its remarkable economy of presentation. Model II was originally worked out in Talcott Parsons, Robert F. Bales, and Edward A. Shils, *Working Papers in the Theory of Action,* Glencoe, Ill.: Free Press, 1953.

the adaptive problem, the goal attainment problem, the integrative problem, and the pattern maintenance or tension management problem.

Clearly, these four social system modalities are quite different from the modalities of objects set forth in Model I. It is also apparent that these system modalities are analytically distinguishable from the specific social relations involved in solving system problems. This immediately suggests problems of over-generalization whose net effect may be to wash out meaningful distinctions. For example, the psychiatrist in his office, the policeman on the beat, and the President's Council of Economic Advisors in session are all concerned with the system modality of pattern maintenance or tension reduction. The differences between social situations of this order, I believe, are greater than their similarities.

Secondly, it should be noted that the four remaining pairs of pattern variables are now harnessed to perform both the orientation function and the evaluation function for the actor. This has the effect of throwing away the orientation categories of Model I, and of destroying whatever usefulness can be attributed to the types of action they delineate.

Table IV—Parsons' Model II of the Social Act[1]

Social System MODALITIES (System Problems)		Actor's EVALUATION of Objects	Actor's ORIENTATION towards Objects
Adaptive	→	Universalism	Specificity
Goal Attainment	→	Performance	Affectivity
Integrative	→	Particularism	Diffuseness
Pattern-maintenance and Tension Management	→	Quality	Neutrality

1. Taken from *Economy and Society*, p. 36. The reader may prefer the earlier and slightly more complex formulation of Model II in *Working Papers in the Theory of Action*, p. 180. There, too, there are only four types of social acts, somewhat differently characterized than presented above.

Furthermore, object modalities disappear as significant features of the social act. Taking their place as triggering mechanisms for the social act is the perception of a system problem in the situation of action. This is equivalent to saying that the policeman on the beat always acts with pattern maintenance and tension management in view, and can only act if this system modality has gained his attention. It would be very hard to square this position with a vast literature, of which Goffman's recent work is an instructive example.[21]

An important feature of Model II is the clearly intended directionality from system modalities to orientation and evaluation by the actor. This

21. Erving Goffman, *The Presentation of Self in Everyday Life*, New York: Doubleday, 1959.

alignment, of course, gives temporal priority to role expectation, determined by the system problem, in establishing the action posture of the person.

Finally and most importantly, it should be noted that Model II stresses the determinant impact of system modalities on the attitudinal orientation of the actor and his categorization of objects. For each type of system problem there is one and only one appropriate orientation posture, and only one way of categorizing objects involved in solving that system problem.

In Model II, moreover, there are only four types of social acts, each uniquely corresponding to a particular type of social system problem. This is indeed an enormous simplification. Perhaps subsequent refinements of Model II will bring this scheme more closely into congruence with the more promising simplifications of Model I.

Parsons has been true to his intentions of developing categorical systems (and ultimately of theoretical systems). In this effort, he strongly emphasizes a typological methodology and displays unique talents of the highest order in labeling the dimensions of his typological boxes and in filling them with perceptive illustrations and content. Perhaps less in his purview has been the analysis of process. Therefore, it is instructive to return briefly to his Model I of the social act and to reconsider it as a paradigm of process. This matter raises, again, the classic problem of Mead, Dewey, Thomas, and even Adam Smith.[22]

Social Act as a Process

Even a brief examination of the social act as a process in terms of Parsons' Model I, as modified, indicates the latter's exceptional utility in delineating the actor in motion.

It is of crucial importance, in considering the social act as a process, to establish a temporal sequence among the parts of the act. Once this sequence is established, we can then consider the act as a stochastic process. For this process in general, each of its stages can be represented as a set of branching alternatives through which the process "goes" to the next stage. If determinant probabilities can be assigned to the alternatives that branch from one stage to the next, then the ultimate probability of a

22. As treated, e.g., in G. H. Mead, *Mind, Self, and Society*, Chicago: University of Chicago Press, 1934; John Dewey, *Human Nature and Conduct*, New York: Holt, 1922; W. I. Thomas, *The Unadjusted Girl*, Boston: Little, Brown, 1923; and Adam Smith, *The Theory of the Moral Sentiments*, 3rd edition, London: 1767.

given final outcome can be specified as the product of the probabilities of the preceding steps of which the product is the result.

It may be assumed that the temporal sequence among the parts of the social act is the following: (1) resolving the relational classificatory modality of the determinant object; (2) establishing evaluations of the object in terms of the pattern variables; and (3) fixing orientation towards the object according to the four-fold classification of orientations. It is not really critical to the argument that this is exactly the sequence of stages of the act. What is essential is that such stages exist which have more than one alternative leading to the next phase of the act.

The discussion here is limited to the situation where the object towards which action is directed is determinant. That is, the actor has resolved the social-non-social object modality choice. In addition, the actor has resolved the choice within that modality in favor of a single type of object. This assumption provides a starting point from which the suggested stages of the social act proceed.

It is now possible to represent graphically the branching alternatives at each stage of the act, as displayed in Table 5. Starting with a fixed

Table V—The Social Act Viewed as a Process Showing the Probability of Each Type of Act for a Single Class of Objects

Temporal Sequence → 1	2	3			
		Actor's ORIENTATION towards Objects			
MODALITIES of Objects	Actor's EVALUATION of Objects	Intellectual	Expressive	Responsible	Instrumental
Classificatory {	Affectivity + Particularism + Quality + Specificity	p_1	p_2	p_3	p_4
	. . . .	. . . .	. . . .	. . . .	. . . .
	. . . .	. . . .	. . . .	. . . .	. . . .
	. . . .	. . . .	. . . .	. . . .	. . . .
	(16 possible combinations)				
	. . . .	. . . .	. . . .	. . . .	. . . .
	. . . .	. . . .	. . . .	. . . .	. . . .
	. . . .	. . . .	. . . .	. . . .	. . . .
	Neutrality + Universalism + Performance + Diffuseness	p_{61}	p_{62}	p_{63}	p_{64}
Relational {	Affectivity + Particularism + Quality + Specificity	p_{65}	p_{66}	p_{67}	p_{68}
	. . . .	. . . .	. . . .	. . . .	. . . .
	. . . .	. . . .	. . . .	. . . .	. . . .
	(16 possible combinations)				
	. . . .	. . . .	. . . .	. . . .	. . . .
	. . . .	. . . .	. . . .	. . . .	. . . .
	. . . .	. . . .	. . . .	. . . .	. . . .
	Neutrality + Universalism + Performance + Diffuseness	p_{125}	p_{126}	p_{127}	p_{128}

object type, and a fixed choice of social-non-social modality, the first branching alternative extends to either a classificatory or rational object modality. The next branching set of alternatives is the determination of one of 16 possible combinations of evaluation for each of the two object modality choices. Finally, for each of these 32 total branches of the act there is a set of four possible orientation postures for the actor.

In principle, two conditions must be met to reach a table of probabilities that would correspond to Table 5. First, we would need measuring instruments to provide empirical indicators of the actor's choices at each of the three choice points in this model of the social act. Second, we would need to be able to express the outcomes in the form of probabilities, at each choice point in the total process.

The problem of empirical indicators for each choice involved in the social act can be solved readily. This may be done by using the actor's own report of introspective data in situations of actual behavior (by methods varying from detailed recall in a depth interview to simultaneous recording by push buttons during the act itself in an experimental situation); or by appropriately designed questionnaires whose purpose is to elicit the actor's bases of choice in a real or contrived situation.

The problem of expressing each outcome of a choice point as a probability has two aspects. There are theoretical grounds for concluding that some of the probabilities are zero, as noted above in the discussion of the revisions of Model I. On the other hand, there are no theoretical reasons for establishing non-zero probability values. Accordingly, we would have to depend on empirical assignment of non-zero values. This means that each branch at a choice point must be included in the instruments of measurement so that empirical probabilities can be derived from any collection of data. Once the probability of each branch at each choice point is empirically established, the probability of an outcome, in the form of the illustrative Table 5, would be the product of the probabilities of the intervening branches leading to the particular outcome.

Following the assumptions on which Table 3 is based, there would be six tables of probabilities like those indicated in Table 5, one for each object class. This procedure yields a theoretical possibility of 768 possible types of social acts. If the non-viable social acts (those having zero probability) are eliminated in accordance with the previous discussion, we would end up with the 640 total types of acts as displayed in Table 3. It is evident that the modified version of Model I, and this reformulation of it as a stochastic process, produce compatible results.

The advantages of viewing the social act as a process are two-fold.

First, we generate a system for predicting particular kinds of acts, knowing the choices made by the actor in each of the stages of the act. In addition, should only portions of the actor's choices be known, it is also possible to state the probabilities of the alternate outcomes that can flow from the known choices. Second, since the system exhaustively describes the set of all possible social acts, the probabilities of the outcomes of any sub-set of acts may be compared.[23]

Both of these advantages are salient for sociological research. The prediction of outcomes from incomplete knowledge of the actor's choices in some steps of the act is relevant to such diverse subjects as forecasting individual academic achievement and prognosis in psychotherapy. The knowledge gained about the probabilities of given acts in relation to all other acts is important in the analysis of any mass phenomenon. In short, the process view of the social act, for which Parsons' Model I is a sophisticated statement, permits prediction in analyzing given acts, or in comparing the probability of occurrence of different acts. This is usually the goal of social investigation.

Actors and Action

We have seen how the categorical system describing the social act, as developed by Parsons and exhibited in the modified Model I, provides a useful and exhaustive typology of human acts. The production of such a typology seems to have been one of Parsons' goals. Its accomplishment is a contribution of significant proportions.

We have also examined the consequences of viewing the categorical system as a statement of the act in process. From this standpoint, we move beyond the typology problem to a consideration of probabilities of the occurrence of a given type of act. This adds to the typological statement the element of prediction.

It should be noted that the step involving prediction is wholly grounded in the preceding development of the typology—an analysis that is consistent with Parsons' desideratum of moving from categorical systems to theoretical systems. The transition between the two kinds of systems involves the sequential ordering of stages of the social act plus

23. The mathematics is fairly involved and beyond the scope of this paper. See, e.g., T. W. Anderson, "Probability Models for Analyzing Time Changes in Attitudes," in P. F. Lazarsfeld, editor, *Mathematical Thinking in the Social Sciences*, Glencoe, Ill.: Free Press, 1954, Chapter 1.

the statement of laws of interaction among the categorical elements of the first system.

It will be remembered that the explicit statement of these laws of interaction, as we encountered them in Model I, take the form of laws of negation. Such laws have the general form, "if this, then *not* that." We have found two laws of this order: quality-performance does *not* apply to non-social objects; if affectivity is chosen, then the choice between particularism-universalism is *eliminated*.

Parenthetically, the possibility has been suggested of affirming laws of interaction of the general form, "if this, then that." For example, if the actor's orientation is expressive action, then he must have chosen the affectivity evaluation of the object of the act.

It should be instructive, and productive of a theoretical system of the social act, to focus on Parsons' categorical system in search of laws of interaction among its elements. It is certain that more laws of both types can be elaborated. Such a search would probably reduce the number of types of acts, perhaps revise the starting categorical system, and, finally, provide powerful models of the social act as a process.

Bibliography

Bibliography of Talcott Parsons

1928

"Capitalism" in Recent German Literature: Sombart and Weber, I.
Journal of Political Economy 36:641–661.

1929

"Capitalism" in Recent German Literature: Sombart and Weber, II.
Journal of Political Economy 37:31–51.

1930

Translation of Max Weber, *The Protestant Ethic and the Spirit of Capitalism*.
London: Allen and Unwin; and New York: Scribners; xi+292 pp.

1931

Wants and Activities in Marshall.
Quarterly Journal of Economics 46:101–140.

1932

Economics and Sociology: Marshall in Relation to the Thought of His Time.
Quarterly Journal of Economics 46:316–347.

1933

Malthus.
Encyclopedia of the Social Sciences 10:68–69.
Pareto.
Encyclopedia of the Social Sciences 11:576–578.

KEY TO SYMBOLS:
* Also in *Essays in Sociological Theory*.
\# Only in *First Edition*, 1949.
† Only in *Revised Edition*, 1954.
⊥ Also in *Structure and Process in Modern Society*, 1960.
° Also in *Social Structure and Personality*, 1964.

1934

   Some Reflections on "The Nature and Significance of Economics."
      Quarterly Journal of Economics 48:511–545.
   Society.
      Encyclopedia of the Social Sciences 14:225–231.
   Sociological Elements in Economic Thought, I.
      Quarterly Journal of Economics 49:414–453.

1935

   Sociological Elements in Economic Thought, II.
      Quarterly Journal of Economics 49:645–667.
   The Place of Ultimate Values in Sociological Theory.
      International Journal of Ethics 45:282–316.
   H. M. Robertson on Max Weber and His School.
      Journal of Political Economy 43:688–696.

1936

   Pareto's Central Analytical Scheme.
      Journal of Social Philosophy 1:244–262.
   On Certain Sociological Elements in Professor Taussig's Thought.
      Jacob Viner (ed.), *Explorations in Economics: Notes and Essays Con-
      tributed in Honor of F. W. Taussig*, New York: McGraw-Hill
      (xii+539 pp.), pp. 352–379.

1937

   The Structure of Social Action.
      New York: McGraw-Hill; xii+817 pp. Reprinted by The Free Press,
      New York, 1949.
   Education and the Professions.
      International Journal of Ethics 47:365–369.

1938

   The Role of Theory in Social Research.
      American Sociological Review 3:13–20. (An address delivered before
      the Annual Institute of the Society for Social Research, at the Univer-
      sity of Chicago, Summer, 1937.)
   *The Role of Ideas in Social Action.
      American Sociological Review 3:653–664. (Written for a meeting on
      the problem of ideologies at the American Sociological Society's annual
      meeting, Atlantic City, N.J., December, 1937.)

1939

   *The Professions and Social Structure.
      Social Forces 17:457–467. (Written to be read at the annual meeting
      of the American Sociological Society in Detroit, December, 1938.)
   Comte.
      Journal of Unified Science 9:77–83.

* See footnote, p. 539.

1940
*Analytical Approach to the Theory of Social Stratification.
American Journal of Sociology 45:841–862.
*Motivation of Economic Activities.
Canadian Journal of Economics and Political Science 6:187–203. [Originally given as a public lecture at the University of Toronto and also published in *Essays in Sociology*, C. W. M. Hart (ed.), and in *Human Relations in Administration: The Sociology of Organization*, Robert Dubin (ed.), 1951.]

1942
Max Weber and the Contemporary Political Crisis.
Review of Politics 4:61–76, 155–172.
The Sociology of Modern Anti-Semitism.
J. Graeber and Stuart Henderson Britt (eds.), *Jews in a Gentile World*, New York: Macmillan, 1942 (x+436 pp.), pp. 101–122.
*Age and Sex in the Social Structure of the United States.
American Sociological Review 7:604–616. (Read at the annual meeting of the American Sociological Society in New York, December, 1941, and republished in several places, notably Logan Wilson and William Kolb, *Sociological Analysis*, and Clyde Kluckhohn and Henry A. Murray, *Personality in Nature, Society and Culture*, 1st and 2nd editions.)
"Propaganda and Social Control.
Psychiatry 5:551–572.
*†Democracy and the Social Structure in Pre-Nazi Germany.
Journal of Legal and Political Sociology 1:96–114.
*†Some Sociological Aspects of the Fascist Movements.
Social Forces 21:138–147. (Written as the presidential address to the Eastern Sociological Society at its 1942 meeting.)

1943
*The Kinship System of the Contemporary United States.
American Anthropologist 45:22–38.

1944
*The Theoretical Development of the Sociology of Religion.
Journal of the History of Ideas 5:176–190. (Originally written to be read at the Conference on Methods in Science and Philosophy in New York, November, 1942.) Reprinted in *Ideas in Cultural Perspective*, Philip Wiener and Aaron Noland (eds.), New Brunswick, N.J.: Rutgers University Press, 1962.

1945
*The Present Position and Prospects of Systematic Theory in Sociology.
Georges Gurvitch and Wilbert E. Moore (eds.), *Twentieth Century Sociology*, A Symposium; New York: Philosophical Library.

*† See footnotes, p. 539.

*The Problem of Controlled Institutional Change: An Essay on Applied Social Science.
  Psychiatry 8:79–101. (Prepared as an appendix to the report of the Conference on Germany after World War II.)
Racial and Religious Differences as Factors in Group Tensions.
  Louis Finkelstein *et al.* (eds.), *Unity and Difference in the Modern World*, A Symposium; New York: The Conference on Science, Philosophy and Religion in Their Relation to the Democratic Way of Life, Inc.

1946

The Science Legislation and the Role of the Social Sciences.
  American Sociological Review 11:653–666.
*†Population and Social Structure (of Japan).
  Douglas G. Haring (ed.), *Japan's Prospect*, Cambridge: Harvard University Press (xiv+474 pp.), pp. 87–114. (This book was published by the staff of the Harvard School for Overseas Administration.)
*Certain Primary Sources and Patterns of Aggression in the Social Structure of the Western World.
  Psychiatry 10:167–181. (Prepared for the Conference on Science, Philosophy, and Religion at its September, 1946, meeting in Chicago, and also published in the volume issued by the Conference.)
Some Aspects of the Relations Between Social Science and Ethics.
  Social Science 22:23–217. (Read at the Annual Meeting of the American Association for the Advancement of Science in Boston, December, 1946.)
Science Legislation and the Social Sciences.
  Political Science Quarterly, Vol. LXII, No. 2, June, 1947. *Bulletin of Atomic Scientists*, January, 1947.
Max Weber: The Theory of Social and Economic Organization.
  Talcott Parsons, editor, and translator with A. M. Henderson; Oxford University Press. #Introduction by Talcott Parsons. Reprinted by The Free Press, New York, 1957.

1948

Sociology, 1941–46.
  Co-author with Bernard Barber. *American Journal of Sociology* 53:245–257.
*#The Position of Sociological Theory.
  American Sociological Review 13:156–171. (Paper read before the annual meeting of the American Sociological Society, New York City, December, 1947.)

1949

Essays in Sociological Theory Pure and Applied.
  New York: The Free Press; xiii+366 pp.

*†# See footnotes, p. 539.

The Rise and Decline of Economic Man.
Journal of General Education 4:47–53.
*†Social Classes and Class Conflict in the Light of Recent Sociological Theory.
American Economic Review 39:16–26. (Read at the meeting of the American Economic Association in December, 1948.)

1950

*†The Prospects of Sociological Theory.
American Sociological Review 15:3–16. (Presidential address read before the meeting of the American Sociological Society in New York City, December, 1949.)
*†Psychoanalysis and the Social Structure.
The Psychoanalytic Quarterly 19:371–384. (The substance of this paper was presented at the meeting of the American Psychoanalytic Association, Washington, D.C., May, 1948.)
The Social Environment of the Educational Process.
Centennial, Washington, D.C., American Association for the Advancement of Science, pp. 36–40. (Read at the AAAS Centennial Celebration, September, 1948.)

1951

The Social System.
New York: The Free Press; xii+575 pp.
Toward a General Theory of Action.
Editor and contributor with Edward A. Shils and others. Cambridge: Harvard University Press; xiii+506 pp. Reprinted, Harper Torchbooks, 1962.
Graduate Training in Social Relations at Harvard.
Journal of General Education 5:149–157.
Illness and the Role of the Physician: A Sociological Perspective.
American Journal of Orthopsychiatry 21:452–460. (Presented at the 1951 annual meeting of the American Orthopsychiatric Association in Detroit.) Reprinted in Clyde Kluckhohn, Henry A. Murray, and David M. Schneider, *Personality in Nature, Society and Culture*, 2nd ed., New York: Knopf, 1953.

1952

°The Superego and the Theory of Social Systems.
Psychiatry 15:15–25. (The substance of this paper was read at the meeting of the Psychoanalytic Section of the American Psychiatric Association, May, 1951, in Cincinnati.) Reprinted in Parsons, Bales, and Shils, *Working Papers in the Theory of Action*, New York: The Free Press, 1953 and 1967.
Religious Perspectives in College Teaching: Sociology and Social Psychology.

°† See footnotes, p. 539.

Hoxie N. Fairchild (ed.), *Religious Perspectives in College Teaching*, New York: The Ronald Press Company (viii+460 pp.), pp. 286–337.

*†A Sociologist Looks at the Legal Profession.
Conference on the Profession of Law and Legal Education, Conference Series Number II, The Law School, University of Chicago, pp. 49–63. (This paper was presented at the first symposium on the occasion of the Fiftieth Anniversary Celebration of the University of Chicago Law School, December, 1952.)

1953

Working Papers in the Theory of Action.
In collaboration with Robert F. Bales and Edward A. Shils. New York: The Free Press; 269 pp. Reissued, 1967.

Psychoanalysis and Social Science with Special Reference to the Oedipus Problem.
Franz Alexander and Helen Ross (eds.), *Twenty Years of Psychoanalysis*, New York: W. W. Norton and Company, Inc., pp. 186–215. (The substance of this paper was read at the Twentieth Anniversary Celebration of the Institute for Psychoanalysis, in Chicago, October, 1952.)

*†A Revised Analytical Approach to the Theory of Social Stratification.
Reinhard Bendix and Seymour M. Lipset (eds.), *Class, Status, and Power: A Reader in Social Stratification*, New York: The Free Press, pp. 92–129.

Illness, Therapy and the Modern Urban American Family.
Co-author with Renée Fox. *Journal of Social Issues* 8:31–44. Reprinted in E. Gartly Jaco (ed.), *Patients, Physicians, and Illness*, New York: The Free Press, 1958.

Some Comments on the State of the General Theory of Action.
American Sociological Review, Vol. 18, No. 6 (December, 1953), pp. 618–631.

1954

°The Father Symbol: An Appraisal in the Light of Psychoanalytic and Sociological Theory.
Bryson, Finkelstein, MacIver, and McKeon (eds.), *Symbols and Values: An Initial Study*, 13th Symposium of the Conference on Science, Philosophy and Religion, New York: Harper & Row, pp. 523–544. (The substance of this paper was read at the meeting of the American Psychological Association in September, 1952, in Washington, D.C.)

Essays in Sociological Theory (revised edition).
New York: The Free Press; 459 pp.

*†° See footnotes, p. 539.

Psychology and Sociology.
John P. Gillin (ed.), *For A Science of Social Man,* New York: Macmillan, pp. 67–102.
°The Incest Taboo in Relation to Social Structure and the Socialization of the Child.
British Journal of Sociology, Vol. V, No. 2 (June, 1954), pp. 101–117.

1955

Family, Socialization and Interaction Process.
With Robert F. Bales, James Olds, Morris Zelditch, and Philip E. Slater. New York: The Free Press; xi+422 pp.
"McCarthyism" and American Social Tension: A Sociologist's View.
Yale Review, Winter, 1955, pp. 226–245. Reprinted under title "Social Strains in America" in Daniel Bell (ed.), *The New American Right,* New York: Criterion Books, 1955.

1956

Economy and Society.
Co-author with Neil J. Smelser. London: Routledge and Kegan Paul; and New York: The Free Press; xxi+332 pp.
Éléments pour une théorie de l'action.
With an introduction by François Bourricaud. Paris: Plon.
⊥A Sociological Approach to the Theory of Organizations.
Administrative Science Quarterly, I (June, 1956), pp. 63–85; II (September, 1956), pp. 225–239.
A Sociological Model for Economic Development.
Co-author with Neil J. Smelser. *Explorations in Entrepreneurial History,* Cambridge, Harvard University Press.

1957

⊥The Distribution of Power in American Society.
World Politics, X (October, 1957), pp. 123–143.
Malinowski and the Theory of Social Systems.
Raymond Firth (ed.), *Man and Culture,* London: Routledge and Kegan Paul.
Man in His Social Environment—As Viewed by Modern Social Science.
Centennial Review of Arts and Science, Michigan State University, Winter, 1957, pp. 50–69.
The Mental Hospital as a Type of Organization.
Milton Greenblatt, Daniel J. Levinson, and Richard H. Williams (ed.), *The Patient and the Mental Hospital,* New York: The Free Press.
Reflexions sur les Organisations Religieuses aux États-Unis.
Archives de Sociologie des Religions, January–June, pp. 21–36.
Sociologia di dittatura.
Bologna: Il Molino.

⊥° See footnotes, p. 539.

1958

⊥Authority, Legitimation, and Political Action.
    C. J. Friedrich (ed.), *Authority*, Cambridge: Harvard University Press.
°The Definitions of Health and Illness in the Light of American Values and Social Structure.
    E. Gartly Jaco (ed.), *Patients, Physicians, and Illness*, New York: The Free Press.
°Social Structure and the Development of Personality.
    Psychiatry, November, 1958, pp. 321–340.
General Theory in Sociology.
    Robert K. Merton, Leonard Broom, and Leonard S. Cottrell, Jr. (eds.), *Sociology Today*, New York: Basic Books.
⊥Some Ingredients of a General Theory of Formal Organization.
    Andrew W. Halpin (ed.), *Administrative Theory in Education*, Chicago: Midwest Administration Center, University of Chicago.
⊥Some Reflections on the Institutional Framework of Economic Development.
    The Challenge of Development: A Symposium, Jerusalem: The Hebrew University.
⊥Some Trends of Change in American Society: Their Bearing on Medical Education.
    Journal of the American Medical Association, May, 1958, pp. 31–36.
⊥The Pattern of Religious Organization in the United States.
    Daedalus, Summer, 1958, pp. 65–85.
The Concepts of Culture and of Social System.
    Co-author with A. L. Kroeber. *American Sociological Review*, October, 1958, p. 582.

1959

An Approach to Psychological Theory in Terms of the Theory of Action.
    Sigmund Koch (ed.), *Psychology: A Study of a Science*, Vol. III, New York: McGraw-Hill, pp. 612–711.
⊥The Principal Structures of Community: A Sociological View.
    C. J. Friedrich (ed.), *Community*, New York: The Liberal Arts Press.
"Voting" and the Equilibrium of the American Political System.
    Eugene Burdick and Arthur Brodbeck (eds.), *American Voting Behavior*, New York: The Free Press.
Durkheim's Contribution to the Theory of Integration of Social Systems.
    Kurt H. Wolff (ed.), *Emile Durkheim, 1858–1917: A Collection of Essays, with Translations and a Bibliography*, Columbus, Ohio: Ohio State University Press.
Implications of the Study.
    (On Marjorie Fiske's "Book Selection and Retention in California Public and School Libraries.") *The Climate of Book Selection*, a sympo-

⊥° See footnotes, p. 539.

sium of the University of California School of Librarianship. Berkeley:
University of California Press.

Some Problems Confronting Sociology as a Profession.
American Sociological Review, August, 1959.

°The School Class as a Social System.
Harvard Educational Review, Fall, 1959. Reprinted in A. H. Halsey,
Jean Floud, and Arnold C. Anderson (eds.), *Education, Economy and
Society,* New York: The Free Press, 1961.

An Approach to the Sociology of Knowledge.
Proceedings, Fourth World Congress of Sociology at Milan, Italy,
September, 1959. Vol. IV.

1960

°Mental Illness and "Spiritual Malaise": The Roles of the Psychiatrist
and of the Minister of Religion.
Hans Hofmann (ed.), *The Ministry and Mental Health,* New York:
Association Press.

Structure and Process in Modern Societies.
(A collection of essays.) New York: The Free Press; 334 pp.

In memoriam
"Clyde Kluckhohn, 1905–1960," *American Sociological Review,* December, 1960.

The Mass Media and the Structure of American Society.
Co-author with Winston White. *Journal of Social Issues,* Vol. XVI,
No. 3, 1960.

Pattern Variables Revisited: A Response to Professor Dubin's Stimulus.
American Sociological Review, August, 1960.

°Toward a Healthy Maturity.
Journal of Health and Human Behavior, Fall, 1960.

Social Structure and Political Orientation.
World Politics, October, 1960. (A review of S. M. Lipset, *Political
Man,* and William Kornhauser, *The Politics of Mass Society.*)

Review of
Max Weber: An Intellectual Portrait, by Reinhard Bendix, *American
Sociological Review,* October, 1960.

1961

Theories of Society.
Co-editor with Edward Shils, Kaspar D. Naegele, and Jesse R. Pitts.
2 Vols., New York: The Free Press.

⊥Some Principal Characteristics of Industrial Societies.
C. E. Black (ed.), *The Transformation of Russian Society Since 1861,*
Cambridge: Harvard University Press.

°The Link Between Character and Society.
Co-author with Dr. Winston White. Seymour Lipset and Leo

°⊥ See footnotes, p. 539.

Lowenthal (eds.), *Culture and Social Character*, New York: The Free Press.

The Contribution of Psychoanalysis to the Social Sciences.
Science and Psychoanalysis, 1961, Vol. IV.

The Cultural Background of American Religious Organization.
The proceedings of the Conference on Science, Philosophy and Religion, 1960.

The Point of View of the Author.
The Social Theories of Talcott Parsons, Max Black (ed.), Englewood Cliffs, N.J.: Prentice-Hall.

The Problem of International Community.
International Politics and Foreign Policy, James N. Rosenau (ed.), New York: The Free Press.

Polarization of the World and International Order.
Preventing World War III, Quincy Wright, William M. Evan, and Morton Deutsch (eds.), New York: Simon and Schuster, 1962. Also in *Berkeley Journal of Sociology*, 1961.

°Youth in the Context of American Society.
Daedalus, Winter, 1961. Reprinted in *Youth: Change and Challenge*, Erik H. Erikson (ed.), New York: Basic Books, 1963.

Some Considerations on the Theory of Social Change.
Rural Sociology, Vol. 26, No. 3, September, 1961.

A Sociologist's View.
Values and Ideals of American Youth, Eli Ginzberg (ed.), New York: Columbia University Press.

Comment on
Llewellyn Gross, "Preface to a Metatheoretical Framework for Sociology," *American Journal of Sociology*, September, 1961.

In memoriam
"Alfred L. Kroeber, 1876–1960," *American Journal of Sociology*, Vol. LXVI, No. 6, May, 1961.

Comment on
William Kolb, "Images of Man and the Sociology of Religion," *Journal for the Scientific Study of Religion*, October, 1961.

Discussion of Trends Revealed by the 1960 Census of Population.
Proceedings of the Section on Social Statistics, American Statistical Association, 1961.

1962

Foreword
to *Herbert Spencer: The Study of Sociology*, University of Michigan Press, Ann Arbor Paperback Series.

In memoriam
"Clyde Kluckhohn, 1905–1960" (with Evon Z. Vogt), *American Anthropologist*, February, 1962. Reprinted as Introduction to a new edition of Kluckhohn's *Navajo Witchcraft*, Boston: Beacon Press, 1962.

° See footnote, p. 539.

Comment on
Dennis Wrong, "The Oversocialized Conception of Man," *Psychoanalysis and Psychoanalytic Review,* Summer, 1962.
Review of
Hurst, *Law and Social Process,* for *Journal of the History of Ideas,* October–December, 1962.
The Aging in American Society.
Law and Contemporary Problems, Winter, 1962.
The Law and Social Control.
Law and Sociology, William M. Evan (ed.), New York: Free Press.
In memoriam
"Richard Henry Tawney, 1880–1962," *American Sociological Review,* December, 1962.
Review of
Paul Diesing, *Reason in Society,* in *Industrial and Labor Relations Review,* July, 1963.
La struttura dell' azione sociale.
Introduzione di Granfranco Poggi. Bologna: Il Molino. (Italian translation of *The Structure of Social Action.*)

1963
Introduction
to Max Weber, *The Sociology of Religion* (translated by Ephraim Fischoff from *Wirtschaft und Gesellschaft*), Boston: Beacon Press, 1963.
Social Strains in America: A Postscript (1962).
The Radical Right, Daniel Bell (ed.), Garden City, N.Y.: Doubleday.
Christianity and Modern Industrial Society.
Sociological Theory, Values, and Sociocultural Change: Essays in Honor of Pitirim A. Sorokin, Edward A. Tiryakian (ed.), New York: The Free Press.
Social Change and Medical Organization in the United States.
Annals of the American Academy of Political and Social Science, March, 1963.
On the Concept of Influence, with rejoinder to comments.
Public Opinion Quarterly, Spring, 1963.
On the Concept of Political Power.
Proceedings of the American Philosophical Society, Vol. 107, No. 3 (June, 1963).
Death in American Society.
The American Behavioral Scientist, May, 1963.

1964
Some Theoretical Considerations Bearing on the Field of Medical Sociology.
Written for a symposium that did not appear. Was published as Chapter 12 in *Social Structure and Personality,* 1964.

The Intellectual: A Social Role Category.
  The Intellectuals: Basic Readings, Philip Rieff (ed.), to be published by Doubleday and later in an Anchor edition.
Social Structure and Personality.
  (A collection of essays.) New York: The Free Press.
The Ideas of Systems, Causal Explanation and Cybernetic Control in Social Science.
  Cause and Effect, Daniel Lerner (ed.), New York: The Free Press, 1965. (Presented at the 4th Hayden Colloquium, Massachusetts Institute of Technology, 1964.)
Evolutionary Universals in Society.
  American Sociological Review, June, 1964.
Max Weber, 1864–1964.
  American Sociological Review, April, 1964.
Sociological Theory.
  Encyclopedia Britannica, 1965.
Some Reflections on the Place of Force in Social Process.
  Internal War: Basic Problems and Approaches, Harry Eckstein (ed.), New York: The Free Press.
Levels of Organization and the Mediation of Social Interaction.
  Sociological Inquiry, Spring, 1964.
Die Juengsten Entwicklungen in Der Strukturell-Funksionalem Theorie.
  Koelner Zeitschrift fuer Soziologie und Sozialpsychologie, 1964, 16, I, pp. 30–49. English version in Haring *Festschrift.*
Youth in the Context of American Society.
  Man in a World at Work, Henry Borow (ed.), Boston: Houghton Mifflin. (Slightly modified version of an article previously written for *Daedalus,* 1961.)
Unity and Diversity in the Modern Intellectual Disciplines: The Role of the Social Sciences.
  Daedalus, Winter, 1965, pp. 39–65.
Evaluation and Objectivity in the Social Sciences: An Interpretation of Max Weber's Contributions.
  (An address delivered at the Weber Centennial, April, 1964.) Published in German with discussion in *Max Weber und die Soziologie Heute,* Otto Stammer (ed.), Tübingen: Mohr, 1965. English version published in the *International Journal of the Social Sciences,* 1965.
Beiträge zur soziologischen Theorie.
  Editor and translator, Dietrich Rüschmeyer; Luchterhand Verlag GmbH.

1965
An American's Impression of Sociology in the Soviet Union.
  American Sociological Review.
Full Citizenship for the Negro American?

Daedalus, November, 1965. Reprinted in *The Negro American*, Parsons and Clark (eds.), 1966.

1966

Societies: Evolutionary and Comparative Perspectives.
Foundations of Modern Sociology Series, Alex Inkeles (general editor), Englewood Cliffs, N.J.: Prentice-Hall.
The Political Aspect of Social Structure and Process.
Varieties of Political Theory, David Easton (ed.), Englewood Cliffs, N.J.: Prentice-Hall.
The Negro American.
Co-editor with Kenneth Clark. Boston: Houghton Mifflin.
Die Bedeutung der Polarisierung für das Sozialsystem: Die Hautfarbe als Polarisierungsproblem.
Militanter Humanismus, Alphons Silbermann (ed.), Frankfurt am Main: S. Fischer Verlag.

1967 and forthcoming

The Nature of American Pluralism.
Religion and Public Education, Theodore Sizer (ed.), Boston: Houghton Mifflin, 1967.
Social Science and Theology.
America and the Future of Theology, William A. Beardslee (ed.), Philadelphia: The Westminster Press, 1967.
The System of Modern Societies.
Englewood Cliffs, N.J.: Prentice-Hall, forthcoming. Companion volume to *Societies: Evolutionary and Comparative Perspectives*, cited above.
Clyde Kluckhohn's Contribution to the Integration of the Social Sciences.
Essays in Anthropology, Evon Vogt and John Fischer (eds.), forthcoming.
Death in American Society.
Co-author with Victor Lidz. A revised and extended version of the article listed under 1963; to appear in *Essays in Self-Destruction*, Edwin Schneidman (ed.), 1967.
The Position of Identity in the General Theory of Action.
The Self in Social Interaction, Chad Gordon and Kenneth J. Gergen (eds.), New York: John Wiley & Sons, forthcoming.
Religion in American Society: Some Recent Developments.
Currents, forthcoming.
Cooley and the Problem of Internalization.
To appear in a book edited by Albert J. Reiss, in honor of the Centennial of Cooley's birth.
Components and Types of Formal Organization.
Presented at a conference at Alderbrook, Washington, in 1965; a volume of papers from the conference will be published by The University of Washington Press, Seattle, 1968.

Readings on Premodern Societies.
 Co-editor with Victor Lidz. Englewood Cliffs, N.J.: Prentice-Hall, forthcoming.
The following articles have been prepared for the *International Encyclopedia of the Social Sciences:*
 Christianity
 Emile Durkheim
 Interaction
 Vilfredo Pareto—Sociological Aspect
 Professions
 Social Systems and Subsystems
 Utilitarians

Index of Authors and Titles

Subject Index